STRESS IN THE MODERN WORLD

STRESS IN THE MODERN WORLD

Understanding Science and Society

VOLUME 1

Serena Wadhwa, Editor

GREENWOOD™

An Imprint of ABC-CLIO, LLC
Santa Barbara, California • Denver, Colorado

Library of Congress Cataloging-in-Publication Data

Names: Wadhwa, Serena, editor.
Title: Stress in the modern world : understanding science and society / Serena Wadhwa, editor.
Description: 1 Edition. | Santa Barbara : Greenwood, 2017. | Includes index.
Identifiers: LCCN 2016023948 (print) | LCCN 2016045695 (ebook) | ISBN 9781610696067 (set : alk. paper) | ISBN 9781440845741 (vol. 1 hardcopy : alk. paper) | ISBN 9781440845758 (vol. 2 hardcopy : alk. paper) | ISBN 9781610696074 (ebook)
Subjects: LCSH: Stress (Psychology) | Stress management.
Classification: LCC BF575.S75 S77333 2017 (print) | LCC BF575.S75 (ebook) | DDC 155.9/042—dc23
LC record available at https://lccn.loc.gov/2016023948

ISBN: 978-1-61069-606-7 (set)
ISBN: 978-1-4408-4574-1 (Vol. 1)
ISBN: 978-1-4408-4575-8 (Vol. 2)
EISBN: 978-1-61069-607-4 (set)

21 20 19 18 17 1 2 3 4 5

This book is also available as an eBook.

Greenwood
An Imprint of ABC-CLIO, LLC

ABC-CLIO, LLC
130 Cremona Drive, P.O. Box 1911
Santa Barbara, California 93116-1911
www.abc-clio.com

This book is printed on acid-free paper ∞

Manufactured in the United States of America

This book discusses treatments (including types of medication and mental health therapies), diagnostic tests for various symptoms and mental health disorders, and organizations. The authors have made every effort to present accurate and up-to-date information. However, the information in this book is not intended to recommend or endorse particular treatments or organizations, or substitute for the care or medical advice of a qualified health professional, or used to alter any medical therapy without a medical doctor's advice. Specific situations may require specific therapeutic approaches not included in this book. For those reasons, we recommend that readers follow the advice of qualified health care professionals directly involved in their care. Readers who suspect they may have specific medical problems should consult a physician about any suggestions made in this book. It should also be noted that the opinions expressed in the contributed chapters do not necessarily reflect those of the editor.

CONTENTS

Part III: Responses to Stress

VOLUME 2

PREFACE

Stress in the Modern World: Understanding Science and Society is a reference book, offering a multifaceted look at a wide array of aspects of stress and the part it plays in all of our lives. It features 47 chapters and 20 personal accounts, arranged in 4 sections:

- Part I explores theories of stress
- Part II describes sources of stress
- Part III examines responses to stress
- Part IV offers personal accounts of stress and stress responses

Part I: Theories of Stress. Although the term *stress* was coined by Dr. Hans Selye and first popularized in the 1950s, the existence of stress in human beings, when understood as a physiological phenomenon, dates back to humans' first appearance on earth. As humans evolved, and eventually sought to understand human behavior, theories and explanations about the nature of stress and its influence on human behavior, personality, and dynamics were developed. Part I offers explorations of cognitive behavioral theories of stress (Chapter 1); developmental explanations (Chapter 2); ecological theories (Chapter 3); diathesis-stress models (showing certain people to have vulnerabilities to stress) (Chapter 4); spiritual theories (Chapter 5); the neuroscience of stress (Chapter 6); and holistic perspectives (Chapter 7). Included in this section are misconceptions about stress (Chapter 8), as it is common for people to make some misleading assumptions about the nature and value of stress. Chapter 9 examines the hormones that activate and participate in the stress response and some of the consequences of the presence of these hormones. The cognitive symptoms and effects of stress , in both the short and long terms are presented in Chapter 10. Chapter 11 discusses the physical (body) and psychological (mind) consequences and effects of stress. Finally, Chapter 12 explores several aspects of stress assessment and measurement, including both psychological and physiological assessments. Many of the chapters in Parts I through III also contain sidebars that give brief overviews of or introductions to related topics.

Part II: Sources of Stress. A variety of things can trigger the stress response. The sources of stress are probably unlimited, because what is perceived as a stressor varies from individual to individual. This part covers a number of the most significant sources of stress, including financial, often cited as the most common source of stress (Chapter 13); socioeconomic, including the effects of poverty and discrimination on psychological and physical health (Chapter 14); social relationships and the happiness and devastation they can cause (Chapter 15); generational and life span issues (Chapter 16); families and their distinctive stresses (Chapter 17); work issues (Chapter 18); technology, both helpful and problematic (Chapter 19); environmental stresses (Chapter 20); academic issues (Chapter 21); caregiving stresses (Chapter 22); and sexuality concerns (Chapter 23).

Part III: Responses to Stress. These chapters focus on the effective and ineffective methods individuals use to cope with stress and discuss trends for current and future ways to manage stress. Effective strategies include attending to the basic human needs that directly affect the ability to manage stress, or which in fact cause stress, such as good nutrition (Chapter 24); physical activity and exercise (Chapter 25); enough deep sleep (Chapter 26); and sufficient relaxation (Chapter 27). The effective strategies of mindfulness and meditation are presented in Chapter 28. Creativity provides resources, usually satisfying, that people can use to better control and enjoy their lives (Chapter 29). Other helpful responses to stress may include the use of complementary and alternative medicine, techniques, and natural substances to manage stress (Chapter 30). The ability to be optimistic and to practice methods that increase this attitude (Chapter 31) may reduce stress; for most people, listening to music and experiencing art and beauty are also significant stress reducers (Chapter 32). Although no medications can eliminate stress (or stress responses), they can help prevent the cognitive and emotional consequences of the stress response and treat symptoms such as headaches, insomnia, and gastrointestinal discomfort (Chapter 33). Writing techniques, such as journaling, can be an effective way to process stress cognitively and understand its place in one's life (Chapter 34); using humor (Chapter 35) as a response to stress is another technique relied upon by many. Other cognitive methods are described in Chapter 36, which describes restructuring to change ineffective and self-defeating attitudes and thoughts into positive methods for handling stress. Language, both verbal and nonverbal, can also be used to better cope to stressors (Chapter 37).

People also employ a great many ineffective and harmful strategies and behaviors to address the stresses in their lives, including substance misuse (both alcohol and drugs; Chapter 38); disordered eating (Chapter 39); self-injury, used as a calming or control mechanism (Chapter 40); and suicide, often the result of chemical imbalances in the brain which cause severe depression (Chapter 41). Other manifestations to serious stress exposure are violence (Chapter 42) and posttraumatic stress disorder (Chapter 43). Chapter 44 focuses on the concept of burnout: how it differs from acute and chronic stress, symptoms of burnout, and what research says about this concept in terms of coping and healing.

Chapter 45 discusses certain psychological stress disorders. The American Psychiatric Association, in its *Diagnostic and Statistical Manual of Mental Disorders, Fifth Edition* (*DSM-5*), lists several stress-related disorders that are considered clinical disorders, indicating that significant distress has been experienced, and that treatment is warranted. This chapter also discusses some of the research on psychological stress disorders.

Chapter 46 explores theory and practice regarding the prevention, management, and reduction of stress, and provides an overview of the research to date. The final chapter in Part III discusses present trends in the study of stress, including the concept of "stressism" developed by Dana Becker, and the future of research on stress.

Part IV features 20 personal accounts, which are just that: personal essays written by real individuals describing their stress, their responses to stress, and how they have learned to cope with the stress in their lives. These accounts are written in the first person and demonstrate how various individuals cope with stress: differently, yet effectively. These vignettes may give readers some ideas for coping with stress in their own lives.

The book ends with an extensive list of recommended books, articles, and websites that will help readers find even more information on stress, its history, its effects, and its management. Lastly, there is a comprehensive index to the entire work.

Fifty-two writers, along with myself, contributed to *Stress in the Modern World*. Nearly all of them are professional mental health counselors and therapists or university faculty who instruct students in the mental health fields. Some are graduate students working on their doctorates. Their specialties and interests range from the science of the central nervous system, to stress effects on other parts of the human body, to the ability of humans to better and more productively live their lives, whether at work, home, or school. I especially want to thank student worker Annetta Jones Morgan, for her initial work on the "Recommended Resources" section; and to Ashley Orendorff, who is pursuing a master's degree in social work, for her efforts on that same section.

Thank you for reading and using this book. I hope that readers will get as much out of it as I put into it.

Stress: An Overview

It is early afternoon as I begin writing this chapter. As I do so, my phone chirps a sound to let me know about incoming emails that may require my attention. Several minutes pass before another sound alerts me to a friend calling. On my computer screen, up pops a reminder about a meeting I have tomorrow and what I need to prepare for it. My eyes reflexively squint as the sun, pouring through the window, suddenly hits them directly. As I lower the shades, I observe that the temperature is becoming warmer in my room. My mind fills with thoughts about the other things that demand my attention, even as I gently shift my focus to what I want to include in this chapter. And while I notice my heart beating a bit faster, my breathing is a bit shallow; at the same time, my focus is a bit sharpened, my attention a bit heightened, and my motivation peaked. It's a paradoxical sense of stress: while my body reacts physically to the experience of having these demands, psychologically it's exhilarating.

Stress is all around us. It is not something we can escape, nor is it something we necessarily want to escape. At any given moment, there are most likely several things competing for our attention and placing demands on our resources. Stress is something we often talk about, and yet we still aren't quite sure what it may be or how to deal with it. This publication explores those topics. It was challenging (maybe stressful?) to decide how to divide this volume about stress and what topics to focus on, as there is an endless supply of subtopics on the subject of stress. Stress seems always to be in the spotlight these days. My conceptualization of stress is that pretty much everything can be connected in one way or another to this concept. In fact, it is estimated that 75 to 90 percent of doctor visits are stress related (as cited in Tsui, 2013; American Institute of Stress, n.d.). With such high rates, it's no wonder that stress has gained prominence in the lives of many people.

Research also reports that we want to learn more about stress. In an article exploring the connection of stress management and health care, Sophie Bethune reported that although about 32 percent of Americans say it's important to talk with their health care providers about stress-related concerns, only 17 percent actually do (Bethune, 2013). According to a report in *Forbes,* Americans spend *billions* on health care problems that may be considered stress related (Blanding, 2015). This suggests two things: (1) a growing concern with how to access resources to manage and reduce stress; and (2) the disconnection of the mind, body, and spirit fields. Given that integrative care appears to be the wave of the future, what does this disconnection mean for individuals, families, communities, and the nation in the present?

This reference work, *Stress in the Modern World,* presents a variety of theories, external and internal triggers of the stress experience, and both ineffective and effective coping mechanisms. The book explores factors relating to increased vulnerability to stress—how individuals assess and appraise something as being a threat or demand—and protective factors.

If someone were to ask you, "What is stress?", what comes to mind? Is it that stress is overwhelming? That stress is your job? Chances are you thought of something that reflects more of a symptom of stress or something that causes stress for you. These aspects are discussed in detail in this book. For now, it is important to understand the definition of stress. Mainly, *stress* is the body's response to a demand or some pressure. An example of this is how the pupils in your eyes adjust as the lighting in your environment shifts. The pupils either dilate or constrict depending on the demands of your visual needs. Stress can be as simple as that.

However, stress in today's world is much more complicated than a pupil change. Although stress responses are still something that occur without your consciously directing attention to them (because these reactions are part of the sympathetic nervous system that regulates and automatically adjusts according to the body's needs), there are other factors that in the modern world influence these occurrences. Hundreds of thousands of years ago, when humans hunted and gathered food, the changes in the body served as an alert system against potential danger. Imagine yourself in those times: You are out happily enjoying the day, gathering berries and firewood. Suddenly you find yourself face to face with a saber-toothed tiger. In a matter of milliseconds, you feel a surge of energy and strength, which occurs to assist you to run faster, hit harder, and think more quickly. Your heart pumps at two to three times the normal rate, sending more blood to your muscles. Blood pressure increases, which prevents you from bleeding to death should you become wounded. Eyes dilate to expand your peripheral vision. Your digestive and immune systems are less effective, as is your sexual functioning, because these

"THE STRESS IN AMERICA" SURVEY

To emphasize the seriousness of stress in American life, since 2007 the American Psychological Association (APA) has conducted an annual survey known as the "Stress in America" survey. The APA is a national association comprising more than 130,000 members (including licensed psychologists, doctoral-level clinicians, students, academics, researchers, clinicians, and consultants).

The survey is distributed within the United States by the Harris Poll group, on behalf of the APA. Questions address common perceived sources of stress, coping mechanisms to manage stress, and the impact of stress on daily living. Each year, surveys explore different aspects of these components. In 2007, the first Stress in America™ survey investigated how people specifically coped with stress, the impact stress had, and sources of stress. In 2008, the survey explored how people perceived themselves managing and experiencing their stress, as well the likelihood of their seeking help. In 2009, the survey asked how stress affected families. Other surveys have asked about children and stress (2010); caregiver health and stress (2011); stress and people with chronic diseases (2012); teenagers and stress (2013); money as a primary stressor (2014); and the impact of discrimination on stress and its connection to poor health (2015).

Each report provides a detailed account of the methodology used in the survey, how many persons responded, and a breakdown of the demographics of the respondents. Survey reports also include key findings that were revealing upon analysis of the data. Some reports analyze information by major cities (Atlanta, Chicago, etc.). These surveys are part of the APA's Public Education Campaign, which started in 1996. The Mind/Body Health Campaign was begun in 2005 as a means to disseminate information on the connection between psychological and physical health, particularly in the areas of stress, heart disease, and obesity. This campaign promotes talking with psychologists, as many psychologists are trained in behavioral and lifestyle changes. The association's public education campaign gives awards to work sites that promote well-being while recognizing performance. More information about the APA and the Stress in America surveys are available at http://www.apa.org/news/press/releases/stress/index.aspx.

systems are not needed right now and the resources can be used elsewhere. In this supercharged moment, you find yourself able to run faster and harder, thus escaping the chance of becoming the tiger's next meal. When you realize you are out of the danger zone, you find a place to rest and do so to restore your exhausted body.

This is a rather efficient and effective system to have, especially in the wake of unexpected and threatening events. Now let's imagine a different scene in the modern world. You are on your first break at work, and you are searching for coffee and donuts. Out of the corner of your eye, you see your boss walking toward you. You pretend you don't see him, but already you feel your heart beating faster and your mouth becoming dry. He calls your name and requests that you to come to his office. Now your system is in full swing. You feel your blood pressure rising. As you follow your boss to his office, you recall a rumor you heard about layoffs due to the company needing to downsize. Now your hearth is beating faster, you start to perspire, your hands become clammy, and your mouth feels like the Sahara Desert. The ancestral "reptilian" part of your brain has a reaction that wants to run or fight, as it seems like a matter of survival, but you cannot do either. As you enter your boss's office, the fight-or-flight response is full blown, and all that energy has no place to go. You are so focused on your thoughts that you barely can hear what your boss is saying. When you ask him to repeat his statement, he tells you that he is considering you for a promotion.

This is a good example of how stress works in today's world. There are two things to keep in mind regarding this scene. Situations that elicit the fight-or-flight response can have a negative effect if too many of them occur. Additionally, when you anticipate that an event will occur, this actually doubles the fight-or-flight response. Nevertheless, there are situations that are considered positive and desirable that still trigger the same fight-or-flight response. A promotion, going on a first date, getting married, and making a big life-changing decision are all situations that are perceived as positive and enlist the stress response for motivating and changing in effective ways. Nelson and Simmons (2005, p. 102) explored this initial concept in the context of workplace stress.

THE PARADOX OF STRESS

When stress is present in small amounts, it provides a "rush" that can be motivational. It can be energizing and stimulating. This can be one of the benefits of stress. Research indicates that an initial increase in stress can increase an individual's performance. A certain amount of stress increases functioning, known as *healthy tension*. Dr. Hans Selye, a pioneer in the research of stress, called this *eustress* (1950). When too much stress is present, lasts too long, or occurs too often, this stress, known as *distress,* can have many deleterious consequences for the brain, mind, body, and emotions. A person's wholeness is affected by the effects of stress.

One of the first steps in managing and reducing stress is developing awareness of what elicits stress for you. These things, commonly known as *stressors,* are anything that causes stress. There are two general categories of stressors, both encompassing various aspects: *External stressors* include human development, health, finances, technology, work, school, family, friends, and your environment. *Internal stressors* include your psychological factors, such as attitude, values, personality, worry, and anticipation levels. *Related stressors* are your lifestyle choices, which are how you sleep, eat, exercise, and so on. Several chapters in this book explore these in more detail.

THE STRESS RESPONSE

When the brain perceives an actual or imagined threat, this initiates the stress response. The first stage is the well-known "fight or flight" stage, also known as the arousal/alarm stage, first discovered and researched by pioneer physiologist Walter B. Cannon during World War I. This is when the body becomes aroused and produces an immediate response to the stress. It's a physiological reaction. It is short term, as it is a temporary disruption of the body's normal state of balance. Once the disruption passes, the body is able to return to its usual homeostasis. Recent literature has proposed the notion of *allostasis,* which is when neurotransmitters, hormones, and other neurophysiological systems maintain stability through change (McEwen, 2004). The fight-or-flight response—the basic survival response—can produce extraordinary strength. In small doses, this stage can be thrilling.

As the fight-or-flight response is initiated, several things occur within the body. The pupils dilate to allow better peripheral vision. An increase in blood's ability to coagulate occurs so that the individual does not quickly bleed to death in the event of becoming wounded. There is a surge of adrenaline, which is mostly responsible for the increased feelings of energy and strength. Additionally, adrenaline increases the metabolism of carbohydrates to give the body extra fuel for immediate use. Blood pressure and blood circulation increase to provide the muscles with more nutrient-enriched blood. An increase of lactic acid occurs, which give the muscles flexibility and energy for action. Other chemicals, such as noradrenaline and other catecholamines, are also released to provide the body with the tools necessary to respond immediately to the stress. If the response to the stress is adequate (i.e., running or fighting), then the body is able to return to homeostasis fairly quickly thereafter.

The second phase of stress is the *intermediate phase,* also known as the *adaptation* or *resistance phase,* in which the stress response continues. Physiologically, changes occur that enable the system to adapt to the prolonged and increased frequency of the stress response. In other words, the body's homeostasis level changes, and this is accepted as normal. As the body adapts to repeated and constant stress, the tolerance for new stress decreases.

WALTER B. CANNON (1871–1945)

Born in 1871 in Prairie du Chien, Wisconsin, Walter Bradford Cannon was one of the most respected scientists of the 20th century. Among other things, he developed the concepts of the fight-or-flight syndrome and homeostasis in the human body. His interest was in the fields of physiology and psychology, and while a student at Harvard Medical School, he pursued initial research about the process of digestion. Cannon was appointed as an instructor in physiology at Harvard, and after that, in 1906, as chairperson of the college's department of physiology, a position he held until his resignation in 1942 ("Who Was Walter Bradford Cannon?," n.d.).

During his time at Harvard, Cannon's research extended the understanding of how the body functions. He studied emotional reactions in animals and how the autonomic nervous system prepares the organism. He invented the phrase *fight-or-flight syndrome,* describing his key finding of the body's reaction to physical or psychological emergencies. He wrote about these observations in *Bodily Changes in Pain, Hunger, Fear and Rage,* published in 1915. During World War I, he joined an Army unit to observe and study the phenomenon of shock. These observations led him to believe that the body strives for "harmonious equilibrium," for which he coined the word *homeostasis* in 1926, building on Claude Bernard's work, representing how the body maintains itself through physiological processes, chemical regulation, and other changes. This biological self-regulation of the organism is a part of the evolutionary process and a key concept in how the body works (Hagen, 1996).

Cannon was also known as a public and political figure. Because he used animals for experimentation, he was somewhat controversial. Although the literature suggests that he was a skilled surgeon and used anesthesia on the animals, protesters criticized his experiments. He also spoke out forcefully about scientists who were being pressured by totalitarian governments abroad. He served as the head of the Committee on Physiology of the National Research Council from its inception in 1916 until his death in 1945. Among his many books is his 1945 autobiography, *The Way of an Investigator.*

The final phase is known as the *exhaustion phase.* This is the chronic form of stress, which is long term. In this phase, the stress response lasts longer, as the body requires additional resources to adapt to the demands made on it. When the body reaches its limit to adapt, so that it cannot cope with the continuing or new demands, the body begins to break down. This happens mainly with continued unexpected stress, a series of stressors, or when acute phases of the stress response accumulate. Changes that may occur in this stage include the depletion of endorphins, the body's "feel good" hormones, which causes the individual to lose the ability to feel pleasure. Other changes include a breakdown in the immune system, which leaves the individual more vulnerable to catching colds, the flu, and other viruses and infections; and developing allergies and autoimmune problems.

SYMPTOMS, SIGNS, AND DISEASES OF STRESS

The effects of stress on the body begin well before one can notice the results. The signs and symptoms of stress are as individualized as fingerprints, because people experience stress differently and to different intensities. Some typical symptoms are behavioral, such as nail biting, frowning, outbursts, decreased productivity, pacing, blaming, and changes in appetite or sleep patterns. Mentally, a person may experience worry, poor memory, lack of focus, and racing thoughts. Emotionally, one may experience anger, fatigue, depression, irritability, or anxiety. Physically, one may experience chest pains, sweating, pain, gastrointestinal problems, headaches, cravings, and a host of other signs and symptoms. Socially, a person may withdraw or cancel plans, stop initiating contact with others, or overinvest in social activities.

At a certain point, the effects of chronic stress do make the body vulnerable to disease. The type, frequency, onset, and other disease-related factors are dependent upon numerous variables: genetics; immune system function; nutrition; coping mechanisms; the use of tobacco, alcohol, or drugs; and a plethora of other factors. Research has linked "stress-induced medical conditions" with chronic stress. The following are just a few of the physical problems that may result: hypertension, strokes, hardening of the arteries, tension headaches, muscular tension, diarrhea, diabetes, arthritis, accelerated aging, insomnia, infertility, decrease in white blood cells, acne, and eczema—among many others.

As the reader will see in this two-volume resource, while the concept of stress itself does not change, what is trending and what is "popular" in terms of causes, coping mechanisms, and other factors, does change. Many variables influence what becomes the focus of stress research; however, because stress will not disappear, research relating to stress will always be needed. There are huge numbers of variables that affect how stress manifests in one person and not another; variables that affect how, for example, losing a job or getting rejected results in actions ranging from the extreme, as in a violent attack on a person or group of people, and/or a suicide; or withdrawal from friends and family; or some unhappiness and distress that eventually change to moving forward. What may become evident is how much of the information seems to overlap. There is a reason for this: as mentioned, much of what is known about stress doesn't change, but as new information is gained, it builds on previous information. The small amount of overlap that exists demonstrates the consistency of research and the remarkable quality of stress, both in the old world and in the modern world.

REFERENCES AND FURTHER READING

American Institute of Stress. (n.d.). Retrieved from http://www.stress.org/.

Bethune, S. (2013). Health-care falls short on stress management. *Monitor on Psychology, 44(4)*, 22. Retrieved from http://www.apa.org/monitor/2013/04/health-care.aspx.

Blanding, M. (2015, January 26). Workplace stress responsible for up to $190b in annual U.S. healthcare costs. *Forbes*. Retrieved from http://www.forbes.com/sites/hbsworking knowledge/2015/01/26/workplace-stress-responsible-for-up-to-190-billion-in-annual -u-s-heathcare-costs/2/#2715e4857a0b2f1c34c6546c.

Brown, T. M., & Fee, E. (2002). Walter Bradford Cannon. *American Journal of Public Health, 92*(10), 1594–1595.

Cannon, W. B. (1915). *Bodily changes in pain, hunger, fear and rage: An account of recent researches into the function of emotional excitement.* New York, NY: D. Appleton.

Cannon, W. B. (1945). *The way of an investigator.* New York, NY: W.W. Norton.

Hagen, J. B. (1996). Walter Cannon and self-regulation in animals. In J. B. Hagen, D. Allchin, & F. Singer (Eds.), *Doing biology* (pp. 95–103). New York, NY: Harper Collins College Publishers.

McEwen, B. S. (2004). Protection and damage from acute and chronic stress: Allostasis and allostatic overload and relevance to the pathophysiology of psychiatric disorders. *Annals of the New York Academy of Sciences, 1032*(1), 1–7.

Nelson, D. L., & Simmons, B. L. (2005). Eustress and attitudes at work: A positive approach. In A. Antoniou & C. Cooper (Eds.), *Research companion to organizational health psychology* (pp. 102–110). Cheltenham, UK/Northampton, MA: Edward Elgar.

Selye, H. (1950). Stress and the general adaptation syndrome. *British Medical Journal, 1*(4667), 1383.

Tsui, A. S. (2013). 2012 presidential address—On compassion in scholarship: Why should we care? *Academy of Management Review, 38*(2), 167–180.

Walter B. Cannon Papers. (2013). American Philosophical Society. Retrieved from http://www.amphilsoc.org/mole/view?docId=ead/Mss.B.C163.1-ead.xml;query=;brand =default.

Who Was Walter Bradford Cannon? (n.d.). Retrieved from http://hms.harvard.edu/depart ments/medical-education/student-services/academic-societies-hms/walter-bradford -cannon-society/walter-bradford-cannon.

Part I
Theories of Stress

Introduction to Part I, Theories of Stress

Stress in the modern world is a broad and vague concept. Although most people know what stress is and what it may look like, the experience of stress can be described from various perspectives. When we consider biological (including the brain physiology), psychological, spiritual, developmental, social, and ecological factors in the experience of stress, these components also suggest a theoretical framework for understanding a part of the larger experience of stress. Part I explores various theories and explanations of the experience of stress. Viewing stress from different vantage points gives depth to our understanding of the complexity of what is termed *stress*. These various vantage points also provide some explanations of how a "stressor" is experienced differently by an individual, as developmental factors, cultural factors, and predispositions will all influence perception.

This section discusses the science of and a variety of theories/explanations about the experience of stress. Chapter 1, on cognitive behavioral explanations of stress, explores the concept of appraisal and how different variables influence perception. Chapter 2 considers how the developmental stage of an individual can contribute to the experience of stress, as the brain and body are developmentally different and thus have different capacities at different stages of life. Chapter 3 explores ecological theories of stress, and how humans adapt to a changing environment and stresses through changing their physiology and behavior. Chapter 4 examines the diathesis-stress model, which explores vulnerabilities in human beings and how these interact with stress to create further vulnerabilities and disorders. It covers the nature-nurture interaction and looks at genetic and other predispositions within the experience of stress. Chapter 5 explores spiritual and religious explanations of the experience of stress. Chapter 6 provides information on the "what and how" of the stress experience from a neurological perspective. Chapter 7 provides a holistic perspective on stress, integrating various factors from previous chapters to account for the whole of the stress experience.

In Chapter 8, many common myths and misconceptions about the experience of stress, and the strategies that individuals may have developed to deal with stress, are examined. Chapter 9 discusses stress hormones: what they are, how they work, and how they may become dysfunctional in the body. Chapter 10 describes how stress affects a person's cognitive abilities and aspects. Chapter 11 explores the mind-body connection and the psychological and physiological impacts of the stress experience. Finally, Chapter 12 considers the assessment of stress, including factors that influence assessments, measures for assessing stress, and other components. This chapter also investigates individual vulnerabilities and predispositions as factors developing from biological and genetic responses to exposure to trauma and stress during certain critical periods of development. Chapter 12 further includes a brief overview of the research to date on the concepts of resiliency and hardiness, and discusses personality factors as components in the appraisal and perception of stress.

While we know that stress is inevitable, how it is understood, explained, and conceptualized does differ among individuals. This section provides a foundation for understanding the experience of stress and what elements may be a part of this experience.

1

Cognitive Behavioral Theories and Explanations of Stress

Samantha Reif

Nothing about the stress epidemic is new to American culture. Stressors have surrounded us throughout history and are referenced in ancient and biblical times. What *has* changed over time is the way experts and laypeople alike conceptualize stress. Modern definitions of stress rely on the lens through which it is viewed, the preconceived notions about its place in our lives, and the presumed importance of the connection between stress and our health and well-being. This chapter reviews cognitive behavioral theories as explanations of stress. Any review of these theories must begin with a closer look at the underpinnings of the cognitive behavioral perspective.

PREMISE OF EARLY BEHAVIOR THEORIES

True behaviorism is based on the premise that personality is built on the sum total of our learned behavior. Individual behaviors are either rewarded or punished as they interact with the environment. This external process is key to predicting behavior. The term *behaviorism* was first coined by John B. Watson, in 1913, to describe the theory that all behaviors are learned through environmental conditioning. The theory of behaviorism posits that only observable behaviors should be studied, and that anyone could be trained to perform any task, regardless of that person's internal processes or capabilities. Strict behaviorists believe that anything is possible with the right conditioning (Watson, 1924).

There are two major types of conditioning: classical and operant. Ivan Pavlov is the father of classical conditioning. Classical conditioning is based on a stimulus-response model of behavior. Pavlov paired an initially neutral stimulus (a bell) with an unconditioned stimulus (meat powder). After consistent pairings, the unconditioned response to food (salivation) became conditioned to the sound of the bell, meaning that the dogs would start to salivate in response to the bell, even in the absence of the food. Pavlovian theory states that behavioral responses can be predicted and controlled through laws of conditioning, and this relatively simple model was used to explain the automatic/nonconscious learning experienced in everyday life (McLeod, 2007). One powerful example of classical conditioning is food aversions. Many people have had the experience of a certain food or taste being paired with a negative experience (e.g., food poisoning), which leads to an immediate visceral response to that food when presented in the future—sometimes as much as years in the future!

Operant conditioning, sometimes also referred to as *instrumental conditioning* or *Skinnerian conditioning*, was introduced by B. F. Skinner in the 1930s. This conditioning represents a method of learning that is contingent on a system of rewards and punishments for behavior. Skinner, being a behaviorist, focused on only external, observable causes of behavior. Skinner did not believe that any internal drives or motivations were important for predicting behavior. Through operant conditioning, an association is made between a behavior and its consequence. Through added reinforcement of close approximations toward the desired behavior, behavior can be shaped through this conditioning process (Skinner, 1938).

As an example of behavior shaping, we can look to the process of teaching children to write their names. Initially, they are praised for anything that resembles the first letter, with expectations, and resultant praise, being raised as progress is made. Some examples of operant conditioning include children who complete their homework to earn the reward of praise or a good grade, or adults in the workplace who complete projects to receive promotions. These demonstrate how the promise of rewards can increase a desirable behavior. However, operant conditioning can also be used to decrease a negative behavior. An adult who acts within the confines of the law, so as to avoid fines or imprisonment, is an example of operant conditioning decreasing a negative behavior.

PREMISE OF EARLY COGNITIVE THEORIES

Whereas behavioral theories describe one method of learning, cognitive theories stem from a learning theory dating back to Piaget and his theorized stages of normal intellectual development. Piaget was the first psychologist to conduct a systematic study of cognitive development. According to Piaget, cognitive development is always sequential, and each stage is associated with a greater ability to understand the complexities of the world (Piaget, 1936). Piaget's theory of cognitive development is based on the precedent that all knowledge is organized into different parts, which he called "schemas." As individuals approach new information, they either assimilate it into their existing schemas, or they change their current schemas to accommodate the new information (Piaget, 1936). This concept laid the groundwork for the role of cognitive processing and reasoning in predicting human behavior and emotion.

Schachter and Singer, in their seminal work on the experience of emotion, demonstrated that cognitive appraisals and interpretations are key to making sense of our internal and external world (1962). They conducted a randomized controlled study in which some individuals were given a shot of epinephrine with varying instructions on what they might experience; these persons were then exposed to a positive (euphoric) or negative (angry) situation, and their reactions compared with those of individuals who had received a shot of saline instead of adrenaline. As predicted, the researchers found that if individuals experience physiological arousal and do not know why, they will label their emotions according to their situation (Schachter & Singer, 1962). Their theory, referred to as the *two-factor theory of emotion* or the *arousal interpretation model,* supports the role of cognition in determining emotion.

Social cognitive theory holds that knowledge acquisition is directly correlated to the observation of models and cognitive expectations resulting from those observations (i.e., If x, then y). As a demonstration of the process of people learning from observing others, Albert Bandura and his colleagues constructed the well-known "Bobo doll" experiments (Bandura, 2007). In these studies, children were exposed to either aggressive or nonaggressive models of either the same or opposite gender as the child. Results determined that the aggressive models played with the doll in an aggressive manner, and the nonaggressive models played with other toys altogether. Children who were exposed to the aggressive models demonstrated more aggressive actions toward the doll. Bandura then constructed a series of experiments to support the notion that the same was true for models presented through media. This research replaced the live model with a video simulation. These studies demonstrate how people reenact behaviors they see in the media. As the subjects are not expecting any actual rewards or punishments for their behavior, but are acting based on assumptions that they will have outcomes similar to those of the model, this exemplifies the importance of outcome expectancies in social cognitive theory.

Further research has revealed that learning is most likely to occur if there is a close identification between the subject and the model, and if the subject has a high level of self-efficacy. *Self-efficacy* is the belief individuals have in their ability to perform a task, and has been found to play a significant role in how goals, tasks, and challenges are approached (Bandura, 2007). There are four main routes by which self-efficacy is acquired: mastery experiences; social modeling; social persuasion; and the interpretation of psychological responses, such as moods, physical reactions, and stress levels (Bandura, 2007). Self-efficacy is also very closely tied to perceptions of and experience of stress, as we will see later in this chapter.

YERKES-DODSON LAW: STRESS AND PERFORMANCE

Developed by Robert Yerkes and John Dodson in 1908, the Yerkes-Dodson Law describes the relationship between arousal and performance. Visually, the arousal and performance relationship appears as an upside-down "U," or bell, and indicates that as arousal for a person increases, performance does as well, which is at the top part of the curve. However, on the way leading up to the curve, when arousal is not high enough, as when a person is bored and has an uninteresting task to perform, performance is poor. On the other side of the curve, leading down, if there is too much arousal the person feels overwhelmed, does not perform well, does not think clearly, and becomes distracted or even physically ill. Both too little and too much arousal are bad for a person's performance.

The application of this law has been studied in relation to many topics, including, for example, weight loss among children who were considered overweight based on their body mass index. Those children with moderate dissatisfaction about their weight performed the best at losing weight, and those children who either had very little concern or the highest concern about their weight performed the worst (Johnston, Moreno, Regas, Tyler, & Foreyt, 2012). Additionally, von Gehlen and Sachse (2015) have researched how increasing arousal (whether through exercise or cognition) can also enhance performance.

The Yerkes-Dodson Law may be applied to stress and performance. Too little stress/arousal in a person's life is not an optimum condition, leading to boredom and dissatisfaction, but too much stress or constant arousal leads to serious and negative psychological and physiological conditions. Thus, a person requires a certain amount of stress to function successfully in the world.

—*Serena Wadhwa*

COGNITIVE BEHAVIORAL INTEGRATION

Although purely behavioral and true cognitive theories may seem in direct opposition to each other from a theoretical perspective, they actually complement each other in clinical and therapeutic applications.

Albert Ellis's rational emotive behavior therapy (REBT) was one of the first cognitive therapies to also incorporate a focus on behavior. REBT is a comprehensive approach to treatment that analyzes behavior, cognitions, and emotions in an interconnected way (Ellis, 2004). The origins of REBT can actually be dated back to

Epictetus, who is quoted as saying that "[m]en are disturbed not by things, but by the view which they take of them" (White, 1983).

According to Ellis, problems are a result of misperceptions and cognitive errors about what is perceived, over- and underreactions to our environment, and dysfunctional patterns of behavior. One of the major principles of REBT is that we label our emotional responses according to our internal evaluations, interpretations, and personal philosophies of life. Rational emotive therapists believe that when people experience unhealthy emotions (e.g., panic, depression, rage), it is typically due to their unrealistic and illogical ideas. A goal of therapy is to identify the irrational philosophies of life that the client believes. REBT interventions work to replace self-defeating philosophies of life with ones that will better serve the person, and help the individual to work toward realistic thinking. Realistic thinking is based on unbiased facts about life, frustration tolerance, and self-acceptance (Ellis, 2004).

Another major figure responsible for the synthesis of cognitive therapies and behavior therapies is Aaron T. Beck (Beck, 1970). Initially Beck's model was referred to as *cognitive theory,* but later it became known as *cognitive behavior theory,* with its clinical application being called *cognitive behavior therapy (CBT).* In CBT, the client and therapist work together to identify and resolve the client's problems. Therapists help clients change their thinking, behavior, and emotional responses through a process of identifying and countering a client's maladaptive thoughts and behavioral responses. Many outcome studies and meta-analyses have found this form of treatment to be effective in treating depression, anxiety disorders, eating disorders, and many other known psychiatric disorders, as well as being applicable to general stress management (Hofmann, Asnaani, Vonk, Sawyer, & Fang, 2012). When individuals are under stress, their perceptions of their environment can become distorted and dysfunctional. The premise of CBT involves testing the validity of these distorted thoughts and restructuring those that are identified as harmful and unrealistic. This process typically results in a reduction of stress and an improvement in behavior (Hofmann et al., 2012).

For the purpose of this chapter, and to determine the cognitive behavioral perspective on stress, we must first create a working definition of *stress.*

WHAT IS STRESS?

Stress is a complex construct—and an overused part of our modern lexicon. Part of the challenge is that stress can mean very different things to different people, at different times, and in different contexts. Stress is not a constant construct that can be doled out in equal magnitude to study participants. The experience of stress is moderated by many cognitive, social, and behavioral factors that can be difficult to identify, describe, and measure. Although the physiological experience is similar for everyone, the way in which this experience is interpreted will vary from individual to individual (Lazarus, 1993).

A COGNITIVE BEHAVIORAL VIEW OF STRESS

The first real introduction of cognitive variables as playing an important role in the experience of and reaction to stress began in the 1950s with R. S. Lazarus, as he and his colleagues moved from a purely stimulus-response (S-R) approach to one that also takes into consideration individual differences of the organism (S-O-R) and how those differences interact with the stimulus and response.

Stress Appraisal and Coping Model

Lazarus's model has been referred to by a number of labels over the years (e.g., cognitive mediational theory, cognitive relational theory, transaction theory of stress), but at its core it has always retained the same emphasis on the two-step appraisal process. Inherent in this process is the interaction of the situational variable of the stressor, the organism variable of perception of the stressor, and expectations about coping mechanisms (Lazarus, 1993).

According to the stress appraisal and coping model laid out by Lazarus, and expanded upon by Folkman and Lazarus, stress is the result of an inequity between one's demands and resources (Lazarus, 1993). Thus, stress is experienced when the pressure of a situation exceeds the ability to cope with what is happening. The actual type, strength, or enormity of the stressor itself is far less important than the way in which it is interpreted. Therefore, individuals, their perceptions of what is "stressful," and what coping mechanisms they are prepared for are going to result in very different outcome experiences from one person to the next. What is significantly stressful to you may be of only minor significance to another.

The two-step appraisal process begins with primary appraisal. The person first determines the degree of relevance of the situation: Does this get in the way of my goals? The person next determines if the stressful situation involves harm or loss, a threat for future harm or loss, or a challenge that can be informative and ultimately helpful. The secondary appraisal process involves assessing the coping mechanisms available to deal with the stressful situation, and may also involve a reappraisal of the situation itself (e.g., determination of changing the stressor). Internal and external coping options will both be assessed. Internal options include constructs such as willpower, fortitude, and the like. External options include such things as social support (Lazarus, 1993).

Coping styles can be classified according to whether they are primarily problem focused or emotion focused (Lazarus, 1993). Problem-focused coping strategies are those we employ when we feel that we can control a situation and can manage the source of the stress. A problem-focused strategy might involve defining the problem, identifying alternative solutions, and learning new strategies for managing the stressor. Emotion-focused coping strategies are typically used when we feel that controlling the situation is not an option, and therefore determine that we must instead control our reaction to or appraisal of the situation. Typical emotion-focused coping strategies include avoidance, denying the impact of a stressor (e.g., "It doesn't matter," "It doesn't really bother me"), acceptance of the negative outcome, seeking of emotional support, expressions of anger (often inappropriate in intensity or direction), or dulling one's affect (often by using or abusing substances).

Models such as the stress appraisal and coping model are considered advances over the earlier stimulus-response models in that they explain the role of individual difference factors in the experience of stress. This accounts for the fluid nature of the appraisal process from one individual to another, and even variances in one individual at two different points in time. The model has been criticized for its interconnection of the primary and secondary appraisal processes, its difficulty in labeling the factors involved in assessing the experience of stress, and its lack of empirical evidence (Steele & Aronson, 1995).

Social Cognitive Theory

The social cognitive theory of stress stemmed from the work of Bandura (Pisanti, 2012), and is consistent with Lazarus's and Folkman's stress and coping theory (Lazarus, 1993). Bandura defined *self-efficacy* as a person's belief about his or her ability to reach a goal. Self-efficacy therefore involves assessment of the demands of the task, and the belief that one has the skills necessary to obtain that goal (Bandura, 2007). People who would describe themselves as efficacious in coping with stress would have strong coping self-efficacy (CSE). Thus, having a high level of CSE can be advantageous in managing stress. During the primary appraisal process, individuals would determine the scope of the problem, its importance to them, and the likelihood of harm, loss, or challenge. During the secondary appraisal, the individuals determine if an outcome is controllable, and whether or not they can implement effective coping strategies. Like general self-efficacy, coping self-efficacy is situation specific. High CSE has been associated with positive stress responses through physiological measures, as well as measures of psychological adjustment, in a range of different studies with varying types of stressors (Kraaij, Garnefski, & Maes, 2002; Bandura, Taylor, Williams, Mefford, & Barchas, 1985). These studies have included stressful life changes such as adjustment to chronic illness, aging, dealing with natural disasters, aggression, and physical assault (Pisanti, 2012). Overall, these studies have supported the role of CSE in predicting the degree to which individuals will develop adaptive responses to both positive stress experiences (those that are ultimately viewed as challenges) and negative ones (those that are viewed as obstacles).

Cognitive Adaptation

The theory of cognitive adaptation was developed by S. E. Taylor in 1983 to describe the process of adjusting to threatening situations. Much of Taylor's research is based in the world of health psychology, and focuses on people's responses to medical conditions. She acknowledges that the majority of people face major life setbacks or challenges at one time or another (e.g., personal illness, death of a family member) and are able to recover from them, and perhaps even prosper following them, without professional help. According to this theory, the adjustment process revolves around three themes: finding meaning in the experience, making an effort to regain mastery over the event, and restoring self-esteem (Taylor, 1983). These processes entail trying to understand the event, determine the significance of the event, gain control over the event (and its likelihood of reoccurrence), and figure out a way to feel good about oneself again.

Inherent in the cognitive adaptation model is the importance of illusions, such as the belief that cancer will not reoccur due to dietary changes. Although Taylor defends the notion of illusions being a productive component of the coping process, one can maintain that *illusion* is merely a term to describe the cognitive lens through which one sees the world (Taylor, 1983). Through a number of cognitive therapy techniques, this lens can be altered to be very adaptive to recovery from threatening events.

Cognitive Activation Theory of Stress

The cognitive activation theory of stress (CATS) explains the stress response within the framework of a neurophysiological activation theory. Stress activates an arousal response and is seen as having some adaptive qualities: increased wakefulness, increased vigilance, and so on. The *stress response* is said to occur whenever there is a disparity between what is expected and what truly exists. The stress response is tantamount to the alarm in a homeostatic system. According to this theory, the physiological experience of stress continues until this disparity is resolved or determined to be unimportant. The reason that this seemingly physiologically based theory is actually considered cognitive in nature is because the result of a stress reaction is based on the cognitive evaluation of expectancies and personal resources (Eriksen & Ursin, 2002).

Self-Regulation Model

The self-regulation model is a model of goal-directed behavior, developed by Carver and Scheier, to study people's ability to cope with chronic illness (Baldwin, Kellerman, & Christensen, 2010). According to this theory, people experience stress

STRESS INOCULATION TRAINING

Developed in the mid-1970s by Dr. Donald Meichenbaum for people suffering from anxiety-related disorders, and grounded in cognitive behavior therapy, stress inoculation training (SIT) is based on the concept of inoculation. The idea of inoculation comes from research on vaccinations, where exposure to a killed or weakened virus stimulates the body to develop the defenses to protect itself from a full attack, thus allowing the organism a better chance to survive. From this perspective, Meichenbaum developed the concept of SIT so that individuals experience small doses of "stress" that help prepare them for full attacks and provide the opportunity to develop resilience (Meichenbaum, 2007).

Another construct of SIT is the notion that, because stress is an individual process, how a person perceives, understands, and subsequently copes with the emotional and psychological aspects of stress will be vastly different from individual to individual. SIT thus is flexible enough to account for these differences. According to Meichenbaum (2007), SIT is based on cognitive behavioral therapy and is an adjunct tool to be used with other interventions.

There are three phases to SIT: (1) education; (2) skill development; and (3) application. In the first phase, the focus is on establishing rapport and developing a "discovery" relationship. This includes various processes and activities focused on the acquisition of knowledge. In the second phase, clients develop skills based on the knowledge they have acquired and practice of these skills both in the clinical setting and outside the clinical setting (Meichenbaum, 2007). Finally, the third phase involves generalizing the newly acquired skills in a variety of contexts. Meichenbaum emphasizes that while SIT is based on knowledge and skills, there is a high narrative component to this intervention and that a basis of its success is clients' reconceptualizations of their understanding of the nature of stress in their lives and their coping abilities.

Although this intervention was initially developed for people with anxiety-related disorders, much of the research on its efficacy has used case studies, nonempirical reports, and studies that lacked appropriate control groups (Saunders, Driskell, Johnston, & Salas, 1996). Thus, Saunders and colleagues did a meta-analysis of studies conducted at the time to determine the efficacy of SIT and the conditions it most effectively treated. Of the 200 studies that addressed SIT, only 70 of these met the criteria set forth by the authors for the meta-analysis. These studies included 1,837 subjects. Their analysis demonstrated that SIT was an effective intervention for anxiety.

—Serena Wadhwa

when they encounter obstacles in reaching their goals, and *coping* is described as any effort toward self-regulation while under stress.

This relationship is influenced by focus and abstraction. The *focus* of a goal is defined as either approach or avoidance. For example, a goal to stay healthy is an approach goal, whereas a goal to avoid lung cancer is an avoidance goal; however, both are directed at certain health behaviors.

According to this model, goals are organized hierarchically, with the more abstract goals (e.g., "stay healthy) at the top, and the more specific, measureable subgoals (e.g., "exercise every other day") lower in the hierarchy. If the onset of stress impedes one's ability to stay focused on a goal, one must create new, lower-order goals that allow continued progress toward the original goal, reassess a goal if it becomes unattainable, or create new goals altogether. Failure to do so will result in stress (Baldwin, Kellerman, & Christensen, 2010).

SUMMARY

Stress can readily be viewed from a cognitive behavioral perspective. To the extent that stress can be quantified, not all stressors will lead to the same reaction in all people, or even in the same person at different times. The manner in which individuals perceive the situation, themselves, and the availability of coping strategies becomes an important factor in determining their response. The interconnectedness of cognitions, emotions, and behaviors is key to the experience of stress as viewed through a cognitive behavioral lens.

REFERENCES AND FURTHER READING

Baldwin, A. S., Kellerman, Q. D., & Christensen, A. J. (2010). Coping with chronic illness. In J. M. Suls, K. W. Davidson, & R. M. Kaplan (Eds.), *Handbook of health psychology and behavioral medicine* (pp. 494–507). New York, NY: Guilford Press.

Bandura, A. (2007). Albert Bandura. In L. Gardner & R. William (Eds.), *A history of psychology in autobiography* (pp. 43–75). Washington, DC: American Psychological Association.

Bandura, A., Taylor, C., Williams, S., Mefford, I., & Barchas, J. (1985). Catecholamine secretion as a function of perceived coping self-efficacy. *Journal of Consulting and Clinical Psychology, 53,* 406–414.

Beck, A. T. (1970). Cognitive therapy: Nature and relation to behavior therapy. *Behavior Therapy, 1,* 184–200.

Ellis, A. (2004). *The road to tolerance: The philosophy of rational emotive behavior therapy.* New York, NY: Prometheus Books.

Eriksen, H. R., & Ursin, H. (2002). Sensitization and subjective health complaints. *Scandinavian Journal of Psychology, 43,* 189–196.

Hofmann, S. G., Asnaani, A., Vonk, I. J. J., Sawyer, A. T., & Fang, A. (2012). The efficacy of cognitive behavioral therapy: A review of meta-analyses. *Cognitive Therapy Research, 36*, 427–440.

Johnston, C. A., Moreno, J. P., Regas, K., Tyler, C., & Foreyt, J. P. (2012). The application of the Yerkes–Dodson law in a childhood weight management program: Examining weight dissatisfaction. *Journal of Pediatric Psychology, 37*(6), 674–679. doi:10.1093/jpepsy/jss040.

Kraaij, V., Garnefski, N., & Maes, S. (2002). The joint effects of stress, coping, and coping resources on depressive symptoms in the elderly. *Anxiety, Stress and Coping, 15*, 163–177.

Lazarus, R. S. (1993). From psychological stress to the emotions: A history of changing outlooks. *Annual Review of Psychology, 44*, 1–21.

McLeod, S. A. (2007). Pavlov's dogs. Retrieved from http://www.simplypsychology.org/pavlov.html.

Meichenbaum, D. (2007). Stress inoculation training: A preventative and treatment approach. *Principles and Practice of Stress Management, 3*, 497–518.

Meichenbaum, D. H., & Deffenbacher, J. L. (1988). Stress inoculation training. *The Counseling Psychologist, 16*(1), 69–90.

Pavlov, I. P. (1927) *Conditioned reflexes: An investigation of the physiological activity of the cerebral cortex* (G. V. Anrep, Trans. & Ed.). London, UK: Oxford University Press.

Piaget, J. (1936). *Origins of intelligence in the child.* London, UK: Routledge & Kegan Paul.

Pisanti, R. (2012). Coping self-efficacy and psychological distress: Results from an Italian study on nurses. *The European Health Psychologist, 14*(1), 11–14.

Rotter, J. (1966). Generalized expectancies for internal versus external control of reinforcements. *Psychological Monographs, 80*(1), Whole No. 609.

Saunders, T., Driskell, J. E., Johnston, J. H., & Salas, E. (1996). The effect of stress inoculation training on anxiety and performance. *Journal of Occupational Health Psychology, 1*(2), 170.

Schachter, S., & Singer, J. (1962). Cognitive, social and physiological determinants of emotional state. *Psychology Review, 69*, 379–399.

Skinner, B. F. (1938). *The behavior of organisms: An experimental analysis.* New York, NY: Appleton-Century.

Steele, C. M., & Aronson, J. (1995). Stereotype threat and the intellectual test performance of African Americans. *Journal of Personality and Social Psychology, 52*, 613–629.

Taylor, S. E. (1983). Adjustment to threatening events: A theory of cognitive adaptation. *American Psychologist, 38*, 1161–1173.

von Gehlen, J., & Sachse, P. (2015). Benefits of distraction. *Social Behavior and Personality, 43*(4), 601–612.

Watson, J. B. (1924). *Behaviorism.* New Brunswick, Canada: Transaction.

White, N. P. (1983). *The handbook of Epictetus.* Indianapolis, IN: Hackett. Retrieved from https://www.google.com/?gws_rd=ssl#q=epictetus+quotes.

Yerkes, R. M., & Dodson, J. D. (1908). The relation of strength of stimulus to rapidity of habit formation. *Journal of Comparative Neurology and Psychology, 18*, 459–482.

2

How Stress Affects Human Development

Joseph Day

INTRODUCTION

Exposure to stress is an essential part of human development. Whether in the form of threats or opportunities (e.g., first day of school, getting married, illness, death of a close relative), stress is a crucial part of every person's life. From a developmental perspective, the nature and frequency of early stress exposure help to structure our later experience of and reactions to stressful situations. For example, the first day of school is often a stressful experience for both parent and child. Several important factors determine how that stress is experienced, including the neurophysiology of both parent and child, the type of attachment that exists between the two, and the environmental context. As noted in later sections, early childhood exposure to stress helps to shape one's neurophysiological stress response. Moderators of this response include both the level of attachment one has with caregivers and the environmental context. Thus, as development proceeds, the type and level of early exposure to stress, the level of attachment to caregivers, and the environmental context help to determine how stress is experienced over the life span.

The stress response system is activated by environmental challenges that ultimately lead to physiological and/or behavioral adjustments (*allostasis*). In both the short and long terms, the stress response system facilitates these adjustments through the coordination of body and brain responses to challenges. Research findings indicate that early exposure to both adverse and supportive environments may elicit "enhanced neurobiological mediated sensitivity to context" (Boyce & Ellis, 2005, p. 271; Del Giudice, Ellis, & Shirtcliff, 2013) suggesting that from an evolutionary perspective the stress response system has the potential to override genetics and cause adaptations according to early life experience, thus playing a central role in brain development and future response to stress.

A brief overview of the neurophysiology of the stress response system enhances understanding of its role and its psychobiology in developmental stages. It also emphasizes the importance of individual differences as a way to approach questions about stress experiences during development and the consequences of those experiences on development.

NEUROPHYSIOLOGY OF STRESS

As described by Claude Bernard and in later research by Walter Cannon and Hans Selye (Cooper, 2008; Selye, 1973), signals of threat to survival or well-being from the environment stimulate a pattern of intricate, highly coordinated responses within the neural circuitry of the brain and the peripheral neuroendocrine pathways that regulate metabolic, immunologic, and other physiological functions. This collection of responses, which is designed to prepare the organism for challenge or threats, is more commonly known as *allostasis*. When we are threatened (whether perceptually or in reality), two distinct but interconnected systems are stimulated.

The first system, known as the sympathetic-adrenal-medullary (SAM) system, is a component of the sympathetic division of the autonomic nervous system, the portion of the nervous system that regulates and controls the glands, muscles, and organs throughout the body. The SAM system releases epinephrine (adrenaline) and norepinephrine from the medulla or center of the adrenal glands (that sit atop the kidneys) and orchestrates the fight-or-flight response (Vollmer, 1996). When these cells are activated, their secretions bind to various receptors in many target organs, which in turn create physiological changes. For example, receptors in the heart and gut cause changes in such things as heart rate, the amount of blood pumped from the heart with each beat, and vasodilation in muscles and constriction of blood vessels in the skin and gut. These changes ensure blood supply to the brain and muscles. Additionally, epinephrine stimulates glycogenolysis (the breakdown of glycogen to glucose), resulting in increased serum levels of glucose and thus energy to fuel defensive responses (Tsapatsaris & Breslin, 1989). The SAM system appears to support alertness, arousal, and narrowing of attention, along with participating in processes that activate the second arm of the stress response system, the hypothalamic-pituitary-adrenocortical system (HPA).

In the adrenal cortex of the adrenal glands, the HPA system produces cortisol, a substance that primarily targets the brain (Bohus, de Kloet, & Veldhuis, 1982). Cortisol differs from epinephrine in several ways. Unlike epinephrine, cortisol production takes longer to get to peak levels, and many of its impacts occur through changes in gene expression (de Kloet, 1991). Thus, cortisol has epigenetic effects, in that over time the accumulation of negative influences, such as stressful life

HANS SELYE (1907–1982)

Hans Selye has been called the "father" of stress. Born in Vienna, Austria, Selye began medical school at the age of 17 at the German University of Prague. His interest in how diseases manifested in individuals and in the effects of certain hormones on the body determined the focus of his work, both as a medical student and while at McGill University in Canada in the early 1930s, where he continued his work as a postdoctoral student. In 1936, he adopted the word *stress* to explain what happens in the body as a result of exposure to various stimuli (temperature, exertion, hormones, etc.), a discovery that he actually stumbled upon as he was seeking data that might identify a new hormone. When the data did not provide evidence of such a hormone, he eventually returned to some ideas he had had as a medical student at Prague, which related to the manifestations and commonalities of symptoms within individuals. Eventually, as he refocused on the data, his research led to what we now know as the "General Adaptation Syndrome" and the identification of stress. The General Adaptation Syndrome describes what happens in the body when stress occurs and hormones and chemicals elicited by the "fight or flight" response produce changes in the body over a period of time. What Dr. Selye also discovered is that if the body is exposed to these hormones and chemicals for a sufficiently long time, physical diseases can result from the chronic exposure.

As Dr. Selye became known for his research, and began speaking on the effects of the hormones on the body and his concept of stress, he later elaborated on the idea of the General Adaptation Syndrome, which moves from the acute fight-or-fight response, to the resistance response, and eventually to the chronic response. He also discovered how these changes make the body more vulnerable to physical diseases, such as heart diseases, sleep problems, skin disorders, and other physical disorders, which he called "diseases of adaptation."

Dr. Selye authored more than 33 books and published more than 1,700 articles. In 1978 he opened The American Institute of Stress, a clearinghouse of information and services related to stress. Selye died in 1982 in Montreal, Canada, at the age of 75.

—*Serena Wadhwa*

circumstances, can determine which genes are turned on either temporarily or permanently. For example, epigenetic effects may help to explain why genetically identical twins, though similar in many ways (including having the same genome), can exhibit different behaviors, skills, health, and achievement in school and in the workplace as a function of their separate exposure to lived experiences (Janusek, Cooper, & Mathews, 2012; Johnstone & Baylin, 2010). The impact of cortisol is slower, but it continues for longer periods (de Kloet, Rots, & Cools, 1996). The role of HPA in the stress response system is complex and not fully understood (Sapolsky, Romero, & Munck, 2000). Its activity seems to support or permit acute fight-or-flight responses, and contradictorily serves to reduce the impact of fight-or-flight reactions. (These hormones are explained in Chapter 9 on stress hormones.)

Connection of the SAM and HPA systems occurs at the level of the hypothalamus, a structure in the brain's limbic system that appears to support a variety of functions, including behavior, motivation, and memory, and may ultimately be responsible for one's emotional life. Thus, SAM and HPA combine autonomic and endocrine functions with behavior and are known to be coordinated by a complex set of brain structures (Gunnar & Vazquez, 2006; Palkovits, 1987). The complexity of these systems and chemical productions influences emotional and cognitive states. The interplay of cognitive capacity, emotional experiences, and physiological reactions are also influenced by the varying demands and pressures throughout the life span.

LEVELS OF STRESS AND CHILDHOOD DEVELOPMENT

Three levels of stress are recognized in childhood: positive, tolerable, and toxic (Shonkoff, Boyce, & McEwen, 2009). Positive stress is an important aspect of healthy development and is seen in the context of stable and supportive relationships that facilitate adaptive responses. Positive stress helps to restore the stress response system to baseline status and is important in the development of preschool milestones such as fine and gross motor skills, language, and cognitive and social skills (Shonkoff et al., 2009).

Tolerable stress denotes a potentially disruptive biological state that is buffered by supportive relationships (caregivers) that facilitate adaptive coping (Shonkoff et al., 2009). For example, death or serious illness of a parent or other loved one, homelessness, or a natural disaster can be precipitants of stress (Shonkoff et al., 2009). Characteristically, tolerable stress occurs within a time-limited period, and within a supportive environment that helps to gives the brain time to recover from potentially damaging effects.

Lastly, toxic stress is characterized by vigorous, recurrent, and/or extended activation of the body's stress response systems in the absence of a supportive caregiving environment (Shonkoff et al., 2009). Extreme poverty, recurrent physical and/or emotional abuse, chronic neglect, severe maternal depression, parental substance abuse, and family violence can all be precipitating events. Toxic stress can disrupt how the brain is wired, affect multiple organ systems, and lead to stress-related disease and intellectual impairment in adulthood. Toxic stress is associated with an increase in childhood exposure to adversity, which leads to chronic, long-term overexposure to cortisol and the other stress hormones that can disturb many of the body's normal processes. This kind of stress is often associated with developmental delays and later chronic health problems, including heart disease, diabetes, substance abuse, and depression.

SOCIAL REGULATION OF STRESS NEUROBIOLOGY

Caregivers

Infant relatedness appears to be affected by the security of the infant-caregiver attachment relationship (Gunnar & Quevedo, 2007). Adult caregivers provide children with close social relationships, which help to modulate and control physiological and behavioral responses to stressors and possibly lay the groundwork for emotional regulation (Stansbury & Gunnar, 1994). Neglect and/or abuse by caregivers or others (toxic stress) have negative effects on the development of secure attachment relationships and can lead to lifelong behavioral and pathophysiological problems, sometimes including hyperreactivity to stress. These effects can be seen in brain structure and function changes and in the risk for later development of depression and posttraumatic stress disorder (PTSD). It is believed that this attachment security is an important mediator of the physiological stress-response system. Research shows that insecure attachment relationships and traumatic family experiences both lead to higher cortisol levels in the children involved. Gunnar and Donzella (2002) reported that toddlers who did not have secure attachments had higher cortisol measurements, in both lab and natural settings. Children who grow up in families where they experience fighting, severe types of punishment, and conflict are also adversely affected, as shown by their cortisol levels, which were compared after traumatic events against less traumatic days (Flinn & England, 1995). Higher cortisol levels have also been shown to predict behavioral problems in school-aged children (Essex, Klein, Cho, & Kalin, 2002), and to indicate both dysfunctional parent attitudes and symptoms of anxiety and depression in the child (Granger, Weisz, & McCracken, 1996), perhaps due to insecure attachments between parents and children.

Adult caregivers and family influences appear to be powerful regulators of the HPA system. It seems clear that when parenting is inadequate and/or is the cause of threat, relationships can be a major source of physiological stress for children, because without the close social relationships provided by the parent the child may have difficulty modulating and controlling physiological and behavioral responses to stressors. Conversely, appropriate caregiving, within the context of positive school and neighborhood experiences, allows children to elicit help by expressing negative emotions without triggering the endocrine component of the stress response, and can prevent elevation in cortisol levels for infants and children even during threatening external events. Thus, developmentally, when children have appropriate caregiving that permits healthier expression of negative emotions, their systems can better moderate the effects of the stress response and diminish the reactivity in future stressful situations.

In general, there appears to be a continuum, on one end of which safe, protected, low-stress environments enhance the development of a stress response system that is responsive to social learning and engagement with the outside world. The child on this end of the continuum is better able to benefit from social resources and opportunities (Del Giudice et al., 2013). These children will rarely experience strong, sustained activation of the SAM and HPA systems; because of the high quality of their environments, they will most likely experience a pattern of low-key, short-lived activations followed by quick recovery. In contrast, for children at the other end of the continuum, reared in extremely dangerous environments categorized by chronic toxic stress, the balance shifts toward low responsiveness to social learning and engagement, especially for males (Boyce & Ellis, 2005; Del Giudice et al., 2013). This informational insulation from environmental signals of threat is an asset, not a weakness, in such circumstances, as it allows insensitivity to threats, dangers, social feedback, and the poor social context. Although this interpersonal style may act to shield the child from social rejection, disapproval, and feelings of shame, the concomitant psychophysiological status promotes the development of manipulative and antisocial characteristics.

LIFELONG CONSEQUENCES: SCHOOL-AGE CHILDREN AND SOCIALIZATION

The stress response system in older children stems from earlier exposure to varying levels of both adverse and supportive environments (as previously discussed) and its reactions to social learning and engagement with the outside world. The school-age child is exposed to more complex environments and contexts, such as school, peer, and adult relationships, which demand the development and use of social skills such as control of behaviors, listening, and taking emotional responsibility. The child's openness to social learning and willingness to engage with the outside world are important factors in the socialization process. Normal development during the school-age years involves the child moving from playing alone to having multiple friends and social groups. Peer interaction and acceptance become increasingly important; however, if the child has been exposed to chronic stress with little or no support, normal socialization is difficult. For children reared in low-stress, supportive environments, the socialization process (developing friendships and dealing with rejection) can be stressful yet positive. However, for children reared in high-stress/low-support environments, these same events may be seen as threatening, leading to avoidance and withdrawal.

Without a supportive context, stress can become chronic and toxic and can have a dramatic effect on learning and social development. Toxic stress can interfere with executive functions such as attention, memory, organization, and integration; over time, it can damage brain cells and shrink main memory structures. The pivotal role of adults in the psychosocial regulation of stress in early childhood has been confirmed by research showing that elevations in cortisol levels in childcare settings are not observed when the child receives individualized, supportive care from care providers (Dettling, Parker, Lane, Sebanc, & Gunnar, 2000). Similarly, Coie, Dodge, and Kupersmidt (1990) found that peer-rejected children produce higher levels of cortisol in the preschool classroom in comparison to average or popular children. In general, these rejected children demonstrated poor social skills and poor emotional regulation, both of which are associated with poorer peer relations and higher cortisol levels (Gunnar, Sebanc, Tout, Donzella, & van Dulmen, 2003). Higher levels of cortisol production have also been found in socially neglected youths who spend hours alone even when they are physically present with peers (e.g., at school; Adam, 2006). Our understanding of the psychosocial pathways by which these youths experience stress is quite rudimentary, though it seems probable that aversive interactions such as social threats and disappointments are negative factors along with poor family, peer, and friendship relationships.

ADOLESCENT TRANSITION

Very little is known about normative variation in the stress response over the adolescent transition. The psychosocial changes associated with the biological processes of puberty may shift the child's stress neurobiology to adult responsive patterns (Spear, 2000). The combination of biological modifications and social transitions creates an increasingly complex milieu that exposes the adolescent to many stressors and challenges. Many of the past explorations of this subject have studied these factors in isolation and have not focused on their interaction.

Examinations of neuroendocrine and cardiovascular responses to performance and peer rejection stressors over the adolescent transition in a normative sample revealed that adolescents showed significantly greater cortisol and stress responses than did children. The primary task of adolescents is identity formation, which allows for the transition from "safe childhood" to a more complex adult world. For adolescents exposed to low stress and high support during earlier stages of development, the increased physiological stress responses may facilitate adaptation to the new challenges of adolescence and adulthood (including the adolescent identity crisis). Conversely, for adolescents exposed to high stress and little support, this shift may tip the balance toward dysregulation of the stress response, and may herald depression and other psychopathology (Baumrind, 1991; Stroud et al., 2009).

ADULTS

The long-term effects of early stress exposure on the brain suggest that early stress exposure can have effects on behavior, physiology, and health that extend into adulthood. Healthy adults who grew up in risky families (i.e., family settings that are punitive, neglectful, highly chaotic, and/or conflict-ridden) displayed increased evidence of changes in the neural mechanisms underlying emotional regulation and threat detection. Hence, being raised in a risky family confers a higher lifetime risk for a range of mental and physical health disorders. Studies suggest that the brain is a living record of stress exposure across the life span. Stress exposure is cumulative over one's lifetime, so as one ages there is increased opportunity for stress effects, psychological insult, and trauma to cause further changes in the brain (other than gray-matter changes observed in normal aging).

CONCLUSIONS

The critical impact of a child's early exposure to adversity cannot be overstated. Environmental impacts such as the chronic stress of poverty can actually affect whether and how genes are expressed, how they are turned on and off, and even whether some are expressed at all. Importantly, stress is not monolithic. The effects of positive stress (e.g., overcoming the challenges and frustrations of learning a new, stimulating task) can be helpful and valuable. In contrast, severe, intense, chronic adversity—toxic stress—can produce harmful effects on the developing brain systems that control adaptation to stressful events. Similarly, interactions with parents, caregivers, and other adults are equally important in shaping the neurophysiology of the stress response and laying down the foundation for later developmental outcomes, from academic performance to mental health and relational skills.

REFERENCES AND FURTHER READING

Adam, E. K. (2006). Transactions among trait and state emotion and adolescent diurnal and momentary cortisol activity in naturalistic settings. *Psychoneuroendocrinology, 31*, 664–679.

Baumrind, D. (1991). Effective parenting during the early adolescent transition. In P. A. Cowan & E. M. Hetherington (Eds.), *Family transitions* (Vol. 2, pp. 111–163). Millsdale, NJ: Lawrence Erlbaum Associates.

Bohus, B., de Kloet, E. R., & Veldhuis, H. D. (1982). Adrenal steroids and behavioral adaptation: Relationship to brain corticoid receptors. In D. Granten & D. W. Pfaff (Eds.), *Current topics in neuroendocrinology* (pp. 107–148). Berlin, Germany: Springer-Verlag.

Boyce, W. T., & Ellis, B. J. (2005). Biological sensitivity to context: I. An evolutionary-developmental theory of the origins and functions of stress reactivity. *Development and Psychopathology, 17*(2), 271–301.

Coie, J. D., Dodge, K. A., & Kupersmidt, J. B. (1990). Peer group behavior and social status. In S. R. Asher & J. D. Coie (Eds.), *Peer rejection in childhood* (pp. 17–59). New York, NY: Cambridge University Press.

Cooper, S. J. (2008). From Claude Bernard to Walter Cannon: Emergence of the concept of homeostasis. *Appetite, 51*(3), 419–427.

de Kloet, E. R. (1991). Brain corticosteroid receptor balance and homeostatic control. *Frontiers in Neuroendocrinology, 12*(2), 95–164.

de Kloet, E. R, Rots, N. Y., & Cools, A. R. (1996). Brain-corticosteroid hormone dialogue: Slow and persistent. *Cellular and Molecular Neurobiology, 16,* 345–356.

Del Giudice, M., Ellis, B. J., & Shirtcliff, E. A. (2013). Making sense of stress: An evolutionary-developmental framework. In G. Laviola & S. Macri, *Adaptive and maladaptive aspects of developmental stress* (pp. 23–43). New York, NY: Springer.

Dettling, A. C., Parker, S. W., Lane, S., Sebanc, A., & Gunnar, M. R. (2000). Quality of care and temperament determine whether cortisol levels rise over the day for children in full-day childcare. *Psychoneuroendocrinology, 25*(8), 819–836.

Essex, M. J., Klein, M., Cho, E., & Kalin, N. H. (2002). Maternal stress beginning in infancy may sensitize children to later stress exposure: Effects on cortisol and behavior. *Biological Psychiatry, 52*(8), 776–784.

Flinn, M. V., & England, B. G. (1995). Childhood stress and family environment. *Current Anthropology, 36*(5), 854–866.

Ge, X., Conger, R. D., & Elder, G. H., Jr. (2001). Pubertal transition, stressful life events, and the emergence of gender differences in adolescent depressive symptoms. *Developmental Psychology, 37*(3), 404–417.

Granger, D. A., Weisz, J. R., & McCracken, J. T. (1996). Reciprocal influences among adrenocortical activation, psychosocial processes, and the behavioral adjustment of clinic-referred children. *Child Development, 67,* 3259–3260.

Gunnar, M., & Donzella, B. (2002). Social regulation of the cortisol levels in early human development. *Psychoneuroendocrinology, 27*(1–2), 199–220.

Gunnar, M., & Quevedo, K. (2007). The neurobiology of stress and development. *Annual Review of Psychology, 58,* 145–173.

Gunnar, M., Sebanc, A. M., Tout, K., Donzella, B., & van Dulmen, M. M. H. (2003). Peer rejection, temperament, and cortisol activity in preschoolers. *Developmental Psychobiology, 43*(4), 346–358.

Gunnar, M. R., & Vazquez, D. (2006). Stress neurobiology and developmental psychopathology. In D. Cicchetti & D. J. Cohen (Eds.), *Developmental psychopathology* (2nd ed., Vol. 2, pp. 533–577). Hoboken, NJ: John Wiley & Sons.

Janusek, L. W., Cooper, D. T., & Mathews, H. L. (2012). Epigenetics and stress: A life course perspective. In V. H. Rice (Ed.), *Handbook of stress, coping, and health: Implications for nursing research, theory, and practice* (2nd ed., pp. 71–96). Thousand Oaks, CA: Sage.

Johnstone, S. E., & Baylin, S. B. (2010). Stress and the epigenetic landscape: A link to the pathobiology of human diseases? *Nature Reviews Genetics, 11*(11), 806–812.

McEwen, B. S. (2007). Physiology and neurobiology of stress and adaptation: Central role of the brain. *Physiological Reviews, 87*, 873–904. doi:10.1152/physrev.00041.2006.

National Scientific Council on the Developing Child. (2010). *Early experiences can alter gene expression and affect long-term development (Working Paper No. 10)*. Retrieved from http://www.developingchild.net.

Palkovits, M. (1987). Organization of the stress response at the anatomical level. In E. R. de Kloet, V. M. Wiegant, & D. de Wied (Eds.), *Progress in brain research* (pp. 47–55). Amsterdam, The Netherlands: Elsevier.

Sapolsky, R. M., Romero, L. M., & Munck, A. U. (2000). How do glucocorticoids influence stress responses? Integrating permissive, suppressive, stimulatory, and preparative actions. *Endocrine Reviews, 21*(1), 55–89.

Selye, H. (1973). The evolution of the stress concept. *American Scientist, 61*(6), 692–699.

Selye, H. (2016). Canadian Medical Hall of Fame. Retrieved from http://cdnmedhall.org/inductees/dr-hans-selye.

Shonkoff, J. P., Boyce, W. T., & McEwen, B. S. (2009). Neuroscience, molecular biology, and the childhood roots of health disparities: Building a new framework for health promotion and disease prevention. *JAMA, 301*(21), 2252–2259.

Spear, L. P. (2000). The adolescent brain and age-related behavioral manifestations. *Neuroscience and Biobehavioral Reviews, 24*(4), 417–463.

Stansbury, K., & Gunnar, M. (1994). Adrenocortical activity and emotion regulation. *Monographs for the Society of Research in Child Development, 59*(2–3), 108–134.

Stroud, L. R., Foster, E., Papandonatos, G. D., Handwerger, K., Granger, D. A., Kivlighan, K. T., & Niaura, R. (2009). Stress response and the adolescent transition: Performance versus peer rejection stressors. *Development and Psychopathology, 21*(1), 47–68.

Tsapatsaris, N. P., & Breslin, D. J. (1989). Physiology of the adrenal medulla. *Urologic Clinics of North America, 16*(3), 439–445.

Vollmer, R. R. (1996). Selective neural regulation of epinephrine and norepinephrine cells in the adrenal medulla—cardiovascular implications. *Clinical and Experimental Hypertension Journal, 18*, 731–751.

3

Ecological Theories of Stress

Tara C. Samples

Ecology is a branch of biological science that studies the interaction of living things in relation to one another. Ecological theory views organism development as a product of dynamic interaction between organism and environment. Each individual organism's genetic expressions, biological processes, and cognitive processes are conceptualized as being shaped and refined by the pressures of living in tension with environmental demands (Del Giudice, Ellis, & Shirtcliff, 2011). Ecological stress theory is a multidisciplinary area of research and study. Biologists, psychologists, sociologists, anthropologists, immunologists, and those in other disciplines study human development in light of the ecological evolutionary stress response. Much of the ecological model of stress is researched via the process of laboratory investigations of organisms that are simpler than humans. Ecologically minded scientists have studied the stress response in one-celled organisms, invertebrates, and vertebrates. In vertebrate studies, much of the laboratory work has been conducted on primates and rodents. In humans, much ecological research has occurred in naturalistic and observational studies of school-aged children.

In contrast to other stress models that conceptualize the etiology of the human stress response as primarily either biological or psychological in nature, ecological theory approaches stress as an interactional process between the environment, the individual's biology, and psychological composition. Viewing development from an evolutionary lens, ecological theory conceptualizes the stress response as central to development and maturation of all living things (Del Giudice, Ellis, & Shirtcliff, 2011). *Stress* is a biological response produced by organisms when facing life threat or homeostasis disruption (Boonstra, 2013). From the ecological view, the stress response is both a catalyst of and an outcome for the complex process of dynamic changes that occur to an individual's biological and psychological characteristics in reaction to environmental factors, both physical and relational (Steinberg, 2012). The ecological view of stress highlights the importance of viewing stress contextually. *Stressors* are defined as events, circumstances, and experiences that activate the hormonal stress response in an individual. Stressors can be neutral, positive, or destructive and can vary in intensity. They can be predictable and usual (such as everyday survival hassles) or unpredictable and traumatic (such as a hurricane or flood) (Boonstra & Fox, 2013). Anticipation of a stress event is enough to produce a stress response in some instances (Boonstra, 2013).

According to ecological stress theory, although the environmental stressor context varies among populations and individuals, potential stressors are everpresent in the environment from conception throughout the life span. The impact of those stressors in facilitating maturation and/or destabilization during an individual's development depends on the contextual interaction of biological and environmental processes (Cohen, Evans, Stokols, & Krantz, 1986).

HISTORICAL CONCEPTUALIZATIONS OF ECOLOGICAL STRESS

The concept of stress impacting and altering the biological development of the individual was first discussed in the realm of biological theory. Selye (1973) proposed that organisms experience a biological stress response when exposed to environmental threats to survival. He further proposed that this biological stress response could result in permanent modification of the biological processes of an organism, as deployment of the stress response would disrupt normal processes of metabolism and cellular repair, thereby creating the potential for irreversible damage if the stress continued for a long enough period of time. In Selye's perspective, stress was the *biological response*—an internal state activated when seeking to ensure survival—that occurred when an organism was placed outside of its ecological niche and under survival threat. He further identified that continuous exposure to stress resulted in three phases: the biparte alarm phase, the resistance phase, and the exhaustion phase (Selye, 1973). In the biparte alarm phase, the organism modifies its biochemical and genetic expression in efforts to respond to the stress, but in doing so affects its growth, repair, and metabolism activities. In the resistance phase, the organism activates further defense mechanisms to endure continuous exposure to the undesirable environmental factors, continuing to reduce growth and repair activities and resulting in further biotransformation. In the final stage, exhaustion, the organism collapses due to the ongoing difficulties with vital cellular function. Selye called this process the General Adaptation Syndrome, which was assumed to occur due to the activation of the stress response as a result of environmental stresses that were perceived to be outside of the normal stress experiences expected in an organism's life cycle. Selye built upon work by Claude

Bernard (1813–1878), who in the mid-19th century proposed the importance of maintaining the stability of the internal body; this idea was in turn refined by Walter Cannon (1871–1945) in his concept of homeostasis, which was defined as the body's natural preference to return to a harmonious state, as well as several other biological and physiological influences. Hans Selye recognized that the body's ability to adapt to changes has a limit, influenced by genetic factors (Selye, 1950).

Nahemow and Lawton (1973) further developed the theoretical basis of the influence of environmental stressors on human development in their Competence-Environmental Press theory. This theory, which was developed to explain the behaviors of geriatric adults, proposed that people adapt more effectively when there is a balance between their behavioral and psychological coping skills and the demands placed upon them by the environment (Nahemow & Lawton, 1973). This theory emphasized that it is important to understand the environmental demands a person is experiencing in order to understand his or her cognitive and behavioral reactions to stress. This theory also emphasized that stressors are not only physiological in nature, but could also result from relational or life-stage-related stressors.

Urie Bronfenbrenner (1974, 1979, 1994) proposed the most comprehensive historical system for understanding the ecological context of development and the role of environmental stress in that development. According to Bronfenbrenner (1979), humans are uniquely different from other organisms in their ability to adapt to, tolerate, and create the ecologies in which they live and develop. He proposed that "human development takes place through processes of progressively more complex reciprocal interactions between an active evolving biopsychological human organism and the persons, objects and symbols in its immediate environment" (Bronfenbrenner, 1994, p. 1644). From this perspective, the stress response is the process of adapting to and reciprocally influencing the environment, all the while producing biological changes in the organism to improve adaptive functioning.

Bronfenbrenner conceptualized a model of development based upon five nested levels of influence. The first level is the Microsystem, which incorporates the genetics and biology of the developing person, as well as the person's race, gender, social roles, interpersonal relationships, and physical environment. In regard to stress on this level, Bronfenbrenner focused much of his work on the influence of relationships such as family, and school and classroom settings, as these affect the biological and personality expression of a developing child. The next level of influence is the Mesosystem, composed of the linkages and processes among the multiple microsystems in which the child resides. This system is illustrated by the example of relationships between school and work, or home and school. Mesosystem factors influence development as a source of both stressors and resources for the developing individual. The Exosystem, the next level of influence, incorporates individuals, policies, and systems that do not have direct influence on the developing individual, but add indirect stress and resources shaping development of biology and personality. For example, the employment practices of a child's parent and the effects of those practices on the home environment shape the parent's and child's experience of security. The next level, the Macrosystem, is further removed from the developing individual, and provides another level of both stressors and resources. This system includes such stressors and resources as cultural belief systems, political freedoms and stability, economic conditions, and material resources available to the developing person. The Macrosystem is largely outside of the developing individual's ability to reciprocally influence (in contrast to previous levels), but still influences developmental processes at the level of the individual. The final subsystem is the Chronosystem, which refers to both the passage of time and the developing individual's context in time. The Chronosystem incorporates not only time-related changes to the individual (developmental milestones, socioeconomic changes, employment, education), but also the events from the passage of time across the specific life span of the individual (wars, droughts, famines, economic collapse, etc.) (Bronfenbrenner, 1977).

According to Bronfenbrenner's model, the individual experiences stress events from all levels. Children's individual development is influenced by their personal psychological characteristics, but also by the support and stress they experience from the nested levels of influence. Additionally, the child, via personality characteristics and developmental demands placed upon caregivers, is also a mechanism of stress, resulting in reciprocal determinism in shaping the child and the environment.

Though not initially part of his theory, in his later years of research Bronfenbrenner proposed that the proximal processes (stressors and resources influencing cognitive, biological, and psychological growth) between the levels of influence were in part responsible for the mechanisms through which genotypes are expressed as phenotypes (Bronfenbrenner, 1994). In regard to stress theory, this influence of ecological environmental stressors upon genetic expression is the mechanism by which stressors from the environment change the biological expression of genetic programming in an individual and also influence future transmission of genetic material to future generations, a process known as *epigenetics*.

MODERN ECOLOGICAL STRESS THEORY

Modern ecological theory of stress continues to build upon early work in focusing upon the biological cascade of changes that occurs in an individual organism when exposed to environmental stress. Current thinking on the stress response in humans (and all vertebrates) is primarily focused on activation of the sympathetic nervous system; more specifically, the hypothalamic-pituitary-adrenocortical (HPA) axis. The HPA axis influences the physical reaction to stress and regulates digestion, immune response, moods, and emotions. Activation of the HPA axis results in the release of glucocorticoids, including cortisol. *Glucocorticoids* are a class of steroid hormones that bind to the glucocorticoid receptors in the brain and nervous system. Glucocorticoids affect many areas of the brain, including the hippocampus, amygdala, and frontal lobes, as well as other organs such as the lungs and liver. Behavioral responses to activation of the HPA axis can include escape or avoidance behaviors, memory effects, concentration effects, altered cognition, and changes in feeding and reproductive behavior. The adaptive suitability of behavioral reactions then in turn increases or decreases goodness of fit in environment and life tasks.

Although same-species animals or humans of similar backgrounds may be exposed to identical threats to survival and homeostasis, the activation of this system is not uniform in all individuals. Activation is very contextual and is influenced by sensitivity to environmental stressors, behavioral experience, psychological threat appraisal, overall stress load, resilience factors, and individual phenotype expression (Steinberg, 2012). Environmental stressors that activate the HPA stress response in one organism may not do so in another (Reeder & Kramer, 2005). Furthermore, the functioning of the HPA axis has been implicated in both the fitness of an individual in adaptation and survival, and, on a larger scale, when adaptive HPA axis effects are widespread across a population of vertebrates, in their overall population growth (Wingfield & Boonstra, 2013). Population effects further elucidate the relationship between an individual's neurochemical response and the larger ecological effects.

In the realm of psychological theory, modern ecological theory is used to explore the stress behaviors of adults and children exposed to potential stress sources across multiple layers of environments. Bronfenbrenner (1979) first proposed that the relational stressors across the five systems of influence shape individual psychological processes, affecting quality of life. One recent application of this idea has been the emergence of resilience studies from the positive psychology movement. The term *resilience* was derived from the physical sciences and was originally used to describe the capacity of a system to return to equilibrium after displacement (Norris, Tracy, & Galea, 2009). In psychological studies, the term has been adapted to refer to an individual's (or group's) ability to thrive during and after stress. The presence of risk factors is required to evaluate the ability to adapt and thrive. Psychological ecological theory argues that the presence of stressors across multiple levels of influence, from everyday survival hassles to trauma exposures, is important for the development of resilience (Ungar, 2011), and that resilience enhances adaptability to overall life experiences. Psychologists and educators apply ecological theory to evaluate levels of stressors and potential interventions that may foster resilience in at-risk children and adults (Swick & Williams, 2006). Genetic and environmental investigations of resilience have become important in investigating environmental and biological factors that influence how individuals survive and thrive through difficult life experiences, such as combat or sexual assault.

Modern ecological stress theory emphasizes the importance of viewing stress as a normative experience that functions as both a dynamic contributor and an obstacle to growth of both individuals and populations. Whereas historical theory has evaluated the role of traumatic stress on biotransformation, modern ecological theory has focused as much research on the process of biotransformations that arise in the face of stress from the everyday hassles of survival (Boonstra & Fox, 2013).

CONCLUSION

According to ecological theory, environmental stressors and the resulting stress response are natural components of every ecological environment, and impact development from conception to death in every organism. All organisms, including humans, adapt to a changing environment through changing their physiology and behavior (Steinberg, 2012). Stressors in the environment provoke the stress response, which is the catalyst for adaptive change. The environmental conditions in which the organism is developing may be predictable (changes such as seasonal weather or developmental milestones) or unpredictable (traumatic), but environmental stressors are part of the natural life cycle (Wingfield & Boonstra, 2013). These stressors provoke a biological stress response that may result in biotransformations at the genetic level. These changes not only modify the adaptation of the individual, but may also alter the transmission of genetic material across generations, resulting in epigenetic transformation.

REFERENCES AND FURTHER READING

Boonstra, R. (2013). The ecology of stress: A marriage of disciplines. *Functional Ecology, 27,* 7–10.

Boonstra, R., & Fox, C. (2013). Reality as the leading cause of stress: Rethinking the impact of chronic stress in nature. *Functional Ecology, 27*(1), 11–23. doi:10.1111/1365-2435.12008.

Bronfenbrenner, U. (1974). Developmental research, public policy and the ecology of childhood. *Child Development, 45,* 1–5.

Bronfenbrenner, U. (1977). Toward an experimental ecology of human development. *American Psychologist, 32,* 515–531.

Bronfenbrenner, U. (1979). *The ecology of human development: Experiments by nature and design.* Cambridge, MA: Harvard University Press.

Bronfenbrenner, U. (1994). Ecological models of human development. In M. Gauvain & M. Cole (Eds.), *Readings on the development of children* (2nd ed., pp. 37–43). New York, NY: Freeman.

Clark, J. D., Rager, D. R., & Calpin, J. P. (1997). Animal well-being II. Stress and distress. *Comparative Medicine, 47*(6), 571–579.

Cohen, S., Evans, G. W., Stokols, D., & Krantz, D. S. (1986). *Behavior, health, and environmental stress.* New York, NY: Plenum Press.

De Kloet, E. R., Joëls, M., & Holsboer, F. (2005). Stress and the brain: From adaptation to disease. *Nature Reviews Neuroscience, 6*(6), 463–475.

Del Giudice, M., Ellis, B. J., & Shirtcliff, E. A. (2011). The adaptive calibration model of stress responsivity. *Neuroscience & Biobehavioral Reviews, 35*(7), 1562–1592.

McEwen, B. S. (2005). Stressed or stressed out: What is the difference? *Journal of Psychiatry and Neuroscience, 30*(5), 315.

Nahemow, L., & Lawton, M. P. (1973). Towards an ecological theory of adaptation and aging. *Environmental Design Research: Selected Papers, 1,* 24.

Norris, F. H., Tracy, M., & Galea, S. (2009). Looking for resilience: Understanding the longitudinal trajectories of responses to stress. *Social Science & Medicine, 68*(12), 2190–2198.

Reeder, D. M., & Kramer, K. M. (2005). Stress in free-ranging mammals: Integrating physiology, ecology, and natural history. *Journal of Mammalogy, 86*(2), 225–235.

Rosch, P. J. (n.d.). Hans Selye: Birth of stress. Retrieved from http://www.stress.org/about/hans-selye-birth-of-stress.

Selye, H. (1950). Stress and the general adaptation syndrome. *British Medical Journal, 1*(4667), 1383.

Selye, H. (1973). The Evolution of the Stress Concept: The originator of the concept traces its development from the discovery in 1936 of the alarm reaction to modern therapeutic applications of syntoxic and catatoxic hormones. *American Scientist, 61*(6), 692–699.

Steinberg, C. (2012). *Stress ecology: Environmental stress as ecological driving force and key player in evolution.* Dordrecht, Germany: Springer. doi:10.1007/978-94-007-2072-5.

Swick, K. J., & Williams, R. D. (2006). An analysis of Bronfenbrenner's bio-ecological perspective for early childhood educators: Implications for working with families experiencing stress. *Early Childhood Education Journal, 33*(5), 371–378.

Ungar, M. (2011). The social ecology of resilience: Addressing contextual and cultural ambiguity of a nascent construct. *American Journal of Orthopsychiatry, 81*(1), 1–17.

Wingfield, J. C., & Boonstra, R. (2013). Ecological processes and the ecology of stress: The impacts of abiotic environmental factors. *Functional Ecology, 27*(1), 37–44. doi:10.1111/1365-2435.12039.

4

Diathesis-Stress Models for Understanding Physiological and Psychological Effects of Stress

Ingrid M. Tiegel

The purpose of this chapter is first to define and examine common definitions of the diathesis-stress model of understanding different vulnerabilities to stress in human beings. It then traces the history of these models as they have been broadly construed, notes paradigm shifts in the model as used in psychology and psychiatry, discusses limitations and provisos to these models, and finally stakes out possible directions for the future, such as the inclusion of specific cultural or subcultural contexts. The changing nature of the stressors that individuals are likely to encounter over time also involves change associated with age, as well as the growing capacities of humans to self-select ecological niches and environments that may protect or exacerbate the nature of experienced stressors.

WHAT IS DIATHESIS STRESS?

Diathesis implies some kind of genetic, congenital, or environmentally produced vulnerability, a predisposition or susceptibility, or a combination of two or more of these factors. Such vulnerability is thought to increase the probability of an overly intense and/or prolonged activation of the sympathetic nervous system (part of the HPA or hypothalamic-pituitary-adrenocortical axis) which taxes or exceeds an individual's ability to adapt or maintain psychological and physiological homeostasis. *Homeostasis* is the body's ability to return to a state of equilibrium and balance. Such vulnerability implies an arousal beyond the usual parameters experienced by individuals of a specific age in a specific culture. A mechanical analogy to the early, rather static, genetic version of a diathesis might be to consider a car with intrinsic design flaws as opposed to a car showing the natural effects of age and use in predicting the probability of a breakdown. In human populations, increased vulnerability to breakdown might be attributed to one or more of the following factors in addition to a possible genetically based susceptibility: adverse prenatal events; effects of infant prematurity; individual differences in temperamental responsiveness to stimulation; early socialization experiences, particularly those revolving around disorganized attachments; exposure to and experience of overwhelming traumatic events at any point in the lifetime; consistent exposure to deprivation or aversive social environments; and/or the construction of faulty cognitive self-schemas or social attributions. Research literature currently gives ever more detailed models of how many of these factors might interact to additively or exponentially increase the probability of individuals succumbing psychologically or physiologically to the effects of stress (e.g., Monroe & Simons, 1991; Hankin & Abramson, 2001).

Stress refers to the activation of one or more stressors on an individual which are sufficiently potent to produce *strain*, meaning a condition that challenges the coping and/or defensive efforts of the individual involved to manage the ensuing arousal of the brain's limbic (emotional) system and in consequence, activation of the sympathetic nervous system. A frequent assumption is that stressors are necessarily negative in nature, but positive stressors (*eustress*) might also create excessive strain. Thus, for example, the experience of a highly desired wedding ceremony can strain many brides' adaptive capabilities.

Evolutionary-based theories assume that the ability to respond to stress is essential for human adaptation to often-changing environments. Deficits in this ability, such as individuals with adrenal insufficiency syndromes (where activation of the sympathetic nervous system is impaired), are at risk for serious complications or even death because of the body's inability to respond adaptively to a physical challenge (National Endocrine and Metabolic Diseases Information Service, 2014). Individual differences in vulnerabilities to stressors might also be invaluable in human evolution to permit adaptation as the characteristics of physical and social environments change. Thus, a constitutional tendency toward inhibition

ALLOSTASIS

Allostasis is a central process for maintaining homeostasis. Allostasis stabilizes the neuroendocrine mechanisms as the body endures chronic stress. When malfunction of this system occurs, the "load," termed *allostatic load*, can lead to dysfunctions within the system (McEwen & Stellar, 1993).

—*Serena Wadhwa*

(frequently linked to the tendency to develop anxiety disorders) might ensure or maximize personal survival in very high-risk physical or social environments, whereas excessive or impulsive risk-taking might not. Additionally, children's and youths' ability to manage stress is necessarily challenged in developmental transitions where they must learn to negotiate changing social expectations and environments. Indeed, in some cultures, deliberate stress-inducing experiences, such as African initiation ceremonies, are important rites of passage; successful mastery of these experiences is necessary to acquire culturally adult status.

Another frequent assumption is that individuals, particularly adults, generally need to perceive stressors as being stressful; thus, the experience of being stressed heavily depends on the "eye of the beholder." Cultural context is also important; the concept of stress might be ubiquitous in a wide variety of contexts. Thus, contemporary American college students may show a particular biased response; they frequently focus on "how stressed" they are both in self-appraisals and in their communications with others. Similarly, American media and pharmaceutical companies pay enormous attention to the topic of stress, which may account in part for the overdiagnosis of anxiety and depressive disorders in America compared to other countries (Demyttenaere et al., 2004).

The diathesis-stress concept as first used in psychology and psychiatry assumed a linear directionality: namely, that a given predisposition or vulnerability had to be present for later stressful events to cause a breakdown in adaptive functioning. More contemporary perspectives have struggled with the issue of directionality and considered either more transactive models or dynamically interactive models.

PARADIGM SHIFTS AND THE HISTORY OF THE DIATHESIS-STRESS MODEL AS APPLIED TO PSYCHOLOGY AND PSYCHIATRY, BROADLY CONSTRUED

The diathesis-stress model in medicine dates back to antiquity (Ingram & Luxton, 2005). It resurfaced in psychiatric and psychological circles in the 1960s when Paul Meehl and others noted the importance of behavioral genetic twin studies for suggesting a strong genetic contribution to the development of severe psychopathology. Thus, a genetically determined neural defect was determined to be a necessary, but not sufficient, condition for schizophrenia to become manifest, usually in young adulthood. To elicit the full-blown syndrome, the appropriate stressors had to exist in addition to this defect. Relatives to the patient might carry the same neural defect and have a schizotypal personality structure, but not experience the kind of stressors that would trigger a psychotic breakdown. Meehl later revised his conception to a more complex polygenetic model (Lenzenweger, 2006). More recently, Walker and Diforio (1997) proposed a neural diathesis-stress model of schizophrenia whereby an abnormality in dopamine neurotransmission, mediated by a cortisol influx produced by stressful events, contributed to psychological breakdown.

The particular line of reasoning shown in these genetic models has continued to this day and has been extended to diathesis-stress models of bipolar disorder and major depression. Recently, twin studies have also been used to track genetic predispositions to depression and to anxiety disorders, including posttraumatic stress disorder (e.g., Koenen, 2007). Further, researchers using twin studies have found mixed results in establishing possible genetic contributions to disorganized attachments in infancy; such attachments are presumed to create a predisposition to posttraumatic stress disorders (Bakermans-Kranenbrug & van IJzendoorn, 2007).

Advocating for a rather linear model of diathesis stress, clinical psychologists in the 1960s were heavily influenced by both a medical model of mental illness and the learning theory tradition in American psychology. The "cognitive revolution" in America in the 1970s permitted inferences of what might be happening in "the black box" (the brain) in accounting for behavior. Only then was it possible for researchers to investigate the role of cognition in predisposing specific vulnerabilities to stress. In explaining individuals' susceptibility to depression, psychiatrist Aaron Beck articulated a prominent cognitive diathesis-stress model, and psychologists such as Martin Seligman moved from learning theory constructs such as "learned helplessness" to more cognitively defined constructs as contributing to increased individual vulnerability for depression (Hankin & Abramson, 2001). Cognitively based expectancies were presumed to facilitate a person's experience of being stressed by events and in turn, excessive experienced stress led to possible depressive reactions. It was presumed that these expectancies originally developed as responses to specific socialization experiences early in childhood, especially when individuals felt thwarted in achievement and social goals.

More recently, stress generation has been added to the cognitive model. Here, maladaptive cognitions are thought to push depressed individuals to behave in ways that produce even more socially based stress, which, in a cascading fashion, contributes to further depressive episodes and maladaptive reactions (Eberhart, Auerback, Bigda-Peyton, & Abela, 2011). Another, more complex cognitive model of depression involves a sensitizing or kindling hypothesis: the individual's neural systems are thought to be altered after an early episode of stress and become more responsive to and sensitized by future stressors (Monroe & Harkness, 2005).

For developmentalists, recent advances in molecular genetic research and technological advances in both cellular laboratory tests and imaging technology allow for much more sophisticated study of the phenotypic expression of genes, of the workings of individual neurons and neuronal circuits in relation to emotional and cognitive behavior, and of the neurotransmitter systems in the central nervous system. As a consequence, newer models of individual vulnerability to stress have been proposed after to findings linked to age-related changes in the interactions of the limbic (emotional) system of the brain with the neocortex (executive functioning). Thus, for example, adolescents' behavioral reactivity to stress is now better understood as their possessing a developmentally immature prefrontal neocortex relative to a more fully developed subcortical limbic system. Similarly, the effects of early adversity and abuse in childhood in permanently altering cortisol release, initiated by the HPA axis in response to stress, are now emphasized (Schore, 2001). Further, infants experiencing disorganized attachments are thought to develop working models (expectancies) about attachments that make them vulnerable to later posttraumatic stress disorder. Disorganized attached infants, when briefly separated from their mothers in the laboratory, show inconsistent and bizarre responses to their mothers during reunions after those separations; such behavior has been correlated with abusive or frightening mothering. In addition, it has been suggested that genetic deficits in the neurotransmitter dopamine D4 receptor system are associated with a tendency toward the formation of disorganized attachments; however, research suggests that environmental factors are probably more significant in early life (Bakermans-Kranenburg & van IJzendoorn, 2007).

Prenatally, random events such as the impact of a virus on a developing embryo or fetus can significantly change crucial structures in the limbic system, long proposed for being at least a contributor to the etiology of schizophrenia. Prenatal events have also been highlighted by another recent reformulation of the diathesis-stress model by developmentalists who emphasize research on the role of epigenetics in the critical prenatal molding of the infant's central nervous system, particularly the right-hemisphere circuits involved in later self-regulation (Schore, 2001). At critical junctures, developing nerve cells of the embryo or fetus can experience an adverse chemical environment created by a flood of hormones and glucocorticoids produced by a highly stressed mother. Thus, ensuing changes in the fetal amygdala and hippocampus can alter the infant's ability to manage stress later in life (Tottenham et al., 2009). Similarly, research has been conducted on the developing neurotransmitter receptors, particularly those related to serotonin, and their relation to creating a vulnerability to later anxiety and depressive disorders, and to dopaminergic receptors in the case of schizophrenia.

LIMITATIONS OF AND PROVISOS TO THE DIATHESIS-STRESS MODELS

Some of the persistent difficulties for diathesis-stress models are first, how to operationally define each of the constructs; and second, how then to interpret the results of studies using inconsistent definitions (Monroe & Simons, 1991). One definition of *diathesis* is a genetic susceptibility based on specifically known or unknown genes or gene arrays, such as when Meehl used the results of twin studies of genetics in his original 1962 argument regarding genetic proclivities toward schizophrenia. He formulated a definition of diathesis as being a neural defect (schizotaxia), which when paired with specific social learning experiences led to a schizophrenic breakdown. Later, Meehl modified his definition of diathesis by including "polygenic potentiators" or other personality dimensions which, when paired with schizotaxia, further potentiated the vulnerability to schizophrenic breakdown (Lenzenweger, 2006).

As already noted, finer-grained definitions of diathesis include epigenetic-based definitions which recognize that specific high-stress events experienced by the pregnant mother are shown to be transmitted through cortisol and hormonal changes to the maternal environment surrounding the developing embryo or fetus and thus affect consequent brain development. Such diathetic changes are thought to have their most significant impact at specific times (Schore, 2001).

Still another operational definition is evident in cognitive diathesis-stress models positing that the diathesis or vulnerability is a learned cognitive expectancy which makes the individual unusually susceptible or reactive to stress. This expectancy is presumably learned through early socialization. In another refinement of the diathesis definition, the Cognitive Stress Generation model holds that already stressed individuals create further environmental stressors through the byproducts of their responses to the original stressors (Eberhart, Auderback, Bigda-Peyton, & Abela, 2011).

Definitions of *stress* are equally problematic (Khoozani & Hadzic, 2010). For example, stress can be biogenic, such as experiencing a physical illness or mishap, or psychogenic, such as experiencing social ostracism. Experience of stress in many, but not all, cases may be predicated on whether an event is evaluated and interpreted as stressful. The cognitive capacity for this evaluation will undoubtedly vary by developmental age. Young children lack cognitive sophistication and may be stressed by a state of physical or emotional insecurity that, because of their immature cognitive abilities, may have different qualities than for an adult. Children may be incapable or inexperienced even at cognitively labeling or identifying their feelings. Thus, social ostracism may be more painfully experienced at certain ages than at others.

Similarly, problems with operationalized definitions of stress have to do with stress being diversely measured. Some researchers may sum significant life events presumed to affect a human's stress reaction (an additive model); others may focus on daily or intermittent hassles. Still others may use physiological measures such as heart rate or cortisol assays. The use of self-report as opposed to more objective instruments also produces inconsistencies that may lead to difficulties in interpretation of findings. The length of exposure to a stressor may also be part of a definition of stress (Khoozani & Hadzic, 2010). For example, formerly institutionalized youngsters show a dose-related association between the amount of time they have spent in an institution during early development and their socioemotional capacities, including dealing with stress (Tottenham et al., 2009).

POSSIBLE FUTURE DEVELOPMENTS

Existing diathesis-stress models are limited by questions about how to establish parameters for what are sufficient conditions for diatheses to become manifest. Are one or more major stressors needed, or is an accumulation (even if intermittent) of daily hassles sufficient for a predisposition to become apparent? Is the particular age of the individual relevant here? Can adaptive failure be considered as being on a single continuum of severity, or are several differing dimensions needed? Are some adaptive failures more heavily dependent on specific genetically based etiologies than others?

How is variability in the manifestations and chronicity of adaptive failure, as frequently seen in schizophrenia and major depression, accounted for? Additionally, where a diathesis is suspected and the possibility for a cascade of further precipitating factors occurs, when and how might it be possible to effectively interfere with or interrupt such a cascade to prevent adaptive failure? Given that many adaptive failures manifest themselves in adolescence or young adulthood, this might be an opportune window to explore further.

Another question is whether diathesis precedes stress, or whether a transactional model is more satisfactory in explaining certain forms of adaptive failure. Cognitive diathesis-stress models of depression suggest the latter (Hankin & Abramson, 2001). In contrast, the kindling hypothesis of depression presumes that previous stress experience may predispose a quicker reaction and greater response to a less potent stressor on future occasions (Monroe & Harkness, 2005).

Much less research has focused on diathesis-stress models that lead to adaptive failures shown by externalizing (acting-out) behaviors; there has been a disproportionate emphasis on models manifested by internalizing behaviors (e.g., anxiety and depression). Additionally, little attention has been paid to the perceptions and learned attributions of the individual growing up in a specific cultural or subcultural context. Opportunities may exist for some individuals to self-select ecological niches which may either be more self-protective or exacerbate the nature of stressors the individuals are likely to encounter over time.

The role of protective factors in the equation is also unclear. Are these factors, such as personality variables, intelligence, sensitive parenting experiences, and successful school experiences (among many others), additive in their effects of preventing adaptive failure, or are there definite limits to their effects? Further, might these factors differ qualitatively in their protective impact in experiences of major life events, as opposed to experiences of cumulative daily hassles; might these also depend upon particular developmental windows of opportunity? Neurovulnerability models suggest the latter (e.g., Thomson, 2004).

Although there are some advantages to the neuro-diathesis models, they share the difficulty of being primarily correlational, rather than causal, explanations in describing the etiology of adaptive failures.

SUMMARY AND CONCLUSIONS

Diathesis-stress models must be viewed in the context of human history and the species' remarkable 2-million-year successful adaptation to a variety of challenging natural and social environments. Impressive in this adaptation is the basic self-righting capacity of humans (Masten, 2001). Yet, while challenges in the physical environment have been relatively easily mastered by modern humans, they continue to struggle to master complex psychological and social environments with a nervous system primarily designed to respond to physical danger. Further, it is common to observe that individuals do not react to common stressors in the same way. Some individuals can maintain psychological homeostasis even under extreme stress (see Monroe & Simons, 1991).

There is great variability in contemporary diathesis-stress models' concepts of adaptive failure and of opportunities for interventions. The need for more dynamic and comprehensive models of the interplay between diathesis and stress that are more inclusive of the possible roles of genetics, epigenetics, constitutional personality variables, developmental timing, and cultural mores is increasingly being recognized. Our beginning analogy of the early diathesis-stress model as a car with potential design flaws should be replaced with that of a dynamically complex living organism possessing a great deal of ongoing plasticity; this organism is in a continual process of seeking to achieve physiological and psychological homeostasis in the context of often rapidly changing physical or social environments. More interactive and dynamic models of the relationship between vulnerability and stressors are already being pursued. The role of epigenetic change and greater sensitivity to developmental changes in individual vulnerability to adaptive challenges is acknowledged (e.g., Thomson, 2004).

Twin studies and molecular studies of genetic alleles related to dopamine expression and the susceptibility to disorganized attachment are suggestive, but not definitive. Such research must be extended to include research on other global communities where alternatives to mother-child attachment prevail (e.g., the Efe in Africa). More attention should also be paid to the increasing possibility for niche-seeking in adulthood; the specific stress characteristics of given environments may provide some individuals with greater selectivity in choosing a specific environment with varying stress characteristics in which to live. Attention to disproportionate cultural emphasis on stress may be helpful; at least some stress is likely to be in the eye of the beholder, and reframing cultural expectations may diminish the actual perception of an event as stressful.

REFERENCES AND FURTHER READING

Bakermans-Kranenburg, & van IJzendoorn, N. H. (2007). Research review: Genetic vulnerability or differential susceptibility in child development: The case of attachment. *Journal of Child Psychology and Psychiatry, 48*(12), 1160–1173.

Demyttenaere, K., Bruffaerts, R., Posada-Villa, J., Gasquet, I., Kovess, V., et al. (2004). Prevalence, severity, and unmet need for treatment of mental disorders in the World Health Organization world mental health surveys. *JAMA, 291*(21), 2581–2590.

Eberhart, N. K., Auderback, R. P., Bigda-Peyton, J., & Abela, J. R. Z. (2011). Maladaptive schemas and depression: Tests of stress generation and diathesis-stress models. *Journal of Social and Clinical Psychology, 30*(1), 75–104.

Hankin, B. L., & Abramson, L. Y. (2001). Development of gender differences in depression: An elaborated cognitive vulnerability-transactional stress theory. *Psychological Bulletin, 12*(6), 773–796.

Ingram, R. E., & Luxton, D. D. (2005). Vulnerability-stress models. In B. L. Hankin & J. R. Z. Abela (Eds.), *Development of psychopathology: A vulnerability-stress perspective* (pp. 32–46). Thousand Oaks, CA: Sage.

Khoozani, E. N., & Hadzic, M. (2010). Designing the human stress ontology: A formal framework to capture and represent knowledge about human stress. *Australian Psychologist, 45*(4), 258–273.

Koenen, K. C. (2007). Genetics of posttraumatic stress disorder: Review and recommendations for future studies. *Journal of Traumatic Stress, 20*(5), 737–750.

Lenzenweger, M. F. (2006). Schizotaxia, schizotypy, and schizophrenia: Paul E. Meehl's blueprint for the experimental psychopathology and genetics of schizophrenia. *Journal of Abnormal Psychology, 115*(2), 195–200.

Masten, A. S. (2001). Ordinary magic: Resilience processes in development. *American Psychologist, 56*(3), 227–223.

McEwen, B. S. (1998). Stress, adaptation, and disease: Allostasis and allostatic load. *Annals of the New York Academy of Sciences, 840*(1), 33–44.

McEwen, B. S., & Stellar, E. (1993). Stress and the individual: Mechanisms leading to disease. *Archives of Internal Medicine, 153*(18), 2093–2101.

Monroe, S. M., & Harkness, K. L. (2005). Life stress, the "kindling hypothesis" and the recurrence of depression: Considerations from a life stress perspective. *Psychology Review, 112,* 417–445.

Monroe, S. M., & Simons, A. D. (1991). Diathesis-stress theories in the context of life stress research: Implications for the depressive disorders, *Psychological Bulletin, 110*(3), 406–425.

National Endocrine and Metabolic Diseases Information Service (NEMDIS), National Institutes of Health (NIH). (2014). Adrenal insufficiency and Addison's disease. Retrieved from https://www.niddk.nih.gov/health-information/health-topics/endocrine/adrenal-insufficiency-addisons-disease/Pages/fact-sheet.aspx.

Schore, A. (2001). The effect of early relational trauma on right brain development, affect regulation, and infant mental health. *Infant Mental Health, 22*(1–2), 201–269.

Thomson, P. (2004). The impact of trauma on the embryo and fetus: An application of the diathesis-stress model and the neurovulnerability-neurotoxicity model. *Journal of Prenatal and Perinatal Psychology and Health, 19*(1), 9–63.

Tottenham, N., Hare, T. A., Quinn, B. T., McCarry, T., Nurse, M., et al. (2009). Prolonged institutional rearing is associated with atypically large amygdala volume and emotional regulation difficulties. *Developmental Science, 13*(1), 46–61.

Walker, E. F., & Diforio, D. (1997). Schizophrenia: A neural diathesis-stress model. *Psychological Review, 104*(4), 667–685.

5

THEORIES OF SPIRITUAL STRESS

Meetu Khosla

Spirituality helps us to understand our minds, our emotions, and our relationship with the transcendent. Spirituality involves a belief in a supreme power of the universe, a sense of interconnectedness with all living creatures, an awareness of the purpose and meaning of life and the development of personal, absolute values. Roof (1999, p. 35) argues that spirituality encompasses four important themes: (1) a source of values and ultimate meaning or purpose beyond the self, including a sense of mystery and self-transcendence; (2) a way of understanding; (3) inner awareness; and (4) personal integration. It has been revealed that visions of spirituality also involve contact with sacred forces, which makes spirituality a powerful and mysterious experience.

The 14th Dalai Lama suggests that spirituality works at two levels. One level simply deals with our emotions, values, experiences, and self in making the present life healthy and happy. The most important mental element for happiness and health is compassion, also known as *karuna* or realization of whole-heartedness. The second level is religion, which means having a belief in love and compassion, selflessness, altruism, and the experience of inner peace, which are all characteristics of spirituality.

DEFINING SPIRITUALITY

Spirituality has most often been defined in terms of individual beliefs and practices related to God or a higher power in the universe, although these beliefs may also be entirely secular (Miller, 1999). It may or may not be affiliated with any particular religion, but it involves a search for higher values, inner freedom, and things that give life meaning (Vergote, 2003). Jernigan (2001, p. 9) defines *spirituality* as "the organization (centering) of individual and collective life around dynamic patterns of meanings, values, and relationships that are trusted to make life worthwhile (or, at least, livable) and death meaningful."

RELIGION AND SPIRITUALITY

There is much debate regarding the conceptual differentiation between religion and spirituality. Ellison (1983) suggests that American religion and spirituality are conceptually different. Spirituality of seeking is more dominant than a *spirituality of dwelling,* which refers to a person finding God within the context of a religious doctrine. *Spirituality of seeking* refers to individuals searching for the divine or the meaning in life and themselves through constantly seeking out information that can help them with immediate needs and problems. The focus in spirituality is on self and not God or the divine. Rose (2001) argues that spirituality does not necessarily promote conformity; rather, the person defines existence, the divine, and morality. These definitions of spirituality may be cultivated apart from religious institutions, beliefs, and practices.

SPIRITUALITY AND SELF

Spirituality is related to self-growth, self-reliance, and the individual's interpretation of what is right and wrong. There is enhanced emphasis on the notion of self, in terms of *self*-growth, *self*-healing, and *self*-actualization. Park, Meyers, and Czar (1998) found that a significant empirical relationship exists between spirituality and self-actualization.

NEW TRENDS IN SPIRITUALITY AND HEALTH

The "new" spiritualities focus less on moral doctrine and more on encouraging personal freedom and the self-definition of truth and morality. They focus on the individual search for meaning and self rather than on traditional religious thoughts. For example, whereas traditional Christianity and other religions are more socially and doctrinally inclined, new spiritualities focus on the experience and power of the individual.

Spirituality helps to foster a feeling of hope among people facing adversity. This positive feeling about resolving crises or being optimistic about problems may not only reduce the probability of future illnesses, but may also increase the life span. The regular practice of prayer and meditation appears to be associated with recovery and abstinence from drugs in anti-addiction programs. Results from several studies indicate that people with strong spiritual beliefs heal faster from surgery, are less anxious and depressed, have lower blood pressure, and cope better with chronic illnesses such as arthritis, diabetes, heart disease, cancer, and spinal cord injury (Burke, Flowers, Graham, & Furr, 2001; Holland, Kash, & Passick, 1998).

Another reason to investigate various theories of spirituality is to help us understand purpose and meaning in life, and how one can interpret one's existence in relation to other people. By understanding inner strength and having spiritual insight, one is better able to withstand any circumstance that may be stressful; spiritual insight will help to manage stress better because one will be able to modify one's thoughts and behaviors to cope with the condition causing stress. By becoming more conscious of our thoughts and the choices that we have, we may then use our inner strength to relax and control the changes in the body as we seek balance and harmony. When we are able to regulate our emotions—primarily the negative ones—we thereby feel more at peace and reduce our arousal levels, bringing the body to a state of equilibrium. This mind-body relation helps to restore balance and cope with stress and makes us more resilient to any future precursors of stress.

Spirituality promotes healthy behavior. Practicing spirituality not only helps to alleviate anxious feelings and promote healing ones, it also positively influences the immune, cardiovascular, hormonal, and nervous systems. It is believed that certain beliefs, attitudes, and practices associated with being a spiritual person influence health. Faith, hope, and forgiveness, and the use of social support and prayer have a noticeable effect on health and healing. It is believed that faith increases the body's resistance to stress; helps women with breast cancer to better cope with stress; enables one to find life more meaningful; and reduces chances of suffering from posttraumatic stress disorder (Khosla, 2012).

SPIRITUALITY AND WELL-BEING

Spiritual practices tend to improve coping skills and induce relaxation. They foster feelings of optimism and hope, while reducing feelings of depression and anxiety. Spiritual well-being conceptualizes human functioning as an integration of the body (*soma*), soul (*psyche*), and spirit (*pneuma*). Spiritual practices enhance physical, mental, and emotional well-being, as well as maximizing the potential for growth and self-actualization. The components of spiritual wellness include meaning and purpose in life, one's intrinsic values, transcendent beliefs, and community or relationships in one's life (Khosla, 2012).

SPIRITUAL PRACTICES

There are many spiritual practices or attitudes that are encouraged for healthy living, such as hope, optimism, compassion, and forgiveness. For example, forgiveness involves a release of hostility and resentment from past experiences that hurt.

Learning to forgive someone who has hurt you in the past not only reduces anger, but also makes you more hopeful and better able to deal with emotions. Forgiveness allows us to move forward without being controlled by past relational difficulties or abuse (Reed & Enright, 2006), thereby enhancing well-being and physical health.

Practical spirituality involves the transformation of the self within the existing culture and society. It is a pathway toward self-realization and the realization of God or a higher power and the surrounding world. It seeks to transform religious pursuits creatively and constructively. Practice involves determining the truth that contains the meaning, experience, and co-realization of life. For example, social engagement in Buddhism, and liberation theology in Islam and Christianity, are examples of how spirituality may manifest itself. In Hinduism, there are many ways in which practical spirituality has manifested itself: the teachings of the Upanishads, the vision and preaching of the Buddha, the *bhakti* movements, the vision of practical Vedanta by Swami Vivekananda, Sri Aurobindo's strivings for Life Divine, and Mahatma Gandhi's experiments with truth and struggle for independence are all examples of practical spirituality.

The *bhakti* movements in the Hindu religion have involved struggle against the domination of caste and gender. They use songs with the themes of unity, self- and social liberation, and enlightenment. The beliefs of Sufism and Sikhism are a result of the transformational dialogue between Hinduism and Islam (Das, 1982). Whether it is Islam, Christianity, Hinduism, or Buddhism, there are notable similarities in preachings and teachings: to explore the underlying goodness in humanity, to unify despite all dissimilarities, to forgive, and to be tolerant and compassionate. The pathway may vary, but the goal is the same, and if one realizes this goal of purity, love, and brotherhood/sisterhood, then there will be peace, happiness, friendship, and sharing.

Swami Vivekananda urges us to realize that the highest idea of mortality and unselfishness goes hand in hand with the highest idea of metaphysical conception, which pertains to the realization that person himself or herself is God: "You are that Impersonal Being: that God for whom you have been searching all over the time is yourself—yourself not in the personal self but in the impersonal" (Vivekananda, 1991, p. 332, as cited in Giri, 2002). Hence, the emphasis is to understand the knowledge that one is divine, one is part of a universal being. This knowledge is the key to human well-being.

As the *Bhagavad Gita* proposes, knowledge to know oneself and one's consciousness is the pathway to happiness on the journey to self-awakening; it is important to let go of the inner suffering, self-pity, and feelings of dejection so that we may gain insight into our inner strength. We must become more sensitive and compassionate toward our inner lives. The darkness of one's ignorance can be dispelled once there is awareness that the immortal *Atman,* or the essential self, is the center of being. This enhances self-confidence and fearlessness to resolve all conflicts.

The quest for spiritual experience involves unifying the fragmented pieces into something that is whole and meaningful. Swami Vivekananda believed that God is present everywhere: He is omnipresent in everything and is more real than our senses. The ontological realism of God (or nature of being of God) is a belief in the reality and experience of God that is quite consistent with epistemological relativism (Bhaskar, 2002). That God is imminent within being, and is the true binder of everything that exists. One has to feel the presence of the divine in society, in one's life, and in this world. God is omnipresent and omnipotent.

What is needed is a transformation of our conceptions of good and bad. The manifestation of good and evil takes many different forms. Swami Vivekananda suggests that the *Vedanta* (the Hindu Indian text) recognizes no sin, it only recognizes error. The greatest error is to say that we are weak. From a Christian perspective, Giani Vattimo (1999) redefined *sin* as a failure in love. Love is unconditional, and we need to overcome integral sins of not being able to love. God is unconditional love. We need to strive, despite our restrictions and shortcomings, to show gratitude, love, and grace; to realize the importance of love in life; to go beyond a facile dualism of good and evil. The real genesis of evil is selfishness. We need to love more than ourselves, to seek higher selves that have the goodness, nobility, and courage to view reality in totality.

PERSPECTIVES ON SPIRITUALITY FROM INDIA

The Upanishads draw a distinction between *Para vidya* (spirituality) and *Apara vidya* (science). The *Mundaka Upanishad* proposes that there are two kinds of knowledge: the higher and the lower. The lower knowledge is the knowledge of the Vedas and of grammar, sciences, and heaven; the higher knowledge is the knowledge that alone reaches the imperishable Being. The information provided in the Upanishad steers advances toward self-realization. *Keno Upanishad* suggests that the end (goals) of life can be attained only if the self is realized while the body lasts. *Katha Upanishad* tells us that unless a person is able to realize the self while the body lasts, he or she must go from life to life through a series of incarnations.

What, then, is the notion of absolute truth or ultimate reality? We can try to understand what goes on inside the mind (the *antahkarana*) to understand the Absolute in us. Maybe we can try to perceive God as the ultimate unifying force between the inner and outer worlds. Descartes (1596–1650) suggested that the *cogito* helps us to understand the conception of God. However, Spinoza (1632–1677) proposed that neither the mind nor reality is primary; rather, God is the creator and end of everything: self-conceived, self-existent, and self-caused.

The *Vedic Rishis* expressed their vision of the Absolute or ultimate reality in the form of hymns, evoking responses at different levels of self-realization, worshipful devotion, and ritual sacrifices. The *Brihadaranayaka Upanishad* talks about the pathways to realize the Absolute or ultimate truth. It was revealed that the *Atman* (the self) should be known, and when this knowledge is achieved, everything in the universe is known. This is so because there is an identity between the *Atman* (self) and the *Brahman* (ultimate reality). The *Mahavakyas* suggest that there are different paths for realization of the Absolute. *Prajnanam Brahma* directs the seeker to meditate on the pure consciousness of the *Brahman* and to merge it with the individual consciousness in the universe. The liberation from material bondage—that is, the attainment of *mukti*—is an endeavor to meditate and realize the Absolute. The inner being is the part of the Absolute, *Ayam Atma Brahman.*

To understand the nature of consciousness, it is important to begin with the states of consciousness—the *avasthatraya* in the Vedantic tradition. The *Brahman* is the *sat* (truth), *cit* (consciousness), and *ananda* (bliss). Particularly important is the *cit svarupa* of *Brahman,* the manifestation of the creator. The internal body, the senses, the *atahkarna,* popularly known as the mind, is endowed with intellect or *Buddhi.* The "I" consists of the *ahankarh,* consciousness, as well as *cit* and *sambrita,* the self. The Vedanta suggests that consciousness is the spiritual force in the *antahkarana* that guides it. *Sankara* refers to the I/Thou issue in the *Adhyasabhasa,* that is, the problem of *Asmat* (self) and *Yusmat* (the other than the self, which includes the mind, senses, body, and the things in the world).

Consciousness provides the *pramanas:* perceptions, inferences, and verbal testimonies. Immediate experience is the core of absolutism, which must be apprehended along with self-realization on the path of spiritual pilgrimage. Sri Aurobindo (1950) views consciousness as being present from the beginning of the cosmic evolution, though initially hidden. Matter is unconscious, but contains the potential for consciousness. Gradually the conscious force evolves. Aurobindo identified the ascending states of consciousness above the ordinary mind, which are difficult to describe. These ascending states, which may be called the spiritual mind, have four sublevels. First is the higher mind: the state of a sage or spiritualized thinker having a Unitarian sense of Being, a dynamic nature capable of forming and using a multitude of aspects of knowledge. It is the mind that is seeking the truth. The next level is the illumined mind that has a greater force of consciousness, to which knowledge appears as a spiritual light. It is like a downpour of inwardly visible light (particularly visual in nature). The third level is the intuitive mind or the intuitional being. At this level, the consciousness of the subject coincides with that of the object. The fourth level is the overmind. It is a power of the cosmic consciousness, a principle of global knowledge, which carries it in a delegated light from the supramental gnosis. The overmind is the highest power of the lower hemisphere. In order to bring about transcendence, the supermind determines the supreme self, determining truth-action and directing the power of manifestation of that transcendence. This nonphysical spiritual state is available to the overmind. One may choose to participate in the divine evolution, with mind and mental humanity transforming within spiritual reality.

Hence, spiritual transformation is primarily the process of growth through the upper layers of the consciousness, of the higher, illumined, intuitive, and overmind. This process continues until it can be experienced frequently and some of the energy from these layers can be brought down to purify the normal mind and the vital and unconscious being.

Gandhi's vision of life involved the spiritual aspects of knowledge, such as interdependence and mutual inclusiveness, which are characterized by the centrality of truth and nonviolence. He motivated seekers to pursue truth in order to experience the spiritual oneness or the unity of being through *ahimsa* (nonviolence), *swaraj* (self-rule), and *satyagraha* (soul or truth force). He always proposed that self-purification leads to self-knowledge, and held that humanity can exist in peace only if truth, morality, and reason work together in harmony toward progress in ethical existence. Hence, he defined Hinduism as a search for truth through nonviolent means. His approach to spirituality was quite liberal and open-minded, as he emphasized reason and moral sense to characterize the essence of *dharma* or religion in the widest sense of spirituality. He suggested that a conscientious seeker of truth will strive for identification with the other through utter humility and self-purification. Without this, the pursuit of truth will not contribute to the state of *sarvodya* (welfare for all). The main essence of his vision was self-purification, without which the observance of *ahimsa* will be merely an empty dream, and it will be impossible to realize God and oneself. Gandhi said that to attain perfect purity, one has to become absolutely passion-free in thought, speech, and action, to rise above the opposing currents of emotions such as love, hatred, attachment, and repulsion (Gandhi, 1927).

PERSPECTIVES ON SPIRITUALITY FROM WESTERN CULTURE

A number of European and American secular psychologists, psychiatrists, and philosophers have written about spirituality and the human search for meaning. The philosopher Carl Jung (1978) believed that spirituality reflected the soul. He believed that when the soul is unable to find a meaning in life, it causes spiritual stagnation, leading to psychoneurosis. He contended that without an inner transcendent experience, human beings lack the resources to withstand the "blandishments of the world" and get in touch with purity of the self. Humanistic psychologist Carl Rogers (1961) felt that people basically have a positive direction toward their true being. In the right conditions, they have the power to reflect and transcend in "fully functioning personality" and flourish. Psychotherapist Viktor Frankl (1978) suggested that the search for meaning is vital to human development. Psychoanalyst and philosopher Erich Fromm (Fromm & Funk, 2003) proposed that humanistic alternatives of development are only a matter of awareness of human being. The goal of life is the fullest development of human powers, specifically those of reason and of love, including the transcending of the narrowness of one's ego. Psychologist Abraham Maslow (1968) referred to the "being values," such as wholeness, goodness, and self-sufficiency, as a part of the human self. These are meta-needs or growth-needs that can be integrated in daily life. Maslow (1971) described such integration in terms of transcendent self-actualization, which carries a spiritual significance in the sacred life. As Nelson (2009, p. 222) notes, "the cognitive structuralist theories developed by Jean Piaget and Lawrence Kohlberg attempted to understand the human person by trying to identify underlying organized structures or schemas of mental activity. Their theories of moral development have been particularly popular, because morality is central to spiritual development, which can be thought of as a kind of learning or change with transformational properties." Nelson also points out the importance of the theologian James Loder, who stated that human development is shaped by both psychological and spiritual transformation. In contrast, Nelson notes that those who rely more on psychological theories believe that spiritual transformation is embedded in human development, and therefore tend to favor psychology over theology (Nelson, 2009, p. 238; Balswick, King, & Reimer, 2005, p. 274).

CONCLUSION

Spirituality helps people acknowledge and work through their feelings, their anxieties, their moral dilemmas, and the emptiness that occurs due to stagnant life patterns. It provides a valuable insight into the self and knowledge of the power of the cosmos that surround the self. Spirituality that leads to freedom may involve relinquishing constant needs for power and control. Spiritual insight helps one to accept the mystery that is inherent in life. One is not only predisposed to a more optimistic approach in life, but also is more grateful and welcoming of what others have to offer. Having a healthy spiritual life helps a person deal with stresses large and small, and can help to prevent mental health problems. If we are to make sense of our emotions, overcome grief, anxiety, and fear of the known and unknown, and realize our desire for happiness, spirituality must be a part of our lives.

REFERENCES AND FURTHER READING

Agamben, G. (1993). *The coming community: Theory out of bounds* (Vol. 1). Minneapolis, MN: University of Minnesota Press.

Aurobindo, S. (1950). *Savitri.* Pondicherry, India: Sri Aurobindo Ashram.

Balswick, J. O., King, P. E., & Reimer, K. S. (2005). *The reciprocating self: Human development in theological perspective.* Downers Grove, IL: InterVarsity Academic Press.
Bhaskar, R. (2002). *From science to emancipation.* Delhi, India: Sage.
Burke, T. M., Flowers, C., Graham, S., & Furr, S. (2001). Religion and spirituality in coping with stress. *Counseling and Values, 46,* 1–13.
Das, C. R. (1982). *Santha sahitya* [literature of the saints]. Bhubanaeswar, Orrisa, India: Sahitya Academy.
Ellison, C. W. (1983). Spiritual well-being: Conceptualization and measurement. *Journal of Psychology and Theology, 11,* 330–340.
Frankl, V. E. (1978). *The unheard cry for meaning: Psychotherapy and humanism.* New York, NY: Simon & Schuster.
Fromm, E., & Funk, R. (2003). *Man for himself: An inquiry into the psychology of ethics.* Abingdon, UK: Routledge [Kindle edition].
Gandhi, M. K. (1927). *An autobiography: The story of my experiments with truth.* Ahmedabad, India: Navajivan Publishing House.
Giri, Anant Kumar (Ed.). (2002). *Conversations and transformations: Toward a new ethics of self and society.* Lanham, MD: Lexington Books.
Holland, J. C., Kash, K. M., & Passick, S. (1998). A brief spiritual beliefs inventory for use in quality of life research on life threatening illness. *Psychooncology, 7,* 460–469.
Jernigan, H. L. (2001). Spirituality in older adults: A cross-cultural and interfaith perspective. *Pastoral Psychology, 49,* 413–437.
Jung, C. G. (1978). *Psychological reflections: A new anthology of his writings, 1905–1961.* Princeton, NJ: Princeton University Press.
Khosla, M. (2012). Affect and well-being: A spiritual perspective. *Research Journal of Social Science and Management, 1*(12), 5–7.
Maslow, A. (1968). *Toward a psychology of being.* New York, NY: Van Nostrand.
Maslow, A. (1971). *The farther reaches of human nature.* New York, NY: Viking.
Miller, G. (1999). The development of the spiritual focus of counseling and counselor education. *Journal of Counseling and Development, 77,* 498–501.
Nelson, J. M. (2009). *Psychology, religion, and spirituality.* New York, NY: Springer.
Park, J. H., Meyers, L. S., & Czar, G. C. (1998). Religiosity and spirituality: An exploratory analysis using the CPI 3-vector model. *Journal of Social Behavior and Personality, 13,* 541–552.
Rama. (1985). *The perennial psychology of Bhagavad Gita.* Honesdale, PA: The Himalayan International Institute of Yoga and Philosophy of U.S.A.
Reed, G. L., & Enright, R. D. (2006). The effects of forgiveness therapy on depression, anxiety, and posttraumatic stress for women after spousal emotional abuse. *Journal of Consulting and Clinical Psychology, 74,* 920–929.
Rogers, C. R. (1961). *On becoming a person: A psychotherapist's view of psychotherapy.* New York, NY: Houghton Mifflin.
Roof, W. C. (1999). *Spiritual marketplace: Baby boomers and the remaking of American religion.* Princeton, NJ: Princeton University Press.
Rose, S. (2001). Is the term "spirituality" a word that everyone uses, but nobody understands what anyone means by it? *Journal of Contemporary Religion, 16*(2), 193–207.

Sankara, A. (1970). *Pancikaranam*. Gujrat, India: Gujrati Printing Press.

Schneiders, S. M. (1998). The study of Christian spirituality: Contours and dynamics of a discipline. *Christian Spirituality Bulletin, 6*(1), 3–12.

Vattimo, G. (1999). *Belief*. Cambridge, UK: Polity Press.

Vergote, A. (2003). Plying between psychology and mysticism. In J. Belzen & A. Geels (Eds.), *Mysticism: A variety of psychological perspectives* (pp. 81–107). Amsterdam, The Netherlands: Rodopi.

Vivekananda, S. (1991). *The complete works of Swami Vivekananda*. Calcutta, India: Advaita Ashram.

Zinnbauer, B. J., Pargament, K. I., Cole, B., Rye, M. S., Butter, E. M., Belavich, T. G., et al. (1997). Religion and spirituality: Unfuzzing the fuzzy. *Journal for the Scientific Study of Religion, 36*, 549–564.

6

THE NEUROSCIENCE OF STRESS

Cynthia Schroeder

> The brain, and the brain alone, is the source of our pleasures, joys, laughter, and amusement, as well as our sorrow, pain, grief, and tears. It is especially the organ we use to think and learn, see and hear, to distinguish the ugly from the beautiful, the bad from the good, and the pleasant from the unpleasant. The brain is also the seat of madness and delirium, of the fears and terrors that assail us by night or by day, of sleeplessness, awkward mistakes, and thoughts that will not come, of pointless anxieties, forgetfulness, and eccentricities.
>
> —*Hippocrates, ca. 400 BCE*

Throughout time, the perception of the role and function of the brain and nervous system has been debated and changed. The Greek philosophers Aristotle and Plato debated whether the heart (cardiocentric) or the brain (cephalocentric) was the controller of the body. Since that time, it has been demonstrated that the central nervous system (CNS, comprised of the brain, brain stem, and spinal cord) controls not only the body, but our emotions and reactions as well.

Within the brain there are a number of different systems, but the limbic system is the most important for stress response. This chapter reviews some of the anatomy of the limbic system, as well as the neurotransmitters involved in stress response. In addition, the neuroscience behind maladaptive responses to stressors, and strategies to maintain the well-being of the brain, are highlighted.

NEUROCIRCUITRY OF STRESS

To understand the neurocircuitry of stress in the brain, it is first necessary to understand the anatomy of the limbic system. The three central components of the limbic system are the hippocampus, the hypothalamus, and the amygdala.

The amygdala is a small, almond-shaped structure located in the center of the brain. Its primary function is interpreting and relaying information having to do with strong emotion (e.g., fear, anxiety). The amygdala receives input of two general types. The first type is from the five senses: taste, touch, olfaction (smell), sight, and hearing. The second type of input is less specific: it is a general sense of physical and emotional status and well-being. The amygdala then has to process and react to this information, sending signals to other areas of the brain (Nolte, 2009).

In addition, the amygdala is crucial for emotion-related learning. This means that if a human is in a stressful or emotional situation, and the amygdala decides how to interpret and react to that stress/emotion, the brain reinforces the response. For example, if a person is being scolded, he may lash out in anger or cry with shame. Whichever reaction occurs is reinforced in the amygdala and thus is more likely to reoccur in a similar situation. This is an important concept when we look at how stress affects the limbic system, and why changing one's reaction is so difficult.

The hypothalamus is a small gland located in front of the amygdala. It is part of the limbic system, and also crucial to the proper functioning of the endocrine system. The endocrine system is a chain of organs and glands that release hormones that travel to other locations in the body; it includes the adrenal glands, pancreas, and gonads. The hypothalamus releases numerous hormones, though corticotropin-releasing hormone (CRH) is the most important when it comes to the reaction of stress. CRH then stimulates the pituitary gland (a gland located in the brain close to the hypothalamus) to release adrenocorticotropic hormone (ACTH). ACTH stimulates the adrenal glands (located on top of the kidneys) to release cortisol. In a stressful event, cortisol lowers immune-system functioning (to save energy and resources), shifts the internal processes of the body to focus on producing energy, and sharpens cognition. This pathway is often referred to as the hypothalamic-pituitary-adrenocortical axis (HPA axis) (Kandel et al., 2013). Cortisol causes the body to store and process glucose differently. Having extremely high levels for a prolonged period can lead to excess storage of body fat as well as muscle wasting. Activation of the HPA axis in this manner is what is commonly referred to as the "fight-or-flight" response or phenomenon.

THE BRAIN

The hippocampus is a small structure behind the amygdala. It often described as resembling a ram's horn or a seahorse because of its small spiral in the middle.

POLYVAGAL THEORY

Polyvagal theory, developed by neuroscientist Stephen Porges, expands the foundation of the role of the nervous system in the classic fight-or-flight response. The polyvagal theory proposes that there are three substructures of the vagus circuit, a major nerve in the parasympathetic nervous system, which influence regulation of the fight-or-flight response. (The parasympathetic nervous system is mostly responsible for restoration and relaxation.) The vagus circuitry includes different paths of functioning. The first pathway conserves metabolic activity; the second distributes energy needed for the mobilization of resources for the fight-or-flight response; the third pathway incorporates relaxed states, promoting the relaxation and restoration responses and imparting a sense of safety (Streeter, Gerbarg, Saper, Ciraulo, & Brown, 2012). This may correlate with studies demonstrating that when we feel love and safety, the perception of threat is reduced (Norman, Lawrence, Iles, Benattayallah, & Karl, 2014).

Thus, when neither fighting nor running is a viable option, the vagus circuitry offers coping mechanisms: one of being present in the face of the initial threat that provides cues of being safe; or a mechanism of not being present in the face of the initial threat that provides cues of not being safe. The behaviors of not being present may include fainting or dissociating, depending on the needs of the individual (see Howes, 2013).

—*Serena Wadhwa*

The hippocampus is often thought of as the memory vault for the brain, as it is involved in processing, storing, and recalling memories. This function is crucial in regard to stress response, because it allows one to form memories, positive or negative, of stressful situations. When a similar situation presents itself, the amygdala recalls the memory, which influences how one responds. In addition to this critical function, it has been shown that stressors presenting themselves as directly harmful to one's survival or health are remembered more vividly than other memories (McEwen, 2000).

Lastly, the limbic system communicates with the frontal cortex of the brain. The frontal cortex is known to be the primary center of critical thinking and evaluation in the brain. The amygdala projects here, delivering information that one becomes conscious of. Before the amygdala sends a signal through this pathway, the person in the situation is not aware of his or her feelings or response. As a result of the processing happening largely on an unconscious level, emotional response to stress is often viewed as reflexive.

Conclusively, in a stressful situation, the amygdala perceives the stress and tries to pull memories from the hippocampus. At the same time, it also stimulates the hypothalamus to prepare the body to enter fight-or-flight mode. When these three structures work together, the limbic system functions very quickly (within milliseconds) to process a response to stress. As the response becomes more rehearsed, it becomes quicker and the neural circuitry becomes stronger for that response—almost reflexive. This is why learning different responses to stressors takes time and practice. The brain has neuroplasticity, or the ability to change and rewire, so a change in response is possible if the new response is practiced and reinforced enough times.

NEUROTRANSMITTERS OF STRESS

Neurotransmitters are chemicals produced within the brain or body that are constantly released to maintain a state of homeostasis, and also to allow one area of the brain to communicate with other areas. There are a plethora of neurotransmitters, but six are extremely important in terms of their function in stress response: epinephrine, norepinephrine, dopamine, serotonin, gamma-aminobutyric acid (GABA), and acetylcholine.

Epinephrine and norepinephrine (also known as adrenalin and noradrenalin) work in conjunction to modulate the fight-or-flight response previously described. Epinephrine is released from the adrenal glands after they are stimulated by ACTH. (Recall that ACTH is released from the pituitary gland after it is stimulated by CRH from the hypothalamus.) Norepinephrine is released in a part of the brain stem called the locus coeruleus. These neurotransmitters together increase heart rate and respiration, slow digestion, dilate the blood vessels to fuel muscles more efficiently, dilate the pupils (though peripheral vision is decreased), and generally prepare the body to prepare to fight or flee (Schmidt & Thews, 1989; Gleitman, Fridlund, & Reisberg, 2004). Norepinephrine specifically prompts vigilant concentration, as opposed to one's normal state of cognitive awareness (Hunt, Keogh, & French, 2006). Once the stressor is removed, the levels of these neurotransmitters decrease and the person returns to a normal state of homeostasis. There is some evidence to support the theory that norepinephrine plays a larger role in returning to homeostasis after a fight-or-flight response than in the actual response, but this is debated. Although the body does return to a state of homeostasis, experiencing this stress response too often can have lasting negative effects, including, for example, headaches, body aches, fatigue, decrease in sexual drive, indigestion, chest pain, anxiety, depression, and sleep problems (Mayo Clinic Staff, 2013).

Dopamine is often thought of as the reward or pleasure neurotransmitter. While it does have that function, it also has other roles in the brain and body. Dopamine has two important roles in stress response in the limbic system.

"Response selection" theory says that when the limbic system has different responses to choose from, it will lower the inhibition of one (using dopamine to do so), making it easier for the person to produce that response. The second role dopamine plays in stress response is rewarding the selected response, making it more likely to be repeated. (Recall that the neural pathway of this response is also strengthened.)

The neurotransmitter serotonin regulates mood and cognitive arousal. Although serotonin is not directly involved in acute stress response, sustained increased amounts of stress can reduce the amounts of serotonin produced in the brain. A reduction in serotonin and norepinephrine has been shown to cause depressive symptoms in humans. A reduction in serotonin and GABA (another neurotransmitter) has been linked to anxiety disorders, including generalized anxiety disorder (GAD) and social anxiety disorder. Depressed serotonin levels generally do not return to normal on their own, but pharmacological treatments are available. Selective serotonin reuptake inhibitors (SSRIs) and serotonin norepinephrine reuptake inhibitors (SNRIs) are two types of medications frequently used to raise serotonin or serotonin and norepinephrine levels in the brain. Using these medications can retrain the brain to increase the amount of serotonin.

GABA (gamma-aminobutyric acid) is a neurotransmitter that functions as the major inhibiter in the brain. This means that it reduces the amount of neuroelectrical activity in the brain. As a result of this, GABA is an excellent pharmacological target for reducing anxiety. Benzodiazepines and barbiturates are two categories of drugs that directly affect the GABA receptors in the brain. Although both will work to alleviate the physiological feeling of anxiety and promote relaxation, benzodiazepines (Valium, Xanax) are currently more commonly used than their cousins the barbiturates (phenobarbital, pentobarbital), because they have increased safety with a reduced risk of overdose.

The neurotransmitter acetylcholine has two categories of functioning. The first is cognitive, allowing for learning, cognitive arousal, and reward. When one's acetylcholine level is increased, attention focuses and cognitive arousal increases. This allows a person to have optimal focus and concentration when presented with a significant stressor. The second function is related to movement of skeletal muscles. Acetylcholine activates at the neuromuscular junction, enabling skeletal muscle to contract and thus allowing a person to move. This is crucial during fight or flight, as one may need to either escape or defend oneself.

Each of these neurotransmitters has its own role and functions, and they are all crucial to maintaining homeostasis on a daily basis. Additionally, each has a vital function when the person is presented with a strong stressor and the body enters a fight-or-flight mode. Whether the task is focusing attention, speeding heart rate, stimulating muscle contraction, or allowing the body to return to normal, each of these neurotransmitters is vital to healthy functioning.

MALADAPTIVE BRAIN RESPONSES TO STRESS

The role of serotonin in depression, or more specifically clinical depression, has already been described to some extent. There is some argument that there are structural differences in the brains of people with clinical depression, as opposed to those without. However, a much more widely accepted theory is that serotonin, norepinephrine, and dopamine are expressed in reduced levels in those with clinical depression. Why this happens is not completely known. Some scientists argue genetics; some argue life events; some argue that it is caused by an overactive endocrine system, specifically the HPA axis. It is believed that an overactive HPA axis stimulates the hypothalamus to release corticotropin-releasing hormone (CRH) too frequently and stimulates the pituitary to release too much adrenocorticotropic hormone (ACTH), which in turn causes the adrenal glands to release epinephrine too frequently, thereby putting the body in a state of fight-or-flight response too often. None of these theories has been conclusively proven yet, but research still continues. Although the cause of clinical depression is not known or agreed upon, the method of treatment that is most widely accepted within the medical community is use of an antidepressant (like the SSRIs or SNRIs previously mentioned) coupled with counseling.

Anxiety is a mood characterized by an overall sense of ill-being, worry, and nervousness. It can become a mental disorder, generalized anxiety disorder (GAD), when it starts to interfere with one's life and increase in intensity. There are three schools of thought on what causes GAD in humans. The first is that parents with anxiety raise children in an anxious environment, thus causing the children to grow up to be anxious. The second is that there is a genetic predisposition to the condition. The third is that the amygdala and hippocampus are overactive, causing the brain to respond too strongly to nonthreatening stimuli. Although it is unknown which of these theories is true, or whether perhaps all are true, there are effective ways to treat anxiety in humans. A few types of pharmaceutical agents are often used. First, as with depression, many people who have GAD show improvement in their symptoms when taking an SSRI or SNRI. Second, for acute anxiety events (often referred to as *anxiety attacks* or *panic attacks*), benzodiazepines have high proven efficacy. Because benzodiazepines increase inhibition in the brain, they can slow the activity and firing in the amygdala and hippocampus. Further, benzodiazepines have a sedative and hypnotic effect. However, benzodiazepines are prescribed with caution, because there is a risk of developing a chemical dependency when taking them.

Posttraumatic stress disorder (PTSD) exhibits after exposure to a traumatic event. The hallmarks of PTSD are anxiety, nightmares, flashbacks, and persistent thoughts about the traumatic event that the person tries to avoid and suppress. Much like anxiety and depression, the exact neurobiological cause of PTSD is highly debated. One of the most popular neurobiological theories is that the amygdala becomes hyperactive in response to the traumatic event. As a result, it triggers the HPA axis too frequently. Some researchers have also shown that people with PTSD have lower amounts of serotonin and dopamine than normal, while they have higher amounts of norepinephrine.

Obviously, it is possible for the brain and body to adapt poorly to chronic or severe stress, but they do not necessarily always do so. Many people who experience chronic stress never develop or struggle with depression, anxiety, or PTSD. It is important to note, though, that there are neurobiological components to these disorders, and that medical help is available for those who need it.

MAINTAINING A HEALTHY BRAIN

After discussing how the brain can be negatively affected by stress, it is crucial to highlight strategies to keep one's brain functioning optimally. Though there is no exact formula guaranteed to maintain health, there are steps one can take to help: rest, exercise, nutrition, and cognitive activities.

The first, and possibly most important thing one can do to help maintain the health of one's brain and nervous system is to maintain a regular sleep schedule of 7 to 8 hours a night. The exact amount of sleep needed varies from individual to individual, but it is imperative to sleep—even though the exact physiological role of sleep is debated. In fact, William Dement, who founded the Sleep Research Center at Stanford University, was quoted as saying, "As far as I know, the only reason we need to sleep that is really, really solid is because we get sleepy" (Brogaard & Marlow, 2015). Some argue that sleep clears toxins from the brain; some researchers argue that it allows the brain and immune system time to recharge and promote healing; some argue that it allows the brain to process and store memories. Although the exact purpose of sleep is unknown, it is certain that sleep is crucial to maintain health. Lack of sleep causes cognitive decline and memory impairment, and it is possibly related to some neurodegenerative disorders. Many scientists also argue that a lack of sleep leads to the impairment in cognitive functioning and reasoning the next day that is called *sleep debt.* This "debt" can accumulate, leading to worsening symptoms.

A second way to help maintain a healthy brain and nervous system is to engage in physical exercise on a regular basis. The cardiovascular benefits of physical exercise are well known, but the neurological benefits are often overlooked. First, physical exercise is shown to reduce the amount of cortisol in the body. Additionally, regular physical exercise is shown to increase cognitive functioning. Physical activity increases serotonin and endorphins in the brain, which are protective against depression and anxiety. Lastly, physical exercise is believed to be protective against neurodegeneration and dementia.

A third way to safeguard the health of the brain is to maintain proper nutrition. The brain is largely composed of fat, and uses glucose as its main source of nutrition. As a result, it is important to ensure consumption of enough fat, carbohydrates, and protein to fuel the brain properly. When one does not eat a balanced diet, headaches are a very common short-term symptom; prolonged consumption of an imbalanced diet can lead to worsening of both cognitive and physical effects.

A fourth way to maintain a healthy nervous system and body is to practice meditation, particularly mindful meditation. This practice goes back thousands of years, but in recent years, neurological research has started to emerge that prove its benefits. People who practice mindful meditation regularly show positive structural differences in their brains. Additionally, it is thought that those who practice mindful meditation show more resilience and resistance to depression and anxiety.

Lastly, there is some evidence that cognitive exercise can improve the overall health of the brain. Cognitive exercise includes any activities that push the brain's abilities, including reading; doing crossword puzzles, jigsaw puzzles, and Sudoku; and playing games. Engaging in these activities is believed to promote neuroplasticity and neural integrity.

Each of these activities is just a small step, but putting them together can help protect the integrity of the brain for a lifetime. In addition, all these activities increase resilience for a person dealing with stress, and aid the brain in returning to its normal state of homeostasis.

CONCLUSION

Stress affects the brain in a number of ways. The limbic system is an integral part of a human's survival, as it stimulates the fight-or-flight response that protects one's well-being and safety. Although the limbic system is part of the brain and nervous system, it is intimately intertwined with the endocrine system, specifically the HPA axis. When this system is activated, there is an effect on a number of neurotransmitters as well, including epinephrine, norepinephrine, serotonin, dopamine, acetylcholine, and GABA. These neurotransmitters are also vital to the maintenance of homeostasis. When they are present in disproportionate amounts, it is possible for depression, anxiety, PTSD, or other problems to develop. These psychological disorders are disruptive and can be debilitating, but treatment options are available. Lastly, a number of strategies are available to help maintain the health and well-being of the brain and nervous system. The brain's complete role in stress and stress response is complex, but it is where the first response to stressors occurs. As the power and functions of the brain become better understood, research continues to look for new strategies to help people cope with stress.

ROBERT ADER AND PSYCHONEUROIMMUNOLOGY

Robert Ader was born in 1932. He received a doctorate in psychology in 1957 and began an academic and research career at the University of Rochester. Ader's interest was within the realm of the body and the mind. At the time of his appointment to the University of Rochester, Ader was free to conduct psychobiological experiments with animals, an area that he particularly wanted to explore. In the early 1970s, while conducting a groundbreaking study, Ader observed the effects of a conditioned taste aversion response in rats. The results of this study indicated that the immune system, once thought to be self-regulating and to function independently, was classically influenced by an immune-suppressing drug that was injected when the rats consumed the sweeter-tasting liquid. With further exposure to this drug, the rats that continued to consume sweetened water demonstrated drastic effects on the immune system, and some animals even died.

This study, along with other research that was available at the time, led Ader to coin the term *psychoneuroimmunology,* which he defined as "the study of the interactions among behavior, neural and endocrine function, and immune processes" (Ader & Cohen, 1993, p. 53). Psychoneuroimmunology developed as a new field within the realm of stress, understanding of how the immune system is influenced by neuronal and endocrine functioning, and how the immune system manifests and affects an organism's behaviors and actions (Ader & Cohen, 1993). Because the nervous system and endocrine system are the primary systems involved in regulation of the stress response and homeostasis (the body's ability to regulate and balance itself), understanding the influence of stress on the immune system and how this increases an individual's vulnerability to disease was an important contribution to the field of stress research. This research has many implications. For example, according to Ader and Cohen (1993), a change in housing conditions of animals can influence antibody responses and increase an animal's susceptibility to disease. Another example is the experience of early separation from mothers, where decreased antibodies were observed in the separated infants.

Ader first used the term *psychoneuroimmunology* in 1981, in his presidential address to the American Psychosomatic Society (Ader, 2000). Ader cited other research that demonstrated similar findings regarding the interactions of behavior and the endocrine, neural, and immune systems. These interactions are clear, and there seems to be bidirectional influence; however, research continues to explore causal links and direct influences (Ader, 2000). Ader emphasized that the interaction of behavior with the endocrine, neural, and immune systems opens multiple pathways through which various factors can influence these systems. We now know that is more than one way that things can happen, as opposed to the original theory of the stress response, which posited only one response to all noxious stimuli (Ader, 2000). Thus, further research and clinical applications continue and are encouraged.

—*Serena Wadhwa*

REFERENCES AND FURTHER READING

Ader, R. (n.d.). *The papers of Robert Ader.* Edward G. Miner Library, University of Rochester Medical Center. Retrieved from https://www.urmc.rochester.edu/libraries/miner/historical_services/archives/Faculty/PapersofRobertAder.cfm.

Ader, R. (2000). On the development of psychoneuroimmunology. *European Journal of Pharmacology, 405*(1), 167–176.

Ader, R., & Cohen, N. (1993). Psychoneuroimmunology: Conditioning and stress. *Annual Review of Psychology, 44*(1), 53–85.

Brogaard, B., & Marlow, K. (2015). *The superhuman mind: Free the genius in your brain.* New York, NY: Hudson Street Press.

Gleitman, H., Fridlund, A. J., & Reisberg, D. (2004). *Psychology* (6th ed.). New York, NY: W.W. Norton.

Howes, R. (2013). Wearing your heart on your face: The polyvagal circuit in the consulting room. *Psychotherapy Networker.* Retrieved from https://www.questia.com/magazine/1P3-3182128061/point-of-view-wearing-your-heart-on-your-face-the.

Hunt, C., Keogh, E., & French, C. C. (2006, August). Anxiety sensitivity: The role of conscious awareness and selective attentional bias to physical thread. *Emotion, 6*(3), 418–428.

Kandel, E. R., Schwartz, J. H., Jessell, T. M., Siegelbaum, S. A., & Hudspeth, A. J. (2013). *Principles of neural science* (5th ed.). New York, NY: McGraw-Hill.

Mayo Clinic Staff. (2013). Stress symptoms: Effects on your body and behavior. Retrieved from http://www.mayoclinic.org/stress-symptoms/ART-20050987.

McEwen, B. S. (2000). The neurobiology of stress: From serendipity to clinical relevance. *Brain Research, 886*(1–2), 172–189.

Nolte, J. (2009). *The human brain: An introduction to its functional anatomy* (6th ed.). Philadelphia, PA: Mosby Elsevier.

Norman, L., Lawrence, N., Iles, A., Benattayallah, A., & Karl, A. (2014). Attachment-security priming attenuates amygdala activation to social and linguistic threat. *Social Cognitive and Affective Neuroscience.* doi:10.1093/scan/nsu127. Retrieved from http://scan.oxfordjournals.org/content/early/2014/11/05/scan.nsu127.

Schmidt, A., & Thews, G. (1989). Autonomic nervous system. In W. Janig (Ed.), *Human physiology* (2nd ed., pp. 333–370). New York, NY: Springer-Verlag.

Streeter, C. C., Gerbarg, P. L., Saper, R. B., Ciraulo, D. A., & Brown, R. P. (2012). Effects of yoga on the autonomic nervous system, gamma-aminobutyric-acid, and allostasis in epilepsy, depression, and post-traumatic stress disorder. *Medical Hypotheses, 78*(5), 571–579.

Vitetta, L., Anton, B., Cortizo, F., & Sali, A. (2005). Mind-body medicine: Stress and its impact on overall health and longevity. *Annals of the New York Academy of Sciences, 1057*(1), 492–505.

7

Holism and Stress: Brain, Mind, and Society

Julia Yang

A multitude of biochemical, physiological, and psychosocial factors interact to contribute to the idiosyncratic and accumulative nature of stress. The adaptation of the total mind-body-social functions in the face of stress has huge impacts on disease and health. Whereas good stress promotes survival, *dis*tress, in contrast, can cause or worsen disease. Perceptions and emotional experiences in all areas of life tasks, as well as relationships at home, school, work, and community, predispose humans either to health or illness. Holism, as postulated in Jan Christian Smuts's philosophy, is profoundly embedded in Adler's theory of treating the whole person. The great Austrian psychologist Alfred Adler (1870–1937) established Individual Psychology in Vienna with the aim of understanding the individual style of life as a part of the whole. Holism and Individual Psychology, when combined with recent insight into neural adaptation, provide a functional conceptual framework for understanding stress. This chapter views stress through the lenses of holism and Individual Psychology, to discuss the roles that the brain, the mind, and society play in stress response and consequences. Although the concept of holism in psychology typically refers to a higher synthesis of body, mind, and spirit, discussions in this chapter pertain to the body-mind-society aspects of stress.

HOLISM

> Both matter and life consist, in the atom and the cell, of unit structures whose ordered grouping produces the natural wholes which we call bodies or organisms. This character or feature of "wholeness" points to something fundamental in the universe, fundamental in the sense that it is practically universal, that it is a real operative factor,

> and that its shaping influence is felt ever more deeply and widely with the advance of Evolution. Holism is the term here coined (from the Greek *holos*—whole) to designate this fundamental factor operative towards the making or creation of wholes in the universe. (Smuts, in Ansbacher, 1994, p. 489)

The term *holism* was coined by South African Jan Christian Smuts (1870–1950) in the book *Holism and Evolution,* published in 1926. Alfred Adler, having already completed his 1922 book on individual psychology, was among the first to acknowledge Smuts's contribution to psychology and their shared view of holism as the key to science (Ansbacher, 1994; Way, 1950). In his article "Holistic Medicine" (written in the 1970s and published in 1997), Rudolf Dreikurs (1897–1972) explained that the concept of holism is in line with works on the science of organisms, Gestalt psychology, the relationship between energy and matter explored in quantum theory, and Einstein's relativity theory. Holism goes beyond the traditional dualist views of opposing systems, such as body and mind, and it goes against the dominant reductionist approaches of studying mind and its elements in medicine and psychology. Smuts argued that "a whole is more than the sum of its parts" (Smuts, in Ansbacher, 1994, p. 489) and that the whole determines the parts (Dreikurs, 1997).

Holism helps us understand how we synthesize our brain-mind-environment activities in the face of stress. First, we must see that the whole of the living organism is characterized by growth and regeneration, which occur by self-modification of the parts themselves. Minds and bodies influence each other through a creative whole of the personality, which Smuts described as the "central synthetic power" (Linden, 1995, p. 257). Therefore, the way one experiences and responds to stress is fundamentally related to one's creative self and the capacity of free self-realization. This self-realization, in Individual Psychology, is a "striving to become a whole" (Adler, in Ansbacher, 1994, p. 491) that involves movement and our ultimate life goals (Udchic, 1984).

In his lecture series at the Long Island College of Medicine, Adler in Stein (2002) called for a "proper" medical psychology which requires "some views about the mind, psyche, soul, spirit, etc." (p. 1). Adler spoke of how bodily illness is influenced by the mind and how mental disturbances are related to some disturbances of the body. Bodily disturbances cannot totally explain symptoms, so Adler (2002) challenged the medical field to attend to how deeply emotions, feelings, or the style of life influence the growth, development, and functioning of the organs. To Adler, all parts of a human's mind and psyche run to the point of a guiding purpose of striving, as a unity, toward completion/the new whole. Specifically, *holism* in Individual Psychology means the dynamic and systematic interconnectedness of thoughts, feelings, and actions and of attitudes and approaches in meeting the demands of love, work, and social relations (Strauch, 2003).

Stress, as understood in holism and Individual Psychology, is interrelated with the biological, psychological, and social factors that influence each individual. To understand stress and its causes and consequences holistically, we must first see the individual as an indivisible living organism composed of physical, chemical, and biological structures, with physiological and psychological mechanisms that are inseparable from the person's outer environment.

STRESS AND THE BRAIN

> Freedom is characteristic of wholes, necessity is characteristic of mechanisms. (Linden, 1995, p. 257)

Stress as a term to describe stimuli received by the brain and body was first used by Hans Selye in 1936, who is most recognized for his studies of stress response or the General Adaptation Syndrome and for his description of the hypothalamic-pituitary-adrenocortical axis (the HPA axis) system of stress response (Cozolino, 2010; Udchic, 1984). In biopsychosocial medicine, *stress* is a term used to define the body's physiological and/or psychological reactions to circumstances that require behavioral adjustment (Nakao, 2010). Previously listed on Axis IV of the *Diagnostic and Statistical Manual of Mental Disorders, 4th edition* (*DSM-IV*; American Psychiatric Association [APA], 1996), stress is recognized in the *DSM-5* in the new category of "Trauma and Stressor-Related Disorders," with a focus on the enduring impacts of life stressors on emotional and physical conditions. Diagnoses include reactive attachment disorder, disinhibited social engagement disorder, posttraumatic stress disorder, acute stress disorder, adjustment disorders, other specified trauma- and stressor-related disorder, and unspecified trauma- and stressor-related disorder (APA, 2013). It is also co-related to "V codes," which are considered nondisordered conditions that often are reflective of a host of psychosocial and environmental issues.

Only within the past two decades have scientific research findings suggested that the mechanisms in the brain correlate with various mental and physical changes when we experience stress. The brain is part of the central nervous system, intricately interconnected with the body via the peripheral nervous system, the spinal cord, and all the signals from the body's physiological processes. In the paradigm of holism, the brain is seen as a system instead of an organ. From of the brain's point of view, stress is a condition where the brain senses a challenge to physical or mental stability that leads to altered activity of systems to meet that challenge.

Two neural circuits are activated when a situation is perceived as stressful. The first is the reflexive fast system operating the communication directly from our senses to the amygdala (De Kloet, Joëls, & Holsboer, 2005; Shin & Liberzon, 2011).

CATEGORIES OF STRESS

Although the physiological response of stress is similar in all people, the perception of whether something is distressing or not will differ from individual to individual. This is how people "categorize" stress. When something is categorized as "good," such as a new job, a raise, a new baby, or a new opportunity, that perception elicits the physiological stress hormones, but the person experiences the stimulus as energizing, motivating, and enticing. Some desire is invested in this particular stimulus (whatever it may be). This is known as *eustress,* a term coined by endocrinologist Hans Selye, which comes from the Greek, "eu," meaning good, and "stress": thus *eustress.* Selye identified eustress as stress that elicits emotions that are positive, happy, and excited, and some form of stimulation. Research indicates that there is benefit to this category of stress, because "positive" stress, while still eliciting the physiological stress response, increases the individual's feelings of excitement, creativity, happiness, and connection, and creates conditions that motivate the person to move forward to achieve or work toward what is wanted.

When there is too much pressure, or when a stimulus becomes "too much," this stress falls into the second category, *distress.* Selye identified that distress causes the individual to experience the physiological symptoms of stress, such as anxiety, a sense of being overwhelmed, and/or some other negatively perceived emotion that accompanies the distressing event. For example, a person with too much work may find herself working more hours, and the pressure to get things done leads to even more hours at the office, less sleep, and less time to do the things that she routinely does to take care of herself. This person may experience an increase in irritability, fatigue, and cognitive lapses (e.g., forgetting things, poor decision making, lack of concentration, focus, etc.). The individual may subsequently engage in behaviors reflecting these emotions and thoughts (choosing ineffective ways to cope with the stress, such as not going to bed at the usual time), and some people in distress will seek ways to escape by indulging in behaviors that avoid facing the stress (drinking, shopping, gambling). Someone who is experiencing distress often lacks the ability to cope with the situation or the skills to solve the presenting problem.

—Serena Wadhwa

The fast mode involves the sympathetic nervous system (SNS), driven by corticotropin-releasing hormone, and the behavioral fight-or-flight response. The second is the simultaneous slow system, the HPA axis, which sends sensory information to the cerebral cortex for contextual evaluation before messages are sent to the hippocampus and then the amygdala. The two stress pathways form interacting signaling networks that underlie the adaptive processes leading to our behavioral, autonomic, and emotional responses to stress.

The autonomic nervous system (ANS) is part of the peripheral nervous system used by the brain for internal adjustments that accompany motions and emotions. It includes the sympathetic nervous system (SNS), the parasympathetic nervous system (PNS), and the enteric nervous system, which together regulate a human's inner world (Wehrenberg & Prinz, 2007). The ANS works by releasing messenger chemicals inside of the body; these chemicals, in turn, act on receptors on target cells that change body functions. There are two types of chemical messengers that can be released. Chemicals released from nerve terminals in body organs are called *transmitters;* the second type, called *hormones,* is released directly into the bloodstream. In *acute stress,* norepinephrine is the main neurotransmitter used by the SNS. Stress-induced sympathetic overactivity has been negatively associated with problems in circulation and in the cardiovascular, digestive, endocrine, and immune systems. *Prolonged stress* can compromise the hippocampus with stress hormones, such as excessive cortisol secreted by the adrenal gland, that affect protein production and cell death. *Chronic stress* is known to have a suppressive effect on immune function, thereby worsening other chronic conditions (Trivieri, 2000). Furthermore, research indicates that mental illness may be associated with genetic and environmental changes in stress-signaling pathways such as the HPA-axis activities (Herbert, 1997).

> We have a brain for one reason and one reason only—and that's to produce adaptable and complex movements. (Wolpert, 2011)

The concepts of *neuroplasticity* (the ability of the brain to change its structure in response to experience) and *neurogenesis* (the development of new neurons and networks across the life span) suggest a new way to connect stress to the brain-mind processes (Cozolino, 2010; Wehrenberg & Prinz, 2007). For example, chronic stress exposure can lead to structural changes in the prefrontal cortex, a brain area that intelligently regulates thoughts, actions, and emotions through extensive connections with other brain regions (Arnsten, 2009). However, our mental processes, such as perceiving, thinking, feeling, and remembering, involve patterns of neural firing via the release of transmitters, and thus can ultimately change the physical structure of the brain (Siegel, 2012, pp. 8-1–8-3). Research has reported that the strength of the neural connection between the prefrontal cortex and hippocampus is decreased in the stressed individual, while the size and strength of the amygdala and orbitofrontal cortex are increased (Hölzel et al., 2010). It is also known that severe trauma and childhood neglect can alter gene expression in the circuit that controls the response to stress and subsequent neural firing that influences brain growth (Siegel, 2012, p. 8-7). According to Deak (2007), exposure to psychological stressors leads to increased expression of pro-inflammatory cytokines and activation of inflammatory-related pathways in the central nervous system.

STRESS AND THE MIND

Our psychic nature is not bound by our organic inheritance, but, on the contrary, what we inherit from humankind is plasticity, freedom, and creativity (Linden, 1995, p. 257). Brain and mind are not the same; each plays a different role in stress. Different stresses can cause the same response, and the same stress can arouse different responses in the same individual under different circumstances. For more than a century, psychology has attempted to define the highly complex nature of the human mind. The brain-mind debates have existed alongside the history of neuroscience. The holistic view of body-mind interaction is most related to the field of psychoneuroimmunology, rooted in Walter Cannon's theory of homeostasis that later influenced Selye's studies of stress (Kelly, Kelly, Crabtree, Gauld, Grosso, & Greyson, 2007). The study of the mind lies at the intersection of many other different disciplines and encompasses a wide spectrum of concepts, such as mental activity, cognition, awareness, will, and consciousness, to name just a few.

> Mind has its conscious illuminated area and its subconscious "field." . . . It is of an intensely holistic unanalyzable character. . . . Through its dual activity of conception and conation, mind forms "purposes" which envisage future situations in experience and make the future an operative factor in the present. Purpose marks the liberation of mind from the domination of circumstances and indicate its free creative activity. (Smuts, in Ansbacher, 1994, p. 489)

> [Mind is] a process that regulates the flow of energy* and information* within our bodies and within our relationships, an emergent and self-organizing process that give[s] rise to our mental activities such as emotion, thinking, and memory. [*The electrochemical energy of the nervous system is carried among neurons. Information is one particular pattern in the movement of energy across time.] (Siegel, 2012, p. 1-1)

> [T]he mind is the product of the activity occurring in the brain at the molecular; cellular; and anatomical levels, which are in turn impacted [by] a person's interpersonal experiences, cultural context, and societal experiences. (Ivey, D'Andrea, & Ivey, 2012, p. 56)

The preceding statements represent perspectives of philosophy, neuroscience, and psychology about the mind. Central to these definitions are aspects relevant to stress and the mind. They are (1) the mind and the brain are different but inseparable; (2) the mind is a subjective process that self-regulates with a purpose; and (3) the mind is developmental, relational, and contextual. The mind functions as the "operative" map, enabling us to perceive and process stressors in relation to our past experiences, thoughts, and feelings in response to our inner world and the outer environment. In the face of the perceived external instability caused by stress, the mind engages in a self-regulation process via the neurocircuitry to appraise the potential harm of the stressor and regain a stable state of equilibrium.

Stress is more than a reaction to external stimuli. It is interrelated with the brain and mind. The subjective operative map and self-organizing ability of the mind can be illustrated by compensation and apperception concepts in Individual Psychology. For example, instead of being victimized by their physical weaknesses, some individuals may compensate with other exceptional gifts, overcome with intentional efforts, and become successful. *Apperception* refers to the ability to appraise, digest, and assimilate new information and build a new whole that works with one's past experiences (Gold, 2005). In other words, one's stress response is an expression of one's values, private logic, goals, and style of life.

> The foremost task of Individual Psychology is to prove this unity in each individual—in this thinking, feeling, acting; in his so-called consciousness and unconsciousness—in every expression of his personality. This unity we call the "life style" of the individual. (Adler, in Linden, 1995, p. 258)

In Adler's Individual Psychology, the term *individual* (*individuell* in German) has the connotation and the denotation of a unity, an indivisible whole (Manaster & Corsini, 1982). To holistic thinkers like Smuts and Adler, stress is the manifestation of one's lifestyle, or personality. To Smuts, personality is fundamentally an organ of self-realization (Ansbacher, 1994). The goal of the whole personality is to achieve more of its creative self (Linden, 1995). We can better understand stress when we see the individual as an indivisible living organism, in its functional totality, responding to that individual's inner and outer environments (Dreikurs, 1997). More specifically, stress is more than a passive response to the environment or heredity; instead, we creatively participate in our stress according to our own apperception, life goals, and experiences over time.

STRESS AND SOCIETY

> It is almost impossible to exaggerate the value of an increase in social feeling. The mind improves, for intelligence is a communal function. (Adler, 1964/1979, p. 79)

We have seen how brain and mind dynamically interact in their influences on stress and stress response. We now must expand our view of stress to include the social perspectives and pros and cons of the consequences stress produces for both the individual and the society. The social meaning of stress is intertwined with the intra- and interpersonal aspects of brain and mind. The interdependent facets of stress parallel what Sperry stated about health: "[P]atterns of thinking and feeling about ourselves and also the quality of our relationships with others and the world either predispose us to health or illness" (1992, p. 486). Recent findings regarding neuroplasticity and mirror neurons provide a biological foundation for Adler's theory of social interest/community feeling and its relationship to health (La Voy, Brand, & McFadden, 2013).

To a large degree, stress is an acquired social problem: we fear failure in a culture that values competition and comparison. Stress is present when there is an absence of social belonging (Siegel, 2012, p. 42-1). Stress and the concomitant lack of social/environmental enrichment can have negative consequences both for the individuals involved and for society at large. We have seen that stress has a major impact on blocking neurogenesis in the hippocampus and on other brain functions, thereby possibly causing physical and mental illness. Stress has prominent effects in social behaviors as well. In groups and communities, exposure to high and/or sustained stress alters the nature of social interactions and individuals' sociability, social dominance, and social aggression. When put in their social and developmental contexts, prevention of and intervention for stress and stress response become an issue of public health and education in the home and the school.

The human brain is open to change and new experiences. Our early experiences shape the neural connections in areas regulating the stress response (Siegel, 2012, p. 9-2). According to Siegel, we first build our social connections and attachments through attunement and reciprocity of processes such as nonverbal social exchanges. There is now a vast literature documenting the social regulation of the HPA axis in humans during early development (Hostinar, Sullivan, & Gunnar, 2013).

> Mirror neurons begin to link observations and actions, allowing us to (a) learn from others by watching them, (b) anticipate and predict actions, (c) activate emotional states supportive of emotional resonance and empathy. (Cozolino, 2010, p. 314)

The discoveries of mirror neurons and the network of resonance circuits (Cozolino, 2014; Siegel, in Badenoch, p. 31, 2008) have far-reaching implications for learning, interpersonal connection and communication, and social development. For good or ill, our social brains help us understand how we are predisposed to recognize and participate in the world around us. Stress, therefore, is both the process and product of social learning that concerns our relationships with others. Research has discovered that caring social relations are reinforced with a rewarding pleasure experience when the neuropeptide oxytocin is produced by neurons that also secrete dopamine (McHenry, Sikorski, & McHenry, 2013). According to these authors, other dopamine-mediated whole-brain experiences include commitment in relationship, the intention to trust, and risk taking. Social support not only buffers stress, it may even moderate genetic and environmental vulnerabilities and confer resilience to stress, possibly via its effects on the HPA system, the noradrenergic system, and central oxytocin pathways (Heinrichs, Baumgartner, Kirschbaum, & Ehlert, 2003; Ozbay, Fitterling, Charney, & Southwick, 2008; Siegel, 2012).

Stress, as part of the human condition, is a question of the creative self and its social adaptability. *Social interest* can be regarded as the extended mind of the individual giving direction to the interconnected brain, mind, and social activities (Siegel, 2012). One knows whether a stress is a good stress that motivates one, or a distress that challenges one's psycho-biological-social well-being, by the degree to which one possesses community feeling or social interest that one is a part of the whole. A supportive social network provides a buffer to stress, whereas social isolation makes one susceptible to stress and stress-related dysfunctions.

SUMMARY

Stress and the stress response are closely connected to each human being's physical and mental health and illness. Describing the complexity of how the physical brain, the mind processes, and the social context interact to influence stress in response to challenging events is beyond the scope of this chapter. This chapter reviewed Smuts's concept of holism that is also embedded in the Individual Psychology of Adler. Both theories anticipated the present-day recognitions by psychoneuroimmunology and neuroscience about how physical health is influenced by thoughts, emotions, attitudes, beliefs, and social relations. Parallels between holism and Individual Psychology were drawn in order to demonstrate the different but interdependent roles the brain, the creative mind, and the social-self play in human stress experience.

REFERENCES AND FURTHER READING

Adler, A. (1964/1979). *Superiority and social interest: A collection of later writings* (H. L. Ansbacher & R. R. Ansbacher, Eds.). New York, NY: W.W. Norton.

American Psychiatric Association. (1996). *Diagnostic and statistical manual of mental disorders, fourth edition.* Washington, DC: American Psychiatric Publishing.

American Psychiatric Association. (2013). *Diagnostic and statistical manual of mental disorders, fifth edition (DSM-5).* Arlington, VA: American Psychiatric Publishing.

Ansbacher, H. L. (1994). On the origin of holism. *Journal of Individual Psychology, 17*(2), 486–492.

Arnsten, A. F. (2009). Stress signalling pathways that impair prefrontal cortex structure and function. *Nature Reviews Neuroscience, 10*(6), 410–422.

Badenoch, B. (2008). *Being a brain-wise therapist: A practical guide to interpersonal neurobiology (Norton Series on Interpersonal Neurobiology).* New York, NY: W.W. Norton.

Cozolino, L. J. (2010). *The neuroscience of psychotherapy* (2nd ed.). New York, NY: W.W. Norton.

Cozolino, L. J. (2014). *The neuroscience of human relationships: Attachment and the developing social brain (Norton Series on Interpersonal Neurobiology)*. New York, NY: W.W. Norton.

Deak, T. (2007). From classic aspects of the stress response to neuroinflammation and sickness: Implications for individuals and offspring. *International Journal of Comparative Psychology, 20*(2), 96–110.

De Kloet, E. R., Joëls, M., & Holsboer, F. (2005). Stress and the brain: From adaptation to disease. *Nature Reviews Neuroscience, 6*(6), 463–475.

Dreikurs, R. (1997). Holistic medicine. *Individual Psychology, 53*(2), 127–205.

Gold, L. (2005). The 2004 H. and R. Ansbacher memorial address. *Journal of Individual Psychology, 61*(1), 3–13.

Heinrichs, M., Baumgartner, T., Kirschbaum, C., & Ehlert, U. (2003). Social support and oxytocin interact to suppress cortisol and subjective responses to psychosocial stress. *Biological Psychiatry, 54*(12), 1389–1398.

Herbert, J. (1997). Fortnightly review: Stress, the brain, and mental illness. *British Medical Journal, 315,* 530–535. Retrieved from http://www.ncbi.nlm.nih.gov/pmc/articles/PMC2127355/pdf/9329310.pdf.

Hölzel, B. K., Carmody, J., Evans, K. C., et al. (2010). Stress reduction correlates with structural changes in the amygdala. *Social Cognitive and Affective Neuroscience, 5*(1), 11–17.

Hostinar, C. E., Sullivan, R. M., & Gunnar, M. R. (2013). Psychobiological mechanisms underlying the social buffering of the hypothalamic–pituitary–adrenocortical axis: A review of animal models and human studies across development. *American Psychological Association, 140*(1), 256–282.

Ivey, A. E., D'Andrea, M. J., & Ivey, M. B. (2012). *Theories of counseling and psychotherapy: A multicultural perspective* (7th ed.). Los Angeles, CA: Sage.

Kelly, E. F., Kelly, E. W., Crabtree, A., Gauld, A., Grosso, M., & Greyson, B. (2007). *Irreducible mind: Toward a psychology for the 21st century.* Lanham, MD: Rowman & Littlefield.

La Voy, S. K., Brand, M. L., & McFadden, C. R. (2013). An important lesson from our past with significance for our future: Alfred Adler's gemeinschaftsgefuhl. *Individual Psychology, 69*(4), 280–293.

Linden, G. W. (1995). Holism: Classical, cautious, chaotic, and cosmic. *Journal of Individual Psychology, 51*(3), 253–265.

Manaster, G. J., & Corsini, R. J. (1982). *Individual psychology: Theory and practice.* Itasca, IL: F. E. Peacock.

McHenry, B., Sikorski, A., & McHenry, J. (2013). *A counselor's introduction to neuroscience.* New York, NY: Routledge.

Myers, J. E., & Sweeney, T. J. (2005). *Counseling for wellness: Theory, research, and practice.* Fairfield, VA: American Counseling Association.

Nakao, M. (2010). Work-related stress and psychosomatic medicine. *Biopsychosocial Medicine, 4*(1), 4.

Ozbay, F., Fitterling, H., Charney, D., & Southwick, S. (2008). Social support and resilience to stress across the life span: A neurobiologic framework. *Current Psychiatry Reports, 10*(4), 304–310.

Shin, L. M., & Liberzon, I. (2011). The neurocircuitry of fear, stress, and anxiety disorders. *FOCUS: The Journal of Lifelong Learning in Psychiatry, 9*(3), 311–334.

Siegel, D. J. (2012). *Pocket guide to interpersonal neurobiology: An integrative handbook of the mind* (Norton Series on Interpersonal Neurobiology). New York, NY: W.W. Norton.

Smuts, J. C. (1926/1986). *Holism and evolution.* Gouldsboro, ME: Gestalt Journal Press (facsimile of 1926 edition by Macmillan).

Sperry, L. (1984). Health promotion and wellness medicine in the workplace: Programs, promises, and problems. *Individual Psychology: Journal of Adlerian Theory, Research & Practice,* 401–411.

Sperry, L. (1992). Recent developments in neuroscience, behavioral medicine, and psychoneuroimmunology: Implications for physical and psychological well-being. *Individual Psychology, 48*(4), 480–487.

Sperry, L. (2003). Psychotherapy and the quest for optimal physical and psychological health. *Journal of Individual Psychology, 59*(1), 94–103.

Stein, H. T. (2002). *The collected clinical works of Alfred Adler* (Vol. 8). Bellingham, WA: Classical Adlerian Translation Project.

Strauch, I. (2003). Examining the nature of holism within lifestyle. *Journal of Individual Psychology, 59*(4), 452–460.

Trivieri, L. (2001). *The American Holistic Medical Association guide to holistic health: Healing therapies for optimal wellness.* New York, NY: John Wiley & Sons.

Udchic, H. V. (1984). Adlerian holism and holistic health. *Individual Psychology: Journal of Adlerian Theory, Research & Practice,* 364–371.

Way, L. M. (1950). *Adler's place in psychology.* London, UK: George Allen & Unwin.

Wehrenberg, M., & Prinz, S. M. (2007). *The anxious brain: The neurobiological basis of anxiety disorders and how to effectively treat them.* New York, NY: W.W. Norton.

Wolpert, D. (2011). The real reason for brains. *TEDGlobal.* Retrieved from http://new.ted.com/talks/daniel_wolpert_the_real_reason_for_brains.

8

MISCONCEPTIONS ABOUT STRESS

Serena Wadhwa

Although the concept of stress is well known across Western cultures, and most individuals have some understanding of what stress is and how it may operate for them, it still remains a mysterious term entangled with misconceptions and illusions. This chapter explores some of the common misconceptions or myths about stress and provides facts that will allow individuals who hold these misconceptions to be able to do something about them, rather than feeling that they are "done" by the stresses.

MISCONCEPTION 1: MY EXPERIENCE OF STRESS IS THE SAME AS YOUR EXPERIENCE

Dr. Hans Selye first discovered the fight-or-flight response back in the 1950s, and defined the stress response as a general, nonspecific response to noxious stimuli (Clark, Rager, & Calpin, 1997). During those times, it seemed that stress was the same for everyone. However, as research into the stress response expanded and experts in various fields, such as psychology, psychobiology, endocrinology, and neurology, among others, explored how different systems interacted and reacted to different influences, it became clear that stress is *not* the same for everyone. The reaction of the body depends on various factors, and although there is a stress reaction (the activation of which also depends on cognitive appraisal, interpretation, recognition of resources, etc.), neither the stress nor the reaction are always the same. For example, some individuals respond to the same stress with a lesser increase of blood pressure or release of the stress hormone cortisol.

What is stress for one person may not be for another. Individuals respond to the same things differently. For example, a multiple-choice exam may be experienced as stressful by one student and neutral by another. As explored in other chapters, the concept of stress is influenced by an individual's personality, biology, coping mechanisms, experiences, cognitive resources and appraisals, the meanings ascribed to experiences, and a host of other factors. This is what makes the experience of stress unique to each person, even when the stressor is the same. Additionally, individuals cope with stress differently. A college student who finds the thought of an upcoming exam to be stressful may turn to avoidance strategies (like procrastination or engaging in potentially destructive behaviors) to cope with the physical, cognitive, and emotional symptoms of the stress. Another individual, however, might use a planned study schedule to manage the perceived stress.

MISCONCEPTION 2: STRESS IS SOMETHING THAT HAPPENS TO US

Andrew Bernstein, author of *The Myth of Stress,* negates the misconception that "stress happens" by pointing out that circumstances themselves do not produce reactions; it's the thoughts and perceptions individuals have that make something stressful. He points out that this is one reason why individuals have different emotional reactions to the same situation (Bernstein, 2010). It's similar to the notion of how individuals can look at the same picture and have different reactions to it, because of different thoughts.

Dr. Cynthia Ackrill (2013), a Fellow of the American Institute of Stress and chair of the Workplace Stress Board through the American Institute of Stress, not only explores the importance of perception in the experience of stress, but also discusses the role of expectation. When perception and expectation are misaligned, stress will result (Ackrill, 2013). Thus, stress is a result of a combination of our thoughts, expectations, and interpretations and not a result of the situation itself.

MISCONCEPTION 3: ONLY BIG THINGS AFFECT US

Because stress depends on how individuals perceive situations, what expectations they have, and how these perceptions and expectations interact with their interpretations of events, even "small" setbacks, events, or situations can trigger strong stress responses in individuals, just as larger and more drastic ones do. Stress experts acknowledge the often-stressful effects of major changes and occurrences (marital, family, employment, residence, etc.). However, most individuals "feel stressed" when they experience a run of minor changes or occurrences: not being able to find the car keys; spilling coffee on oneself while already running late; getting a flat tire; forgetting important papers at home; forgetting one's wallet; not getting to an appointment on time; bad road traffic; and so on. Though none of these events is life-threatening, the body still experiences a physical reaction—the stress reaction—to these "emergencies," and when another "emergency" is piled on top, the body and the individual do not have the opportunity to recover or return to some level of restorative functioning. Thus, as Ackrill puts it, "The 'little' stress reactions tax every system in our bodies and rapidly drain our energy and brainpower" (2013, p. 3).

Another piece of this misconception is that all "stress is bad." There are some conflicting thoughts on this. Selye's research suggested that positive activities (such as physical activity) also produce the same physiological reaction as negative activities (such as being chased by an animal). Thus, he developed the concept of *eustress* to explain this idea. Some people misperceive stress as something that motivates and helps them move forward; when they are experiencing stress about something such as a difficult deadline, they are motivated. However, according to Bernstein (2010), this is inaccurate, as stress is not actually what's good for you. Research indicates that stress itself, when unmanaged, contributes to the manifestation of a number of medical conditions (Cohen, Janicki-Deverts, & Miller, 2007)—some claim as much as 75 percent of them (Abdou, Higashiguchi, Horie, Kim, Hatta, & Yokogoshi, 2006). Likewise, a high percentage of doctor visits may be related to stress: in some estimates, between 60 percent and 80 percent of them are (Avey, Matheny, Robbins, & Jacobson, 2003). Bernstein proposes that what we are "misperceiving" is that we are motivated by being *stimulated,* not by the stress we are experiencing. The focus, therefore, is what is providing stimulation and motivation, not the stress itself.

Nevertheless, there is some research to the contrary. According to early research by Rosalind Forbes (1979), and research on peak performance relating to optimal stress (Ackrill, 2013), it is the perception of the situation and our abilities that influence an optimal balance. Once that becomes misaligned, stress is experienced.

MISCONCEPTION 4: WE KNOW WHEN WE ARE STRESSED

We like to believe that we know when we are stressed; however, the truth is that most individuals are unaware of their stress reactions. Part of the reason for this is how the brain works in keeping survival to just that: survival. When the brain believes that imminent danger is present, it enters a primitive mode; this fight-or-flight survival mode keeps a tunnel-vision focus on survival. In this mode, the higher level of the triune human brain, the neocortex, which controls thinking, reasoning, decision making, and other similar abilities, does not have the opportunity to do what it normally does. Thus, the individual operates from what is sometimes called the reptilian brain, an older and more primitive part of the brain.

Another part of the reason for this inability or unawareness is that the human body constantly regulates itself to maintain homeostasis without involvement of the conscious mind. For example, when the external temperature changes, your body adjusts to maintain a steady body temperature. This is not something you do consciously or pay any attention to; although you may be aware of the sensation of feeling cold or hot, you do not directly tell your body to turn on the cooling system or turn on the heating system to regulate the temperature. Similarly, most individuals are not aware of the effects that long-term stress has on them until they experience obvious ill effects, by which time serious damage may have already occurred (Porensky, n.d.; Ackrill, 2013).

We experience physiological changes in response to stress, regardless of whether we are aware of them or not. Much of this is automatic (for example, breathing and heart rate). Although we may become aware of some of these symptoms/changes on some level, it's impossible to recognize or know all of them. Your focus then becomes only on these natural physiologically changes occurring in response to something. Thus, many people may fall prey to the misconception that they are "okay," either because they are not aware of the symptoms actually occurring, the symptoms occur insidiously, or the individuals only pay attention to symptoms that seem to arise from or be affecting other areas (e.g., anxiety disorders).

MISCONCEPTION 5: STRESS IS INEVITABLE, SO YOU MIGHT AS WELL LIVE WITH IT

Although an individual may experience situations that exceed his or her coping capacity or resources available to effectively handle them, or that challenge the person's perceptions or emotional tolerance, the notion that stress is inevitable is unhealthy. A constant sense of imminent gloom and doom is immobilizing and tends to lead to passive and ineffective coping mechanisms. Additionally, it lends credence to the belief that "stress" is the explanation for all of life's problems (Wheaton & Montazer, 2010). Bernstein (2010) offers the perspective of looking for "[s]omething you're not bothered by that other people are. . . . [T]hey can't imagine not feeling stress, but you know that this isn't so." This refers to the fact that what a person believes about a situation creates the conditions of what he or she is able to do, and whether the person will be passive or active in responding. Research also suggests that the energy levels an individual experiences come from his or her emotions, and that emotions stem from what the person believes.

Woodson Merrell, MD, author of *The Source,* focuses on the notion that "living" with stress is different from believing you have control of it. This is known as an internal *locus of control,* which research demonstrates has a positive effect on an individual's self-esteem, self-efficacy, disease prevention, and coping with stress. According to Merrell, "the more control you perceive yourself to have over the stressful situation, the less damaging the stress will be" (2008, p. 33). This sense limits the "doom and gloom" perception and opens a space for individuals to recognize that effectively coping and healing from the effects of stress are possible and necessary. Merrell likens stress to a "gateway drug" to more serious problems, such as various diseases, distressing emotional states, and destructive coping mechanisms and behaviors.

MISCONCEPTION 6: I DON'T KNOW HOW TO RELAX, AND IF I DO, I WON'T BE PRODUCTIVE

Children are an example of play and productivity. They go to school at various ages, learn various things, do "work," and still have time to play, rest, and take care of business. Bernstein (2010) comments that adults get so used to stress, they forget what life was like without the experience of stress. So, it's not that people do not know how to relax; rather, often it may relate more to forgetting the experience or not recognizing that there is a different way. As discussed in other chapters, the experience of stress tends to constrict one's focus to whatever demands/pressure/threat is looming. Once a person finds and utilizes tools that remind him or her about the experience of relaxation, the chances of jump-starting the process of relaxation increase, whether the tools used are cognitive, spiritual, emotional, behavioral, or social.

MISCONCEPTION 7: STRESS AND ANXIETY ARE THE SAME

As discussed here and in previous chapters, stress is a basic biological and physiological response to change. It is a response experienced in all living species, as life is about change (Hafen, Karren, Frandsen, & Smith, 1996). Once the threat of danger has passed, the response ceases and the organism returns to the state of homeostasis. This has been demonstrated in living species. Thus, after a stress experience, there is a return to some "normal" state of bodily functioning.

Anxiety, however, is an experience that often does not have an identifiable trigger. Even though individuals may experience anxiety in relation to day-to-day activities and future-oriented planning, the conceptualization of anxiety is different from that of stress. Humans are the only species that experiences anxiety. Anxiety is a result of excessive and often negative thoughts relating to the future and the physiological sensations and effects accompanying those thoughts. In the *Diagnostic and Statistical Manual of Mental Disorders, 5th Edition* (American Psychiatric Association, 2013), used by psychiatrists, psychologists, and counselors, anxiety is classified into several disorders that cause distress in an individual. Each of these anxiety-related disorders has identifiable criteria, and to meet these clinical definitions the problems must be present for a certain period of time. Stress, however, due to the complexities of individual factors (such as biology, personality, genetics, environment, health, etc.) can manifest in a myriad of such idiosyncratic ways that often an individual needs help to determine if symptoms are related to stress or something else. (See Chapter 12 on assessing stress.)

MISCONCEPTION 8: THE SAME TECHNIQUES WORK FOR EVERYONE; IF IT'S PROVEN, IT WILL WORK

When Hans Selye first developed the General Adaptation Syndrome back in 1936, this may have been true. In the 21st century, we've come a long way toward understanding the idiosyncratic functioning of the stress response and the influences of biology, neurology, cognitions, emotions, actions, chemicals, environments, and other factors that play a part not only in the triggering of the stress response, but, equally importantly, in the manifestation of a stress and whether it is experienced as stress. The American Psychological Association states that a comprehensive program is what will work. Stress management techniques are not cookie-cutter approaches, and even research studies include information on method and designs.

MISCONCEPTION 9: YOU CAN LIVE IN A STRESS-FREE WORLD

Wheaton and Montazer (2010) explored varieties of stress that exist across the life span and how distinct stress experiences interrelate and affect current and future stress experiences. In other words, given an individual's experience growing up, that individual may not be aware of what was stressful, or know that experiences of stress influenced his or her vulnerability to stress in the future.

Change is constant, and stress is part of the adaptation to change to maintain homeostasis. Hafen et al. state, "The very process of living entails change" (1996, pp. 43–44). Therefore, it is unrealistic to believe that a stress-free world is possible. As indicated in this chapter and elsewhere, by developing the knowledge and skills to effectively cope with stress and/or heal from stress-related problems, an individual can learn to lessen the damaging effects of stress in his or her world.

REFERENCES AND FURTHER READING

Abdou, A. M., Higashiguchi, S., Horie, K., Kim, M., Hatta, H., & Yokogoshi, H. (2006). Relaxation and immunity enhancement effects of γ-aminobutyric acid (GABA) administration in humans. *Biofactors, 26*(3), 201–208.

Ackrill, C. (2013). 10 Costly myths about stress you can't afford to believe. Retrieved from http://www.cynthiaackrill.com/wp-content/uploads/2013/11/10-Costly-Myths.-Contentment-Jan-2013.pdf.

American Psychiatric Association. (2013). *Diagnostic and statistical manual of mental disorders, 5th edition (DSM-5)*. Washington, DC: American Psychiatric Association.

Avey, H., Matheny, K. B., Robbins, A., & Jacobson, T. A. (2003). Health care providers' training, perceptions, and practices regarding stress and health outcomes. *Journal of the National Medical Association, 95*(9), 833.

Bernstein, A. (2010). 8 deadly myths about stress. Retrieved from https://www.psychologytoday.com/blog/the-myth-stress/201005/8-deadly-myths-about-stress.

Clark, J. D., Rager, D. R., & Calpin, J. P. (1997). Animal well-being II. Stress and distress. *Comparative Medicine, 47*(6), 571–579.

Cohen, S., Janicki-Deverts, D., & Miller, G. E. (2007). Psychological stress and disease. *JAMA, 298*(14), 1685–1687.

Forbes, R. (1979). *Corporate stress*. New York, NY: Doubleday Books.

Hafen, B. Q., Karren, K. J., Frandsen, K. J., & Smith, N. L. (1996). *Mind/Body health: The effects of attitudes, emotions, and relationships*. Boston, MA: Allyn & Bacon.

Porensky, E. K. (n.d.). Stress management: Part I—Stress and health. Retrieved from https://ccme.osu.edu/WebCastsFiles/562The%20Management%20of%20Stress%20-%202.pdf.

Merrell, W. (2008). *The source*. New York, NY: Free Press.

Miller, L. H., Smith, A. D., & Rothstein, L. (1994). *The stress solution: An action plan to manage the stress in your life*. New York, NY: Pocket Books.

Wheaton, B., & Montazer, S. (2010). Stressors, stress, and distress. In T. Scheid & T. Brown (Eds.), *A handbook for the study of mental health: Social contexts, theories, and systems* (pp. 171–199). Cambridge, UK: Cambridge University Press.

9

Stress Hormones

Ioulia Maimari

Stress may be defined as any situation that tends to disturb the equilibrium between a living organism and its environment. Research has demonstrated that the neuroendocrine "fight-or-flight" response can be activated in human beings by numerous and diverse psychological influences, including varied psychosocial stimuli (Everly & Lating, 2013). In modern life, there are many stressful situations (work pressure, school examinations, etc.), psychosocial stresses, and physical stresses due to trauma, surgery, and various medical disorders (Ranabir & Reetu, 2011). Stress can lead to changes in the serum level of several hormones, including glucocorticoids, catecholamines, growth hormone, and prolactin. Some of these changes are necessary for activation of the fight-or-flight response that readies one for self-protection (Ranabir & Reetu, 2011).

EPINEPHRINE AND NOREPINEPHRINE

Epinephrine (also known as adrenaline or adrenalin) is a hormone and neurotransmitter. It is produced in the medulla of the adrenal glands; from there it is released into the bloodstream and attaches at the ends of sympathetic nerve fibers, where it serves as a chemical mediator for conveying the nerve impulses to effector organs.

Epinephrine itself does not reach the brain; rather, it affects the brain by stimulating a small island of gray matter in the base of the brain, the brain stem, which forwards the message to the locus coeruleus. The locus coeruleus is the site where the brain cells that produce the "twin" of epinephrine reside. This brain-based twin is called *norepinephrine* (or noradrenaline) (Andreasen, 2004); it is a precursor of epinephrine that is secreted by the adrenal medulla and is a widespread central and autonomic neurotransmitter. Both epinephrine and norepinephrine are also used as neurotransmitters by some nerve cells to communicate with other cells. However, very little epinephrine is used in this way.

Norepinephrine is a catecholamine synthesized from dopamine by dopamine β-hydroxylase. It is released from the adrenal medulla into the blood as a hormone, but it also acts as a neurotransmitter in the central nervous system and sympathetic nervous system, where it is released from noradrenergic neurons. The actions of norepinephrine are carried out via its binding to adrenergic receptors. Norepinephrine is the principal transmitter of most postganglionic sympathetic fibers and of the diffuse projection system in the brain that arises from the locus coeruleus (Norepinephrine, n.d.). The locus coeruleus releases norepinephrine by direct pathways to both the amygdala and the hippocampus. In this way, the limbic brain and the physical body (other than the nervous system) are co-activated during the stress response (Andreasen, 2004).

There is a continuous low level of activity of the sympathetic nervous system resulting in release of norepinephrine into the circulation. Epinephrine release is increased only at times of acute stress. Currently it is thought that norepinephrine serves primarily to assist epinephrine, as the ratio of these two chemical substances released at neural synapses is 5:1 epinephrine to norepinephrine during a stress response. The effects of epinephrine and norepinephrine are very short, lasting only a few seconds. Because of their rapid release from neural endings, as well as their rapid influence on targeted organ tissues, the effects of the sympathetic nervous system are categorized as immediate (Seaward, 2008).

Epinephrine and norepinephrine can trigger various responses depending on the types of cells they are acting upon. However, the overall effect of both is to prepare the body for the fight-or-flight response in times of stress—that is, for vigorous and/or sudden action.

Epinephrine affects the peripheral nervous system through stimulation and inhibition. It affects the central nervous system by enhancing respiration and increasing muscle activity. Key actions of epinephrine include increasing the heart rate, increasing blood pressure, expanding the air passages of the lungs, and dilating the pupil in the eye. It also stimulates smooth muscle cells and blood vessels in organs and tissues throughout the body to redistribute blood to the skeletal muscles, in order to enhance the force of muscle contractions. Epinephrine is also part of the endocrine system's regulation of insulin. It alters the body's metabolism so as to maximize blood glucose levels (primarily for the brain), and suppresses the immune system.

Norepinephrine affects parts of the brain that control attention and responses. Along with epinephrine, norepinephrine also underlies the fight-or-flight response by directly increasing heart rate and triggering the release of glucose from energy stores. Norepinephrine causes almost all blood vessels in the body to dilate, while (as mentioned earlier) epinephrine restricts smaller blood vessels in the liver and kidneys, thereby increasing blood flow to skeletal muscle. Norepinephrine can also suppress neuroinflammation when released diffusely in the brain from the locus coeruleus.

In the short term, Both epinephrine and norepinephrine benefit the immediate reaction of a human organism to any kind of perceived danger. A fight-or-flight response triggered in this fashion served the aim of survival of the species for millions of years. Then as now, facing danger would lead to muscle tension, increased heart rate and blood pressure, shallow and rapid breathing, and dilated pupils. This entire panoply of changes, which occur when a person faces danger, help mobilize the human body to either fight the threatening situation or get away from it. When the organism actually fights or runs, the tension that was built up is released. As soon as the danger is over (assuming that survival was achieved), the body returns to homeostasis, its normal state.

In the long term, epinephrine and norepinephrine benefit the survival of our species not only by preparing us for a physical fight-or-flight reaction, but also by preparing us to prevent or handle difficult situations occurring in daily life. Moderate amounts of stress in daily life can promote concentration and improve performance under pressure; furthermore, stress stimulates us to maintain an energetic, alerted, and motivated status to face all kinds of challenges.

However, epinephrine and norepinephrine can also provoke various negative effects. In the short term, they can cause increased arterial blood pressure; a moderately increased blood supply to the brain; increased heart rate and cardiac output; increased stimulation of skeletal muscles; increased plasma free fatty acids, triglycerides, and cholesterol; increased release of endogenous opioids; decreased blood flow to the kidneys and the gastrointestinal system; and decreased blood flow to the skin (Everly & Lating, 2013). In the longer term, especially if persistent, these same actions and effects can lead to acute or chronic diseases. They can cause increased risk of hypertension, thrombosis formation, angina pectoris attacks, arrhythmias, sudden death from lethal arrhythmia, myocardial ischemia, myocardial fibrillation, and myocardial infarction (Everly & Lating, 2013).

CORTISOL

While the inner parts of the adrenal glands release epinephrine, other parts of those glands are also activated by the stress response and send out the neuroendocrine transmitter cortisol. *Cortisol* is a steroid hormone, more specifically a glucocorticoid, produced by the zona fasciculata of the adrenal cortex. It is released in response to stress and a low level of blood glucose. Cortisol is the primary hormone responsible for the stress response, and its main function is to restore homeostasis following exposure to stress. It is at its highest levels in the morning.

Cortisol encourages an increase in blood sugar and stimulates the metabolic pathway that synthesizes glucose from oxaloacetate. The presence of cortisol triggers the expression of enzymes critical for the metabolic pathway called *gluconeogenesis,* which causes this increase in glucose production. It also stimulates glycogen synthesis in the liver, decreasing blood sugar levels. Cortisol thus regulates the level of glucose throughout the bloodstream (Randall, 2012).

During a stress response, the endocrine system sends a message through a series of checkpoints, including the hypothalamus and pituitary gland, which use the messengers corticotropin-releasing factor (CRF) and adrenocorticotropic hormone (ACTH). As the adrenal glands increase cortisol production, the hypothalamus controls the levels and the pituitary gland normalizes the quantity by sending control signals to the adrenal glands (Andreasen, 2004). As Aronson notes, "Cortisol prepares the body for a 'fight or flight' response by flooding it with glucose, supplying an immediate energy source to large muscles. It inhibits insulin production in an attempt to prevent glucose from being metabolized, favoring its immediate use, and narrows the arteries while the epinephrine increases heart rate, both of which force blood to pump harder and faster" (Aronson, 2009, p. 38).

In the moment, cortisol helps the body deal with threatening situations. Cortisol (along with epinephrine) is best known for its involvement in the fight-or-flight response and temporary increase in energy production, at the expense of processes that are not required for immediate survival. Cortisol also affects ion transport, the immune response, and even memory-related mechanisms (Randall, 2012). Cortisol provides the body with glucose by getting protein via gluconeogenesis in the liver. The resulting biochemical and hormonal imbalances resolve due to a hormonally driven inhibitory (negative) feedback loop (Aronson, 2009), in which cortisol participates by blocking the secretion of corticotropin-releasing hormone, preventing the hypothalamic-pituitary-adrenocortical (HPA) axis interactions. However, acute and chronic stress and frequent or long-term cortisol exposure may have several negative effects, some of which may be severe.

In the short term, the effects of the glucocorticoids, in apparent response to stressful stimuli, include increased glucose production (gluconeogenesis), exacerbation of gastric irritation, increased urea production, increased release of free fatty acids into systemic circulation, increased susceptibility to arteriosclerotic processes, increased susceptibility to nonthrombotic myocardial necrosis, thymicolymphatic atrophy (demonstrated in animals only), suppression of immune mechanisms, exacerbation of herpes simplex, increased ketone body production, appetite suppression, and associated feelings of depression, hopelessness, helplessness, and loss of control (Everly & Lating, 2013). High levels of stress, even over relatively short periods and in vastly different contexts, tend to produce similar results: prolonged healing times, reduction in ability to cope with vaccinations, and heightened vulnerability to viral infection (Randall, 2012).

In the long term, chronic stress may result in prolonged secretion of cortisol. This constant cortisol exposure associated with chronic stress causes more problems. Along with decreased thyroid function and accumulation of abdominal fat, which itself has implications for cardiovascular health symptoms (Randall, 2012), cortisol can also promote fluid and salt retention. If the HPA system is activated frequently, adverse health outcomes such as hypertension (from salt retention) and impaired immune function (from excess cortisol) may result (Mertz, n.d.).

White blood cells respond by downregulating their cortisol receptors. This in turn reduces the cells' capacity to respond to anti-inflammatory signals and allows cytokine-mediated inflammatory processes to flourish. Stress may thereby contribute

GHRELIN AND CHRONIC STRESS

Ghrelin is a hormone that plays a role in appetite and weight: its function appears to be to increase the appetite. It is released in the stomach and promotes the accumulation of fatty tissue in the abdominal area, which is known to be harmful to health. Research also suggests that this hormone plays a part in stress-related eating habits, as this hormone increases during times of physiological stress (Schellekens, Finger, Dinan, & Cryan, 2012), and studies show that stressed individuals may subsequently also gain weight. These findings led researchers to explore this as a potential avenue for obesity treatment options.

Although these explorations have not yet resulted in favorable outcomes, another discovery surfaced. Subsequent research led to the discovery that the increased levels of ghrelin released during chronic stress can predispose the brain to posttraumatic stress disorder (PTSD). Thus, drugs that were initially developed to help with the obesity epidemic are now being studied for their effects in preventing PTSD (Massachusetts Institute of Technology, 2013). In further research, findings linked chronic stress, the release of ghrelin and growth hormone, and the reinforcement of fear-based memories in the amygdala, which is a process similar to that suspected to occur in PTSD (Meyer, Burgos-Robles, Liu, Correia, & Goosens, 2013). This research demonstrates how sensitive the amygdala is to the release of ghrelin during times of chronic stress, which may reinforce fear-based reactions. The findings also suggest that this may lead to a way to reduce or prevent excessive fear during chronic stressful life events. Further research is necessary in this area (Meyer et al., 2013).

—*Serena Wadhwa*

to diseases involving excessive nonspecific inflammation (e.g., multiple sclerosis, rheumatoid arthritis, coronary heart disease) (Segerstrom & Miller, 2004).

Moreover, during stress response, the pituitary gland responds to CRF by releasing ACTH to stimulate the adrenal glands to secrete the stress hormone cortisol. According to Thakur et al. (2014, p. 3), "The cross talk between gut microbiota, the immune system and the brain-gut axis plays an important role in the modulation of the stress response of the gut in the context of the development of different gastrointestinal disorders."

Excessive exposure to high cortisol levels may impair cognition. Many cortisol receptors are located in the hippocampus, a region of the brain highly related to memory. Although normal cortisol levels have no adverse effects on the hippocampus, excess cortisol overwhelms the hippocampus and can cause atrophy; in studies with elderly subjects, those with elevated cortisol levels showed significant memory loss resulting from hippocampal damage, though the age range at risk is unclear (Randall, 2012).

Elevated cortisol levels related to prolonged stress can also cause or exacerbate erectile dysfunction, and disrupt normal ovulation and menstrual cycles. Furthermore, excess cortisol production may hamper optimal production of the androgenic sex hormones, which are produced in the same glands as cortisol and epinephrine (Weinstein, 2004).

Cushing's syndrome is a severe disease characterized by dangerously high cortisol levels. Those afflicted with Cushing's experience rapid weight gain, hyperhidrosis, and hyperkalemia, along with various psychological and endocrine problems (Randall, 2012).

The classic fight-or-flight reaction is based mostly on the three major hormones discussed so far. However, more hormones may interact in the stress processes, including the following:

Vasopressin. This hormone regulates blood volume, as well as water volume in cells, and is stimulated during stress. Acute stress can lead to rapid release of vasopressin from the paraventricular nucleus of the hypothalamus, along with CRH (Ranabir & Reetu, 2011).

Gonadotropins. The release and circulation of these hormones, produced in the pituitary gland, can be suppressed by stress. This can affect a woman's normal menstrual cycle, and long-term exposure to stress can lead to significant impairment of the reproductive function (Ranabir & Reetu, 2011).

Thyroid hormones. The levels of thyroid hormones tend to be decreased during stress, which inhibits the thyroid-stimulating hormone (TSH) through the action of glucocorticoids on the central nervous system (Ranabir & Reetu, 2011).

Growth hormone. The growth hormone (GH) level is increased anywhere from 2 to 10 times normal during acute physical stress. In psychological stress, however, GH responses are not often observed, and in long-term psychosocial stress, there can be deficiencies in the secretion of GH (Ranabir & Reetu, 2011).

Prolactin. This hormone, which stimulates breast growth and milk production in women, can increase or decrease with stress. A recent study of the response of prolactin to psychological stress showed inconsistent results, with increased, decreased, and unchanged levels of prolactin (Lennartsson & Jonsdottir, 2011; Ranabir & Reetu, 2011).

Insulin. Insulin levels may decrease during stress and, combined with antagonistic hormones, can cause stress-induced hyperglycemia (Ranabir & Reetu, 2011).

REFERENCES AND FURTHER READING

Andreasen, N. C. (2004). *Brave new brain: Conquering mental illness in the era of the genome.* New York, NY: Oxford University Press.

Aronson, D. (2009). Cortisol—Its role in stress, inflammation, and indications for diet therapy. *Today's Dietitian, 11*(11), 38. Retrieved from http://www.todaysdietitian.com/newarchives/111609p38.shtml.

Everly, G. S., Jr., & Lating, J. M. (2013). *A clinical guide to the treatment of the human stress response* (3rd ed.). New York, NY: Springer.

Konturek, P. C., Brzozowski, T., & Konturek, S. J. (2011). Stress and the gut: Pathophysiology, clinical consequences, diagnostic approach and treatment options. *Journal of Physiology and Pharmacology, 62*(6), 591–599.

Lennartsson, A. K., & Jonsdottir, I. H. (2011, November). Prolactin in response to acute psychosocial stress in healthy men and women. *Psychoneuroendocrinology, 36*(10), 1530–1539. doi:10.1016/j.psyneuen.2011.04.007.

Massachusetts Institute of Technology. (2013, October 15). Ghrelin, a stress-induced hormone, primes the brain for PTSD. *ScienceDaily.* Retrieved May 25, 2014, from www.sciencedaily.com/releases/2013/10/131015191405.htm.

Mertz, H. (n.d.). *Stress and the gut.* UNC Center of Functional GI & Motility Disorders. Retrieved from http://www.med.unc.edu/ibs/files/educational-gi-handouts/Stress%20and%20the%20Gut.pdf.

Meyer, R. M., Burgos-Robles, A., Liu, E., Correia, S. S., & Goosens, K. A. (2013). A ghrelin–growth hormone axis drives stress-induced vulnerability to enhanced fear. *Molecular Psychiatry, 19,* 1284–1294.

Norepinephrine. (n.d.). In PubChem Open Chemistry Database. PubChem CID 439260. Retrieved from http://pubchem.ncbi.nlm.nih.gov/compound/norepinephrine.

Ranabir, S., & Reetu, K. (2011). Stress and hormones. *Indian Journal of Endocrinology and Metabolism, 15*(1), 18–22.

Randall, M. (2012). The physiology of stress: Cortisol and the hypothalamic-pituitary-adrenal axis. *Dartmouth Undergraduate Journal of Science.* Retrieved from http://dujs.dartmouth.edu/fall-2010/the-physiology-of-stress-cortisol-and-the-hypothalamic-pituitary-adrenal-axis#.VDuQnvmSz0T).

Schellekens, H., Finger, B. C., Dinan, T. G., & Cryan, J. F. (2012). Ghrelin signaling and obesity: At the interface of stress, mood and food reward. *Pharmacology & Therapeutics, 135*(3), 316–326. doi:10.1016/j.pharmthera.2012.06.004.

Seaward, B. L. (2008). *Managing stress: Principles and strategies for health and well being.* London, UK: James and Bartlett.

Segerstrom, S. C., & Miller, G. E. (2004). Psychological stress and the human immune system: A meta-analytic study of 30 years of inquiry. *Psychological Bulletin, 130,* 601–630.

Thakur, A. K., Shakya, A., Husain, G. M., Emerald, M., & Kumar, V. (2014). Gut-microbiota and mental health: Current and future perspectives. *Journal of Pharmacology and Clinical Toxicology, 2*(1), 1016.

Weinstein, R. (2004). *The stress effect.* New York, NY: Avery-Penguin Group.

10

Cognitive Symptoms and Effects of Stress

Gage Stermensky II and Robert R. Moss

Although the brain is a protected and complex organ, cognitive symptoms resulting from stress can be detrimental to individuals in many ways. For purposes of this chapter, *stress* is defined as an individual's perception that environmental demands exceed the individual's adaptive capacity (Cohen, Janicki-Deverts, & Miller, 2007). If one thinks of the brain as a computer, stress overload on the brain can cause wiring and software glitches, as well as allowing intrusion of viruses. The more frequently these glitches occur, the more damaged the software and hardware become over time.

The brain is an incredibly complex system. This chapter provides a brief exploration of the effects of stress on cognitive functioning. The chapter begins with an overview of the brain, followed by a review of the short- and long-term effects of stress on cognition. The chapter concludes with an exploration of the clinical biopsychological model as it relates to cognitive stress.

AREAS OF THE BRAIN AFFECTED BY STRESS

The two brain systems activated by stress are the autonomic nervous system (ANS), which controls the fight-or-flight response, discussed in other chapters in Part I; and the hypothalamic-pituitary-adrenocortical (HPA) axis. The HPA axis responds less quickly than the ANS. Once activated, the brain proceeds to compare the current stress to past stressful events, creating arousal, alertness, and the perceived need to respond by the human. The first subcortical structures activated are the amygdala and hypothalamus, followed by efferent activity to other areas of the brain and spinal cord (Schwabe, Wolf, & Oitzl, 2010).

The major areas of the brain affected by stress are the prefrontal cortex, the amygdala, the hippocampus, the HPA axis, and the sympathetic-adrenal-medullary (SAM) system. The various parts of the brain communicate through neurotransmitters. Two major factors related to stress involve the release of the neurotransmitter norepinephrine and the neuromodulating hormone cortisol. Research supports a role for each of these substances in the cognitive sequelae of stress (Schwabe et al., 2010; Stahl, 2013).

The initial release of the hormones causes a normal, protective response to stress. However, prolonged exposure to these hormones or stress causes the brain to become conditioned to the stress response. This has been proposed to contribute to the experience of anxiety, panic attacks, posttraumatic stress disorder, and other anxiety disorders (Stahl, 2013). Part of the conditioning involves the brain storing memories related to the stressful events, which can then become associated with other stimuli encountered on a day-to-day basis (Carlson, 2013; Moss, 2013a). Table 10.1 contains information, based on prior research, related to the proposed effects of stress on major areas of the brain affected by stress.

Based upon the described mechanisms, some neurons may become overexcited and eventually stop functioning (they die). Once a neuron receives a message, calcium is admitted into the cell membrane through an excitatory neurotransmission.

Table 10.1 Cognitive Symptoms and Effects of Stress

Area	Responsibilities	Effects of Stress
Hippocampus	Memory, learning, emotional regulation	Volume reduction (long-term) and inability to regulate HPA axis stress response
Amygdala	Emotional regulation, visual processing of emotions	Signals other parts of the brain to react to stress through neurotransmitter communication
Prefrontal cortex (PFC)	Cognitive control, behavior inhibition, working memory, executive functioning	Reduction in size and permanent structural changes (long-term); behavioral, emotional, and cognitive regulation impairment (short-term)
HPA axis	Regulation and production of cortisol	Inability to moderate the effects of stress on day-to-day functioning (long-term); amplified production and release of cortisol (short-term)
SAM system	Regulation of physiological processes associated with the stress response	Inability to effectively regulate physiological systems associated with the stress response

Repeated excitations can potentially overload the neurons with calcium. This causes the neurons to be unable to function in the manner they are supposed to, resulting in the previously mentioned cell death (Szydlowska & Tymianski, 2010). The long-term effects of cortisol can also cause the brain to age more rapidly. In addition, long-term cortisol exposure makes the human brain more susceptible to strokes, Alzheimer's disease, and other dementias (National Institute of Mental Health [NIMH], 2013). In fact, the effects of cortisol and related neurotransmitter changes are associated with the most common mental health disorders in the United States.

Anxiety disorders (18.1%) and mood disorders (8.1%) are the most prevalent mental health disorders in the United States (NIMH, 2013). Depression, which affects nearly 7 percent of adults in the United States, has a strong relationship to cortisol and stress exposure (NIMH, 2013). One of the primary biological indicators of depression is elevated cortisol levels in the blood. It has been proposed that serotonin, the neurotransmitter most commonly associated with depression, is not the cause of depression (Schatzberg et al., 2013). Instead, it has been argued that depression is primarily caused by neurochemical and anatomical changes related to the stress response (Schatzberg et al., 2013). As one can see, there is a pervasive belief that cortisol and the stress response can lead to neurological changes contributing to mental health problems. Depression can cause sleeping problems, over- or undereating, psychomotor retardation, suicidal thoughts, guilt, lack of interest in activities, and lethargy/decreased levels of energy. The reduced energy and interest in activities can cause individuals to lack the motivation needed to perform activities that ameliorate stress, subsequently exacerbating their depression.

LONG-TERM VERSUS SHORT-TERM EFFECTS OF STRESS ON THE BRAIN

There are stark contrasts between the long-term and short-term effects of stress on the human brain. Some of the short-term effects of stress may display positive effects on cognitive functioning. For example, stress has been shown to increase emotional memory capacity during acute, stressful (or traumatic) situations (Buchanan & Lovallo, 2001; Lupien, McEwen, Gunnar, & Heim, 2009). In addition, memory consolidation during acute period of stress is suggested to be improved due to amplified cortisol levels (Ackermann, Hartmann, Papassotiropoulos, de Quervain, & Rasch, 2013). Lastly, working memory and learning have been shown to be amplified in the PFC due to heightened cortisol levels (Yuen et al., 2009). Such reactions are adaptive from an evolutionary standpoint, and can save lives. Improvements in memory can assist soldiers and parents with tasks, or even assist students in preparing for examinations while taking notes in class.

However, negative effects of acute stress on cognition have also been shown to occur. Short-term cortisol level increases are correlated with impairment in memory and cognitive functioning such as working memory, memory recall, and the ability to regulate behavior, thoughts, and emotions (Ackermann et al., 2013; Arnsten, 2009; Qin, Hermans, van Marle, Luo, & Fernández, 2009). Hypotheses regarding the causes of these impairments include the PFC, lateral cortex, and associated neuronal connections being used for other purposes during short-term stress. The use of these areas of the brain for attending to the stress may impair performance on tasks involving other executive functioning, such as cognitive flexibility, working memory, and set-shifting (Qin et al., 2009). Similar effects may result in symptomology of individuals with various psychiatric disorders, such as reported memory and concentration problems. Plessow et al. (Plessow, Fischer, Kirschbaum, & Goschke, 2011) found impairment in cognitive flexibility and control that was parallel with the time of the HPA axis stress response. *Cognitive flexibility* is the ability of the brain to attend to different tasks and environmental demands simultaneously, and to develop new responses or ways of thinking about the environment. For example, let's say you are standing at a bus stop, but decide to walk across the street to get a cup of coffee, and must dodge an oncoming vehicle while doing so. The brain is able to attend to multiple environmental demands simultaneously. Stress has been demonstrated to impair this ability. Although the short-term and acute effects of stress on the brain are readily apparent, the long-term effects may cause more functional impairment that is less reversible.

Stress starting in childhood has been shown to be especially detrimental to cognitive functioning. Several studies demonstrate the effects of prolonged stress starting in childhood. Whether the cause is poverty or abuse, short-term and working memory impairment were positively correlated with heightened cortisol activity and stress in childhood (Evans & Shamberg, 2009; Ivy et al., 2010; Pechtel & Pizzagalli, 2011). Early-life stress has been found to hamper development of brain regions associated with executive functioning and higher-order cognitive capabilities, as well as affective functioning (Pechtel & Pizzagalli, 2011). The amygdala has been shown to be especially vulnerable to early-life stress, which has been linked to later-life anxiety and psychotic disorders. Chronic stress has also been shown to decrease the size and functionality of the hippocampus (Ivy et al., 2010). Excessive cortisol activity and release for prolonged periods of time in one's early years have caused memory impairments lasting into adulthood, which are also associated with hippocampus atrophy (Ivy et al., 2010).

The prefrontal cortex demonstrates profound dendrite connection and neuronal restructuring as a result of chronic stress (Lupien et al., 2009). The PFC plays a major role in planning, executing, and coordinating behavior, social interactions and inhibitions, and emotion. It is also involved in many forms of psychopathology and mood disorders, including panic disorder, generalized anxiety disorder, depression, posttraumatic stress disorder, and addiction (NIMH, 2013). By definition, mental health disorders cause impairment in one's day-to-day functioning.

Depending upon the specific diagnosis, one can see changes in memory, inability to cope with environmental demands, or heightened anxiety that does not allow one to meet employment, relationship, educational, or other psychosocial demands. In conjunction with these neuroanatomical changes related to stress, humans demonstrate impaired ability to mediate day-to-day stress, as well as educational, occupational, and psychosocial relationships (Holmes & Wellman, 2009). Some studies have demonstrated the possible reversibility of some of the effects of stress on the hippocampus and PFC over time. In addition, Liston, McEwen, and Casey (2009) have demonstrated psychosocial stress impairment of attentional control and disrupted functional connectivity in the frontoparietal networks of subjects who were compared to a matched group of low-stress controls. However, when assessed a month later, after a period of reduced stress, the formerly stressed group showed no difference from the control group in the behavioral task performance and functional magnetic resonance imaging (fMRI) results. The authors concluded that the PFC likely contains components of high plasticity.

THE CLINICAL BIOPSYCHOLOGICAL MODEL

A new theoretical view based on a brain model appears capable of explaining several aspects of cognitive problems associated with stress. The clinical biopsychological model (Moss, 2007, 2010, 2013a) is based on a physiological theory of learning and memory (Moss, 2006, 2013b; Moss, Hunter, Shah, & Havens, 2012). The model proposes that there are predictable patterns in the types and manner of processing in various cortical regions, and suggests that processing in one region may interact with other regions both intrahemispherically and interhemispherically. This section briefly discusses how the model explains the manner in which stress leads to cognitive changes, including impaired retrieval of information and working memory, and deficits in attentional set-shifting and cognitive flexibility.

The clinical biopsychological model posits that the basis for learning and memory involves higher cortical functioning, which relies on information stored in columnar circuits. For the purposes of this chapter, each *column* is a group of a few thousand neurons that represent a specific information bit. Strengthening of the synaptic connections among the columns is the manner in which new memories are formed. Strengthening occurs due to recurrent activity in the circuit, which leads to changes such as increased neurotransmitter storage, which then increases information transfer from one column to the next. Acute stress leads to SNS activation and the release of norepinephrine. This occurs due to input from the thalamus and the cortex to the amygdala which, via its connections, activates the sympathetic ganglia and adrenal medulla. With the increased arousal, columnar circuit activation increases, and this is theorized to lead to enhanced memory.

To understand the other stress effects on cognitions, the theory uses an explanation of three dimensions: internal–external, action–reception, and global–analytic processing. Internal and self-referential processing involve the medial areas of the cortices, whereas external or environmental processing involves the lateral cortices. The medial cortical areas receive input from and provide input to subcortical structures, including those in the affective systems highlighted by Panksepp (2010) that he called the "core self." However, external stimulus information is processed and coded in the lateral cortex. In experimental tasks that involved working memory, set-shifting, and cognitive flexibility, the lateral cortical regions were required. The higher the stress load, particularly if self-referential aspects are involved, the more likely it is that the medial regions will be activated and interfere with activities in the lateral cortex. This is consistent with the findings in a study by Qin et al. (2009).

The two cortices are viewed as semi-independent functioning minds. Within the suggested parallel-processing design, the side that can best respond to an ongoing situation is the one that assumes control of the ensuing response. Both hemispheres receive similar sensory input. The left cortex processes sensory information in a detailed manner, resulting in its being slower than the right. The right cortex processes the information much faster, but in a global, less detailed manner. This allows for faster responses if confronted with outside danger, thus suggesting that this side is best equipped to respond and will assume behavioral control when a person is in a negative emotional state. Right cortical activation is expected to be most pronounced when an individual is stressed and pressured. There is exchange of information between the sides, although frontal lobe interactions are often inhibitory in nature. This is necessary to inhibit or prevent competing behavioral responses from opposing hemispheres.

The left cortex is the primary handler of highly detailed verbal language functions. The left posterior areas are involved in understanding spoken language, while the left frontal lobe controls production of spoken language. Thinking verbally and forming interpretive schemas are left frontal cortical processes, referred to as the "verbal interpreter" (Moss, 2013a). In contrast, the right cortex is involved in many less detailed, more global functions, including nonverbal emotional analyses and responses. The right posterior areas are involved in understanding emotional behaviors shown by others, as well as storage of external (e.g., sight, sound) and internal (e.g., visceral responses) sensory memories tied to emotions. The right frontal lobe is involved in emotional expressions.

The rapid processing in the right hemisphere allows for faster response patterns. With stressful situations creating negative emotional responses, the right frontal area is quickly activated, with inhibitory influence on the left frontal lobe. In situations resulting in inhibition of the left lateral ventral frontal activity, the perceived symptom would be impairment of one's verbal-thinking ability. This can result in problems accessing verbally based information (e.g., test phobics knowing the material but being unable to access it due to anxiety while being tested) and impaired attention to details. It does not matter if the right hemisphere's excitatory receptive sensory processing is the result of new internal or external stressors; the activation of the right frontal lobe and its inhibitory influence on the left frontal lobe occurs in either case. Impaired retrieval of left-hemisphere verbal information and set-shifting is the result.

SUMMARY

Cognitive neuroscience recognizes that the cognitive effects of stress can be debilitating at times. Many areas of the brain are affected by stress exposure. The primary areas are the hippocampus, HPA axis, SAM, prefrontal cortex, and amygdala. There are stark differences between long-term and short-term exposure to stress in relation to resulting cognitive impairments. Short-term stress exposure can amplify some aspects of cognition, whereas long-term exposure can cause overexcitation and possibly even neuron death. Stress may contribute to the development of mental health disorders, such as depression, posttraumatic stress disorder, generalized anxiety disorder, panic disorder, and many others. Cortisol is the main hormone linked to stress and adverse effects on the brain, such as premature aging and increased susceptibility to dementia, Alzheimer's disease, and other results of cognitive atrophy.

A contemporary theory, the clinical biopsychological model, offers a novel view on the effects of stress that is consistent with emerging views that brain circuits are probably the level at which various psychiatric problems are produced. This model explains the cognitive effects of stress based on interconnected cortical areas. The model also demonstrates how stress can increase cognitive functioning under some conditions (e.g., enhanced memory under acute stress) and impair cognitive functioning in other circumstances (e.g., limited ability to address environmental needs, day-to-day functioning, and impairments in executive functioning).

REFERENCES AND FURTHER READING

Ackermann, S., Hartmann, F., Papassotiropoulos, A., de Quervain, D., & Rasch, B. (2013). Associations between basal cortisol levels and memory retrieval in healthy young individuals. *Journal of Cognitive Neuroscience, 25*(11), 1896–1907. doi:10.1162/jocn_a_00440.

Arnsten, A. (2009). Stress signalling pathways that impair prefrontal cortex structure and function. *Nature Reviews Neuroscience, 10*(6), 410–422. doi:10.1038/nrn2648.

Buchanan, T., & Lovallo, W. (2001). Enhanced memory for emotional material following stress-level cortisol treatment in humans. *Psychoneuroendocrinology, 26*(3), 307–317.

Carlson, N. R. (2013). *Physiology of behavior* (11th ed.). Boston, MA: Pearson/Allyn & Bacon.

Cohen, S., Janicki-Deverts, D., & Miller, G. (2007). Psychological stress and disease. *JAMA, 298*(14), 1685–1687.

Evans, G., & Schamberg, M. (2009). Childhood poverty, chronic stress, and adult working memory. *Proceedings of the National Academy of Sciences of the United States of America, 106*(16), 6545–6549. doi:10.1073/pnas.0811910106.

Holmes, A., & Wellman, C. (2009). Stress-induced prefrontal reorganization and executive dysfunction in rodents. *Neuroscience and Biobehavioral Reviews, 33*(6), 773–783. doi:10.1016/j.neubiorev.2008.11.005.

Ivy, A., Rex, C., Chen, Y., Dubé, C., Maras, P., Grigoriadis, D., . . . Baram, T. (2010). Hippocampal dysfunction and cognitive impairments provoked by chronic early-life stress involve excessive activation of CRH receptors. *Journal of Neuroscience: The Official Journal of the Society for Neuroscience, 30*(39), 13005–13015. doi:10.1523/JNEUROSCI.1784-10.2010.

Liston, C., McEwen, B., & Casey, B. (2009). Psychosocial stress reversibly disrupts prefrontal processing and attentional control. *Proceedings of the National Academy of Sciences of the United States of America, 106*(3), 912–917. doi:10.1073/pnas.0807041106.

Lupien, S., McEwen, B., Gunnar, M., & Heim, C. (2009). Effects of stress throughout the lifespan on the brain, behaviour and cognition. *Nature Reviews Neuroscience, 10*(6), 434–445. doi:10.1038/nrn2639.

Moss, R. A. (2006). Of bits and logic: Cortical columns in learning and memory. *Journal of Mind and Behavior, 27*, 215–246.

Moss, R. A. (2007). Negative emotional memories in clinical practice: Theoretical considerations. *Journal of Psychotherapy Integration, 17*, 209–224.

Moss, R. A. (2010). Clinical biopsychology: Could a grand theory actually exist to allow true psychotherapy integration? *Independent Practitioner, 30*, 67–71.

Moss, R. A. (2013a). Psychotherapy and the brain: The dimensional systems model and clinical biopsychology. *Journal of Mind and Behavior, 34*, 63–89.

Moss, R. A. (2013b). A roadmap to the cerebral cortices. *The Neuropsychotherapist, 2*, 114–117. doi: 10.12744/tnpt(2)114–117.

Moss, R. A., Hunter, B. P., Shah, D., & Havens, T. (2012). A theory of hemispheric specialization based on cortical columns. *Journal of Mind and Behavior, 33*, 141–172.

National Institute of Mental Health. (2013). *Health and education statistics*. Retrieved from https://www.nimh.nih.gov/health/index.shtml.

Panksepp, J. (2010). The affective brain and core consciousness: How does neural activity generate emotional feelings? In M. Lewis, J. M. Haviland–Jones, & L. F. Barrett (Eds.), *Handbook of emotions* (pp. 47–67). New York, NY: Guilford Press.

Pechtel, P., & Pizzagalli, D. (2011). Effects of early life stress on cognitive and affective function: An integrated review of human literature. *Psychopharmacology, 214*(1), 55–70. doi:10.1007/s00213-010-2009-2.

Plessow, F., Fischer, R., Kirschbaum, C., & Goschke, T. (2011). Inflexibly focused under stress: Acute psychosocial stress increases shielding of action goals at the expense of reduced cognitive flexibility with increasing time lag to the stressor. *Journal of Cognitive Neuroscience, 23*(11), 3218–3227. doi:10.1162/jocn_a_00024.

Qin, S., Hermans, E., van Marle, H., Luo, J., & Fernández, G. (2009). Acute psychological stress reduces working memory-related activity in the dorsolateral prefrontal cortex. *Biological Psychiatry, 66*(1), 25–32. doi:10.1016/j.biopsych.2009.03.006.

Schatzberg, A., Keller, J., Tennakoon, L., Lembke, A., Williams, G., Kraemer, F., . . . Murphy, G. (2013, October 2). HPA axis genetic variation, cortisol and psychosis in major depression. *Molecular Psychiatry*. PMID: 24166412. Database: MEDLINE.

Schwabe, L., Wolf, O. T., & Oitzl, M. S. (2010). Memory formation under stress: Quantity and quality. *Neuroscience and Biobehavioral Reviews, 34*(4), 584–591. doi:10.1016/j.neubiorev.2009.11.015.

Stahl, S. M. (2013). *Stahl's essential psychopharmacology: Neuroscientific basis and practical applications* (4th ed.). New York, NY: Cambridge University Press.

Szydlowska, K., & Tymianski, M. (2010). Calcium, ischemia and excitotoxicity. *Cell Calcium, 47*(2), 122–129. doi:10.1016/j.ceca.2010.01.003.

Yuen, E. Y., Liu, W., Karatsoreos, I. N., Feng, J., McEwen, B. S., & Yan, Z. (2009). Acute stress enhances glutamatergic transmission in prefrontal cortex and facilitates working memory. *PNAS: Proceedings of the National Academy of Sciences of the United States of America, 106*(33), 14075–14079. doi:10.1073/pnas.0906791106.

11

The Mind-Body Connection and Stress

Ioulia Maimari and Serena Wadhwa

Rene Descartes laid the foundation for the idea of mind-body separation in Western civilization. Although vast amounts of research over the past century have proven that the mind and body are interdependent, several other discoveries regarding this connection demonstrate the effects of stress on the body and subsequently the mind, and vice versa. Hence, no book on stress is complete without some discussion of the mind-body connection. The following is a brief synopsis of key knowledge regarding the mind-body connection and stress. In essence, evidence of how the body maintains harmony when systems are balanced and functioning together provides a foundational understanding of the mind-body connection.

The concept and study of the mind-body connection can be traced back to early works of Hans Selye and Walter Cannon and follow-up studies from Rahe, documenting how major life events contribute to illness (Jacobs, 2001). Research conducted by Beecher (1955) further demonstrated a mind-body connection, as *placebos* (fake medications with no active ingredients) provided some therapeutic benefits to the users even though there was no active medication. This led to the conclusion that a person's mindset, expectations, beliefs, and so on can influence body states (Vittetta, Anton, Cortizo, & Sali, 2005).

Further evidence of how other systems react to assist in maintaining harmony and balancing the body was developed when research in psychoneuroimmunology expanded (see Chapter 6). This field of study explores the relationships among stress, the immune system, and health, and has yielded additional research and studies on how the body's physical systems are affected by various states in the mind. Pioneers in this field include Drs. Janice Kiecolt-Glaser and Ronald Glaser.

Readers can refer to Kiecolt-Glaser, McGuire, Robles, and Glaser (2002) for further information and resources.

Various studies confirm the hazards and deleterious effects of chronic stress on the cardiovascular system, the digestive system, sleep, the immune system, the respiratory system, and other systems in the body (McEwen, 2008; Glaser & Kiecolt-Glaser, 2005; Hamilton-West, 2011), which can precipitate or contribute to the development of diseases such as cancer, heart disease, insomnia, infertility, and others. Research has also demonstrated how the mind's effects on the immune system, as well as other body systems, influence the onset and maintenance of colds, allergies, cognitive decline, and other problems.

The mind-body connection also accounts for the influence of personality variables; for example, how different traits may impact physical and mental health. Chapter 12, on stress assessment, also explores this concept, because assessment provides a basis for understanding how a demand is perceived as being addressed or not addressed in relation to how and when a recovery period occurs. Research in the area of the mind-body connection contends that individuals with the same medical disorder will fare differently due to personality factors, protective factors, and individual appraisal of events (Vittetta et al., 2005). Much research demonstrates linkages not just among physiological systems (Hamilton-West, 2011), but among psychological systems as well (see Chapter 12 for further exploration of this topic).

In addition to the effects of stress and chronic stress on various health issues, research is also exploring how stress affects our very DNA (see Epel et al., 2004). The results of some of Epel et al.'s work suggest that stress, when it is not managed, can affect the aging process and actually change our genetics.

PHYSIOLOGICAL EFFECTS OF STRESS

Stress is a condition that is present in daily life. Moderate amounts of stress can help us concentrate and perform under pressure; some stress can keep us energetic, alert, and motivated to face all kinds of challenges. Although stress is a physiological reaction of the human body, its effects are also psychological, cognitive, and behavioral.

Stress is the physiological response of the human body to a perceived threat. In other words, it is the body's mechanism to protect itself: it activates a fight-or-flight response with the aim of either fighting the danger or fleeing from it. During whichever of these actions is chosen, the tension that has built up in the body gets released. As soon as the danger is gone (assuming that the individual survived), the body returns to homeostasis, its normal state.

Today the threats are more often emotional or psychological than physical. Although these threats may exist only in a person's way of thinking or perceptions, the body does not know the difference. In any given moment, the human brain perceives and analyzes various events in the surrounding environment. Some of them may be categorized as dangerous. As a result, the body activates the stress response, preparing for fight or flight. However, because threats nowadays are rarely physical, there is no way to release or extinguish the accelerated stress response, because the human body does not distinguish between physical and psychological threats. This can result in both physiological and psychological symptomatology.

External factors are not the only cause of stress. It can also be self-generated, for example, through excessive thought and analysis of past or anticipated situations or through irrational, pessimistic thoughts regarding one's life.

The situations and events that are perceived as threats and cause stress are known as *stressors*. Usually stressors are considered to be something negative, such as an exhausting work schedule or a problematic relationship. However, a highly demanding situation or the need for a sudden adjustment under new conditions can also be positive, such as getting married, buying a house, going to college, or receiving a promotion, though these conditions are nevertheless sometimes perceived as stressful. Some of these stressors trigger an acute stress response, in which the fight-or-flight response activates, meets the demand, and dissipates into a recovery stage. Acute stress is a brief reaction to a response. Physiologically, a cascade of hormones and chemicals is released in the brain and body to assist in meeting the immediate threats/demands (Chapter 9 on stress hormones explores this in more detail). These hormones and chemicals have the physiological effect of increasing energy, glucose availability, and ability to meet the stressor or threat head-on. Basically, the body prepares itself to survive. Once the threat or stressor subsides, the body reverts to its previous state. This is the recovery stage.

However, when stressed over a busy schedule, an argument with a friend, a mountain of bills, or eviction from a home, the body reacts just as strongly as when facing a physical life-or-death situation. If one constantly has many responsibilities and worries, the emergency stress response may be activated most of the time. The longer the human body is in an activated mode, the harder it is to shut off or deactivate. This makes stress a chronic condition (chronic stress), where demands seem never-ending and there is little to no recovery stage.

The body has physiological reactions to the constant and consistent demands placed on it. When acute stress becomes chronic stress, can the psychological effects of this also be detrimental? According to some research, yes. According to Lupien, McEwen, Gunnar, and Heim (2009), some of this may be related to *when* an individual is exposed to this kind of stress. However, it is known that chronic stress affects cortisol levels, and that these levels affect brain development; it also appears that chronic stress in adults can contribute to the experience of clinical disorders. Thus, an individual may be clinically depressed, experience stressful life events, and be more vulnerable to the effects of the stress. Some of the symptoms experienced in chronic stress and in the anxiety and depression include lethargy, low energy levels or restlessness, insomnia, oversleeping, lack of appetite or overeating, loss of interest in pleasurable activities, increased breathing, and rapid heartbeat. Some of these symptoms occur as part of the stress response as well: the fight-or-flight response typically manifests in rapid heartbeat, shallow, rapid breathing, increased alertness, and so on, as previously described. However, an individual may not be distressed psychologically while experiencing these physiological symptoms.

Physiologically, long-term exposure to stress can lead to serious health problems. Chronic stress disrupts nearly every system in the body. An individual experiencing chronic stress constantly has a host of additional chemicals and hormones being released into the body to sustain the bodily response to the apparently constant threat. Some individuals end up with poorer health outcomes as a result of these physiological effects (Jackson, Knight, & Rafferty, 2010), which can cause symptoms such as headaches, high blood pressure, chest pain, heart palpitations, skin rashes, and loss of sleep. Chronic stress may also suppress the immune system, increase the risk of heart attack and stroke, contribute to infertility, and speed up the aging process. Long-term stress can even rewire the brain, leaving one more vulnerable to mental disorders such as anxiety and depression. Physiologically, the presence of such chemicals also affects the plasticity of certain structural portions of the brain. These changes have subsequent effects on physiological functioning, cognitive functioning, and emotional regulation (McEwen & Morrison, 2013).

Psychological Effects

Psychological effects of stress nowadays are rather complex. Modern society and the increasingly fast pace of life have created several stressors that our ancestors did not have to deal with. Daily stressors, microstressors, and major life events are often common triggers for symptoms of stress and even anxiety disorders. This is the caveat regarding the psychological effects of stress: Something considered threatening will have a different effect than something considered a challenge. Chapter 12 explores the concept of appraisal and assessment; that is, how an individual's perception and interpretation of a situation contribute to the individual's belief as to whether or not he or she can adequately meet the demands presented. The effects of stress are not dichotomous, heads-or-tails issues; rather, there is an insidious progression to the psychological effects of stress, which can range from being bored to being overwhelmed. There are experiences of low, moderate, and high stress, and each type affects functioning in some way, whether beneficial or detrimental (Mohan, Sharma, & Bijlani, 2011). There is even an effect from denial.

PAIN

In a 2012 survey, about 126 million people in the United States reported pain (Nahin, 2015). The financial cost of pain ranged from $560 to $635 billion in 2010, a total representing the costs of medical treatment plus the costs of reduction in worker productivity (Gaskin & Richard, 2012). *Pain* has traditionally been defined as "an unpleasant sensory and emotional experience that is associated with actual or potential tissue damage or described in such terms of such damage" (International Association for the Study of Pain, n.d.). The traditional view of pain, while subjective, is derived from a biological model: that is, having a point of injury or damage, and requiring that something be done to or at the site of pain to provide relief. However, in the past couple of decades, research has demonstrated that pain is more complicated than this. There are psychological, social, and environmental factors that complicate the biological manifestations of pain (Gonzales, Martelli, & Baker, 2000; Sturgeon & Zautra, 2013). Additionally, the understanding of pain as a phenomenon different from nociception (the transmission of a pain impulse from activated sensory nerves), and the recognition that acute pain is different from chronic pain (which activates the prefrontal and limbic systems), complicate the issue.

Pain affects an individual's ability to function, concentrate, and make decisions, and is detrimental to other aspects of quality of life (Gaskin & Richard, 2012). Because pain requires treatment (traditionally, medical treatment), there is additional interference with the person's ability to live a day-to-day life without the worry, fear, or consequences of pain.

Pain can be exacerbated if the pain sensations are viewed as threatening, demanding, or pressuring in some way. As a result of this perception, the stress response is activated, preparing the body to fight or flee. For some individuals, the chemical and hormone releases elicited by the stress response can cause further perceived injury. Individuals may thus "learn" to fear pain sensations: they anticipate that the pain will become worse, so they may try to avoid the pain or anything that might trigger it. Roelofs, Boissevain, Peters, de Jong, and Vlaeyen (2002) call this *pain catastrophizing*.

Another way the experience of pain can become cyclic is when individuals who have pain conceal it. One study showed that people who concealed their pain not only had less tolerance for pain, they experienced higher pain intensities (Uysal & Lu, 2011).

—*Serena Wadhwa*

Psychologically, denial operates as a defense mechanism when the reality of something is overwhelming to the psyche and in facing that reality the psyche might "break." Thus, denying an overwhelming reality, though self-deceiving, may or may not help temporarily in weathering a storm. Other factors also contribute to the outcome, of course. However, it is possible that in denying the initial factor of stress, the psychological effects of that stress are avoided; that is, the individual "avoids" a potential disruption to his or her mental and emotional balance. This is not always ideal, but the fact remains that this can provide some cushion against the detrimental effects of facing an overwhelming stressor head-on. Ramachandran (1996) explores this phenomenon in relation to medical patients' explanations about their medical conditions and how they rationalize right- and left-hemisphere injuries.

Nonetheless, psychological pressure can result from chronic stress when emotions are not expressed. The suppression of certain emotions, often as a result of misconceptions relating to "handling stress," can have detrimental effects. For example, Slavin-Spenny, Lumley, Thakur, Nevedal, and Hijazi (2013) explored the effects of emotional expression and emotional reduction approaches to pain. Although there were no significant differences in the approaches themselves, these researchers did find that expressing emotions, being direct about needs and wants, and utilizing relaxation techniques were effective in reducing both the psychological effects of stress and the resulting physical effects (e.g., headaches). It is well known that the avoidance of discussing certain thoughts, feelings, and experiences results in those things becoming more cemented in one's day-to-day experience. Individuals who struggle with clinical depression, for example, find it more difficult to be proactive about the condition if they are not expressing their thoughts, feelings, and experiences, as opposed to a person who is actively seeking support and resources.

So, while some avoidance of a stressful reality may be beneficial in maintaining a sense of control and competency, the psychological effects of stress will manifest themselves at some point. A cyclic pattern may also ensue. The complexity of the stress response, both acute and chronic; the influences of chemicals and hormones; the availability of coping mechanisms (whether effective or ineffective); the methodology of decision making; and appraisal and cognitive functionality all play a role in the psychological effects that appear. For example, when individuals face a challenging or demanding situation, there is less self-control over consumption of tempting foods (Maier, Makwana, & Hare, 2015). It is well known that stress can not only affect decision-making ability, but also can distort the reality one perceives.

Another consideration to be examined, as part of the discussion of the psychological effects of stress, is some research explores the notion of distress activating the stress response (Glaser & Kiecolt-Glaser, 2005) and reducing the parasympathetic response (Clays et al., 2011). When the body does not function at its peak, it becomes more vulnerable to both the effects of stress and the onset of psychological distress. This can result in a vicious cycle.

Hormones can have a huge influence on how one perceives what is happening. Consider the effects of adrenaline: the experience of the individual can be either ready to take on the world or panic and restlessness. Each of these scenarios creates different psychological effects as well. An individual who experiences a "bring it on" attitude may be psychologically ready, willing, and able to face whatever challenges are coming, whereas an individual who is experiencing sensations interpreted as panic or restlessness may become afraid, worried, or apprehensive. Each of these psychological states creates reactive loops that trigger further thoughts, sensations, chemical releases, brain states, moods, and so forth.

Not only are the effects of stress on decision-making ability well known, it is also known that stress affects cognitive functioning in general (see Chapters 1 and 36 on cognitive and behavioral theories and how ineffective or harmful ways of thinking can be restructured). One example of this, to further explore the psychological effects of stress, emerges from research by Mohan, Sharma, and Bijlani (2011). The increase in glucocorticoids leads to deficits in memory and attention, thus impairing performance. When enough stress is present for the individual to cause the body to initiate the release of glucocorticoids, that individual's performance and confidence in his or her ability to perform may be reduced. Additionally, when a person does not perform as he or she expected or does not believe that he or she met other people's expectations, the perceived failure can lead to feelings of guilt and shame, which act as internal stressors—the experience of which can further impair performance. This too can easily become a vicious cycle.

TYPES OF STRESS

In addition to acute and chronic stress, the Australian Psychological Society (2012) identifies another distinct type of stress according to the duration of the symptoms: *episodic acute stress*. This kind of stress seems similar to chronic stress; the difference is that within experiences of episodic acute stress, it seems that there is crisis after crisis to be dealt with. In chronic stress, stressors are a continued, consistent presence.

SHORT-TERM PSYCHOLOGICAL EFFECTS OF STRESS

In the short term, during a stressful situation and for the first few weeks after the stressful event occurs, several psychological effects may manifest. Anxiety is one of the main symptoms. *Anxiety* is the process during which a person becomes scared and apprehensive of what lies ahead. It is among the many adverse effects of stress, and often manifests itself in physical problems such as pain, dizziness, and panic attacks (Groberman, 2012). Muscular tension and restlessness may also be experienced. Anxiety is accompanied by physiological reactions that often closely resemble those of the fight-or-flight response. For example, individuals who experience anxiety often report physical symptoms of heart palpitations, sweating, or shortness of breath ("Anxiety disorders and stress," n.d.). However, because anxiety does not typically have a cause similar to that of stress (where the onset is caused by something perceived as threatening or demanding), anxiety is considered a legitimate mental health disorder. People who experience symptoms similar to those of anxiety when presented with a stressor typically can reduce the perceived threat, demand, or pressure that was initiating or exacerbating the subsequent physical and emotional symptoms. With anxiety, this is not always the case.

FREUD AND HIS PSYCHODYNAMIC THEORIES OF STRESS

Another way of studying and managing stress is found in psychodynamic therapies, based in Sigmund Freud's psychodynamic approach. The fundamental psychodynamic theory assumes that maladaptive or unwanted behavior is caused by unconscious drives and processes, so therapy focuses on fostering insight and/or corrective experiences. In specific terms, struggle with internal conflicts, whether subconscious, unconscious, or conscious, leads to conflicts and to the experience of anxiety and other manifestations of these competing demands. The id, ego, and superego, which play specific roles in an individual's psyche, may each present some of these competing demands. For example, the id (known mostly for its instant gratification desires) may want something and want it now, a demand that runs up against the superego's demands in its role of regulation of behavior/morality (for example, you should not have ice cream for breakfast). As a result of this internal conflict, stress may be experienced, and may manifest in emotional, physiological, and other symptoms. Other theories within the psychodynamic framework focus on the relationship of the individual to the "object" and the subsequent stress that results from loss of or interactions with this object (Kaslow et al., 1998). Coping with these symptoms (including potential loss) involves exploring the conflicts that exist and finding some resolution, which may sometimes result in unhealthy coping mechanisms (Andreasen, 2011). Some of the literature involving psychodynamic concepts in stress resolution comes from Horowitz's research (see Horowitz, 1986), which explores how identifying some of these competing pressures can provide relief.

—*Serena Wadhwa*

Each case is different and stressors vary widely. As a result, there are a variety of symptoms of different intensities and durations. However, if stressors or symptoms persist for a long period of time, more and more severe effects occur. Sometimes the physiological effects may cause changes in the brain that affect personality and emotions.

LONG-TERM PSYCHOLOGICAL EFFECTS OF STRESS

If stressors are too strong and too persistent in individuals who are biologically vulnerable because of age, genetic, or constitutional factors, stressors may lead to diseases (Schneiderman, Ironson, & Siegel, 2005). However, the psychological symptoms of stress vary according to the kind of stressors, their intensity, and their persistence. Effects of stress, such as extensive worry and anxiety, may be followed by depressive symptoms; mood swings; feelings of guilt, hopelessness, or powerlessness; low self-esteem or low self-worth; irritability, resentment, or angry outbursts; increased cynicism; isolation, avoidance of social encounters, or lack of interest in activities; feeling overwhelmed or unable to be happy; and cognitive effects such as difficulties with concentration and memory.

PSYCHOLOGICAL EFFECTS OF CHRONIC STRESS DURING CHILDHOOD

According to Schneiderman et al. (2005), childhood exposure to maltreatment/abuse takes a heavy toll on children and adolescents, whether their exposure was to violence, abuse (sexual, physical, emotional, or neglect), and/or divorce/marital conflict. The negative effects may include dysregulation of affect, provocative behaviors, avoidance of intimacy, and disturbances in attachment. Shonkoff et al. (2012) discuss three types of childhood stress responses, each affecting how the individual copes with stress later in life because of the physiological disruptions in development. The first is a positive stress response, produced when the child has support to help him or her cope with an acute stressor. The next is a tolerable stress response, produced when the child has support to cope with a life-changing event, such as a major threat to safety and security. Finally, there is a toxic stress response, which arises when the child has minimal to no protective factors to cope with stress.

The Adverse Childhood Experience Study (ACES) examines the effects of severe stressors and how these experiences affect brain development, thus influencing later-life experiences, as long-lasting neurobiological effects and other physiological challenges increase the risk for additional physiological and psychological disorders. This landmark study, which is still ongoing, is finding a number of physical results from childhood stress, including obesity, diabetes, heart disease, and sexually transmitted diseases, among others. Schneiderman et al. (2005) explored how various toxic stress experiences in early life increase vulnerability to mental health disorders, poor school performance, low social support, and other undesirable outcomes. The experience of stress may also affect a child's "set point" of homeostasis or allostasis, thus increasing vulnerability to stressors and stress-related disorders later in life.

EFFECTS OF CHRONIC STRESS DURING ADULTHOOD

Stress has been linked with depression. During adulthood, first depressive episodes often develop following the occurrence of a major negative life event (Schneiderman et al., 2005). Furthermore, there is evidence that stressful life events can cause the onset of depression. A study of 13,006 patients in Denmark, diagnosed with depression in their first psychiatric admissions, uncovered a correlation between these individuals and significant life stressors (e.g., divorce) compared with matched control groups (Kessing, Agerbro, & Mortensen, 2003). Other research has suggested that the consistent and continuous stress of a medical diagnosis increases the risk of depression. In one study, one-fourth of individuals diagnosed with cancer met criteria for clinical depression (McDaniel et al., 1995).

Studies suggest that individuals who experience chronic stress may adopt behaviors that further increase vulnerability to additional physiological and psychological stress and outcomes (Schneiderman et al., 2005). Several studies show that in stressful environments, individuals tend to engage in risky health behaviors like smoking, drinking, and impulsive behaviors (Schneiderman et al., 2005; McEwen, 2012; Lovallo, 2013).

SUMMARY AND FUTURE CONSIDERATION

As explained in this chapter, the physiological and psychological effects of stress can be both short term and long term. These effects vary from person to person. How a stressor will affect a particular person depends on various factors, such as the person's age, his or her predisposition and coping skills, and so on. There are many possible symptoms, and each may vary in intensity and duration. If stressors or symptoms persist for a long period of time, more—and more severe—effects may occur.

There is a high likelihood that in the near future, due to the modern lifestyle, more people will suffer from the effects of stress enough to exhibit symptoms. Researchers all around the world will keep studying stress and effective coping strategies. Stress is a dynamic, multidimensional, and complex subject. There can be little doubt that a lot has been learned, even though each increment of progress seems to spawn multiple new questions.

Today, a vast amount of information is available, and most people have the ability to access most of them at any given time. Knowledge and self-observation can help each and every one of us to recognize our personal stressors and stress effects, in order to seek possible solutions or assistance (see also Chapter 45, "Psychological Stress Disorders").

REFERENCES AND FURTHER READING

American Psychiatric Association. (2000). *Diagnostic and statistical manual of mental disorders, fourth edition, text revision (DSM-IV-TR)*. Washington, DC: American Psychiatric Publishing.

Andreasen, N. C. (2011). What is post-traumatic stress disorder? *Dialogues in Clinical Neuroscience, 13*(3), 240.

Anxiety disorders and stress. (n.d.). American Psychological Association. Retrieved from http://www.apa.org/divisions/div12/rev_est/anxiety.html.

Australian Psychological Society. (2012). *Understanding and managing stress*. Melbourne, Australia: The Australia Psychological Society Limited.

Beecher, H. (1955). The powerful placebo. *JAMA, 159*(17), 1602–1606. doi:10.1001/jama.1955.02960340022006.

Brom, D., Kleber, R. J., & Defares, P. B. (1989). Brief psychotherapy for posttraumatic stress disorders. *Journal of Consulting and Clinical Psychology, 57*(5), 607.

Centers for Disease Control and Prevention (CDC). (2016). ACES study. Retrieved from http://www.cdc.gov/violenceprevention/acestudy/.

Clays, E., De Bacquer, D., Crasset, V., Kittel, F., de Smet, P., Kornitzer, M., Karasek, R., & De Backer, G. (2011, February). The perception of work stressors is related to reduced parasympathetic activity. *International Archives of Occupational and Environmental Health, 84*(2), 185–191. doi:10.1007/s00420-010-0537-z.

Epel, E. S., Blackburn, E. H., Lin, J., Dhabhar, F. S., Adler, N. E., Morrow, J. D., & Cawthon, R. M. (2004). Accelerated telomere shortening in response to life stress. *Proceedings of the National Academy of Sciences of the United States of America, 101*(49), 17312–17315.

Gaskin, D. J., & Richard, P. (2012). The economic costs of pain in the United States. *The Journal of Pain, 13*(8), 715–724.

Gebhart, G. F. (2000). Scientific issues of pain and distress. In National Research Council (US) Committee on Regulatory Issues in Animal Care and Use, *Definition of pain and distress and reporting requirements for laboratory animals: Proceedings of the workshop held June 22, 2000* (pp. 22–30). Washington, DC: National Academies Press.

Glaser, R., & Kiecolt-Glaser, J. K. (2005). Stress-induced immune dysfunction: Implications for health. *Nature Reviews Immunology, 5*, 243.

Gonzales, V. A., Martelli, M. F., & Baker, J. M. (2000). Psychological assessment of persons with chronic pain. *NeuroRehabilitation, 14*(2), 69–83.

Green, B. L. (1996). Traumatic stress and disaster: Mental health effects and factors influencing adaptation. In F. L. Mak & C. Nadelson (Eds.), *International review of psychiatry* (pp. 177–211). Washington, DC: American Psychiatric Press.

Groberman, A. (2012). Difference between stress and anxiety. Retrieved from http://www.psyweb.com/articles/anxiety/difference-between-stress-and-anxiety.

Hamilton-West, K. (2011). *Psychobiological processes in health and illness*. London, UK: Sage.

Horowitz, M. J. (1986). Stress-response syndromes: A review of posttraumatic and adjustment disorders. *Psychiatric Services, 37*(3), 241–249.

International Association for the Study of Pain. (n.d.). Retrieved from http://www.iasp-pain.org/index.aspx.

Jackson, J. S., Knight, K. M., & Rafferty, J. A. (2010). Race and unhealthy behaviors: Chronic stress, the HPA axis, and physical and mental health disparities over the life course. *American Journal of Public Health, 100*(5), 933–939.

Jacobs, G. D. (2001). The physiology of mind-body interactions: The stress response and the relaxation response (vol. 7, pg S83, 2001). *Journal of Alternative and Complementary Medicine, 7*(1), 83–92; erratum published, *Journal of Alternative and Complementary Medicine, 8*(2), 219.

Kaslow, N. J., Reviere, S. L., Chance, S. E., Rogers, J. H., Hatcher, C. A., Wasserman, F., . . . Seelig, B. (1998). An empirical study of the psychodynamics of suicide. *Journal of the American Psychoanalytic Association, 46*(3), 777–796.

Kessing, L. V., Agerbro, E., & Mortensen, P. B. (2003). Does the impact of major stressful life events on the risk of developing depression change throughout life? *Psychological Medicine, 33,* 1177–1184.

Kessler, R. C., Sonnega, A., Bromet, E., Hughes, M., & Nelson, C. B. (1995). Posttraumatic stress disorder in the National Comorbidity Survey. *Archives of General Psychiatry, 52,* 1048–1060.

Kiecolt-Glaser, J. K., McGuire, L., Robles, T. F., & Glaser, R. (2002). Psychoneuroimmunology: Psychological influences on immune function and health. *Journal of Consulting and Clinical Psychology, 70*(3), 537.

Lovallo, W. R. (2013). Early life adversity reduces stress reactivity and enhances impulsive behavior: Implications for health behaviors. *International Journal of Psychophysiology, 90*(1), 8–16.

Lupien, S. J., McEwen, B. S., Gunnar, M. R., & Heim, C. (2009). Effects of stress throughout the lifespan on the brain, behaviour and cognition. *Nature Reviews Neuroscience, 10*(6), 434–445.

Maier, S. U., Makwana, A. B., & Hare, T. A. (2015). Acute stress impairs self-control in goal-directed choice by altering multiple functional connections within the brain's decision circuits. *Neuron, 87*(3), 621–631.

McDaniel, J. S., Musselman, D. L., Porter, M. R., Reed, D. A., & Nemeroff, C. B. (1995). Depression in patients with cancer: Diagnosis, biology and treatment. *Archives of General Psychiatry, 2,* 89–99.

McEwen, B. S. (2008). Central effects of stress hormones in health and disease: Understanding the protective and damaging effects of stress and stress mediators. *European Journal of Pharmacology, 583*(2), 174–185.

McEwen, B. S. (2012). Brain on stress: How the social environment gets under the skin. *Proceedings of the National Academy of Sciences, 109*(suppl. 2), 17180–17185.

McEwen, B. S., & Morrison, J. H. (2013). The brain on stress: Vulnerability and plasticity of the prefrontal cortex over the life course. *Neuron, 79*(1), 16–29.

Mills, H., Reiss, N., & Dombeck, M. (2008). *Mental and emotional impact of stress.* Retrieved from https://www.mentalhelp.net/articles/types-of-stressors-eustress-vs-distress/.

Mohan, A., Sharma, R., & Bijlani, R. L. (2011). Effect of meditation on stress-induced changes in cognitive functions. *Journal of Alternative and Complementary Medicine, 17*(3), 207–212.

Nahin, R. L. (2015). Estimates of pain prevalence and severity in adults: United States, 2012. *Journal of Pain, 16*(8), 769–780.

Ramachandran, V. S. (1996). The evolutionary biology of self-deception, laughter, dreaming and depression: Some clues from anosognosia. *Medical Hypotheses, 47*(5), 347–362.

Roelofs, J., Boissevain, M. D., Peters, M. L., de Jong, J. R., & Vlaeyen, J. W. (2002). Psychological treatments for chronic low back pain: Past, present and beyond. *Pain Reviews, 9*(1), 29.

Schneiderman, N., Ironson, G., & Siegel, S. D. (2005). Stress and health: Psychological, behavioral, and biological determinants. *Annual Review of Clinical Psychology, 1,* 607–628.

Shonkoff, J. P., Garner, A. S., Siegel, B. S., Dobbins, M. I., Earls, M. F., McGuinn, L., . . . Wood, D. L. (2012). The lifelong effects of early childhood adversity and toxic stress. *Pediatrics, 129*(1), e232–e246.

Slavin-Spenny, O., Lumley, M. A., Thakur, E. R., Nevedal, D. C., & Hijazi, A. M. (2013). Effects of anger awareness and expression training versus relaxation training on headaches: A randomized trial. *Annals of Behavioral Medicine, 46*(2), 181–192.

Sturgeon, J. A., & Zautra, A. J. (2013). Psychological resilience, pain catastrophizing, and positive emotions: Perspectives on comprehensive modeling of individual pain adaptation. *Current Pain and Headache Reports, 17*(3), 1–9.

Trauma. (n.d.). American Psychological Association. Retrieved from http://www.apa.org/topics/trauma.

Uysal, A., & Lu, Q. (2011). Is self-concealment associated with acute and chronic pain? *Health Psychology, 30*(5), 606.

Van Houdenhove, B., & Egle, U. T. (2004). Fibromyalgia: A stress disorder? *Psychotherapy and Psychosomatics, 73*(5), 267–275.

Vitetta, L., Anton, B., Cortizo, F., & Sali, A. (2005). Mind-body medicine: Stress and its impact on overall health and longevity. *Annals of the New York Academy of Sciences, 1057*(1), 492–505.

What is a placebo? (n.d.). Retrieved March 13, 2016, from http://www.drugs.com/article/placebo-effect.html.

12

Factors in Assessing and Measuring Stress

Serena Wadhwa

The subject of stress assessment is vast. Many factors contribute to the understanding of how stress is assessed, how to measure it, and what do to with the data derived from assessment and measurement. Many articles, books, and other resources on this topic are available, and provide more in-depth information about the enormous number of factors involved in the assessment and measurement of stress. This chapter provides a brief view into some of these factors, how they are included in assessment and measurement, and what influences they exert.

Stress is a challenging thing to measure. When the term *stress* surfaced in the mid-19th century, Cartesian beliefs about the separation of body and mind led researchers to try to measure the "experience" of stress via the physiological response and the chemicals and hormones released during this process. For example, it is now well known that cortisol is a highly important factor in stress, and cortisol level was one of the measurements made to assess the stress reaction. More recently, biofeedback (see Chapter 30) has become an assessment tool, using physiological feedback to allow the individual to "see" and explore what is happening inside the body and brain in reaction to certain stimuli.

This chapter describes some common factors involved in the assessment and measurement of stress.

VULNERABILITIES/PERSONALITY TRAITS/TEMPERAMENT

Vulnerabilities

An individual who is vulnerable (reactive) to stress is influenced by genetic, biological, and physiological factors. Research demonstrates when a fetus is growing in the womb, many factors affecting the mother during that time will also have an impact on the growing fetus. The intensity of the stressors experienced by the mother has consequences for the physical and neurological development of the growing fetus (Schetter & Tanner, 2012). Such influences on neurological development have been demonstrated to affect the child's ability to regulate attention, and to cause behavioral and emotional struggles as well as cognitive problems. Additionally, vulnerabilities influence dispositions and other factors, as explained later.

Although a full discussion is well beyond the scope of this chapter, it is necessary to be mindful of the influence that these physiological vulnerabilities may have on an individual's reactions to his or her experience of stress. An individual who is more prone to "stress reactivity" may find stress to be more challenging, depending on environmental, social, and family factors that provide either effective or ineffective/harmful means of coping with stressors. Readers are encouraged to explore the references at the end of this chapter for more in-depth analysis of this topic.

Personality Traits

Research explores how certain trait constructs influence our perception of what is threatening, demanding, or pressuring (Hamilton-West, 2011). Earlier research examined how "Type A" personalities—individuals who characteristically had traits of impatience, competitiveness, and hostility—were more prone to cardiovascular disease. Recent research suggests that hostility is probably the factor contributing most to the development of heart disease, because it affects the person's perceived vulnerability, leading him or her to perhaps see situations and interactions as more threatening than they actually are, or constantly engages the person in the reactive state of the fight-or-flight response (Miller, Smith, Turner, Guijarro, & Hallet, 1996; Sloan et al., 2001). One's biology, genetics, and brain structure also contribute to the development of vulnerabilities, personality traits, temperament, and the like (Hollenstein & Lougheed, 2013).

Temperament

Temperament refers to individuals' traits that contribute to the relationships they have in the world, the types of experiences they may or may not have, and how they function in various unexpected and expected situations, in addition to other factors (Strelau, 1996; Hollenstein & Lougheed, 2013). The underlying structural blueprints of temperament lead to the development of an attachment style, which is also dependent upon the caregivers in the child's environment. There is a bidirectional relationship among these various factors, which all have an influence on the child's development of stress coping mechanisms, vulnerabilities, and the like.

Attachment Styles

There is much research demonstrating that attachment styles influence how an individual responds or reacts to stress (Mikulincer & Florian, 1998; Powers, Pietromonaco, Gunlicks, & Sayer, 2006; Fraley, Roisman, Booth-LaForce, Owen, & Holland, 2013). Attachment styles, whether secure, avoidant, anxious, or disorganized, carry certain predispositions contributing to the development of internal resources and ways of organizing information about the world, which subsequently can either be protective factors in the experience of stress, or contribute to vulnerabilities.

APPRAISAL

Chapter 1 explores the stress appraisal and coping model developed by Lazarus, providing an overview of this model and its relationship to the perception and evaluation of stress. However, it is imperative to recognize that when it comes to assessing stress, an individual's interpretation and perceptual evaluation of the trigger will have the most bearing upon how the individual reacts and what the individual

DEPRIVATIONAL STRESS

Being deprived of something can be stressful, particularly if it's something essential to one's general well-being. According to Meerlo, Sgoifo, and Suchecki (2008), depriving oneself of regular sleep has deleterious consequences for one's cognitive functioning. Chronic deprivation can change the neural pathways within the brain and body and result in different consequences down the road. In another study that focused on social deprivation (Chugani, Behen, Muzik, Juhász, Nagy, & Chugani, 2001), Romanian orphans, both infants and children, were observed to have cognitive, physical, and social deficits and brain abnormalities. One study demonstrated that when young rats are deprived of their mothers during a specific period of development, they are at increased risk of developing an animal version of schizophrenia (Ellenbroek & Cools, 2002). The authors suggest that this deprivation, due to its stressful nature, creates a fertile field for chemical reactions to run rampant within the body and influence mental and emotional symptoms. In another study, by Teicher, Andersen, Polcari, Anderson, Navalta, and Kim (2003), the authors determined that deprivation of care (maltreatment) not only influenced brain development, but also had an impact on subsequent development of psychological disorders.

consequentially experiences. One aspect of this evaluation is whether something is identified as an obstacle or as a threat. An obstacle (which may also be a *challenge*) tends to be viewed with frustration, as something that is getting in the way of achievement of a goal, whereas a threat is perceived with an immediate or anticipatory sense of harm. The perception of something being frustrating or threatening will also be influenced by one's sense of *control* (see the next section) and *predispositions* (as reviewed earlier). In this process, once the frustration/threat aspect is determined, the person's reaction or response to the stressor occurs. When conflict is present, resources for coping will also be a factor in the response. Chapter 1 explores coping styles. In addition to problem-focused coping and emotion-focused coping, reactions to conflicts generally fall into two categories: approach or avoidance (Roth & Cohen, 1986). Four categories related to approaching or avoiding the objects of conflict exist: approach-approach; approach-avoidance; avoidance-approach, and avoidance-avoidance. Readers are encouraged to review Chapter 1 on this topic and use the resources listed there for further information.

CONTROL

The perception of control influences one's reactions and responses to stress. Individuals who have a "hardy" personality generally experience stress without dire effects on health and well-being. Kobasa (1979) suggests that one of the characteristics of hardiness in these individuals is a sense of control over things. Locus of control, whether external or internal, generally influences the perception of stress. Regardless of the physiological reactions, when an individual believes things will work out, stress has a different effect. Resilient individuals—those who tend to be able to respond to and cope with stressors effectively—also usually have a sense of internal control.

Control depends on more than whether an individual has a sense of control over the stressor (Cohen, 1980). Learned helplessness is also a factor. This is similar to resignation: The individual believes that nothing can be done, perhaps even in the face of some signal that change could occur. Within the context of stress and stressors, an individual's experience of inability to avoid or escape what is happening by personal agency has a significant impact on the assessment of stress events.

MEASUREMENTS

Originally developed in the 1960s by Holmes and Rahe (1967), the Life Event Scale is one of the best-known instruments for assessing stress levels. It has demonstrated validity and reliability. This checklist predetermined how intense an event was, based on how much disruption and reorganization it required from the individual. Other self-report measures include assessments of job characteristics, symptoms experienced, personality factors, and so on. Some researchers, however, contend that these measures are actually more stress profiling (see Briner, 1997), as they do not directly or accurately measure stress itself. Briner notes that many of these "assessments" do not offer an operational definition of *stress;* thus, it becomes more difficult to know if something is "stressful" or a different option is desired. He further argues that affect and cognitions may not be accurately reported, as these are not necessarily experienced at the time of the measurement.

Some rating scales also do not account for individual differences, such as many of the personality and temperament factors mentioned earlier. Another piece that may be missing is the relationship existing between the individuals and what is considered stressful or not. Humans are relational and our brains are wired for connection. Assessments in the modern world are beginning to take these qualities into account. What has been missing, according to some research, is recognition of the influence of contextual contexts, like politics and sociocultural threads, that affect stress assessments (Pollock, 1988; Barley & Knight, 1992).

Assessment of stress relies on many factors and can no longer be considered a yes/no dichotomy. As the modern world introduces new developments and experiences rapid change, how individuals perceive events will factor into rated levels of stress and how stress will be measured.

REFERENCES AND FURTHER READING

Barley, S. R., & Knight, D. B. (1992). Toward a cultural theory of stress complaints. *Research in Organizational Behavior, 14,* 1–48.

Briner, R. B. (1997). Improving stress assessment: Toward an evidence-based approach to organizational stress interventions. *Journal of Psychosomatic Research, 43*(1), 61–71.

Chugani, H. T., Behen, M. E., Muzik, O., Juhász, C., Nagy, F., & Chugani, D. C. (2001). Local brain functional activity following early deprivation: A study of postinstitutionalized Romanian orphans. *Neuroimage, 14*(6), 1290–1301.

Cohen, S. (1980). Aftereffects of stress on human performance and social behavior: A review of research and theory. *Psychological Bulletin, 88*(1), 82–108.

Ellenbroek, B. A., & Cools, A. R. (2002). Early maternal deprivation and prepulse inhibition: The role of the postdeprivation environment. *Pharmacology Biochemistry and Behavior, 73*(1), 177–184.

Fraley, R. C., Roisman, G. I., Booth-LaForce, C., Owen, M. T., & Holland, A. S. (2013). Interpersonal and genetic origins of adult attachment styles: A longitudinal study from infancy to early adulthood. *Journal of Personality and Social Psychology, 104*(5), 817–838.

Hamilton-West, K. (2011). *Psychobiological processes in health and illness.* London, UK: Sage.

Hollenstein, T., & Lougheed, J. P. (2013). Beyond storm and stress: Typicality, transactions, timing, and temperament to account for adolescent change. *American Psychologist, 68*(6), 444–454.

Holmes, T. H., & Rahe, R. H. (1967). The social readjustment rating scale. *Journal of Psychosomatic Research, 11*(2), 213–218.

Kobasa, S. C. (1979). Stressful life events, personality, and health: An inquiry into hardiness. *Journal of Personality and Social Psychology, 37*(1), 1–11.

Meerlo, P., Sgoifo, A., & Suchecki, D. (2008). Restricted and disrupted sleep: Effects on autonomic function, neuroendocrine stress systems and stress responsivity. *Sleep Medicine Reviews, 12*(3), 197–210.

Mikulincer, M., & Florian, V. (1998). The relationship between adult attachment styles and emotional and cognitive reactions to stressful events. In J. A. Simpson & W. S. Rholes (Eds.), *Attachment theory and close relationships* (pp. 143–165). New York, NY: Guilford Press.

Miller, T. Q., Smith, T. W., Turner, C. W., Guijarro, M. L., & Hallet, A. J. (1996). Meta-analytic review of research on hostility and physical health. *Psychological Bulletin, 119*(2), 322–348.

Pollock, K. (1988). On the nature of social stress: Production of a modern mythology. *Social Science and Medicine, 26*(3), 381–392.

Powers, S. I., Pietromonaco, P. R., Gunlicks, M., & Sayer, A. (2006). Dating couples' attachment styles and patterns of cortisol reactivity and recovery in response to a relationship conflict. *Journal of Personality and Social Psychology, 90*(4), 613–628.

Roth, S., & Cohen, L. J. (1986). Approach, avoidance, and coping with stress. *American Psychologist, 41*(7), 813–819.

Schetter, C. D., & Tanner, L. (2012). Anxiety, depression and stress in pregnancy: Implications for mothers, children, research, and practice. *Current Opinion in Psychiatry, 25*(2), 141–148. doi:10.1097/YCO.0b013e3283503680.

Sloan, R. P., Bagiella, E., Shapiro, P. A., Kuhl, J. P., Chernikhova, D., Berg, J., & Myers, M. M. (2001). Hostility, gender, and cardiac autonomic control. *Psychosomatic Medicine, 63*(3), 434–440.

Strelau, J. (1996). The regulative theory of temperament: Current status. *Personality and Individual Differences, 20*(2), 131–142.

Teicher, M. H., Andersen, S. L., Polcari, A., Anderson, C. M., Navalta, C. P., & Kim, D. M. (2003). The neurobiological consequences of early stress and childhood maltreatment. *Neuroscience and Biobehavioral Reviews, 27*(1–2), 33–44.

Part II
Sources of Stress

Introduction to Part II, Sources of Stress

Part I explored various theories and explanations of the experience of stress. Understanding stress from a theoretical and conceptual framework allows different perspectives on how the experience of stress can occur for an individual. With a variety of factors influencing the experience, it's no wonder there is some curiosity about how individuals appraise a thought, feeling, or situation as being an experience of stress, and how that appraisal affects what the body undergoes. There is some research supporting the notion that the body can undergo a physical *reaction*, whereas the mind and emotional systems can *respond*. When individuals experience demands or threats, their physiological reactions may be very similar, but their cognitive, emotional, and behavioral responses to the demand or threat can be vastly different. One person may have gastrointestinal issues that are exacerbated when stress is present; another individual may catch more colds. One individual may respond with fear while another responds with confusion. Some people respond to stresses in a way that is aligned physically, mentally, and emotionally. Some theorists believe the appraisal factor plays a large role in what comes next. However, not only are the physical and psychological manifestations of stress different for individuals, what is actually perceived as a stressor is different as well.

Stressors are things that elicit the stress response. How an individual perceives or appraises something that happens in the moment is based on a variety of factors. When an individual perceives a threat, the act of perception is influenced by developmental factors, cultural and social factors, life experiences, genetics, vulnerabilities, and other aspects. While we know that stress is inevitable, how it is assessed, appraised, evaluated, and manifested does differ from individual to individual. In essence, Part II provides a second level of investigation into the complexity of the experience of stress.

This section explores stressors, those "things" which, based upon one's perception, appraisal, interpretation, and the like, impose additional demands both psychologically and physiologically. Although it is possible that any "thing," person, or place can potentially be stressful, it is both impossible and not useful to list every single one of these. This section therefore explores 11 general categories of potential stressors. Subsections of general categories explore the who, what, when, how, and why factors surrounding these stressors.

Chapter 13 focuses on finances and money, which are primary issues that individuals find stressful in the modern world. Not having enough money, or having too much debt, or not having enough resources for retirement: all these are concerns that many people struggle with. Chapter 14 focuses on socioeconomic stressors, which are closely related to the factors explored in Chapter 13, but most affect those raised in poverty, with poor education and employment opportunities, and disproportionately affect people of color. Chapter 15 explores social stressors, including relationships and loneliness. Chapter 16 discusses developmental and life span stressors. Although many subjects could be included in this section, this chapter focuses on stressors related to parenting, generational aspects, and culture. Chapter 17 details stressors relating to family and how the family unit and family members (nuclear and extended) can be sources of stress. Chapter 18 focuses on work, including the work environment and work roles. Chapter 19 examines technology and technology-related matters, including how technology can be both a stressor and a benefit. Chapter 20 discusses environmental stressors, including aspects in the natural environment and the individual's environment, such as weather, pollution, and urban versus rural settings, as well as lifestyle factors. Chapter 21 focuses on academic stress, including the stress that college students experience during their first year and beyond. Chapter 22 covers the stress involved in caregiving; taking care of others, in addition to handling one's own responsibilities, can be demanding and extract additional emotional and resources from an individual. Finally, Chapter 23 explores sexuality as a stressor, including aspects of identity, orientation, and sexual behavior.

As evidenced by this overview, one can generate an almost endless list of the many stressors encountered in the modern world. Some of the more general categories are explored in the chapters in this part, with additional but brief consideration given to other factors that may also act as potential stressors.

13

Financial Sources of Stress

Serena Wadhwa

INTRODUCTION

According to the "2014 Stress in America Survey," about 72 percent of Americans experienced stress about money at least some of the time (American Psychological Association [APA], 2015). Money is all too often an uncomfortable topic to discuss, yet we think about it often, according to the survey. This chapter explores how money and its related aspects can be a source of stress for many individuals. Perceptions of money are influenced by both external factors (e.g., recessions) and internal factors (e.g., not placing a high value on material items). Other variables, such as culture, ethnicity, gender, marriage status, and occupation, among many others, also affect how money influences the experience of stress. The full scope of these factors is beyond what can be explored here, but this chapter provides an overall introduction to these factors and supplies resources for further exploration. Variables that have been discovered to reduce the perception, experience, and/or reaction of stress can be changed. Finally, this chapter also explores strategies for managing financial distress.

Financial stress is also known by many other names in the literature. Prawitz et al. (2006) cited authors who have used terms such as economic stress, financial strain, and so on. Thus, the study of one's economic status is not a new field. According to the "2015 Stress in America Survey" conducted by the American Psychological Association, money is the number-one source of stress. How does money become a source of stress? There are several ways. According to Prawitz et al. (2006, p. 35), *financial distress* is an "individual's reaction to the financial condition." Given this definition, it is clear that one's financial condition may be affected by many factors.

HAVING A CYCLIC MINDSET FOR FINANCES

While Americans do believe in saving, in the United States the rate of savings overall is less than 5 percent. Because finances continue to be a stressor for many individuals, Tam and Dholakia (2013) explored the question of how to help individuals save more money. Their research found that only 38 percent of employees took advantage of automated payroll deductions to fund a savings plan. Tam and Dholakia studied the application of a cyclic model of time to see what effect this would have on the amount of savings, and found that participants saved about 82 percent more during a two-week period. What accounted for this increase? The researchers indicate that cyclic mindsets include a fairly concrete, present-focus plans, which increases the belief that saving now is easier than saving later. Those who tried the cyclic model focused more on making routines and habits repeat as necessary, rather than having a linear view of saving as something to do later, or down the road. See Tam and Dholakia for additional details about this study and approach.

Financial behaviors contribute to financial distress (Sages, Britt, & Cumbie, 2013), and fall within three general themes, explored in the following section: individual characteristics, the availability of resources, and financial knowledge.

THEMES

Individual characteristics include age, gender, ethnicity, and other personal factors. Other relevant individual factors that contribute to the experience of financial distress include coping mechanisms (for example, if a person tends to be impulsive and therefore may impulsively spend money), personality factors, and even vulnerability to being emotionally swayed (for example, when you're tired and are not cognitively fully present or engaged). On average, men make more money than women do. Thus, men may have enough to pay the bills they incur, whereas women in general worry about whether they will have enough (Anthes & Most, 2000; Chen & Volpe, 2002). Older individuals tend to have more effective financial behaviors and make better money decisions, which may have a positive effect on stress levels. Other studies explored ethnicity factors and found that African Americans had higher credit-card balances and struggled to make payments (as cited in Sages, Britt, & Cumbie, 2013).

Debt is another huge factor in the assessment of financial stress (Norvilitis et al., 2006). The more debt individuals incur, the more distress they may experience, particularly if they do not have the means to pay off that debt. The type of debt that one incurs can also make a difference on the intensity of one's financial distress. For example, some individuals may experience more pressure to pay off a debt to a bookie than a debt to a family member; or to make their mortgage payment rather than a payment on a high-interest credit-card balance.

Individuals at higher income levels tend to demonstrate *financially responsible behavior,* which is defined by Perry and Morris (2005) as "the respondent's self-assessed propensity to budget, save money, and control spending." This behavior also includes paying bills on time, which tends to decrease the distress individuals may experience, as they will not incur additional fees, get collection calls, or receive overdue notices in the mail because account balances were not paid or paid on time. Thus, having the resources to pay one's debts is another factor in financial distress. When individuals apply for loans, they usually must report the amount of debt they have, what income they receive, and what their net worth is. An individual experiences financial distress when he or she is trying to get out of debt and is unable to secure the resources to do so.

Mistry, Lowe, Benner, and Chien (2008) examined the differences between meeting basic family needs and making discretionary purchases, and how these differences contribute to financial distress. For some parents, the lack of ability to meet basic needs affects their sense of self-worth, and this can manifest in various adverse behaviors. The Mistry et al. study also explored how parents—mothers in particular—seek resources and income to meet basic needs and accommodate discretionary financial purchases. In essence, these mothers spend additional time seeking ways to secure extra income, and the result is obtaining resources that allow them to make purchases that they have budgeted for: both day-to-day expenses and nonessential expenses (birthday gifts, eating out, etc.). According to the authors, this allows mothers to feel a sense of pride and accomplishment.

Another portion of the literature relating to financial distress explores lack of financial knowledge (Sages, Britt, & Cumbie, 2013; Perry & Morris, 2005). Perry and Morris (2005) note that financial knowledge comes from both informal sources (parents, friends, family members, etc.) and formal sources (classes, seminars, workshops, books, etc.), and state that the lack of solid financial knowledge can result in poor decisions or a decision to do nothing, which subsequently can keep people stuck. An example of this is lack of investment knowledge. Although most individuals recognize that wise investing can be an effective step in obtaining additional financial resources, their lack of solid knowledge prevents them from acting.

The notion of eventual retirement is involved in many financial decisions. Individuals who lack knowledge about investments, for example, may not be able to build funds for their future. A lack of knowledge about financial resources and the current economy also creates underlying financial distress (Howlett, Kees, & Kemp, 2008). In the United States, it appears that many individuals are not saving what they need to for a comfortable future. According to Howlett et al. (2008), there are several factors that may explain this. One factor is that individuals have a hard time regulating impulses; thus, money that can be used today for living expenses or nonessentials is spent, rather than saved or contributed to a separate retirement account (like an individual retirement account or a 401(k)). This harks back to the notion of short-term pleasure versus long-term security." Another factor relates to the aforementioned lack of knowledge. Howlett et al. (2008) state that becoming financially literate requires individuals to have the "knowledge, skills, and habits to successfully manage [their] money." In a study conducted by the authors, when participants received some basic information about how 401(k) plans worked, there was some increased commitment to invest money in this type of retirement account, thus decreasing some of the distress about future income.

What about the economy? How does this play a part in financial distress? When uncertainty exists within the economy, individuals are less willing to spend money, and thus cut back on spending. This further depresses the economy, which further affects individual spending, and so on (Hakkio & Keeton, 2009; Davig & Hakkio, 2010). The authors indicate that when there is this much uncertainty in the economy, it becomes more challenging for individuals and families to get the credit and loans they need to move forward and come out ahead rather than lag behind in their finances, as banks and other creditors increase the standards for taking out loans, mortgages, credit, refinancing, and the like. This further adds to the distress that individuals and families experience as they try to get out of poor or uncertain financial situations—and, as discussed in other chapters, individuals react to their stress and distress in a variety of ways.

FINANCES AND RELATIONSHIPS

Finances can be a significant source of stress within relationships (Zimmerman & Roberts, 2012; Conger, Rueter, & Elder, 1999). Many researchers have explored how financial pressures affect the quality of marital relationships. As discussed, financial distress affects an individual in a number of ways and areas, so if the distressed individual is in a relationship, there will be some impact on the relationship as well.

One finding in the literature is that the topic of money is seldom discussed among couples (see Zimmerman & Roberts, 2012). There is evidence suggesting that when topics of distress are not discussed, there are subsequent adverse effects on the distressed person. Pennebaker (1997) acknowledges that the process of identifying and discussing a problem with another person helps one to heal from distress. This is true of finances and financial stress as well. In a relationship, when finances are a source of distress but are not being acknowledged as such, a barrier is created for the individual. Conger and colleagues (see review in Conger, Rueter, &

Elder, 1999) demonstrated that financial strain increases negative behaviors within relationships and decreases positive ones. When couples are experiencing distress relating to financial strain, which increases emotional distress, it has a resulting consequence of increasing marital conflict and marital distress.

Britt, Grable, Nelson Goff, and White (2008) take this one step further. In their study, they discuss the plausibility of a contention that the difference between the perception of financial behaviors and the reality of financial behaviors is a factor that is seldom addressed, but influences the distress relating to financial strain between couples and satisfaction. In their study, they concluded that this perceptual influence does have an impact on the satisfaction level within the relationship. Thus, how one perceives the financial behaviors of the significant other within a relationship can affect how satisfied one is within the relationship. A partner who spends money without consulting the other increases dissatisfaction within the relationship, often creating the perception or feeling of secrecy or lack of commitment.

COLLEGE STUDENTS

An overview of the literature indicates that financial distress among college students is significant. Students typically incur debt during their college years, and those who go on to advanced education in their chosen professions usually see even higher debt. Research indicates that the effects of financial distress negatively affect academic performance and cognitive abilities, often stimulating reconsideration of academic pursuits and having other deleterious consequences (see Archuleta, Dale, & Spann, 2013; Xiao, Tang, & Shim, 2009). Thus, this period for a young adult is an important time, as financial decisions can make an impact not only on present circumstances but also on future opportunities. Taking out credit cards and/or loans to supplement lifestyle and academic living expenses can quickly amount to thousands or hundreds of thousands of dollars of debt. Most students do not realize the immensity of these loans until after graduation, when they are required to start making payments. Students may also not be aware that student loans are often exempt from discharge in bankruptcy and other financial relief programs.

MANAGING FINANCIAL DISTRESS

Seeking financial therapy or financial counseling is often an effective way to reduce the experience of distress relating to finances. According to Sages, Britt, and Cumbie (2013), this step can help one develop optimal financial habits that remain throughout one's adult life. It is known that financial distress does affect physical and mental health (Kim, Garman, & Sorhaindo, 2003). Those authors' literature review provided an overview of the damage that financial distress—the stress one experiences when not meeting financial responsibilities, needs, wants, or obligations—can do to one's physical health. The effects may also manifest as social and psychological stress.

One means of managing financial distress is credit counseling. Individuals go to credit counselors to seek information about behavioral changes relating to financial decisions. Individuals may be advised to refrain from using credit cards, to create and follow budgets, not to apply for new credit or loans, and so on (Kim, Garman, & Sorhaindo, 2003). Another avenue for financially distressed individuals is debt relief programs, in which a counselor intervenes on an individual's behalf to negotiate payments to creditors. The individual then makes one payment each month to the debt relief program, which systematically distributes that amount to the creditors. In a study by Kim et al. (2003), there was some evidence that credit counseling changed participants' financial behaviors.

Another means of reducing financial distress is education. Fox, Bartholomae, and Lee (2005) explored three educational programs that consumers can take part in to increase their knowledge base. First, there are programs that address general, broad topics of financial management such as budgeting and credit. Second, there are programs that address retirement and savings; third are educational programs that address home ownership and purchase of a home. As discussed earlier, a lack of knowledge in these areas tends to increase an individual's distress levels, which often subsequently manifest in other consequences for the individual. One way to manage potential effects is to obtain the knowledge needed to take the necessary steps toward choices that are in one's best financial interests.

If one is in a relationship, Zimmerman and Roberts (2012) suggest that both relationship partners take a course together. According to their research, when couples who were experiencing marital distress over finances enrolled in a financial management course together, they demonstrated improved relationship quality and implementation of financial recommendations. So, not only did the couples find some financial relief and lessen their distress, they found a means of improving their relationship quality, as they were able to spend more time together and were learning something as well. Making financial decisions together was also found to allow couples to develop a level of intimacy in an area that they may not have shared before. This allows relationship partners to experience one another in new ways and bring a new dimension to the relationship.

Seeking financial counseling is another option. As discussed in Britt, Grable, Nelson Goff, and White (2008), perceptual differences in financial behaviors can increase dissatisfaction in relationships and cause couples more distress and strain. With the guidance of a financial counselor, relationship partners can review spending behaviors openly and honesty, plan budgets, and make concessions for individual needs and wants as appropriate.

Another strategy, which is actually a necessity, is communication. As discussed with regard to relationships, one of the factors that increases distress for both an individual and the couple is the simple fact that finances are not discussed. Chapter 37 in Part III explores communication and effective ways to communicate as a means to decrease stress. Pennebaker (1997) also explores writing as a means of healing; writing may be an effective coping strategy and hints that it may be a means to utilize to relieve financial distress. One may write about one's distress related to finances, or write a letter to one's significant other, or write about finances in general.

Securing financial resources is another option. As discussed in the study by Mistry, Lowe, Benner, and Chien (2008), individuals who do not make enough to meet basic needs are often able to draw upon several resources to supplement their incomes or stretch their existing income. The study discussed how mothers utilized charities, side jobs, friends, and other family members. Layaway options are another possibility. The authors also discussed price-comparison shopping, use of planned budgets, and saving and credit accounts as means of managing financial distress. In their study, the authors reported that the participants found these strategies effective.

CONCLUSION

Financial stress, or stress related to money, is a pervasive theme for many Americans. As indicated, individuals struggle with saving money, being able to meet basic needs, and having money to spend on discretionary items. Many individuals do not know enough about finances and financial matters, which further contributes to the stress they experience. Much of the research suggests that gaining information about the basics of finances, and learning about investment, retirement options, and home buying and home ownership, can significantly reduce one's experience of stress. For couples, the perception of financial behaviors is often quite different from the reality of their spending behaviors. Communicating clearly about spending habits, debts, and income is a means of potentially decreasing this distress and increasing relationship satisfaction. College students should explore options relating to sources of income; monitor their spending habits; and know both the total amount and terms of the loans they take out and what repayment options exist. Students can explore work-study programs, credit for live experiences, and other incentives that may reduce loan obligations, as well as scholarship opportunities. They should also comparison-shop in terms of program prices and fees at different colleges and universities, as academic facilities may offer different incentives and/or pricing. Other, more general, resources for managing financial distress include seeking credit counseling, entering debt repayment programs, getting guidance on budget planning, communicating about finances, and developing general awareness about the economy and one's habits. These strategies have been demonstrated to assist in reducing some of the stress and distress related to finances.

REFERENCES AND FURTHER READING

American Psychological Association (APA). (2015). Stress in America survey. Retrieved from https://www.apa.org/news/press/releases/stress/2014/stress-report.pdf.

Anthes, W. L., & Most, B. W. (2000). Frozen in the headlights: The dynamics of women and money. *Journal of Financial Planning-Denver, 13*(9), 130–143.

Archuleta, K. L., Dale, A., & Spann, S. M. (2013). College students and financial distress: Exploring debt, financial satisfaction, and financial anxiety. *Journal of Financial Counseling and Planning, 24*(2), 50–62.

Britt, S., Grable, J. E., Nelson Goff, B. S. N., & White, M. (2008). The influence of perceived spending behaviors on relationship satisfaction. *Journal of Financial Counseling and Planning, 19*(1), 31–43.

Chen, H., & Volpe, R. P. (2002). Gender differences in personal financial literacy among college students. *Financial Services Review, 11*(3), 289.

Conger, R. D., Rueter, M. A., & Elder, G. H. (1999). Couple resilience to economic pressure. *Journal of Personality and Social Psychology, 76*(1), 54–71.

Davig, T., & Hakkio, C. S. (2010). What is the effect of financial stress on economic activity? *Economic Review,* 35–62.

Fox, J., Bartholomae, S., & Lee, J. (2005). Building the case for financial education. *Journal of Consumer Affairs, 39*(1), 195–214.

Hakkio, C. S., & Keeton, W. R. (2009). Financial stress: What is it, how can it be measured, and why does it matter? *Economic Review,* 5–50.

Howlett, E., Kees, J., & Kemp, E. (2008). The role of self-regulation, future orientation, and financial knowledge in long-term financial decisions. *Journal of Consumer Affairs, 42*(2), 223–242.

Kim, J., Garman, E. T., & Sorhaindo, B. (2003). Relationships among credit counseling clients' financial wellbeing, financial behaviors, financial stressor events, and health. *Journal of Financial Counseling and Planning, 14*(2), 75–87.

Mistry, R. S., Lowe, E. D., Benner, A. D., & Chien, N. (2008, February). Expanding the family economic stress model: Insights from a mixed-methods approach. *Journal of Marriage and Family, 70,* 196–209.

Norvilitis, J. M., Merwin, M. M., Osberg, T. M., Roehling, P. V., Young, P., & Kamas, M. M. (2006). Personality factors, money attitudes, financial knowledge, and credit-card debt in college students. *Journal of Applied Social Psychology, 36*(6), 1395–1413.

Pennebaker, J. (1997). Writing about emotional experiences as a therapeutic process. *Psychological Science, 8*(3), 162–166.

Perry, V., & Morris, M. (2005). Who is in control? The role of self-perception, knowledge, and income. *Explaining Consumer Financial Behavior: The Journal of Consumer Affairs, 39*(2), 299–313.

Prawitz, A. D., Garman, E. T., Sorhaindo, B., O'Neill, B., Kim, J., & Drentea, P. (2006). InCharge financial distress/financial well-being scale: Development, administration, and score interpretation. *Journal of Financial Counseling and Planning, 17*(1), 34–50.

Sages, R. A., Britt, S. L., & Cumbie, J. A. (2013). The correlation between anxiety and money management. *The College Student Journal, 47,* 1–11.

Tam, L., & Dholakia, U. (2013). Saving in cycles: How to get people to save more money. *Psychological Science, 25*(2), 531–537. Retrieved from University of Woolongong, Research Online at http://ro.uow.edu.au/cgi/viewcontent.cgi?article=1317&context=buspapers.

Xiao, J. J., Tang, C., & Shim, S. (2009). Acting for happiness: Financial behavior and life satisfaction of college students. *Social Indicators Research, 92*(1), 53–68.

Zimmerman, K. J., & Roberts, C. W. (2012). The influence of a financial management course on couples' relationship quality. *Journal of Financial Counseling and Planning, 23*(2), 46–54.

14

Socioeconomic Status and the Stress Process

Lydia Falconnier, Judy Berglund, and Quenette L. Walton

Gandhi stated that poverty is the worst form of violence (Funiciello, 1993). This statement brings to mind an image of people living in societies where poverty is dire and drastic for individuals with severely limited opportunities. In the United States, we like to believe that the kind of poverty that Gandhi saw on a regular basis in his society doesn't exist in ours. But poverty is a relative concept that has consequences in any context and in any country. In 2012, the percentage of people living in poverty in the United States was the highest reported in 52 years, with 46.5 million people—15 percent of the population—living in poverty (U.S. Census Bureau, 2010). In addition, the United States Department of Agriculture (USDA) estimated that in 2010, 14.5 percent of all families experienced food insecurity (the condition of having difficulty in providing enough food for all family members). According to the U.S. Census Bureau, these poverty levels can be attributed to increases in unemployment and underemployment rates (U.S. Census Bureau, 2010). This brief presentation of the statistics makes it clear that poverty is indeed an issue in the United States, and is connected to the number and extent of stressors an individual experiences, including such stressors as unemployment, financial strain, and food insecurity.

Sociologists have focused extensively on the role of socioeconomic status (SES) in determining the level of stress individuals experience over the life span. In particular, Leonard Pearlin's "stress process" paradigm (Pearlin, Menaghan, Lieberman, & Mullan, 1981) has guided much of the empirical work in this area for the past 30 years. Pearlin argues that stress is not randomly distributed among populations; instead, social stratification inherently entails inequalities in the possession of power, privilege, and prestige that pervade the structure of daily existence and reach into every critical area of people's lives. In Pearlin's work, social stress is considered to have three major conceptual domains, all of which are profoundly affected by SES. The first domain is the *sources of stress,* which can include contextual stressors, discrete life events, chronic strains, discrimination stress, and traumatic stress. Second is the *mediators or moderators of stress,* those resources such as coping, social support, and personal mastery that protect individuals from the consequences of stressful experiences. The third domain is the *manifestations of stress,* or stress outcomes, which can range from changes in microbiological substrates to overt emotional and behavioral expressions. The most commonly studied manifestations of stress based on the stress process paradigm are health and mental health outcomes, although there is also more recent work in the areas of health outcomes, allostatic load, stress biomarkers, role entries and exits, achievement inequality (e.g., dropping out of school, teenage pregnancy, crime, work performance), and inequality in life outcomes, including socioeconomic outcomes.

An extensive body of research documents differences by SES in mental health and health outcomes, with lower SES consistently found to be associated with higher rates of health and mental health problems. Pearlin's (1999) stress process paradigm posits mechanisms by which SES affects these measured outcomes. He argues that SES determines the context of individuals' lives, the stressors to which they are exposed, and the resources they have at their disposal to mediate the consequences of stress. An extensive body of research has documented the pervasive influence of SES in each of these three areas. This chapter starts with a brief review of the literature linking SES with health and mental health outcomes. It then reviews the literature on how SES affects individuals' contexts, exposure to other stressors, and personal and social resources.

MANIFESTATIONS OF STRESS

The seminal research documenting an association between SES and stress outcomes is found in the "Whitehall studies." In 1978, Marmot, Rose, Shipley, and Hamilton investigated the social determinants of health among 17,530 British civil servants. They found an inverse relationship between SES, as measured by grade of employment, and adverse health outcomes. Specifically, results illustrated that the health outcomes of individuals follow a social gradient, where the higher the social position of the individuals, the better their health. The follow-up, Whitehall II, study (Marmot et al., 1991) found that income was an even better predictor of health outcomes than was occupation. Specifically, it found that lower income was associated with an increased risk for a range of diseases, including heart disease, lung disease, and depression. They also examined how individuals' workplaces and social environments contributed to their social gradient in health. Following these early studies, researchers have documented a consistent link between exposure to social stress and multiple chronic health problems (Turner, 2010). In addition, higher levels of stress exposure have consistently been shown to mediate the effect of SES on mental health outcomes (Turner & Avison, 2003).

Depression is the mental health outcome that has received the most attention in the stress process research. This body of literature establishes both the link between depression and SES (Lorant et al., 2003) and the link between depression and particular stressors understood to be more prevalent among lower-SES individuals, including inadequate financial resources and unemployment or job loss (McLeod, 2013). This empirical work supports the theory that the relationship between SES and depression can be explained by greater exposure to stressful life experiences for lower-SES individuals).

In particular, Matthews and Gallo (2011) show support for all three domains of the stress process paradigm. They argue that with lower SES comes a heightened risk of exposure to stressors, such that exposure to chronic stressors over the life course results in biological and psychological costs to lower-SES individuals. In addition, they argue that with lower SES also comes reduced access to and erosion of resources that might mediate the effects of stress, such as coping, social support, and mastery, which are themselves social products resulting from individuals' socially determined positions.

The effects of childhood poverty have been widely researched; living in poverty has been found to negatively affect children in a variety of ways, including emotional development, self-esteem, psychosocial adjustment, and educational attainment in addition to poorer health and mental health outcomes. Whereas research on adults has focused on perceived financial strain, work conditions, and chronic stressors to explain the association of SES with mental health problems, research on children has focused more on family process variables (McLeod, 2013).Phillips (2012) found that adolescents from poor families experienced more personal problems related to major life events and daily living, more hopelessness regarding their future possibilities, and lower self-esteem than their peers in higher-income families. Phillips proposed a model based on this research that fits closely with the Pearlin (1999) model, arguing that poor children experience stigma and marginalization related to their poverty, which leads to low self-esteem. In addition, they experience a limited opportunity structure and stress from exposure to negative life events and chronic strain.

Conger, Wallace, Sun, Simons, McLoyd, and Brody (2002) found that economic strain from income loss negatively affected parental and spousal well-being, as well as parenting behaviors. These adult outcomes in turn affected children's outcomes. Thus, the stressors that affected parents also indirectly affected their children's mental and physical health. Some research has even suggested that the relationship between poverty-related stress and psychopathological symptoms is stronger for the children than for the parents (Wadsworth & Santiago, 2008).

DISEASES OF ADAPTATION

Dr. Hans Selye's General Adaptation Syndrome concept posits that organisms experiencing pressures or demands (in other words, stresses) need to adapt to them; otherwise, those organisms are in danger. Selye also recognized that the body's ability to adapt to changes has a limit which is influenced by genetic factors (Selye, 1950).

Another component of the General Adaptation Syndrome is that of "diseases of adaptation." Selye discovered that organisms will sometimes develop certain diseases in the course of adjusting to stressors that exist within the environment (more recent research indicates that precipitating stressors can also be internal). For example, when blood pressure is consistently increased as a function of the alarm (stress) reaction, and the alarm happens repeatedly or continuously, the body adapts to this increased blood pressure as the "homeostatic" level. It becomes the new normal for that organism's body. Selye proposed that this process occurs in several physical diseases; subsequent research in later decades has demonstrated that stress contributes to the manifestation of many chronic diseases and to many acute illnesses. Stress has also been linked to numerous doctor visits and flare-ups of various medical conditions. For people who have low socioeconomic status, continual stress, whether due to dangerous neighborhoods, fear of eviction, and/or worry about the future, can lead to cardiovascular disease; chronic anxiety disorders, including depression; and other serious health problems.

—Serena Wadhwa

CONTEXTS

A number of contexts related to the stress process have received attention in the literature, including macroeconomic problems, schools, and families. However, the preponderance of the literature linking context to elements of the stress process has focused on neighborhood context and the workplace.

Neighborhood socioeconomic disadvantage appears to both increase individuals' exposure to stressors and restrict access to social, psychological, and material resources. A number of studies have shown an association between neighborhood disadvantage and stress outcomes (including depression, anxiety, psychological distress, and reduced cognitive functioning) over and above the effect of individual SES (Aneshensel, 2010; Hill & Maimon, 2013). This neighborhood context, for lower-SES individuals, may include lack of transportation, crowded or substandard housing, and lack of needed access to shopping, programs, and services, safe entertainment and leisure activities, and quality schools and employment opportunities.

Some research suggests that although higher SES may protect some families from neighborhood disadvantage, the relationship between SES and neighborhood disadvantage may be moderated by race. In particular, despite increased racial integration and suburbanization, middle-class African Americans continue to have limited residential options. Because of this, middle-class and affluent African Americans may not be protected from neighborhood disadvantage, despite their class status (Schulz et al., 2006).

Some research has focused on the role of social disorder in increasing stress in neighborhoods. Massey and Denton (1993) describe a mutually reinforcing process that increases neighborhood disorder over time. They show that neighborhoods characterized by concentrated poverty tend to show signs of physical decay, which is associated with public deviance. This increased public deviance leads residents to stay inside their homes and limit contact with neighbors, leading to reduced social cohesion and social control.

Ross and Mirowsky (2001) examine the mechanisms by which neighborhood disorder arises. They suggest that (1) limited opportunities for youth in disadvantaged neighborhoods lead youth to leave school and engage in deviant activities; (2) a lack of institutional resources that would bind neighbors together leads to reduced social cohesion, (3) this results in a lack of informal social controls that help maintain order, and (4) over time, deviance becomes increasingly normative.

Workplace stress may play an important role in contributing to overall stress and poor physical and mental health outcomes. A number of different diseases have been related to stress in the workplace; most common are coronary heart disease, musculoskeletal disorders (Marmot, Siegrist, & Theorell, 2006), and mental illness, especially depression (Siegrist & Marmot, 2004). Several studies have documented stress outcomes associated with working in occupations that allow little autonomy or control (McLeod, 2013), which tend to be lower-status occupations.

STRESSORS

Pearlin (1999) argues that lower SES also heightens the risk of exposure to stressors. These include discrete life event stressors (e.g., losing a job or getting a divorce), chronic stressors (e.g., ongoing financial difficulties), "nonevent" stressors (disparities between an individual's goals and hopes and the ability to achieve them), discrimination stressors, and traumatic stressors.

Early research on the stress process focused on discrete life events. However, it quickly became apparent that similar life events could have dramatically different impacts on individuals in different socioeconomic positions, due to the process of stress proliferation. *Stress proliferation* refers to new or "secondary" stressors that

SOCIOLOGICAL THEORIES AND EXPLANATIONS OF STRESS

Sociological theories examine the impact of social circumstances on an individual's well-being. Sociologists study social factors related to responses and reactions to social conditions and social structures (social support, gender, community, etc.).

According to Scheid and Brown (2010), understanding of the stress and well-being that people experience requires understanding of their reactions to the social conditions in which they live. Knowledge and understanding social roles, limitations, and structures of these circumstances contribute to the overall conceptualization of the experience of stress. For example, someone who has a variety of social stressors (limited work opportunities, being a sole caregiver, being in a minority group, etc.) faces different challenges than an individual who has other social constructs in place.

—Serena Wadhwa

arise as a result of the "primary" stressors, defined as the stressors to which an individual is initially exposed. For example, losing a job could lead to ongoing financial difficulties, marital conflict, and/or losing one's home. Socioeconomic status is instrumental in determining the extent of secondary stressors arising from any given primary stressor. For example, the proliferation of secondary stressors resulting from a job loss is likely to be considerably greater for individuals with limited education, savings, and marketable skills.

RESOURCES THAT MODERATE THE EFFECT OF STRESSORS

Differences in the pattern and extent of stress proliferation based on SES may be one factor in explaining individual differences in the impact of stressors. However, the majority of research that has examined these individual differences has focused on differences in personal resources. Resources that have consistently been shown to moderate the stressful consequences of stressors on individual outcomes include coping behaviors, social support, and individuals' self-concept of mastery, each of which varies by socioeconomic status.

Coping behaviors are behaviors that individuals use to prevent or avoid stress or its consequences. These could include changing the situation leading to the stressors (problem-focused coping) or changing the meaning of the stressors to reduce their threat (emotion-focused coping). Coping is the most extensively studied personal resource. Unfortunately, from a sociological perspective, very little of this research has focused on the social context of coping. Specifically, very few investigations into coping have investigated possible differences in coping repertoires between groups differing in SES, instead focusing on coping as a personal characteristic of individuals.

There are, however, some findings related to social context and coping which suggest that the choice or effectiveness of problem-focused or emotion-focused coping depends on whether a person's actions can influence or change the outcome. In an early study examining problem-focused and emotion-focused coping, Pearlin and Schooler (1978) found that problem-focused coping strategies were more effective in domains where people had more control (marriage and family), whereas emotion-focused strategies were more effective in domains where individuals had less control (work and finances). They found that the emotion-focused strategy of devaluing the importance of work or money was particularly effective for individuals who had chronic difficulties with finances and work. Extending this research to specifically address the issue of coping and SES, Caplan and Schooler (2007) found that lower SES was associated with a greater use of emotion-focused coping and a lesser use of problem-focused coping with financial strains. Thoits (2010), in an extension of these findings, established the role of "compensatory coping" in managing persistent difficulty with important roles. Using compensatory coping, individuals not only devalued the importance of the stressful domain, but also invested their time and energy in alternative, more rewarding, roles.

Social support is the second resource documented to buffer the impact of social stress. Similar to coping resources, social support is also influenced by an individual's social context. Individuals' social networks are likely to include others who share a similar SES, experience similar hardships, and have similar resources to cope with those hardships. Thus, these networks may be strained in times of difficulty for lower-SES individuals.

Pearlin (1999) defines *mastery* as individuals' understanding of their ability to control the forces that affect their lives. Mastery, or a belief in personal control, has been consistently associated with low levels of psychological distress. Individuals' perceptions of mastery are shaped by objective experiences of control over meaningful events and circumstances in life. The opportunity for these types of experiences is, of course, greatly influenced by one's place in a socially stratified society. Socioeconomic status has been consistently and positively related to a sense of mastery and control, with higher levels of education, family income, individual income, job status, and control at work each independently increasing levels of mastery (Ross & Mirowsky, 2013).

Socioeconomic status is implicated at every level of the stress process. As reviewed in this chapter, it determines the context of individuals' lives; the extent, duration, and proliferation of the stressors they encounter; and the personal and social resources available to mitigate the consequences of the stressors encountered.

REFERENCES AND FURTHER READING

American Psychological Association. (2016). Health disparities and stress. Retrieved from http://www.apa.org/topics/health-disparities/fact-sheet-stress.aspx.

Aneshensel, C. S. (2010). Neighborhood as a social context of the stress process. In W. R. Avison, C. S. Aneshensel, S. Schieman, & B. Wheaton (Eds.), *Advances in the conceptualization of the stress process: Essays in honor of Leonard I. Pearlin* (pp. 35–52). New York, NY: Springer.

Caplan, L. J., & Schooler, C. (2007). Socioeconomic status and financial coping strategies: The mediating role of perceived control. *Social Psychology Quarterly, 70,* 63–78.

Clark, J. D., Rager, D. R., & Calpin, J. P. (1997). Animal well-being II. Stress and distress. *Comparative Medicine, 47*(6), 571–579.

Conger, R., Wallace, L., Sun, Y., Simons, R., McLoyd, V., & Brody, G. (2002). Economic pressure in African American families: A replication and extension of the family stress model. *Developmental Psychology, 38,* 179–193.

De Kloet, E. R., Joëls, M., & Holsboer, F. (2005). Stress and the brain: From adaptation to disease. *Nature Reviews Neuroscience, 6*(6), 463–475.

Funiciello, T. (1993). *Tyranny of kindness: Dismantling of the welfare system to end poverty in America.* New York, NY: Atlantic Monthly Press.

Hill, T. D., & Maimon, D. (2013). Neighborhood context and mental health. In C. S. Aneshensel, J. C. Phelan, & A. Bierman (Eds.), *Handbook of the sociology of mental health* (pp. 479–501). New York, NY: Springer.

Lorant, V., Deliège, D., Eaton, W., Robert, A., Philippot, P., & Ansseau, M. (2003). Socioeconomic inequalities in depression: A meta-analysis. *American Journal of Epidemiology, 157,* 98–112.

Marmot, M. G., Rose, G., Shipley, M., & Hamilton, P. J. S. (1978). Employment grade and coronary heart disease in British civil servants. *Journal of Epidemiology and Community Health, 32,* 244–249.

Marmot, M. G., Siegrist, J., & Theorell, T. (2006). Health and the psychosocial environment at work. In M. Marmot & R. Wilkinson (Eds.), *Social determinants of health* (pp. 97–130). Oxford, UK: Oxford University Press.

Marmot, M. G., Smith, G. D., Stansfeld, S., Patel, C., North, F., Head, J., . . . Feeney, A. (1991). Health inequalities among British civil servants: The Whitehall II study. *Lancet, 337,* 1387–1393.

Massey, D. S., & Denton, N. A. (1993). *American apartheid: Segregation and the making of the underclass.* Cambridge, MA: Harvard University Press.

Matthews, K. A., & Gallo, L. C. (2011). Psychological perspectives on pathways linking socioeconomic status and physical health. *Annual Review of Psychology, 62,* 501–530.

McEwen, B. S. (2005). Stressed or stressed out: What is the difference? *Journal of Psychiatry and Neuroscience, 30*(5), 315.

McLeod, J. D. (2013). Social stratification and inequality. In C. S. Aneshensel, J. C. Phelan, & A. Bierman (Eds.), *Handbook of the sociology of mental health* (pp. 229–253). New York, NY: Springer.

Pearlin, L. I. (1999). The stress process revisited: Reflections on concepts and their interrelationships. In C. S. Aneshensel & J. C. Phelan (Eds.), *Handbook of the sociology of mental health* (pp. 395–415). New York, NY: Kluwer Academic/Plenum Publishers.

Pearlin, L. I., Menaghan, E. G., Lieberman, M. A., & Mullan, J. T. (1981). The stress process. *Journal of Health and Social Behavior, 22,* 337–356.

Pearlin, L. I., & Schooler, C. (1978). The structure of coping. *Journal of Health and Social Behavior, 19,* 2–21.

Phillips, T. (2012). An exploration of the triarchic model of poverty. *Journal of Poverty, 16,* 220–231.

Ross, C. E., & Mirowsky, J. (2001). Neighborhood disadvantage, disorder, and health. *Journal of Health and Social Behavior, 42,* 258–276.

Ross, C. E., & Mirowsky, J. (2013). The sense of personal control: Social structural causes and emotional consequences. In C. S. Aneshensel, J. C. Phelan, & A. Bierman (Eds.), *Handbook of the sociology of mental health* (pp. 379–402). New York, NY: Springer.

Scheid, T. L., & Brown, T. N. (2010). *A handbook for the study of mental health: Social contexts, theories, and systems.* Cambridge, UK: Cambridge University Press.

Schulz, A. J., Israel, B. A., Zenk, S. N., Parker, E. A., Lichtenstein, R., Shellman-Weir, S., & Klem, A. B. L. (2006). Psychosocial stress and social support as mediators of relationships between income, length of residence and depressive symptoms among African American women on Detroit's eastside. *Social Science and Medicine, 6,* 510–522.

Selye, H. (1950). Stress and the general adaptation syndrome. *British Medical Journal, 1*(4667), 1383.

Siegrist, J., & Marmot, M. (2004). Health inequalities and the psychosocial environment—two scientific challenges. *Social Science and Medicine, 58,* 1463–1473.

Thoits, P. (2010). Compensatory coping with stressors. In W. R. Avison, C. S. Aneshensel, S. Schieman, & B. Wheaton (Eds.), *Advances in the conceptualization of the stress process: Essays in honor of Leonard I. Pearlin* (pp. 23–34). New York, NY: Springer.

Turner, R. J. (2010). Understanding health disparities: The promise of the stress process model. In W. R. Avison, C. S. Aneshensel, S. Schieman, & B. Wheaton (Eds.), *Advances in the conceptualization of the stress process: Essays in honor of Leonard I. Pearlin* (pp. 3–21). New York, NY: Springer.

Turner, R. J., & Avison, W. R. (2003). Status variations in stress exposure: Implications for the interpretation of research on race, socioeconomic status and gender. *Journal of Health and Social Behavior, 44,* 499–505.

U.S. Census Bureau. (2010). *Income, poverty, and health insurance coverage in the United States.* Washington, DC: Author.

Wadsworth, M. E., & Santiago, C. D. (2008). Risk and resiliency processes in ethnically diverse families in poverty. *Journal of Family Psychology, 22,* 399–410.

15

The Impact of Social Relationships on Stress

Raven Lynn Badger

A number of social factors influence stress. Friendships, romantic partnerships, marriage, and family are a few of the social influences discussed in this chapter, although relationship dynamics are not explored in detail. Rather, the dynamics of how social aspects of living create stress in life are introduced and examined.

Conceptualizations of stress usually involve the following elements: a state of arousal resulting either from the presence of socioenvironmental demands that tax the ordinary adaptive capacity of the individual or from absence of the means to attain sought-after ends, such as goals, career, relationships, intimacy, and basic needs (Pearlin, 1983, Menaghan, 1983). External circumstances that challenge or obstruct are labeled *stressors; stress* refers to the internal arousal. Sometimes, social relationships can impede individuals' ability to reach their goals or get their intrinsic needs met. Thus, stress is not an inherent attribute of external conditions, but emanates from discrepancies between those characteristics and conditions of the individual—his or her needs, values, perceptions, resources, and skills. So, people's response to stress is moderated in part by their ability to adapt to new situations based on available resources and their coping strategies, such as self-efficacy. Some people are able to navigate stressful relationships with ease; others struggle with challenges that are out of the realm of their lived experiences.

Social influences are governed by matters of structure, organizations, roles, and other social constructs (e.g., gender, marriage). Elements within social relationships that have been studied include the quality of relationships and the frequency of contact (social isolation). Research has consistently reported that quality, rather than quantity, is more important in terms of stress-ameliorating effects. Negative social interactions and social isolation are associated with depression and suicide

(Chou, Liang, & Sareen, 2011; Holma, Melartin, Haukka, Sokero, & Isometsa, 2010). Negative marriage quality and perceived marital dissatisfaction are risk factors for a major depressive episode and can create stress in an individual's life (Overbeck et al., 2006). In a 10-year study on social relationships and depression, strained relationships with spouses/partners and family members (but not friends) increased the risk of depression (Teo, Choi, & Valenstein, 2013). Teo et al. (2013) also found that social isolation, or frequency of contact, was not predictive of increased risk of depression. It appears that the romantic partnership exerts the most power with relation to predicting risk of depression, compared to family members or friends. Thus, the subjective or perceived components of social relationships are more critical to one's health than objective characteristics of one's social network. This finding is consistent not only for mental health outcomes, but also for some physical health manifestations of stress, including heart disease, disability, and mortality.

SOCIAL SUPPORT AND SOCIAL STRAIN AS CONTRIBUTORS TO STRESS

Other research has examined the role of social support and social strain and its effects on social relationships (partner/spouse, family, and friends) (Walen & Lachman, 2000). Definitions of *social support* vary, but usually include the perceived availability of support, actual support, density of network, frequency of network contact, and composition of the network, for example. Social support definitions include whether a person's social needs (affection, approval, sense of belonging, security, identity, and esteem) are met through interactions with others. *Social strain* refers to an individual experiencing psychological distress (resentment, anger) caused by network members or by having reservations about a social relationship (Rook, 1992). Relationships and attachment, social aspects of friendship, and changes in social stressors over the life span are discussed here.

ATTACHMENT STYLE AND STRESS RESPONSES

Attachment style is a psychological term for how we relate to other people along three psychological dimensions: relationship closeness, anxiety, and dependence. The primary purpose of the attachment system is to increase the likelihood that vulnerable individuals will survive the numerous perils and dangers of childhood (Bowlby, 1969). Life stressors activate the attachment system, so experiencing fear, anxiety, or other forms of distress triggers attachment responses. From an evolutionary standpoint, attachment helps people to survive; from a psychological standpoint, attachment functions to reduce fear responses so that people can reach goals in life and perform everyday tasks. Attachment models are developed across the life span in response to how people are treated by significant attachment figures (e.g., parents, friends, romantic partners), and are said to shape the expectations, attitudes, and beliefs that a person holds for future relationships (Bowlby, 1973, 1980).

Once working models are developed, they guide how people orient themselves to their attachment figures and the interpersonal world around them, particularly in stressful situations (Simpson & Rholes, 2012). For instance, if a person's past schema has taught her that she can count on her partner for support in stressful situations, she is said to have a secure attachment style. Such persons are able to disengage from attachment responses to conduct everyday tasks instead of focusing on coping with fear in their relationships.

The two other dimensions of attachment that underpin romantic relationships are well documented by researchers (e.g., Brennan, Clark, & Shaver, 1998; Fraley, Waller, & Brennan, 2000). Avoidance, the first dimension, affects the ability for intimacy and emotional closeness to occur in relationships. People who are avoidant tend to be more emotionally independent and less connected to their relationships. The second dimension, anxiety, affects how appreciated people feel in a relationship and the degree to which they fear abandonment. Anxious styles typically react by getting as emotionally close as possible to their partners, to the point of enmeshment. Secure individuals score low on avoidance and anxiety, which means that they are not overly insecure in their relationships. Secure people tend to feel relatively comfortable with their partners; they do not exhibit negative coping strategies in order to maintain this closeness and trust, and do not worry about being abandoned.

These attachment styles have significant impacts on how individuals cope with stress in relationships on numerous levels. In fact, having a high avoidance or anxiety style in itself contributes stress to a relationship, due to the coping methods used by these individuals as they seek to navigate their fears and insecurities. These dimensions are explored in more detail as close relationships (friends, family, romantic) are discussed from a developmental perspective.

RELATIONSHIPS IN ADOLESCENCE

In adolescence, peer relationships, especially close friendships and romantic relationships, surpass parents' influence as social support for many young people. Peer acceptance and peer crowd affiliation become extremely important (Prinstein & La Greca, 1999). Although by age 16, a majority of adolescents report having had a romantic relationship of some kind (Carver, Joyner, & Udry, 2003), it appears that close friendships are even more important. Friendships provide a special form of support in weathering problems with peer acceptance or approval and can even protect mental health by lowering levels of anxiety (La Greca & Lopez, 1998;

Vernberg, Abwender, Ewell, & Beery, 1992). Support from close friends has been associated with positive self-esteem and better psychosocial adjustment (e.g., Buhrmester, 1990).

IMPACT OF PARENT-CHILD RELATIONSHIPS ON STRESS

One of the tasks of adolescence is to develop a sense of autonomy in the world. In the process of establishing more mature and equal relationships with one's parents, it is common for stressful interactions to occur (Branje, van Doorn, van der Valk, & Meeus, 2009). The ability of parents to successfully interact with and allow children to develop into autonomous and mature young adults affects the levels of stress that occur within the parent-child relationship. Parental involvement that does not support developing youth autonomy, parenting styles that are authoritative in nature, and parents who are critical and overbearing create environments that can result in increased stress responses of children and adolescents.

Research on families has shown that conflicts are normal aspects of family relations and have a clear function in the development of autonomy (Laursen, Coy, & Collins, 1998; Steinberg, 2001). Overall, adolescents often experience stress with parents and have disputes with their friends about diverse issues, with levels of peer-related stress being lower than parent-related stress (Laursen & Hafen, 2010). Part of the reason for this involves relationship dynamics: parent-child relationships are obligatory and hierarchical, so the power structure is not equal. These dynamics invite conflict as a result of the power differential. In contrast, peer relationships are voluntary and more egalitarian. Thus, power imbalance in parent-child relationships creates conditions that lead to more conflict as a normal part of adolescent development.

INFLUENCES OF FRIENDSHIP ON STRESS

Most individuals have a number of social networks that can either enhance or detract from their lives. Friendships that are based on self-serving motivations, or ones that are abusive in nature, contribute greatly to daily stress (Sword & Zimbardo, 2013). *Friendships* are relationships between two peers and are healthiest when a balance between reciprocating needs and interests exist. When the needs of one person are overlooked and a power imbalance exists, the potential for negative feelings to take over is likely—and this creates stress.

Unhealthy relationship dynamics can occur when one person is unsupportive, emotionally draining, unrewarding, stifling, demanding, and generally negative. Most friendships wax and wane over time, with one or the other person needing support or assistance from the other. The unhealthy aspects of friendships occur

SUPPORT

Support in this context refers to the social encouragement provided by an individual's network of friends, family members, and peers. This "social support" has been studied as a buffer and protection from the negative effects of stress (Thoits, 2011). According to Lakey and Orehek (2011) and Park et al. (2013), certain characteristics of support make it effective. These characteristics include factors like listening, empathy, praise, encouragement, and compassion. Through these means, social support provides both an escape from and a reinforcement to counter stressful parts of life. This kind of support creates a space where acceptance and comfort exist, providing a sense of belonging to the person; supportive networks provide resources that can decrease the consequences of the stress that the individual initially experiences. Supportive networks can also provide fortification for a person so that he or she can cope with pressure or demands; they also may provide options as to how to do this, thus assisting with problem-solving (Vosvick, 2012).

—*Serena Wadhwa*

when the more demanding individual consistently exhibits abusive behavior and unrealistic expectations. Being the recipient of this type of relationship creates anxiety and higher stress responses. These unhealthy relationship dynamics can occur in friendships, work-related circumstances, families, and romantic partnerships.

EARLY RELATIONSHIPS

Dating, which usually starts when a person is around 14 to 15 years old, typically stems from socializing in mixed-gender groups (Connolly, Craig, Goldberg, & Pepler, 1999; Feiring, 1996), and like friendships, involves support and companionship. In addition, dating relationships also involve romantic passion, commitment, and sexual intimacy. Although not much research has examined this issue, a positive romantic relationship during adolescence might provide an important source of support and contribute in positive ways to adolescents' mental health. However, a negative experience with romantic relationships can be significantly upsetting (La Greca & Harrison, 2005). According to Davila et al. (2004), teenagers with negative experiences in romantic relationships report higher levels of depressive symptoms than those without these experiences. There is also some evidence that depressed adolescents tend to seek out less positive romantic partners (Daley & Hammen, 2002).

LIFE SPAN CONSIDERATIONS FOR SOCIAL RELATIONSHIPS

Age can moderate the effects of social support. Across the life span, people experience transitions to adulthood, career, family, retirement, and old age. Transitions between relationships can create stress. For example, if individuals relocate when changing jobs, their social circles become smaller, so the lack of social relationships can create stress; entering a new romantic relationship and getting married, although an exciting time, can be stressful; the birth of children creates stress related to changing family roles and subsequent role strain. Younger persons in their 20s typically have a larger friend network and fewer family members compared to older adults (Levitt, Weber, & Guacci, 1993). The highest amount of social support is typically given to one's social network in midlife, as greater demands are being made of the individual, such as family, work, raising children, and so on (Carstensen, 1991).

Aging tends to be associated with shrinking social networks, but friendships may be increasingly important as support becomes less available through other avenues due to death of a romantic partner, spouse, family members, or friends. Although the lessening of close relationships for older adults was initially thought to be associated with social isolation and loneliness, older adults who have friendships are more likely to confide in peers, as those peers are more likely to provide needed support with regard to the aging process, and older adults may find greater support from close social relationships (Schnittker, 2007). Peers may also be chosen as support providers, rather than family members of the aging individual taking on this ascribed and often obligatory role (Adams & Blieszner, 1995).

Older adults tend to find more happiness and positive emotions from social interactions such as marriages, friendships, and relationships with children than do younger and middle-aged adults (Birditt & Fingerman, 2003; Charles & Piazza, 2007; Rook, 2003). Reports from older adults also suggest fewer conflicts in relationships and fewer problematic relationships (Fingerman, Hay, & Birditt, 2004), as well as fewer arguments and disagreements with others (Almeida & Horn, 2004). Even when there are conflicts, older adults seem to be able to regard their spouses more positively (Levenson, Carstensen, & Gottman, 1994) and with less anger and negative emotion (Blanchard-Fields & Coats, 2008).

AGING IMPROVES SOCIAL RELATIONSHIP DYNAMICS

The reasons for increases in social support with aging are varied, and include purposeful social restructuring, positivity bias, social expertise, and avoidance of conflict. Older adults seem to have a cognitive bias, not observed in younger adults, to move toward positivity and happier experiences and away from less happy ones (Luong, Charles, & Fingerman, 2011; Charles, Mather & Carstensen, 2003). Older adults may have the ability to overlook problems with social partners because they also rely on those people for emotional support and intimacy (La Greca & Harrison, 2005). Older adults may make judgments in a more complex or sophisticated way than younger people do (Hess, 2006). It is also found that older adults, because they have more experience, are able to identify and avoid social partners who are difficult and problematic (Blanchard-Fields, 2007; Hess, 2005). Finally, because of their experiences, older adults are more practiced and expert at relationships, and thus are able to make better choices not only in deciding with whom they will have relationships, but also in how they choose to act in those relationships.

REFERENCES AND FURTHER READING

Adams, R. G., & Blieszner, R. (1994). An integrative conceptual framework for friendship research. *Journal of Social and Personal Relationships, 11,* 163–184.

Adams, R. G., & Blieszner, R. (1995). Aging well with friends and family. *American Behavioral Scientist, 39,* 209–224.

Almeida, D. M., & Horn, M. C. (2004). Is daily life more stressful during middle adulthood? In O. G. Brim & C. D. Ryff (Eds.), *How healthy are we? A national study of well-being at midlife* (pp. 425–451). Chicago, IL: University of Chicago Press.

Birditt, K. S., & Fingerman, K. L. (2003). Age and gender differences in adults' emotional reactions to interpersonal tensions. *Journals of Gerontology: Psychological Sciences, 58B,* 237–245.

Birditt, K. S., Fingerman, K. L., & Almeida, D. M. (2005). Age differences in exposure and reactions to interpersonal tensions: A daily diary study. *Psychology and Aging, 20,* 330–340.

Blanchard-Fields, F. (2007). Everyday problem solving and emotion: An adult developmental perspective. *Current Directions in Psychological Science, 16,* 26–31.

Blanchard-Fields, F., & Coats, A. H. (2008). The experience of anger and sadness in everyday problems impacts age differences in emotion regulation. *Developmental Psychology, 44,* 1547–556.

Bowlby, J. (1969). *Attachment and loss: Vol. 1: Attachment.* New York, NY: Basic Books.

Bowlby, J. (1973). *Attachment and loss: Vol. 2: Separation: Anxiety and anger.* Middlesex, UK: Penguin Books.

Bowlby, J. (1980). *Attachment and loss: Vol. 3: Loss: Sadness and depression.* Middlesex, UK: Penguin Books.

Branje, S., van Doorn, M., van der Valk, I., & Meeus, W. (2009). Parent–adolescent conflicts, conflict resolution types, and adolescent adjustment. *Journal of Applied Developmental Psychology, 30,* 195–204.

Brennan, K. A., Clark, C. L., & Shaver, P. R. (1998). Self-report measurement of adult romantic attachment: An integrative overview. In J. A. Simpson & W. S. Rholes (Eds.), *Attachment theory and close relationships* (pp. 46–76). New York, NY: Guilford Press.

Buhrmester, D. (1990). Intimacy of friendship, interpersonal competence, and adjustment during preadolescence and adolescence. *Child Development, 61*(4), 1101–1111.

Carstensen, L. L. (1991). Selectivity theory: Social activity in life-span context. In K. Schaie & M. P. Lawton (Eds.), *Annual review of gerontology and geriatrics* (Vol. 11, pp. 195–217). New York, NY: Springer.

Carstensen, L. L., Fung, H. H., & Charles, S. T. (2003). Socioemotional selectivity theory and the regulation of emotion in the second half of life. *Motivation and Emotion, 27,* 103–123.

Carver, K., Joyner, K., & Udry, J. R. (2003). National estimates of adolescent romantic relationships. In P. Florsheim (Ed.), *Adolescent romantic relationships and sexual behavior: Theory, research, and practical implications* (pp. 291–329). New York, NY: Cambridge University Press.

Charles, S. T., Mather, M., & Carstensen, L. L. (2003). Aging and emotional memory: The forgettable nature of negative images for older adults. *Journal of Experimental Psychology: General, 132,* 310–324.

Charles, S. T., & Piazza, J. R. (2007). Memories of social interactions: Age differences in emotional intensity. *Psychology and Aging, 22,* 300–309.

Chou, K. L., Liang, K., & Sareen, J. (2011). The association between social isolation and DSM-IV mood, anxiety, and substance use disorders: Wave 2 of the National Epidemiologic Survey on Alcohol and Related Conditions. *Journal of Clinical Psychiatry, 72*(11), 1468–76.

Connolly, J. A., Craig, W., Goldberg, A., & Pepler, D. (1999). Conceptions of cross-sex friendships and romantic relationships in early adolescence. *Journal of Youth and Adolescence, 28*(4), 481–494.

Daley, S., & Hammen, C. (2002). Depressive symptoms and close relationships in late adolescence: Perspectives from dysphoric young women, their best friends, and their romantic partners. *Journal of Consulting and Clinical Psychology, 70,* 129–141.

Davila, J., Steinberg, S., Kachadourian, L., Cobb, R., & Fincham, F. (2004). Romantic involvement and depressive symptoms in early and late adolescence: The role of a preoccupied relational style. *Personal Relationships, 11,* 161–178.

Feiring, C. (1996). Concepts of romance in 15-year-old adolescents. *Journal of Research on Adolescence, 6*(2), 181–200.

Fingerman, K. L., Hay, E. L., & Birditt, K. S. (2004). The best of ties, the worst of ties: Close, problematic, and ambivalent relationships across the lifespan. *Journal of Marriage and Family, 66,* 792–808.

Fraley, R. C., Waller, N. G., & Brennan, K. A. (2000). An item-response theory analysis of self-report measures of adult attachment. *Journal of Personality and Social Psychology, 78,* 350–365.

Hess, T. M. (2005). Memory and aging in context. *Psychological Bulletin, 131,* 383–406.

Hess, T. M. (2006). Adaptive aspects of social cognitive functioning in adulthood: Age-related goal and knowledge influences. *Social Cognition, 24,* 279–309.

Holma, K. M., Melartin, T. K., Haukka, J., Sokero, T. P., & Isometsa, E. T. (2010). Incidence and predictors of suicide attempts in DSM-IV major depressive disorder: A five-year prospective study. *American Journal of Psychiatry, 167*(7), 801–808.

La Greca, A. M., & Harrison, H. M. (2005). Adolescent peer relations, friendships, and romantic relationships: Do they predict social anxiety and depression? *Journal of Clinical Child and Adolescent Psychology, 34*(1), 49–61.

La Greca, A. M., & Lopez, N. (1998). Social anxiety among adolescents: Linkages with peer relations and friendships. *Journal of Abnormal Child Psychology, 26*(2), 83–94.

Lakey, B., & Orehek, E. (2011). Relational regulation theory: A new approach to explain the link between perceived social support and mental health. *Psychological Review, 118*(3), 482–495. doi:10.1037/a0023477.

Laursen, B., Coy, K. C., & Collins, W. A. (1998). Reconsidering changes in parent-child conflict across adolescence: A meta-analysis. *Child Development, 69,* 817–832.

Laursen, B., & Hafen, C. A. (2010). Future directions in the study of close relationships: Conflict is bad (except when it's not). *Social Development, 19,* 858–872.

Levenson, R. W., Carstensen, L. L., & Gottman, J. M. (1994). The influence of age and gender on affect, physiology, and their interrelations: A study of long-term marriages. *Journal of Personality and Social Psychology, 67,* 56–68.

Levitt, M. J., Weber, R. A., & Guacci, N. (1993). Convoys of social support: An intergenerational analysis. *Psychology and Aging, 8,* 323–326.

Luong, G., Charles, S. T., & Fingerman, K. L. (2011). Better with age: Social relationships across adulthood. *Journal of Social and Personal Relationships, 28*(1), 9–23.

Menaghan, E. G. (1983). Individual coping efforts: Moderators of the relationship between life stress and mental health outcomes. In H. B. Kaplan (Ed.), *Psychosocial stress: Trends in theory and research* (pp. 157–191). New York, NY: Academic.

Overbeck, G., Vollebergh, W., de Graaf, R., Scholte, R., de Kemp, R., & Engels, R. (2006). Longitudinal associations of marital quality and marital dissolution with the incidence of DSM-III-R disorders. *Journal of Family Psychology, 20,* 284–291.

Park, J., Kitayama, S., Karasawa, M., Curhan, K., Markus, H. R., Kawakami, N., . . . Ryff, C. D. (2013). Clarifying the links between social support and health: Culture, stress, and neuroticism matter. *Journal of Health Psychology, 18*(2), 226–235.

Pearlin, L. I. (1983). Role strains and personal stress. In H. B. Kaplan (Ed.), *Psychosocial stress: Trends in theory and research* (pp. 3–32). New York, NY: Academic Press.

Prinstein, M. J., & La Greca, A. M. (1999). Linkages between mothers' and children's social competence, and associations with maternal adjustment. *Journal of Clinical Child Psychology, 28,* 197–210.

Rook, K. S. (1992). Detrimental aspects of social relationships: Taking stock of an emerging literature. In H. O. Veiel & U. Baumann (Eds.), *The meaning and measurement of social support* (pp. 157–169). New York, NY: Hemisphere.

Rook, K. S. (2003). Exposure and reactivity to negative social exchanges: A preliminary investigation using daily diary data. *Journals of Gerontology: Psychological Sciences and Social Sciences, 58B,* 100–111.

Schnittker, J. (2007). Look (closely) at all the lonely people: Age and the social psychology of social support. *Journal of Aging and Health, 19,* 659–682.

Simpson, J. A., & Rholes, W. S. (2012). Attachment, stress, and romantic relationships. *Advances in Experimental Social Psychology, 45,* 279–328.

Steinberg, L. (2001). We know some things: Parent-adolescent relationships in retrospect and prospect. *Journal of Research on Adolescence, 11,* 1–19.

Sword, R., & Zimbardo, P. (2013). Toxic relationships. *Psychology Today.* Retrieved from https://www.psychologytoday.com/blog/the-time-cure/201308/toxic-relationships

Teo, A. R., Choi, H., & Valenstein, M. (2013). Social relationships and depression: Ten-year follow-up from a nationally representative study. *PLOS One, 8*(4), 1–7.

Thoits, P. A. (2011). Mechanisms linking social ties and support to physical and mental health. *Journal of Health and Social Behavior, 52*(2), 145–161.

Vernberg, E. M., Abwender, D. A., Ewell, K. K., & Beery, S. H. (1992). Social anxiety and peer relationships in early adolescence: A prospective analysis. *Journal of Clinical Child Psychology, 21,* 189–196.

Vosvick, M. (2012). *Heterosexist harassment and rejection, emotional social support and perceived stress in a lesbian, gay and bisexual sample* (unpublished doctoral dissertation). University of North Texas, Denton, TX.

Walen, H. R., & Lachman, M. E. (2000). Social support and strain from partner, family, and friends: Costs and benefits for men and women in adulthood. *Journal of Social and Personal Relationships, 17,* 5–30.

16

Generational and Life Span Stresses

Serena Wadhwa

Stresses relating to generational and life span factors vary. These factors can include age, life span tasks, generational struggles, differences with mainstream culture, and parenting. Although many such factors exist, this chapter explores a few of them in detail: acculturation, parenting, and generational differences.

It's no secret that being a parent brings much joy and is also stressful. There's no handbook on how to be a parent; there is nothing like the owner's manual that a new car buyer receives upon getting a new car. As the theory on human developmental stressors noted, there are many stressors relating to maturity and development tasks, and overlaying them are the influences of social, family, and economic demands and pressures that influence these generational and life span spaces.

As a parent, the stress an individual experiences will influence how that person parents, and how he or she responds to the child. If a partner is involved (whether this person is the spouse, biological parent, stepparent, or other), one parent's stress affects the other's mood, affect, and parental style as well (Ponnet et al., 2013). Parental stress can also result when parents have different styles of parenting (for example, when one is less demanding than the other). Ponnet et al. (2013) explore how these styles can be stressful, especially when conflict is present, which can confer additional stress for one or both parents. Some parents may also experience stress as a result of the role limitations inherent in being a parent.

Parenting stress is defined as the psychological and physical burdens imposed by parenting responsibilities (see Nam, Wikoff, & Sherraden, 2015; Ponnet et al., 2013). Parenting stress has consequential effects of lowered self-esteem/efficacy, risks for depression/anxiety, and diminution of satisfaction in the parenting role. When there is low "work" satisfaction, doubt and feelings of incompetency can also be stressful and may both exacerbate existing stress and cause new stress (see Chapters 17 and 18).

Ethnic background can also affect parental stress. Research indicates that ethnic minorities, on average, tend to struggle with limited economic resources, environmental stressors, and social/relational limitations as they try to raise children (see Chapter 14 on socioeconomic conditions). It is noteworthy to mention that research also suggests that there are stressors specific to those of different ethnic backgrounds as a result of living in a different culture. Low economic resources, lack of supporting environments, and material hardships are factors that increase distress for mothers, thus affecting how they parent and what coping mechanisms they may utilize (Nam et al., 2013).

Stepparenting is another type of parenting role, which raises different stressors as a new family, roles, rules, and responsibilities are negotiated within the new family structure (Shapiro, 2014). With the role and title of a stepparent, often no clear expectation, rules, roles, or boundaries are defined. These roles are typically developed and negotiated through the relational process, but, because of the uncertainty involved, stress is often present. Some stepparents may not feel like "real" parents, or may feel threatening to the biological parent(s). *Stepparent,* as the title suggests, is a nontraditional role, with its own implications. This role can be stressful for individuals depending on other contextual factors (e.g., religious beliefs, possible social stigmas, etc.). Trying to uphold traditional values in a nontraditional way requires adaptation, mediation, and flexibility. In a study conducted by Shapiro (2014), stepparents holding traditional gender roles reported higher levels of parenting stress. Thus, when it comes to generational/life span stressors, one thing that becomes evident is that when individuals were born; where they were raised; and the generational values they embody (beliefs, values of that era), particularly relating to gender roles, can also be stress factors. Being flexible may be a protective factor (Shapiro, 2014).

Parenting is also influenced by many other circumstances. These include infidelity; infertility issues (including when a couple with children from other relationships or marriages wants to have a child together, yet finds they are struggling with getting pregnant); addictions; separations necessitated by work or military deployment; marital discord; domestic violence; abuse; attachment styles; and a host of other factors.

Chapter 2, on developmental explanations of stress, provides a basis for recognition of additional stressors specifically related to the life span. For example, tasks explicit to developmental stages can become stressful depending on numerous factors. In addition, the individual's temperament, attachment style, coping mechanisms, support, conditioning, and genetic vulnerabilities greatly affect what is perceived and embodied as stressful. Ecologically (see Chapter 3), contextual factors of the larger community, and religious/spiritual connections, all play a part in how developmental tasks are experienced, as well as how intensely the experience may be felt.

For example, consider the generation of millennials. Like the terms *baby boomer* and *Gen X, millennial* (sometimes called *Gen Y*) is a term commonly used for individuals born during a certain time frame and growing up and living in the embodied culture. Each group delineated by one of these terms shares variations of age, social culture, economic differences, political differences, and global circumstances (for example, baby boomers lived through the Vietnam War and its aftermath, whereas Gen Y or millennials are dealing with the global issue of terrorism). Each group experiences its own challenges and struggles.

Millennials are the group of individuals born in the early 1980s up until the late 1990s, roughly speaking. According to Atkinson (2004), these younger adults make up about 20 percent of the population and generally come from parents who are more educated, affluent, and ethnically diverse (as cited in Bland, Melton, Welle, & Bigham, 2012). In the modern world, many developmental tasks are potentially placing more demands and pressure on the people in this group, and coping mechanisms are varied for this special group of individuals. Many of the youngest millennials are beginning college or career schools, which in the modern world, entails pressures and demands that may be perceived as more stressful, due to the nature of family, social, community, and national culture. Certainly costs of college have shot way up in recent years, with students and/or parents loaded down with many thousands of dollars in debt by the time of graduation. Students struggle with more uncertainty, ways of thinking and doing that are different from traditional college classrooms, and different options in major life choices (Hales, 2009). Life in college has its own set of stressors that compound these generational factors (see Chapter 21).

Despite several positive factors millennials possess, they tend to be a highly stressed group, due to heavy schedules and demands/pressures to excel. Additionally, technology allows these young people to experience global mishaps and challenges much more personally and regularly than previous generations. Parents of millennials, on average, have fewer children, thus making it easier for parents to be available to do more for their children in helping them through problems, which can become detrimental for the young person's development of stress coping strategies. In one study, Bland et al. (2012) found that social support was an effective and helpful stress reducer. Having support, however, is different from having someone do something for you, as so-called helicopter parents have a tendency to do when their children face problems at school or even in jobs.

Millennials are in the developmental stage of early adulthood. The contextual family, economic, and social factors of this life stage affect the degree to which these individuals experience pre-existing stressors. Millennials, because of the fact that they were born and raised in the modern world of technological growth and dependency, are importantly affected by stresses created by technology. Researchers study how different generations of individuals encounter unique stressors, most of which relate to changes in society, broader culture, and other wide-ranging influences (e.g., the economy, wars).

Retirement, another example of a generational/life span stressor, has its own set of stressors, particularly when ineffective coping mechanisms have been established. For example, if one spouse is retired or stays at home, this can influence the retirement of the other. Sometimes spouses will need to negotiate their own plans based upon influences of the other (Smith & Moen, 1998). If there is minimal preparation regarding expectations, management of time and finances, and so on, these factors, as other chapters suggest, can create experiences of distress as well as experiences of eustress. If someone who is retiring has planned finances, activities, and the like to occupy the additional time retirement provides, it may be experienced as a welcomed opportunity.

COACHING

Coaching is a growing profession that took hold in the early 21st century. According to Bresser and Wilson (2006), the profession as known today in personal development and business emerged from sports in the 1970s to the 1990s. In essence, *coaching,* sometimes called *life coaching,* aims at empowering individuals through self-directed learning, enhanced performance, and personal growth (Bresser & Wilson, 2006). Because there is presently no governing board for people who work as coaches, anyone can call himself or herself a coach. While this leads to challenges in the field in terms of credentialing, ethics, guidelines, and other factors, certifications are available to demonstrate areas of competence.

Coaching differs from therapy, counseling, and mentoring in several ways. According to Hart, Blattner, and Leipsic (2001), one difference is that coaching focuses on present potential, whereas therapy often focuses on past injuries to promote healing. Another difference is that therapy "talk" revolves around emotional processing, whereas coaching "talk" revolves around action plans.

Coaching affords several benefits. Among these, Bresser and Wilson (2006) include: (1) personal growth; (2) enhanced leadership skills; (3) higher quality of life; (4) improved communication/relationships; and (5) sustainable forms of personal development. Coaching also provides benefits for teams and organizations, which are mostly variations of those listed for individuals.

Though full discussion is beyond the scope of this chapter, other generational/life span stressors include acculturation stress and major life transitions (e.g., caregiving for parents or a spouse; going to college; starting a family; identifying a career; negotiating relationships). Readers are referred to resources within this book and in the "Resources" section for additional information on these other stressors (e.g., Laszloffy, 2002; Padilla, Alvarez, & Lindholm, 1986; Wanka, Kolland, & Psihoda, 2015; Mitchell, 2014; Hou, Kim, & Wang, 2016; Pease, 2013).

REFERENCES AND FURTHER READING

Anderson, M. C., Dauss, C., & Mitsch, B. F. (2002). The return-on-investment of executive coaching. In J. J. Phillips & D. Mitsh (Eds.), *In action: Coaching for extraordinary results* (pp. 9–22). Alexandria, VA: ASTD.

Atkinson, M. L. (2004). Advice for (and from) the young at heart: Understanding the millennial generation. *Guidance and Counselling, 19*(4), 153–157.

Bland, H. W., Melton, B. F., Welle, P. D., & Bigham, L. E. (2012). Stress tolerance: New challenges for millennial college students. *College Student Journal, 46*(2), 362–375.

Bresser, F., & Wilson, C. (2006). What is coaching? In J. Passmore (Ed.), *Excellence in coaching: The industry guide* (pp. 9–25). London, UK: Kogan Page.

Hales, D. (2009). *An invitation to health* (13th ed.). Belmont, CA: Wadsworth/Cengage Learning.

Hart, V., Blattner, J., & Leipsic, S. (2001). Coaching versus therapy: A perspective. *Consulting Psychology Journal: Practice and Research, 53*(4), 229–237.

Hou, Y., Kim, S. Y., & Wang, Y. (2016). Parental acculturative stressors and adolescent adjustment through interparental and parent–child relationships in Chinese American families. *Journal of Youth and Adolescence, 45*(7), 1466–1481. doi:10.1007/s10964-016-0441-2.

Laszloffy, T. A. (2002). Rethinking family development theory: Teaching with the Systemic Family Development (SFD) model. *Family Relations, 51*(3), 206–214.

Mitchell, B. A. (2014). Generational juggling acts in midlife families: Gendered and ethnocultural intersections. *Journal of Women and Aging, 26*(4), 332–350.

Nam, Y., Wikoff, N., & Sherraden, M. (2015). Racial and ethnic differences in parenting stress: Evidence from a statewide sample of new mothers. *Journal of Child and Family Studies, 24*(2), 278–288.

Padilla, A. M., Alvarez, M., & Lindholm, K. J. (1986). Generational status and personality factors as predictors of stress in students. *Hispanic Journal of Behavioral Sciences, 8*(3), 275–288.

Pease, J. (2013). Mental Health Outcomes of First Generation College Students: Is Generational Status Associated with Increased Risk for Depression and Anxiety? *Electronic Theses and Dissertations,* Paper 900. Retrieved from http://digitalcommons.du.edu/cgi/viewcontent.cgi?article=1899&context=etd.

Ponnet, K., Mortelmans, D., Wouters, E., Van Leeuwen, K., Bastaits, K., & Pasteels, I. (2013). Parenting stress and marital relationship as determinants of mothers' and fathers' parenting. *Personal Relationships, 20*(2), 259–276.

Shapiro, D. (2014). Stepparents and parenting stress: The roles of gender, marital quality, and views about gender roles. *Family Process, 53*(1), 97–108.

Smith, D. B., & Moen, P. (1998). Spousal influence on retirement: His, her, and their perceptions. *Journal of Marriage and the Family, 60*(3), 734–744.

Wanka, A., Kolland, F., & Psihoda, S. (2015). Job strain and coping among ageing baby boomers. *Zeitschrift fur Gerontologie und Geriatrie, 48*(6), 511–516.

17

Families and Stress

Janis Clark Johnston

Stress in the family may not begin with an obvious alarm. Most family situations start with stress fumes before a critical time when distress flames erupt. However, definitions of stress include times of positive challenges in family life, and some tolerable levels of distress have lessons for family members. It is the toxic level of distress that has the potential to scald or burden a child in later life.

THE FAMILY "FIREHOUSE"

Endocrinologist Hans Selye made the word *stress* a household staple, suggesting that life would be boring without stress. Many positive family situations entail stress. Selye labeled positive stress as *eustress* and negative stress as *distress*. He created the word *stressor* to describe the stimulus or event that precipitates a stress response (Selye, 1974). Examples of positive stressors in the family are a child's piano recital or sporting event, and a parent's new job. Family distress ranges from community natural disasters like Hurricane Katrina, to inside-the-family reactions to death or illness of a loved one, to juggling a myriad of everyday decisions and deadlines. Parents need to learn how to detect smoke before their own reactions, and/or their child's stress reactions, blaze out of control.

Smoke-Detector Parents

Stress occurs when the demands of one's life, or one's *expectations* of those demands, exceed one's ability to cope with them. Our expectations are powerful in every situation; however, we may expect the worst when the worst outcome might not happen. Our working definition of stress in the family includes stressors arising from both the realities of difficult situations and personal expectations and perceptions that something is a stressor. Psychologist Megan Gunnar (2009), who studies stress and coping in infants and children, outlines three levels of stress and their accompanying physiological responses:

1. Positive—Brief increases in heart rate, mild elevations in stress hormone levels
2. Tolerable—Serious, temporary responses, buffered by supportive relationships
3. Toxic—Prolonged activation of stress response systems in the absence of protective relationships

Research by psychologist Shelley Taylor (2006) finds that having protective "befriending" relationships can benefit females under stress. The social-bonding hormone, oxytocin, is part of a female's stress response; oxytocin may lead females to "tend" children and "befriend" others, rather than fight or flee when stressed. Oxytocin is enhanced by estrogen, so men may not experience a similar protectiveness.

Stress Hazards for Children

Examples of toxic stress in children include neglect, abuse, exposure to violence, mental illness, substance abuse, homelessness, high mobility, incarceration of a family member, and death of a relative. For adults, death of a spouse is considered more stressful than any other situation on the Holmes-Rahe Life Stress Inventory (McLeod, 2010). Toxic stressors, also called adverse childhood experiences (ACEs), are detrimental to children. ACEs are major risk factors for illness, a poor quality of life, and even an early death in adulthood. The ACE Study (2003) of 17,000 health maintenance organization (HMO) members from Kaiser Permanente Health Appraisal Clinic in San Diego is an ongoing collaboration with the Centers for Disease Control and Prevention (CDC). Results from a 10-question survey show astonishing linkages to adult lives of childhood trauma in families (including verbal, physical, or sexual abuse; an incarcerated, mentally ill, or substance-abusing family member; domestic violence; or absence of a parent because of divorce or separation). Reactions to severe and/or chronic childhood traumas produce stress hormones that affect an individual's overall development.

Epidemiologist Robert Anda from the CDC and internist Vincent Felitti from Kaiser Permanente developed a simple scoring system for the ACE survey. A person without any toxic childhood stressors receives a score of zero. One who experiences verbal abuse repeatedly during his or her childhood, but has no other childhood traumas, receives a score of 1 point. If one experiences verbal abuse as well as physical abuse, lives with a mentally ill parent, and has another parent who abuses drugs, the ACE score is 4 points. Compared with people with zero ACEs, those with ACEs of 4 have a 240 percent greater risk of hepatitis, are 390 percent more likely to have chronic obstructive pulmonary disease (emphysema or chronic bronchitis), and a 240 percent higher risk of getting a sexually transmitted disease. As dangerous as a four-alarm fire requiring extra firefighting equipment, individuals scoring 4 ACEs are twice as likely to be smokers, 12 times more likely to have attempted suicide, 7 times more likely to be alcoholic, and 10 times more likely to have injected street drugs (ACE Study, 2003).

Furthermore, people with high ACE scores are more likely to be violent, and to have more marriages, more broken bones, more drug prescriptions, more depression, more auto-immune diseases, and more work absences. Unexpectedly, results from these 17,000 individuals showed that 1 in 6 people had 4 or more ACEs, and 1 in 9 had an ACE score of 5 or more. These participants were "average" Americans! Eighty percent were white (including Latino), 10 percent were black, and 10 percent were Asian. They were middle-class and middle-aged (an average age of 57), and 74 percent were college-educated. Because they were members of Kaiser Permanente, they all had jobs and access to health care. Fight, flight, or freeze stress hormones can help a person at an intersection when a fire truck is coming too fast; however, toxic results occur with multiple and/or ongoing stress reactions. Childhood distress smolders for a long time.

Alarm Fires on Average Days

Whereas adverse childhood traumas wreak havoc within a family, less intense situations provoke distress on "average" days. Family-life specialist Doris Curran researched perennial, everyday family stressors. She surveyed 450 parents (men and women, including married couples and single parents), asking them to rank

CHILD ABUSE PREVENTION AND TREATMENT ACT

The Child Abuse Prevention and Treatment Act (CAPTA) was enacted in 1974 by the federal government, and it has been amended several times throughout its history (most recently, as of this writing, in 2010). This law provides funding for the prevention and treatment of child abuse as well as for research purposes (see www.childwelfare.gov). According to Childhelp.org (n.d.), at www.childhelp.org, more than 3 million reports of child abuse are made every year: approximately one report every 10 seconds.

—*Serena Wadhwa*

stressors (out of a list of 25) in their family. Although there was some variance between men and women on items, everyone checked "Economics/finances/budgeting" as their top stressor. Other highly ranked stressors in these individuals' current families were the following: "Children's behavior/discipline/sibling fighting"; "Insufficient couple time"; "Communicating with children"; "Insufficient 'me' time"; "Intimate relationship (communication, friendship, sex)"; "Insufficient family playtime"; "Overscheduled family calendar"; "Unhappiness with work situation" (only men and single mothers); "Lack of shared responsibility in the family" (only women); "Guilt for not accomplishing more" (only women); and "Self-image/self-esteem/feelings of unattractiveness" (only women) (Curran, 1985). Notice how many of these timeless stressors relate to a perception of "not enough" time or communication issues.

Susan (6), Oliver (7), Ellen (35), and Larry (40)

Seven-year-old Oliver receives a detention for not listening at school. When his teacher calls his home early the next morning, her stressful message spirals into *take-away-TV-home-detention-for-a-week,* on top of the school's punishment. The already hectic morning of trying to get two youngsters out of the house, along with two working parents (one of whom "hates" the job), adds alarming yelling. During the hustle-and-bustle, Oliver sneaks to the family room to watch TV commercials of children eating instead of eating his own cereal; Susan dresses her doll instead of dressing herself. Each child receives a spanking. Each parent blasts blaming words at the other to detail what the "other" does *not* do well. Larry and Ellen give mixed messages to their children about what *to do,* since all of their words focus on *what not to do.* A silent alarm about an impending marital separation does not reach awareness. No family member seems aware that no one has gotten enough sleep. Foggy functioning matches the outside foggy weather, but both parents admit that it is an "average" day in the family firehouse.

Oliver comes to psychotherapy expressing anger about not getting TV rights. He rumbles around the office like a firefighter who needs to break down a door in a darkened home. Oliver grumbles under his breath; the scowl on his face puffs out his cheeks. He huffs loudly before sitting down to draw a picture of a boy with glasses and one arm shorter than the other: "This is Arthur. He is a fun character and funny. He is in fifth grade. He has a sister. Sometimes Arthur's family goes on vacations. And sometimes Arthur does not listen to his mom. The end." Upon questioning, Oliver sighs sadly and tells about the part of him that does *not* listen to Mom: "He has to get along with his sister or he'll get in trouble. He gets grounded for a week." Oliver slumps in his chair as if he expects perpetual distress.

When family members do not meet their basic energy needs, stress responses can ripple throughout the family. Often, when basic energy needs for sleep and nutrition go unmet, there are challenges in meeting other basic needs throughout the day, especially those involving discipline, creativity, belonging, and ability (Johnston, 2013). Ellen and Larry are as energy-challenged as Oliver. When already-stressed parents receive bad news from their child's school, their energy supplies plummet from half-full to empty. *Stress ennui,* or a mental and physical state of giving up, can take over. Some children are so demanding of energy that a spouse's needs are overlooked; spouses need to watch for times when they overinvest in a child and underinvest in the partner. Meeting everyone's needs in the family takes time management skills.

When Oliver's parents establish energizing family rituals that help everyone with healthy habits in eating, sleeping, and exercise, they are better able to establish morning discipline in the home, reducing distress for everyone. Oliver and Susan are taken to the grocery store where they are given a few choices of healthy breakfast items. Each child picks two kinds of cereal that are pre-approved by their mother. Bedtimes become consistent so that everyone can get up earlier. Morning TV becomes the whole family engaging in exercise for 15 minutes with the aid of a video.

Cultural Flashpoints

Many different stressors can ignite stress hormones in family members. However, the very definition of *family* has become a cultural flashpoint. Today's definition of *family* is not limited to people who are descendants of a common ancestor, as that definition leaves out adopted children and foster children. Families today are challenged by cultural disagreements over issues such as immigration and separations caused by fleeing family members, and same-gender couples who desire both conjugal love and the experience of raising children together. Legal decisions can have an enormous impact in reducing or increasing distress in families.

Another cultural flashpoint concerns the definition of *safety.* In post-9/11 America, terrorist attack fears smolder. Closer to home, uncertainty surrounds a rising number of soldiers coming home from military service with posttraumatic stress disorder (PTSD). The frightening number of school shootings changes concepts of safety in education for both children and parents. In addition to routine fire drills in schools, now there are naturalistic school shooting drills that alert—and expose—children to stressors that seem unbelievable to them. School psychologist Scott Poland understands the possibility of a serious stress response to such drills: naturalistic drills could exacerbate distress for students with pre-existing traumas (Aronowitz, 2014).

Gun violence incidents, especially prevalent in urban areas, often have linkages to poverty in families (Thompson, 2013). According to the Children's Defense Fund *State of America's Children Report* (2014), 1 in 5 children was poor in 2012; 40 percent, or 7.1 million children, lived in *extreme poverty,* defined in a family of four as having a maximum annual income of $11,746. More than two-thirds of the impoverished children lived in families where one or more family members worked, but full-time minimum wages could not pay the fair market rent for a two-bedroom rental and leave enough money for food, utilities, and other necessities in any U.S. state. Nearly 1.2 million public school children were homeless in 2011–2012. When cultural outside-of-the-house stressors are critical or scary for children, it becomes even more important for parents to provide stable energy levels inside the home. What happens when there is no home?

Work: The Family Load-Bearing Wall

Sigmund Freud said it best when he captured the essence of communal life as "work, which was created by external necessity, and the power of love" (2010, p. 55). Love relationships can involve stress in numerous ways, but family members' work also incorporates multiple stressors. Job layoffs, firings, unemployment, and sometimes retirement, can distribute distress to the entire family. Even among parents with good jobs, dual-career couples and single parents strain to juggle work/home demands. Some family-friendly companies offer remedies. A report on the "2014 Best Companies to Work For" found that 86 percent offer their employees some type of flexible schedule, including working from home one or more days a week. Research finds that employees who telecommute are 13.5 percent more productive and quit at half the rate of office-based workers. Offering a flexible schedule leads to a 45 percent drop in turnover. Job-sharing is another flex-time asset for working parents; 51 percent of Best Companies offer job-sharing where two people split a single position (Rafter, 2014).

Few parents can land a job in one of the "best companies"—and even for those who do, there are money stressors. Cultural historian Riane Eisler looks at our culture as one that currently supports overconsumption: "we are culturally obsessed with getting, buying, building—and wasting things, as a substitute for the satisfactory emotional relationships that are denied by the child-raising styles and the values of adults in the present system" (1987, p. 196). Some parents, and teens with their budding independence, seek an escape route from pressure-filled lives. "More" seems better, although the maintenance of all the "stuff" they buy can become yet another stressor. Shopping occurs at any hour of the day, not just when shopping malls are open. In addition to sleep-deprived shoppers, paperless money makes it easy for family members to be driven consumers today. For too many, credit-card debt threatens workers' load-bearing wall of financial health.

Much stressful "stuff" today is "in the cloud," or digital stress. Although the Digital Age has time-saving advantages, some family members connect more to electronic devices than to people. Not only do parents carry work home in their pockets or pocketbooks, but their recreation too is digital. People of all ages spend inordinate amounts of time online instead of with family members in the next—or even same—room. How often can one find people sitting at the same table in a restaurant texting someone other than the person right in front of them? There is less talking on phones and more texting. Blogging is the new form of social support. Romantic breakups are tweeted and apologies appear on Facebook instead of face-to-face. M.I.T. Technology and Society Specialist Sherry Turkle (2011) argues that instead of furthering intimate relationships with others, the reliance upon technology for engagement actually leaves family members with considerable solitude.

Time Commitment and Response Time

Sociologist Robert Putnam (2000) noticed a generational decline in almost all forms of civic engagement, including disconnection in the form of fewer get-togethers with friends. Loneliness and disengagement from social life are further stressors. Volunteering and/or engaging in social support in one's community can enhance well-being, but a time commitment is required, and time commitments are an issue in every family. With half of all marriages breaking up in America, family life in the new millennium is more in need of networks of engagement and support than ever. Where is the support for couples in making their marriage work? Where is the advocacy for making childrearing a high priority in life?

The community firehouse has a team of firefighters at the ready; one lone firefighter cannot tackle major blazes very effectively. Parents have the ability to put out stress-caused fires, especially if they befriend supportive networks. However, parents' response time to handle stressful situations may not be immediate. All caretakers lug a storied history of meeting and not meeting particular basic needs throughout their lifetime. Many of their life stories reflect missed opportunities and failed problem solving in meeting basic energy, discipline, creativity, belonging, and ability needs. Adults may not respond to their own childhood stressors until they have a child of their own.

Awareness and acceptance of one's own childhood needs—some met and some unmet—raise empathy for stress reactions in children. The end goals for all effective childrearing include having children absorb lessons in family values and learn creative problem solving to reach their potential. Satisfying basic needs starts with meeting the energy needs of good nutrition, enough sleep, and regular exercise to accomplish anything well. As demonstrated in Ellen and Larry's stress-filled morning, caretaker-child needs require careful commitment and timely responses. Children, as well as parents, may fulfill basic needs on stress-free days. On distress-filled days, family members often fall into a collapse zone of disorder, tumble into the "blues," and end up feeling apathetic (Johnston, 2013).

Fire (Distress) Prevention

All stages of family life, including pregnancy and birthing, contain eustress and/or distress. Distress reduction and prevention training offered in group settings, whether for prenatal parents, empty-nest parents, or grandparents, can alleviate the solitude and loneliness too many adults experience today. Caretakers need training on causes of adverse consequences in the family. For example, it is unbelievable in the "modern world" that some parents and school districts continue to discipline children by spanking, when the advice of pediatricians and authors of childrearing books take strong stands against this damaging practice. Distress reduction and prevention require physiological as well as psychological training. How adults role-model taking excellent care of bodies, as well as minds, has meaning for future generations. When caretakers overcome the constant bombardment of messages from the culture that do not match healthy values for their family, they teach children to think for themselves.

The young child requires help in verbalizing his or her stress story; Oliver rumbled and grumbled his distress initially. Caretakers can learn how to identify nonverbal signs and signals of a child in distress. Part of any distress-reduction training for a parent is learning to become a change agent (Sood, 2013). When biological parents are absent, it is hoped that other caring adults can commit to taking care of a given child. Early family attachment relationships are powerful regulators of children's stress systems (Gunnar, 2009). Similarly, early childhood education and intervention programs enhance lifelong health, as well as prepare youth to meet their ability potential. Remedial efforts in distress reduction are much more costly than preventive intervention in the first years of life.

Distress prevention for children requires caring adults who are aware of their *present* connection moments with a child and can relate one interaction at a time (Johnston, 2013). Actually, maintaining a focus on the present moment is good for parents too. Psychologists Matthew Killingsworth and Dan Gilbert (2010) created a smartphone app at a psychology lab at Harvard that allowed 2,250 volunteer app users (ages 18 to 88) to track how happy they were at various times of the day. Overall, 46.9 percent of the time the participants' minds were *not* focused on their present activities; overwhelmingly, their "non-present" thoughts were "unpleasant." Such findings confirm what many people have discovered through the ages: *be here now*. Commit to time to be present with family members. Train for resilience together in the family firehouse.

SUMMARY

A visit to the local fire station provides inspiration for handling family distress. The morning shift appears relaxed until one crew member bellows, *"Train, train,*

train!" Several firefighters grab equipment and scurry toward a door. They train their reactions over and over so that everyone has the same expectations in a crisis. Some therapists believe that families may need a loudspeaker making a morning announcement in the family firehouse: "*Train, train, train!*" Firefighters extend their training to children by visiting schools for "fire prevention week." Perhaps counselors, therapists, and physicians could visit school classrooms and PTA meetings for "distress prevention week." All family members could benefit from reviewing tips for having safe and productive days.

REFERENCES AND FURTHER READING

Adverse Childhood Experiences Study (ACES). (2003, April). Origins and essence of the study. *ACE Reporter, 1*(1), 1–4.

Aronowitz, N. W. (2014, February 14) Do school shooting drills go too far? Experts weigh in. *NBC News*. Retrieved from http://www.nbcnews.com/news/us-news/do-school-shooting-drills-go-too-far-experts-weigh-n30836.

Childhelp.Org. (n.d.). Child abuse statistics and facts. Retrieved from https://www.childhelp.org/child-abuse-statistics.

Children's Defense Fund. (2014). *The state of America's children 2014 report*. Retrieved from http://www.childrensdefense.org/child-research-data-publications/state-of-americas-children/overview.html.

Child Welfare Information Gateway. (2011). *About CAPTA: A legislative history*. Washington, DC: U.S. Department of Health and Human Services, Children's Bureau.

Curran, D. (1985). *Stress and the healthy family*. San Francisco, CA: Harper & Row.

Eisler, R. (1987). *The chalice and the blade: Our history, our future*. San Francisco, CA: Harper & Row.

Freud, S. (2010). *Civilization and its discontents* (J. Strachey, trans. & ed.). New York, NY: W.W. Norton.

Gunnar, M. (2009, October 9). The impact of toxic stress on brain development and health [PowerPoint presentation]. Retrieved from http://www.house.leg.state.mn.us/comm/docs/MeganGunnarPowerpoint.pdf.

Johnston, J. C. (2013). *It takes a child to raise a parent: Stories of evolving child and parent development*. Lanham, MD: Rowman & Littlefield.

Killingsworth, M. A., & Gilbert, D. T. (2010, November 12). A wandering mind is an unhappy mind. *Science, 330*(6006), 932. Retrieved from http://www.sciencemag.org/content/330/6006/932.abstract.

McLeod, S. (2010). Stressful of life events. Retrieved from http://www.simplypsychology.org/SRRS.html.

Putnam, R. D. (2000). *Bowling alone: The collapse and revival of American community*. New York, NY: Simon & Schuster.

Rafter, M. V. (2014, January 22). Best companies offer employees more flexible work options. Retrieved from http://reviews.greatplacetowork.com/blog/best-companies-offer-employees-more-flexible-work-options.

Selye, H. (1974). *Stress without distress: How to use stress as a positive force to achieve a rewarding life style.* New York, NY: J. B. Lippincott.

Sood, A. (2013). *The Mayo Clinic guide to stress-free living.* Boston, MA: Da Capo.

Taylor, S. E. (2006). Tend and befriend: Biobehavioral bases of affiliation under stress. *Association for Psychological Science, 15*(6), 273–277. Retrieved from http://pathwayshrc.com.au/wp-content/uploads/2013/02/Tend-and-Befriend-beobehavioral-Bases-of-Affiliation-Under-Stress.pdf.

Thompson, C. A. (2013, January 7). Poverty a trigger for gun violence. *Detroit Legal News.* Retrieved from http://www.legalnews.com/detroit/1371274.

Turkle, S. (2011). *Alone together: Why we expect more from technology and less from each other.* New York, NY: Basic Books.

18

Understanding Work Stress

Julia Yang

Stress is a term used to describe humans' physiological and/or psychological reactions when we perceive danger to our physical, emotional, or mental safety. Work-related problems have been identified in numerous research studies as the major stressor of our lives. Although stress is inherent in our daily lives, chronic or excessive stress can be costly to both the individual and the workplace. Our responses to stress are idiosyncratic and have much to do with the dynamics within the individual, work group, and the organization. In this chapter, several perspectives concerning work stress are highlighted. The following discussions include (1) the nature of work, work-related stress, and stressors; (2) psychological and vocational barriers that contribute to work stress; (3) the phenomenon of workplace bullying/mobbing; (4) the challenges of a protean career; and (5) spirituality and work stress.

WORK: WHAT IS IT?

To some individuals, *work* often means a professional position or a job as a means of making a living (i.e., financial security). For others, *work* may mean an occupation, career, or vocation that has social, psychological, and spiritual purposes. Career development theories provide explicit assumptions about and perspectives on work. For example, from the developmental framework, work is a journey from birth to death and the totality of all the life roles we play in all life settings. From the social-cognitive perspective, work is a person-centered pathway through life (i.e., preoccupational, occupational, and postoccupational) in which we find expression of our love for life and for the commonwealth (Yang & Waller, 2005).

The theoretical concept of social interest in Adlerian Individual Psychology proposes that work is a life task inseparable from love and social relations. Work is the most central life task for an individual's survival, family provision, and maintenance of social living. Occupation can be looked at as "any kind of work which is useful to the community" (Dreikurs, cited in Yang, Milliren, & Blagen, 2010, p. 92). When we work, we do not work alone. Problems of work surface when we over- or under-work to safeguard against failures and when we fail to cooperate and contribute to the society to which we belong.

Work is a process that may allow the individual to find his or her calling and embark on a journey that is "markedly spiritual, introspective, and highly personal" (Agenlian, cited in Yang, Milliren, & Blagen, 2010, p. 48). Conditions of work are capable of generating in us feelings of passion, pride, desire, curiosity, fear, frustration, anger, hurt, and hostility, many of which contribute to our work stress. In times of pain and loss caused by work, these emotional experiences are expressions and reflections of our spiritual yearning for meaning and healing. Spiritually speaking, work, as a life task, can connect one's deepest inner self to one's community, society, and the largeness of life.

WORK-RELATED STRESS AND STRESSORS

According to the U.S. National Institute for Occupational Safety and Health, *work stress* is "the harmful physical and emotional responses that occur when the requirements of a job do not match the capabilities, resources, or needs of the worker" (Nakao, 2010, p. 2). The *Diagnostic and Statistical Manual of Mental Disorders, Fifth Edition* (*DSM-5;* American Psychiatric Association [APA], 2013) allows work stress to be considered as a risk factor in posttrauma syndrome disorder. The *DSM IV-TR* (APA, 2000) gave examples of occupational problems that are stressful: unemployment, threat of job loss, stressful work schedule, difficult working conditions, job dissatisfaction, job change, and discord with boss or co-workers. A review of work-stress literature suggests that stress occurs in many work circumstances, such as a poor fit between the worker and the work environment, unbalanced work demands and support, work overload, role conflicts, family and work interface, work safety, inadequate leadership and management, and (according to Leka, Griffiths, & Cox, 2003) poor organization of work and systems.

Most recent literature related to work stress uses the theoretical model of job demands and job resources (JD-R) developed by Bakker and Demerouti (2007). *Job demands* refer to mental, emotional, and physical and other social efforts/skills for meeting the job requirements. Job demands have direct impact on the worker's strain and negative organizational outcomes. *Job resources* refer to elements like social support, autonomy, and feedback that reduce job demands, facilitate achievement of the work goals, and stimulate personal growth. Job resources enhance motivation and engagement and thus positive organizational outcomes. Work stress happens when we attempt to meet the job demands with limited job resources. The authors propose that the development of job strain and job motivation depend on the interaction of job demands and job resources. For example, job resources would have buffer effects and moderate job demands, resulting in fewer stress responses, and even promote motivation and positive organizational outcomes. The JD-R model provides a framework describing how job demands and resources influence motivation and strain. Readers are encouraged to review the visual model in Bakker and Demerouti (2007, p. 313).

Stressors are events or conditions that cause stress. Leka, Griffiths, and Cox (2003), in the third document of a series called *Protecting Worker's Health,* by the World Health Organization, provide a comprehensive overview of stressors with respect to work content and work context. As an example, one stress might be the tasks of the job, if these are repetitive, challenging, and so on. According to Leka et al., these stressors are results of poor work organization that includes poor work design, poor management, and unsatisfactory working conditions.

Research has shown that occupational stressors are correlated with physical, psychological, and behavioral symptoms (Nixon, Mazzola, Bauer, Krueger, & Spector, 2011). Among the physical symptoms are gastrointestinal problems, sleep disturbances, backaches, headaches, eye strain, loss of appetite, and fatigue. Work-related stress can have emotional consequences that include anxiety, irritability, lack of confidence, low self-efficacy, anger, hostility, isolation, alienation, depression, lack of motivation and meaning, depression, and so forth. Behaviorally, the stressed worker may engage in more substance use/abuse (cigarettes, alcohol, and other drugs), absenteeism, indecision or bad decisions, poor effectiveness, social aggression, and other symptomatic behaviors that have negative impact on both the worker and the organization.

PSYCHOLOGICAL AND VOCATIONAL BARRIERS

Relevant to this discussion of work stress and stressors are psychological and vocational barriers that hinder career development and attainment. Work is often regarded as the main pathway to success, which is defined by wealth and social status, especially in capitalistic societies. We work hard to meet job demands and overcome our fear of defeat as we seek job retention and advancement. Our work problems mostly stem from our psychological need to safeguard against failures. These problems are exacerbated by workplace cultures that are autocratic and punitive. The challenges of economy upheavals and unemployment only bring further devastation to many who are stressed and distressed by fears from within and without. In our social living, we generally fear not being good enough, making mistakes, disapproval, rejection, "not making it," and failure. At work, we specifically fear defeat, not being perfect or good enough, not being in control, not achieving intrinsic goals or extrinsic rewards, isolation, lack of fairness, and lack of meaning.

> We develop negative work attitudes when we attempt to avoid dealing with fears of work. Instead of meeting work challenges with courage, the discouraged workers are drawn to the side shows of timidity, procrastination, laziness, indecisiveness, entitlement, victimization and a lack of motivation. Basically what these behaviors manifest are inadequacies in the individuals who under work to avoid the perceived threat of failures. (Yang, Milliren, & Blagen, 2010, p. 40)

We can deepen our understanding of work stressors by looking at the work climate that is directly related to the "shadows of leadership" in the workplace described by Palmer (1999). If leaders feel insecure about their own identities, they may create work settings that deprive other people of their identities as a way of defending the leaders' own. The workplace would value competition over cooperation, and hierarchy over equality, if leaders harshly believe that employees must "do or die." Leaders may favor control and autocracy when they assume that ultimate responsibility for everything rests with them and they fear chaos. Some leaders allow fear to foreclose the potential for worker creativity, ingenuity, and change by imposing rigid rules and procedures. Lastly, when they lack the courage to face their own failures and losses, some leaders will fear change. Such leadership fosters various layers of discouragement and frustration in the workplace that stem from perceptions and actions that are based on fear.

The consequences of our fears at work are our "minus feelings" and inadequacies that conflict with our own ideals about ourselves and careers. To compensate for these negative feelings, we overwork or avoid work so as not to appear defeated. We become discouraged workers who often express such complaints as fatigue, stress, lack of vitality, self-doubt, role overload and role conflict (at home and work), lack of personal control, and weak self-efficacy. Strong self-efficacy helps us to better deal with life's hurdles and facilitates our management of the inner challenges that influence our vocational intentions, choices, and performances. In contrast, weak self-efficacy limits our interaction with our work environment and leaves us at risk of other negative experiences at work.

In addition to the internal fears the individual may have about work, exogenous, external, and contextual factors may interact to restrict or override personal endeavor at times, and thus bring about stress and stress responses. Vocational barriers can be conceived of as "events or conditions, either within or in [one's] environment, that make career progress difficult" (Swanson & Woitke, 1997, p. 434). When examined in the cultural and societal contexts, vocational barriers are reflections of the dynamic interaction between the individual and the environment. Race, gender, class, education, sexual orientation, differing abilities, and many other value-laden cultural factors embedded in individuals, families, institutions, and social systems can impede the individual's career and educational choices and progress (e.g., Yang, 1991; Yang, 2009).

Vocational barriers, according to social cognitive career theory, are paradoxically a part of career development. From the social learning theoretical perspective,

EMPLOYEE ASSISTANCE PROGRAMS

Employee assistance programs (EAPs) were created in the 1950s and 1960s when alcohol abuse programs began to be offered in federal agencies as a means to help employees whose productivity levels were worsening due to alcohol abuse (Normington, 2012). However, not until the 1970s were these programs made official (U.S. Department of Agriculture, n.d.). Programs offered expanded to include comprehensive services, including legal and financial assistance. Counseling services began to be provided. Typically, these services are offered for a limited number of sessions and free of charge, as employers recognize that EAPs provide services that offer support and assistance while individuals are either still working, on a medical leave, or need some initial assessments. These services may be useful for employees who are struggling with signs or symptoms related to stress. Additionally, some EAPs even branch out and provide assistance to managers and supervisors, offering knowledge and skill-based training to increase their ability to work effectively with their employees. Normington (2012) makes note of one example of this: after the 9/11 terrorist attacks occurred, there was an increase in on-site grief counseling and training.

EAPs offer confidentiality, a critical factor in trusting the services enough to use them. Aside from the usual limits of confidentiality (harm to self or others or abuse), EAPs adhere to the same ethics pertaining to confidentiality as other helping professionals. Thus, dialogues with counselors are private, and reports are not given to the employee's supervisor. The only time information is released is if the employee signs a consent form permitting the release or if there is a limit on confidentiality.

With the use of technology, EAPs are offering new ways to make services accessible and information available. EAPs are finding ways to use technology and media as a means to reach younger generations, as issues that individuals struggle with still have to be addressed. Most larger companies or organizations offer EAP access, and employees can inquire about these resources through the human resources department.

—Serena Wadhwa

vocational barriers and chance events (i.e., happenstances) can be opportunities for those who can learn from seemingly negative events and respond with curiosity, persistence, flexibility, optimism, and risk-taking (Mitchell, Levin, & Krumboltz, 1999). Happenstances are no longer viewed as random events, but as growth opportunities.

WORKPLACE BULLYING AND MOBBING

Work problems, which are already challenging given the possible fears and stressors mentioned earlier, are intensified when other issues such as discrimination and workplace bullying/mobbing also exist. Often the fears individuals have at the workplace are manifested in collective attitudes of "better than" or "less than." These attitudes, along with people's drive for status, power, and privilege, reinforce the problems of work harassment, discrimination, oppression, and microaggressions. *Discrimination at work* refers to a showing of difference or favoritism in treatment and overt behavior directed toward a person or group of people that is different from the individual's behavior toward others. Oppression at the workplace is best recognized as an abuse of power. According to Sue, "Microaggressions are brief, everyday exchanges that send denigrating messages to certain individuals because of their group membership" (Sue, 2010, p. 24). He indicated that the psychological consequences of microaggressions in the workplace include anxiety, paranoia, depression, sleep difficulties, lack of confidence, feelings of worthlessness, intrusive cognitions, helplessness, loss of drive, and false positives. (False positives generally indicate that something is present when it's not. For example, some work drug screens may show opiate use after a person eats a poppy seed muffin.)

According to Balducci, Fraccaroli, and Schaufeli (2011), the phenomenon of *workplace bullying* involves prolonged exposure to frequent hostile behaviors at work, and it can lead to stress reactions. Duffy and Sperry (2012) list specific elements of workplace bullying: presence of aggressive behavior and/or negative actions such as harassing, offending, excluding, negatively affecting a person's tasks, repeated bullying behaviors, power imbalance, victim being unable to easily defend self, and negative work consequences; most often these elements are present for a long period of time. *Mobbing* is bullying by a group, not just by an individual or two. With the additions of intention to harm and organizational complicity, the phenomenon becomes *workplace mobbing,* a serious issue and a form of persecution, humiliation, and degradation that leads victims to experience many negative health, psychological, relational, and career/work consequences.

> Fear—which is not unreasonable—binds people to silence. Take the fate of whistleblowers, people in an organization who publicly reveal its misdeeds. Studies of

whistleblowers in business find they are typically motivated not by vengeful or selfish motives, but by a lofty one: loyalty to the ethics of their profession or to the organization's avowed mission and principles. Yet most are victimized by the organization—fired, persecuted, sued—rather than thanked. (Goleman, 1998, p. 284)

Aggressive elements are embedded in organizational cultures that persistently permit and reward workplace abuses (Duffy & Sperry, 2012; Goleman, 1998; Sperry, 2009). According to these authors, regardless of how the victims respond to the abuses (i.e., fight or flight), victims suffer from the negative impacts of workplace mobbing on their careers and families. The victims experience a wide range of short-term and long-term health consequences that injure/threaten their physical and psychological well-being, including PTSD symptoms and sudden death.

SEXUAL HARASSMENT

Sexual harassment falls into two categories. The first type, known as *quid pro quo harassment,* includes the notion of verbal or physical sexual conduct as a condition of employment, or perhaps as a condition of receiving good grades in an education setting. The contact may involve unwelcome sexual advances or requests. In the second type, known as *hostile work environment harassment,* an employee finds that unwelcome conduct, comments, or other verbal/physical occurrences at the workplace create an abusive and oppressive work setting. It is not the intention that is the focus of sexual harassment; rather, it is the actual behavior that is unwelcome (Pryor & Fitzgerald, 2003). Thus, although sexual harassment is subjective, people who report these incidents need to be able to demonstrate that other individuals who share similar characteristics also find or would find the behavior to be offensive or unwelcome (Pryor & Fitzgerald, 2003). Research has documented the detrimental effects of workplace sexual harassment on individuals. For example, Schneider, Swan, and Fitzgerald (1997) present research from several authors that demonstrates the negative effects of sexual harassment on the well-being of employees, including decreased morale, increased absenteeism, and decreased relationships with co-workers. As those who have experienced sexual harassment can attest, it causes an extremely stressful and markedly less productive work environment.

—*Serena Wadhwa*

THE PROTEAN CAREER AS NEW STRESS

In the book *The Psychology of Courage: An Adlerian Handbook of Healthy Social Living,* the author and her associates wrote about the new stressors of the protean career era (Yang, Milliren, & Blagen, 2010). Proteus, the god of sea in Greek mythology, was known to be changeable, but could not commit to a single form, for safety lest he be seized and chained. In existential psychology, the dilemma of the "Protean Man" is best described as ambivalence created by the incessant need for change to continuously reflect the changing world and meet the need for identity and belonging. *Protean career* is a concept capturing what is characteristic of the fast and vast personal and environmental changes in the 21st century. The evolution to protean career from transitional institutional career was first noted by Hall in 1976. The career orientation highlights differences of values, attitudes, and success formula between the traditional and the protean career orientations. An example is traditional careers following an institutional structure, whereas protean paths are more autonomous and free.

We are faced with new worries and fears when we make the transition from the traditional concept of work to a protean career. The pathways by which we pursue job attainment, satisfaction, and retention are under scrutiny, changing both values and how issues of work and family interface. Contextual barriers to one's development exist, and require systemic interventions. In the face of unpredictable changes, a protean career calls for workers who are self-directed, value driven, and adaptable.

> [T]he protean concept encompasses any kind of flexible, idiosyncratic career course, with peaks and valleys, left and right turns, moves from one line of work to another, and so forth. Rather than focusing outward on some ideal generalized career "path," the protean career is unique to each person—a sort of career fingerprint. (Hall & Mirvis, 1996, p. 21)

While the intriguing concept of protean career liberates us from external control of our work lives, imparting a sense of vitality and freedom, the unprecedented idea of protean career development also brings a new set of stressors, as we now encounter more fears of an unknown, uncharted future. Answering the new challenges of the protean career requires us to counter our fears with creative power and courage as we train ourselves to be adaptable and to imagine possible resolutions. Our fear is a gift when we can listen to it, not exaggerate it, and use it to facilitate change.

WORK SPIRITUALITY

Discussion of work spirituality is necessary, as work stress continues to exist in the face of the normal yet tenuous work conditions and, sometimes, crises such as sudden losses and changes. In the workplace, we are accustomed to letting function and performance efficiency dominate our understanding of work. Interestingly, the emotional complaints regarding work life, such as emptiness, meaninglessness, vague depression, a loss of values, yearning for personal fulfillment, and a hunger for spirituality are, for the most part, ignored. Feelings of work difficulties often are indications of a quest for meaning and spiritual direction (Yang, Milliren, & Blagen, 2010).

Spirituality is often regarded as a journey of finding meaning, breath that brings us to life, and a space for sacred connections. Work, often seen as a secular space, is in fact a spiritual pathway through life in which we find expression of our selves and our love for life and the commonwealth (Yang & Waller, 2005). Although spirituality is a unique and subjective experience, the literature reveals a noticeable trans-theoretical pattern showing that spiritual fulfillment evolves from such elements as centeredness, connectedness, being, believing, belonging, becoming, and transcendence.

Sandberg and Yang (2006) indicate that there are benefits of spirituality for individuals who share courage and hope, especially in times of work-related transitions and adversities. These authors learned from the career transitioners whom they observed that attending to work spirituality "brought out sources of energy, encouraged creativity and communication, affirmed ethical and moral behaviors, promoted the efficiency of problem solving, and unleashed their potentials" (p. 27).

SUMMARY

The goal of this chapter was not to cover the total spectrum of models that explain work stress and stress management, but rather to examine some conceptual frameworks that facilitate a broad understanding of the causes and consequences of work stress. The author first presented theoretical concepts that are related to work, work stress, and stressors. She also approached the topic of work stress from the perspectives of psychological and vocational barriers, workplace bullying and mobbing, and the impacts of a protean career, as well as how work spirituality gives meaning to work stress and recovery.

REFERENCES AND FURTHER READING

American Psychiatric Association. (2000). *Diagnostic and Statistical Manual of Mental Disorders, Fourth Edition-Text Revision.* Washington, DC: Author.

American Psychiatric Association. (2013). *Diagnostic and Statistical Manual of Mental Disorders, Fifth Edition.* Washington, DC: Author.

Bakker, A. B., & Demerouti, E. (2007). The job demands-resources model: State of the art. *Journal of Managerial Psychology, 22*(3), 309–328.

Balducci, C., Fraccaroli, F., & Schaufeli, W. B. (2011). Workplace bullying and its relation with work characteristics, personality, and post-traumatic stress symptoms: An integrated model. *Anxiety, Stress & Coping, 24*(5), 499–513.

Definition of sexual harassment. (2010). California Department of Fair Employment and Housing. Retrieved from http://www.dfeh.ca.gov/Publications_StatLaws_SexHarrass.htm.

Dreikurs, R. (1989). *Fundamentals of Adlerian psychology.* New York, NY: Greenberg.

Duffy, M. P., & Sperry, L. (2012). *Mobbing: Causes, consequences, and solutions.* Oxford, UK: Oxford University Press.

Employee assistance programs for a new generation of employees. (n.d.). Retrieved May 21, 2015, from http://www.dol.gov/odep/documents/employeeassistance.pdf.

Goleman, D. (1998). *Working with emotional intelligence.* New York, NY: Random House Digital.

Hall, D. T. (1976). *Careers in organizations.* Glenview, IL: Scott Foresman.

Hall, D. T., & Mirvis, P. H. (1996). The new protean career: Psychological success and the path with a heart. In D. T. Hall (Ed.), *The career is dead—long live the career: A relational approach to careers* (pp. 15–45). San Francisco, CA: Jossey-Bass.

Leka, S., Griffiths, A., & Cox, T. (2003). *Work organisation and stress: Systematic problem approaches for employers, managers and trade union representatives* (Protecting Workers' Health Series. No. 3). Geneva, Switzerland: World Health Organisation.

Mitchell, K. E., Levin, A. S., & Krumboltz, J. D. (1999). Planned happenstance: Constructing unexpected career opportunities. *Journal of Counseling and Development, 77,* 115–124.

Nakao, M. (2010). Work-related stress and psychosomatic medicine. *BioPsychoSocial Medicine, 4*(1), 4.

Nixon, A. E., Mazzola, J. J., Bauer, J., Krueger, J. R., & Spector, P. E. (2011). Can work make you sick? A meta-analysis of the relationships between job stressors and physical symptoms. *Work & Stress, 25*(1), 1–22.

Normington, M. (2012). How to set up an employee assistance program. Retrieved May 21, 2015, from http://www.bizjournals.com/bizjournals/how-to/human-resources/2012/01/how-to-set-up-an-employee-assistance.html?page=all.

Palmer, P. J. (1999). *Let your life speak. Listening for the voice of vocation.* San Francisco, CA: Jossey-Bass/Wiley.

Pryor, J. B., & Fitzgerald, L. F. (2003). Sexual harassment research in the United States. In S. Einarsen, H. Hoel, D. Zapf, & C. Cooper (Eds.), *Bullying and emotional abuse in the workplace: International perspectives in research and practice* (pp. 79–100). London, UK: Taylor & Francis.

Sandberg, D., & Yang, I. (2006). Spirituality at work: Usefulness of analogy and questions. *Illinois Counseling Association Journal, 154*(1, Special Issue), 17–28.

Savickas, M. (2005). *Career construction theory.* Conference paper presented at American Counseling Association Annual Convention, April, Atlanta, GA.

Schneider, K. T., Swan, S., & Fitzgerald, L. F. (1997). Job-related and psychological effects of sexual harassment in the workplace: Empirical evidence from two organizations. *Journal of Applied Psychology, 82*(3), 401–415.

Sperry, L. (2009). Mobbing and bullying: The influence of individual, work group, and organizational dynamics on abusive workplace behavior. *Consulting Psychology Journal: Practice and Research, 61*(3), 190–201.

Stoltz, K. B., Wolff, L. A., Monroe, A. E., Farris, H. R., & Mazahreh, L. G. (2013). Adlerian lifestyle, stress coping, and career adaptability: Relationships and dimensions. *Career Development Quarterly, 61*(3), 194–209.

Sue, D. W. (Ed.). (2010). *Microaggressions and marginality: Manifestation, dynamics, and impact.* Hoboken, NJ: John Wiley & Sons.

Swanson, J. L., & Woitke, M. B. (1997). Theory into practice in career assessment for women: Assessment and interventions regarding perceived barriers. *Journal of Career Assessment, 5*(4), 443–462.

U.S. Department of Agriculture. (n.d.). Employee assistance program. Retrieved from http://www.aphis.usda.gov/mrpbs/publications/new_employee_orientation/downloads/GIPSA_Employee_Assistance_Program.pdf.

Yang, J. (1991). Career counseling of Chinese American women: Are they in limbo? *Career Development Quarterly, 39*(4), 350–359.

Yang, J. (2009). Awakening the hidden dragon: Career development and organizational consulting with Chinese. *Career Planning and Adult Development Journal, 24*(4, Special Issue), 44–51.

Yang, J., Milliren, A., & Blagen, M. (2010). *The psychology of courage: An Adlerian handbook for healthy social living.* New York, NY: Routledge/Taylor & Francis.

Yang, J., & Waller, B. (2005). Transforming a work life into a life work. *Illinois Counseling Association Journal, 153*(1, Special Issue), 21–31.

19

Technology and Stress

Serena Wadhwa

Technology occupies a vast territory, particularly in the 21st century. With advances in technology every year, technology offers a paradoxical purpose: It often serves as a convenience and therefore may relieve stress, but it may just as often be a cause of stress (a *stressor*).

Here are three scenarios:

- Tom connects with his friends who live thousands of miles away on a regular basis, yet struggles to say "Hello" to or communicate with the individuals he passes by every day in his neighborhood, and the few he sees at the store, post office, and other community areas.
- An entrepreneur, who owns a flourishing business, hears the "chirp" of her phone, letting her know that emails are coming in that require her attention; she feels that she has to respond, even though as she is in the middle of enjoying date night with her partner.
- Watching children's videos on an iPad has become a ritual for little Joan, as her mother tends to household chores.

Each scenario is different, and yet the common element is of some form of technology being interwoven in the day-to-day life of these individuals.

What is technology? *Technology* is usually defined as "the use of science in industry, engineering, etc., to invent useful things or to solve problems," or "the practical application of knowledge especially in a particular area" (Merriam-Webster Online, n.d.). Breaking this definition down, there are two parts: The first is the recognition of how science and other fields of knowledge are utilized to develop solutions to challenges facing society. The second part of this definition focuses on the application of knowledge. Thus, technology provides tools as a means of making something possible, or making things easier, more convenient, or more accessible. We have many examples of technology throughout history. To begin with, during the Stone Age, technology consisted of the development of tools to help in the process of hunting and gathering food and using fire. Moving from the Stone Age throughout human history, one can find numerous advances in technology fitting with the times. The discovery or invention of medications, art forms, transportation, electronics, communications, treatments to improve mental, physical, emotional health, and a variety of other technologies demonstrate the importance of technology as an evolutionary tool. In the modern world, technology such as computers, the Internet, and medicines commonly and directly affects how we shop, cook, communicate, and live. As technology advances, so does our species . . . or is it the other way around?

In the modern world, technology is most often thought of in terms of electronics, including computers, phones, and televisions; and other machines, especially at worksites like factories or medical facilities. Even watches have been adapted to serve as more than time-telling devices: they can connect the user to phone calls; track pieces of information; and perform other functions typically expected of a personal computer. Computers and the Internet are perhaps the most widely recognized modern-day technological advancement. At the end of the 20th century (around the 1980s), technology in this sense was not as widely used as it is today. In fact, according to the U.S. Census Bureau report (Day, Janus, & Davis, 2005), an average of only 8.2 percent of households owned a computer back in the mid-1980s. Today, in the 21st century, that number is closer to 83 percent (File & Ryan, 2014). This signifies a change in the nation's perspective about the meaning, use, and impact of technology in day-to-day living as well as within our work and social environments. It also signifies a change in the accessibility of this technology to individuals, because the more accessible something is which is desired and projected as a life enhancement, the more people are going to want to try it and use it for themselves. As technology (particularly electronic-based) became more accessible and affordable for many socioeconomic classes, many people bought it. This technology has made things more convenient and the modern world much "smaller." What follows is a synopsis of many of the ways in which technology has contributed to the modern world, as both a life enhancer and a life stressor.

COMMUNICATION

Technology contributes to the ability to easily communicate with others. There is research that measures the modes and frequency of communication via technological means (email, texting, etc.) and compares this to how individuals communicated prior to the availability of modern technology (phone, mail, telegraph, etc.), and this research shows a definite surge in technological communication. However, some researchers debate the comparability of these communications: they claim that although communication among individuals has increased, the quality of those communications is different, being more impersonal or nonpersonal. Some point out that use of technology limits certain aspects of communication that were possible (and common) in face-to-face interactions. Another factor often explored, when it comes to the effects of technology on communication, is how the Internet, while a source of information and connection to other parts of the world, actually diminishes socialization (skills and opportunities) and the development of intimate connections with others (Kraut et al., 1998). These authors traced this diminution to the introduction of the television set, which, while providing entertainment and serving as a resource in the 1950s, also reduced the need for interactions with neighbors. A paradox is thus presented: Although technology provides a means of instantly and frequently communicating with others, it also changes and limits those communications in some ways.

In a sense, technology can be viewed both as a source of stress and as a means of managing that stress. When it comes to the subject of communication, it's not uncommon to see individuals on their phones or tablets communicating basic minutiae of day-to-day life many times during the day. We use technology as a way of communicating in an instant when we are delayed in getting to an event or some scheduled gathering, to reduce our stress and/or others' stress about where we are or when we will arrive. We use technology to let others know where we are when we arrive, for convenience and notification purposes. Technology helps with this.

Technology opens the gates for individuals to communicate easily with others. This can occur with family and friends living long distances apart; for example, in other countries, or different cities, as travel may be challenging due to lack of transportation or funding for transportation. Individuals who live further away from family and friends generally communicate more frequently via technological means than those who do not. However, often this contact comes with the expectation that recipients of these communications will respond rather quickly. In other words, technology becomes a "burden due to the constant availability" of individuals (Gemmill & Peterson, 2006). Being present for others, and responding to others practically immediately, are unspoken expectations raised by the advancements of technology. These can increase perceptual demands and pressures, thus creating stress for many individuals. Communication, then, can seem burdensome, due to the consistent interruptions and perceived need to respond immediately. Tarafdar, Gupta, and Turel (2013) compiled statistics suggesting that about 43 percent of the smartphone users surveyed found that having a smartphone (which allows access to email and options to text-message rather than call) was stressful, due to

UNDERSTANDING TECHNOLOGY TOOLS TO REDUCE STRESS

Technology is often blamed for increased stress levels, but technology itself doesn't increase stress. In fact, it is almost always a lack of knowledge and training in effective use of technological tools for their identified purposes that creates stress. Tools facilitate the execution of a task. We can complete the task without the tool, but the tool certainly simplifies and often vastly reduces the challenge at hand. Once we step back and look at technology as a tool instead of a magic wand to the finish line, we can begin to understand its purpose and its role in stress.

When our technology changes, such as when a computer's operating system is updated, we experience higher stress levels, partially due to the uncertainty of how to execute previously well-known, simple tasks. We now must stop and think through how to execute the routine task we formerly performed quickly and easily. Although the new steps may be just as simple, or even more efficient, we do not have an unconscious competency for enacting those steps—at least not yet. This ambiguity and uncertainty add layers of complexity, which can ultimately increase stress.

When users take the time to learn, practice, and eventually master the steps to use the new operating system (or new technological tool), their actions soon become as habitual as they once were with the previous system. However, when the user does not take the time needed to learn the new processes, this lack of knowledge prolongs the time needed to complete the task, and stress levels increase as users wade through the confusing execution of processes they once performed quickly and easily. Allowing time for training and better comprehension of the use of the tool and its functionality will help users find the best use of the tool for the situation at hand, all the while reducing stress as tasks can be completed efficiently and effectively.

—*Joelyne Marshall*

the pressure to constantly check emails and messages. Sixty percent of those surveyed indicated that they are unable to go an hour without checking their devices (Tarafdar, Gupta, & Turel, 2013). What once was a life enhancer—providing a means of instant communication and accessibility at any time of the day or night—may thus turn into a life stressor: being subjected to constant interruptions of others needing or wanting something; not having one's own space and time to relax, restore, or rest; "being on" 24 hours a day; and quite possibly one's own perceived "need" to respond to incoming texts and emails while engaged with other tasks, whether pleasure or work. Disruptions, then, themselves become stressors; when one is focused on a task or an activity, the constant pull and interruption of something else can add unnecessary demands and distract from a flow of thoughts/creativity/productivity.

MANAGING TIME

The modern world is full of activities relating to the perception of a fulfilling and holistic life. The desire to do things to enhance one's quality of life—and to some extent, to extend the quantity of years available—becomes more evident with each advance in technology. Individuals buy gadgets to record/store shows, songs, and so on to watch and listen to later, as they may not have the "time" to engage with the source of entertainment at that exact moment. Individuals download various applications (apps) for their smartphones to set reminders, create lists, and locate stores, restaurants, and other places. Americans can now pack more into a day in the modern world than could have been conceived of 50, 40, or even 30 years ago. Yet, in a study cited by Flaskerud and Flaskerud (2013), about half of Americans reported that they don't have the time to do what they want, and 40 percent experience frequent stress. Although we have more time-saving devices, we seem to have less free or leisure time (Flaskerud & Flaskerud, 2013). Thus, the paradoxical dilemma of technology is created: While we can do more by "saving time," there is more pressure to get more done. This creates a *time urgency,* which in essence is another experience of stress resulting from additional pressures and demands placed upon the individual. Another example of the paradoxical dilemma results from the time-saving convenience of having information at one's fingertips. Technology easily brings quick information at the push of a button, rather than having to wait to go to the library, contact someone, or wait on the telephone. However, the ability to save time by going online sometimes results in an individual spending more time online, as the location and means of access to the desired information may not be immediately obvious or clear—and the potential for distractions is vast (Tarafdar, Gupta, & Turel, 2013).

WORK SETTINGS

There is evidence that use of technology in the workplace aims at improving productivity and cost-effectiveness and enhancing innovation (Tarafdar, Tu, Ragu-Nathan, & Ragu-Nathan, 2007). Technology has made most work conditions efficient and accessible from both the work and home environment. This allows individuals to access work-related material from their personal computers, work computers, or hand-held devices. It also allows 24-hours-a-day communication with other employees about new developments, issues, or concerns. Although there are business-related advantages to being constantly "on" from a work perspective, research also indicates that there is another side: the costs of such arrangements.

According to Soylu and Campbell (2012), the increase in computer use for work-related tasks has led to a concomitant increase in carpal tunnel syndrome, which includes symptoms of tingling, numbness, and pain, due to the pressure placed on the median nerve in the wrist. The increase in carpal tunnel syndrome for employees, according to Soylu and Campbell (2012), can also lead to other physical injuries, cause psychological distress, increase difficulty with concentration, and possibly pose other cognitive challenges. It is also true that the repetitive physical movement involved in using a keyboard can causes physical stress to the fingers, hands, and even arms. These issues can have to counterproductive outcomes when employees must take time off work to attend to the care and management of these symptoms. The study authors suggest that about 25 percent of computer users experience some adverse physical consequences from continued use.

Tarafdar, Tu, Ragu-Nathan, and Ragu-Nathan (2007) identify several negative consequences from technology in the workplace. Aside from computers being foreign territory for many individuals of older generations, the constant change in technology can be frustrating and overwhelming in itself. New software, hardware, applications, systems, and devices can become a daunting experience for some people, leading to stress and anxiety.

Another consideration the authors posit is that technology changes the role of the individual at work. With the increase in information available and work production expected, individuals have to learn more information and be aware of what is available and where. This creates a multitasking perspective, in that people now often operate on several systems at once (email, documents, videoconferencing), all of which take concentration and energy. The brain is able to focus only on one task at a time; thus, attempted multitasking for many individuals causes strain and stress.

MULTITASKING

Technological advancements and conveniences provide numerous opportunities for multitasking, which many believe is an efficient way to work. The concept of multitasking has actually been studied for many decades. Several factors influence whether or not an individual can actually be successful at paying attention to two or more separate tasks at the same time. Some tasks require different resources and are of different levels of complexity. Some tasks may be more habitual than others, and therefore may not require as much thought or effort (Salvucci & Taatgen, 2008).

More importantly, research suggests that the brain does not really focus on both tasks at the same time; it actually switches attention from one task to the other and back again (Rosen, 2008), which can cause increased stress and activate the release of more stress-related hormones into the body. This can be a negative effect of multitasking attempts, particularly if the individual is not aware of the potential consequences. Subsequently, multitasking can contribute to the loss of short-term memory, making it challenging to retain information, study, or (for example) to remember the names of people you have just met. When you multitask, your focus is divided, and that subsequently affects your ability to learn material, process information, and retain information for the future.

Wallis (2006) describes some of the concerns with this concept for the younger generation. When one is multitasking, it usually requires more time to get the tasks done; completing tasks by focusing on one task at a time actually allows each task to be completed more quickly, sometimes in half the time. Most young adults, because they are accustomed to multitasking, may not allow themselves the rest and recovery periods their bodies and brains need to recuperate. Someone who has a hard time going 30 minutes without checking the phone or going on social media may actually be conditioning his or her brain to remain highly activated to fill in that "space" (Wallis, 2006).

Another concern with multitasking is the ability to stay in the present. When a person is in a meeting or listening to a lecture or in a movie theater, and at the same time checking emails, reviewing sports scores, or surfing the Web, that person is not present to what is actually happening in real time. It's more challenging to become intimate, or focused on what you are doing at the time, with whoever you are with, or in whatever setting you are in, if you're distracted.

Tarafdar, Tu, Ragu-Nathan, and Ragu-Nathan (2007) introduced the term *technostress* to describe the problems with constantly learning new technology and multitasking. *Technostress* is stress created by information and computer technology. Another study, conducted by Lee, Chang, Cheng, and Lin (2015), found that technostress may also be related to certain personality traits. In that study, Lee et al. discovered that certain personality traits increase one's experience of technostress: one's locus of control, social interaction anxiety, and the need for "touch." Participants were both traditional cell phone users and smartphone users, with those individuals who had smartphones turning out to be more apt either to have more of the personality traits studied; or, as a result of these traits, to have bought the smartphone. The study suggested, for example, individuals who are more "touch oriented" touch gadgets and items as they walk into a store, and perhaps engage in touch as a means of avoiding boredom. Additionally, this want/need for physical touch among individuals often leads to the purchase of smartphones with "touch screen" options, thus inducing a compulsion to keep "touch-screening" the phone.

Within the health and human services field, the use of technology has also created controversy. Technology has transformed care of patients in the medical field, as well as opening doors for additional forms of communication. For counselors, psychologists, and psychiatrists, among others, technology provides the ability to reach many patients or clients to collaborate on health- and wellness-related concerns and outcomes.

CONCLUSION

Technology serves individuals in a variety of ways, through increasing communication, acting as a time-saving device, and assisting in the workplace, with a variety of benefits to the user. At the same time, technology brings its own set of challenges to the table. As the modern world continues to advance, the ways in which technology works to benefit and/or disadvantage users will continue to develop.

REFERENCES AND FURTHER READING

Day, J. C., Janus, A., & Davis, J. (2003). *Computer and internet use in the United States: 2003* (Current Population Reports). Retrieved from http://www.census.gov/prod/2005pubs/p23-208.pdf.

File, T., & Ryan, C. (2014). *Computer and internet use in the United States: 2013* (American Community Survey results). Retrieved from http://www.census.gov/content/dam/Census/library/publications/2014/acs/acs-28.pdf.

Flaskerud, J. H., & Flaskerud, J. H. (2013). Western cultural notions of time and stress. *Issues in Mental Health Nursing, 34*(7), 558–561.

Gemmill, E. L., & Peterson, M. (2006). Technology use among college students: Implications for student affairs professionals. *Journal of Student Affairs Research and Practice, 43*(2), 482–502.

Kraut, R., Patterson, M., Lundmark, V., Kiesler, S., Mukopadhyay, T., & Scherlis, W. (1998). Internet paradox: A social technology that reduces social involvement and psychological well-being? *American Psychologist, 53*(9), 1017–1031.

Lee, Y. K., Chang, C. T., Cheng, Z. H., & Lin, Y. (2015). Helpful-stressful cycle? Psychological links between type of mobile phone user and stress. *Behaviour & Information Technology*, 1–12.

Merriam-Webster Online. (n.d.). s.v. Technology. Retrieved from http://www.merriam-webster.com/dictionary/technology.

Parker, A. (2009, February 13). *Case study: DIRECTV.* Association for Talent Development (AST). Retrieved from https://www.td.org/Publications/Newsletters/Learning-Circuits/Learning-Circuits-Archives/2009/02/Case-Study-DIRECTV.

Rosen, C. (2008). The myth of multitasking. *The New Atlantis, 20*(Spring), 105–110.

Salvucci, D. D., & Taatgen, N. A. (2008). Threaded cognition: An integrated theory of concurrent multitasking. *Psychological Review, 115*(1), 101–130.

Snehansu, K. (2013, August 4.) Technology increases productivity for students and teachers. *EdTechReview (ETR)*. Retrieved from http://edtechreview.in/trends-insights/insights/476-technology-increases-productivity-for-students-and-teachers.

Soylu, A., & Campbell, S. S. (2012). Physical and emotional stresses of technology on employees in the workplace. *Journal of Employment Counseling, 49*(3), 130–139.

Tarafdar, M., Gupta, A., & Turel, O. (2013). The dark side of information technology use. *Information Systems Journal, 23*(3), 269–275.

Tarafdar, M., Tu, Q., Ragu-Nathan, B. S., & Ragu-Nathan, T. S. (2007). The impact of technostress on role stress and productivity. *Journal of Management Information Systems, 24*(1), 301–328.

Wallis, C. (2006). The multitasking generation. *Time Magazine, 167*(13), 48–55.

Williams, O. (2013, October 21). Can technology relieve stress at work? *Small Business /Chron.com*. Retrieved from http://smallbusiness.chron.com/can-technology-relieve-stress-work-59503.html.

20

ENVIRONMENTAL STRESS

Serena Wadhwa

Environment, as discussed in this chapter, means all that is around a person, including the natural environment (climate, nature) and any physical surroundings (office, house, cities).

The environment contains many potential stressors that, paradoxically, may also serve as buffers to the effects of stress. Although many of the factors explored in this chapter relate to how one's environment can present stressful experiences, situations, and so on, it is important to recognize that some of these can also serve as effective coping mechanisms against stress. For example, various lifestyle factors can contribute to the experience of stress for many individuals, and these same lifestyle factors, when modified, can become useful allies in protecting the individual from the effects of stress.

LIFESTYLE

An individual's lifestyle can affect stress levels. Research has demonstrated that various lifestyle factors, such as volunteer service, connections with nature, exercise, and nutrition, among others, can be both stressors (contributing to stressful experiences) and stress relievers. Walsh (2011) explored several lifestyle changes that were demonstrated by research to provide mental health and wellness benefits to the body and the mind; he also explored lifestyle changes that provide some economic and community advantages. In addition to reviewing some of these lifestyle changes and how they benefit an individual, he also alluded to other benefits, such as reductions in medical costs, time off work, potential reduction in medication use, and increases in social connections. Walsh focused on the benefits of various lifestyle changes also covered in this book: exercise (physical activity, in Chapter 25); nutrition (Chapter 24), relaxation (Chapter 27), and social relationships (Chapter 15) are a few of these.

NATURE

We often spend the majority of the day indoors; if we are outdoors, more than likely we are contained within a particular space with limited natural light and exposure to the natural elements. Walsh (2011) cites several environmental psychology studies showing that an individual's minimal exposure to the natural environment contributes to sleep and mood disruptions. It is well known that disruptions in sleep can affect and also impair cognitive functioning, including functioning in self-regulating behaviors. *Technostress* (a term discussed in Chapter 19) is one of the many afflictions occurring as a result of the increase in technology use and limited time outdoors. There are even commercials addressing concerns raised by the fact that most youth spend more time with video games than outdoors, and the impact this may have on development. One study suggested that the sounds of rippling water have a strong relaxing effect on individuals due to the connection with nature, movement, and "subconsciously seek[ing of] connection with all that is alive and vital" (Kim, Kim, & Myoung, 2011, as cited in Thoma, La Marca, Brönnimann, Finkel, Ehlert, & Nater, 2013). Recent publications have also warned of a nature deficit that especially affects children, who, due to demands on their time from various after-school activities, overworked and overprotective parents, or living in urban settings, are no longer able to go out into woods, parks, or other natural settings.

Nevertheless, nature can also be a source of stress. Nature can be unexpected in terms of weather, natural disasters, and climate changes, which can subsequently affect livestock, ecological operations, crops, and other aspects of existence. Some areas experience high heat indexes, which can cause certain physical conditions; other areas face repeated tornadoes and water-related calamities. Some research also suggests that weather changes can influence various medical conditions, such as fibromyalgia (Bennett, Jones, Turk, Russell, & Matallana, 2007).

RELATIONSHIPS

Cultivating positive and supportive relationships is a cornerstone of mental health and hence of stress management. Given the stressors and structure of the modern world, several theorists have explored the notion of social isolation, one of the best-known facets of which is the aspect of social capital, as put forth by Robert Putnam (see Walsh, 2011; Post, 2005). *Social capital* refers to the amount and quality of social networks a person has (friends, family, etc.). Putnam believes that this kind of capital, like the monetary kind, provides a strong basis for psychological as well as physical health and well-being (see, e.g., Putnam, 2000).

RELIGIOUS AND SPIRITUAL INVOLVEMENT

In a meta-analysis of 724 studies, about 476 demonstrated a positive correlation between religious and spiritual involvement and mental health (Koenig, McCullough, & Larson, 2001, as cited in Walsh, 2011). Many individuals use faith and prayer, as well as meditation, as a means to find strength, reflect, and develop certain values and principles central to managing and reducing stress. For example, many religious and spiritual paths discuss cultivation of love and forgiveness as a means of restoring one's mental health and balance.

SERVICE

Volunteering, doing something for others, and random acts of kindness are examples of service and contribution to others. Altruism is a concept that has been studied for many years. Research indicates that significant benefits accrue when an individual does something for another person, without a sense of duty, obligation, or attachment to some outcome (Post, 2005; Walsh, 2011). Service to others in these contexts provides an outlet and ways to focus attention on something other than the stressors the individual may normally experience. People also report feeling better after volunteering for some difficult cause about which they care (for example, helping in a program for abused children), because it gives them more agency; that is, they feel that they are doing something to assist in making things better. This may particularly help people who feel that in their jobs or daily lives they are not normally providing useful services. Many people find that, in various contexts, helping others does help them feel better. A related finding is the feeling expressed by many volunteers that they have received more from the person(s) being assisted than the other way around.

PHYSICAL STRESSES FROM WORK AND HOME ENVIRONMENTS

Many people face physical stressors, including unpleasant or dangerous physical conditions such as crowding, too much or constant noise, bad construction of housing or workplaces, poor ventilation or heating/cooling systems, air pollution, dangerous amounts of lead or other substances in water, exposure to chemicals, and other issues. Even being employed in work areas with little or no natural light can be stressful. Some people have physical jobs in construction that can be dangerous and hazardous. Laborers on farms, as well as those supervising them (including farmers), are exposed to bad physical conditions, dangerous equipment

ENVIRONMENTAL TOBACCO SMOKE

Environmental tobacco smoke (ETS) is also known as *passive smoke*. Research indicates that exposure to this kind of smoke may be more toxic than actually smoking the cigarette or cigar. According to Mohammad (2015), studies indicate that the concentration of toxic substances in ETS may be higher than in the original vehicle. Additionally, ETS tends to include smaller particles of these substances, which allows the toxic materials to penetrate deeper into the body (see Mohammad, 2015, for a review). Additional studies indicate that passive smoke increases respiratory issues for children, especially asthma (Kobayashi et al., 2014), and increases the risk of respiratory problems in older adults as well (Almirall et al., 2014).

and chemicals, and intense heat or cold. Miners of all types are repeatedly exposed to hazards. Although there are federal as well as local laws to protect employees from harm, often conditions go unreported or are unresolved due to fears of job loss. Although some offices now are designed to provide more pleasant, safer, and even fun surroundings for employees, many workplaces continue to contribute to stress.

Living in housing that is in poor repair, with peeling paint, leaky roofs, broken windows, faulty plumbing, lack of hot water, no access to air conditioning in the summer and poor heating in the winter, is stressful. Living in high-crime areas leads to chronic stress. As discussed in Chapter 14, people in low socioeconomic conditions who face stress routinely have far more health problems than people who do not.

COMMUTING AND TRANSPORTATION

According to the United States Census Bureau, approximately 86 percent of workers commuted to work by car in 2013 (McKenzie, 2015), with most of these individuals commuting alone. On average, this is about 4–10 percent of waking time for an individual (see Olsson, Gärling, Ettema, Friman, & Fujii, 2013). One effect of this is an increase in the time it takes to get to work. This is not caused simply by the number of commuters; it also depends on the distance traveled to work, limitations on public transportation options within a particular area, and other variables. Commuter stress exists regardless of the mode of transportation (other modes include train or bus). Bicycling and walking to work, however, usually have benefits, because these modes are variations of physical activity. Literature suggests that the longer commutes these days may take time away from social activities, physical activities (Evans & Wener, 2006), reflection, sleep, and other effective coping mechanisms of coping with stress (which other chapters have explored in terms of reducing, managing, or preventing stress). An occupation in transportation (for example, driving a bus) tends to increase susceptibility to health issues and early mortality, more than other occupations (Evans & Carrère, 1991). The authors looked at other factors playing a role in this, including a demanding schedule and being responsible for the safety of numerous people, for instance (Evans & Carrère, 1991). Traffic carries its own stressors, including congestion and pollution. Other research has indicated that the complexity of the commute (Wener, Evans, Phillips, & Nadler, 2003) and vehicular crowding also increase the experience of stress.

REFERENCES AND FURTHER READING

Almirall, J., Serra-Prat, M., Bolíbar, I., Palomera, E., Roig, J., Carandell, E., . . . Study Group of Community-Acquired Pneumonia in Catalan Countries (PACAP). (2014). Passive smoking at home is a risk factor for community-acquired pneumonia in older adults: A population-based case–control study. *BMJ Open, 4*(6), e005133.

Bennett, R. M., Jones, J., Turk, D. C., Russell, I., & Matallana, L. (2007). An internet survey of 2,596 people with fibromyalgia. *BMC Musculoskeletal Disorders, 8*, 27. doi:10.1186/1471-2474-8-27.

Centers for Disease Control and Prevention (CDC). (2014). Stress . . . at work (DHHS (NIOSH) Publication Number 99–101). Retrieved from http://www.cdc.gov/niosh/docs/99-101/.

Evans, G. W., & Carrère, S. (1991). Traffic congestion, perceived control, and psychophysiological stress among urban bus drivers. *Journal of Applied Psychology, 76*(5), 658–663.

Evans, G. W., & Wener, R. E. (2006). Rail commuting duration and passenger stress. *Health Psychology, 25*(3), 408–412.

Evans, G. W., Wener, R. E., & Phillips, D. (2002). The morning rush hour predictability and commuter stress. *Environment and Behavior, 34*(4), 521–530.

Kim, Y. K., Kim, S. M., & Myoung, H. (2011, April). Musical intervention reduces patients' anxiety in surgical extraction of an impacted mandibular third molar. *Journal of Oral & Maxillofacial Surgery, 69*(4),1036–1045. doi:10.1016/j.joms.2010.02.045.

Kobayashi, Y., Bossley, C., Gupta, A., Akashi, K., Tsartsali, L., Mercado, N., . . . Ito, K. (2014). Passive smoking impairs histone deacetylase-2 in children with severe asthma. *CHEST Journal, 145*(2), 305–312.

McKenzie, B. (2015, August). Who drives to work? Commuting by automobile in the United States: 2013 (American Community Survey Reports). Retrieved from http://www.census.gov/hhes/commuting/files/2014/acs-32.pdf.

Mohammad, Y. (2015). Passive smoking interference with wheezing and asthma: Short review of current knowledge. *Pulmonology and Respiratory Research, 3*(1), 2.

Olsson, L. E., Gärling, T., Ettema, D., Friman, M., & Fujii, S. (2013). Happiness and satisfaction with work commute. *Social Indicators Research, 111*(1), 255–263.

Post, S. G. (2005). Altruism, happiness, and health: It's good to be good. *International Journal of Behavioral Medicine, 12*(2), 66–77.

Putnam, R. D. (2000). *Bowling alone: The collapse and revival of American community.* New York, NY: Simon & Schuster.

Thoma, M. V., La Marca, R., Brönnimann, R., Finkel, L., Ehlert, U., & Nater, U. M. (2013). The effect of music on the human stress response. *PloS One, 8*(8), e70156.

Walsh, R. (2011). Lifestyle and mental health. *American Psychologist, 66*(7), 579–592.

Wener, R. E., Evans, G. W., Phillips, D., & Nadler, N. (2003). Running for the 7:45: The effects of public transit improvements on commuter stress. *Transportation, 30*(2), 203–220.

21

Academic Stress in High School and College Students in the United States

Yoo Jung Kim

WHAT IS ACADEMIC STRESS?

Given the level of academic workload and social obligations typically expected in high school and college, many students find themselves struggling to cope with difficult situations that often seem insurmountable or overwhelming, such as courseload, extracurricular activities, and social obligations.

Academic stress in the United States is also inextricably linked to a variety of challenges specific to student life. Among college students, these hurdles include—but are not limited to—struggling with the academic workload, being preoccupied with accruing student debt, adjusting to a new environment, living up to expectations set by family members, being away from home, dealing with social pressures such as drinking and drug use, and underlying psychological issues.

HOW PREVALENT IS ACADEMIC STRESS IN THE UNITED STATES?

At first glance, it may appear reasonable to conclude that students struggling to graduate or to pass their courses are the most likely candidates to experience academic stress. However, even students who perform at a high level are not immune to academic stress. High-achieving high school students may see grades as a means of gaining acceptance into highly selective universities, and thus place a greater emphasis on getting perfect grade-point averages, much to the detriment of their mental and emotional well-being. College students may also see their academic performance as a means of maintaining their academic scholarships, scoring sought-after internships, being selected for lucrative jobs in a competitive market after graduation, applying to highly selective graduate and professional programs, or meeting social and familial expectations.

In fact, a significant number of students struggle with academic stress, and some find their collegiate careers adversely affected by it. According to a 2006 survey of 97,357 college students conducted by the American College Health Association, the most significant health impediment to a student's academic performance was academic stress, which was ranked above other common stressors such as depression or alcohol use. Nearly a third of the college students sampled reported that academic stress had resulted in noncompletion of a course, course withdrawal, or low grade (Hoban, 2007).

SOURCES OF ACADEMIC STRESS AND OTHER RELATED STRESS

Students face academic stress from a variety of sources. Among high school students, 70 percent reported that "they often or always feel stressed by their schoolwork," and 56 percent reported "often or always worrying about grades, tests, and college acceptance" (Conner, Pope, & Galloway, 2009).

Unfortunately for these students, academic stress often persists well beyond high school graduation. College students, especially freshmen, are especially prone to stress because of the major transition between high school and college life. Moreover, by far the greatest source of stress for college students stemmed from their coursework. In a 1991 study, researchers surveyed 100 undergraduates from a mid-sized Midwestern university. Ross, Niebling, and Heckert found that the top two causes of academic stress were dealing with increased workload in college and receiving a lower grade than anticipated (Ross et al., 1999). As students make the transition from high school to college, many find that they are not sufficiently prepared to tackle the rigors of university coursework.

Ross et al. (1999) also discovered that academic stress is magnified by interpersonal, intrapersonal, and environmental pressures commonly found in college life, as well as expectations from peers and family members. Students who pursue interpersonal relationships may be distracted from their academic workload. Students enrolled in courses that assign grades based on a cumulative class curve may find themselves comparing their performance with that of their peers. College also offers a greater variety of extracurricular activities, which may distract students from their academics, as do part-time and full-time jobs. Some students may be preoccupied with the thought of accruing debt in college and—in order to get their degree on time or earlier than usual—perceive their examinations as a potentially high-risk endeavor. Finally, high expectations from parents in the context of academic success can pose a significant stressor for students.

IMPLICATIONS OF ACADEMIC STRESS FOR STUDENTS

Academic stress is common in high schools and college campuses, and it can have some serious implications for both levels of students, especially if the students find themselves ill-prepared to cope. Academic stress may deleteriously affect student performance in high-stakes situations, keep students from graduating, fuel stimulant abuse, and foster academic dishonesty.

First, a primary adverse effect of academic stress is that it can compromise student performance by impairing working memory, a cognitive system that allows the person to store information for the short term (Baddeley, 1992). In brief, working memory can be conceptualized as a mental cache of Post-It notes. These notes carry information that is immediately relevant to the task at hand. However, if a student's working memory is taxed, his or her performance in the task begins to suffer—the relevant Post-It notes are displaced. Because of effects such as these, educational psychologists believe that in stressful situations—such as taking a midterm or a final exam—students must learn ways to disregard their performance-based anxieties and devote their working memory to tackling the test efficiently.

To test this hypothesis, University of Chicago researcher Sian L. Beilock devised a controlled, high-stakes testing environment. Beilock asked the low-stakes group "simply to try their best on a math test"; the high-stakes group members were offered money if they were able to perform at a high level, thereby simulating a situation in which students must reach a prescribed grade to maintain their academic scholarships. The high-stakes group was also told that the results of their tests might be evaluated by others. This situation simulated real-life situations in which students' self-image may be dependent partially on the perceived opinion of their professors, friends, and family members (Beilock, 2008).

Beilock showed that high-pressure situations increased participants' perception of pressure and—despite external incentives to do well—actually ended up diminishing test performance on average. In accordance with the original hypothesis, Beilock's results suggest that in high-pressure situations, students' working memory is taxed so that less of it is available to be used for the task at hand (Beilock, 2008).

Second, academic stress can also keep students from graduating high school or college. In 2013, researchers from the Michigan Department of Education and Texas A&M University compiled data from several national studies spanning more than five decades to figure out why students dropped out of high school. Out of the top 10 reasons, "Was getting poor grades/failing in school" ranked third, with 38 percent overall frequency; "Could not keep up with schoolwork" ranked fifth, with 32.1 percent overall frequency (Doll, Eslami, & Walters, 2013).

Unfortunately, earning their high school diplomas and matriculating into college did not mean that students were immune from academic stress further on in their academic careers. In the United States, 40 percent of full-time four-year college students fail to earn a bachelor's degree within six years, and many never complete their education. In a 2009 public agenda report for the Bill & Melinda Gates Foundation, "With Their Whole Lives Ahead of Them: Myths and Realities about Why So Many Students Fail to Finish College," researchers asked more than 600 adults aged 22 to 30 why they did not or were unable to complete their postsecondary education. The reason "I needed a break from school" was selected by 54 percent of the respondents, 21 percent of whom listed it as a major reason and 33 percent of whom listed it as a minor reason. Furthermore, the reason "Some of the classes were too difficult" was selected by 34 percent of all survey responders, 10 percent of whom listed it as a major reason and 24 percent of whom listed it as a minor reason (Johnson & Rochkind, 2009).

Third, academic stress fuels stimulant abuse among college students. Stimulants such as Adderall, Concerta, Vyvanse, and Ritalin are drugs commonly prescribed to patients with attention deficit hyperactivity disorder (ADHD) as performance and cognitive enhancers. However, more and more healthy students are turning to these drugs in hopes of augmenting their ability to handle their academic challenges.

A 2014 survey conducted by the Partnership for Drug-Free Kids sampled 1,621 participants between the ages of 18 and 25. The organization reported that the misuse and abuse of prescription drugs are becoming normalized, as students take advantage of the stimulants to juggle their academic, work, and social responsibilities. Fifty percent of the young adults surveyed reported that they abused prescription stimulants to study or improve academic performance, with 64 percent of the students self-reporting that they believed the drugs actually helped them improve their academic performance. The study also found that young adults perceived the misuse of prescription stimulants as less risky than abusing prescription painkillers, cigarettes, or alcohol. Researchers surmised that students minimize their concern about long-term harm in exchange for short-term gains in their academic scores (Feliz, 2014). In short, students find themselves willing to misuse prescription drugs to more efficiently manage their academic workload.

Finally, academic stress may push students toward academic dishonesty. According to the "2012 Report Card on the Ethics of American Youth," a survey of 23,000 U.S. high school students conducted by the Josephson Institute Center for Youth Ethics, 52 percent of high school students admitted to cheating on a test at school in the previous year, with 24 percent stating that they cheated "only once" and 28 percent stating "two or more times." Furthermore, 32 percent of students admitted to "plagiarizing an Internet document for a classroom assignment," and 74 percent admitted to copying another student's homework (Josephson Institute of Ethics, 2012).

The numbers became even more concerning following college matriculation. According to a survey conducted by former Rutgers University business professor

Don McCabe, out of 18,177 undergraduates, 33 percent self-reported committing academic misconduct in their classes by "learning what is on a test from someone who has already taken it"; 16 percent admitted to using a "false excuse to delay taking a test"; and 11 percent stated that they had copied "from another student on a test/exam without their knowledge" in the past year (McCabe, 2005). Moreover, a 2009 survey revealed that out of 273 alumni, more than 81 percent self-reported engaging in some form of cheating during college (Yardley, 2009).

In a forum sponsored by Stanford University's Program in Ethics and Society, panelists linked academic dishonesty to the pressure that students face to value grades over actual education, learning, and creativity (Palmer, 2005). Through academic stress created by a misplaced emphasis on grades, many students opt to cheat themselves out of a true education.

ADDITIONAL ACADEMIC STRESS FOR UNDERREPRESENTED MINORITIES

Underrepresented minorities face additional sources of academic pressure, both inside and outside of the classroom setting. For instance, negative stereotypes can turn into real stumbling blocks for underrepresented minority students, who are "at risk of confirming, as self-characteristic, a negative stereotype about one's group," a phenomenon that psychologists refer to as a *stereotype threat* (Steele & Aronson, 1995). Stereotype threats can adversely affect a student's academic performance by providing disincentives; for instance, an underrepresented minority student who believes that those from his or her race, ethnicity, or gender are "typically not good at math" is more likely to have problems in a math course. In this sense, the stereotype—as untrue as it may be—is realized as a destructive, self-fulfilling prophecy.

Furthermore, according to the Higher Education Research Institute at UCLA, many underrepresented minorities matriculate into college with a lower high school GPA, fewer years of high school math and science coursework, and more concerns about financing their education than non-underrepresented students, making it more difficult for minority students to make the transition to college life. Underrepresented minorities also spend more hours working during high school and are more likely to work full-time during college and have less time to devote to their education. Yet another challenge faced by these students may include a lack of role models (Hurtado, Newman, Tran, & Chang, 2010). Taking all of these factors together, these psychological and economic realities pose additional academic hurdles for underrepresented minorities in college.

HOW STUDENTS CAN TACKLE ACADEMIC STRESS

Fortunately, students can effectively manage their stress by adopting proven methods such as applying time management skills, keeping a stress journal, and maintaining a sense of self-affirmation. For instance, researchers who surveyed 249 full-time undergraduate students at a midwestern university observed that "time management behaviors had a greater buffering effect on academic stress than leisure satisfaction activities." Students who employed time management strategies—or merely perceived that they had control over their own schedules—reported fewer physical and psychological symptoms of stress. Moreover, students who felt they had a better handle on time control typically demonstrated a positive self-image and performed better on tests (Misra & McKean, 2000). The researchers suggested that advisors should "emphasize participation in time management seminars" to equip students with skills that can help them to improve their academic performance and effectively manage stress.

Furthermore, researchers have also demonstrated that students who wrote down their worries on paper ahead of the test were able to think less of their worries during the test and free up working memory, thereby helping the students to focus on the tasks at hand (Ramirez & Beilock, 2011).

Finally, especially in the context of high-stakes testing situations, students can also better manage stress through self-affirmation. In a 2013 study, researchers tested 73 undergraduate students who were asked to complete "30 difficult remote associate problem-solving items." Research participants in the self-affirmation condition were asked to rank values that were important to them and to elaborate on why their most highly ranked value was important to them. Students who performed the self-affirmation exercise improved over students who admitted to being chronically stressed for a month before the test was administered. Researchers suggested that the exercise helped students to protect their self-image while undergoing a difficult task, thereby allowing those individuals to manage the resulting stress effectively (Creswell, Dutcher, Klein, Harris, & Levine, 2013).

Overall, academic institutions offer a myriad of support services for individuals struggling with stress, and students can take the initiative to take advantage of those resources, such as academic counselors, psychological or health services, academic or learning skills centers, and the like.

CONCLUSION

Stress is an inevitable part of school, as well as life in general. However, if a student cannot cope effectively with academic stress and other related stressors, the accumulated psychological burden can result in deleterious consequences, ranging from a lack of focus in high-stakes testing situations to dropping out of high school or college. Because academic stress is a ubiquitous issue among students in the United States, high schools and institutions of higher educations are uniquely suited to help students manage stress and mitigate its impact. If students are taught to adopt and wield the skills they need to conquer academic stress, the same techniques will help them to tackle other demanding situations later in their lives.

REFERENCES AND FURTHER READING

Baddeley, A. (1992). Working memory. *Science, 255*(5044), 556–559.

Beilock, S. L. (2008). Math performance in stressful situations. *Current Directions in Psychological Science, 17*(5), 339–343.

Conner, J., Pope, D., & Galloway, M. (2009). Success with less stress. *Health and Learning, 67*(4), 54–58.

Creswell, J. D., Dutcher, J., Klein, W., Harris, P., & Levine, J. (2013). Self-affirmation improves problem-solving under stress. *PloS* one, *8*(5), e62593. doi:10.1371/journal.pone.0062593.

Doll, J. J. Eslami, Z., & Walters, L. (2013). Understanding why students drop out of high school, according to their own reports. *SAGE Open, 3*(4). doi:10.1177/2158244013503834.

Feliz, J. (2014, November 13). New survey: Misuse and abuse of prescription stimulants becoming normalized behavior among college students, young adults. *Partnership for Drug-Free Kids.* Retrieved from http://www.drugfree.org/newsroom/adhd-survey-2014.

Hoban, M. (2007). American College Health Association National College Health Assessment Spring 2006 reference group data report (abridged). *Journal of American College Health, 55*(4). Retrieved from http://www.acha-ncha.org/docs/JACH%20January%202007%20SP%2006%20Ref%20Grp.pdf.

Hurtado, S., Newman, C. B., Tran, M. C., & Chang, M. J. (2010). Improving the rate of success for underrepresented racial minorities in STEM fields: Insights from a national project. *New Directions for Institutional Research, 148,* 5–15.

Johnson, J., & Rochkind, J. (2009). With their whole lives ahead of them: Myths and realities about why so many students fail to finish college (Public Agenda Report). Retrieved from http://www.publicagenda.org/files/theirwholelivesaheadofthem.pdf.

Josephson Institute of Ethics. (2012, November). 2012 report card on the ethics of American youth. Retrieved from https://charactercounts.org/wp-content/uploads/2014/02/ReportCard-2012-DataTables.pdf.

McCabe, D. L. (2005). Cheating among college and university students: A North American perspective. *International Journal for Educational Integrity, 1*(1). Retrieved from http://www.ojs.unisa.edu.au/index.php/IJEI/article/view/14.

Misra, R., & McKean, M. (2000). College students' academic stress and its relation to their anxiety, time management, and leisure satisfaction. *American Journal of Health Studies, 16*(1), 41–51.

Palmer, B. (2005, February 23). Pressure for good grades often leads to high stress, cheating, professors say. *Stanford News*. Retrieved from http://news.stanford.edu/news/2005/february23/cheat-022305.html.

Ramirez, G., & Beilock, S. L. (2011). Writing about testing worries boosts exam performance in the classroom. *Science, 331*(6014), 211–213.

Ross, S. E., Niebling, B. C., & Heckert, T. M. (1999). Sources of stress among college students. *Social Psychology, 61*(5), 841–846.

Schwartz, A. J. (2006). College student suicide in the United States: 1990–1991 through 2003–2004. *Journal of American College Health, 54*(6), 341–352.

Steele, C. M., & Aronson, J. (1995). Stereotype threat and the intellectual test performance of African Americans. *Journal of Personality and Social Psychology, 69*(5), 797–811.

Yardley, J., Domenech Rodriguez, M. M., Nelson, J., & Bates, S. C. (2009). True confessions?: Alumni's retrospective reports on undergraduate cheating behaviors. *Ethics and Behavior, 19*(1), 1–14.

22

Caregiver Stress

Rachel Dubrow

Questions about how to provide care for others who are declining in their level of functioning, and whether or not to seek out assistance from others, are not unfamiliar and frequently become a topic of conversation and a source of stress. Most caregivers must find new ways to define their roles, cope with added stressors, and learn more effective ways to work through problems that arise in caregiving. This chapter explores the historical significance of caregiving, defines and describes the types of caregiver stress, explains ways of coping with caregiver stress, and concludes with a brief look at caregiving in the future.

HISTORICAL SIGNIFICANCE OF CAREGIVING

Newbern (1994) argued that throughout history, women have assumed the caregiving role for those around them. Their ability to provide this care proved to be essential during the most trying times in United States history, from the period of colonial America, the time of slavery and the Civil War, and through the Great Depression and World Wars I and II. Although most of this role centered on providing medical care, women also educated future generations in an attempt to pass along knowledge, skill, and expertise. As a result, some caregiving approaches and rituals rooted in historical methods are often combined with more modern medicine and treatments.

DEFINING CARE

Care is a cyclical long-term process that evolves over time. Every person will require care at different times in life, depending on his or her needs and abilities;

many people will also assume the caregiving role. Infants and young children require care that is centered on the individual and is unidirectional, meaning the child is the recipient and the caregiver is the provider. The primary caregiver is often a mother, father, grandparent, or guardian. As the child grows and matures, this network of caregivers expands to include teachers, clergy, extended family, friends of the family, and other children (Talley & Montgomery, 2013).

When children become adults, they may have children of their own and/or have to care for an aging parent or family member, and thus become caregivers themselves. This dual role of caring for oneself and others is shaped by past experiences and the needs of care recipients. Gonzalez, Polansky, Lippa, Walker, and Feng (2011) report common sociodemographic factors that affect how one provides care (age, gender, education level, ethnicity, employment, income, and the type of relationship to the individual receiving care), and note that each factor affects the caregiving dynamic in a unique way. For example, family caregivers will approach caretaking responsibilities differently than a caregiver who is employed by an outside agency, because of the relationship they have with the care recipient.

As the needs of the care recipient change, caregivers may choose to utilize community- or agency-based supports to provide additional care and services. Examples of these supports include adult day care, skilled nursing facilities, federally funded housekeeping or meal programs, subsidized caretaking services in the home, and respite care at an extended care facility. All of these supports offer distinct services to those in need, but are often based on the financial resources of the care recipient and any outside contributions. The choice to involve individuals outside the family to provide care is personal and involves both coordination and participation by the care recipient.

TYPES OF CAREGIVER STRESS

According to Son et al. (2007), caregivers are more likely to experience negative health outcomes as a result of their role than those who do not assume a caregiving role. This can add a heightened level of stress as caregivers balance their own medical care needs in addition to the needs of the care recipient. Consequently, caregivers are referred to as the "hidden patients," as they may face multiple physical and emotional effects of providing care to others over a period of time (Schulz & Beach, 1999; Gonzalez et al., 2011).

Physical

Providing physical care to another individual can cause varying levels of physical stress. Caregivers who provide homemaking services (cooking, cleaning, etc.) may experience fatigue and physical soreness, especially if they simultaneously have to provide this service for themselves and their families. Performing personal care duties, such as assisting with bathing, dressing, and/or mobility, incontinence, and other medical conditions can create different levels of physical stress for the caregiver. Caregivers risk physical injury while performing these duties, which is largely dependent on physical strength and ability. Utilizing assistive devices, such as walkers, wheelchairs, and bedside commodes, may assist caregivers and lessen the physical impact of providing care.

Additionally, caregivers often perceive that their physical health is worse than that of non-caregivers. Individuals who consistently experience chronic and intense stress will place more physical demands on their bodies, which may lead to chronic diseases such as high blood pressure (hypertension) and an elevation in cholesterol levels (Clark, Bond, & Hecker, 2007).

Financial

Care provision for an individual across the life span has several financial dimensions and must be considered for services that family members are unable to provide, such as medical, social, and educational activities, as well as pharmaceutical and therapeutic services. These considerations may add pressure, especially when money is limited, because they directly impact how the care recipient's needs are prioritized. In these cases, extended family and/or outside service agencies often become involved as a way of trying to decrease the stress of making financially based decisions on behalf of a care recipient (Strawbridge, Wallhagen, Shema, & Kaplan, 1997).

Environmental

Caregivers and care recipients must consider the environment in which care will take place. The unique needs of each care recipient must be met in order for that person to remain in a safe environment that is conducive to care. To illustrate, if an individual requires a ramp or railing for safety, that equipment must be installed as soon as possible. If in-home supervision is required, caregivers will have to be secured and trained on the specific needs of the care recipient, housing will have to be arranged, and the new surroundings may have to be adjusted for an outside caregiver.

Families often take on the responsibility of caring for a family member in their homes, for reasons of convenience and comfort. When this happens, the same principles apply in regard to meeting the care recipient's needs and ensuring safety in the home. The dual adjustment for both the caregiver and care recipient is an integral part of making the caregiving arrangement successful. However, if caregivers move away from their families, there may be a period of sadness and guilt or worry.

Readiness

Deciding to become a caregiver

Assuming the caregiving role can be emotionally stressful, and individuals must consider their emotional state before deciding to do so. It is helpful for potential caregivers to evaluate their readiness to take on additional responsibilities, such as driving the care recipient to doctors' appointments, purchasing groceries, and assisting with bathing, dressing, and feeding. Sometimes care recipients feel uncomfortable with opposite-sex caregivers providing intimate care, such as bathing and dressing, and these issues must be considered as well. Furthermore, caregivers need to think about what they are capable of doing and what may require additional assistance. Recognizing these limits provides a framework for potential caregivers to use in the decision-making process.

Adjusting to the caregiving role

Individuals often feel overwhelmed in the early stages of care provision because of the sudden shift in focus from caring for oneself to providing care for others. Aneshensel, Pearlin, Mullan, Zarit, and Whitlatch (1995) describe the varying levels of care provision, ranging from providing informal care for a relative who is largely independent but has some mild or moderate cognitive impairment, to providing continuous care for a relative who has a terminal illness or moderate to severe cognitive impairment. Due to personal characteristics and infirmities, each care recipient will have a different level of dependency on the caregiver. The emotional impact of this depends on each individual and ranges from mild to severe symptoms of distress.

Care recipients may exhibit adjustment behaviors, which include isolation, anger, or disorientation, in response to having a caregiver in their homes or moving to a new home. Gonzalez et al. (2011) explain that caregivers must consider the objective indictors of stress, such as the care recipient's behavior and the reaction to having another individual assist with daily living activities. Moreover, caregivers have their own subjective experience of providing care, in which they contemplate the perceived emotional burden of these stressors. The combination of the care recipient's response and the caregiver's perception can cause emotional distress for both individuals involved. This may be exacerbated by the relationship the caregiver and care recipient had with each other before and during the initiation of care.

Social

Balancing social responsibilities can be difficult for caregivers. Being a caregiver can be socially stressful because of how potentially isolating it may be at times, especially if the care recipient requires 24-hour care. The physical and emotional exhaustion of providing care leaves less time for caregivers to focus on themselves and their families. As a result, anger and resentment may build up toward the care recipient, because this individual is viewed (consciously or unconsciously) as the cause of the social isolation (Knussen et al., 2008).

Grief

Care recipients and caregivers alike may experience grief as the care recipient's condition deteriorates, especially if they have a close relationship with one another. Each individual will likely go through different phases of the grief process, ranging from denial to anger to acceptance. As a result, the relationship between the care recipient and caregiver can change as one or both experience this process. Caregivers might experience positive feelings of gratitude, acceptance, and appreciation during their time with the care recipient and often reflect on this during the grieving process. Furthermore, the level of emotional intimacy during the grieving process depends on the relationship between the caregiver and care recipient (spouse, parent, child, sibling, or extended family), and grieving may begin before the care recipient passes away.

Mental attitude and approach

A caregiver's mental attitude and approach directly affect his or her stress levels. Knussen et al. (2008) describe the relationship between caregiver stress and coping by explaining that caregivers experience lower stress levels when they take a problem-solving approach to care. This includes tackling daily challenges as they occur and accepting the current situation as it is. Creating steadfast daily routines helps both parties as well. For example, caregivers who are continually struggling to feed a care recipient will have lower stress levels if they problem-solve when the issue arises and alter their feeding approach instead of avoiding the feeding issue altogether.

Using positive coping skills instead of avoidance may provide a sense of control for the caregiver, which can also alleviate some anxiety. Examples of positive coping skills for both caregiver and care recipient include practicing relaxation exercises, doing daily physical exercise, and taking up hobbies to stay both intellectually and interpersonally stimulated, both of which also help combat depression.

Circumstantial depression often afflicts care recipients as well, as they cope with the changes in their conditions and their increased need for assistance. Depression can lead to further neurodegeneration in care recipients with dementia, which poses a challenge for care recipients and caregivers alike (Knussen et al., 2008). The emotional needs of the care recipient may affect the mental attitude of the caregiver, which, in turn, will impact both individuals' overall mental health.

Mental health

As mentioned earlier, caring for a relative poses emotional challenges. Caregivers may find that they are experiencing symptoms of depression, such as feeling hopeless, helpless, or worthless, or that they have lost interest in their own activities, as a result of providing continuous care. Many caregivers turn to family or friends for emotional support and guidance. When these symptoms become intense, they may also seek professional mental health care from a psychotherapist and/or psychiatrist.

Substances such as alcohol or recreational drugs are sometimes used as a coping skill, and may become an issue if the caregiver uses them to excess or grows dependent on them. Precautions should be taken to ensure that the caregiver is able to appropriately provide necessary care and not endanger the care recipient. If substance use does become an issue, caregivers should consider an alternative arrangement for care and seek mental health treatment until they are able to safely carry out the necessary caregiving tasks.

COPING WITH CAREGIVER STRESS

BURNOUT

Caregiver burnout is a common issue among caregivers. *Burnout* in caregiving is defined as physical and emotional exhaustion as a result of providing care for someone else; it often occurs when caregivers try to provide care for others without taking into account their own physical and emotional needs (Clark, Bond, & Hecker, 2007). When this happens, the risk of health complications increases and the caregiver's ability to care for the care recipient, such as a relative in need, may be compromised. As a result, there may be an increase in elder abuse and neglect, ranging from not providing adequate care to physical harm to financial exploitation. Because of this, caregivers often seek out support groups, many of which are sponsored by nonprofit agencies such as the Alzheimer's Association, or local hospitals.

Seeking either short- or long-term care options may help alleviate the stress of providing continual care. This may involve asking other family members to assist with caregiving tasks and using social support for emotional well-being. It may also include utilizing skilled nursing facilities for respite care, or short-term care that may or may not include physical, occupational, or speech therapies. Adult day care is also an option for some care recipients if they qualify for specialized programming, such as memory care, and can provide caregivers some relief during the day. Furthermore, private-duty caregivers can provide relief to familial caregivers if financial means are available.

Sharing the Caregiving Role with a Sibling

One way to alleviate caregiving stress is to enlist assistance from other relatives, specifically siblings. Merrill (1997) explains the network that siblings often form depending on the relationship they have with each other. This network may be useful in coordinating how care is provided, developing a schedule of when care is provided and by whom, and offering emotional support throughout the caregiving process. In contrast, siblings who do not have this network may find themselves feeling more alone, isolated, or facing conflict (Merrill, 1997). This is why it is important to reach out to additional relatives or family members for support as needed.

Working Caregivers

Neal and Wagner (2002) state that "working caregivers, like their non-working counterparts, are providing essential long-term services to older adults who otherwise would be dependent upon public or private formal systems of care" (p. 1). As a result, working caregivers often have a dual role of being an employee and caregiver simultaneously. For some, the caregiving role involves daily check-ins for relatives in need or stopping by to prepare meals after work. For others, it involves more constant care, which raises a serious question as to whether the caregiver can continue to do both. The rise in healthcare costs often influences whether continuing to work is a necessity.

Statistics show that working caregivers provide levels of care to the care recipients similar to those who are not working. However, male working caregivers typically provide less care than their female counterparts. Additionally, Neal and Wagner (2002) state that working caregivers are more likely to care for elderly parents than they are for their spouses, due to finances. Working caregivers in the "sandwich generation" are also tasked with caring for their children and older relatives simultaneously (Neal & Wagner, 2002). The needs of the care recipient and finances are often the deciding factors in whether a caregiver can continue to hold a job.

Assuming this dual role has both positive and negative effects on the well-being of the caregiver. Some caregivers believe that working provides a respite from caring for a relative during the day, in addition to financial gains. In contrast, some find that the added caregiving responsibility leads to more social isolation and possible loss of communal support (Son et al., 2007; Neal & Wagner, 2002). The stress of work and caregiving is also known to increase the likelihood of health problems and must be considered as well.

Providing Care to an Ill Child

Parents with an ill child face unique caregiving stressors depending on the nature of the illness. If a child is sick for a short period of time, parents might find the caregiving role less stressful than if the child has a long-term illness or one that is terminal in nature. The multiple responsibilities that parents generally have, such as working, providing for other children in the home, and maintaining a relationship with a significant other, often take precedence over self-care. Over time, parents may feel burnt out and lose focus on living a healthy lifestyle, which includes eating a balanced diet, exercising, and utilizing individual psychotherapy and support groups that focus on caring for an ill child. Seeking assistance from others for running errands may be helpful for parents who must manage multiple children's schedules (Canning, Harris, & Kelleher, 1996).

Providing Care to a Terminally Ill Relative

The relationship a caregiver has with a terminally ill relative may not change as a result of the diagnosis and prognosis. However, the caregiver's role may shift from providing more physical care to being an emotional support for the relative. If hospice care is involved, the hospice agency will provide additional support to the caregivers in addition to the care recipient, which often decreases stress levels throughout the dying process.

Providing Care to a Relative with Memory Loss

Caring for a relative with memory loss poses unique challenges, for both the care recipient and the caregiver, because of how this condition manifests itself (Knussen et al., 2008). In the early stages of memory loss, care recipients might recognize their cognitive decline and become frustrated, sad, or angry. As a result, they may project these emotions onto the caregiver, causing tension in the caregiving relationship. Care recipients may also feel resentment toward their caregivers due to the significant strain and burden that stem from becoming a care recipient with reduced adaptive functioning. Requiring care signifies their diminished capacity to care for themselves, role change, and loss of independence. Thus, care recipients may experience subsequent feelings of bereavement, such as emotional withdrawal, sadness, denial, shame, agitation, and helplessness. They might even blame their caregivers for their situations. Furthermore, caregivers who watch their relatives go through a cognitive decline may also feel similar emotions and may want to seek guidance from a mental health professional.

As the memory loss progresses, caregivers may experience a change in caregiving tasks. For example, they may have to provide continence care for an incontinent relative or put in more caregiving hours if the care recipient becomes prone to wandering. This often causes fear and frustration for caregivers, especially if they do not provide 24-hour supervision or if they work during the day and care is delegated to a different caregiver or agency. Caregivers will often seek respite care for their relatives or decide to place them in a skilled nursing facility that has a memory care unit to ensure safety and provide some emotional relief from the stress of providing this care routinely.

CAREGIVING CONSIDERATIONS FOR THE FUTURE

There is a high likelihood that current adults will have longer life spans, given the significant medical advances that have occurred over the past century. This, in combination with fluctuating birth rates, may lead to an increased need for caregiving support over time. Although caregiving stressors will likely remain much the same, the ways in which they are handled by caregivers, care recipients, and outside agencies may change over time due to family dynamics and the economy (Jacobs, 2006). Families that were once able to care for their relatives may find that they cannot continue to meet this need, or realize that they will need to seek outside agency support. The state of the economy will continue to impact the decisions caregivers and care recipients make in regard to access to care and emotional well-being. Though the precedent of providing care will not change, care delivery may change, and caregivers and care recipients alike will be directly affected.

REFERENCES AND FURTHER READING

Aneshensel, C. S., Pearlin, L. I., Mullan, J. T., Zarit, S. H., & Whitlatch, C. J. (1995). *Profiles in caregiving: The unexpected career.* San Diego, CA: Academic Press.

Canning, R., Harris, E., & Kelleher, K. (1996). Factors predicting distress among caregivers to children with chronic medical conditions. *Journal of Pediatric Psychology, 21*(5), 735–749.

Clark, M., Bond, M., & Hecker, J. R. (2007). Environmental stress, psychological stress and allostatic load. *Psychology, Health and Medicine, 12*(1), 18–30.

Gonzalez, E. W., Polansky, M., Lippa, C. F., Walker, D., & Feng, D. (2011). Family caregivers at risk: Who are they? *Issues in Mental Health Nursing, 32*(8), 528–536.

Jacobs, B. J. (2006). *The emotional survival guide for caregivers.* New York, NY: he Guilford Press.

Knussen, C., Tolson, D., Brogan, C., Swan, I., Stott, D., & Sullivan, F. (2008). Family caregivers of older relatives: Ways of coping and change in distress. *Psychology, Health and Medicine, 13*(3), 274–290.

Merrill, D. M. (1997). *Caring for elderly parents: Juggling work, family, and caregiving in middle and working class families.* Westport, CT: Auburn House.

Neal, M. B., & Wagner, D. L. (2002). Working caregivers: Issues, challenges, and opportunities for the aging network. *National Family Caregiver Support Program Issue Brief* 1–31.

Newbern, V. B. (1994). Women as caregivers in the South, 1900–1945. *Public Health Nursing, 11*(4), 247–254.

Schulz, R., & Beach, S. (1999). Caregiving as a risk factor for mortality. *Journal of the American Medical Association, 282,* 2215–2219.

Son, J., Erno, A., Shea, D., Femia, E., Zarit, S., & Stephens, M. (2007). The caregiver stress process and health outcomes. *Journal of Aging and Health, 19,* 871–887.

Strawbridge, W. J., Wallhagen, M. I., Shema, S. J., & Kaplan, G. A. (1997). New burdens or more of the same? Comparing grandparent, spouse, and adult-child caregivers. *The Gerontologist, 37*(4), 505–510.

Talley, R. C., & Montgomery, R. J. V. (2013). Caregiving: A developmental, life-long perspective. In R. C. Talley & R. J. V. Montgomery (Eds.), *Caregiving across the lifespan: Research, practice, policy* (pp. 3–10). New York, NY: Springer.

23

SEXUALITY AND STRESS

Raven Lynn Badger

Sexuality is linked to stress in numerous ways. Before those connections are discussed, though, it is important first to have a definite conceptualization of *sexuality*. There are several ways in which sexuality can be viewed, and these views are based on a myriad of variables. Sex or sexuality is often conceptualized as the act of intercourse. Sex can also be viewed as a person's biological makeup: if someone is born with XX chromosomes, and has a vulva, clitoris, vagina, labia, uterus, and ovaries, that person is typically referred to as female; if someone is born with XY chromosomes, and has a penis, scrotum, and testicles, the person is usually referred to as male. If a person is born with other variations of chromosomes, that person's biological sex will be impacted in numerous ways, such as atypical sexual development, infertility or sterility, and accompanying psychological and social-emotional stressors.

We live in a society that is sexually secretive, sexually ignorant, and sexually traumatized (James, 2012). Living in this world of negative sexual perceptions contributes greatly to the stress that surrounds sexuality. Other sexuality-related causes of stress include, but are not limited to, having negative self-image, relationships, the inability to reproduce, acquiring sexually transmitted infections (STIs) or HIV, infidelity in committed relationships, rape, incest, sexual harassment, sexual dysfunctions, sexual orientation, intimacy issues, and lack of knowledge about sexual techniques. Incorporating a broad spectrum of sexuality provides a more comprehensive picture of how complex the relationships are between external sexual events or nonevents (e.g., first sexual experience, rape, infertility) and subsequent psychological responses to external events.

Causality surrounding stress and sexuality is not one-way. What results has commonly been referred to as "the chicken or the egg" syndrome—that is, what came first? In some cases, stress impacts sex, sexuality, or sexual health. In other cases, sexuality issues can create an environment of stress based on social conditions or societal expectations. An important factor is knowledge of how inextricably linked stress and sexuality can be at times. The remainder of this chapter describes sex-related stress by explaining the most commonly recognized associations of stress and stress-related events to some of the aforementioned sexuality variables. Both causal and bidirectional linkages are explored (again, the chicken and the egg).

SEXUAL IDENTITY AS A STRESSOR

The concept of social stress extends stress theory by suggesting that conditions in the social environment, not only personal events, are sources of stress that may lead to mental and physical ill effects (Ranabir & Reetu, 2011). Social stress might therefore be expected to have a strong impact in the lives of people belonging to stigmatized social categories, including categories related to socioeconomic status, race/ethnicity, gender, or sexuality. According to these formulations, prejudice and discrimination related to low socioeconomic status, racism, sexism, or homophobia—much like the changes precipitated by personal life events that are common to all people—can induce changes that require adaptation and can therefore be conceptualized as stressful (Allison, 1998; Clark, Anderson, Clark, & Williams, 1999; Meyer, 1995; Pearlin, 1999).

The lived experiences of sexual minorities are often accompanied by daily stigma and discrimination based on societal expectations of human sexual behavior and gender. Lesbian, gay, and bisexual individuals often experience what has been termed *minority stress*. Minority stress posits that groups of people who are not the majority in a culture (usually groups defined by race, ethnicity, and/or gender) experience discrimination based on their minority status and that the effects of minority stress can lead to adverse mental health outcomes. In developing the concept of minority stress, researchers' underlying assumptions have been that minority stress is unique—that is, minority stress is an addition to the general stressors that are experienced by all people, and therefore stigmatized people must make an adaptation effort above that required of similar others who are not stigmatized; chronic—that is, minority stress is a phenomenon that occurs over the life span and does not remain stable over time in society; and socially based—that is, it stems from social processes, institutions, and structures beyond the individual rather than individual events or conditions. With regard to lesbian, gay, bisexual, and transgender (LGBT) persons, the experiences of sexual prejudice are stressful and can result in adverse health outcomes (Cochran, 2001; DiPlacido, 1998; Herek, 2000; Mays & Cochran, 2001; Meyer, 1995).

Processes related to LGBT persons and minority stress include external stressors from life events, internal perceptions and acceptance of one's sexual identity, expectations of negative events and the vigilance this requires, and the concealment of one's sexual identity. Hiding sexual orientation from others can be utilized as a coping strategy, but can take an emotional toll on the person's psyche as a result. Some mediators for ameliorating sexual minority stress include identification with the "larger" group identity to sustain cohesiveness and solidarity, coming out to safe and supportive people, and developing a sense of self-acceptance (Hershberger & D'Augelli, 1995). Internalized stress from sexual identity and living in a culture that is not welcoming to LGBT identity can create numerous health and mental health problems, including negative self-image and internalized homophobia (a form of self-loathing).

OBESITY, NEGATIVE BODY IMAGE, AND STRESS

Body image is a component of sexuality and can be defined as how individuals' perceptions of their bodies affects their sexual response and relationships (James, 2012). Negative body image can lead to stress-related conditions. The construct of body image has been defined as a multidimensional attitude toward one's body that includes perceptual, affective, and cognitive components. However, the current emphasis of research concerning body image is on shape, weight, and the degree to which individuals are satisfied with their appearance (Cash, Ancis, & Strachan, 1997).

The links between sexuality and obesity have been well documented. In a 2006 study that examined the impact of obesity on sexual health outcomes (e.g., sexual satisfaction, sexual activity) of more than 12,000 individuals, several significant findings were noted (Nauert, 2010). Obese women were more likely to experience unintended pregnancy due to their lack of contraceptive use when compared to women of healthy body mass index (BMI), even though the obese sample had fewer sexual partners. This finding is explained in terms of social desirability: women were willing to put themselves at risk in order to be more desirable to available sex partners. Obese women were also five times as likely to have met their partner on the Internet, more likely to have an obese partner, and less likely to view sex as important for personal life balance. The authors suggested that social pressure, low self-esteem, and concerns about body image may help explain these findings. Obesity can also result in infertility and difficulty in conceiving, which in and of itself creates stress (Norman, 2010).

For men, obesity was associated with higher rates of sexually transmitted infections (STIs), fewer sexual partners, and erectile dysfunction. Obese men were 70 percent less likely to have had more than one sexual partner in a 12-month period than normal-weight men, and were two and one-half times more likely to experience erectile dysfunction. Obese men under the age of 30 were found to have higher rates of STIs than normal-BMI men under age 30. Studies have linked abdominal obesity to erectile dysfunction, especially in older men. They suggest that having a BMI of 28 increased a man's risks of developing erectile dysfunction by 90 percent (Harvard Men's Health Watch, 2011). Losing weight, in contrast, is linked to improvement in symptoms. Obesity in men is also directly linked to low frequency of sexual intercourse.

Obesity, negative body image, and sexuality are inextricably linked and illustrate the "chicken and egg" syndrome, with each both contributing to and being exacerbated by stress. It appears that sexual health risks associated with obesity are linked in part to stress-related factors. Negative self-image can contribute to weight gain, obesity, and sexual risk-taking in both men and women (Nauert, 2010). Stress, in particular chronic stress, can affect a person's metabolism, deplete hormones that discourage weight gain, and contribute to poor health outcomes.

Of course, individuals need not be obese to hold negative perceptions of their bodies. The prevalence of body dissatisfaction is being termed a *normative discontent* (Forman & Davis, 2005). What this suggests is that it is an extremely common trait—at any age—to be anxious about the body to some degree. Societal influences include the media, peer influence, and family, as well as shifts in cultural norms over time. Media plays a big role in perpetuating myths concerning beauty and attractiveness, particularly for young adolescent women. These influences can result in stress when individuals do not feel that they meet these perceived societal norms. Negative body image and body dissatisfaction have been implicated as being both stressful and risk factors for various forms of psychopathology, including depression, anxiety, and disordered eating (Forman & Davis, 2005).

REPRODUCTIVE ISSUES AND STRESS

Sexuality issues related to reproduction can result in stress. In psychological literature, *stressors* are defined as events and conditions (e.g., sexual abuse, death of a romantic partner, infertility) that cause change and that require the individual to adapt to the new situation or life circumstance. Stress researchers have studied traumatic events, eventful life stressors, chronic stress, and role strains, as well as daily hassles and even nonevents as varied components of stress (Dohrenwend, 2000).

Examples of nonevents are life events that are expected to occur in the life span, but due to their inability to manifest are stressful by not happening; infertility is a primary example. Fertility issues take a psychological and emotional toll on people who want families, but are unable to conceive due to biological circumstances. The process of fertility counseling and treatment is stressful, given the often lengthy process of testing and evaluating both partners, the invasiveness of treatment, and subsequent failures to conceive. The strength of attachment to the idea of bearing children can create great distress in both men and women and over time chronic stress can exacerbate infertility.

Chronic stress can impact the pituitary gland, which controls the thyroid, adrenal glands, and ovaries. When the ovaries are not functioning properly, a woman's menstrual cycle is adversely affected. Her menstrual cycle may become irregular, or she may experience amenorrhea (absence of menstruation). If the menstrual irregularities are stress-induced, fertility problems are typically not permanent, and the reduction of stress can reverse fertility outcomes. In males, there can be decreased sperm count and motility. Ejaculatory disorders, impotence, and low sperm count may be associated with psychological factors in male infertility (Chrousos, 2009).

Women, in particular, are vulnerable to numerous adverse mental health outcomes as a result of being diagnosed as infertile, such as depression, alcoholism, and, in rare cases, suicide. There is a great societal pressure for women to reproduce; in fact, many religions have historical roots originating from a procreative view of sex—that is, that sexual intercourse should be for the purpose of reproducing, nothing more. Some strict religious traditions continue in this belief. This historical view of the role of women in societies may contribute to a deep internal sense of shame when faced with the nonevent of infertility. A sense of sexual shame can bring with it numerous mental health risks, if left untreated, which contribute to sexual dysfunction, lack of sexual desire, intimacy problems, and relationship avoidance.

SEXUALITY AND SEXUAL TRAUMA

Sexuality can be impeded by sexual trauma in ways similar to fertility (e.g., sexual dysfunctions, depression, intimacy problems). The effects of sexual trauma can last a lifetime and affect individuals' abilities to form healthy relationships and thrive. Factors that impact the severity of stressful outcomes include the type of sexual trauma, the severity of the experience, the chronic nature of the trauma (whether it was a one-time event, or occurred repeatedly over years), age of onset, and the survivor's ability to be resilient and find supportive resources. So, individuals' experiences of sexual trauma can result in stress when attempting to heal from negative events, and adversely affect their ability to form healthy and trusting relationships.

Early sexual trauma can profoundly affect the course of a person's sexual development. These traumas, depending on their nature, severity, and age of onset, can create dysfunctional patterns of behavior, ranging from sexual dysfunction and anxiety, to sexual compulsivity and re-enacting, to disturbing sexual thoughts and obsessions. Traumatic events, whether acute or chronic, can disrupt an individual's ability to form healthy relationships with important persons in the individual's environment (Spaccarelli, 1994). Sexual dysfunctions and compulsive sexual behaviors are often unconscious defense strategies employed by an individual to regulate the stress and anxiety around intimacy. A man who was sexually abused as a child may experience continued stress and develop erectile dysfunction as a result; similarly, a woman with past sexual trauma may experience dyspareunia (painful sex) as a result of stress when thinking about being sexual with a partner. Sexual trauma can result in stress-induced outcomes; psychotherapy can be utilized in the discovery and healing process.

LIBIDO AND STRESS

What is libido? Terms that are synonymous with libido include sexual appetite, sexual impulse, sexual interest, desire, and sexual drive (Levin, 1994). *Libido* is a Latin word that means "desire." Libido differs from sexual arousal in that sexual desire pertains to an attitude toward an object, whereas sexual arousal is a state of being in which specific feelings are usually associated with the genitals. These two terms are distinguishable from one another, as it is possible to have sexual desire without arousal and sexual arousal without desire. Libido is what motivates a person to obtain sex with a focus toward that goal. It is a subjective experience accompanied by physiological changes, many of which are in preparation for sexual behavior (Bancroft, 1988). A useful working definition is that *sexual desire,* or *libido,* is "normally an activated, unsatisfied mental state of variable intensity, created by . . . external (via sensory modalities) or internal stimuli (e.g. fantasy, memory, cognition) that induces a feeling of a need or want to partake of sexual activity (usually with the subject of desire) to satisfy the need" (Levin, 1994, p. 131).

Low libido can result in stress, particularly for men, who are traditionally viewed as the sexual initiator or aggressor in relationships. The inability to initiate sex in a relationship or the lack of desire to be sexual in men is often internalized as the belief that "I am less of a man if I am not as sexual as my partner thinks I should be." Important components of the ability to experience libido are a person's mood and the interactions of hormones. Chronic stress can impact the production and metabolism of cortisol, a stress-related hormone. If high levels of cortisol persist for a prolonged period of time, they suppress sex hormones. Decreases in androgen and estrogen production due to chronic stress can impact libido in both men and women (Graziottin, 2000). Lower quantity of sex hormones equals lower libido. Depression, anxiety, and chronic stress may interfere with the central pathways of sexual response, reducing not only libido, but the quality of sexual functioning as well. For both men and women, many antidepressants can in turn have side effects of low sex drive.

Women can be equally impacted by low desire/libido. There is increasing pressure in our culture for women to be sexual, orgasmic, and desirable in addition to the traditional role of being available to please their partners and meet the partner's sexual needs. If low libido impedes sexual relations, women can internalize the message and feel inadequate, which results in stress. Alternatively, high libido in women can also create stress. Traditionally, highly sexual women are viewed negatively in our culture, garnering such labels as "slut," "whore," or "promiscuous." The U.S. cultural double standard regards high libido as being a desirable trait in men but a negative trait in women; this is true in many other cultures as well. For women experiencing a stressful emotional state resulting from high libido, a heightened sense of self-loathing or depression might result, and induce negative behaviors such as drinking or other destructive coping mechanisms.

CONCLUSION

Stress—in particular, chronic stress—can create an environment that contributes to negative sexual consequences; in turn, negative sexual experiences can influence the experience of stress. While there are certainly other sexuality and stress-related links, some of the more common connections and their etiologies were presented in this chapter. Part of the journey to positive sexual health, and recognition of sources of stress, includes a broad knowledge of sexuality issues, coping strategies for stress that enhance sexual health, a positive regard for self and sex, reduction of stress through behavior change, and elimination of negative emotions. Stress is part of life; it cannot be eliminated. Understanding the ways in which sexuality can be stressful provides individuals with opportunities to take control of their sexual health.

REFERENCES AND FURTHER READING

Allison, K. W. (1998). Stress and oppressed social category membership. In J. K. Swim & C. Stangor (Eds.), *Prejudice: The target's perspective* (pp. 145–170). San Diego, CA: Academic Press.

Bancroft, J. (1988). Sexual desire and the brain. *Journal of Sex and Marital Therapy, 3*(11), 11–27.

Cash, T. F., Ancis, J. R., & Strachan, M. D. (1997). Gender attitudes, feminist identity, and body images among college women. *Sex Roles, 37,* 433–447.

Chrousos, G. P. (2009). Stress and disorders of the stress system. *Nature Reviews Endocrinology, 5,* 374–381.

Clark, R., Anderson, N. B., Clark, V. R., & Williams, D. R. (1999). Racism as a stressor for African Americans: A biopsychosocial model. *American Psychologist, 54,* 805–816.

Cochran, S. D. (2001). Emerging issues in research on lesbians' and gay men's mental health: Does sexual orientation really matter? *American Psychologist, 56,* 931–947.

DiPlacido, J. (1998). Minority stress among lesbians, gay men, and bisexuals: A consequence of heterosexism, homophobia, and stigmatization. In G. M. Herek (Ed.), *Stigma and sexual orientation: Vol. 4. Understanding prejudice against lesbians, gay men, and bisexuals* (pp. 138–159). Thousand Oaks, CA: Sage.

Dohrenwend, B. P. (2000). The role of adversity and stress in psychopathology: Some evidence and its implications for theory and research. *Journal of Health and Social Behavior, 41,* 1–19.

Forman, M., & Davis, W. N. (2005). Characteristics of middle-aged women in inpatient treatment for eating disorders. *Eating Disorders, 13,* 231–243.

Graziottin, A. (2000). Libido: The biologic scenario. *Maturitas: The European Menopause Journal, 34*(S1), S9–S16.

Harvard Men's Health Watch. (2011). Obesity: Unhealthy and unmanly. Retrieved December 1, 2013 from http://www.health.harvard.edu/newsletters/Harvard_Mens_Health_Watch/2011/March/obesity-unhealthy-and-unmanly.

Herek, G. M. (2000). The psychology of sexual prejudice. *Current Directions in Psychological Science, 9,* 19–22.

Hershberger, S. L., & D'Augelli, A. R. (1995). The impact of victimization on the mental health and suicidality of lesbian, gay, and bisexual youth. *Developmental Psychology, 31,* 65–74.

James, R. (2012). *Sexuality and addiction: Making connections, enhancing recovery.* Westport, CT: Praeger.

Kyrou, I., & Tsigos, C. (2009). Stress hormones: Physiological stress and regulation of metabolism. *Current Opinion in Pharmacology, 9,* 787–793.

Levin, R. J. (1994). Human male sexuality: Appetite and arousal, desire and drive. In C. Legg & D. Boot (Eds.), *Human appetite: Neural and behavioural bases* (pp. 127–164). New York, NY: Oxford University Press.

Mays, V. M., & Cochran, S. D. (2001). Mental health correlates of perceived discrimination among lesbian, gay, and bisexual adults in the United States. *American Journal of Public Health, 91,* 1869–1876.

Meyer, I. H. (1995). Minority stress and mental health in gay men. *Journal of Health and Social Behavior, 36,* 38–56.

Meyer, I. H. (2001). Why lesbian, gay, bisexual, and transgender public health? *American Journal of Public Health, 91,* 856–859.

Nauert, R. (2010). Obesity influences sexual health. Retrieved December 13, 2013, from http://psychcentral.com/news/2010/06/17/obesity-influences-sexual-health/14684.html.

Norman, J. E. (2010). The adverse effects of obesity on reproduction. Retrieved December 1, 2013, from http://www.reproduction-online.org/content/140/3/343.full.pdf.

Norris, J., Masters, N. T., & Zawacki, T. (2004). Cognitive mediation of women's sexual decision making: The influence of alcohol, contextual factors, and background variables. *Annual Review of Sex Research, 15,* 258–297.

Pearlin, L. I. (1999). Stress and mental health: A conceptual overview. In A. V. Horwitz & T. L. Scheid (Eds.), *A handbook for the study of mental health* (pp. 161–175). New York, NY: Cambridge University Press.

Ranabir, S., & Reetu, K. (2011). Stress and hormones. *Indian Journal of Endocrinology and Metabolism, 15*(1), 18–22.

Seagraves, R. T., & Balon, R. (2003). *Sexual pharmacology: Fast facts.* New York, NY: Norton.

Spaccarelli, S. (1994). Stress, appraisal, and coping in child sexual abuse: A theoretical and empirical review. *Psychological Bulletin, 116*(2), 340–362.

Part III
Responses to Stress

Introduction to Part III, Responses to Stress

The chapters in Part III explore various mechanisms, both effective and ineffective, for coping with stress. Effective coping mechanisms assist with management, reduction, and prevention of the impacts of stress; however, many people develop less helpful responses that do little or nothing to reduce stress, may actually exacerbate it, and in extreme applications can have disastrous and even fatal consequences.

The previous part (Part II) covered an array of factors, including people, circumstances, events, and experiences, that potentially elicit the stress response, known as *stressors*. Some people may experience work, family, economic, parenting, social, environmental, and technological stressors all within a day. Thus, it's easy to see how stress can become a chronically experienced condition. As explored in Parts I and II of this text, when the pressures and demands from stressors exceed one's coping ability, the experience can be overwhelming, resulting in chronically high levels of stress hormones. Without any recovery or relief, these hormones wear down bodily systems and leave both body and mind vulnerable to potential damage and disease.

Coping, as defined by Roth and Cohen (1986, p. 1), "is the cognitive and emotional activity that is oriented either towards or away from threat." As a result, *approach-oriented coping*, which later became known as *problem-focused coping*, is task oriented and views a stressor as something that can be changed and managed. Strategies that fall into this category include actions such as activity/task pacing, distraction, and problem solving. *Avoidance-oriented coping*, also known as *emotion-focused coping*, views a stressor as an unchanging factor. Thus, reactions are more emotionally based; individuals tend to respond to the stressful situation or task by using distraction. This may be by using a social support network, engaging in pleasurable or pleasant activities, or by other means of distraction. Engagement of various distorted thought patterns (for example, using wishful thinking or catastrophizing; Smith, Lumley, & Longo, 2002) also falls into this category. Although coping mechanism are usually separated into approach/avoidance styles, Lazarus (1993) views coping mechanisms as also being process or style oriented, as other factors can determine which mechanism(s) will be employed. For example, Lazarus provides examples of how different emotions not only elicit different coping styles and mechanisms, but also may serve different intentions and goals from an individual perspective than from a couple or group perspective (Lazarus, 1993).

Chapter 1, in Part I, presented the different categories of coping, specifically emotional-focused coping and problem-solving coping. Each of these categories may include both effective and ineffective coping mechanisms. For example, to relieve stress, some individuals may turn to alcohol or drugs, or avoidance and other such behaviors; these strategies and mechanisms, though possibly helpful in the short term, usually prove ineffective in the long term. Hundreds of coping mechanisms exist, but this part provides in-depth information on 20 of the most common coping mechanisms/responses (both effective and ineffective). Chapters 24 to 37 discuss effective responses; Chapters 38 to 42 and several sidebars focus on ineffective coping mechanisms.

Chapter 24 examines nutrition and the various nutrients that are necessary to the functioning of the body, both during times of rest and in times of stress. Chapter 25 explores various components of physical activity and how physical activity assists in preventing, reducing, and managing stress; it also provides some suggestions on using this coping mechanism appropriately. Chapter 26 focuses on sleep: how the quantity and quality of sleep affect stress and how sleep is in turn affected by the experience of stress. Chapter 27 discusses relaxation and includes several methods commonly used to create a relaxed state. Chapter 28 describes meditation and mindfulness, the differences between them, and benefits derived from practice of these techniques. It also offers suggestions for using meditation and mindfulness as coping tools. Chapter 29 shows how creativity can be affected by stress, and also enhanced and utilized as a tool to reduce stress. Chapter 30 explores complementary and alternative medicine and describes various healing strategies that can be used as ways to manage stress and improve wellness. Chapter 31 explores optimism: what it is, how it works, and how it can be brought more deliberately into one's life to help one cope with stress. Chapter 32 briefly discusses music and art as effective tools in coping with stress. This chapter also provides suggestions on how to use both art and music for stress reduction, and describes how they can be employed simultaneously. Chapter 33 considers the types of medications that may be effective for those struggling with stress. Chapter 34 explains how writing can be incorporated into one's coping regimen. Chapter 35 discusses humor and how it can used as a healthy coping mechanism. Chapter 36 explores cognitive restructuring, which involves identifying thought patterns that lead to stress and options for restructuring ineffective and harmful thoughts. Finally, Chapter 37 focuses on language, and how the energy and power of words, as well as the nonverbal aspects of language, can utilized to cope with stress.

The rest of the chapters in Part III focus on ineffective methods of coping with stress. Chapter 38 deals with on substance misuse. It's important to note that this chapter doesn't focus on "using" per se; rather, it investigates how individuals who use mood-altering substances to cope with stress may find themselves misusing those substances, due to the nature of the drugs and certain behaviors. The chapter acknowledges the complexity of substance use and lists the factors involved in the development of severe substance use disorders. Chapter 39 discusses eating disorders. Whereas nutrition as an effective coping mechanism is described in Chapter 24, Chapter 39 explains how eating (or restriction of food intake) can spiral out of control when used as a means of coping with stress and unhappiness. This chapter focuses on various subtypes of eating disorders, factors leading to the development of eating disorders, and treatment and recovery. Chapter 40 examines self-injury, which includes behaviors such as cutting as a coping method to relieve stress, and differentiates self-injury from suicide; Chapter 41, dealing specifically with suicide, focuses on thoughts and actions relating to the intent to kill oneself. This chapter also explores factors contributing to the thoughts and desire underlying and prompting this behavior. Chapter 42 discusses the use of violence to deal with stress, outlining the combination of anger and the inability to control it in the progression to violence. Sadly, this kind of behavior often begins in childhood when a child witnesses or is a victim of violence by adults. Chapter 43 describes posttraumatic stress disorder (PTSD), best known for the toll it has taken on those in the military who have experienced the extreme stresses of trauma and violence. As the chapter notes, the condition of PTSD can also develop in anyone, of any age or circumstance, who has experienced trauma and violence.

In Chapter 44, the often-misunderstood phenomenon of burnout is explored. The literature and research reviewed in this chapter tend to explain burnout in terms of emotional exhaustion, depersonalization, and a decreased sense of personal achievement, but the chapter extends the discussion to include the concept of compassion fatigue, and conceptualizes burnout as a physical exhaustion that occurs as a result of chronic stress and a depletion of bodily resources. Chapter 45 presents clinical disorders that relate to stress, as a means of understanding how some of the factors covered in this text can push one's capacity to cope beyond one's limit, to the point where dysfunction sets in.

The remaining chapters discuss other ways to address stress as a whole. Chapter 46 explores the concepts of prevention, management, and reduction of stress. Many of the strategies discussed individually in the preceding chapters on coping are placed within the context of general and more effective plans for response to stress. Finally, Chapter 47 describes moving forward in our knowledge of stress: what research is currently being done and what is trending. Because stress will continue to be present (perhaps in ever-increasing amounts) if the world evolves as it has been doing, there will continue to be a need to understand how stress affects us in body, mind, and spirit.

REFERENCES AND FURTHER READING

Lazarus, R. S. (1993). Coping theory and research: Past, present, and future. *Psychosomatic Medicine, 55*(3), 234–247.

Roth, S., & Cohen, L. J. (1986). Approach, avoidance, and coping with stress. *American Psychologist, 41*(7), 813.

Smith, J. A., Lumley, M. A., & Longo, D. J. (2002). Contrasting emotional approach coping with passive coping for chronic myofascial pain. *Annals of Behavioral Medicine, 24*(4), 326–335.

24

Nutrition and Stress

Heather Shannon, with Jonathan Fenton

FOOD HISTORY AND CONTROVERSY

Nutrition is a much debated and controversial field in the United States. Over the years, experts have touted many different ways of eating. As we learn more, the new advice seems to contradict the old, making it tough to tell what we can really believe. Much of this is because nutrition is a fairly young and rapidly evolving science.

Current schools of wisdom also contradict each other. The Paleo Diet suggests eating more protein, while vegan and vegetarian wisdom suggests that consuming fewer animal products is better for health and longevity. Who is right? The facts are not clear, and the various studies done in this area are limited because they frequently do not take into account the quality of the foods being studied. Are meats detrimental because they are meat, or are they detrimental because most meats contain hormones, antibiotics, and pesticides? Are vegetarians really healthier if they eat lots of cheese or processed soy foods, or do the supposed benefits apply only if they stick to a whole foods diet? Will eating more protein help our mental health, or are these effects more dependent on our bodies' ability to digest and utilize the protein we're already eating? These are questions that continue to be asked, though research has yielded no definitive answers so far.

In terms of how nutrition affects mental health, we know even less. Historically, the U.S. healthcare system has viewed each component of the human body as separate. It was widely held that nutrition affected the physical body, whereas mental health was based on less tangible things like thoughts and feelings that originate from in the brain. Now many experts know better. Emotions are actually stored in the cells of our bodies. Mental health is intricately linked with the digestive system, where 95 percent of one's serotonin is produced (White, 2013). When we're stressed, we deplete our B vitamins more quickly than usual, and we also need the B vitamins that produce more happy and calming neurotransmitters like serotonin and GABA to help us feel normal (Somer, 1995). If we aren't relaxed while eating, we don't break down nutrients as well, and this again makes it harder for our bodies to assimilate those nutrients. Rather than being separate components of wellness, mental and physical health are actually one and the same, and have equal impact on the effectiveness of nutrition.

CULTURAL EFFECTS ON FOOD AND BODY IMAGE

American culture encourages a distorted view of food and body, which unfortunately sets up an unhealthy stress cycle. Fashion and fitness magazines and websites portray often unrealistic ideals of what our bodies should look like, and flash headlines advertising tips and tricks that will help you lose that last bit of weight or tone that last flabby muscle. The diet industry is a multibillion-dollar machine churning out websites and books aimed at telling us the latest gimmicky way we can shed fat and achieve our goals for good—if we just buy the promoter's or author's products. It certainly raises a red flag as to the goals of these authors: Are they trying to help us, or just trying to make money? Are these individuals and companies really all that different from most of the processed food industry? Regardless, these diets and weight loss products still capture plenty of interest, attention, and money. The implication is that once you achieve the right body, you'll be acceptable, so just keep buying more books and products and magazines and videos and working on your unacceptability until then. Readers try to adopt the tips and tricks they read about, which are usually not sustainable in the long run, and certainly are not tailored for their individual biochemistry. Inevitably we give up—typically a sensible choice—but then often blame ourselves for failure, which can cause diminished self-esteem and a greater sense of cognitive dissonance and stress. This cycle continues endlessly, with more attempts to get our bodies how they "should" be and more "failures" along the way. A cycle of compulsive dieting and obsession with food and body may ensue for some folks, leading to a very stressful way of life. In fact, in a study of female dieters, calorie restriction was shown to *increase* the stress hormone cortisol, as well as the participants' sense of perceived stress (Tomiyama et al., 2010).

Media, family culture, obsessive dieting, and genetics can sometimes create the perfect storm and lead to emotional eating and eating disorders such as anorexia, bulimia, and binge eating (Stice, Presnell, & Spangler, 2002). The scope of eating disorders is covered elsewhere (Chapter 39); the point here is that a compulsion concerning food may develop as a way to deal with stress and exert control in a world in which people may not feel they have much control. Compulsions and addictions are ways for individuals to cope with overwhelming stress, especially when individuals do not have other supportive resources to meet their true needs. The physiological effects of sugary foods can provide a temporary mental boost, but those effects are short-lived and eventually lead to a cycle of shame and continued overeating. The effects on blood sugar of this type of eating contribute to further physical cravings for sweet foods. Thus, stress can lead to unhealthy nutrition and vice versa.

A HEALTHIER APPROACH TO FOOD AND STRESS

Nature is smart—sometimes smarter than we are—and it provides an abundance of nutrient-rich whole foods to nourish our bodies. Consuming whole foods, eating plenty of vegetables (especially leafy greens), and reducing sugar are a few points on which most nutritional experts concur. Starting with these behaviors can help our bodies return to optimal function on both a physical and an emotional level. Not only will smart food choices affect our bodies' ability to produce neurotransmitters to make us feel good, our physical ailments will reduce, leaving us feeling more energized and more resilient to stress.

Whole Foods

What is a whole food?

A *whole food* is something that came from the earth and is as nature intended. It's unprocessed and unrefined. Some examples include sweet potatoes, black beans, eggs, almonds, pumpkin seeds, broccoli, apples, basil, and so on. Some other foods that are minimally processed are also generally considered whole foods, such as brown rice (the hull is removed) and certain cuts of meat. Normally, though, once the food is altered in some way, it is no longer considered a whole food. For example, canned fruit, white rice, and boxed potatoes are no longer considered "whole" because of the processing they've undergone. To clear up a few misconceptions about what constitutes a whole food: cooked foods can still be considered whole foods, as can conventional produce. The term *whole food* should not be confused with the term *organic,* which refers to nonuse of pesticides, genetically modified organisms (GMOs), hormones, and antibiotics in foods.

Vegetables

Most notably, vegetables are the most nutritionally dense food group, so we get the best bang for our nutritional buck here. They far exceed even fruits in terms of fiber, vitamins, minerals, and phytonutrients (beneficial plant substances that may help prevent disease) per calorie and have little to no sugar. Leafy greens are the best bet in this category, far outperforming the rest of their vegetable counterparts in terms of nutritional benefits and detoxifying properties.

Sugar

These are some sobering facts about sugar and sweeteners:

- According to the U.S. Department of Agriculture (USDA, 2003), the average American consumes more than 150 pounds of added sugar per year. On a daily basis, that's 355 calories or 24 teaspoons. The American Heart Association recommends anywhere from 6–9 teaspoons per day, depending on caloric intake.
- The average American also consumes 24 pounds of artificial sweeteners per year (USDA, 2003).
- The average American consumes only 8 pounds of broccoli per year (USDA, 2003).
- Overconsumption of sugar is linked to diabetes, weight gain, cancer, and heart disease (Kiecolt-Glaser, 2010).
- Overconsumption of artificial sweeteners is also linked to an increase in diabetes, weight gain, and possibly cancer (Kiecolt-Glaser, 2010).
- Both sugar and artificial sweeteners have been proven to have addictive qualities. Eating even a small amount creates a craving for more (Somer, 1995). Quitting cold turkey might lead to withdrawal symptoms such as fatigue, headaches, and/or mood swings (Avena, 2007).

The Sugar Solution

One of the most helpful concepts for understanding the effects of sugar on the body is the glycemic index. This rating of foods that contain carbohydrates helps explain the impact on blood sugar as well as resulting mood swings, energy crashes, and food cravings. Choosing lower-glycemic foods helps to smooth out blood sugar levels throughout the day and is one of the best ways to maximize productivity, stabilize mood, and minimize cravings for unhealthy items. According to some studies, the fluctuation in blood glucose resulting from consuming highly refined carbohydrates results in a worsened mood (Dog, 2010).

When sugar is a problem, going "cold turkey" may work for some, but a gradual approach may work best for most people. This gradual approach can be viewed as baby steps or like moving up the rungs of a ladder. On the bottom rung are soda, artificial sweetener, and processed candy and baked goods. Moving up a rung, there is juice instead of soda and regular sugar instead of artificial sweetener. The next rung might offer 100 percent fruit juice, and baked goods sweetened with fruit and natural sweeteners that have trace minerals and a lower glycemic index.

FOOD AND NEUROTRANSMITTERS

When one examines good mental health and stress management, it is helpful to think of food as providing the building blocks the body needs to balance the levels of neurotransmitters like serotonin, dopamine, norepinephrine, and GABA that regulate mood.

Serotonin is a neurotransmitter that makes us feel both happy and calm, essentially fighting off stress and helping regulate sleep and appetite. Ninety percent of serotonin is found in the gut, *not* the brain (as many would believe). However, the serotonin in the gut cannot travel to the brain due to the blood-brain barrier. The body creates serotonin from tryptophan (or 5-HTP), an amino acid, and uses B vitamins in that process. It has been shown that increasing the ratio of tryptophan to phenylalanine and leucine increases levels of serotonin, as does eating a low-protein, carbohydrate-rich diet. However, eating a carb-rich diet—especially one composed of simple, sugary carbs—produces more insulin and can lead to problems with obesity, diabetes, and lower serotonin in the long run. Tryptophan can also be found in protein-rich foods, but a high-protein diet has been shown to reduce levels of serotonin in the body. According to one study, vegetarians reported significantly fewer negative emotions despite reduced levels of omega-3 fat consumption. Although there are many mediating factors, vegetarians' carbohydrate intake is almost certainly higher than that of omnivores. Additionally, vegetarians may be more likely to make mindful choices about what they are eating and choose more antioxidant-rich produce (Beezhold, Johnston, & Daigle, 2010). The important thing to note here is that neurotransmitter production and regulation is a complicated system, and there are many checks and balances built into our bodies to maintain balanced levels of neurotransmitters. That said, each person has unique biochemistry; it is important to pay attention to how various foods and supplements affect the particular individual, rather than making sweeping generalizations. Of note, it has also been found that more muscular individuals have higher serotonin levels. When consuming a meal of carbohydrate and tryptophan, insulin is released and stimulates muscles to use up the other amino acids, thus reducing the competition for tryptophan.

GABA (gamma-aminobutyric acid), a calming neurotransmitter, is created from inositol and vitamins B3, B6, and B12. Think of GABA like the brakes on a car: it helps the body to slow down and relax. The amino acid L-theanine also helps the body produce GABA. L-theanine can be found in some teas, but not in high enough dosages to be considered therapeutic. Studies show that 50 to 200 mg can be effective in having a calming effect, but there is little research on the smaller amounts found in teas (Challem, 2007). Other amino acids—glutamine and taurine—are also helpful in GABA production. Caffeine and unhealthy fats can inhibit the production of GABA and increase dopamine, which is an excitatory neurotransmitter—more like the car's accelerator—related to addictive behaviors.

KEY NUTRIENTS FOR MENTAL HEALTH

B vitamins come in different chemical forms. Each person's unique genetics determines the form of B vitamins that is most usable by his or her body (e.g., methylated, hydroxylated, etc.). B vitamins are depleted during times of increased stress, but we need them even more during stressful times to help us produce serotonin and GABA. Because they are water soluble, B vitamins do not build up in our bodies and are typically safe to take in supplement form. Stough et al. (2011) found that a 90-day course of B multivitamin supplementation correlated with a significant decrease in workers' perception of stress in the workplace.

Our brains run largely on healthy fats, and omega-3 fatty acids deserve special mention, as they are linked to strong mental health and reduced risk of depression. Fish—especially salmon and tuna—and flaxseed are commonly known food sources of omega-3s, as is cod liver oil. However, because there are relatively few safe food sources, many people choose to take supplements to meet their dietary needs. It's important to know that not all sources of omega-3s are created equal. Many fish are contaminated with mercury, so it's best to research which varieties are safest to consume. Flaxseed is a good source of omega-3, but also contains ALA (alpha linolenic acid), and our bodies are only able to convert about 10 percent of that into DHA (docosahexaenoic acid), a usable form of omega-3. When choosing an omega-3 supplement, safety and usability are also important factors to consider. It is not the quantity of fish oil, but the amount of DHA and EPA (eicosapentaenoic acid) that are important to look at when choosing a product. The recommended quantity of omega-3s varies among health and medical professionals; it is important for patients to consult their own providers when choosing how to meet their individual needs.

Vitamin D has been linked to many health benefits, not the least of which is improved mental health and reduced risk of depression (Durson, 2010). Vitamin D levels of less than 25 or 30 ng/mL (nanograms/milliliter) are considered low; optimal levels are in the 50–80 ng/mL range. Unprotected sun exposure is a good way to get vitamin D, but the torso—which is usually covered—does the best job of converting sunlight into vitamin D. In contrast, the face—the most exposed part of the body—does the worst job of conversion. Many people live at latitudes where their sun exposure cannot possibly give them enough vitamin D, especially during the winter. Additionally, vitamin D is available in only a few food sources, such as cod liver oil, shrimp, and eggs. Because many people cannot get adequate D3 from sun or food sources, this important nutrient is often one to supplement.

Magnesium levels may be inversely associated with levels of depression (Jacka et al., 2009). Stress, caffeine, sugar, and alcohol all deplete magnesium, which is helpful in producing serotonin and GABA. Low levels of magnesium are linked to anxiety, restless leg syndrome, and cramping. Good whole-food sources of magnesium include green leafy vegetables, pumpkin seeds, and black beans. Magnesium citrate supplements are often recommended for those suffering constipation, but magnesium glycinate is a gentler option for those with normal bowel movements or tending toward production of loose stools.

DIGESTION

The serotonin that is so critical to managing stress and maintaining a balanced mood is primarily found in the digestive tract rather than in the brain. This is a great reminder that mind and body are a single combined system rather than two separate systems. Mental and physical health are in constant interaction and can either support each other or work to the detriment of each other.

Maintaining a healthy digestive system is a great way to help keep stress in check. Many people have heard about the importance of probiotics for health. Unfortunately, long-term use of antibiotics—even years in the past—can have a negative impact on the digestive microbiome, because they kill the good bacteria along with the bad. Probiotics help maintain a balanced digestive system and prevent bad bacteria and yeast from overgrowing. Because serotonin is produced in the gut, probiotics also have a positive impact on mental health; they have been found to reduce anxiety levels in chronic fatigue sufferers (White, 2013). Probiotics may be found in fermented foods such as sauerkraut, miso, tempeh, pickles made without vinegar, and supplements.

Dairy products such as yogurt and kefir are perhaps the best-known foods that contain active probiotics, but most people gradually lose the ability to digest lactose after the age of 2, and there is research linking dairy to sinus problems. In addition to those with lactose intolerance, many people have sensitivities or allergies to the proteins found in dairy—casein and whey—which contribute to uncomfortable digestive symptoms and sometimes systemic reactions. An elimination diet can help determine if dairy is a problem in terms of digestion or other symptoms.

FOOD SENSITIVITIES

Although antibiotics are often effective at killing bad bacteria, they kill the good bacteria with them. When the good bacteria are killed off, it leaves room for bacterial infections and/or overgrowth of *Candida* yeast. These conditions can cause dysbiosis or intestinal permeability—referred to as *leaky gut syndrome* in alternative medicine circles—that allows food particles to pass through before being fully broken down (Brown, Decoffe, Molcan, & Gibson, 2012). The body identifies these particles as toxic invaders and attacks them with antibodies. Eventually the antibodies build up and the person develops systemic reactions to certain foods that may come on immediately after consumption or up to two days later. Symptoms may include bloat, excessive gas, diarrhea, fatigue, and puffiness/swelling, among others. Like autoimmune conditions, these food sensitivities contribute to stress levels due to the chronic physical ailments as well as the added difficulty of following a restrictive diet. Because nutrients are not absorbed as well by the wounded intestines, the body may also have more difficulty in producing feel-good neurotransmitters like serotonin and GABA. Healing the gut in the case of intestinal permeability involves eliminating sensitive foods for a period of time and often taking targeted nutrients. This protocol should be supervised by a doctor and/or nutritionist who is familiar with this condition. Treatment can help reduce or eliminate symptoms and may allow an individual to safely reintroduce certain food items.

MINDFUL EATING: A HEALTHY RELATIONSHIP WITH FOOD

In addition to making smart food choices, how we consume our food can be impactful in managing stress. *Mindfulness* refers to pure awareness and experiencing without judgment or striving. *Mindful eating* means bringing this gentle awareness to food choices and our sensory experience as we eat food. Here are some questions that can help increase awareness and presence when eating. Remember, the goal is not to judge, but simply to notice.

- Where is the food being consumed?
- Are other activities going on at the same time?
- Are you feeling distracted or thinking about something other than your meal as you eat?
- What does the food look like?
- What does the food smell like?
- Is there an emotional reaction to the food? If so, what is it?
- What physical movements are necessary during the eating process?
- Do you feel relaxed or hurried as you eat?
- What side of your mouth does the food move to?
- How quickly or slowly are you chewing before you swallow?
- What sounds do you notice as you chew?
- What does the food taste like?
- How do you feel physically and emotionally after eating this food?

We may not always have time to be quite this conscious of the eating process, but the answers to these questions can help guide choices that contribute to well-being. Maybe we notice feeling more stressed when we have to eat in a hurry, and are able to come up with a solution to the time crunch. Or perhaps we notice a greater sense of enjoyment when eating with friends or partaking of certain foods. Mindfulness is a way to become more fully present to one's experiences with food without labeling them as good, bad, right, or wrong. Mindfulness-based stress reduction (MBSR) programs have been proven effective in helping participants reduce perceived distress in their lives (van Aalderen et al., 2012).

CURRENT STATUS AND FUTURE POSSIBILITIES

Although American culture still generally dictates a focus on appearance rather than health, there is a growing movement of health leaders who are advocating for a positive relationship with food and body. Research has been clear that 95 percent of diets fail, processed foods are generally not healthy, and most people do not eat enough vegetables (Somer, 1995). While large food manufacturers continue striving to make processed foods addictive so they can make a profit, many health coaches, integrative nutritionists, personal trainers, farmers, and holistic doctors are advocating for a return to whole, unprocessed foods and treating our bodies with love rather than disdain.

There is a new, exciting movement starting in the mental health community that looks at a person's unique makeup through genetic testing and recommends courses of nutrients based on individual genetic mutations and resultant biochemical insufficiencies or excesses in the body. This field opens up much hope for sufferers of mental illness to receive effective treatment without the side effects of many of today's pharmaceutical drugs. This genetic perspective also allows people to let go of thinking that mental illness is a character defect and understanding that much of mental health comes from the genetic cards we are dealt at birth.

SUMMARY

Stress can be difficult for anyone and everyone to deal with, but nutritional choices provide several opportunities for better coping. Giving ourselves the proper nutrients we need for optimal biochemistry makes us more resilient to stress, by helping us maximize serotonin and GABA production. Research suggests that making certain food choices, and eating a whole-foods, low-sugar, plant-rich diet, and using targeted supplementation in consultation with a healthcare professional can be effective. Eating according to the glycemic index helps to maintain energy levels and reduce cravings, both of which can be sources of stress when eating poorly. This approach also helps to keep blood sugar stable and reduce mood swings. Addressing digestive dysfunction and food sensitivities can help to alleviate physical symptoms and thereby reduce physical sources of emotional stress. Healthy digestion is also directly linked to serotonin levels and a positive mood. Lastly, taking a mindful approach to our choices and experiences involving food can help us notice patterns that are working well for us with our diet and others that are no longer serving us.

REFERENCES AND FURTHER READING

Avena, N. M. (2007). Examining the addictive-like properties of binge eating using an animal model of sugar dependence. *Experimental and Clinical Psychopharmacology, 15*(5), 481–491. doi:10.1037/1064-1297.15.5.481.

Beezhold, B. L., Johnston, C. S., & Daigle, D. R. (2010). Vegetarian diets are associated with healthy mood states: a cross-sectional study in Seventh Day Adventist adults. *Nutritional Journal, 9*(26), 1–8.

Brown, K., Decoffe, D., Molcan, E., & Gibson, D. L. (2012). Diet-induced dysbiosis of the intestinal microbiota and the effects on immunity and disease. *Nutrients, 4*(11), 1552–1553.

Challem, J. (2007). Finding your food-mood solution. *Better Nutrition,* 52–55.

Dog, T. L. (2010). The role of nutrition in mental health. *Alternative Therapies, 16*(2), 42–46.

Durson, S. M. (2010). Vitamin D for mental health and cognition. *Canadian Medical Association Journal, 182*(17), 1886. doi:10.1503/cmaj.110–2125.

Jacka, F. N., Overland, S., Stewart, R., Tell, G. S., Bjelland, I., & Mykletun, A. (2009). Association between magnesium intake and depression and anxiety in community-dwelling adults: The Hordaland health study. *Australian and New Zealand Journal of Psychiatry, 43*(45), 45–52.

Kiecolt-Glaser, J. K. (2010). Stress, food and inflammation: Psychoneuroimmunology and nutrition at the cutting edge. *Psychosomatic Medicine, 72,* 365–369.

Pollan, M. (2006). *The omnivore's dilemma.* New York, NY: Penguin.

Somer, E. (1995). *Food and mood: The complete guide to eating well and feeling your best.* New York, NY: Henry Holt.

Stice, E., Presnell, K., & Spangler, D. (2002). Risk factors for binge eating onset in adolescent girls: A 2-year prospective investigation. *Health Psychology, 21*(2), 131–138.

Stough, C., Scholey, A., Lloyd, J., Spong, J., Myers. S., & Downey, L. A. (2011). The effect of 90-day administration of a high dose vitamin B-complex on work stress. *Human Psychopharmacology: Clinical and Experimental, 26,* 470–476.

Tomiyama, A. J., Mann, T., Vinas, D., Hunger, J. M., DeJager, J., & Taylor, S. E. (2010). Low calorie dieting increases cortisol. *Psychosomatic Medicine, 72,* 357–364. doi:10.1097/PSY.0b013e3181d9523c.

U.S. Department of Agriculture. (2003). *Agriculture fact book 2001-2002.* Retrieved from http://www.usda.gov/documents/usda-factbook-2001-2002.pdf.

van Aalderen, J. R., Donder, A. R. T., Giommi, F., Spinhoven, P., Barendregt, H. P., & Speckens, A. E. M. (2012). The efficacy of mindfulness-based cognitive therapy in recurrent depressed patients with and without a current depressive episode: A randomized controlled trial. *Psychological Medicine, 42*(5), 989–1001. doi:10.1017/S0033291711002054.

White, D. (2013, January). What your gut says about your health. *Fitness Magazine.* Retrieved from http://www.fitnessmagazine.com/health/body/head-to-toe/digestive-system-health.

25

Physical Activity and Stress

Serena Wadhwa

In the 21st century, physical activity is one of the strongest recommendations for health—for many reasons. With obesity (and its related diseases) common, and growing concerns about the physical effects of stress on the mind-body unit, more and more individuals are turning to physical activity as a means of reducing stress, increasing health, and reaping additional benefits for the psyche. Nevertheless, the flood of information and opinions, hype, and research available about this particular coping mechanism makes it challenging to separate fact from fiction. Because the depth and breadth of information on physical activity is more than can be covered within a single chapter, this chapter focuses on what physical activity is, the benefits of engaging in forms of physical activity, components of physical activity, and an overview of the research on this topic.

According to the Office of Disease Prevention and Health Promotion, about 80 percent of Americans do not meet the guidelines for physical activity (www.healthypeople.gov). This percentage refers to the number of individuals at risk for developing various medical issues and vulnerability to psychological effects. Some experts note that "quick fixes" are often sought for existing aliments, rather than professional collaboration on preventive efforts (see Lewis & Hennekens, 2015). Physical activity can go a long way toward preventing physical and psychological struggles. In a search conducted online (using Google Scholar), about 600,000 publications surfaced with a date range of 2005 to 2010. From 2011 to 2016 (which, at the time of this writing, was in the beginning of the year), 953,000 publications were tagged. Though there are likely several reasons for this number of publications (such as the inception of Michelle Obama's "Let's Move" initiative, beginning in 2010; health benefits; federal funding for research; etc.), the surge in publications demonstrates the increased interest in knowledge, skills, and the application of physical activity.

DEFINITION AND MYTHS

What exactly is physical activity? *Physical activity* is a collective term that includes both exercise and any other movement. According to Blair, Cheng, and Holder (2001), *physical activity* is often used interchangeably with *physical fitness,* but the two are not equivalents and do not represent the same concept. The authors point out that *physical fitness* is the physical activity patterns (sustained movement, exercise) that occurred over recent weeks and/or months. To meet the definition of physical fitness, the level of physical activity (activities that are physical, requiring movement and expenditure of energy) should meet the health guidelines promulgated by the U.S. Department of Health and Human Services (Powell, Paluch, & Blair, 2011). The most recent Physical Activity Guidelines (PAGs) for Americans were developed in 2008. According to the Department of Health and Human Services, recommendations are provided for children (6 years old and above), adolescents, adults, and older adults. For adults, the recommended amount of endurance (aerobic) activity is a minimum of 150 minutes of moderate-intensity activity and 2 or more days of muscle-strengthening activities per week. The PAGs indicate that the more activity an individual gets, the more benefits will be yielded, including benefits relating to health and medical issues and psychological, mental, and emotional issues. Although the definition of *physical activity* encompasses movement, the guidelines indicate that both aerobic and muscle-building activities are needed for optimal health.

COMPONENTS OF PHYSICAL ACTIVITY

Physical activity simply indicates movement, so there are additional components to the notion of physical fitness. For example, *muscular strength* refers to the ability of muscles to exert force; *muscle endurance* is the ability of a muscle or a group of muscles to sustain the exertion of force or repeated contractions. *Flexibility* is the ability to use muscles and joints to the full range of movement. Finally, *stamina* refers to cardiovascular endurance: the body's ability to get rid of wastes, deliver necessary nutrients, and maintain oxygen. These four components of physical activity are targeted through stretching, increasing the heart rate, strength training and toning, and other activities.

Powell, Paluch, and Blair (2011) discuss four questions regarding physical activity to which the literature often gives varied and variable answers. These questions are: How much physical activity? What kind? How often? How intense? Powell et al. demonstrated that different responses to these questions yield different health outcomes. The first question addresses how much physical activity one should do. What the authors discovered in their research was that daily durations did not matter much as long as the weekly total amounts were consistent. Another significant finding was that even light-intensity activities yield some benefits, as compared to sedentary activities. One study reported that interrupting sedentary activity with light activity for one minute or less can yield some benefits (Healy et al., 2008).

Myths

Kylie Ball (2015) explores common myths relating to physical activity. One myth Ball describes is the belief that existing evidence-based practices, which are based on theory and proven strategies, work for everyone (Ball, 2015). This is not the case, as individual factors do influence outcomes relating to engaging in physical activity. For example, the common theory that anyone can do physical activity is not necessarily realistically applicable to individuals working several jobs to make ends meet. These individuals invest most of their energy in work and convenience and what is good for the family. "Healthy" does not always equal the best choice for all involved. Additionally, risk factors (economic, environment, genetics) necessitate innovation and creative application.

According to the World Health Organization (WHO), there are many additional myths. A common belief is that one needs a lot of time for physical activity and that one need not be concerned about physical activity until later in life ("Myths of physical activity," n.d.). Current guidelines recommend 30 minutes of physical activity a day, and it is generally fairly easy to schedule this within one's day-to-day activities. The sooner one understands (and internalizes) the benefits of incorporating physical activity into one's life and the risks of not doing so, the more effective it is for one's overall health.

Other myths include the following:

1. Myth: You need a large amount of energy to incorporate physical activity. Reality: The fact is that only by expending energy does one increase it.
2. Myth: It takes much planning and effort to get started. Reality: It doesn't require lengthy periods, as current guidelines indicate to start slowly and build up to 30 minutes of activity 5 days a week or more.
3. Myth: Only target one area to work on. Reality: Doing whole-body activities, whether cardiovascular or muscle strengthening, provides more benefits and creates less stress on the body.
4. Myth: "No pain, no gain." Reality: Pain during an activity may indicate that you are stressing an injury or causing another one. However, soreness is different, as it is felt after activities (particularly strenuous ones), and it is normal unless it continues for more than a couple of days.

Another common misconception that Ball (2015) discussed is the lack of physical activity and motivation among economically disadvantaged people. Research, according to Ball, shows that many economically disadvantaged individuals are overweight or obese. There is a belief that individuals at low economic status do not engage in physical activity, due to status, motivation, or other reasons. However, Ball cited a study in which economically disadvantaged women consistently participated in a project providing both strategies and suggestions to increase better eating. These incentives and suggestions were provided within the women's central day-to-day environment: using the grocery store in which they normally purchased groceries and providing access to recipes, loyalty points, and small reductions in price. According to Ball (2015, p. 142), these study results suggest that there is "a high degree of interest among low-income groups in nutrition promotion strategies and if offered the right program, these groups are not inevitably hard to reach." The same is likely to be true of physical activity.

BENEFITS

While there are many myths about physical activity, and it is prudent to be cautious about them, research demonstrates the benefits of physical activity in many areas of life.

Psychological and Emotional

The benefits of physical activity are numerous, according to consistent research. In an article posted in the *Monitor on Psychology,* Weir (2011) describes the journey of psychologists in recommending physical activity to patients who struggle with clinical disorders and day-to-day stresses of life. Blumenthal et al. (2007, cited in Weir's article) reported that individuals who are active tend to be less depressed than inactive individuals, and those who stopped a physical activity program tended to sink deeper into their depression than those who continued their programs. Thus, a vicious cycle ensues, in which physical activity may be of benefit to the individual, yet the person doesn't "feel like" engaging in physical activity due to the depression. In one study, 47 percent of individuals who originally met the criteria for major depressive disorder were in remission after 4 months of supervised exercise. This means these individuals no longer met the criteria for major depressive disorder (Blumethal et al., 2007).

In a study conducted by Smits, Berry, Rosenfield, Powers, Behar, and Otto (2008), the authors demonstrated the use of physical activity to combat anxiety. The symptoms of physical activity (sweating, shallow breathing, etc.), are similar to the symptoms experienced during anxiety and panic attacks, or *anxiety sensitivity.* The study looked at the effects of incorporating physical activity as a means of managing anxiety symptoms, since physical activity creates similar symptoms. Results indicated that participants experienced less anxiety when involved in a physical activity routine.

Other research yields similar findings. In one meta-analysis, Tkachuk and Martin (1999) examined studies focusing on the effects of physical activity on depression, anxiety, developmental disabilities, schizophrenia, somatoform disorders (which are physical symptoms with no organic origin and do not result from substance use or from another mental illness, according to the *DSM-IV-TR* [American Psychiatric Association, 2008]), pain disorders, and substance use disorders. Among other things, the analysis concluded that physical activity as a behavioral intervention demonstrated significant impact on these disorders, though to varying degrees. The authors' suggestions for adding physical activity to the treatment of these disorders included collaborating with exercise physiologists, getting medical clearance for activity, and establishing some guidelines.

Emotionally, there are also positive benefits to physical activity. When a positive effect is present, it reduces the intensity of other symptoms. For example, Kishida and Elavsky (2014) demonstrated that participants experiencing menopause adapted to their symptoms more effectively as a result of physical activity routines.

Physical

Lewis and Hennekens (2015) report that lack of physical activity accounts for 22 percent of heart disease; 22 percent of colon cancer; and 12 percent of diabetes, hypertension, and other diseases. Siscovick, Laporte, and Newman (1985) also demonstrated the effects of physical activity on various medical conditions. Blair, Cheng, and Holder (2001) conducted a meta-analysis of 67 articles relating to physical activity. They concluded that some physical activity increases the life span and decreases the risk for coronary heart disease, cardiovascular disease, stroke, and colon cancer. Another meta-analysis, by Powell, Paluch, and Blair (2011), reported decreased risk of early death, stroke, type 2 diabetes, breast and colon cancer, excessive weight gain, and loss of cognitive functioning. These authors noted that the type of activity performed will cause specific physiological changes, resulting in specific bodily adaptations. Thus, certain functioning may increase in capacity, efficiency, and coordination. Other benefits included improvements in muscular and bone strength, endurance, and posture; decreased inflammation; and increased immune functioning.

Sleep

As Chapter 26 (on sleep) explains, many individuals struggle with sleep. Approximately 70 million people in the United States suffer from chronic sleep loss or a

ENDORPHINS

Endorphins are naturally occurring peptide neurotransmitters that are produced in two brain regions of vertebrates: the pituitary gland and the hypothalamus (a deep brain structure). The chemical structure of endorphins is similar to that of morphine, and the brain has opioid receptors to which endorphins bind when released. People engaged in intense activity, such as recreational or competitive runners, often speak of an "endorphin high," a feeling of euphoria and pleasure.

Both pain and pleasure can be affected by endorphin release. Thus, when someone stubs a toe or engages in a pleasurable activity, endorphins are released into the brain. The amount of endorphins released will depend on the intensity of the stressful or pleasurable experience.

In the short term, endorphins released during a stressful experience assist the body and mind in dealing with the sensation of pain. When the pituitary gland is signaled that a pain sensation is present, endorphins are released, bind with the opioid receptors in the brain, and reduce the perception of pain (Sprouse-Blum, Smith, Sugai, & Parsa, 2010). The individual also experiences fewer effects of stress.

When someone participates in a sustained physical activity that is considered enjoyable, the release of endorphins enhances the experience, giving the individual a sense of euphoria and energizing feelings. Some scientists believe that endorphins can enhance the immune system, lower blood pressure, and have anti-aging effects. Prolonged exercise has been linked with increased endorphins, improved mood, and overall positive sense of well-being. Such findings have also occurred with laughter and forms of body pressure, such as massage (Dunbar et al., 2011).

sleep disorder. Research results suggest that individuals who engage in physical activity fall asleep faster and stay asleep longer (Bushman, 2013).

Environmental

Lewis and Hennekens (2015) report that the lack of physical activity accounts for 2.4 percent of healthcare costs, which equates to about $24 billion a year. The cost of sedentary lifestyles includes increased risks, not only of developing medical conditions, but also of becoming reliant on medications and other means of support.

Motivation for Activities

How does one increase motivation to engage in physical activity, both aerobic and muscle strengthening? Researchers explore what motivates and sustains individual engagement with physical activity routines and practices. Research conducted by Anshel and others explores the link between values and level of engagement. For example, in one study conducted by Anshel and Kang, the authors discuss how "changing exercise behavior. . . is difficult because it's accompanied by long-held feelings and attitudes that may reflect an array of barriers, negatively held perceptions, and unpleasant past experiences" (Anshel & Kang, 2007b, p. 87). As a result, the exercise patterns are not usually connected with one's core values. Anshel and colleagues studied the effects of connecting one's negative habits (e.g., not engaging in exercise/physical activity) with one's values and found that when the disconnect is not acceptable, change happens. For example, if one of my values is to live long enough to help others with managing their stress and understanding how stress affects them physically, taking care of myself physically will be important to me. In terms of physical activity, how and what I engage in may play a role in the representation of this value. I may engage in some forms of activity to see how they affect me; I may engage more vigorously, or I may develop a plan of action and engage others to hold me accountable. Whatever the plan, the goal, according to Anshel, is the connection of values to negative habits. To test this theory, the authors examined the application of this intervention for 41 faculty/staff members at a university (Anshel & Kang, 2007b). The results of this study revealed that the intervention based on this theory not only improved physical activity patterns, but was also connected to positive and improved lifestyle changes.

Cognition and motivation play a large role in an individual's attempts at physical activity. Laforge, Rossi, Prochaska, Velicer, Levesque, and McHorney (1999) concluded that an individual's perceptions of the benefits of regular exercise and/or the severity of the negative health consequences of sedentary lifestyles can be shifted to increase motivation for increased physical activity. It is not uncommon to hear individuals make statements relating to the lack of motivation or the inability to perform when it comes to "working out." Thus, this study provides some significant evidence that a shift in perception can potentially shift behavior. A more recent study examined motivational effects in sedentary behaviors, as American adults average about 7.7 hours a day in sedentary modes (defined as activities requiring minimal energy expenditures, as cited in Conroy, Maher, Elavsky, Hyde, & Doerksen, 2013). Both automatic (impulsive) and controlled (reflective) types of motivation were studied, and this research showed that controlled (reflective) motivational processes regulated sedentary behaviors. In other words, intention is important.

Another example of how even slight changes can impact one's stress levels and/or quality of life is provided by a study measuring the effects of posture. Nair,

Sagar, Sollers III, Consedine, and Broadbent (2015) examined whether postural interventions can reduce the stress response. The authors demonstrated that posture affects cognitions and subsequent emotions, expressions, and health.

Thus, emerging research indicates the importance of intention and connection when developing and sustaining a physical activity routine. Once these aspects are clarified for the individual, the habit of regular physical activity becomes more conscious and enjoyable.

Research also suggests that there are ways to increase one's daily or weekly physical activity. The President's Council on Fitness and Sports recommends that individuals first check with their primary care physicians to determine if they are medically able to engage in most types of physical activity. Some suggestions for low-impact physical activity include parking further away from the entrance (to the office, store, restaurant, etc.) in the parking lot; if using public transportation, get off a few blocks before your destination; use stairs rather than an elevator; take breaks during the day and walk around the block, office, or inside your residence; do a thorough house cleaning or carry groceries to and from the car. These are suggested small steps in beginning to improve your activity routine and increase physical activity overall.

For individuals who may want to begin a more intense routine and include both aerobic and muscle-strengthening activities, first finding enjoyable physical activities goes a long way. Swimming, jogging, dance, sports, walking, hiking, bicycling, weight lifting or weight training, group classes at gyms, personal training at gyms, yoga, Pilates, and seasonal-weather outdoor activities are just some of the activities that may be appealing. Blair et al. (2011) stress the importance of starting slowly for individuals who have been sedentary, so the body can adapt accordingly. Jumping into a program without adequate preparation and patience may cause unforeseen and unwanted consequences.

CONCLUSION

Interest in physical activity as a behavioral intervention to prevent, manage, and reduce symptoms relating to medical conditions, psychological disorders, and stress-related effects is on the rise. Efforts such as Michelle Obama's "Let's Move!" campaign have stimulated research into the effects of physical activity. Research provides ample evidence for the benefits of physical activity, locally, nationally, and globally. Activities requiring muscle strength and endurance, stamina, and flexibility are important parts of building an integrated coping mechanism. Recognizing ill-supported beliefs relating to physical activity, and developing routines that connect with one's individual values, may also enhance motivation to initiate and sustain a physical activity routine.

REFERENCES AND FURTHER READING

American Psychiatric Association. (2000). *Diagnostic and statistical manual of mental disorders, fourth edition, text revision.* Washington, DC: Author.

Anshel, M. H., Brinthaupt, T. M., & Kang, M. (2010). The disconnected values model improves mental well-being and fitness in an employee wellness program. *Behavioral Medicine, 36*(4), 113–122.

Anshel, M. H., & Kang, M. (2007a). An outcome-based action study on changes in fitness, blood lipids, and exercise adherence, using the disconnected values (intervention) model. *Behavioral Medicine, 33*(3), 85–100.

Anshel, M. H., & Kang, M. (2007b). Effect of an intervention on replacing negative habits with positive routines for improving full engagement at work: A test of the disconnected values model. *Consulting Psychology Journal: Practice and Research, 59*(2), 110–125.

Ball, K. (2015). Traversing myths and mountains: Addressing socioeconomic inequities in the promotion of nutrition and physical activity behaviours. *International Journal of Behavioral Nutrition and Physical Activity, 12,* 142. http://doi.org/10.1186/s12966-015-0303-4.

Blair, S. N., Cheng, Y., & Holder, J. S. (2001). Is physical activity or physical fitness more important in defining health benefits? *Medicine and Science in Sports and Exercise, 33*(6 Suppl.), S379–S399.

Blumenthal, J. A., Babyak, M. A., Doraiswamy, P. M., Watkins, L., Hoffman, B. M., Barbour, K. A.,. . . Hinderliter, A. (2007). Exercise and pharmacotherapy in the treatment of major depressive disorder. *Psychosomatic Medicine, 69*(7), 587–596.

Boucher, C. (n.d.). Top 9 fitness myths—Busted! Retrieved October 20, 2015, from WebMD: http://www.webmd.com/fitness-exercise/top-9-fitness-myths-busted.

Bushman, B. A. (2013). Exercise and sleep. *ACSM's Health & Fitness Journal, 17*(5), 5–8.

Conroy, D. E., Maher, J. P., Elavsky, S., Hyde, A. L., & Doerksen, S. E. (2013). Sedentary behavior as a daily process regulated by habits and intentions. *Health Psychology, 32*(11), 1149–1157.

Dunbar, R. I., Baron, R., Frangou, A., Pearce, E., van Leeuwin, E. J., Stow, J., . . . Van Vugt, M. (2011). Social laughter is correlated with an elevated pain threshold. *Proceedings of the Royal Society B: Biological Sciences, 279*(1731), 1161–1167. doi:10.1098/rspb.2011.1373.

Healy, G. N., Dunstan, D. W., Salmon, J., Cerin, E., Shaw, J. E., Zimmet, P. Z., & Owen, N. (2008). Breaks in sedentary time: Beneficial associations with metabolic risk. *Diabetes Care, 31,* 661–666.

Kishida, M., & Elavsky, S. (2014). Daily physical activity enhances resilient resources for symptom management in middle-aged women. *Health Psychology, 34*(7), 756–764.

Laforge, R. G., Rossi, J. S., Prochaska, J. O., Velicer, W. F., Levesque, D. A., & McHorney, C. A. (1999). Stage of regular exercise and health-related quality of life. *Preventive Medicine, 28*(4), 349–360.

Lewis, S. F., & Hennekens, C. H. (2015). Regular physical activity: Forgotten benefits. *American Journal of Medicine, 129*(2), 137–138. doi:10.1016/j.amjmed.2015.07.016.

Myths of physical activity. (n.d.). Retrieved October 20, 2015, from World Health Organization website: http://www.who.int/dietphysicalactivity/factsheet_myths/en.

Nair, S., Sagar, M., Sollers III, J., Consedine, N., & Broadbent, E. (2015). Do slumped and upright postures affect stress responses? A randomized trial. *Health Psychology, 34*(6), 632–641. doi:10.1037/hea0000146.

Physical Activities Guidelines Advisory Committee. (2008). *2008 Physical activity guidelines for Americans*. Washington, DC: U.S. Department of Health & Human Services. Retrieved from http://health.gov/paguidelines/pdf/paguide.pdf.

Powell, K. E., Paluch, A. E., & Blair, S. N. (2011). Physical activity for health: What kind? How much? How intense? On top of what? *Public Health, 32*(1), 349–365. doi:10.1146/annurev-publhealth-031210-101151.

President's Council on Fitness and Sports. (n.d.). Home page. Retrieved September 2015 from http://www.fitness.gov.

Siscovick, D. S., Laporte, R. E., & Newman, J. M. (1985). The disease-specific benefits and risks of physical activity and exercise. *Public Health Reports, 100*(2), 180–188.

Smits, J. A., Berry, A. C., Rosenfield, D., Powers, M. B., Behar, E., & Otto, M. W. (2008). Reducing anxiety sensitivity with exercise. *Depression and Anxiety, 25*(8), 689–699.

Sprouse-Blum, A. S., Smith, G., Sugai, D., & Parsa, F. D. (2010, March). Understanding endorphins and their importance in pain management. *Hawaii Medical Journal, 69*(3), 70–71.

Tkachuk, G. A., & Martin, G. L. (1999). Exercise therapy for patients with psychiatric disorders: Research and clinical implications. *Professional Psychology: Research and Practice, 30*(3), 275–282.

Weir, K. (2011). The exercise effect. *Monitor on Psychology, 42*(11), 48–52.

26

Sleep and Stress

Kirsten Levin Belzer

INTRODUCTION

Sleep is a building block of good health. Because sleep is a natural and necessary bodily function, too little sleep creates significant problems and additional stress on both body and mind. This chapter explores why and how we sleep; how a lack of sleep creates distress in various ways; and how sleep can be improved, thus reducing stress and improving general health and well-being.

Adults sleep less than they ever have. In the 1950s, Americans slept an average of 8 to 9 hours per night (Kripke, Simons, Garfinkel, & Hammond, 1979). A National Sleep Foundation poll in 2011 showed that the average American adult sleeps 6 hours and 55 minutes. Surely, our bodies have not evolved that much in the past six decades that we would need one to two fewer hours of sleep than our grandparents! This inadequate amount of sleep leads to increased negative medical and mental health consequences and has become a significant public health problem, according to the U.S. Centers for Disease Control and Prevention ("Insufficient Sleep," 2014). Increasing use of technology and expectations of employers are some of the possible causes often blamed for the decreasing amounts of sleep. According to the National Sleep Foundation (2013), the development of this widespread sleep deprivation is most likely the effect of external factors, such as the need to be at work or school earlier than one's internal body clock would dictate and the need for more workers to hold more than one job, or extra responsibilities due to cuts in staff, and shift work. For more than 60 percent of the population, work start times are too early to allow adequate, restorative sleep (Roenneberg, 2012).

Sleeping may be viewed by some as a sign of weakness (Wehrenberg, 2008). While this biased perception against sleep has seemed to increase in recent times, it dates back throughout history. Napoleon allegedly said, "Six hours' sleep for a man, seven for a woman, and eight for a fool." Thomas Edison claimed that sleep was a waste of time. These two historical figures, however, may have been a part of a very small percentage of humans who naturally require fewer hours sleep than most. Albert Einstein, in contrast, required at least 10 hours' sleep for peak performance (Roenneberg, 2012). Most people fall somewhere between the extremes.

Sleep deprivation can lead to a host of mental, physical, emotional, and even social troubles. Mentally, the sleep-deprived may suffer from memory problems, difficulty concentrating, and symptoms similar to those of attention deficit and hyperactivity disorder. Car accidents may often be a result of too little sleep, according to the National Institute of Health. Physically, inadequate sleep more than doubles the risk for cardiovascular disease. Other effects of too little sleep include increased risk of type 2 diabetes, hallucinations, severe yawning, impaired immune system, increased heart rate variability, muscle aches, and tremors. One researcher suggests that sleep is at least as important for energy regulation as it is for brain function, as our metabolic functions and insulin signaling mechanisms are affected by sleep (Broussard et al., 2012). Sleep deprivation increases one's risk of obesity and diabetes. In addition to our metabolisms slowing, when we are tired we naturally reach for the nearest carbohydrate and overeat, according to a recent study from Uppsala University (2013). Long-term sleep deprivation can lead to gaining significant weight; one study found that children who slept more ate less (Hart et al., 2013). Most recently, inadequate sleep has been found to affect cancer growth by decreasing the immune system's ability to fight cancer and increasing the speed of tumor growth (Easton, 2014). Emotionally, a general sense of stress and irritability results from sleep deprivation, and anxiety and depression can develop or increase (Edelberg & Hough, 2006). Socially, one of the first functions to go as a consequence of too little sleep are social skills, as being polite, patient, or gracious can be difficult when one is feeling irritable, tired, and not fully rested (Roenneberg, 2012).

WHY WE SLEEP AND HOW SLEEP PROTECTS US

Sleep experts are not yet clear on why we sleep, though they believe sleep serves many vital functions. Scientists don't know exactly where in the brain sleep occurs. One theory is that sleep is controlled by a wide network of neural networks dispersed throughout the brain (Northwestern University Feinberg School of Medicine, 2016). Recently, however, researchers were able to identify a causal link between neuron activity in the lateral hypothalamus and one stage of sleep: rapid eye movement (REM) sleep, a sleep state described in more detail later in this chapter (Douglas Mental Health University Institute, 2013). Sleep is also governed by the pineal gland, melatonin secretion, and a person's unique biological circadian rhythm (Wehrenberg, 2008). How long we sleep and at what time of day we naturally are tired or awake is governed by our genes and is called one's *chronotype*. Some people have a later or earlier chronotype, shifting their innate circadian rhythms from those of the average person by up to several hours (Roenneberg, 2012).

Sleep seems to confer both short- and long-term benefits. In the short term, sleep helps us function the next day, have energy, and remain alert to complete our daily tasks. In the long term, good sleep may offer some protection from illness, as it supports the immune system. A link has been shown between inadequate sleep and development of type 2 diabetes and cardiovascular disease due to inflammatory responses, according to a study from the University of Helsinki in Finland (2013). Researchers at the university deprived healthy young adult male subjects of sleep, having them sleep just 4 hours a night for 5 days. At the end of those days, the scientists looked at blood samples and found indicators of differences in how genes were expressed in those deprived of sleep and a control group of those who were not. The sleep-deprived showed an inflammatory response, with more antigens that produce the body's defense mechanisms, leading to an increase in allergic and asthmatic responses. Adequate sleep helps our bodies by keeping inflammatory responses low. Cardiovascular disease and diabetes are conditions related to inflammatory responses in the body. Long-term sleep deprivation creates changes in the body's immune system and can lead to chronic inflammation, putting people at risk of serious illness. Studies of the sleep-deprived also show increased heart rate and blood pressure (Tochikubo, Ikeda, Miyajima, & Ishii, 1996), and blood samples show differences in C-reactive protein, a marker of inflammation that is a risk factor for coronary artery disease (Meier-Ewart et al., 2004). The development of diabetes and obesity is also related to the impaired glucose tolerance found in the significantly sleep-deprived (Spiegel, Tasali, Leproult, & Van Cauter, 2009).

In demonstrating how sleep affects the immune system, a recent study tried to induce a cold in 150 subjects by administering nasal drops of a rhinovirus. Participants who received 7 hours or less sleep were almost three times more likely to develop a cold than those who slept 8 hours or more (Roenneberg, 2012). Sleep quality in this study was found to be even more important than duration, with those reporting less than 93 percent of the optimal sleep quality having a five-and-a-half times increased chance of catching the cold.

Sleep is vital for survival itself. Appropriate levels of sleep appear necessary for the nervous system, including the brain, to work properly. Some experts believe sleep is the time during which neurons repair themselves. Without this break and time to rejuvenate, neurons may lack the energy to function properly when the person is awake. Many of the body's cells also increase protein production during deep sleep. Proteins are needed for cell repair from stress.

WHEN AND HOW WE SLEEP AND THE STAGES OF SLEEP

The main factors that determine when we fall asleep are our individual internal, genetically determined timing or chronotype and the amount of sleep pressure we experience: essentially, a state of feeling a need to fall asleep (Roenneberg, 2012). How long one has been awake, one's body temperature, one's biological clock, and how dark it is help determine how much sleep pressure one feels. Women tend to have earlier chronotypes than men from the teen years until late middle age, when men and women begin to synchronize more around when they fall asleep (Roenneberg, 2012).

There are five stages of sleep, and the brain cycles between these stages. As sleep begins, brainwaves slow in frequency as the person moves from wakefulness to sleep. The cycles through the five stages typically recur three to five times per night, according to the Northwestern University Feinberg School of Medicine (2016).

Stage One: This stage, typically lasting 5 to 10 minutes, is the transition between wakefulness and sleep. The brainwaves continue to slow in frequency, and arousing the person from sleep becomes more difficult. It is not uncommon for people in this sleep stage to experience strange and vivid sensations called hypnogogic hallucinations. A sense of a sudden fall is an example of such hallucinations. If awakened during this period, the individual may not even believe that he or she had been asleep.

Stage Two: Heart rate begins to slow and body temperature decreases during this approximately 20-minute sleep stage. There are bursts of rapid brainwave activity.

Stage Three: Deep, slow brainwaves, called *delta waves,* begin as sleep deepens.

Stage Four: This deep-sleep stage is often known as *delta sleep,* and lasts approximately 30 minutes.

Stage Five or REM sleep: This is a lighter stage of sleep, during which a person's eyes move back and forth rapidly. Brainwaves may be similar to those of the waking state. Heart rate and respiration become irregular. Most muscles become paralyzed and any outside stimulus causes a greater response. Most dreaming is believed to occur during REM sleep. REM sleep may last up to an hour.

SLEEP ACROSS THE LIFE SPAN

At different ages and stages in life, one's needs for sleep change. Newborns tend to sleep 16 hours or more per day. Toddlers can need between 10 and 12 hours of sleep. Children and adolescents need 9 to 10 on average, and the need for sleep is slightly less for adults. Older adults often sleep more or less than younger adults, for a variety of reasons and depending on their health. Because many elderly adults are not outside much, and therefore do not receive much full sunlight, their sleep pattern may be different than when they were younger. Increased depression and anxiety can also affect the sleep of the elderly.

Individual circadian rhythms change throughout one's life, too. Whether one is an early or late chronotype, adolescence brings a later sleep onset. This lateness of onset peaks at age 20 and then begins to gradually shift to an earlier time of the night. Progressively thinking high schools have experimented with changing the morning start time to later in the day, and had quite positive results on academics and behavior (Roenneberg, 2012).

Sleep Myths

- Myth 1: We need 8 hours of sleep each night. Reality: Each person's sleep needs differ. One way of knowing whether you are sleeping enough is if you are able to awaken without an alarm clock each morning feeling refreshed (Roenneberg, 2012). Genetic background has also been found to determine how much sleep one needs.
- Myth 2: More sleep is better. Reality: A person's own innate biological clock determines just how much sleep is optimal. Studies have shown that too much sleep may be detrimental to health, too. Some people may need only 4 hours sleep, although this percentage of the population is extremely small, at less than 1 percent (Roenneberg, 2012).
- Myth 3: You can make up for lost sleep on the weekends or days off. Reality: Varying one's sleep schedule can throw off the natural circadian rhythm, making it more difficult to have a sufficient night of sleep on a regular basis (Wehrenberg, 2008).
- Myth 4: If you can't sleep, just lie there and wait to fall asleep again. Reality: In the past, and in some cultures, sleeping in two shorter blocks of perhaps 4 hours each with a break of a few hours or even more in between was the norm, particularly in warm cultures where working in the heat of the day decreased productivity and taking a long nap made sense (Roenneberg, 2012). Thus, there can be flexibility in how one receives the necessary sleep. Today, there is an expectation that we should sleep in a solid 8-hour block, which may not fit for all people. If one awakens in the middle of the night and is not sleepy, it can be helpful to get out of bed and do something relaxing, such as reading a book in fairly soft light (Edelberg & Hough, 2006). Others find that if they awaken and cannot fall back to sleep, writing a list of what they are worrying about can help contain those worries until they are in a state during which they can actively manage them or take needed action.
- Myth 5: Sleep is a purely a matter of discipline. Reality: Because each person's chronotype (the tendency to fall asleep late or early combined with how much sleep is needed) is genetically innate, usually discipline has little to do with the amount of sleep someone needs.

RECOMMENDATIONS TO HELP ACHIEVE BETTER SLEEP

Sleep hygiene, a term recently coined to describe how people can take care of their sleep through positive sleep-related habits, can include the following recommendations:

- Sleep in total darkness. Throughout the millions of years humans have walked the earth, people slept in complete darkness. Only the relatively recent invention of electricity changed that. Our brains are designed to sleep most deeply in complete darkness. Yet many of us, especially those who live in cities, are chronically exposed to light pollution, meaning our bedrooms are never completely dark, despite window blinds and curtains. Technology also affects almost all of us. The seemingly small amount of light emitted by a digital clock does not allow the brain to experience the deepest sleep possible. Complete dark signals the brain to produce the important sleep-deepening hormone melatonin, essentially letting the brain know that it is night and time to sleep. If the brain does not experience complete darkness, it is not signaled to produce the optimal amount of melatonin. Turn off, or at least block, any electronic device that emits even a small amount of light. Turn the alarm clock to face away. Use an eye mask to further block any light; there are a variety of fits and types.
- See daylight. Surprisingly enough, just as having complete darkness at night is vital, researchers have also found that experiencing daylight during the daytime hours is also crucial to deep sleep later in the day. Such light helps our brains sync with the rhythms of the day and night and keep our own circadian rhythms on a 24-hour cycle. The daylight during the day also helps our brains to produce the melatonin essential for sleep at night. Researchers at the American Academy of Sleep Medicine (2013) found that people who worked within sight of windows slept better than those without access to daylight during the day. Also, spending 2 or more hours outside each day can help people who naturally fall asleep later than others to be able to fall asleep an hour earlier than usual (Roenneberg, 2012). For those who are sleep deprived due to having to rise early for work or school, this means one hour less sleep deprivation, helping to improve learning ability, immune system, health, mood, and social skills.
- Use a white-noise machine. For many people, sounds can awaken the brain or not allow them to receive the deepest possible sleep. The amygdala, a part of the brain that helps signal danger, works even while we are sleeping and responds to changes in sound, as well as smell and light (Wehrenberg, 2008). Thus, the brain wakes up when it notices any changes. White-noise machines, also called sound conditioners, can be soothing and can help eliminate the amygdala response; they are easily found online for less than $50.
- Exercise. Exercising during the day, not too close to bedtime, helps one to sleep that night. The National Institute of Health recommends moderate exercise 20 to 30 minutes a day, no closer than 5 to 6 hours before bedtime, to help achieve a good night's sleep. Exercise helps people sleep soundly through the night (Roenneberg, 2013).

Exercise helps boost serotonin levels, relieve stress, and increase sleep pressure (Edelberg & Hough, 2006).

- Don't smoke. In a 2013 study out of the University of Florida and Research Triangle Park, smokers were found to have much more difficulty falling and staying asleep than nonsmokers (McNamara et al., 2014). Those who stopped smoking were able to improve their sleep patterns. Smokers often sleep lightly and awaken too early due to nicotine withdrawal, according to the National Institute of Neurological Disorders and Stroke (www.ninds.nih.gov; see also Edelberg & Hough, 2006). Unfortunately, sleep deprivation has been shown to increase the likelihood of smoking. For those whose internal biological clock and external social clock (school or work starting times, for example) are less than an hour different, 15 to 20 percent are smokers. For those whose external clocks are more than 5 hours out of sync with their internal clocks, 60 percent are smokers (Roenneberg, 2012).
- Control room temperature. Humans typically sleep best in a cool temperature, though extreme cold can adversely affect sleep.
- Avoid caffeine, especially after 5:00 or 6:00 p.m. As a stimulant, caffeine naturally keeps us awake, and its effects can last for hours, especially for people who are more sensitive to it. Many medications, such as painkillers designed to combat migraines, contain a large amount of caffeine (Edelberg & Hough, 2006). Those who are naturally prone to anxiety and/or panic attacks may be extra sensitive to the stimulating effects of caffeine and may need to avoid caffeine completely, or certainly after noon (Wehrenberg, 2008).
- Avoid alcohol. Alcohol consumption keeps the brain in the lighter stages of sleep and robs one of the deep sleep needed to feel fully refreshed. Some people may be "sleep-sensitive" to alcohol, which may feel relaxing at first, but can reduce the quality of sleep (Edelberg & Hough, 2006).
- Avoid electronic screens within 1 hour of bedtime. The blue light emitted by computer monitors, cell phones, and TV screens confuses the brain into thinking it's daytime, as blue light is similar to sunlight. This light doesn't allow production of the optimal amount of melatonin to take us into the deepest levels of sleep. Reading a book by low light is a much better option than being online before bedtime.
- Take a warm bath. The warmth of the water can help soothe muscles and stimulate oxytocin, a hormone that promotes relaxation (Wehrenberg, 2008).
- Plan for awake times. If you typically awaken with worries, planning—before going to bed—a neutral topic on which to focus can help shift the mind from anxiety and stress to a more relaxed state (Wehrenberg, 2008). Paradoxically, as disturbed sleep leads to stress, stress can lead to disturbed sleep.
- Stay on the same sleep schedule. Sleeping at the same time each day, including weekends, helps the body stay in a pattern that allows for the deepest sleep. Sleep is part of the natural rhythm of the body (Wehrenberg, 2008).
- Avoid foods that raise blood sugar. Eating refined carbohydrates, such as baked goods, pasta, white bread, and sugary foods, in the evening may awaken you within a few hours with hypoglycemia, which is low blood sugar (Edelberg & Hough, 2006).

In conclusion, although how and when we fall asleep may be beyond our full control, there are many steps people can take to improve the quality of their sleep, which ultimately can improve their health and overall well-being.

REFERENCES AND FURTHER READING

American Academy of Sleep Medicine. (2013, June 3). Study links workplace daylight exposure to sleep, activity and quality of life. *ScienceDaily.* Retrieved February 4, 2014, from www.sciencedaily.com/releases/2013/06/130603114000.htm.

Broussard, J., Ehrmann, D., Van Cauter, E., Tasali, E., & Brady, M. (2012). Impaired insulin signaling in human adipocytes after experimental sleep restriction: A randomized, crossover study. *Annals of Internal Medicine, 157*(8), 549–557. doi:10.7326/0003-4819-157-8-201210160-00005.

Douglas Mental Health University Institute. (2013, October 2). Researchers identify the neural circuits that modulate REM sleep. *ScienceDaily.* Retrieved February 8, 2014, from www.sciencedaily.com/releases/2013/10/131002125514.htm.

Easton, J. (2014, January 27). Fragmented sleep accelerates cancer growth. *University of Chicago Medicine.* Retrieved from http://news.uchicago.edu/article/2014/01/27/fragmented-sleep-accelerates-cancer-growth.

Edelberg, D., & Hough, H. (2006). *The triple whammy cure.* New York, NY: Free Press.

Hart, C. N., Carskadon, M. A., Considine, R. V., Fava, J. L., Lawton, J., Raynor, H. A., . . . Wing, R. (2013, December). Changes in children's sleep duration on food intake, weight, and leptin. *Pediatrics, 132*(6), e1473-1480. doi:10.1542/peds.2013–1274.

Insufficient sleep is a public health epidemic. (2014, January 13). Retrieved from Centers for Disease Control and Prevention website, http://www.cdc.gov/features/dssleep/.

Kripke, D., Simons, R., Garfinkel, L., & Hammond, E. (1979). Short and long sleep and sleeping pills: Is increased mortality associated? *Archives of General Psychiatry, 36,* 103–116.

McNamara, J. P., Wang, J., Holiday, D. B., Warren, J. Y., Paradoa, M., Balkhi, A. M., . . . McCrae, C. S. (2014). Sleep disturbances associated with cigarette smoking. *Psychology, Health & Medicine, 19*(4), 410–419.

Meier-Ewert, H. K., Ridker, P. M., Rifai, N., Regan, M. M., Price, N. J., Dinges, D. F., & Mullington, J. M. (2004). Effect of sleep loss on C-reactive protein, an inflammatory marker of cardiovascular risk. *Journal of the American College of Cardiology, 43*(4), 678–683.

National Sleep Foundation. (2013). *White paper: How much sleep do adults need?* Retrieved from http://sleepfoundation.org/sleep-polls-data/white-papers/how-much-sleep-do-adults-need.

Northwestern University Feinberg School of Medicine. (2016). Center for Circadian and Sleep Medicine. Retrieved from http://www.feinberg.northwestern.edu/sleep/about.html.

Randall, D. K. (2012, September 23). Rethinking sleep. *The New York Times,* p. SR1.

Roenneberg, T. (2012). *Internal time: Chronotypes, social jet lag and why you're so tired.* Cambridge, MA: Harvard University Press.

Spiegel, K., Tasali, E., Leproult, R., & Van Cauter, E. (2009). Effects of poor and short sleep on glucose metabolism and obesity risk. *Nature Reviews Endocrinology, 5*(5), 253–261.

Tochikubo, O., Ikeda, A., Miyajima, E., & Ishii, M. (1996). Effects of insufficient sleep on blood pressure monitored by a new multibiomedical recorder. *Hypertension, 27*(6), 1318–1324.

University of Helsinki. (2013, October 23). New links between sleep deprivation, immune system discovered. *ScienceDaily*. Retrieved February 3, 2014, from www.sciencedaily.com/releases/2013/10/131023183908.htm.

Uppsala Universitet. (2013, February 20). Lack of sleep? Keep away from the buffet. *ScienceDaily*. Retrieved February 8, 2014, from www.sciencedaily.com/releases/2013/02/130220084701.htm.

Wehrenberg, M. (2008). *The ten best-ever anxiety management techniques*. New York, NY: W.W. Norton.

27

Relaxation and Stress

Serena Wadhwa

Relaxation is a challenging term to define, as the subjective meaning of this word can have well over hundreds of variations (Smith, 2007), as well as encompassing many states of relaxation. Smith proposes that relaxation can occur psychologically, physically, and neurologically. Although Smith (2007) was one of the earliest to propose that relaxation can be categorized into various groups, much like food groups, he also noted that not all relaxation strategies work for everyone.

What, then, does *relaxation* mean? In an online Google search, *relaxation* is defined as "the state of being free from tension and anxiety; recreation or rest. . . ; the loss of tension." In physics, it is "the restoration of equilibrium following disturbance."

These definitions are examples of a wide array of meanings; however, many of them involve a relationship to recovery. In the stress literature, *recovery* is a period of time needed for the body and other systems to return to a prestress level. For example, after the fight-or-flight response is elicited by a perceived threat or demand, and resources have been mobilized to fight or flee the threat or resources have been actively engaged to meet the needs of the demand, there is a recovery period during which the body returns to homeostasis. Other research demonstrates similar results in relation to meeting work demands. For example, Korpela and Kinnunen (2011) explore how resources are "used up" at work, therefore leaving little to spare once the individual leaves work. Thus, low-effort activities at home are a primary way to help with restoration of the energy dissipated. Relaxation may also be thought of as a state where no further demands are placed upon the systems.

The idea of recovery is important, as it occurs only when minimal additional demands are placed upon the system. Without a recovery period, the body and regulatory systems have less of a chance of recuperating and returning to some prestress level. Without the recovery period, the body also becomes more vulnerable to disease. Meditation and sleep are two strategies relating to relaxation discussed elsewhere in this book.

Working with these definitions, and recognizing relaxation as a multiple state, provides a framework within which to understand the various coping mechanisms categorized as relaxation. We can understand that physiological relaxation will be different from psychological relaxation, and so forth. It may also provide a contextual framework for understanding how some of these mechanisms work as a path to relaxation.

It is also worth noting that there is a field known as *relaxation therapy*. According to Kaspereen (2012), relaxation therapy works to reduce body tension and restore the individual's energy. As previously explained, stress can drain one's physiological, cognitive, social, emotional, and energy resources and interfere with effective decision making and productivity. Kaspereen (2012) notes that relaxation therapy uses a person's internal resources.

Numerous items, activities, therapies, and pursuits fit under the umbrella of relaxation (e.g., yoga, meditation, mindfulness, etc.). This chapter presents an overview and small sample of what is available.

LEISURE

It is well documented that leisure can be an effective coping mechanism for stress. There are several ways to define *leisure:* Leisure can be time left over from obligations, voluntarily pursued activities, or involvement with activities that provide internal rewards (Qian, Yarnal, & Almedida, 2014; Csikszentmihalyi & LeFevre, 1989; Sonnentag & Zijlstra, 2006). However, different activities are considered leisure based on one's perception, meaning, values, and other internal and external factors. What may be relaxing for one individual may not be so for another.

The concept of leisure has changed over history. Some researchers (Haller, Hadler, & Kaup, 2013) propose a concept of "time stress" and explore how it relates to additional pressures of finding things to enjoy—which is not what leisure is about, as leisure should ideally not be based on time limits. Leisure as relaxation takes the form of activities enjoyed by the individual and usually draws upon other resources not needed in a stress situation (Sonnentag & Zijlstra, 2006). For example, an activity such as talking with a friend on the phone does not require the same effort, resources, and energy as talking to someone in a business meeting. The concept relates to fun, in that some creativity, spontaneity, joy, and/or laughter are experienced. Meta-analyses report the positive effects of leisure (Qian et al., 2014), and while a description of the efforts to understand the mechanisms of these effects is beyond the scope of this chapter, it is well known that engaging oneself in activities one enjoys, purely for the fun and joy of it, can reduce stress levels.

BREATHING

Deep breathing brings in more oxygen and allows the body to become more relaxed, thus countering the effects of stress. The body cannot be in a state of tension and relaxation at the same time, as this state of contrasting demands does not allow the body to work efficiently and maintain homeostasis or effectively cope with any additional demands. *Breathing practice* refers to voluntary changes in rate, pattern, and quality of respiration (Brown, Gerbarg, & Muench, 2013). The effects of regulated breathing on the body and mind are well documented (see Brown et al., 2013).

The "relaxation response," a strategy developed by Herbert Benson in the 1970s, is one of the best-known and most-used relaxation techniques. Martin (2008) explored how use of the relaxation response confers many benefits, including counteracting the effects of stress, inducing anti-oxidation and anti-inflammatory shifts. He refers to the relaxation response as "break[ing] the train of everyday thought" (p. 32). The relaxation response consists of nine steps, which include using a word, cultivating a specific attitude, and using the breath to activate the parasympathetic system, which oversees restoration and relaxation. Readers are referred to *The Relaxation Response,* by Herbert Benson (2000), as well as Davis, Eshelman, and McKay (2008), for additional information.

HERBERT BENSON (1935–)

Born in Yonkers, New York, in 1935, Herbert Benson went to medical school at Harvard University and graduated in 1961. He held various appointments up to 1987, when he returned to Harvard and then, in 1988, founded and became the president of the Mind/Body Medical Institute of Harvard Medical School in 1988. While he has a varied and accomplished career, he is best known for bringing the relaxation response into the spotlight in the mid-1970s. The relaxation response is known to decrease the symptoms of the fight-or-flight response, which include increased heart rate; rapid, shallow breathing; and increased blood pressure. When the relaxation response is elicited, these symptoms are slowed down and/or lowered. Research has demonstrated the efficacy of this technique in reducing the fight-or-flight response and "turning on" the response to relax and slow down. Additional benefits of the relaxation response that have been demonstrated include decreased pain, tension, and stress hormone amount and activity; increased energy and immune-system functioning; improved sleep; and others. Benson's book *The Relaxation Response,* originally published in 1975, was a bestseller and taught millions of readers how to relax. It introduced readers to the benefits of relaxation and techniques to elicit this response. He showed that there are many ways to elicit relaxation; thus, there is a way for each person to relax. However, there are many paths to the destination of relaxation: What will work for one person may not necessarily work for another.

Herbert Benson wrote many books, focusing not only on the healing benefits of the relaxation response, but also on the possible healing benefits of belief and faith. Although he led clinical trials in this latter area, these studies were not as conclusive as those testing the relaxation response.

AUTOGENIC TRAINING

Developed in the earlier part of the 1900s by Johannes Heinrich Schultz, a German psychiatrist, autogenic training utilizes verbal "commands" to induce a relaxed state. The phrase *autogenic* means "self-regulating"; thus, the individual doing autogenic training is actually learning to control functions normally regulated by automatic means. The use of certain words (popular ones include "warm" and "heavy") suggest to the brain conditions resembling a relaxed state. Individuals repeat these phrases during a session, as a means of retraining the brain to "listen" to the person and shift physiological arousal accordingly. Autogenic training is similar to hypnosis and is a self-induced process. Liza (2011) provided some research reviewing the effectiveness of this relaxation technique.

GUIDED IMAGERY

Although the concept of imagery appears in many forms, especially esoteric, spiritual, and religious varieties of experience, the use of guided imagery as a coping mechanism relating to stress began in the 19th century. *Guided imagery* is the use of images relating to an individual's specific needs and stressors. For example, in pain management, individuals may be guided to imagine a wrench loosening the tension on the head, much like a wrench loosens the nuts on a bolt. Research demonstrates the effectiveness of guided imagery in various contexts (see, e.g., Reibel, Greeson, Brainard, & Rosenzweig, 2001; Jallo, Ruiz, Elswick, & French, 2014; Liza, 2011; Menzies, Lyon, Elswick Jr., McCain, & Gray, 2014).

PROGRESSIVE MUSCULAR RELAXATION

Progressive muscular relaxation (PMR) focuses on developing awareness about the difference between a physiological tensed state and a physiological relaxed state; this awareness then affects the thoughts, feelings, behaviors, and neurological systems within the individual. PMR was developed in the 1930s by Jacobson (Vancampfort et al., 2013) and adapted in the 1940s by Wolpe for stress reduction. By focusing on tensing and relaxing the muscles, an individual can learn to differentiate between these two states and, when he or she becomes aware of a tense sensations, can engage in PMR to begin the process of systematically relaxing the muscles. Typically, a person will tense and relax various muscle groups in a bottom-up approach (such as from the feet) or top-down approach (from the head), depending on the philosophy of the facilitator. Much research has been conducted regarding the effects of this technique on stress (Isa, Moy, Adbul Razack, Zainuddin, & Zainal, 2013; Schröder, Heider, Zaby, & Göllner, 2013).

YOGA AND OTHER FORMS OF MOVEMENT

Yoga, which trains the mind and body to work together in a mindful, spiritual, and physical practice, and which features formal breathing techniques along with certain exercises that calm the mind, has been found to be helpful as a relaxation method (Woodyard, 2011). It is often recommended to people with anxiety and stress problems (see Chapter 30 on complementary and alternative medicine). According to Wang et al. (2014), *qigong* is another form of movement proven to have some benefits on stress levels. Another study found that gum chewing can induce relaxation. According to Smith (2009), chewing gum as a means of inducing relaxation was actually studied by Hollingsworth back in the late 1930s. Gum chewing was demonstrated to moderate the effects of acute stress reactions and keep the alertness attuned, despite other present distractions competing for attention (Sasaki-Otomaru et al., 2011).

OTHER METHODS

Many people find that massage is relaxing, as is soaking in warm or hot water. Others find the aftereffects in the body of vigorous physical activity, such as running, hiking, swimming, biking, skiing, snowboarding, or spinning or other aerobic activities, to be highly relaxing and to provide a sense of well-being. Research has found that intense physical activity does indeed stimulate the release of endorphins, neurotransmitters in the brain that help to create good feelings. Nonphysically specific activities such as artistic creation, whether painting, sculpting, drawing, or craft or building activities, can be so engrossing as to be relaxing.

Dance, as well as creating music, singing, and seriously listening to music may have similar relaxation effects. Research demonstrates the effectiveness of art and music as relaxation strategies (depending on the type of art or music); this subject is covered further in Chapter 29, on creativity; Chapter 32, on music and art; and Chapter 28, on mindfulness and meditation.

BOREDOM

Finally, a brief note about boredom, which can be related to relaxation. Human beings and other animals need the right balance of stress and relaxation from stress. Too much leisure and relaxation may lead to boredom; too little stimulation, such as working at an unchallenging job, or taking an unchallenging course at school, will also lead to boredom. According to Haller, Hadler, and Kaup (2013), *boredom* is the negative experience or feeling that arises from monotonous activities or from the lack of stimulation and challenges. The same authors researched boredom to determine what factors contributed to the experience. Their study confirmed the outcomes of other studies: age (younger individuals generally), being unemployed, or having fewer skills; and living in larger households were factors consistent with those found in other studies to determine boredom. Vogel-Walcutt, Fiorella, Carper, and Schatz (2012) differentiate between state and trait boredom. *Trait boredom* is a person's propensity or likelihood to experience lack of interest; *state boredom* usually arises due to a combination of low arousal and the subjective experience of dissatisfaction, although no clear operational definition can be determined from the literature. While there is research relating to boredom in the academic and work setting, according to March (2005), rather than staying present in the real world, many people choose distraction to escape it. With technology providing the opportunity for almost any desire or interest to be gratified, it becomes more challenging to be satisfied, which can certainly influence the experience of boredom.

REFERENCES AND FURTHER READING

Benson, H. (n.d.). Retrieved from http://www.relaxationresponse.org.

Benson, H. (1976/2000). *The relaxation response* (rev. ed.). New York, NY: HarperCollins.

Brown, R. P., Gerbarg, P. L., & Muench, F. (2013). Breathing practices for treatment of psychiatric and stress-related medical conditions. *Psychiatric Clinics of North America, 36*(1), 121–140.

Csikszentmihalyi, M., & LeFevre, J. (1989). Optimal experience in work and leisure. *Journal of Personality and Social Psychology, 56*(5), 815–822.

Davis, M., Eshelman, E. R., & McKay, M. (2008). *The relaxation and stress reduction workbook* (6th ed.). Oakland, CA: New Harbinger Publications.

Haller, M., Hadler, M., & Kaup, G. (2013). Leisure time in modern societies: A new source of boredom and stress? *Social Indicators Research, 111*(2), 403–434.

Isa, M. R., Moy, F. M., Abdul Razack, A. H., Zainuddin, Z. M., & Zainal, N. Z. (2013). Impact of applied progressive deep muscle relaxation training on the level of depression, anxiety and stress among prostate cancer patients: A quasi-experimental study. *Asian Pacific Journal of Cancer Prevention, 14*(4), 2237–2242.

Jallo, N., Ruiz, R. J., Elswick, R. K., & French, E. (2014). Guided imagery for stress and symptom management in pregnant African American women. *Evidence-Based Complementary and Alternative Medicine, 2014*, 840923. doi:10.1155/2014/840923.

Kaspereen, D. (2012). Relaxation intervention for stress reduction among teachers and staff. *International Journal of Stress Management, 19*(3), 238–250.

Korpela, K., & Kinnunen, U. (2011). How is leisure time interacting with nature related to the need for recovery from work demands? Testing multiple mediators. *Leisure Sciences, 33*(1), 1–14.

Liza, V. (2011). Stress management techniques: evidence-based procedures that reduce stress and promote health. *Health Science Journal, 5*(2), 74–89.

March, T. (2005). The new WWW: Whatever, whenever, wherever. *Educational Leadership, 63*(4), 14–19.

Martin, S. (2008, October). Relaxation: The power of the relaxation response. *Monitor on Psychology, 39*(9), 32–33.

McCallie, M. S., Blum, C. M., & Hood, C. J. (2006). Progressive muscle relaxation. *Journal of Human Behavior in the Social Environment, 13*(3), 51–66.

Menzies, V., Lyon, D. E., Elswick Jr., R. K., McCain, N. L., & Gray, D. P. (2014). Effects of guided imagery on biobehavioral factors in women with fibromyalgia. *Journal of Behavioral Medicine, 37*(1), 70–80.

Qian, X. L., Yarnal, C. M., & Almeida, D. M. (2014). Using the Dynamic Model of Affect (DMA) to examine leisure time as a stress coping resource: Taking into account stress severity and gender difference. *Journal of Leisure Research, 46*(4), 483–505.

Reibel, D. K., Greeson, J. M., Brainard, G. C., & Rosenzweig, S. (2001). Mindfulness-based stress reduction and health-related quality of life in a heterogeneous patient population. *General Hospital Psychiatry, 23*(4), 183–192.

Sasaki-Otomaru, A., Sakuma, Y., Mochizuki, Y., Ishida, S., Kanoya, Y., & Sato, C. (2011). Effect of regular gum chewing on levels of anxiety, mood, and fatigue in healthy young adults. *Clinical Practice and Epidemiology in Mental Health, 7*, 133–139.

Schröder, A., Heider, J., Zaby, A., & Göllner, R. (2013). Cognitive behavioral therapy versus progressive muscle relaxation training for multiple somatoform symptoms: Results of a randomized controlled trial. *Cognitive Therapy and Research, 37*(2), 296–306.

Smith, A. P. (2009). Chewing gum, stress and health. *Stress and Health, 25*(5), 445–451.

Smith, J. (2007). The psychology of relaxation. In P. M. Lehrer, R. L. Woolfolk, & W. E. Sime (Eds.), *Principles and practice of stress management* (3rd ed., pp. 38–56). New York, NY: Guilford Press.

Sonnentag, S., & Zijlstra, F. R. (2006). Job characteristics and off-job activities as predictors of need for recovery, well-being, and fatigue. *Journal of Applied Psychology, 91*(2), 330–350.

Vancampfort, D., Correll, C. U., Scheewe, T. W., Probst, M., De Herdt, A., Knapen, J., & De Hert, M. (2013). Progressive muscle relaxation in persons with schizophrenia:

A systematic review of randomized controlled trials. *Clinical Rehabilitation, 27*(4), 291–298.

Vogel-Walcutt, J. J., Fiorella, L., Carper, T., & Schatz, S. (2012). The definition, assessment, and mitigation of state boredom within educational settings: A comprehensive review. *Educational Psychology Review, 24*(1), 89–111.

Wang, C. W., Chan, C. H., Ho, R. T., Chan, J. S., Ng, S. M., & Chan, C. L. (2014). Managing stress and anxiety through qigong exercise in healthy adults: A systematic review and meta-analysis of randomized controlled trials. *BMC Complementary and Alternative Medicine, 14*(8). doi:10.1186/1472-6882-14-8.

Williams, D. A., & Carey, M. (2003). You really need to relax: Effective methods. Retrieved from http://www.med.umich.edu/painresearch/patients/Relaxation.pdf.

Woodyard, C. (2011). Exploring the therapeutic effects of yoga and its ability to increase quality of life. *International Journal of Yoga, 4*(2), 49–54. doi:10.4103/0973-6131.85485.

28

Mindfulness and Meditation for Reducing Stress

Rae Louise Mazzei

INTRODUCTION

Mindfulness refers to the process of being aware in the moment. Thoughts, feelings, and physical sensations are simply experienced for what they are in the present. Additionally, mindfulness relates to being emotionally open to the moment. *Meditation* is a focusing activity that incorporates mindfulness. Many research studies examining mindfulness and meditation have shown that regular use of these practices can lead to lower levels of stress (Lane, Seskevich, & Pieper, 2007; Prasad, Wahner-Roedler, Cha, & Sood, 2011; Singh, Sharma, & Talwar, 2012).

MINDFULNESS

Mindfulness involves sustained consciousness and a state of awareness. People often become enmeshed with their thoughts and feelings, which trigger emotional distress. The internal dialogue of the mind often produces noisy chatter. The mind becomes distracted, shifting focus away from the present experience. When this occurs, thoughts often become worries, concerns, distractions, and judgments, causing additional demands and pressure on the individual. Mindfulness encourages a practical focus on noticing one's current state with a detached and open attitude. Perceptions that enter into awareness are not evaluated as good or bad. Ultimately, mindfulness is an ability to attend in a specific manner.

Practicing mindfulness can be an effective coping strategy for minimizing stress. Rather than dwelling on automatic thoughts and disturbing emotions, one can stay connected to the present and be freed from stressful cognitions and feelings. Mindfulness practice allows an immediate connectedness to one's psychological and somatic experience situated in the environment. A Vietnamese Buddhist monk, Thich Nhat Hanh (2009), describes mindfulness as "touching life deeply in every moment" (p. ix). He encourages practicing mindfulness while participating in everyday activities, such as breathing, walking, eating, and talking. Jon Kabat-Zinn (1990), who popularized mindfulness practices in the Western world, defined *mindfulness* as "paying attention to the present moment in a nonjudgmental manner" (p. 2).

There are three primary forms of mindfulness: sensory, body, and emotional. *Sensory mindfulness* refers to paying attention to the moment using the senses of taste, touch, smell, and hearing. Mindful eating is an effective way to access sensory mindfulness. For example, when eating a piece of chocolate, the individual notices how it tastes, the flavors it releases into the mouth, and how it smells. *Body mindfulness* refers to noticing any physical sensations in the body. For instance, pain is viewed with curiosity and inquisitiveness rather than a desire for avoidance. *Emotional mindfulness* is the way in which thoughts and feelings are accepted for what they are. By utilizing sensory, body, and emotional mindfulness, an individual may experience a reduction in stress. The focus is on present-moment awareness rather than distressing cognitions.

Cognitive change that occurs when an individual detaches from thoughts and emotions (for example) is one of the mechanisms of mindfulness that leads to stress reduction (Baer, 2006). Cognitive change occurs because thoughts and emotions are not taken for reality. Consequently, an individual does not become entangled with his or her thinking. When a thought arises, such as "I am a bad person" or "I cannot handle this," it is not seen as the truth. With mindfulness, there is no need to change or avoid these disturbing thoughts. Having a nonjudgmental and detached perspective can reduce stress created by an attachment to thinking and feeling. Thus, stress is less likely to be triggered by negative thoughts. Cognitive change happens when an individual understands that thoughts and emotions are not reflections of reality or self-worth.

ORIGINATION OF MINDFULNESS

The term *mindfulness* originated from ancient texts that were translated into English starting about a century ago (Mace, 2008). The overall concept of mindfulness is derived from ancient languages of Pali and Sanskrit (Mace, 2008). In 1910, Rhys Davids identified the Pali word *sati* to be "attention" or "contemplation." Other Pali terms, such as *appamada,* refer to present watchfulness (Thera, as cited in Mace, 2008). While the concept of mindfulness originated in Eastern religious practices, most notably Buddhism, the spiritual aspect of mindfulness can be found in Jewish, Christian, and Muslim faiths (Mace, 2008). More recently, theorists have secularized mindfulness to appeal to the general public. Thus, mindfulness is not meant to conflict with any religious beliefs or practices; rather, mindfulness can be thought of as a particular set of skills.

Buddhism incorporated mindfulness concepts from the ancient languages. Although Buddhism is comprised of multiple schools, certain philosophical tenets apply to the religion as a whole. Buddhism teaches that life is full of suffering, but that an enlightened path can lead to the liberation from this suffering. Many Buddhist teachers believe that mindfulness practice is one way in which liberation occurs (Mace, 2008). The Buddha identified the Four Noble Truths that summarize the notion of suffering, or *dukkha* (Bodhi, 1984). The premise of the Four Noble Truths is that suffering has an origin, that life is filled with suffering, that suffering can end, and that a path exists to end suffering (Bodhi, 1984). To address the Four Noble Truths, Buddhist philosophy teaches the Noble Eightfold Path as a spiritual path toward enlightenment. The Noble Eightfold Path refers to the "right view, right intention, right speech, right action, right livelihood, right effort, right mindfulness and right connection" (Bodhi, 1984, p. 12). Mindfulness is embodied in the Four Noble Truths and the Noble Eightfold Path. Thus, through mindfulness practice, one can achieve spiritual wisdom (*panna*).

RESEARCH FINDINGS ON MINDFULNESS

Over the past decade, mindfulness has become a widely studied area. Since 1980, research studies on mindfulness have significantly increased (Black, 2010). A meta-analytic review of 23 research studies showed that mindfulness can be an effective intervention in the treatment of several mental and medical disorders, including stress-related disorders (Baer, 2006). Research findings on utilization of mindfulness in individuals with stress revealed a significant reduction in the ratings of perceived stress (Caldwell et al., 2010). Similarly, studies examining anxiety, mood disorders, and eating disorders demonstrated improvements in psychological functioning.

Researchers have developed questionnaires to assess mindful activity. The Mindfulness Attention and Awareness Scale (MAAS) (Brown & Ryan, 2003) is a 15-item self-report questionnaire that assesses mindful states over time. The assessment focuses on present-moment attention. Questions assess the level of experiencing emotions in the present, engaging in behaviors without paying attention, and noticing feelings of physical tension. The Kentucky Inventory of Mindfulness Skills (Baer, Smith, & Allen, 2004) is another questionnaire widely utilized to assess mindfulness attributes, such as observing and acceptance.

MINDFULNESS IN PRACTICE

In recent years, mindfulness has become a popular concept in Western culture. Although mindfulness derived from religious practices, it has been incorporated secularly into mental health treatment (Kabat-Zinn, 2006). Many schools of psychology promote self-awareness and open-mindedness. More recently, theoretical orientations have incorporated aspects of mindfulness into their therapeutic models. Mindfulness-Based Stress Reduction (MBSR; Kabat-Zinn, 1990), Mindfulness-Based Cognitive Therapy (MBCT; Segal, Williams, & Teasdale, 2002), Acceptance and Commitment Therapy (ACT; Hayes & Strosahl, 2004), and Dialectical Behavioral Therapy (DBT; Linehan, 1993) are some of the main theories that utilize mindfulness. These mindfulness-based interventions encourage present-moment awareness and acceptance as a means to enhance psychological flexibility, with the aim of reducing distress. Engaging in the practice of these models has the potential to reduce stress in individuals.

PRACTICE MINDFULNESS

One of the best ways to understand mindfulness is by engaging in practice. The following instructions are meant to provide experimental insight into mindfulness.

1. Find a quiet and safe place to practice. This place should be free of distractions.
2. Sit comfortably and balanced, keeping your back upright and straight. Gently close your eyes.
3. Bring awareness to your breathing, noticing each exhalation and each inhalation. Bring attention to the way breathing feels and notice any physical sensations with each breath. You can concentrate on the air moving in through the nose or attend to the overall process of breathing. There is no need to control your breathing in any way.
4. Whatever thoughts, emotions, or sensations occur, simply notice and accept them, allowing them to be there without resistance. If you have a thought, just notice that thought. If you have a feeling, just simply notice that feeling. You can even label that thought, such as "I'm noticing that I am having a thought about. . . ." Do not judge your experience. When you feel distracted, bring your attention back to your breathing and focus on each inhalation and each exhalation. Try to bring an attitude of curiosity, compassion, and patience to your experience.
5. After 10 minutes, bring your awareness to your body and the room.
6. Allow your eyes to open; reflect on your experience.

MEDITATION

Origins of Meditation

A large variety of meditative practices have emerged from the world religions, including Buddhism, Taoism, Sufism, Judaism, Christianity, Hinduism, and

Shamanism. Meditation is a central practice in many of these religions. Multiple forms of meditation originated from these religious practices, similar to the history of mindfulness. In fact, meditation can be seen as a formal practice of mindfulness. Meditation promotes mindfulness skills by utilizing techniques to expand self-awareness. Thus, mindfulness can be achieved through meditation practice. Meditation encompasses sustained awareness, contemplation, and focus through specific methods. From a scientific perspective, meditation is seen as a physiological state that produces physical and mental relaxation and emotional balance. Many practitioners find that meditation brings about spiritual insight and a higher state of consciousness. Additionally, thoughtless awareness can lead to positive emotions, including serenity and tranquility. The long-term effects of meditation are thought to be therapeutic and spiritually enlightening. Some individuals report that meditation brings a deep sense of inner peace or bliss. The heightened state of awareness can produce a feeling of oneness or a transcendental experience, which is an ultimate source of subjective awareness.

Meditation is related to but different from daydreaming, hypnosis, praying, and relaxation techniques (Perez-De-Albeniz, 2000). Meditation is practiced in a state of awakened consciousness, unlike the semiconscious trance produced by hypnosis. Not everyone is able to meditate effectively. Meditation requires the ability to be self-disciplined and to harness one's attention. Furthermore, meditation, similar to mindfulness, may be contraindicated when psychosis is present, because it can act as a stressor (Kuijpers, van der Heijden, Tuinier, & Verhoeven, 2007).

Types of Meditation

There are many different types of meditation; it is not considered a religion. Some may utilize meditation as part of a religious practice, though meditation can be practiced from a secular perspective as well. Most meditative practices fall on a continuum between mindfulness meditation and concentration meditation (Perez-De-Albeniz, 2000). In mindfulness meditation, the meditator sits comfortably still and initially focuses on an object or process, such as the breath, a feeling, a sound, a mantra, or a visualization. The mind maintains attention to the present experience and any intruding thoughts or feelings are experienced in a detached manner. Whatever is not the focus of attention is simply noticed without becoming involved in it. Distractions such as physical discomfort, extraneous noises, or intense emotions are simply noticed, without becoming overly involved in them or shutting them out. The meditator becomes aware of whatever is most present in the moment and an attitude of openness and willingness is fostered.

In Chinese *qigong* meditation, the individual visualizes the body's energy, or *qi*, circulating around the body until it is dispersed (Perez-De-Albeniz, 2000). Vipassana meditation is a type of insight meditation (Delmonte, 1985). The vipassana practice of Theravada Buddhism emphasizes pure attention to the in-and-out breath. This form of meditation focuses on the connection between the mind and body through self-observation and insight.

Zazen meditation, a practice of Zen, is thought to be one of the more difficult forms of meditation (Fontana, 2002). In this meditation, concentration is focused on thinking. Unlike other meditations in which thoughts simply pass through one's mind, the meditator carefully watches his or her thoughts without becoming distracted by them. There is no explicit purpose or intention in Zazen. An analogy to Zazen meditation is an individual standing on the side of a stream, where leaves are floating down the stream. All leaves, no matter their size or color, are seen with the same objectivity and without judgment. This type of meditation is thought to reduce suffering caused by an entanglement with negative thoughts.

In concentration meditation, the meditator's mind is to remain focused on an object or process for the duration of the meditation. The mind is brought to a state of rest and tranquility by paying attention to a single stimulus. Concentration is an essential component of this type of meditation. It is a form of disciplined and sustained attention on a particular stimulus. When the meditator concentrates, the mind becomes free of distractions and worries. In this sense, meditation promotes meta-cognition, that is, awareness about thinking. Through concentration, the mind becomes clearer and sharper and distractions become minimal. When attention wanders from the point of focus, the meditator is to bring awareness back to the object or process. For example, a meditator may concentrate on a candle flame, watching the light flicker and change colors. The flame is noticed for what it is, without any expectations or engagement in thinking processes. A sense of serenity and tranquility may result from this disciplined practice. Buddhist Samatha meditation is an example of concentration meditation, as concentration is focused on the breath.

Tai chi is a unique form of moving meditative practice. Chang San-feng, a Chinese Taoist living in the 13th century, is thought to have developed the practice; however, some think that this practice may date back to the seventh century (Fontana, 2002). Tai chi relies on a sequence of slow, deliberate movements. Concentration is focused on every aspect of movement. A common style of tai chi involves a practitioner moving around on a floor or area no more than 10 square feet for approximately 10 to 20 minutes. Through precise postures and movements, the meditator harnesses internal energy, or *ch'i* (*qi*), allowing it to be balanced throughout the body. Thus, tai chi is a way to practice meditation while moving. Yoga is another form of moving meditation. In yoga, the practitioner performs a series of movements and postures while focusing on breathing. Each movement is attended to with a contemplative mindset.

Within Christianity, *centering prayer* is a form of meditation originating from Catholic mysticism (Knabb, 2012). Centering prayer focuses on prayer as a means to connect with God (Knabb, 2012). This type of prayer allows the practitioner to be present with God. Typically, a prayer word becomes the object of focus. Whenever the mind wanders or becomes distracted, the individual gently returns to concentrating on the prayer word (Knabb, 2012).

Some meditative practices focus on different types of breathing. Most often, meditators breathe naturally; however, there are a number of special breathing techniques. Pranayama, which is also utilized in yoga, allows the meditator to control breathing in such a way as to transform physical energy into spiritual energy (Fontana, 2002). In Transcendental Meditation, a mantra is utilized which is repeated silently with the intention to achieve a state of heightened consciousness (Lowe, 2011). Typically, it is practiced for about 15–20 minutes, sometimes multiple times per day. Most of the mantras originate from Indian Tantric traditions. Transcendental Meditation was introduced in the 1950s by Maharishi Mahesh Yogi (1918–2008). Numerous peer-reviewed studies have demonstrated physiological, psychological, and behavioral changes due to Transcendental Meditation practice.

Research Findings on Meditation

Over the past 60 years, many electrophysiological studies have examined experienced practitioners in order to study meditative states and the impact that meditation had on brainwave activity. Dunn, Hartigan, and Mikulas (1999) examined the electroencephalographic patterns of novice meditators to examine the difference between relaxation and meditation states. For the relaxation condition, participants simply closed their eyes and relaxed. During concentration meditation, individuals focused on breathing with closed eyes. In the third condition, participants practiced mindfulness meditation, allowing whatever came to mind to be there freely without judgment. Concentration meditation and mindfulness produced a higher level of alpha amplitude in the parietal and occipital brain areas than relaxation. In contrast, relaxation showed higher means of amplitude in the lower-frequency bands of delta compared to meditation and mindfulness. Cahn and Polich (2006) reviewed neuroimaging research and cited numerous studies with similar findings of increased alpha amplitude during meditation. In addition, studies have shown that meditation improves physiological effects related to stress, including slowing of the heart rate, increased cerebral flow, and decreased respiration (Perez-De-Albeniz, 2000). Meditators have been found to have increased parasympathetic activity, necessary for relaxation, compared to nonmeditators. After practicing a mantra meditation, participants in one study showed a decrease in perceived stress after just 15 to 20 minutes of practice (Lane, Seskevich, & Pieper, 2007). In another study, advanced practitioners of Hatha yoga, a form of meditative practice, reported reduced stress levels after engaging in yoga (Brisbon & Lowery, 2011). Thus, meditation has been found to be an effective technique to reduce perceived stress in individuals.

Practice Mindfulness Meditation

There are numerous ways to practice meditation. Focusing on one's internal state while breathing, walking, reading, or repeating a mantra are just some simple ways to practice meditation. As mentioned earlier, mindfulness meditation is a type of meditation that encourages open-mindedness. For an experience of mindfulness meditation, here are some common directions.

1. Find a quiet and safe place to meditate, which is free of any distractions.
2. Sit comfortably and balanced, keeping your back upright and straight. If you are on the floor, you may sit with your legs crossed and your hands on your lap. You may place your hands, palms up, on the thighs. You can use cushions to help you remain balanced and comfortable. Keep your eyes open.
3. Take a couple of deep breaths and begin to focus on your experience.
4. Focus your attention on whatever stimulus comes into awareness, such as an object in the room. Notice all the features of this object, such as the shape, color, and smell. Calmly attend to the image. If an impulse, thought, or emotion arises, attempt to notice it without reacting to it. Do not try to push it outside of your consciousness. Simply allow it to be there, while paying attention to the image. Bring an attitude of acceptance and openness to your experience.
5. After 10 minutes, bring your awareness to your body and the room.
6. Allow your eyes to open; reflect on your experience. Notice any differences in your emotional state after meditating. If you felt any stress prior to the meditation, notice how it has changed.

CONCLUSION

There are multiple practices of mindfulness and meditation, many originating from Eastern religious practices. Mindfulness and meditation are increasingly being utilized as therapeutic techniques to reduce stress and improve well-being. These practices are intended to bring about a state of calmness and a slowing of the mind's internal cognitions. Stress is reduced by disengaging from intense thoughts and emotions. Research in the field of mindfulness and meditation has demonstrated the positive neurological and physiological effects of regular practice.

REFERENCES AND FURTHER READING

Altman, D. (2010). *The mindfulness code: Keys for overcoming stress, anxiety, fear and unhappiness.* Novato, CA: New World Library.

Baer, R. (2006). Mindfulness training as a clinical intervention: A conceptual and empirical review. *Clinical Psychology: Science and Practice, 10*(2), 125–143.

Baer, R., Smith, G., & Allen, K. (2004). Assessment of mindfulness by self-report: The Kentucky inventory of mindfulness skills. *Assessment, 11*(3), 191–206.

Black, D. (2010). Mindfulness research guide: A new paradigm for managing empirical health information. *Mindfulness, 1*(3), 174–176. Retrieved from http://www.ncbi.nlm.nih.gov/pmc/articles/PMC3124867/.

Bodhi, B. (1984). *The noble eightfold path: Way to the end of suffering.* Kandy, Sri Lanka: Buddhist Publication Society.

Brisbon, N., & Lowery, G. (2011). Mindfulness and levels of stress: A comparison of beginner and advanced hatha yoga practitioners. *Journal of Religion and Health, 50*(4), 931–41. doi:http://dx.doi.org/10.1007/s10943-009-9305-3.

Brown, K. & Ryan, R. (2003). The benefits of being present: Mindfulness and its role in psychological well-being. *Journal of Personality and Social Psychology, 84*(4), 822–848. doi:10.1037/0022-3514.84.4.822.

Cahn, B. R., & Polich, J. (2006). Meditation states and traits: EEG, ERP, and neuroimaging studies. *Psychological Bulletin, 132*(2), 180–211. doi:10.1037/0033-2909.132.2.180.

Caldwell, K., Harrison, M., Adams, M., Quin, R. H., & Greeson, J. (2010). Developing mindfulness in college students through movement-based courses: Effects on self-regulatory self-efficacy, mood, stress, and sleep quality. *Journal of American College Health, 58*(5), 433–442.

Delmonte, M. (1985). Meditation and anxiety reduction: A literature review. *Clinical Psychology Review, 5,* 91–102.

Dunn, B. R., Hartigan, J. A., & Mikulas, W. L. (1999). Concentration and mindfulness meditations: Unique forms of consciousness? *Applied Psychophysiology and Biofeedback, 24*(3), 147–165.

Fontana, D. (2002). *The meditator's handbook: A complete guide to Eastern and Western techniques.* London, UK: HarperCollins.

Hanh, T. (2009). *Happiness: Essential mindfulness practices.* Berkeley, CA: Prallax Press.

Hayes, S., & Strosahl, K. (Eds.). (2004). *A practical guide to acceptance and commitment therapy.* New York, NY: Springer.

Kabat-Zinn, J. (1982). An outpatient program in behavioral medicine for chronic pain patients based on the practice of mindfulness meditation: Theoretical considerations and preliminary results. *General Hospital Psychiatry, 4*(1), 33–47. doi:10.1016/0163-8343(82)90026-3.

Kabat-Zinn, J. (1990). *Full catastrophe living.* New York, NY: Bantam Dell.

Kabat-Zinn, J. (2006). Mindfulness-based interventions in context: Past, present, and future. *Clinical Psychology: Science and Practice, 10*(2), 144–156.

Knabb, J. J. (2012). Centering prayer as an alternative to mindfulness-based cognitive therapy for depression relapse prevention. *Journal of Religion and Health, 51*(3), 908–924. doi:10.1007/s10943-010-9404-1.

Kornfield, J. (2008). *Meditation for Beginners.* Boulder, CO: Sounds True.

Kuijpers, H., van der Heijden, F., Tuinier, S., & Verhoeven, W. (2007). Meditation-induced psychosis. *Psychopathology, 40*(6), 461–464. doi:10.1159/000108125.

Lane, J., Seskevich, J., & Pieper, C. (2007). Brief meditation training can improve perceived stress and negative mood. *Alternative Therapies in Health and Medicine, 13*(1), 38–44.

Linehan, M. (1993). *Cognitive-behavioral treatment of borderline personality disorder.* New York, NY: Guilford Press.

Lowe, S. (2011). Transcendental meditation, vedic science and science. *Nova Religio, 14*(4), 54–76. doi:10.1525/nr.2011.14.4.54.

Ma, S., & Teasdale, J. (2004). Mindfulness-based cognitive therapy for depression: Replication and exploration of differential relapse prevention effects. *Journal of Consulting and Clinical Psychology, 72*(1), 31–40. doi:10.1037/0022-006X.72.1.31.

Mace, C. (2008). *Mindfulness and mental health: Therapy, theory and science.* New York, NY: Routledge.

Monaghan, P., & Viereck, E. (2011). *Meditation—the complete guide: Techniques from East and West to calm the mind, heal the body, and enrich the spirit.* Novato, CA: New World Library.

Perez-De-Albeniz, A. (2000). Meditation: Concepts, effects and uses in therapy. *International Journal of Psychotherapy, 5*(1), 49–58.

Prasad, K., Wahner-Roedler, D., Cha, S., & Sood, A. (2011). Effect of a single-session meditation training to reduce stress and improve quality of life among health care professionals: A "dose-ranging" feasibility study. *Alternative Therapies in Health and Medicine, 17*(3), 46–49.

Segal, Z., Williams, J., & Teasdale, J. (2002). *Mindfulness-based cognitive therapy for depression: A new approach to preventing relapse.* New York, NY: Guilford Press.

Singh, Y., Sharma, R., & Talwar, A. (2012). Immediate and long-term effects of meditation on acute stress reactivity, cognitive functions, and intelligence. *Alternative Therapies in Health and Medicine, 18*(6), 46–53.

Sipe, W., & Eisendrath, S. (2012). Mindfulness-based cognitive therapy: Theory and practice. *Canadian Journal of Psychiatry, 57*(2), 63–69.

Yogani. (2005). *Deep meditation: Pathway to personal freedom.* Nashville, TN: AYP Publishing.

29

Creativity and Stress Management

Erin Conway

Recently, researchers have begun to look at creativity and how it could play a role in the management of stress and the promotion of emotional well-being. Art therapy, which encompasses a myriad of creative techniques such as music therapy, drama therapy, and dance therapy (some of which are covered in later chapters), has been suggested as a successful adjunctive therapy for adolescents who suffer from depression, anxiety, and grief (Karkou, 2010). Additionally, art therapy has been used as a technique to help enhance nonverbal expression in autistic children and to help increase emotional understanding in youth with learning disabilities. Movement or dance therapy promotes multisensory experiences, which can help individuals who suffer from chronic pain due to a medical illness and can help foster the articulation of emotions in young children (Tortora, 2009). When used in conjunction with traditional psychotherapies, art therapy can add components that help foster mental, emotional, and physical well-being.

The *Merriam-Webster Dictionary* (n.d.) defines *creativity* as "the ability to make new things or think of new ideas." Howard Gardner (1993) defined *creativity* as a person's ability to create something or raise awareness within a certain domain in a way that begins as innovative and unique, but is eventually seen as a great achievement by the public. To further expand on Gardner's idea of creativity, Csikszentmihalyi (1996) suggested that creativity happens when three separate elements are merged within one individual. The first element requires certain personality characteristics to be present within the individual: namely, talent and ambition. The second element says the individual must work within an area that is recognized by a particular culture, such as the arts or music; the third element says the individual's work must be recognized and judged by people who are considered to be experts on the subject within the culture (Csikszentmihalyi, 1996). Therefore, being different is not necessarily the same as being creative.

Gardner's initial definition of creativity and the creative process led to many other organizations generating their own definitions of creativity. For example, the National Advisory Committee for Cultural and Creative Education (NACCCE) defined *creativity* as a process involving imagination that eventually leads to a product that is original and valuable (Ofsted, 2010). Ofsted, the Office for Standards in Education, Children's Services and Skills, in the United Kingdom, further expands on the NACCCE's definition by saying that creativity should inspire individuals to "question and challenge, make connections, see relationships, speculate, keep options open while pursuing a line of inquiry and reflect critically on ideas, actions and results" (2010). Although many people think of creativity only in relation to artistic ability, creativity itself is actually a very broad term that is open to interpretation.

CREATIVITY THEORY

A new theory is emerging from creativity research that provides a general hypothesis regarding how creativity affects human beings. The hypothesis states that human beings have the instinctive ability to be creative and the desire to express their creativity. When given the opportunity to express creativity through daily activities, a significant positive effect is seen in the individual's health and well-being (Schmid, 2005). Creativity theory is founded on what is called an "open systems model" (Schmid, 2005). The idea behind an open systems model is that "the open system increasingly becomes what it does" (Schmid, 2005, p. 10); therefore, the more you do something the better you become at doing it. Using this framework to understand creativity, one could argue that the more people practice being creative, the better they will become at producing creativity.

If we examine our roots as human beings, there is ample evidence to suggest that creativity aided in the survival of the human race. We solved problems, developed new inventions to help with daily tasks, and devised a way to communicate with each other, which continues to evolve even to this day. We also shared our achievements with other people. There is a kind of excitement that comes from finding out you could do something for the first time, and as human beings we want to share that excitement, and usually the details of how we were able to reach the new achievement, with others. Additionally, in the past, it was apparent that our ancestors were more social than we are currently, which probably aided in the spread of new ideas. Great emphasis was placed on accomplishing daily tasks as a group, rather than individually (Schmid, 2005). By working as a group to constantly evolve and solve problems, human beings may have innately cultivated and fostered a desire for creativity.

THE NEUROSCIENCE OF CREATIVITY

What exactly is creativity in relation to the brain? We have a general idea of what creativity is as a process and a definition; however, the impact that creativity has on the brain is still pretty much a mystery. However, recent research into how creativity is manifested within the brain has suggested that creativity involves particular brain pathways associated with higher brain functions (Dietrich, 2004). Dietrich's research into the specific neural pathways that are linked to creativity speculated that there are many different types of creativity, each controlled by a separate neural pathway. Thus, to understand how creativity may affect an individual's ability to manage stress, it is important to understand how the brain "produces" creativity.

Although creativity is typically seen as a process or an act, it has been suggested that creativity is also an essential component in information processing. Much of the current literature focuses on creativity and its role within various subcontexts of human functioning, such as emotional, social, and psychological contexts (Dietrich, 2004). Recent research has expanded this view of creativity to include other processes, such as problem solving and creative thinking, and has begun to include the study of cases found in history involving individuals who have demonstrated extraordinary creativity (Dietrich, 2004). The view that creativity is a mysterious process meant only for individuals who are artistically gifted is gradually being replaced by a more concrete understanding of the creative process. Creativity is a mental function and is therefore grounded in basic neuroscience, which posits that creativity is a result of higher brain function, as mentioned earlier. It has been stressed in the research that creativity is the result of many psychological processes, including information processing and emotional regulation, and thus different types of creativity will overlap with each other, regardless of the pathway(s) from which they originated (Dietrich, 2004). As our understanding of the brain and how the brain functions increases, it is likely that our understanding of how creativity may affect emotional and psychological well-being will also increase.

THE ROLE OF THE PREFRONTAL CORTEX IN CREATIVITY

The prefrontal cortex—the main brain structure identified as controlling the production of creativity and the brain structure that is responsible for most higher brain functions—is believed to generate creativity in three steps. First, the prefrontal cortex brings a thought into the working memory and thus raises awareness of the thought (Dietrich, 2004). Following the awareness of a thought, the prefrontal cortex engages other higher brain functions to produce creativity. Examples of higher brain functions include increasing the ability to pay attention, employing applicable memories, organizing necessary information, and promoting abstract thinking. Lastly, the prefrontal cortex initiates action toward the intended goal, which in this case is to produce the product of the creative idea (Dietrich, 2004). Thus, the prefrontal cortex fosters creative insight, but it is merely the first step in the creative process. As we discuss later in this chapter, creativity does not stop at the brain.

Another theory about creativity and brain activity is that creativity involves two modes of information processing: spontaneous and deliberate (Dietrich, 2004). Many researchers have noted that creativity occurs when the brain is in a state of unfocused attention (Dietrich, 2004; Howard-Jones & Murray, 2003); that is, creativity happens automatically and effortlessly. However, some researchers argue against the idea that creativity is a spontaneous cognitive process. They believe creativity is more deliberate and is caused by systematic problem solving, and argue that creative acts present within our history are evidence of how arduous trial and error can also produce creativity (Dietrich, 2004). Regardless of whether creativity happens as a result of a spontaneous or a deliberate act, researchers do agree that creativity may play a large role in the management of stress.

EVERYDAY CREATIVITY

Much of the current research focuses on what is called *eminent creativity,* a term used to describe the work of highly talented and groundbreaking thinkers, such as Steve Jobs. Little research addresses what effect everyday creativity may have on the role of stress management. Researchers have suggested that studying how everyday creativity affects physical and mental well-being could be invaluable when trying to promote good self-care and create a healthier society (Grace, Gandolfo, & Candy, 2008). The idea that one must be a genius in order to achieve true creativity may have stifled the progression of research into everyday creativity. Some experts hope to promote the idea that creativity is a spectrum and source of coping, instead of the idea that creativity is inherent and you either have creativity or you do not (Grace et al., 2008).

Further supporting the idea that creativity is found in everyday activities, Schmid (2005) believes that the chance to be creative happens on a daily basis. She states that simple activities, such as work, raising children, choosing an outfit for the day, or even helping a friend with a problem require creativity. Therefore, creativity cannot be limited to a single idea or process that happens at a specific moment or when the brain is distracted. Additionally, Schmid (2005) says that creativity is a necessary part of evolution; without creativity, we as a human race would not be able to make advancements in technology, science, or the arts.

Traditionally, successful creativity was assessed based on the outcome: a product, an idea, or a behavior. However, the feelings associated with the self-expression that is involved in producing the creative outcome have not been widely studied

CREATIVE ACTIVITIES FOR STRESS MANAGEMENT

These techniques have been used for stress management.

1. Taking a walk. Walking releases muscle tension and stimulates endorphins, which are associated with good feelings.
2. Working on a do-it-yourself project. Doing something like painting a picture frame, building a piece of furniture, or finding a way to clean up a shabby item already owned can be enjoyable.
3. Cooking without a recipe. Even if it ends up tasting bad, it's often fun to experiment with ingredients and cooking techniques.
4. Playing. Even without children to join in, playing a game can be therapeutic.

(Schmid, 2005). Indeed, creativity does not end with the generation of an idea and the eventual outcome, but also involves the process by which the outcome is achieved. If one uses chaos theory to understand creativity, it is possible to believe that creativity is a nonlinear process that requires the individual to go above and beyond previous experiences in order to generate a new and more meaningful experience. In short, being creative requires imagination, specific knowledge about a certain subject, and possession of the skills needed to implement ideas to achieve a desired outcome (Schmid, 2005). Creativity as a process involves discovery, not only of individual talent, but also of one's inner self. The creative process stimulates positive emotions and causes good feelings, which in turn promote a healthy well-being (Schmid, 2005).

The research that is available regarding everyday creativity indicates that creativity is actually a tool for survival. Human beings are constantly evolving; therefore, they need to be able to adapt to new environments, new people, and new technology. In order to adapt to ever-changing surroundings, we as humans must be creative in our thinking and in our lifestyle (Schmid, 2005). In fact, it has been suggested that the mental health and well-being of individuals who do not practice creativity on a regular basis are likely worse because they do not have an opportunity to express their inner selves (Schmid, 2005). It has been proposed that the increase in the prevalence of mental illness over the past decade may be directly related to a lack of opportunities to express creativity.

Another trend within the current research on creativity is that it has been limited to the achievements of men, due to gender roles that previously existed within society. Grace et al. (2008) noted that more often than not, men have been recognized for their creative achievements, which has caused the creative accomplishments of women to go unrecognized. This inequality among men and women has suppressed research into how the creative process affects and is expressed by women. The research that is available regarding creativity and women suggests that women display creativity in several aspects of their lives, including "relationships, work, personal interests, aesthetics, and their appearance" (Grace et al., 2008). The research into creativity as a spectrum does not stop with the desire to understand creativity in women. In fact, researchers have suggested exploration of how creativity affects everyone's daily life in order to understand how creativity is used to manage stress (Grace et al., 2008).

CREATIVITY AND SOCIAL AND EMOTIONAL WELL-BEING

A study conducted using a community art program found that producing a social environment with the common goal of creating something increased self-confidence in the participants and generally made people feel better, both physically and emotionally (Grace et al., 2008). Creative writing has been shown to be effective in improving the mental and physical health of individuals diagnosed with eating disorders and of individuals who suffer from severe, chronic pain. Moreover, research has shown that engaging in creative activities can help geriatric individuals cope with aging, cognitive decline, illness, and the death of friends. Therapists who work with children who have experienced trauma have found that creative play is effective in helping the children understand the trauma and their fears surrounding the trauma, and can help these children build better social skills (Grace et al., 2008). It appears that creativity is not limited by age, race, gender, or sexual orientation, and that it is not the mystical or exceptional process it was thought to be in the past.

Expanding on the view that creativity should be viewed as a spectrum rather than an inherent trait, as mentioned previously, recent research has investigated other forms of creativity and the benefit these other forms may have on human well-being. One study focused on urban private gardens in the United Kingdom; these gardens make up 15.6 percent of the total land in the United Kingdom (Dunnett & Qasim, 2000). Gardening is viewed as one of the most prevalent free-time activities and is enjoyed by more than 10 million citizens of the United Kingdom. Urban gardens are believed to have a positive effect on an individual's spiritual and psychological well-being, in addition to providing a space that is visually beautiful. Urban gardens are viewed as the best place to have social gatherings, and provide contact with wildlife and nature that may not occur in other areas (Dunnett & Qasim, 2000). Further elaborating on creativity encompassing more aspects of daily life, research has looked into the role that humor plays in reducing stress, promoting team unification within the workplace, motivation, the generation of ideas, and the release of frustration by venting (Lyttle, 2006). Humor is covered in more detail later in this book.

CONCLUSION

Creativity has had many definitions throughout history and still continues to be a subject on which research is scarce. Advances in neuroscience and our understanding of the brain continue to increase the possibilities for new research regarding how creativity affects the management of stress. Although the prefrontal cortex is assumed to play a major role in the development and implementation of creativity, not much is known about the involvement of other areas of the brain and how creativity may affect different neural pathways. Additionally, given another view of creativity as a way to process information, future research may focus on how creativity affects an individual's ability to understand certain situations, such as trauma.

Many experts agree that promoting creativity can be extremely beneficial in managing stress. Learning more about everyday creativity and how it affects stress levels in a variety of individuals seems to be where the research is most lacking. Creativity encourages individual autonomy, self-awareness, future-oriented thinking, and the desire to take a risk; when individuals' confidence and self-esteem increase, they may be able to function better not only as individuals, but also as part of a larger group within society. When you are trying to manage your stress, paint a picture, move around to some music, start your own garden, write a short story, or tell a joke. Creativity is limited only by the limitations you place on yourself.

REFERENCES AND FURTHER READING

Buchalter, S. I. (2009.) *Art therapy: Techniques and applications.* London, UK: Jessica Kingsley Publishers.

Csikszentmihalyi, M. (1996). *Creativity, flow and the psychology of discovery and intervention.* New York, NY: HarperCollins.

Dietrich, A. (2004). The cognitive neuroscience of creativity. *Psychonomic Bulletin and Review, 11,* 1011–1026.

Dunnett, N., & Qasim, M. (2000). Perceived benefits to human well-being of urban gardens. *International Issues in Human Horticulture, 10,* 40–45.

Frankfort, D. (2000). *Calming crafts: Relaxing crafts to inspire your creativity.* San Francisco, CA: Nitty Gritty Productions.

Gardner, H. (1993). *Frames of mind: The theory of multiple intelligences* (2nd ed.). London, UK: Fontana Press.

Grace, M., Gandolfo, E., & Candy, C. (2008). Crafting quality of life: Creativity and well-being. *Journal of the Association for Research on Mothering, 11,* 239–250.

Hass-Cohen, N., & Carr, R. (2008). *Art therapy and clinical neuroscience.* London, UK: Jessica Kingsley Publishers.

Howard-Jones, P. A., & Murray, S. (2003). Ideational productivity, focus of attention, and context. *Creativity Research Journal, 15,* 153–166.

Karkou, V. (2010). *Arts therapies in schools: Research and practice.* London, UK: Jessica Kingsley Publishers.
Lyttle, J. (2006). The judicious use and management of humor in the workplace. *Business Horizons, 50,* 239–245.
Malchiodi, C. A. (2012). *Art therapy and health care.* New York, NY: Guilford Press.
Merriam-Webster Dictionary. (n.d.). s.v. creativity. Retrieved from http://www.merriam-webster.com/dictionary/creativity.
Ofsted (Office for Standards in Education Children's Services and Skills). (2010). *Learning: Creative approaches to raise standards.* London, UK: Author.
Schmid, T. (Ed.). (2005). *Promoting health through creativity.* London, UK: Whurr Publishers.
Tortora, S. (2009). Dance/movement psychotherapy in early childhood treatment. In S. Chaiklin & H. Wengrower (Eds.), *The art and science of dance/movement therapy: Life is dance* (pp. 159–180). New York, NY: Routledge.

30

Complementary and Alternative Medicine for Managing Stress

Cheryl L. Mejta

CONCEPT OF STRESS

John is walking at a leisurely pace through the forest. It is a pleasant day. He is enjoying the warmth of the sun, the gentleness of the wind, the smell of the pine trees, the chirping of the birds, and the peaceful solitude. Then, from behind the trees, he hears a rustling sound. Out from the trees run two bear cubs, with their mother close behind. Startled, John stops in his tracks. His heart begins to race, his breathing intensifies, and his shirt becomes wet from perspiration. He also notices a surge in his energy levels, propelling him to run in the other direction.

Ann is on her way to her sociology class to take her mid-term exam. She actively participated in the class, responding to the instructor's questions and engaging in discussions with other students. She kept up with her assignments and she studied for several days. As she approaches the classroom to take the exam, her heart begins to pound, her breathing quickens, she begins to perspire, and she feels ill. Despite how well prepared she is for the exam, she wants to run back home, fearing that she will fail.

Joe is a vice president for a large communications firm. The firm is merging with a larger communications organization. He is responsible for several critical projects related to the merger of these two organizations. Additionally, he is a new father to a 3-month-old daughter. To meet their childcare needs, he and his wife opted for opposite work schedules; he works days and she works nights as a nurse. With the impending merger, Joe knows that he may lose his job if he does not successfully complete these projects. He also is overwhelmed with his responsibilities as a father. He has begun to have heart palpitations, headaches, and difficulties sleeping.

In each of the preceding examples, the person is experiencing a stress reaction to a perceived threat in his or her environment. In John's case, the threat is of a physical nature: a possible attack by a bear. Ann and Joe, in contrast, are experiencing threat of a psychological nature. Ann is anticipating possible failure on her exam, challenging her sense of herself as a competent person. Joe is experiencing stress related to his fears about being unable to meet his job and family responsibilities.

Stress refers to the emotional and physical reaction to a situation in which the person feels threatened and unable to effectively cope with or respond to the threat (McLeod, 2010; NCCIH, 2013). Originally coined by Walter Cannon (1915), the term *stress* was linked to the fight-or-flight response. When an organism encounters a threat, an adaptive survival mechanism kicks in, propelling the organism either to flee from the situation or to prepare to fight. Although less commonly discussed, freezing is another reaction to a threatening situation used by some animals (e.g., opossums) as well as some people.

COMPONENTS OF THE STRESS RESPONSE

There are three components of the stress response: a cognitive interpretation, an emotional and physiological reaction, and a behavioral response. The cognitive interpretation, described by McLeod (2010), includes determining if the threat is real and assessing one's competency to effectively respond to the threat. If the threat is perceived to be real, an emotional response (fear and anxiety) may be elicited and a physiological reaction is evoked (Selye, 1978). (Note that the situation need not actually be a threat; the person only needs to *perceive* the situation as threatening.) This physiological reaction involves activation of the sympathetic nervous system, which prepares the person physiologically to respond to the threat by increasing heart rate, respiration, blood pressure, and perspiration; decreasing digestive activity; releasing glucose for energy; and suppressing the immune response. The behavioral response involves the person dealing directly with the threat (fighting), retreating from the threat (fleeing), or becoming immobilized (freezing). Instead of responding behaviorally to the threat, the person may respond emotionally, continuing to experience anxiety and tension. This latter emotional reaction may occur if the person feels unable to effectively eliminate or escape the threat. Once the threat has passed, the parasympathetic nervous system is engaged, returning the person to a more balanced and relaxed physiological state by decreasing heart rate, respiration, blood pressure, and perspiration.

CONSEQUENCES OF STRESS

Although the concept of stress has a negative connotation in our society, the stress response is critical to our survival, preparing us to respond to physical and psychological threats within our environment. Without this ability, we would be unable to protect ourselves against threats. Not only does stress have survival value, it can also help us perform optimally: Too much stress, and the person feels overwhelmed; too little stress, and the person feels bored (the Yerkes-Dodson curve).

Stress becomes maladaptive when it is prolonged and chronic. The normal physiological changes that occur with acute stress can have health consequences if they are sustained, as occurs with continued threat and chronic threat stress (Helvie, 1999). Under chronic stress, increase in blood pressure may develop into hypertension; increase in glucose level may develop into diabetes; increase in heart rate may develop into an arrhythmia; and suppression of the immune system may develop into an immune or autoimmune disorder. To avoid negative health consequences, it is critical for the body to return to a state of homeostasis (a balanced physiological state) once the threat is over. When in a constant state of stress or threat, the body is unable to sustain its physiological readiness to respond, and adverse health consequences are likely to ensue.

FOCAL POINTS OF STRESS MANAGEMENT INTERVENTIONS

Stress management interventions may focus on one or several of the components of a stress reaction. The intervention may focus on: (1) altering the perception and interpretation of the threat (cognitive component); (2) increasing a sense of self-efficacy and competency to respond to the threat (cognitive component, behavioral components); (3) addressing the emotional and/or physiological reactions to stress (emotional/physiological component); (4) addressing the physical symptoms/health conditions emerging from stress (health consequences); (5) developing more effective behavioral responses to eliminate, manage, or avoid the threat or stress (behavioral component); and (6) establishing a lifestyle that prevents or minimizes stress (stress prevention).

The types and focus of stress interventions are very different depending upon whether one is using a Western or allopathic medical paradigm, an alternative medical paradigm, or a complementary mind-body approach.

Preventing and Managing Stress: Medical Paradigms

Medical paradigms are comprehensive systems of health care encompassing perspectives on health, illness, and disease that include: (1) a philosophy and beliefs about the causes and etiology of illness and disease; (2) diagnosis of symptoms using specific diagnostic procedures; (3) determination of the origin or cause of the illness or disease; (4) implementation of specific treatment approach and methods; and (5) treatment goals. There are two major categories of medical systems:

allopathic, Western, or traditional medicine; and alternative or nontraditional medicine, which includes all other systems other than allopathic. These medical systems differ critically in their understanding and interpretation of stress-related symptoms, their diagnostic methods, their treatment approaches, and their treatment goals.

Allopathic or Western Medical System

Allopathic medicine is a biologically and evidence-based system focused upon the body (viewed as separate and distinct from the mind), its anatomical structures, its physiological processes, and pathophysiology. The allopathic physician would obtain a medical history, conduct a medical exam, perform diagnostic procedures, and order laboratory tests to identify and treat the illness/disease caused by stress (*Mosby's Medical Dictionary*, 2009). If the person's symptoms are an acute physiological reaction to stress, the physician is likely to prescribe a medication, such as an anti-anxiety drug, to manage those symptoms. If the person's symptoms are a physiological reaction to chronic stress, the physician is likely to treat the medical conditions caused by the stress (e.g., hypertension, diabetes, cardiovascular disease), using medications. The physician also may advise the patient to reduce the stress by relaxing, getting more sleep, exercising, and eating better. However, this advice is rarely accompanied with recommendations about how to accomplish these things. Allopathic medicine is less focused on the initial causes of the stress and more focused on the medical conditions resulting from the stress. The treatment goal is limited to eliminating or reducing stress-related symptoms and accompanying medical problems.

Alternative and Complementary Medical Systems

Alternative medical systems differ from the allopathic medical system in their views about the relationship between the body and mind, etiological theories about illness and disease, interpretation of symptoms, diagnostic methods, treatment approaches, and treatment goals. While there are several alternative medical systems, most notably Ayurvedic medicine and traditional Chinese medicine, they share some basic philosophical tenets about the nature of humans, causes of illness and disease, and goals of treatment. Some common tenets and beliefs are: (1) belief in the interrelationship among the mind, body, spirit, and nature; (2) belief in a vital life force or energy; (3) belief that energetic balance leads to health and energetic imbalances produce illness and disease; (4) belief in the healing power of nature and the body's ability to heal itself; (5) belief in treating the root cause(s) of illness and disease, not just their symptoms; (6) goal of treatment is to restore health, not just alleviate symptoms; (7) health is restored by achieving energetic balance; (8) emphasis on maintaining health and preventing disease; and (9) belief that treatment must be individualized based upon the person's unique constitution and energetic patterns (Micozzi, 2001; *Mosby's Medical Dictionary*, 2012).

Ayurvedic medicine

Ayurveda is an ancient medical system that originated in India more than 5,000 years ago. Ayurveda is a comprehensive and complex system requiring lengthy study to fully understand. Nevertheless, one can gain a cursory understanding of this ancient healing tradition by exploring its underlying philosophy, theory of disease, and approach to healing.

The philosophy underlying Ayurvedic medicine is rooted in observations of nature. So, some of the terms used to explain phenomena in the universe refer to relationships, qualities, and processes of observable elements and events found in nature. A key concept is that all things in the universe are interconnected and emerge from *prana*, the basic life force or energy. Prana energy is the building blocks of nature from which the five basic elements, also called *tattwa*, arise. The five basic elements of nature are earth, air, fire, water, and space. Ayurveda looks to the qualities of these elements, the relationships among them, and their interconnectedness to describe the universe.

As a part of nature, human beings are created from the same prana energy and basic elements as are all other living things. Within the human body, the basic elements are transformed into three primary *doshas* or life forces: *vata*, *pitta*, and *kapha*. A person's body constitution, determined at conception, may be one of these primary doshas, or more frequently, a combination of these doshas: *vata-pitta*, *vata-kapha*, or *pitta-kapha*. Another important concept is that the body, mind, and spirit interact, affecting the body's constitution or doshas. A person is healthy when the body's constitution or doshas are in balance. When the body's constitution or doshas are imbalanced, normal functioning is disrupted, leading to disease and dysfunction.

Several factors can contribute to dosha imbalance and disease. As previously mentioned, the mind, body, and spirit are interconnected, with imbalances in one area affecting the other areas. Mental and emotional imbalances may lead to lifestyle imbalances (poor eating, sleeping, alcohol or drug use habits) affecting the physical body and resulting in stress-related diseases from dosha imbalances.

To understand the origin, path, and manifestation of the imbalance, an Ayurvedic physician will conduct a comprehensive diagnostic examination that includes: (1) a physical examination of the body; (2) personal and family history; (3) analyses of the patient's pulse, tongue, and face; and (4) analysis of the patient's urine. Through this diagnostic process, the Ayurvedic physician intends to identify the causative factors of the disease; identify early signs and symptoms of disease; analyze presenting signs and symptoms of disease to determine the manifestation, route, and origins of the disease; and assess the pathogenesis of the disease (e.g., how the dosha imbalance created disease). Within Ayurveda, treatment can be effective even if the specific disease remains unnamed.

Ayurvedic treatment is individualized with the goal of re-establishing the body's dosha balance. Initially, the patient may go through a precleansing procedure called *purva-karma* to begin removing toxins from the body, through ingestion of medicated oil and heat to promote sweating. Following this precleansing procedure, the patient may undergo additional treatment procedures. Shodhanam therapy is designed to further remove toxins, relieve stress, and balance the doshas through forced vomiting, forced purging, medicated enemas, sinus cleaning, and blood detoxification. Shamana therapy focuses on creating a balanced state and alleviating disease symptoms by stimulating the appetite, aiding digestion, controlling hunger and thirst, exercising, sun bathing, and breathing fresh air. Pathya Vyavastha therapy is designed to enhance treatment effects through diet and activity.

In addition to achieving balance among the doshas, Ayurvedic medicine also seeks to prevent disease. Nidan Parijarjan therapy focuses on changing lifestyles that promote disease (e.g., smoking, drinking). Rasayana therapy is designed to strengthen the body and immunity. Satvajaya therapy focuses on creating mental balance and health through counseling, meditation, and other similar interventions.

For more information, contact the National Institute of Ayurvedic Medicine (2008).

Traditional Chinese medicine (TCM)

Traditional Chinese medicine (TCM) is a medical system that originated in China more than 3,000 years ago. As with other alternative medical systems, TCM is comprehensive and complex, requiring lengthy study to fully understand and practice. However, one can gain an appreciation of this medical system by reviewing its philosophy and core tenets, its views of health and disease, its treatment goals and approaches, and its effectiveness in treating health conditions.

Ancient Chinese philosophy serves as the foundation of TCM and has its origins in observations of nature. Five theories, in particular, underlie TCM principles and practices: (1) theory of holism; (2) theory of yin and yang; (3) theory of *qi;* (4) meridian theory; and (5) five-phase theory.

The theory of holism is the belief that everything in the universe, including human beings, is interconnected. As a part of nature, human beings are affected by and affect their environment. Furthermore, human beings are viewed as whole, with mind, body, and spirit inter-related and inseparable. A change in one part will affect other parts.

The theory of yin and yang holds that everything in the universe, including human beings, is comprised of opposing but complementary forces. These forces are intertwined and inseparable, with one unable to exist without the other. A fundamental concept of yin-yang is balance, equilibrium, interdependence, and interrelatedness. Some examples of these forces are light-dark and hot-cold.

Qi (also spelled *chi*) denotes the concept of life force or vital energy. It is similar to the Ayurvedic concept of prana. Qi moves through the body, in a constant state of change, through medians or channels. Qi is responsible for most physiological functions needed to maintain a person's health. Disease or illness is the result of a blockage of qi, resulting in an excess of qi in one region and a corresponding deficiency in another region.

The theory of medians purports that there are internal and external channels in the body through which qi flows. There are 12 major medians, 6 yin and 6 yang, that connect to 12 vital organs. Along these major channels are 361 specific and highly charged trigger or pressure points. There also are many ancillary points. These are the points used in many of TCM treatments (e.g., acupuncture, acupressure). Stimulating these points will result in movement of the qi. Which points are selected for therapeutic stimulation is based upon the source and cause of the imbalance.

The theory of the five elements is based upon ancient philosophy and is used to explain the physical universe. The five elements are water, fire, wood, metal, and earth. The human body, including its physiology and pathology, and its relationship to nature, is described using these terms. Elements are found in the natural environment, and they move and shift in relationship to one another.

Similar to Ayurvedic medicine, TCM attributes the cause of disease and illness to imbalances resulting from impediments to the flow of qi. The TCM physician will conduct a diagnostic examination to differentiate energetic imbalances with specific reference to four opposite qualities: yin or yang, hot or cold, energy excess or deficiency, and interior or exterior. The diagnostic examination will consist of a medical history, observations of the patient, tongue diagnosis, and pulse diagnosis.

The goal of TCM treatment is to re-establish energetic balance, to restore health, and to strengthen the immune system to prevent disease. Treatment may focus on the symptoms of the disease, the causes of the disease, or both. Treatment methods may include acupuncture or acupressure, herbal medicine, qi gong, tai chi, Chinese psychology, massage or tua na, dietary changes, and exercise.

Preventing and Managing Stress: Mind-Body Approaches

As noted earlier, medical systems or paradigms are comprehensive approaches to the understanding, diagnosis, and treatment of illness and disease. Within complementary and alternative medicine (CAM), however, there also are single practices and approaches often applied separate from but sharing a common philosophy with other medical systems, most notably the belief that the mind and body are inseparable. These practices and approaches are often categorized as *mind-body interventions*. Mind-body interventions focus on altering physical and biochemical functioning by using methods that change mental activity or body processes.

The focal point of mind-body stress management interventions tends to be: (1) the cognitive component, affected by altering the person's interpretation of the event and/or the person's assessment of his or her ability to respond to the stressor; (2) the emotional or physiological component, changed by altering responses to the stressor; and/or (3) the behavioral components, influenced by developing more effective behavioral and/or emotional responses to the stressor.

Field (2009) reviewed the research on CAM therapies that are commonly used to treat psychological and medical conditions. She concluded that there was some evidence to support use of the following techniques in addressing stress: aromatherapy, biofeedback, exercise, imagery, massage therapy, meditation, music therapy, and progressive muscle relaxation (see also Barnett, Shale, Elkins, & Fisher, 2014).

Cognitive-Focused Stress Management Techniques

Cognitive stress management techniques focus upon ignoring, changing, or reinterpreting our perceptions of stress or its triggers; and changing our sense of competency in handling the stressful event. These techniques include cognitive restructuring, guided imagery, meditation, hypnosis, skill development, and behavioral rehearsal.

Cognitive restructuring

Cognitive restructuring attempts to change the person's perception or interpretation of an event from being stressful to being neutral or nonstressful. Koopsen and Young (2009) identified two personality traits related to increased stress: pessimism and victimization. The pessimistic person tends to view things from a negative perspective; that is, the glass is half empty. The person who feels victimized tends to see himself or herself as a target for negative things, with the person helpless to change these circumstances. In cognitive restructuring, the therapist asks the person to reappraise the situation using a more objective and realistic frame. Changing a negative perspective might include looking at the glass as half-full rather than half-empty, listing those things for which one is grateful, seeing what is working, or viewing the situation as a challenge. Alternatively, a person can reassess the likelihood of an event occurring to him or her. Changing a victimization perspective might include exploring how the person might change, alter, or prevent an event. It might also include seeing that others, besides the person, are impacted by an event. Someone who views a rained-out event as something that "always" happens to him or her might be asked to consider how many other people were also impacted by the rainout.

By reappraising a situation, the mind does not encode the event as stressful. As a result, the stress-related biological and physiological changes do not occur, as there is no threat to which the person needs to respond.

Meditation

Meditation is rooted in ancient cultures, especially Asian religious practices (Micozzi, 2001), and it may be the oldest of the mind-body techniques (Kessler,1999). There are several different types of meditation. One form, Transcendental Meditation, was introduced into Western culture in the 1960s by Mararisi Mahesh Yogi. A currently very popular form of meditation, mindfulness meditation, has been used to alleviate stress and stress-related illness. Jon Kabat-Zinn (2003) is a well known practitioner of and researcher in mindfulness meditation. Meditation increases the capacity for self-observation (Kessler, 1999). Across all meditation approaches, the mind focuses its attention actively on a specific experience (e.g., breathing), word or phrase (e.g., *om*) or passive observation of thoughts or experiences. Ospina et al. (2007) described the main components of meditation as breathing, mantra (sound, word, phrase), relaxation, intentional self-regulation of attention, and belief in metaphysical concepts. Typically, people are asked to meditate twice a day (usually in the morning and evening) for 20 to 30 minutes.

In a review of research on the effects of mindfulness meditation on stress, Chiesa and Serretti (2009) concluded that people who practiced this form of meditation significantly reduced their stress levels. Another study on mindfulness meditation showed that cortisol levels (stress hormone) are lower in people who meditate.

Meditation may redirect attention from a stressful event so that the person does not get "hooked" by or stuck on the event. Meditation may also directly affect the autonomic nervous system, reducing activity in the sympathetic nervous system (involved in the stress response) and increasing activity in the parasympathetic nervous system (involved in the relaxation response).

Guided imagery

Imagery underlies many of the cognitively based stress management techniques. *Imagery* is a thought or mental picture that invokes a visual, auditory, tactile, olfactory, proprioceptive, and/or kinesthetic sensation (Horowitz, 1983). The use of guided imagery as a stress reduction technique is based upon the premise that we can alter our experience, including physiological reaction, by bringing specific images into our minds that are incompatible with stress reactions.

Micozzi (2001) notes that there are three components to a guided imagery intervention: (1) evaluative or diagnostic imagery; (2) rehearsal, and (3) therapeutic intervention. In evaluative imagery, the person is asked to describe, in emotional and sensory terms, the experience of an event that he or she wants to alter. For example, a person might describe a tension headache as a vice squeezing the head, making him want to scream. In rehearsal imagery, the person is asked to mentally rehearse the reaction in a stress-inducing event. For example, an athlete may mentally rehearse hitting a home run before she goes up to bat in a tied ball game. In therapeutic imagery, the person is taught to modify existing images in order to change stress-associated sympathetic nervous system activation. In response to a negative, stress-producing image, patients may be asked to imagine themselves in a place where they are totally at peace. Simonton and Matthews-Simonton (1978) indicated that imagery is most effective when the person creates the image using as many sensory modalities as possible in a dynamic way.

Field (2009) reviewed the research on the effects of imagery. She concluded that imagery is effective in reducing stress, lowering negative and raising positive moods, and improving health scores (pp. 105–106).

Hypnosis

Hypnosis also originated in ancient civilizations, where it was used in spiritual and healing rituals. In the 18th century, Franz Anton Mesmer introduced the concept of animal magnetism: the belief that all people possessed an invisible fluid transmissible through the body and capable of healing others. This was the precursor to modern clinical hypnosis. The term *hypnosis,* meaning "sleep" in Greek, was coined in the 19th century by Braid.

Hypnosis, as defined by the American Society of Clinical Hypnosis, is "a state of inner absorption, concentration, and focused attention" (www.asch.net). When in a hypnotic state, the person has a heightened focus on his or her internal state, while external events fade into the background. The person does not lose contact with what is occurring externally; rather, these external events just become muted while internal states become highlighted. There are several components of the hypnotic state: (1) absorption or selective attention; (2) dissociation; and (3) suggestibility (Micozzi, 2001; Jensen, Adachi, Tome-Pires, Lee, Osman, & Miro, 2015). Selective attention requires shifting focus from the external environment to one's internal environment. Dissociation involves remaining aware of one's external environment while detaching or disconnecting from it. *Suggestibility* refers to one's willingness to suspend one's own thoughts and images while being receptive to another person's suggested images.

There are several ways to induce an hypnotic state. In one technique, the person is asked to roll the eyeballs toward the back of the head. Another technique asks the person to place the index fingers, facing each other, at eye level. The person is asked to let the index fingers move toward each other, without intentionally forcing them. When they touch, the person is asked to close the eyes. Sometimes visual cues, such as imagining that one is riding down an elevator, are used to deepen the person's trance state. A hypnotic state can be induced in several seconds.

Once the person is in a hypnotic state, the clinical hypnotist uses imagery to help the person enter into a calm, relaxed state. Usually, the imagery used evokes all of the senses. For example, "Imagine yourself at the beach. You hear the waves lapping up on shore. You smell the salty air. You feel a light and warm breeze on your skin. You see seagulls gliding across the deep blue sky."

When trying to prevent or reduce the experience of stress, often it is enough to have the person imagine a situation is which he or she is totally relaxed, without a concern in the world, at peace, one with the environment. However, the clinical hypnotist may also present ideas or suggestions to the patient while the patient is in the hypnotic state. For example, the clinical hypnotist may ask the person to imagine successfully handling a threatening situation, and take the person through various steps leading to success. Contrary to images of people doing silly things when in an hypnotic state, the hypnotized person will not do anything against his or her beliefs, values, or comfort; the patient never fully relinquishes control to the hypnotist.

At the conclusion of the session, the clinical hypnotist takes the person out of the hypnotic state in various ways. The hypnotist may count backward from 10, asking the person to open the eyes at one. Or, the hypnotist may suggest that the elevator is moving back up and when it reaches the top, the person should open the eyes.

The American Society of Clinical Hypnosis (ASCH) lists anxiety and stress as conditions for which hypnosis is useful. In a discussion of the effects of hypnosis, Micozzi (2001, pp. 228–229) reported a decrease in sympathetic nervous system activity, including lower blood pressure and heart rate, following hypnosis.

Body-Focused Stress Management Techniques

Therapies that focus directly upon altering the biological and physiological response to stress include relaxation, biofeedback, and massage therapies.

Relaxation training

Just as imagery is the foundation for many cognitive techniques used to manage stress, relaxation is the foundation for many cognitive and body-focused techniques used to reduce stress. Relaxation is based on the physiological impossibility of the body being in a tense and relaxed state simultaneously: muscles are either contracted (as in the tense state) or flaccid (as in a relaxed state). In relaxation training, people are instructed to alternate their breathing, contract and relax their muscles, and attend to the sensations in the body (Kessler, 1999). Through this process, the person learns to voluntarily relax specific muscle groups. It is thought that a person who is physiologically relaxed will also experience affective or emotional relaxation (Kessler, 1999).

Benson (1975), one of the original proponents of the relaxation response, found that people who practiced relaxation showed physiological changes, including reduced heart rate, metabolism, and blood pressure. Pawlow and Jones (2002) also found that people who were trained in relaxation reported lower levels of heart rate, anxiety, and perceived stress compared to people who just sat quietly.

Biofeedback

In the late 1960s, Neal Miller suggested that people might be able to consciously control physiological functions (e.g., blood pressure, body temperature, heart rate) traditionally thought of as being under the involuntary control of the autonomic nervous system (ANS). As medical technology advanced, enabling researchers to measure physiological function, an extensive research literature evolved examining the effectiveness of biofeedback in treatment of a variety of conditions (Miller, 1985).

The ANS is responsible for monitoring and enacting bodily processes that occur automatically, without the individual giving conscious thought or intention to either the process or the activation thereof. For example, the ANS directs the eyelids to blink to lubricate the eye and prevent it from drying out and debris from coming in. *Biofeedback* is the practice of making this process more conscious by using certain instruments. A person gains moment-to-moment knowledge about what physiological changes are occurring at the time and how he or she can use this information to help regulate a condition (Gartha, 1976). More recently, the Association for Applied Psychophysiology and Biofeedback has developed a similar definition, and listed the types of physiological processes that the individual can monitor: brainwaves, heart function, breathing, muscle activity, and skin temperature (among others). Thus, individuals interested in using biofeedback have an instrument that specifically measures the physiological process recommended for monitoring. This may be based on the medical or psychological condition in which the individual wants to see some improvement. There are some subsequent changes to thoughts, feelings, and behaviors as a result of these physiological changes (Association for Applied Psychophysiology and Biofeedback, 2011).

Research suggests that regulating the fight-or-flight response can help prevent stress-related disorders in the long run. When the body experiences chronic hyperarousal, this sets the stage for development of various diseases (heart disease, high blood pressure, etc.) and maladaptive behavioral patterns (insomnia, drinking, etc.) as the body is adapting, adjusting, or accommodating to meet the demands (Fehring, 1983). According to the research, biofeedback provides information so that the individual can intentionally change the physiological response (for example, slowing down the breath) so that an optimal state is achieved. In a comprehensive meta-analysis, Lehrer, Carr, Sargunaraj, and Woolfolk (1994) compared the effects of biofeedback to other modes of regulation (autogenics, progressive muscular relaxation, meditation methods, and cognitive methods.) Though results were mixed, and the researchers cautioned readers about some of the limitations of the meta-analysis, overall there was some general consensus that for various somatic conditions (blood pressure and hypertension; Raynaud's disease; dysmenorrhea, asthma, peptic ulcer, irritable bowel syndrome, and headaches) and behavioral conditions (insomnia; anxiety disorders; anger and aggression; depression; substance abuse; and schizophrenia), results were positive for the effects of biofeedback.

Yucha and Montgomery (2008) also provide a comprehensive document, submitted in part for support of coverage of biofeedback by insurance companies. The document provides research and information about biofeedback and the various conditions it has been used to treat. It also provides information about evidence-based practices and the efficacy of biofeedback.

There are five common forms of biofeedback, differentiated based upon the instrumentation used and the physiological function measured: (1) electromyographic biofeedback (EMG), used to measure muscle tension; (2) thermal biofeedback, used to measure skin temperature; (3) electrodermal biofeedback, used to measure sweat activity; (4) finger pulse, used to measure pulse rate and force; and (5) breathing biofeedback, used to measure breath rate, volume, rhythm, and location (Micozzi, 2001, pp. 230–231). A more recent form of biofeedback is neurofeedback, used to measure brainwave activity. ANS indicators of stress include increased muscle tension, low skin temperature, increased sweat activity, increased pulse rate and force, and increased breath rate, volume, and rhythm. A person can learn to alter these ANS responses through biofeedback, moving from a stressed to a relaxed state.

Yucha and Gilbert (2004) reviewed studies examining the efficacy of biofeedback in treating a range of health conditions. Each condition was assigned a level of efficacy based upon the strength of the evidence supporting its effectiveness for treating that condition. Although "stress" was not a specific category in this study, conditions reflecting stress, such as anxiety, hypertension, headache, and insomnia, were included categories. Biofeedback was found to be efficacious in treating anxiety, hypertension, and headache and probably efficacious in treating insomnia. Overall, biofeedback appears to be safe and effective for treating stress-related conditions.

Massage therapy

Massage is an ancient healing practice that uses a variety of physical techniques to manipulate soft tissue and muscles. There are two major categories of massage: (1) Western, which includes Swedish, Esalen, and holistic types; and (2) Eastern, which includes Ayurvedic, Chinese (*tui na*), and Japanese (*shiatsu*) types of massage. Eastern massage types tend to be one treatment method, among many others, used in alternative medical systems. The goal of massage in these medical systems is to move vital energy (*qi, prana*). Western types of massage tend to focus on soothing and calming the body.

Massage is based upon the theory that the body's muscles and tissues require the unimpeded flow and drainage of blood, as well as the drainage of lymph, for optimum function (rule of artery) (Micozzi, 2011, pp. 211–217). An imbalance in the flow and drainage of blood and lymph will lead to muscle and tissue tightness. Massage thus acts to restore balance to the flow and drainage of blood and lymph, reducing tightness and pain.

There are many different massage techniques. The following are the five basic techniques: effleurage, petrissage, friction, tapotement, and vibration (Micozzi, 2011). *Effleurage,* the most commonly used, involves gliding strokes with light pressure. *Petrissage* involves kneading with deeper and more rapid motion. *Friction* involves deeply applied motion with greater pressure. *Tapotement* involves a rapidly repeated chopping motion using the sides or palms of the hands. *Vibration* typically involves the use of a vibrator or oscillator moved around the body.

Stress is one of the conditions recommended for massage by the American Massage Therapy Association (AMTA). The AMTA summarized research showing that massage therapy lowered levels of cortisol, a hormone associated with stress, by as much as 53 percent. Research findings also showed that massage reduced blood pressure, increased neurotransmitters associated with lesser anxiety, and decreased neurotransmitters associated with greater anxiety (AMTA, 2016).

Moraska, Pollini, Boulanger, Brooks, and Teitlebaum (2010) reviewed studies that examined the physiological effects of massage. They found decreases in cortisol, blood pressure, and heart rate, all correlated with stress, after a single massage session. Moyer, Rounds, and Hannum (2004) conducted a meta-analysis of the research literature on massage therapy, and concluded that massage therapy can be effective in reducing stress-related physiological correlates, although more than one massage therapy session may be required for this effect.

Emotional Freedom Technique (EFT)

Emotional Freedom Technique (EFT) was developed in the mid-1990s by Gary Craig, an engineer who was studying energy therapy. EFT involves a sequential "tapping" process on certain meridian points on the body and face. Included in this process are verbal statements that fit with the particular issue the individual is working on. Craig originally developed this as a self-help technique, but in the past decade it has become a systematic process for which individuals can obtain certification as practitioners. According to Craig, the theory works with energy paths within the body: the "tapping" of certain points opens up the paths that have been blocked by distressing events. It is a controversial treatment. Some have questioned its effectiveness and lack of supporting peer-reviewed research, describing any positive results as coming from a placebo effect, because the person being tapped is expecting to get better. Nevertheless, some research has shown that veterans with posttraumatic stress disorder (PTSD) can be helped with EFT treatment.

Reflexology

Reflexology is a practice of applying pressure to various points on the hands and feet (Bauer, 2012). This practice has existed for thousands of years. According to the International Institute of Reflexology, illustrations from many countries and dating back as far as 4,000 BCE portray individuals working on others' feet.

Modern reflexology was developed in the early 1930s by physiotherapist Eunice Ingham, based on the works of Dr. Fitzgerald. Fitzgerald was an ear, nose, and throat specialist and through his work, discovered how applying pressure to various points in the zone associated with an injury reduced the pain and, in some cases, the cause of the injury. Fitzgerald wrote about zone theory, which was later refined and developed by a Dr. Riley.

Zone therapy, according to Horton (n.d.), a licensed reflexologist, works on the premise that there are 10 lengthwise zones throughout the body. As a result, every part of the body is connected to one or more of these zones, all of which end at the feet. This differs from massage in that reflexology uses the thumb and forefinger to remove blocks in the nerve pathways, thus allowing energy to flow freely (Wang, Tsai, Lee, Chang, & Yang, 2008). In a systematic review, Wang et al. (2008) concluded that while reflexology did not demonstrate efficacy for several medical conditions, many patients seek out reflexology as a treatment adjunct, which may not be subject to benefits research. There are studies, however, indicating that reflexology has positive effects on various medical conditions and overall results (Bisson, 2008; Quinn, Hughes, & Baxter, 2008; Wilkinson, Lockhart, Gambles, & Storey, 2008).

Tai Chi

Tai chi, "supreme ultimate force," combines a self-defense art form with slow rhythmic movements, which are mindfully practiced. Originating from China, tai chi is based on the principles of yin and yang, a central concept in Taoist philosophy (Sandlund & Norlander, 2000). Many styles of tai chi exist, and each form consists of performing a series of postures or movements in a smooth and consistent way. There are five styles (Beginners Tai Chi, 2015). The Yang style is most commonly practiced, although it has more than 20 variations, based on the technique or the location of the originator. The Wu style has three variations and focuses on small, compact movements. The third style is the Chen style, practice of which is limited; it is more physically demanding than the other forms and more complex, appealing more to younger individuals and athletes. A fourth style is the Hao style. This style is rare in the West, as its focus is on increasingly small movements and internal chi (energy) movements. Finally, the combination style is a mix of other forms and variations of other martial arts.

The benefits of tai chi have also been studied in a variety of contexts. According to a systematic review and meta-analysis by Wang, Bannuru, Ramel, Kupelnick, Scott, and Schmid (2010), several benefits of tai chi practice were evident in the research, notably the positive effects of reduced stress, anxiety, and depression and enhanced mood. Other studies demonstrate benefits relating to improved balance functioning, reduction in blood pressure, improved aerobic capacity, and improved flexibility (Kuramoto, 2006). It is also beneficial because it is inexpensive (no equipment needed), although a good teacher is important; it can be done just about anywhere; and it does not require high-impact exercise, making it a good choice for older adults.

Yoga

Yoga is a 5,000-year-old Indian practice focused on attaining relaxation, physical fitness, and a healthy lifestyle. In the United States, yoga did not become popular until the 1960s, when people began exploring alternative health practices. The word *yoga* comes from Sanskrit and means "union" of different aspects of the person, especially the union of the mind and body The philosophy upon which yoga is based is that "everything is supplied from within the individual" (American Yoga Association, 2006). Yoga focuses on three primary techniques: physical exercise, because the body enables us to work and evolve; breathing, because it is the source of life; and meditation, because this soothes the mind (American Yoga Association, 2006). There are eight steps in classical yoga: (1) *yama* or restraint and moral behavior; (2) *niyama* or observance of healthy habits; (3) *asana* or physical exercise and posture; (4) *pranayama* or breathing exercises; (5) *pratyahara* or sense withdrawal and preparation for meditation; (6) *dharana* or concentration; (7) *dhyana* or meditation and contemplation; and (8) *samadhi* or higher consciousness and essential nature of self. As practiced in the United States, physical exercise (step 3), breathing exercises (step 4), and preparation for meditation (step 5) tend to be the focus of yoga.

There are hundreds of types of yoga, with the best known being hatha yoga, raja yoga, jnana yoga, bhakti yoga, and karma yoga. The techniques used in these different types of yoga have evolved across centuries and were passed on through demonstration and dialogue (American Yoga Association, 2006). Hatha yoga is the most commonly practiced in the United States.

Yoga has been studied extensively and found to be effective in managing stress. Specifically, yoga has been found to promote physiological effects associated with relaxation (reduced heart rate and blood pressure, muscle relaxation, and reduced stress hormones such as GABA and cortisol). There is strong evidence supporting the use of yoga in reducing blood pressure. There is moderate evidence supporting the use of yoga in reducing anxiety and enhancing quality of life ("Yoga for anxiety and depression," 2009).

Schell, Allolio, and Schonecke (1994) compared physiological and quality-of-life indicators between a control group and a yoga group. They found significantly decreased heart rate, increased life satisfaction, reduced stress, and improved mood among those in the yoga group compared to those in the control group. The American Yoga Association (2006) suggests that yoga reduces stress and anxiety by helping the person access inner strength, build coping skills, release tension from muscles, and flood the body with blood, oxygen, and nutrients.

CONCLUSION

Complementary and alternative medicine consists of diverse medical systems, health practices, and health products that are not included in allopathic or Western medicine (http://nccih.nih.gov). This chapter discussed ancient and alternative medical paradigms (Ayurvedic and traditional Chinese medicine) that are comprehensive and complex systems of health focused on achieving and maintaining health, as opposed to only eliminating symptoms. It also discussed some specific CAM mind-body interventions focused upon changing the perception and interpretation of stress, enhancing a sense of competency in dealing with stress, and altering the physiological effects of stress. Although more research should be conducted, several of these approaches hold promise in reducing stress and its associated emotional, physiological, and health consequences.

REFERENCES AND FURTHER READING

American Massage Therapy Association (AMTA). (2016). Retrieved from www.amtamassage.org.

American Society of Clinical Hypnosis (ASCH). (2015). Retrieved from www.asch.net.

American Yoga Association. (2006). What is yoga? Retrieved December 31, 2014, from www.americanyogaassociation.org/general.html#WhatisYoga.

Association for Applied Psychophysiology and Biofeedback. (2011). Retrieved from http://www.aapb.org/i4a/pages/index.cfm?pageid=1.

Barnett, J., Shale, A., Elkins, G., & Fisher, W. (2014). *Complementary and alternative medicine for psychologists*. Washington, DC: American Psychological Association.

Bauer, B. (2012). What is reflexology? Can it relieve stress? Retrieved May 25, 2015, from http://www.mayoclinic.org/healthy-lifestyle/consumer-health/expert-answers/what-is-reflexology/faq-20058139.

Beginners Tai Chi. (2015). Retrieved from http://www.beginnerstaichi.com.

Benson, H. (1975). *The relaxation response*. New York, NY: Morrow.

Bisson, D. (2008). Reflexology. In M. Weintraub, R. Mamtani, & M. Mixozzi (Eds.), *Complementary and integrative medicine in pain management* (pp. 201–214). New York, NY: Springer.

Cannon, W. (1915). *Bodily changes in pain, hunger, fear and rage: An account of recent researches into the function of emotional excitement*. New York, NY: D. Appleton.

Chambers Clark, C. (Ed). (1999). *Encyclopedia of complementary health practice*. New York, NY: Springer.

Chiesa, A., & Serretti, A. (2009). Mindfulness-based stress reduction for stress management: A review and meta-analysis. *Journal of Alternative and Complementary Medicine, 15*(5), 593–600.

Energy Arts. (2016). Tai chi. Retrieved from http://www.energyarts.com/tai-chi.

Fehring, R. J. (1983). Effects of biofeedback-aided relaxation on the psychological stress symptoms of college students. *Nursing Research, 32*(6), 362–366.

Field, T. (2009). *Complementary and alternative therapies research.* Washington, DC: American Psychological Association.

Gartha, I. V. (1976). What is biofeedback? *Canadian Family Physician, 22,* 105.

Helvie, C. (1999). Mind-body connection. In C. Chambers Clark (Ed.), *Encyclopedia of complementary health practice* (pp. 29–30). New York, NY: Springer.

History of reflexology. (n.d.). Retrieved May 25, 2015, from http://www.reflexology-usa.net/history.htm

Horowitz, M. (1983). *Image formation.* New York, NY: Jason Aronson.

Horton, C. T. (n.d.). Getting a grip with reflexology. Retrieved May 25, 2015, from http://www.geocities.ws/CollegePark/Library/9858/reflexology.html.

International Institute of Reflexology. (n.d.). History. Retrieved from http://www.reflexology-usa.net/history.htm.

Jensen, M., Adachi, T., Tome-Pires, C., Lee, J., Osman, Z., & Miro, J. (2015). Mechanisms of hypnosis: Toward the development of a biopsychosocial model. *International Journal of Clinical Experimental Hypnosis, 63*(1), 34–57.

Kabat-Zinn, J. (2003). Mindfulness-based interventions in context: Past, present and future. *Clinical Psychology, 10,* 144–156.

Kessler, R. (1999). Mind-body approaches. In C. Chambers Clark (Ed.), *Encyclopedia of complementary health practice* (pp. 27–28). New York, NY: Springer.

Kong, D. S., Lim, L. J., & Oon, C. H. (1989). Biofeedback and stress management strategies. *Annals of the Academy of Medicine, Singapore, 18*(3), 261–265.

Koopsen, C., & Young, C. (2009). *Integrative health: A holistic approach for health professionals.* Burlington, MA: Jones & Bartlett Learning.

Kuramoto, A. M. (2006). Therapeutic benefits of Tai Chi exercise: Research review. *WMJ-MADISON, 105*(7), 42.

Lehrer, P. M., Carr, R., Sargunaraj, D., & Woolfolk, R. L. (1994). Stress management techniques: Are they all equivalent, or do they have specific effects? *Biofeedback and Self Regulation, 19*(4), 353–401.

McLeod, S. (2010). Attribution theory. Retrieved November 30, 2014, from http://ww.simplypsychology.org/attribution-theory.html.

Micozzi, M. (2001). *Fundamentals of complementary and alternative medicine* (2nd ed.). New York, NY: Churchill Livingstone.

Miller, N. E. (1985, February). Rx: Biofeedback. *Psychology Today, 19*(2), 54–59.

Moraska, A., Pollini, R., Boulanger, K., Brooks, M. Z., & Teitlebaum, L. (2010). Physiological adjustments to stress measures following massage therapy. *Evidence-Based Complementary and Alternative Medicine, 7*(4), 409–418.

Mosby's Medical Dictionary (8th ed.). (2009). St. Louis, MO: Mosby Elsevier.

Mosby's Medical Dictionary (9th ed.). (2012). St. Louis, MO: Mosby Elsevier.

Moyer, C. A., Rounds, J., & Hannum, J. W. (2004). A meta-analysis of massage therapy research. *Psychological Bulletin, 130*(1), 3–18.

National Center for Complementary and Integrative Health (NCCIH). (2013). Retrieved from https://nccih.nih.gov

National Center for Complementary and Integrative Health (NCCIH). (2015). Tai chi and qi gong: In depth. Retrieved from https://nccih.nih.gov/health/taichi/introduction.htm#hed1.

National Institute of Ayurvedic Medicine. (2008). Retrieved from www.panchakarma.com/the-national-institute-of-ayurvedic-medicine-new-york-usa-p-342.html.

Ospina, M., Bond, K., Karkhaneh, M., Tjosvold, L., Vandermeer, B., Liang, Y., . . . Klassen, T. (2007). *Meditation practices for health: State of the research* (Evidence Report/Technology Assessment No. 155). Rockville, MD: University of Alberta Evidence-Based Practice Center, Agency for Healthcare Research and Quality.

Pawlow, L., & Jones, G. (2002). The impact of abbreviated progressive muscle relaxation on salivary cortisol. *Biological Psychology, 60*(1), 1–16.

Quinn, F., Hughes, C. M., & Baxter, G. D. (2008). Reflexology in the management of low back pain: A pilot randomized controlled trial. *Complementary Therapies in Medicine, 16*(1), 3–8.

Sandlund, E. S., & Norlander, T. (2000). The effects of Tai Chi Chuan relaxation and exercise on stress responses and well-being: An overview of research. *International Journal of Stress Management, 7*(2), 139–149.

Schell, F. J., Allolio, B., & Schonecke, O. W. (1994). Physiological and psychological effects of Hatha-Yoga exercise in healthy women. *International Journal of Psychosomatics, 4*(1–4), 46–52.

Scott, J. (2008, Winter). Emotional freedom technique. *Counselling at Work, 9,* 9–12.

Selye, H. (1978). *The stress of life.* New York, NY: McGraw-Hill.

Simonton, O. C., & Matthews-Simonton, S. (1978). *Getting well again.* New York, NY: Bantam Books.

Wang, C., Bannuru, R., Ramel, J., Kupelnick, B., Scott, T., & Schmid, C. H. (2010). Tai Chi on psychological well-being: Systematic review and meta-analysis. *BMC Complementary and Alternative Medicine, 10*(1), 23.

Wang, M. Y., Tsai, P. S., Lee, P. H., Chang, W. Y., & Yang, C. M. (2008). The efficacy of reflexology: Systematic review. *Journal of Advanced Nursing, 62*(5), 512–520.

Wilkinson, S., Lockhart, K., Gambles, M., & Storey, L. (2008). Reflexology for symptom relief in patients with cancer. *Cancer Nursing, 31*(5), 354–360.

Yerkes, R. M., & Dodson, J. D. (1908). The relation of strength of stimulus to rapidity of habit formation. *Journal of Comparative and Neurological Psychiatry, 18,* 459–482.

Yoga for anxiety and depression. (2009). Harvard Mental Health Letter, Harvard Health Publications. Retrieved from http://www.health.harvard.edu/mind-and-mood/yoga-for-anxiety-and-depression.

Yucha, C., & Gilbert, C. (2004). Evidence-based practice in biofeedback and neurofeedback. *Applied Psychophysiology and Biofeedback.* Retrieved from https://www.aapb.org/files/public/Yucha-Gilbert_EvidenceBased2004.pdf.

Yucha, C., & Montgomery, D. (2008). *Evidence-based practice in biofeedback and neurofeedback.* Wheat Ridge, CO: AAPB.

STRESS IN THE MODERN WORLD

STRESS IN THE MODERN WORLD

Understanding Science and Society

VOLUME 2

Serena Wadhwa, Editor

GREENWOOD™

An Imprint of ABC-CLIO, LLC
Santa Barbara, California • Denver, Colorado

Library of Congress Cataloging-in-Publication Data

Names: Wadhwa, Serena, editor.
Title: Stress in the modern world : understanding science and society / Serena Wadhwa, editor.
Description: 1 Edition. | Santa Barbara : Greenwood, 2017. | Includes index.
Identifiers: LCCN 2016023948 (print) | LCCN 2016045695 (ebook) | ISBN 9781610696067 (set : alk. paper) | ISBN 9781440845741 (vol. 1 hardcopy : alk. paper) | ISBN 9781440845758 (vol. 2 hardcopy : alk. paper) | ISBN 9781610696074 (ebook)
Subjects: LCSH: Stress (Psychology) | Stress management.
Classification: LCC BF575.S75 S77333 2017 (print) | LCC BF575.S75 (ebook) | DDC 155.9/042—dc23
LC record available at https://lccn.loc.gov/2016023948

ISBN: 978-1-61069-606-7 (set)
ISBN: 978-1-4408-4574-1 (Vol. 1)
ISBN: 978-1-4408-4575-8 (Vol. 2)
EISBN: 978-1-61069-607-4 (set)

21 20 19 18 17 1 2 3 4 5

This book is also available as an eBook.

Greenwood
An Imprint of ABC-CLIO, LLC

ABC-CLIO, LLC
130 Cremona Drive, P.O. Box 1911
Santa Barbara, California 93116-1911
www.abc-clio.com

This book is printed on acid-free paper ∞

Manufactured in the United States of America

This book discusses treatments (including types of medication and mental health therapies), diagnostic tests for various symptoms and mental health disorders, and organizations. The authors have made every effort to present accurate and up-to-date information. However, the information in this book is not intended to recommend or endorse particular treatments or organizations, or substitute for the care or medical advice of a qualified health professional, or used to alter any medical therapy without a medical doctor's advice. Specific situations may require specific therapeutic approaches not included in this book. For those reasons, we recommend that readers follow the advice of qualified health care professionals directly involved in their care. Readers who suspect they may have specific medical problems should consult a physician about any suggestions made in this book. It should also be noted that the opinions expressed in the contributed chapters do not necessarily reflect those of the editor.

Contents

Part II: Sources of Stress

Part III: Responses to Stress

VOLUME 2

Part IV: Personal Accounts

Preface

Stress in the Modern World: Understanding Science and Society is a reference book, offering a multifaceted look at a wide array of aspects of stress and the part it plays in all of our lives. It features 47 chapters and 20 personal accounts, arranged in 4 sections:

- Part I explores theories of stress
- Part II describes sources of stress
- Part III examines responses to stress
- Part IV offers personal accounts of stress and stress responses

Part I: Theories of Stress. Although the term *stress* was coined by Dr. Hans Selye and first popularized in the 1950s, the existence of stress in human beings, when understood as a physiological phenomenon, dates back to humans' first appearance on earth. As humans evolved, and eventually sought to understand human behavior, theories and explanations about the nature of stress and its influence on human behavior, personality, and dynamics were developed. Part I offers explorations of cognitive behavioral theories of stress (Chapter 1); developmental explanations (Chapter 2); ecological theories (Chapter 3); diathesis-stress models (showing certain people to have vulnerabilities to stress) (Chapter 4); spiritual theories (Chapter 5); the neuroscience of stress (Chapter 6); and holistic perspectives (Chapter 7). Included in this section are misconceptions about stress (Chapter 8), as it is common for people to make some misleading assumptions about the nature and value of stress. Chapter 9 examines the hormones that activate and participate in the stress response and some of the consequences of the presence of these hormones. The cognitive symptoms and effects of stress , in both the short and long terms are presented in Chapter 10. Chapter 11 discusses the physical (body) and psychological (mind) consequences and effects of stress. Finally, Chapter 12 explores several aspects of stress assessment and measurement, including both psychological and physiological assessments. Many of the chapters in Parts I through III also contain sidebars that give brief overviews of or introductions to related topics.

Part II: Sources of Stress. A variety of things can trigger the stress response. The sources of stress are probably unlimited, because what is perceived as a stressor varies from individual to individual. This part covers a number of the most significant sources of stress, including financial, often cited as the most common source of stress (Chapter 13); socioeconomic, including the effects of poverty and discrimination on psychological and physical health (Chapter 14); social relationships and the happiness and devastation they can cause (Chapter 15); generational and life span issues (Chapter 16); families and their distinctive stresses (Chapter 17); work issues (Chapter 18); technology, both helpful and problematic (Chapter 19); environmental stresses (Chapter 20); academic issues (Chapter 21); caregiving stresses (Chapter 22); and sexuality concerns (Chapter 23).

Part III: Responses to Stress. These chapters focus on the effective and ineffective methods individuals use to cope with stress and discuss trends for current and future ways to manage stress. Effective strategies include attending to the basic human needs that directly affect the ability to manage stress, or which in fact cause stress, such as good nutrition (Chapter 24); physical activity and exercise (Chapter 25); enough deep sleep (Chapter 26); and sufficient relaxation (Chapter 27). The effective strategies of mindfulness and meditation are presented in Chapter 28. Creativity provides resources, usually satisfying, that people can use to better control and enjoy their lives (Chapter 29). Other helpful responses to stress may include the use of complementary and alternative medicine, techniques, and natural substances to manage stress (Chapter 30). The ability to be optimistic and to practice methods that increase this attitude (Chapter 31) may reduce stress; for most people, listening to music and experiencing art and beauty are also significant stress reducers (Chapter 32). Although no medications can eliminate stress (or stress responses), they can help prevent the cognitive and emotional consequences of the stress response and treat symptoms such as headaches, insomnia, and gastrointestinal discomfort (Chapter 33). Writing techniques, such as journaling, can be an effective way to process stress cognitively and understand its place in one's life (Chapter 34); using humor (Chapter 35) as a response to stress is another technique relied upon by many. Other cognitive methods are described in Chapter 36, which describes restructuring to change ineffective and self-defeating attitudes and thoughts into positive methods for handling stress. Language, both verbal and nonverbal, can also be used to better cope to stressors (Chapter 37).

People also employ a great many ineffective and harmful strategies and behaviors to address the stresses in their lives, including substance misuse (both alcohol and drugs; Chapter 38); disordered eating (Chapter 39); self-injury, used as a calming or control mechanism (Chapter 40); and suicide, often the result of chemical imbalances in the brain which cause severe depression (Chapter 41). Other manifestations to serious stress exposure are violence (Chapter 42) and posttraumatic stress disorder (Chapter 43). Chapter 44 focuses on the concept of burnout: how it differs from acute and chronic stress, symptoms of burnout, and what research says about this concept in terms of coping and healing.

Chapter 45 discusses certain psychological stress disorders. The American Psychiatric Association, in its *Diagnostic and Statistical Manual of Mental Disorders, Fifth Edition* (*DSM-5*), lists several stress-related disorders that are considered clinical disorders, indicating that significant distress has been experienced, and that treatment is warranted. This chapter also discusses some of the research on psychological stress disorders.

Chapter 46 explores theory and practice regarding the prevention, management, and reduction of stress, and provides an overview of the research to date. The final chapter in Part III discusses present trends in the study of stress, including the concept of "stressism" developed by Dana Becker, and the future of research on stress.

Part IV features 20 personal accounts, which are just that: personal essays written by real individuals describing their stress, their responses to stress, and how they have learned to cope with the stress in their lives. These accounts are written in the first person and demonstrate how various individuals cope with stress: differently, yet effectively. These vignettes may give readers some ideas for coping with stress in their own lives.

The book ends with an extensive list of recommended books, articles, and websites that will help readers find even more information on stress, its history, its effects, and its management. Lastly, there is a comprehensive index to the entire work.

Fifty-two writers, along with myself, contributed to *Stress in the Modern World*. Nearly all of them are professional mental health counselors and therapists or university faculty who instruct students in the mental health fields. Some are graduate students working on their doctorates. Their specialties and interests range from the science of the central nervous system, to stress effects on other parts of the human body, to the ability of humans to better and more productively live their lives, whether at work, home, or school. I especially want to thank student worker Annetta Jones Morgan, for her initial work on the "Recommended Resources" section; and to Ashley Orendorff, who is pursuing a master's degree in social work, for her efforts on that same section.

Thank you for reading and using this book. I hope that readers will get as much out of it as I put into it.

Stress: An Overview

It is early afternoon as I begin writing this chapter. As I do so, my phone chirps a sound to let me know about incoming emails that may require my attention. Several minutes pass before another sound alerts me to a friend calling. On my computer screen, up pops a reminder about a meeting I have tomorrow and what I need to prepare for it. My eyes reflexively squint as the sun, pouring through the window, suddenly hits them directly. As I lower the shades, I observe that the temperature is becoming warmer in my room. My mind fills with thoughts about the other things that demand my attention, even as I gently shift my focus to what I want to include in this chapter. And while I notice my heart beating a bit faster, my breathing is a bit shallow; at the same time, my focus is a bit sharpened, my attention a bit heightened, and my motivation peaked. It's a paradoxical sense of stress: while my body reacts physically to the experience of having these demands, psychologically it's exhilarating.

Stress is all around us. It is not something we can escape, nor is it something we necessarily want to escape. At any given moment, there are most likely several things competing for our attention and placing demands on our resources. Stress is something we often talk about, and yet we still aren't quite sure what it may be or how to deal with it. This publication explores those topics. It was challenging (maybe stressful?) to decide how to divide this volume about stress and what topics to focus on, as there is an endless supply of subtopics on the subject of stress. Stress seems always to be in the spotlight these days. My conceptualization of stress is that pretty much everything can be connected in one way or another to this concept. In fact, it is estimated that 75 to 90 percent of doctor visits are stress related (as cited in Tsui, 2013; American Institute of Stress, n.d.). With such high rates, it's no wonder that stress has gained prominence in the lives of many people.

Research also reports that we want to learn more about stress. In an article exploring the connection of stress management and health care, Sophie Bethune reported that although about 32 percent of Americans say it's important to talk with their health care providers about stress-related concerns, only 17 percent actually do (Bethune, 2013). According to a report in *Forbes,* Americans spend *billions* on health care problems that may be considered stress related (Blanding, 2015). This suggests two things: (1) a growing concern with how to access resources to manage and reduce stress; and (2) the disconnection of the mind, body, and spirit fields. Given that integrative care appears to be the wave of the future, what does this disconnection mean for individuals, families, communities, and the nation in the present?

This reference work, *Stress in the Modern World,* presents a variety of theories, external and internal triggers of the stress experience, and both ineffective and effective coping mechanisms. The book explores factors relating to increased vulnerability to stress—how individuals assess and appraise something as being a threat or demand—and protective factors.

If someone were to ask you, "What is stress?", what comes to mind? Is it that stress is overwhelming? That stress is your job? Chances are you thought of something that reflects more of a symptom of stress or something that causes stress for you. These aspects are discussed in detail in this book. For now, it is important to understand the definition of stress. Mainly, *stress* is the body's response to a demand or some pressure. An example of this is how the pupils in your eyes adjust as the lighting in your environment shifts. The pupils either dilate or constrict depending on the demands of your visual needs. Stress can be as simple as that.

However, stress in today's world is much more complicated than a pupil change. Although stress responses are still something that occur without your consciously directing attention to them (because these reactions are part of the sympathetic nervous system that regulates and automatically adjusts according to the body's needs), there are other factors that in the modern world influence these occurrences. Hundreds of thousands of years ago, when humans hunted and gathered food, the changes in the body served as an alert system against potential danger. Imagine yourself in those times: You are out happily enjoying the day, gathering berries and firewood. Suddenly you find yourself face to face with a saber-toothed tiger. In a matter of milliseconds, you feel a surge of energy and strength, which occurs to assist you to run faster, hit harder, and think more quickly. Your heart pumps at two to three times the normal rate, sending more blood to your muscles. Blood pressure increases, which prevents you from bleeding to death should you become wounded. Eyes dilate to expand your peripheral vision. Your digestive and immune systems are are less effective, as is your sexual functioning, because these

"THE STRESS IN AMERICA" SURVEY

To emphasize the seriousness of stress in American life, since 2007 the American Psychological Association (APA) has conducted an annual survey known as the "Stress in America" survey. The APA is a national association comprising more than 130,000 members (including licensed psychologists, doctoral-level clinicians, students, academics, researchers, clinicians, and consultants).

The survey is distributed within the United States by the Harris Poll group, on behalf of the APA. Questions address common perceived sources of stress, coping mechanisms to manage stress, and the impact of stress on daily living. Each year, surveys explore different aspects of these components. In 2007, the first Stress in America™ survey investigated how people specifically coped with stress, the impact stress had, and sources of stress. In 2008, the survey explored how people perceived themselves managing and experiencing their stress, as well the likelihood of their seeking help. In 2009, the survey asked how stress affected families. Other surveys have asked about children and stress (2010); caregiver health and stress (2011); stress and people with chronic diseases (2012); teenagers and stress (2013); money as a primary stressor (2014); and the impact of discrimination on stress and its connection to poor health (2015).

Each report provides a detailed account of the methodology used in the survey, how many persons responded, and a breakdown of the demographics of the respondents. Survey reports also include key findings that were revealing upon analysis of the data. Some reports analyze information by major cities (Atlanta, Chicago, etc.). These surveys are part of the APA's Public Education Campaign, which started in 1996. The Mind/Body Health Campaign was begun in 2005 as a means to disseminate information on the connection between psychological and physical health, particularly in the areas of stress, heart disease, and obesity. This campaign promotes talking with psychologists, as many psychologists are trained in behavioral and lifestyle changes. The association's public education campaign gives awards to work sites that promote well-being while recognizing performance. More information about the APA and the Stress in America surveys are available at http://www.apa.org/news/press/releases/stress/index.aspx.

systems are not needed right now and the resources can be used elsewhere. In this supercharged moment, you find yourself able to run faster and harder, thus escaping the chance of becoming the tiger's next meal. When you realize you are out of the danger zone, you find a place to rest and do so to restore your exhausted body.

This is a rather efficient and effective system to have, especially in the wake of unexpected and threatening events. Now let's imagine a different scene in the modern world. You are on your first break at work, and you are searching for coffee and donuts. Out of the corner of your eye, you see your boss walking toward you. You pretend you don't see him, but already you feel your heart beating faster and your mouth becoming dry. He calls your name and requests that you to come to his office. Now your system is in full swing. You feel your blood pressure rising. As you follow your boss to his office, you recall a rumor you heard about layoffs due to the company needing to downsize. Now your hearth is beating faster, you start to perspire, your hands become clammy, and your mouth feels like the Sahara Desert. The ancestral "reptilian" part of your brain has a reaction that wants to run or fight, as it seems like a matter of survival, but you cannot do either. As you enter your boss's office, the fight-or-flight response is full blown, and all that energy has no place to go. You are so focused on your thoughts that you barely can hear what your boss is saying. When you ask him to repeat his statement, he tells you that he is considering you for a promotion.

This is a good example of how stress works in today's world. There are two things to keep in mind regarding this scene. Situations that elicit the fight-or-flight response can have a negative effect if too many of them occur. Additionally, when you anticipate that an event will occur, this actually doubles the fight-or-flight response. Nevertheless, there are situations that are considered positive and desirable that still trigger the same fight-or-flight response. A promotion, going on a first date, getting married, and making a big life-changing decision are all situations that are perceived as positive and enlist the stress response for motivating and changing in effective ways. Nelson and Simmons (2005, p. 102) explored this initial concept in the context of workplace stress.

THE PARADOX OF STRESS

When stress is present in small amounts, it provides a "rush" that can be motivational. It can be energizing and stimulating. This can be one of the benefits of stress. Research indicates that an initial increase in stress can increase an individual's performance. A certain amount of stress increases functioning, known as *healthy tension*. Dr. Hans Selye, a pioneer in the research of stress, called this *eustress* (1950). When too much stress is present, lasts too long, or occurs too often, this stress, known as *distress,* can have many deleterious consequences for the brain, mind, body, and emotions. A person's wholeness is affected by the effects of stress.

One of the first steps in managing and reducing stress is developing awareness of what elicits stress for you. These things, commonly known as *stressors,* are anything that causes stress. There are two general categories of stressors, both encompassing various aspects: *External stressors* include human development, health, finances, technology, work, school, family, friends, and your environment. *Internal stressors* include your psychological factors, such as attitude, values, personality, worry, and anticipation levels. *Related stressors* are your lifestyle choices, which are how you sleep, eat, exercise, and so on. Several chapters in this book explore these in more detail.

THE STRESS RESPONSE

When the brain perceives an actual or imagined threat, this initiates the stress response. The first stage is the well-known "fight or flight" stage, also known as the arousal/alarm stage, first discovered and researched by pioneer physiologist Walter B. Cannon during World War I. This is when the body becomes aroused and produces an immediate response to the stress. It's a physiological reaction. It is short term, as it is a temporary disruption of the body's normal state of balance. Once the disruption passes, the body is able to return to its usual homeostasis. Recent literature has proposed the notion of *allostasis,* which is when neurotransmitters, hormones, and other neurophysiological systems maintain stability through change (McEwen, 2004). The fight-or-flight response—the basic survival response—can produce extraordinary strength. In small doses, this stage can be thrilling.

As the fight-or-flight response is initiated, several things occur within the body. The pupils dilate to allow better peripheral vision. An increase in blood's ability to coagulate occurs so that the individual does not quickly bleed to death in the event of becoming wounded. There is a surge of adrenaline, which is mostly responsible for the increased feelings of energy and strength. Additionally, adrenaline increases the metabolism of carbohydrates to give the body extra fuel for immediate use. Blood pressure and blood circulation increase to provide the muscles with more nutrient-enriched blood. An increase of lactic acid occurs, which give the muscles flexibility and energy for action. Other chemicals, such as noradrenaline and other catecholamines, are also released to provide the body with the tools necessary to respond immediately to the stress. If the response to the stress is adequate (i.e., running or fighting), then the body is able to return to homeostasis fairly quickly thereafter.

The second phase of stress is the *intermediate phase,* also known as the *adaptation* or *resistance phase,* in which the stress response continues. Physiologically,

WALTER B. CANNON (1871–1945)

Born in 1871 in Prairie du Chien, Wisconsin, Walter Bradford Cannon was one of the most respected scientists of the 20th century. Among other things, he developed the concepts of the fight-or-flight syndrome and homeostasis in the human body. His interest was in the fields of physiology and psychology, and while a student at Harvard Medical School, he pursued initial research about the process of digestion. Cannon was appointed as an instructor in physiology at Harvard, and after that, in 1906, as chairperson of the college's department of physiology, a position he held until his resignation in 1942 ("Who Was Walter Bradford Cannon?," n.d.).

During his time at Harvard, Cannon's research extended the understanding of how the body functions. He studied emotional reactions in animals and how the autonomic nervous system prepares the organism. He invented the phrase *fight-or-flight syndrome,* describing his key finding of the body's reaction to physical or psychological emergencies. He wrote about these observations in *Bodily Changes in Pain, Hunger, Fear and Rage,* published in 1915. During World War I, he joined an Army unit to observe and study the phenomenon of shock. These observations led him to believe that the body strives for "harmonious equilibrium," for which he coined the word *homeostasis* in 1926, building on Claude Bernard's work, representing how the body maintains itself through physiological processes, chemical regulation, and other changes. This biological self-regulation of the organism is a part of the evolutionary process and a key concept in how the body works (Hagen, 1996).

Cannon was also known as a public and political figure. Because he used animals for experimentation, he was somewhat controversial. Although the literature suggests that he was a skilled surgeon and used anesthesia on the animals, protesters criticized his experiments. He also spoke out forcefully about scientists who were being pressured by totalitarian governments abroad. He served as the head of the Committee on Physiology of the National Research Council from its inception in 1916 until his death in 1945. Among his many books is his 1945 autobiography, *The Way of an Investigator.*

changes occur that enable the system to adapt to the prolonged and increased frequency of the stress response. In other words, the body's homeostasis level changes, and this is accepted as normal. As the body adapts to repeated and constant stress, the tolerance for new stress decreases.

The final phase is known as the *exhaustion phase.* This is the chronic form of stress, which is long term. In this phase, the stress response lasts longer, as the body requires additional resources to adapt to the demands made on it. When the body reaches its limit to adapt, so that it cannot cope with the continuing or new demands, the body begins to break down. This happens mainly with continued unexpected stress, a series of stressors, or when acute phases of the stress response accumulate. Changes that may occur in this stage include the depletion of endorphins, the body's "feel good" hormones, which causes the individual to lose the ability to feel pleasure. Other changes include a breakdown in the immune system, which leaves the individual more vulnerable to catching colds, the flu, and other viruses and infections; and developing allergies and autoimmune problems.

SYMPTOMS, SIGNS, AND DISEASES OF STRESS

The effects of stress on the body begin well before one can notice the results. The signs and symptoms of stress are as individualized as fingerprints, because people experience stress differently and to different intensities. Some typical symptoms are behavioral, such as nail biting, frowning, outbursts, decreased productivity, pacing, blaming, and changes in appetite or sleep patterns. Mentally, a person may experience worry, poor memory, lack of focus, and racing thoughts. Emotionally, one may experience anger, fatigue, depression, irritability, or anxiety. Physically, one may experience chest pains, sweating, pain, gastrointestinal problems, headaches, cravings, and a host of other signs and symptoms. Socially, a person may withdraw or cancel plans, stop initiating contact with others, or overinvest in social activities.

At a certain point, the effects of chronic stress do make the body vulnerable to disease. The type, frequency, onset, and other disease-related factors are dependent upon numerous variables: genetics; immune system function; nutrition; coping mechanisms; the use of tobacco, alcohol, or drugs; and a plethora of other factors. Research has linked "stress-induced medical conditions" with chronic stress. The following are just a few of the physical problems that may result: hypertension, strokes, hardening of the arteries, tension headaches, muscular tension, diarrhea, diabetes, arthritis, accelerated aging, insomnia, infertility, decrease in white blood cells, acne, and eczema—among many others.

As the reader will see in this two-volume resource, while the concept of stress itself does not change, what is trending and what is "popular" in terms of causes, coping mechanisms, and other factors, does change. Many variables influence what becomes the focus of stress research; however, because stress will not disappear, research relating to stress will always be needed. There are huge numbers of variables that affect how stress manifests in one person and not another; variables that affect how, for example, losing a job or getting rejected results in actions ranging from the extreme, as in a violent attack on a person or group of people, and/or a suicide; or withdrawal from friends and family; or some unhappiness and distress that eventually change to moving forward. What may become evident is how much of the information seems to overlap. There is a reason for this: as mentioned, much of what is known about stress doesn't change, but as new information is gained, it builds on previous information. The small amount of overlap that exists demonstrates the consistency of research and the remarkable quality of stress, both in the old world and in the modern world.

REFERENCES AND FURTHER READING

American Institute of Stress. (n.d.). Retrieved from http://www.stress.org/.

Bethune, S. (2013). Health-care falls short on stress management. *Monitor on Psychology, 44(4)*, 22. Retrieved from http://www.apa.org/monitor/2013/04/health-care.aspx.

Blanding, M. (2015, January 26). Workplace stress responsible for up to $190b in annual U.S. healthcare costs. *Forbes*. Retrieved from http://www.forbes.com/sites/hbsworkingknowledge/2015/01/26/workplace-stress-responsible-for-up-to-190-billion-in-annual-u-s-heathcare-costs/2/#2715e4857a0b2f1c34c6546c.

Brown, T. M., & Fee, E. (2002). Walter Bradford Cannon. *American Journal of Public Health, 92*(10), 1594–1595.

Cannon, W. B. (1915). *Bodily changes in pain, hunger, fear and rage: An account of recent researches into the function of emotional excitement*. New York, NY: D. Appleton.

Cannon, W. B. (1945). *The way of an investigator.* New York, NY: W.W. Norton.

Hagen, J. B. (1996). Walter Cannon and self-regulation in animals. In J. B. Hagen, D. Allchin, & F. Singer (Eds.), *Doing biology* (pp. 95–103). New York, NY: Harper Collins College Publishers.

McEwen, B. S. (2004). Protection and damage from acute and chronic stress: Allostasis and allostatic overload and relevance to the pathophysiology of psychiatric disorders. *Annals of the New York Academy of Sciences, 1032*(1), 1–7.

Nelson, D. L., & Simmons, B. L. (2005). Eustress and attitudes at work: A positive approach. In A. Antoniou & C. Cooper (Eds.), *Research companion to organizational health psychology* (pp. 102–110). Cheltenham, UK/Northampton, MA: Edward Elgar.

Selye, H. (1950). Stress and the general adaptation syndrome. *British Medical Journal, 1*(4667), 1383.

Tsui, A. S. (2013). 2012 presidential address—On compassion in scholarship: Why should we care? *Academy of Management Review, 38*(2), 167–180.

Walter B. Cannon Papers. (2013). American Philosophical Society. Retrieved from http://www.amphilsoc.org/mole/view?docId=ead/Mss.B.C163.1-ead.xml;query=;brand=default.

Who Was Walter Bradford Cannon? (n.d.). Retrieved from http://hms.harvard.edu/departments/medical-education/student-services/academic-societies-hms/walter-bradford-cannon-society/walter-bradford-cannon.

31

OPTIMISM AND STRESS

Thomas C. Anderson

The concept of optimism seems to exemplify the familiar expression "what's old is new again." It is not difficult to imagine ancient peoples and cultures noticing that some among them saw the world and their future in a consistently positive way, while others seemed frightened or hesitant about the future. Thus, it is difficult to identify a true beginning to optimism. Some of the first organized thoughts on optimism came from the German mathematician and philosopher Gottfried Wilhelm von Leibniz. In an attempt to reconcile the struggles of life with the idea of an all-powerful and benevolent God, Leibniz suggested that the world is and always will be the best possible combination of events and outcomes that could be assembled given the limitations of men and the world. This view was criticized by influential and more pessimistic philosophers like Friedrich Nietzsche.

HISTORICAL EVOLUTION OF THE CONCEPT OF OPTIMISM

In American psychology, the concept of optimism has a history of going in and out of focus. William James was one of the early advocates for optimism and the power of interpretation. James pointed out that the mind often interprets physiological events (e.g., sweating palms, rapid heartbeat, etc.) and gives them meaning (e.g., I am afraid, this is dangerous, etc.). In some ways his work was a precursor to cognitive therapy as well as optimism. James noted the pragmatic and powerful impact that either positive or negative thoughts could have in shaping people and their lives. He observed the tendency for people to struggle due to how they perceive situations: "Pessimism leads to weakness, optimism to power" (James, 1902, p. 84).

The role of cognitions and optimism was largely eclipsed by world events and an increased focus on psychoanalysis and behaviorism. Sigmund Freud is often credited with being the father of psychoanalysis. By the time of his death in 1939, Freud had established himself as a well-known pessimist and a man who valued reason and knowledge above all else. Freud recognized the power of thinking both for understanding and for self-deception. Freud saw optimism as a type of psychological crutch based upon hope and illusion. For Freud, religion was a prime example of an optimistic illusion passed down through the generations. Optimism in Freud's world was a tool useful for managing the masses but never to be confused with something healthy.

In the late 1940s, as America began to recover from the Second World War, the importance of diagnosis and treatment of mental illnesses became increasingly obvious. The focus of psychology shifted from understanding the unconscious and defense mechanisms toward understanding how the environment affected mental health and behavior. It was this shift that led to the advancement of behaviorism. Behaviorism (Skinner, 1938) was predominately focused on what could be observed (e.g., behaviors) and what things either increased or decreased the observed behaviors. This emphasis on observable behaviors drew focus away from explorations of the roles of cognitions and optimism.

Cognitive Psychology

The concept of optimism was lost in the tide for several decades. This began to change with the advent of cognitive psychology. Coming from a background and training in psychoanalysis, Aaron Beck (1967) noticed that depressed patients were often subject to floods of negative thoughts. He grouped the content of these depressive thoughts into negative ideas about themselves, the world, and the future. Beck and other cognitive theorists reintroduced the importance of what a person thought into psychology, as they began to study and catalog the relevance of cognitions. The idea arose that what happened to a person was not nearly as important as what that person thought about what happened.

Learned Helplessness

Drawing upon the work of Beck and other cognitive psychologists, Martin Seligman and his colleagues (Seligman & Maier, 1967) began to study learned helplessness. Their initial work used dogs as subjects. They discovered that when dogs were exposed to uncontrollable shocks, they passively endured the shocks more than dogs who had learned strategies for stopping the shocks. In effect, the dogs exposed to uncontrollable and negative events learned to be helpless. Parallels between dogs and humans were quickly noticed and learned helplessness became the subject of study in humans. One of the key mediating variables in human learned helplessness is cognition. If people believe there is/is not a way to manage a difficult situation, they are less/more likely to develop learned helplessness. Subsequent researchers began to wonder, "If we can teach people to feel helpless, can we teach them to be the opposite?" This marked a transition from diagnosing and fixing problems to attempting to improve the lives of people.

Positive Psychology

The combination of the increased emphasis on cognition and a renewed interest in the development of human potential contributed to the development of positive psychology and the study of optimism. *Positive psychology* is a term created by Martin Seligman and Mihaly Csikszentmihalyi (2000). The objective of positive psychology was the development of research, treatment, and discussion focused on what helps people become increasingly healthy and improves the quality of their lives. The formation of the positive psychology movement ushered in a renewed interest in the concept of optimism. Researchers began to systemically define and research the basic questions: "What is optimism? How does it impact human development?" (See more on positive psychology in the sidebar at the end of this chapter.)

WHAT IS OPTIMISM?

There are many definitions of *optimism,* but two seem the most prevalent in the literature: explanatory style and dispositional optimism. Optimism as an explanatory style was initially espoused by Martin Seligman and his colleagues. Drawing from his work on learned helplessness, Seligman (1991, p. 4) explained the differences between optimism and pessimism:

> The defining characteristics of pessimists are that they tend to believe bad events will last a long time, will undermine everything they do and are their own fault. The optimists, who are confronted with the same hard knocks of this world, think about misfortune in the opposite way. They tend to believe defeat is just a temporary setback, that its causes are confined to this one case. The optimists believe defeat is not their fault.

There are three dimensions in Seligman's definition of optimism: internal vs. external, stable vs. unstable, and global vs. specific. Optimists view negative events as being of external origin (meaning they are beyond a person's control); they are relatively unstable (temporary) and specific (limited to only a small slice of life). Optimists explain positive events in the opposite direction compared to negative events. They view positive events as being of internal origin (due to one's own efforts), relatively permanent (the event is bound to last a long time), and global (likely to be found in many places). This explanatory style results in positive feelings.

Dispositional Optimism

Dispositional optimism (Scheier, Carver, & Bridges, 1994) is often conceptualized as a relatively stable trait that nevertheless likely differs from person to person. The central attribute of dispositionally optimistic people is their belief that positive things will happen with significantly greater frequency than negative things.

WHERE DOES OPTIMISM COME FROM?

Although there is some literature suggesting that optimism may be inherited, most research (Peterson, 2000; Carver, Scheier, Miller & Fulford, 2009) points to the notion that optimism is something that can be learned and/or shaped. "Where does optimism come from?" is a question pursued by a variety of researchers.

Heritability

Is it possible that optimism, like eye color or height, is genetically based? When one considers that optimism is a relatively complex series of thoughts, beliefs, and emotions that inspire an even more complex series of actions, it is hard to see a fully genetic source for optimism. Despite this complexity, research done on twins suggests a genetic link in explanatory style (Schulman, Keith, & Seligman, 1993). Researchers discovered that explanatory styles are more similar in identical twins than in fraternal twins. The increased genetic similarity of identical twins is assumed to account for the increased similarity in twins' explanatory style. Though the genetic mechanism responsible for transmitting explanatory styles is unclear, there does seem to be a moderate genetic connection in the development of an optimistic or pessimistic explanatory style.

The notion of optimism having a genetic origin is also supported by the work of David Buss (1989). Buss's evolutionary psychology suggests that certain traits (such as optimism) have been adaptive for our human ancestors. These traits allowed early humans to be more successful in survival and mating; thus, those traits were more likely to be passed along from generation to generation. To support this theory, Buss began looking for attributes held to be consistently attractive for men and women. Research across a variety of cultures has found that women typically find men with some optimistic personality characteristics attractive. Optimistic men were found to be more likely to take risks (believing that a positive outcome will follow), be happier, and be less affected by stress. Similarly, Buss found that men prefer women who have certain traits associated with optimism. Men are attracted to women who are less anxious, more easygoing, and seemingly healthy. He also noted that men are more likely to overestimate their own attractiveness. This optimistic appraisal of themselves leads them to strive to obtain greater numbers and quality of mating partners than their actual level of attractiveness would indicate as being appropriate. Buss and others argue that optimistic people likely had a developmental edge that contributed to the flourishing of optimism in later generations. This hypothesized proliferation in optimism would eventually help advance the human species. Buss theorizes that optimistic humans would strive to achieve status, accomplish difficult tasks, and work toward ever more unlikely goals because they were fueled by an optimistic belief in a positive outcome. It is this striving for difficult goals that would advance the interests of the human species as a whole.

Development of Optimism

Despite evidence suggesting a genetic origin for optimism, most research assumes that the environment plays a major role in shaping and developing an explanatory style. Research on environmental impact on optimism tends to focus on parenting, trauma, and other areas associated with social learning. Whether through modeling, genetics, or social learning, it turns out that certain types of environments tend to produce more optimistic children.

Impact of Parenting on Optimism

There is limited and somewhat conflicting information about the impact of parents on the development of optimism in children. Some research shows a positive correlation between a mother's explanatory style and her children's explanatory style. These studies show that optimistic mothers seemed to transfer their explanatory style to both their female and male children. Other studies found no such link in styles between mothers and their children. Interestingly, no link has been found between paternal explanatory style and the explanatory style of children, related to optimism.

A 2007 study (Baldwin, McIntyre, & Hardaway, 2007) examined the relationship between perceived parenting styles and levels of optimism in adolescent college students. The study compared the impact of having authoritative or authoritarian parenting styles on the development of dispositional optimism in college-age adolescents. Authoritative parents were described as having rules, consistent consequences, and high expectations. They tend to be responsive to their children's needs, forgiving of mistakes, and warm and loving. Authoritarian parents were described as "strict": They have high expectations; they demand that rules be followed, often without explaining reasons therefor; are punishing when children fail and often unresponsive to their needs. Having authoritative parents was predictive of adolescent optimism. If taken at face value, the likely implication of the somewhat limited research on parenting is that optimism is sometimes conveyed to children from parents. What variables contribute to or hinder this transference is not well understood.

Impact of Trauma on Optimism

It is not possible to live in a world without stress. The impact of stress on optimism is still being investigated, but optimism seems to thrive in environments where there is enough stress to learn resilience, but not so much stress as to be overwhelming. Children exposed to stressful events that eventually lead to positive resolutions are more likely to develop optimistic explanatory styles (Seligman, 1991). Still, having too much stress can be a hindrance to the development of optimism. Children exposed to the same stressors but who never have a positive resolution are more likely to develop pessimistic explanatory styles. Optimism seems to fade in environments where stress is not only present but unrelenting and/or seemingly out of a person's control.

It seems that optimism is impacted not only by the duration of stress, but also by the severity of the stress. Research on children exposed to single-incident traumatic events that could not be controlled show higher rates of pessimism. The literature (Brodhagen & Wise, 2008; Seligman, 1991) shows that children exposed to the death of a parent, a single incident of sexual abuse or incest, or even the divorce of parents all display elevated pessimism scores. Not surprisingly, children exposed to chronic or reoccurring stressors such as physical, sexual, or emotional abuse also tend to show higher rates of pessimism (Cerezo & Frias, 1994). Similarly, homes where there are high levels of discord or substance abuse among the parents tend to result in reduced optimism and increased pessimism in children (Perez-Bouchard, Johnson, & Ahrens, 1993). It seems that children raised in stable, safe, and caring environments are more likely to develop optimism (Franz, McClelland, Weinberger, & Peterson, 1994).

Impact of Optimism on Managing Stress

Regardless of how it is defined, when it comes to managing stress, optimism seems to provide a buffering effect across a wide range of stressors. This buffering seems to extend to both mental health and physical health. The method of buffering seems to be some combination of indirect and direct impact on stress.

Optimism and Health

Physical health issues are a significant source of stress, both for the ailing and those who love and care for them. Whether measured by expectational style or dispositional attitude, optimism seems to have a positive impact on a person's health. Examples of improved health for optimistic people are relatively consistent in the literature. Optimistic people seem to have significantly fewer and less impactful coronary issues. Studies (Kim, Park, & Peterson, 2011; Kubzansky, Sparrow, Vokonas, & Kawachi, 2001) on stroke and coronary disease patients show that optimism is associated with significantly greater life expectancy than for pessimistic people. Patients scoring high on optimism and undergoing heart surgery were found to have fewer postsurgical complications. Similar results have been found with other health issues. For example, patients with certain types of advanced cancer who scored high on optimism showed lower mortality rates than pessimistic patients. In general, optimistic patients seem to have fewer health problems and to live longer than pessimistic patients.

HOPE

What is hope? Referenced throughout history, hope appears in stories from Greek mythology to early accounts in the Jewish and Christian religions. The notion that something good can occur from a not-so-good situation was a central theme in ancient cultures (Snyder, Feldman, Taylor, Schroeder, & Adams, 2000). The authors note that as the times changed and evolved, so did the definition of *hope*. In the late 1950s and early 1960s, hope was thought of more as the perception that goals can be achieved (Snyder et al., 2000). Research by Snyder (1998) recognized that hope was a complex interweaving of goals, pathways, and agency.

Research suggests that individuals with higher levels of hope are more proactive than their low-hope counterparts (Snyder et al., 2000), thus contributing to acts of prevention that aim at increasing better outcomes in the future. Additionally, individuals with high levels of hope have positive emotions and a different energy, as they bring with them a history of past goal achievements and successes (Snyder & Lopez, 2007). In terms of stress, individuals who have high levels of hope usually perceive obstacles to goal achievement as challenges and something to work through, whereas individuals with low levels of hope may not see options.

—*Serena Wadhwa*

Can Optimism Be Harmful?

Despite the generally helpful impact of optimism on health, there is literature exploring the question, "Is there a downside to optimism?" Not all research shows optimism having a buffering effect on illness. Research done by Schofield and her colleagues (Schofield et al., 2004) on optimism and lung cancer found no improvement in mortality rates for patients with high scores for dispositional optimism. Similarly, other studies have shown some increased risk-taking behavior associated with unrealistic optimism. These types of findings raise another question: Can some optimism be unrealistic and ultimately harmful? Some theorists suggest that unrealistic optimism may cause people to spend their efforts on ineffectual or inappropriate treatments. It may cause people to feel chronically "let down" due to frequently getting statistically expected but un-hoped-for news. In the case of terminal illness, unrealistic optimism may cause patients to prioritize their remaining time poorly and miss opportunities to spend time with family or opportunities for closure.

The literature suggests that pessimistic people with life-threatening illnesses tend to be more realistic in their appraisal of situations than optimistic people in the same circumstances. A study by Tomakowsky and her colleagues (Tomakowsky, Lumley, Markowitz, & Frank, 2001) perhaps best summarizes the risks and rewards of optimism versus pessimism. This group examined the impact of two types of optimism (optimistic explanatory style and dispositional optimism) on HIV-infected men. They found that elevated rates of optimism were related to greater sense of subjective well-being and fewer demonstrated symptoms, even though higher rates of optimistic explanatory style were related to a poorer immune status (lower CD4). The study also found that dispositional optimism had no impact on immune status. In short, it seems that although health may not always be positively affected by optimism, people almost always feel physically better when they are optimistic.

Optimism and Mental Health

A person's expectations for the future (optimism vs. pessimism) seem to have important implications for mental health. A growing body of research has begun to show that optimism and pessimism are important predictors of positive affective states, satisfaction with life, and depression. Research on cancer patients (Carver et al., 1993) shows significantly lower rates of depression for optimistic patients. Even in studies where rates of mortality were not improved by optimism, patients reported higher rates of subjective well-being. These results have been replicated for people dealing with a wide range of physical illnesses (Hart, Vella, & Mohr, 2008). Optimistic people managing chronic illnesses such as multiple sclerosis, HIV, or heart disease all demonstrate lower rates of depression and increased satisfaction with life.

Optimism, as measured by the Life Orientation Test-Revised (LOT-R), has been shown to be negatively related to depression, pain, and fatigue in veterans (Segovia, Moore, Linnville, Hoyt, & Hain, 2012). Optimism seems to play an important role in reducing feelings of hopelessness and isolation, and is associated with lower suicidal ideation and fewer suicide attempts. In the face of natural disaster and trauma, optimistic people are less likely to develop anxiety or posttraumatic symptoms and to have shorter duration of symptoms when they do develop. Pessimists have been shown to be more likely to feel helpless, be hopeless about the future, and give up.

How Does Optimism Affect Stress?

How optimism affects mental and physical health is not entirely understood. There is evidence that optimism has both direct and indirect benefits for health. Indirect benefits of optimism seem to revolve around aspects of Seligman's expectancy theory. Optimistic people believe that stressful situations are within their control, are temporary, and do not impact all aspects of their lives. What people expect from the future affects what they do and how they attempt to solve problems.

Life-Enhancing Behaviors

Because optimists believe that things are in their control and the future will be positive, they seem to engage in more life-improving behaviors. Optimistic beliefs seem to contribute to increased rates of exercise and follow-through on medical treatments. It is this sense of control and hope for the future that are often credited with causing optimistic people with health issues to drink less, smoke fewer cigarettes, and utilize a wider variety of coping skills more frequently than pessimistic people with the same conditions. All of these behaviors seem to have a positive impact on health, which in turn seems to promote or increase optimism and reduce feelings of stress.

Impact of Optimism on the Body

Interesting research has begun to be conducted to find the direct physiological impact of optimism on stress, mental health, and physical health. There have been studies (Sharot, Riccardi, Raio, & Phelps, 2007) showing different patterns of brain functioning in optimistic thinkers compared to pessimistic thinkers. Researchers looking at functional MRI scans of subjects who were engaged in optimistic thinking showed greater utilization of the rostral anterior cingulated cortex (RACC) and the right amygdala. Neuroscientists have begun to speculate that the RACC and the amygdala may play an important role in mitigating the impacts of negative emotional responses. The exact reason for and the full implications of these differences in brain utilization are still being explored. Additionally, several studies have shown that levels of CD-4 cells (helper cells) tend to be higher in optimistic people with a variety of illnesses. A related project (Ebrecht et al., 2004) looked at postbiopsy men who were studied throughout their treatment. In the biopsy stage, these men were grouped into "fast healing" and "slow healing" groups. The fast-healing group scored significantly higher than the slow healers on optimism. Increasingly, researchers are exploring the relationship between how a person thinks about the future and that person's physical health.

Coping Strategies

Among the ways optimism seems to affect stress is through improved coping skills. There is considerable research showing that optimistic people tend to participate more actively in their own treatment and to utilize different problem-solving strategies. Carver, Scheier, and Weintraub (1989) point out that optimistic people are more active and solution-focused problem solvers; that is, optimistic people utilize more planning to solve problems and actively restrain themselves from problematic behaviors. They are more likely to accept the "truth" of a situation and seek instructional help on resolving problems. They are more likely to reframe a problem that cannot be solved as something to be learned from. Compared to pessimists, optimists are less likely to focus on venting emotions or managing their emotions through the installation of hope via wishful thinking or distractions. Pessimists seem to be more likely to deploy passive problem-solving strategies. They tend to be more likely to utilize denial, to become disengaged or physically avoidant, and to utilize drugs or alcohol to cope with stress.

How Do People Develop Optimism?

There are theorists (Seligman, 1991) who believe optimism is something one can develop. One of the first points made by Seligman and others is that learning how to stop being pessimistic is not the same thing as learning to be optimistic. Seligman suggests that learning to be optimistic is accomplished with his ABCs (Adversity, Beliefs, and Consequences) approach. Seligman credits the mechanics of his approach to the psychologist Albert Ellis. He describes A as recognizing and accepting Adversity (e.g., I failed a test at school). Once the adversity has been accepted, a person must become increasingly aware of the resulting series of Beliefs. These beliefs can range from optimistic (e.g., this is not going to last forever; this is just one test) to pessimistic (e.g., my life is over and I am so stupid for letting this happen). Finally, a person needs to become aware of the Consequences of the beliefs (e.g., I become angry, hopeless, and leave school).

Once one is aware of the ABCs, the chore becomes dealing with the beliefs and the resulting consequences. Seligman offers two broad strategies: either disputing or distracting. Disputing strategies involve challenging, reframing, and distancing oneself from beliefs. Distraction techniques involve using cognitive distractions (e.g., screaming "Stop!" internally) and physical interventions such as snapping a rubber band on the wrist to drive focus toward the sensation and away from beliefs and consequences. Learning to be optimistic is associated with greater satisfaction with life and having a sense of purpose. For Seligman, cultivating optimism is meant to be a type of inoculation against depression and stress. Compared to control groups, study participants who learned optimism skills were about half as likely to develop moderate or severe depression while in treatment. After 2 years, children taught these skills had only 22 percent as many depressive episodes as the control group.

Future Directions

The study of optimism is incomplete. Is there more than one type of optimism? What is the definition of *optimism?* How does optimism affect a person's health? Why do some people develop optimism while others in the same situation do not? Despite the need for greater clarity and further investigation, there seems to be a growing body of literature suggesting that optimism can play an important role in mitigating the negative impact of stressful events and living a fuller and more productive life.

POSITIVE PSYCHOLOGY

Martin Seligman pioneered positive psychology in the late 1990s. As the president of the American Psychological Association at that time, Seligman reminded APA members that psychology's "other" areas had been forgotten, one of which included optimizing strengths. Focusing on the themes of prevention and therapy created favorable conditions for moving away from the concepts of *disease, weakness,* and other such negative-connotation words. Positive psychology focuses on human strengths and values. It looks at the "other side" of what is typically the subject of psychology. The focus of positive psychology is on human strengths, resilience, and prevention and enhancement. How does this relate to stress? Recognizing the two categories of stress, and how these categories can affect an individual's mind, body, and spirit when it comes to a stress experience, positive psychology emphasizes the emotional states and coping mechanisms that will create states that contribute to eustress, or an overall positive stress experience.

For example, gratitude is a state that can create or cultivate a positive space when stress is experienced, and is considered one of the strengths by positive psychology. Gratitude is linked with several other positive emotions, such that the experience and expression of gratitude may lead an individual to experience these other positive emotions as well. Cultivating gratitude tends to increase a person's sense of appreciation, love, courage, faith, and several other strengths that are pivotal in the field of positive psychology. Interestingly, some physiological changes occur with the experience of appreciation (Snyder & Lopez, 2007).

Positive psychology is based on scientific evidence, and a quick article search yielded more than 2 million articles at the time of this writing. Referring back to the concepts of primary and secondary prevention, positive psychology looks at increasing desired behaviors while preventing or decreasing undesired ones and increasing interventions for behaviors that already exist. (Therapy usually fits in this category, as it assists individuals when they find that they are unable to manage things that are occurring in their lives and need to find new solutions to the problems they have.) Another area of concentration in positive psychology is that of increasing functioning and life satisfaction, whether through pleasure or goal attainment (Snyder & Lopez, 2007). Positive psychology views relationship development as a primary means of emotional enhancement. Relationships can be with people, work, leisure, hobbies, spiritual aspects, or any number of other connections that bring enjoyment, pleasure, or satisfaction. Positive psychology looks at how to broaden one's perspective when experiencing stress and how to shift from the tunnel vision of a tense and overwhelming experience to an experience of resilience, strength, contentment, and satisfaction.

—*Serena Wadhwa*

REFERENCES AND FURTHER READING

Baldwin, D. R., McIntyre, A., & Hardaway, E. (2007). Perceived parenting styles on college students' optimism. *College Student Journal, 41*(3), 550–557.

Beck, A. T. (1967). *The diagnosis and management of depression.* Philadelphia, PA: University of Pennsylvania Press.

Brodhagen, A., & Wise, D. (2008). Optimism as a mediator between the experience of child abuse, other traumatic events and distress. *Journal of Family Violence, 23,* 403–411.

Buss, D. (1989). Sex differences in human mate preferences: Evolutionary hypotheses tested in 37 cultures. *Behavioral and Brain Sciences, 12,* 1–49.

Buss, D. (1999). Human nature and individual differences: The evolution of human personality. In L. Pervin & O. John (Eds.), *Handbook of personality: Theory and research* (2nd ed., pp. 31–56). New York, NY: Guilford Press.

Carver, C. S., Pozo, C., Harris, S. D., Noriega, V., Scheier, M. F., Robinson, D. S., . . . Clark, K. C. (1993). How coping mediates the effect of optimism on distress: A study of women with early stage breast cancer. *Journal of Personality and Social Psychology, 65,* 375–390.

Carver, C. S., Scheier, M. F., Miller, C. J., & Fulford, D. (2009). Optimism. In S. Lopez & C. R. Snyder (Eds.), *Oxford handbook of positive psychology* (2nd ed., pp. 303–312). New York, NY: Oxford University Press.

Carver, C. S., Scheier, M. F., & Weintraub, J. K. (1989). Assessing coping strategies: A theoretically based approach. *Journal of Personality and Social Psychology, 56,* 267–283.

Cerezo, M. A., & Frias, D. (1994). Emotional and cognitive adjustment in abused children. *Child Abuse and Neglect, 18,* 923–932.

Ebrecht, M., Hextall, J., Kirtley, L. G., Taylor, A. M., Dyson, M., & Weinman, J. (2004).Perceived stress and cortisol levels predict speed of wound healing in healthy males adults. *Psychoneuroendocrinology, 29,* 798–809.

Franz, C. E., McClelland, D. C., Weinberger, J., & Peterson, C. (1994). Parenting antecedents of adult adjustment: A longitudinal study. In C. Perris, W. A. Arrindell, & M. Eisemann (Eds.), *Parenting and psychopathology* (pp. 127–144). San Diego, CA: Academic Press.

Gillham, J., Shatté, A., Reivich, K., & Seligman, M. E. P. (2001). Optimism, pessimism, and explanatory style. In E. Chang (Ed.), *Optimism and pessimism: Implications for theory, research, and practice* (pp. 53–75). Washington, DC: American Psychological Association.

Hart, S. L., Vella, L., & Mohr, D. C. (2008). Relationships among depressive symptoms, benefit-finding, optimism, and positive affect in multiple sclerosis patients after psychotherapy for depression. *Health Psychology, 27*(2), 230–238. doi:10.1037/0278-6133.27.2.230.

James, W. (1902). *The varieties of religious experience: A study in human nature.* Retrieved from https://worldu.edu/library/william_james_var.pdf.

Kim, E. S., Park, N., & Peterson, C. (2011). Dispositional optimism protects older adults from stroke: The health and retirement study. *Stroke: Journal of the American Heart Association, 42*(10), 2855-2859. doi:10.1161/STROKEAHA.111.613448.

Kubzansky, L. D., Sparrow, D., Vokonas, P., & Kawachi, I. (2001). Is the glass half empty or half full? A prospective study of optimism and coronary heart disease in the normative aging study. *Psychosomatic Medicine, 63,* 910–916.

Perez-Bouchard, L., Johnson, J. L., & Ahrens, A. H. (1993). Attributional style in children of substance abusers. *American Journal of Drug and Alcohol Abuse, 19,* 475–489.

Perilloux, C., Fleischman, D. S., & Buss, D. M. (2011). Meet the parents: Parent-offspring convergence and divergence in mate preferences. *Personality and Individual Differences, 50*(2), 253–258.

Peterson, C. (2000). The future of optimism. *American Psychologist, 55,* 44–55.

Peterson, C., Seligman, M. E. P., & Vaillant, G. (1988). Pessimistic explanatory style as a risk factor for physical illness: A thirty-five year longitudinal study. *Journal of Personality and Social Psychology, 55,* 23–27.

Peterson, C., & Steen, T. (2009). Optimistic explanatory style. In S. Lopez & C. R. Snyder (Eds.), *Oxford handbook of positive psychology* (2nd ed., pp. 313–322). New York, NY: Oxford University Press.

Rogers, C. (1961). *On becoming a person: A therapist's view of psychotherapy.* London, UK: Constable.

Scheier, M. F., Carver, C. S., & Bridges, M. W. (1994). Distinguishing optimism from neuroticism (and trait anxiety, self-mastery, and self-esteem): A re-evaluation of the Life Orientation Test. *Journal of Personality and Social Psychology, 67,* 1063–1078.

Schofield, P., Ball, D., Smith, J. G., Borland, R., O'Brien, P., Davis, S., . . . Joseph, D. (2004). Optimism and survival in lung carcinoma patients. *Cancer, 6,* 1276–1282.

Schulman, P., Castellon, C., & Seligman, M. E. P. (1989). Assessing explanatory style: The content analysis of verbatim explanations and the Attributional Style Questionnaire. *Behaviour Research and Therapy, 27,* 505–512.

Schulman, P., Keith, D., & Seligman, M. E. P. (1993). Is optimism heritable? A study of twins. *Behavior Research and Therapy, 6,* 569–574.

Segovia, F., Moore, J. L., Linnville, S. E., Hoyt, R. E., & Hain, R. E. (2012). Optimism predicts resilience in repatriated prisoners of war: A 37-year longitudinal study. *Journal of Traumatic Stress, 25,* 330–336.

Seligman, M. E. P. (1991). *Learned optimism.* New York, NY: Alfred Knopf.

Seligman, M. E. P. (2002). Positive psychology, positive prevention, and positive therapy. In C. R. Snyder & S. Lopez (Eds.), *Handbook of positive psychology* (pp. 3–12). New York, NY: Oxford University Press.

Seligman, M. E. P. (2012). *Flourish: A visionary new understanding of happiness and well-being.* New York, NY: Atria.

Seligman, M. E. P., & Csikszentmihalyi, M. (2000). Positive psychology: An introduction. *American Psychologist, 55,* 5–14.

Seligman, M. E. P., & Maier, S. F. (1967). Failure to escape traumatic shock. *Journal of Experimental Psychology, 74,* 1–9.

Sharot, T., Riccardi, A. M., Raio, C. M., & Phelps, E. A. (2007). Neural mechanisms mediating optimism bias. *Nature, 450*(7166), 102–105.

Skinner, B. F. (1938). *The behavior of organisms: An experimental analysis.* Oxford, UK: Appleton-Century.

Snyder, C. R. (1998). Hope. In H. S. Friedman (Ed.), *Encyclopedia of mental health* (pp. 421–431). San Diego, CA: Academic Press.

Snyder, C. R., Feldman, D. B., Taylor, J. D., Schroeder, L. L., & Adams, V. H. (2000). The roles of hopeful thinking in preventing problems and enhancing strengths. *Applied and Preventive Psychology, 9*(4), 249–269.

Snyder, C. R., & Lopez, S. J. (2007). *Positive psychology: The scientific and practical explorations of human strengths.* Thousand Oaks, CA: Sage.

Taylor, S. E., Kemeny, M. E., Reed, G., Bower, J., & Gruenewald, T. L. (2000). Psychological resources, positive illusions and health. *American Psychologist, 55,* 99–109.

Tedeschi, R. G., & Calhoun, L. G. (1996). The posttraumatic growth inventory: Measuring the positive legacy of trauma. *Journal of Traumatic Stress, 9*(3), 455–471.

Tomakowsky, J., Lumley, M. A., Markowitz, N., & Frank, C. (2001). Optimistic explanatory style and dispositional optimism in HIV-infected men. *Journal of Psychosomatic Research, 51*(4), 577–587.

Zullow, H., Oettingen, G., Peterson, C., & Seligman, M. E. P. (1988). Pessimistic explanatory style in the historical record: Caving LBJ, presidential candidates and East versus West Berlin. *American Psychologist, 43*, 673–682.

32

Music and Art: Their Relationship to Stress

Serena Wadhwa

Music and art are two strategies often used as ways to manage and reduce stress. This chapter explores these approaches separately.

MUSIC

What is *music?* Music itself is a broad topic and means different things to different people. How does it relate to sound, and noise, and what we sense in our environment? How does it become a stressor or act as a mechanism to cope with stress? What does the literature say about the notions that sound and music can be connected to stress? This chapter explores these questions, and provides some suggestions from the research about incorporating music as a coping mechanism; it also investigates differences between music therapy and music for stress relief, the physical and psychological effects of music on the individual, and the profession of music therapy.

SOUND

To understand the nuances of music, both as a coping mechanism and as a source of stress, we must first understand the sense of sound. According to Don Campbell, author of *The Mozart Effect,* "The word *health* comes from Old English *hal,* the root word signifying whole, healing, hale, and inhaling. *Heal,* in Northern Middle English, means 'to make sound,' to become healthy again. We use the word *sound*—a synonym for health and wholeness—to signify basic vitality and unshakeable foundation for whatever we do" (1997, p. 10). Campbell also notes that our identity, our persona, and even the word *person* originate from the Greek roots of *per son,* which means "the sound passes through" (1997, p. 11). Thus, sounds and the music springing from these are an integrated part of human workings.

So, what is sound? How is it utilized? Sound is measured in frequency and intensities. *Frequency* is the depth or height of a sound—the *pitch*—measured in hertz, which focuses on the wave vibrations (Campbell, 1997, p. 32). Normal hearing falls in the range of 16,000 to 20,000 hertz. Environmental and cultural elements do play a role in the ability of an individual to hear. According to Campbell (1997), there is a group of people in Africa (the Maabans) who can hear a whisper from 90 feet away. Sound can also affect how the brain operates. Alfred Tomatis, a French physician, studied the ear, including the workings of sound, hearing, listening, and when these events occur. Part of his research concluded that high-frequency sounds (3,000 to 8,000 hertz and above) resonate in the brain and affect thinking, spatial perception, and memory.

Sounds can be "music" to one's ears, or sounds can be stressful. The vibration of a sound determine the frequency and pitch. Campbell (1997) calls these *charging* and *releasing effects,* as sounds can enhance the body and movement, directing the energy in a certain way; or sound can interfere with the body, causing distress to both body and mind.

Music has been around for centuries and can be traced back to antiquity in many cultures and traditions. Music in Eastern Indian and Buddhist traditions, created by chanting, was used to alter the physical and mental states of participants. As a form of healing, there is some evidence that the stringing-together of sounds that we call *music* dates back to primitive tribal cultures (Taylor, 1997). In both Judaism and Christianity, there is a story that young David used the harp to soothe King Saul's soul. In Greek mythology, Apollo was known as the god of music. Throughout many cultures and religions, music has been a means of communication and expression of feeling (Yehuda, 2011), as well as an aid to memory.

WHAT IS MUSIC?

How does understanding the basics of sound apply to music? Music is known to affect both the central nervous system and the autonomic nervous system (Thoma, Ryf, Mohiyeddini, Ehlert, & Nater, 2012; Wang, Sun, & Zang, 2014), two parts of the body that play a significant role in the experience of stress. As noted in previous chapters, the central nervous system consists of the brain and spinal cord; the autonomic nervous system regulates internal functions central to your life without you having to control it. The autonomic nervous system consists of the sympathetic and parasympathetic systems. You may have heard of the sympathetic system in relation to the fight-flight-or-freeze response and your parasympathetic system in relation to the rest-and-restore (rest-and-digest) response. The limbic system, which is regulated by the autonomic nervous system, is where emotions are primarily created, regulated, and triggered.

So, what is music? Is it just a sound or silence? A string of sounds and silence strategically placed? Yes; according to the *Merriam-Webster Dictionary* (n.d.), *music* is the "science or art of ordering tones or sounds in succession, in combination, and in temporal relationships to produce a composition having unity and continuity; vocal, instrumental, or mechanical sounds having rhythm, melody, or harmony."

EFFECTS OF MUSIC

Research has demonstrated the benefits of music in a variety of contexts. A full exploration of these benefits is well beyond the scope of this chapter (that subject alone would take a book or two), so this chapter provides a small sampling of the research on how music physiologically and psychologically benefits users. For example, in one study conducted by Thoma, La Marca, Brönnimann, Finkel, Ehlert, and Nater (2013), the authors listed several benefits of music discovered through research. They found that music can improve mood; distract one from the experience of stress and from negative thought states; reduce anxiety; and enhance a sense of meaning, among other things. Other research demonstrates the benefits of music for improved sleep (Wang et al., 2014); increases in the metabolism; positive effects on respiration and muscular activity; and decreases in blood pressure and heart rate (Yehuda, 2011). Other research has shown that music can affect brainwaves. Music can connect one with forces outside of oneself: the community and the culture (Harvey, 1991) as well as spiritual and mystical forces. Music has also been demonstrated to provide pain relief (Michel & Chesky, 1995; Bernatzky, Strickner, Presch, Wendtner, & Kullich, 2012). In other studies, music has been found to increase endorphins (the feel-good chemicals) and enhance the functioning of the immune system (Charnetski, Brennan, & Harrison, 1998; Bernatzky et al., 2012), by increasing hemoglobin production (stress decreases hemoglobin levels). Music has also been noted to facilitate symmetrical operations, improve concentration, and enhance intuitive and creative abilities (Campbell, 1997).

Fancourt, Ockelford, and Belai (2014) provide a meta-analysis on research from 1953 to 2013 on the psychoneuroimmunology effects of music. Their study collected results consistently showing that music positively affects the nervous system, immune functioning, and the regulation of other processes in the body.

VARIATIONS OF MUSIC

Because music is so broadly defined and various factors affect the production of music (instruments available, creativity/imagination, culture, traditions, etc.), transmission of music can occur in a variety of ways. For example, music can be live, performed or played by an individual or group. Music can also be recorded and listened to at will. It can be produced by a single instrument or voice, or a large complement with many instruments and voices, or any combination in between. It may or may not include lyrics. Music may be transmitted by active participation or passive listening.

In a meta-analysis conducted by Nilsson (2008) of 42 previous studies, "soothing music" was described as music that averaged about 60–80 beats per minute. This correlates to the brain frequency of alpha waves (6–8 and 12–13 hertz [Hz]), and has the potential to be experienced as a hypnotic state. These alpha waves are present when we are relaxed and awake.

Numbers on the frequency of beta brainwaves are varied, but it is generally recognized that beta waves have a frequency of 12–14 Hz and 20-30 Hz. Beta brainwaves are usually present during active, awakened states. The higher the frequency of the wavelength range, the more active and involved the mind and emotions are.

Theta brainwaves, which are between 4 Hz and 8 Hz, are usually related to peak creative moments, sleep, and meditation. Finally, delta waves, usually between 0.5 Hz and 3 Hz, reflect deeper sleep and unconsciousness. There is minimal research regarding the effects of music on these states, which already reflect deep levels of relaxation.

Studies have also suggested that music can affect the chemical levels in the brain. For example, dopamine and serotonin, both present in the brain's reward system, may be released in response to pleasing music (Yehuda, 2011).

Music can be a stress reliever or a stress trigger. For example, "technomusic," a type of music popular with certain groups, has been demonstrated to induce the release of cortisol, a common hormone signifying the presence of stress. The higher the cortisol level in the body, the more stress it is believed the individual is experiencing. Additionally, how music is experienced (whether as stressful or relaxing) may depend on several factors. Yehuda (2011) explored how culture may be a factor affecting the different reactions to music and the different styles of music that exist. This may also influence the effectiveness of music as an intervention; culture does influence preference, experience, and familiarity (Yehuda, 2011). In another study—one of the first of its kind—nature's rippling-water sounds were used (Thoma et al., 2013). In this study, what was significant was the finding that individuals who had been largely detached from nature responded more favorably to the natural sound of rippling water.

Music can deeply affect our emotions, and this effect can occur in several ways. Emotions can be expressed *through* music and *in* music (Hiller, 2015; Bodner & Gilboa, 2006; Davies, 1980). It is also common knowledge that music can induce emotions and have an effect on the brain (Daly et al., 2015). What this means is that what we choose to listen to affects what we may experience emotionally. We may choose music that matches what we are feeling and expresses it for us, as well as music to shift what we are experiencing. Thus, it seems logical that music would also affect a person's experience of stress. When an individual is feeling overwhelmed and distressed, music may be a strategy that allows the person to breathe and stay open. A person may also make music as a means of reducing distress. For example, some individuals may start to beat on the desk with a pencil or their fingers; this "drumming" occurrence is a means of discharging some of their distress. However, some research demonstrates that making music is not always effective for emotional regulation, and also indicates that this may also be influenced by the gender of the individual (Carlson et al., 2015). Additionally, musicians, music therapists, and other individuals who resonate with the experience of producing music may also be experiencing a state of flow, as described by Kapitan about art therapy (Kapitan, 2013). *Flow,* as conceived of the psychologist Mihaly Csikszentmihalyi, is defined as complete absorption in an activity that diverts the perception of time and increases energy (Kapitan, 2013). The state of flow can also be a distress reducer for many individuals.

WHAT IS MUSIC THERAPY?

Music therapy (MT) is often categorized as a complementary and alternative therapy, which, according to the National Center for Complementary and Integrative Health, consists of "diverse medical and health care systems, practices and products that are not presently considered part of conventional medicine" (NCCIH, n.d.). As one part of this category, music therapy helps the client in promoting health by using music experiences, and exploring the relationships that develop through them as a dynamic force of change. MT became a profession after World War II and includes improvisation, songs, and listening to music (see Lee & Thyer, 2013). In the field of mental health, MT has three approaches: (1) active or receptive; (2) level of structure; and (3) focus of therapeutic attention.

Lee and Thyer (2013) conducted a meta-analysis of nine studies supporting the use of music therapy with adults having various mental health issues. The outcomes suggested that music therapy usually enhanced outcomes more than psychotherapy alone. Overall, the study demonstrated that MT yields positive results, although further research was suggested.

How exactly does the music in music therapy work? According to research, there are several reasons for its effectiveness. First, the area of the brain that responds to music is regionally different from that for speech and language reception. Music taps into a different part of the brain, and the response to it is not usually verbal or linguistic. Music stimulates the right side of the brain, encouraging bilateral activity and exchange between brain hemispheres. Research suggests that when information and experiences stay within one hemisphere, they are not as integrated as they could be and thus are perceived as "different." Bilateral stimulation allows this dual-hemispheric processing.

Music serves as a powerful memory aid and reminder. We tend to remember things with a strong emotional pull, and songs and music create this pull in our lives. Finally, in the areas of cognition and memory, research suggests that rhythm can affect how we remember and how our cognitions function. Campbell (1997) focused on other factors that align how music works with the body and brain's natural attunement. The first factor in the way that music therapy works is called *entrainment*. This is similar to being "in sync" with each other. The *iso* principle is the second factor, which is like a wave, carrying a listener from one state to another. Finally, *diversion* focuses on the use of music to distract from pain and discomfort.

A large variety of music, from many cultures, can be utilized in this healing modality. There is also a variety of methods of using music to relieve stress. For example, one can use music with guided imagery; breathing exercises, or other meditative forms.

SUGGESTIONS

Although you may not be considering a career change or desire to learn a new subject, based on the information provided, there are several things you can do to use music as a stress reduction tool, whether for yourself or your clients. Campbell (1997) offers several of these:

- Gregorian chant can assist in the reduction of stress.
- Slower Baroque music creates a mentally stimulating environment.
- Romantic music, in general, can evoke compassion, sympathy, and love.
- Mantra chants (for example, Aum, Aum Namah Shivaya) can help achieve a meditative state.

ART

What is Art?

According to Curl (2008), *art* is a flexible medium encompassing a wide range of methods. In a general sense, art consists of creative production by means of painting, woodworking, sculpture, drawing, print making, collage making, and other expressions; and, in a broader sense, writing, dancing, and music, among other forms of creative endeavor.

Effects of Art

Art generally tends to be an aesthetic experience. Of course, the type of art that is experienced as aesthetically pleasing will vary from person to person. In

FLOW

In the 1990s, Mihaly Csikszentmihalyi, an American positive psychologist, developed his theory on the concept of flow. In his book on the topic, he defined *flow* as an immersion into an experience of effortless action, and responses that are appropriate to the goal (Csikszentmihalyi, 1997a, 1997b). Other characteristics of the flow state include: (1) intense, focused concentration in the present moment; (2) loss of sense of self; (3) loss of sense of time; (4) a sense of being in control; and (5) a sense that the process is the reward (Nakamura & Csikszentmihalyi, 2002). The authors write that flow has been experienced by individuals in various disciplines, including the arts, sciences, medicine, sports, and others. The intentional, focused concentration/attention is a defining element of flow, and the state of consciousness is affected by what the individual is focusing this attention on. Evidence suggests that consequences of this sustained activity state include enjoyment, loss of the sense of time, and feedback from the activity.

Obstacles to the experience of flow include the level of the challenge involved in the activity, the skill level of the individual, and the individual's sense of control (Ghani & Deshpande, 1994). Another obstacle, according to Csikszentmihalyi (1997b), is created by the challenge to control attention and develop the discipline to do what needs to be done. Finally, he noted that the goal an individual intends to focus his or her attention upon can potentially become an obstacle, depending on the nature of that goal.

general, though, the allure of most forms of art tends to be beauty, ability to express and elicit emotions, appreciation for the execution of the artwork, and some interpretation of and/or ability to communicate meaning (Leder, Carbon, & Ripsas, 2006; Jakesch & Leder, 2009; Leder, Gerger, Dressler, & Schabmann, 2012).

WHAT IS ART THERAPY?

Like music therapy, art therapy is a variation of psychotherapy that uses an individual's ability to express himself or herself through art media and visual forms (Halužan, 2012). Art media may include paints, pens and pencils, crayons, chalk, clay, and many other substances. The philosophical premise of art therapy is based on the idea that individuals tend to embody experiences in nonverbal formats. As a result, when individuals express their experiences in images and abstract, creative forms, additional means and modes of communication become available.

According to Halužan (2012), all sensory modes are activated, thus increasing perception by the individual about the piece of art created. There is a sense of reduced distress; hence, art therapy may be very useful for individuals experiencing distress as a result of pressures and demands placed on them by day-to-day or unexpected experiences—that is, stress.

Art therapy has many benefits. In addition to providing a safe way to express what may be difficult or even impossible to express verbally (Halužan, 2012), art therapy can have an effect on mood (Curl, 2008) and instill confidence in the individual about expression.. Being a creator is also a benefit, due to the investment in the process and outcome of the creative effort. Curl (2008) argues that creating art allows for freedom and choice, which often assist when an individual is experiencing distress. Using art as an expression of what is experienced during distressing times may then have the benefit of shifting one's perception and the amount of control one believes oneself to have. Additionally, as some other research suggests (see Chapter 29 on creativity), art therapy can also increase an individual's creativity, which may have a systematic effect on problem-solving abilities. A state of "flow" may develop as a result of creating and releasing something (Caddy, Crawford, & Page, 2012). Caddy et al. (2012) summarize other benefits revealed by in the research into art therapy, such as increasing participants' self-worth and esteem and providing a means of distraction from negative emotions and thoughts. General improvements in participants' ratings of well-being have also been found (Crone et al., 2013).

USING ART FOR STRESS REDUCTION

How can people use art as a stress reduction tool? Some suggestions include setting time aside to write in a journal, color in a coloring book (popular adult coloring books are widely available), dance, draw, paint, use a mandala, engage in a craft, develop a collage of some sort, and use various media for expression (e.g., crayons, markers, clay, glitter).

CONCLUSION

Since humans are in essence part of "sound," it is important to understand the concept of sound as both a means of distress and a means of relaxation. With the transformation of sound into music, music can be used as a healing art and as an effective coping mechanism. Additionally, art therapy may provide an effective coping mechanism for some people. This chapter gave a number of suggestions on how to use sound, music, and art for stress reduction and management, and highlighted key factors in the therapeutic aspects of music and art.

REFERENCES AND FURTHER READING

Bernatzky, G., Strickner, S., Presch, M., Wendtner, F., & Kullich, W. (2012). Music as non-pharmacological pain management in clinics. In R. MacDonald, G. Kreutz, & L. Mitchell (Eds.), *Music, health, and wellbeing* (pp. 257–275). Oxford, UK: Oxford University Press.

Bodner, E., & Gilboa, A. (2006). Emotional communicability in music therapy: Different instruments for different emotions? *Nordic Journal of Music Therapy, 15*(1), 3–16.

Caddy, L., Crawford, F., & Page, A. C. (2012). "Painting a path to wellness": Correlations between participating in a creative activity group and improved measured mental health outcome. *Journal of Psychiatric & Mental Health Nursing, 19*(4), 327–333.

Campbell, D. (1997). *The Mozart effect: Tapping the power of music to heal the body, strengthen the mind, and unlock the creative spirit.* New York, NY: Avon.

Carlson, E., Saarikallio, S., Toiviainen, P., Bogert, B., Kliuchko, M., & Brattico, E. (2015). Maladaptive and adaptive emotion regulation through music: A behavioral and neuroimaging study of males and females. *Frontiers in Human Neuroscience, 9.* http://dx.doi.org/10.3389/fnhum.2015.00466.

Charnetski, C., Brennan, F. X., & Harrison, J. F. (1998). Effect of music and auditory stimuli on secretory immunoglobulin A (IgA). *Perceptual and Motor Skills, 87*(3f), 1163–1170.

Crone, D. M., O'Connell, E. E., Tyson, P. J., Clark-Stone, F., Opher, S., & James, D. V. (2013). "Art Lift" intervention to improve mental well-being: An observational study from UK general practice. *International Journal of Mental Health Nursing, 22*(3), 279–286.

Csikszentmihalyi, M. (1997a). *Finding flow: The psychology of engagement with everyday life.* New York, NY: Basic Books.

Csikszentmihalyi, M. (1997b). Finding flow. Retrieved June 2, 2015, from http://wiki.idux.com/uploads/Main/FindingFlow.pdf.

Curl, K. (2008). Assessing stress reduction as a function of artistic creation and cognitive focus. *Art Therapy, 25*(4), 164–169.

Daly, I., Williams, D., Hallowell, J., Hwang, F., Kirke, A., Malik, A., . . . Nasuto, S. J. (2015). Music-induced emotions can be predicted from a combination of brain activity and acoustic features. *Brain and Cognition, 101,* 1–11. doi:10.1016/j.bandc.2015.08.003.

Davies, S. (1980). The expression of emotion in music. *Mind, 89*(353), 67–86.

Fancourt, D., Ockelford, A., & Belai, A. (2014). The psychoneuroimmunological effects of music: A systematic review and a new model. *Brain, Behavior, and Immunity, 36,* 15–26.

Ghani, J. A., & Deshpande, S. P. (1994). Task characteristics and the experience of optimal flow in human-computer interaction. *Journal of Psychology, 128*(4), 381–391.

Harvey, A. W. (1991). Music in attitudinal medicine. In D. Campbell (Ed.), *Music: Physician for times to come* (pp. 186–196). Wheaton, IL: Quest Books.

Halužan, M. (2012). Art therapy in the treatment of alcoholics. *Alcoholism, 48*(2), 99–105.

Hiller, J. (2015). Aesthetic foundations of music therapy: Music and emotion. In B. L. Wheeler (Ed.), *Music therapy handbook* (pp. 29–39). New York, NY: Guilford Press.

Jakesch, M., & Leder, H. (2009). Finding meaning in art: Preferred levels of ambiguity in art appreciation. *Quarterly Journal of Experimental Psychology, 62*(11), 2105–2112.

Kapitan, L. (2013). Art therapy's sweet spot between art, anxiety, and the flow experience. *Art Therapy, 30*(2), 54–55.

Leder, H., Carbon, C. C., & Ripsas, A. L. (2006). Entitling art: Influence of title information on understanding and appreciation of paintings. *Acta Psychologica, 121*(2), 176–198.

Leder, H., Gerger, G., Dressler, S. G., & Schabmann, A. (2012). How art is appreciated. *Psychology of Aesthetics, Creativity, and the Arts, 6*(1), 2–10.

Lee, J., & Thyer, B. A. (2013). Does music therapy improve mental health in adults? A review. *Journal of Human Behavior in the Social Environment, 23*(5), 591–603.

Michel, D. E., & Chesky, K. S. (1995). A survey of music therapists using music for pain relief. *The Arts in Psychotherapy, 22*(1), 49–51.

Merriam-Webster Dictionary. (n.d.). s.v. music. Retrieved from http://www.merriam-webster.com/dictionary/music.

Nakamura, J., & Csikszentmihalyi, M. (2002). The concept of flow. In C. R. Snyder & S. J. Lopez (Eds.), *Handbook of positive psychology* (pp. 89–105). Oxford, UK: Oxford University Press.

National Center for Complementary and Integrative Health. (n.d.). Retrieved from https://nccih.nih.gov.

Nilsson, U. (2008). The anxiety- and pain-reducing effects of music interventions: A systematic review. *AORN Journal, 87*(4), 780–807.

Spintge, R., & Droh, R. (1989, October). Music medicine. In *Conference Proceedings from the Sixth International MusicMedicine Symposium,* Annenberg Center for Health Sciences at Eisenhower Rancho Mirage, CA.

Taylor, D. B. (1997). *Biomedical foundations of music as therapy.* St. Louis, MO: MMB Music.

Thoma, M. V., La Marca, R., Brönnimann, R., Finkel, L., Ehlert, U., & Nater, U. M. (2013). The effect of music on the human stress response. *PloS* one, *8*(8), e70156.

Thoma, M. V., Ryf, S., Mohiyeddini, C., Ehlert, U., & Nater, U. M. (2012). Emotion regulation through listening to music in everyday situations. *Cognition & Emotion, 26*(3), 550–560.

Vaitl, D., Birbaumer, N., Gruzelier, J., Jamieson, G. A., Kotchoubey, B., Kübler, A., . . . Sammer, G. (2005). Psychobiology of altered states of consciousness. *Psychological Bulletin, 131*(1), 98–127.

Wang, C. F., Sun, Y. L., & Zang, H. X. (2014). Music therapy improves sleep quality in acute and chronic sleep disorders: A meta-analysis of 10 randomized studies. *International Journal of Nursing Studies, 51*(1), 51–62.

Yehuda, N. (2011). Music and stress. *Journal of Adult Development, 18*(2), 85–94.

33

Medications for Stress Management

Doug Smith

When people seek stress relief, they may try active approaches such as yoga, self-hypnosis, or exercise, but many hope to find their solution differently—in the form of a pill. Although no medications eliminate external sources of stress, they can help prevent the cognitive and/or emotional consequences of the stress response or treat symptoms that stem from physiological reactions to stress, such as headaches, insomnia, and gastrointestinal discomfort. External and internal (psychological) stress has been implicated in symptoms such as depressed mood and anxiety, and these may also be mitigated through the use of certain medications. Following the medical stricture, "First, do no harm," caution is important with medication use to avoid adding to, compounding, or creating further stress. This chapter provides an overview of the different medication categories and how they work in the human system to prevent, manage, or alleviate stress-related symptoms.

MEDICATIONS AND STRESS PREVENTION

Benzodiazepines

When an individual is aware that a certain situation is stressful, such as flying in an airplane, going to the dentist, playing the piano in front of a live audience (performance anxiety), or attending a cocktail party, the situation can be discussed with a psychiatrist to consider whether medication may be an effective management option. This may be particularly useful for anticipated situations that occur infrequently but cause great distress. A *phobia*, persistent fear of an object or situation that causes the sufferer to go to great lengths to avoid it, is one example. These situations cause anxiety, an increased heart rate, tremulousness, dizziness, and other symptoms of acute stress. Such symptoms may be lessened with use of the antianxiety class of drugs known as *benzodiazepines*. The most common of these are Ativan (lorazepam), Xanax (alprazolam), and Valium (diazepam). Taken as prescribed by a physician, 30 to 60 minutes prior to the event, they can decrease overall anxiety for the several hours needed by preventing a full sympathetic nervous system stress reaction. Benzodiazepines bind receptors in multiple sites within the brain, most particularly in the limbic system (emotions), and enhance the effects of gamma-aminobutyric acid (GABA), the major inhibitory neurotransmitter chemical in the human central nervous system. More specifically, benzodiazepines bind to a specific site on the GABA receptor and increase its efficiency by increasing the frequency with which the chloride channel opens. Chloride ions carry a negative charge, and their increasing concentration hyperpolarizes the post-synaptic neuron. Hyperpolarization is the electrical equivalent of making it less excitable or "calmer." In effect, this short-circuits the physiological stress reaction and prevents the potentially negative effects of that stress, such as the inability to perform in front of a live audience due to fear.

Benzodiazepines tend to be well tolerated, and usually have minimal side effects, such as dizziness, drowsiness, decreased concentration, decreased alertness, decreased reflexes, decreased memory, and the like. However, these potential side effects, if severe enough, may inadvertently decrease the individual's ability to perform effectively, thereby creating a self-fulfilling prophecy and potentially increasing future anxiety in similar situations. For example, if a graduate student is about to give a public speech and takes Ativan to prevent overwhelming anxiety, but takes too much and feels sleepy and loses his train of thought during the presentation, he may not come across as an effective orator—or may even blow the talk completely. If he is aware of this poor performance, or learns that audience members thought he did not do a good job, he may be even more anxious the next time he has to give a talk. This longer-term effect is a psychological reaction to the experience he had, not a direct biochemical effect of the medication itself.

Another potential problem with benzodiazepines is that the brain develops tolerance to their pharmacologic effect, so a higher dosage is needed to achieve the same amount of the desired calming effect. This, combined with the fact that many people enjoy the calming effect, makes benzodiazepines addictive. Individuals then do not want to discontinue use of the medication, due to the potentially severe physiological withdrawal effects, such as tremors, agitation, insomnia, seizures, and even death, or due to the psychological fear of returning to a state of anxiety. In effect, this means that benzodiazepines can become a source of stress instead of an effective treatment for anxiety (Ashton, 2005; Greenblatt & Shader, 1978).

GABA, THE NERVOUS SYSTEM, AND STRESS

GABA, or gamma-aminobutyric acid, is an inhibitory neurotransmitter. Several types of receptor sites have been identified in the brain; when a neurotransmitter binds to a specific site, certain effects occur (and different effects occur when the same neurotransmitter binds to a different site, or a different neurotransmitter binds to the same site). GABA is known to play a role in both central nervous system functioning and disorders, mood disorders, and certain health conditions (Abdou, Higashiguchi, Horie, Kim, Hatta, & Yokogoshi (2006).

Under homeostasis, GABA tends to regulate the functioning of the amygdala. The amygdala (from the Greek for "almond shape") is a mass of neurons that plays a major role in the processing of aversive memories (Liu et al., 2014). Although the exact mechanisms are currently unknown, GABA tends to inhibit the amygdala during homeostasis. During the stress response, GABA levels are depleted, and the amygdala may be activated. Researchers have determined that there are primary differences between tonic and phasic GABA inhibition. The effects of stress on maladaptive tonic GABA inhibition of the amygdala potentially influence the persistence of "anxious" symptoms and possibly play a role in the manifestation of other disorders (Liu et al., 2014). Additionally, the experience of excitable symptoms may contribute to an individual's experience of what some label as "anxiety." When participants in a study were given oral doses of GABA, brainwave measurements suggested that they experienced a relaxing effect (Abdou et al., 2006).

What this suggests is that the neurotransmitter plays a role in maintaining the relaxation stage. Several pharmacological developments have been based on this knowledge, including medications to treat anxiety, seizures, and mood disorders. However, several categories of these medications (for example, the benzodiazepines and barbiturates) can be addictive (Julien, 1995; Kalat, 2001).

Other research suggests that the type of stressor influences the type of GABA mechanism (inhibitory or releasing), thereby influencing memory and learning processes (Skilbeck, Johnston, & Hinton, 2010). There is also evidence indicating that acute stress in adulthood influences and alters the number of GABA receptor sites in the brain, which impacts the adult's experiences of anxiety (Skilbeck et al., 2010).

—Serena Wadhwa

Antidepressants

Stress has been associated with a subjective decrease in mood, decreased energy, decreased sleep, decreased appetite, decreased concentration, psychomotor agitation, and a decreased enjoyment in life—all of which may be symptoms that occur in isolation or as part of a depressive episode (American Psychiatric Association, 2013). Thus, antidepressants (another large category of medications) are frequently prescribed to reduce the effects of stress.

There are several classes of antidepressants, each based on the neurotransmitter action(s) enhanced by the drugs. For example, selective serotonin reuptake inhibitors (SSRIs) increase the amount of serotonin at the level of the neuronal synapse. Serotonin is found in many areas of the brain, particularly in the raphe nuclei in the brainstem and reticular formation, which send neuronal projections throughout the brain, including the frontal cortex, cerebellum, and amygdala. Examples of SSRIs include Prozac (fluoxetine), Paxil (paroxetine), Luvox (fluvoxamine), and Zoloft (sertraline). SSRIs mediate and modulate brain pathways that affect memory, anxiety, mood, aggression, and appetite, to name just a few. Because the nervous system in the gastrointestinal tract also contains serotonin, side effects of SSRIs may include nausea, diarrhea, change in appetite, and dyspepsia, along with brain side effects such as headache, insomnia or somnolence, dizziness, sexual dysfunction, sweating, or increased thoughts of suicide.

Another category of antidepressants is selective serotonin and norepinephrine (another neurotransmitter) reuptake inhibitors (SNRIs). Effexor (venlafaxine) is one example. These medications can also cause side effects, including gastrointestinal disturbance, sexual dysfunction, increased risk of suicide, and headaches, among others.

These two categories of medications do not have the potential for addiction and have a low-severity side effect profile. However, they carry a warning about a potential increase in suicide risk (as do all antidepressant medications) and can have bothersome side effects.

Tricyclics

Tricyclic antidepressants (TCAs) are named for their three-ring molecular structure. They inhibit norepinephrine and serotonin reuptake by blocking the chemical transport processes that reabsorb these neurotransmitters within the neuronal synapse. Because they also block acetylcholine and histamine receptors, these medications tend to have more bothersome side effects than SSRIs and SNRIs, including sedation, blurred vision, constipation, dry mouth, lethargy, weight gain, heart electrical changes, and sexual dysfunction, among many other possibilities. As a result, they tend to be prescribed for stress-related symptoms only after a trial of an SSRI or SNRI has not been beneficial. One example of a TCA is Elavil (amitriptyline), which has been in use in the United States for about 60 years. Others include Pamelor (nortriptyline), Tofranil (imipramine), and Norpramin (desipramine). These drugs are generally prescribed specifically to treat depressive illness and have not been widely researched for use in the treatment of anxiety or other stress-related symptoms.

MAOIs

The monoamine oxidase inhibitors (MAOIs), such as Marplan (isocarboxazid), Nardil (phenelzine), and Parnate (tranylcypromine), are rarely used as first-choice antidepressants due to the potential to cause sudden and extreme, potentially fatal, episodes of high blood pressure (greater than 180/120) when certain foods such as aged cheese and wine are ingested. These medications block the enzyme monoamine oxidase, which acts naturally in the brain to catalyze the chemical process that breaks down the monoamine neurotransmitters, including serotonin, norepinephrine, and dopamine. The positive effect of this is to increase the availability of the neurotransmitters known to affect mood and anxiety. The negative effect, which occurs because MAOIs cannot be broken down when ingested with certain fermented foods, is a sudden excess of those same chemicals elsewhere in the body that causes a hypertensive crisis; norepinephrine (noradrenaline) is the chemical released in the fight-or-flight response alongside adrenaline, which is also not broken down in the presence of an MAOI. Serotonin syndrome (excessive serotonin) may also occur. Under a physician's direction, and after education about which foods to avoid, MAOIs are prescribed to individuals who have not responded to other classes of antidepressant medication, or have bipolar depression or atypical depressive episodes. MAOIs can be very effective at treating these conditions.

Wellbutrin

Wellbutrin (bupropion) is currently the only norepinephrine and dopamine reuptake inhibitor (NDRI) currently in use as an antidepressant; it can be administered in standard, sustained-release, or extended-release forms. Mainly by inhibiting the reuptake of dopamine, and to a lesser extent norepinephrine, it has good effectiveness against the symptoms of depression and some effectiveness against those of anxiety. It is also a nicotine receptor blocker, and is sold as Zyban (bupropion) as an effective aid for smoking cessation. Its most common side effects include headache, dry mouth, weight loss, nausea, and insomnia.

All of the drugs in the antidepressant classes may help individuals to cope with stress and stress-related symptoms, as they increase availability of key neurotransmitters in the brain and lead to microscopic changes within the brain that allow it to function at a more optimal capacity and maintain an effective homeostatic balance. While the medications may not eliminate all of the effects of stress, they tend to decrease those effects to a point that allows the individual to use other coping mechanisms more effectively. That combination, sometimes with the addition of psychotherapy, affords the best chance of optimal functioning in daily life.

MEDICATIONS FOR SPECIFIC SHORT-TERM STRESS-RELATED SYMPTOMS

Apart from prevention, when anxiety symptoms arise from stress, medication may help to decrease the severity of a symptom or eliminate it altogether. The mechanisms for this were detailed previously. The symptomatic action of antidepressants may take from one to eight weeks to develop, and therefore they are rarely useful to help ameliorate stress-related symptoms immediately or in the short term. Due to their rapid onset of action, the most commonly prescribed class of medication for this purpose is benzodiazepines.

Taken by mouth, the main effects of benzodiazepines are often felt within 60 minutes, with some beneficial effects felt within as little as 10 minutes. Due to their chemical properties, they are absorbed into the bloodstream almost completely (bioavailability 90 percent) and reach the brain quickly. When anxiety is intermittent and brief—hours as opposed to days—then Xanax (alprazolam) or Ativan (lorazepam) are commonly prescribed. These medications reach peak effectiveness very quickly, but tend to be eliminated by the body relatively quickly as well. When anxiety tends to be present for most of the day, medications with a longer half-life (i.e., that remain in the bloodstream longer before being cleared out of the body by the liver or kidneys), such as Valium (diazepam) and Klonopin (clonazepam), are often more effective. None of the benzodiazepines are safe when used with alcoholic beverages. Another caution is that benzodiazepine use can lead to tolerance, such that the patient will require higher doses in order to get the same calming effect over time. Caution must be used to prevent and watch for signs of addiction.

BETA-BLOCKERS

A different medication option is the beta-blocker class. Acting on beta-adrenergic receptors within the sympathetic nervous system, which mediate the body's fight-or-flight response to a stressor, beta-blockers prevent the action of the two main endogenous catecholamines, epinephrine (adrenaline) and norepinephrine (noradrenaline). As a result, this category of medications is mostly used to treat high blood pressure and other cardiovascular conditions.

Inderal (propranolol), a nonselective beta-adrenergic receptor blocker, is most commonly prescribed for performance anxiety. Taken in small doses (for example, before giving a piano recital or a lecture), this medication may decrease the tremors of hands or voice, sweating, and rapid heartbeat caused by the situational anxiety that triggers the sympathetic nervous system and the resulting symptoms. Blocking those physical manifestations can lead to an effective performance despite ongoing anxiety. For example, an opera singer has anxiety and related symptoms when she performs in front of a large live audience. The performance anxiety triggers her sympathetic nervous system, the action of which manifests in symptoms (such as sweating, a rapid heartbeat, and shallow breathing) that distract her and damage the performance.

As one mechanism of action, a beta-blocker prevents epinephrine (adrenaline), released in the fight-or-flight response, from activating beta-adrenergic receptors in the heart, thereby keeping the heart rate from climbing. With respect to stress-related symptoms, beta-blockers act mainly peripherally on the cardiovascular system and likely not directly on the brain or central nervous system (Bourgeois, 1991). Hence, beta-blockers are not typically used for general stress-related disorders, but they can be very effective in short-term performance situations. Beta-blockers are not addictive like benzodiazepines, but can still cause side effects, such as sexual dysfunction, orthostatic hypotension, fatigue, and insomnia. The latter three can add to or cause stress, as opposed to decreasing it, if they inadvertently make it more difficult for the individual to function at his or her peak. Apart from orthostatic hypotension, many of the side effects are likely related to beta-blocker effects on the central nervous system.

SUMMARY

The human stress response is mediated through chemicals in the body and in the brain that act on specific receptors in those areas. Specifically, the fight-or-flight response of the sympathetic nervous system uses adrenaline and noradrenaline, which can cause a racing heart or tremors of body or voice when beta-receptors are activated; brain excitation through stress can lead to an increased release of excitatory neurotransmitters in the brain; and stress over time may decrease the availability of neurotransmitters such as serotonin, dopamine, or norepinephrine in the limbic system. These areas may be targeted with beta-blockers, benzodiazepines, and antidepressant medications, respectively. Beta-blockers, such as propranolol, can decrease or eliminate the tremors and other undesirable sympathetic nervous system responses to stressful conditions such as stage fright. Benzodiazepines, such as lorazepam and diazepam, increase the effectiveness of the neurotransmitter GABA and thereby help quiet the brain and decrease anxiety. Antidepressants, most particularly those in the SSRI and SNRI categories, increase the availability of the neurotransmitters serotonin and/or norepinephrine within the neuronal synapses and, after a week to a number of weeks, lead to microscopic physical brain changes that may decrease symptoms of both anxiety and depressive disorders. None of the medications can actually eliminate sources of stress, and all of these medications may have side effects that can cause stress rather than ameliorating it, so treatment under the direction of a psychiatrist is necessary.

REFERENCES AND FURTHER READING

Abdou, A. M., Higashiguchi, S., Horie, K., Kim, M., Hatta, H., & Yokogoshi, H. (2006). Relaxation and immunity enhancement effects of γ-aminobutyric acid (GABA) administration in humans. *Biofactors, 26*(3), 201–208.

American Psychiatric Association. (1994). *Diagnostic and statistical manual of mental disorders* (4th ed.). Washington, DC: Author.

American Psychiatric Association. (2013). *Diagnostic and statistical manual of mental disorders* (5th ed.). Washington, DC: Author.

Ashton, H. (2005). The diagnosis and management of benzodiazepine dependence. *Current Opinion in Psychiatry, 18*, 249–255.

Bostwick, J. R., Casher, M. I., & Yasugi, S. (2012). Benzodiazepines: A versatile clinical tool. *Current Psychiatry, 11*(4), 55–63.

Bourgeois, J. (1991). The management of performance anxiety with beta-adrenergic blocking agents. *Jefferson Journal of Psychiatry, 9*(2), 13–28.

Ferguson, J. M. (2001). SSRI antidepressant medications: Adverse effects and tolerability. *Primary Care Companion: Journal of Clinical Psychiatry, 3*(1), 22–27.

Greenblatt, D., & Shader, R. (1978). Dependence, tolerance, and addiction to benzodiazepines: Clinical and pharmacokinetic considerations. *Drug Metabolism Reviews, 8*(1), 13–28.

Julien, R. M. (1995). *A primer of drug action: A concise, nontechnical guide to the actions, uses, and side effects of psychoactive drugs.* New York, NY: WH Freeman/Times Books/Henry Holt.

Kalat, J. W. (2001). *Biological psychology.* Belmont, CA: Wadsworth/Thomson Learning.

Kaplan, A. (2011, October 5). Antidepressants: Lifesavers—or active placebos? *Psychiatric Times.* Retrieved from http://www.psychiatrictimes.com/articles/antidepressants-lifesavers%E2%80%94or-active-placebos.

Liu, Z. P., Song, C., Wang, M., He, Y., Xu, X. B., Pan, H. Q., . . . Pan, B. X. (2014). Chronic stress impairs GABAergic control of amygdala through suppressing the tonic GABAA receptor currents. *Molecular Brain, 7*, 32.

Physicians' Desk Reference. (2014). Montvale, NJ: PDR Network.

Pigott, H. E., Leventhal, A. M., Alter, G. S., & Boren, J. J. (2010). Efficacy and effectiveness of antidepressants: Current status of research. *Psychotherapy and Psychosomatics, 79*, 267–279.

Skilbeck, K. J., Johnston, G. A., & Hinton, T. (2010). Stress and GABAA receptors. *Journal of Neurochemistry, 112*(5), 1115–1130.

34

Writing as a Means of Stress Management

Raven Lynn Badger

Stress is unavoidable, so being able to cope with stress in healthy ways can help alleviate associated problems. There are a multitude of studies that provide evidence of writing as a conduit for achieving physical and psychological benefits (Smyth, 1998). Writing is an effective method for assisting many individuals with reducing the effects of stress. Writing can be cathartic; that is, it can allow people to put their feelings on paper and process negative emotions they may be experiencing. Writing also assists in developing effective coping mechanisms related to stressors. This chapter explores several types of writing methods that have been shown to reduce stress and improve health outcomes.

WRITING AND COPING

Coping has been defined as cognitive and behavioral efforts to master, tolerate, or reduce external and internal demands and conflicts (Folkman & Lazarus, 1980). Methods of coping include eliminating or avoiding the stressor, changing the meaning of the situation, and managing states of stress arousal (Pearlin & Aneshensel, 1986). Rather than being emotion focused, coping is categorized as problem focused. Processing emotion through "talk" therapy and/or through various forms of writing as a method to achieve problem solving has been proven an effective conduit for reducing stress.

Numerous studies have reported evidence that writing about traumatic events or personal stressors is associated with improvements in physical and mental health (Meads, 2003; Smyth, 1998). Reductions in distress have been noted in the following areas by writing about traumatic or stressful events: lessening depression; positive changes in immune function; improvements in self-reported health; improved psychological well-being, physiological, and general functioning; and fewer illness-related visits to a medical provider (Meads, 2003). Journal writing and expressive writing are two of the writing methods most utilized, in numerous settings, for stress reduction and as coping techniques.

JOURNAL WRITING

Journaling was a term coined for the practice of keeping a diary or journal that explores thoughts and feelings surrounding the events of one's life (Anderson & MacCurdy, 2000). Journaling, as a stress management and self-exploration tool, is not the same as simply recording the happenings in one's life, like keeping a log. To be most helpful, people must write in detail about feelings and cognitions related to stressful events, as one would discuss topics in therapy (Ullrich & Lutgendorf, 2002).

Journaling is a good problem-solving tool; a person can often grapple with a problem and come up with solutions more easily on paper. Journaling about traumatic events can aid in the processing and release of emotions involved, and allow a richer exploration of associated emotions. Both hemispheres of the brain are involved in the process of journaling, so the experience becomes fully integrated in a person's mind (Ullrich & Lutgendorf, 2002). This kind of writing allows people to clarify their thoughts and feelings, thereby gaining valuable self-knowledge.

Identifying stress is an important component of learning how to manage stress. One method for identifying stress involves tracking everyday stressors. Keeping a stress journal can be one way to do this. When journaling to identify stressors, keep the following in mind: (a) How did you feel while experiencing the stressor? (b) What did you do to cope with it? (c) What caused the stress? and (d) What did you do to make yourself feel better? (Smith & Segal, 2014). This type of journaling will aid a person in learning about his or her daily routines, associated stressors, and current coping mechanisms. If negative coping strategies are being employed, having journal entries that illustrate those current coping methods will help people identify patterns in their stress responses, allowing for conscious thought processes, or cognition, to aid in developing healthier methods for coping with stressors.

Journal writing has been used as a personal tool to aid in stress reduction, as well as in multiple therapeutic settings and in such situations as job-related training and occupation; as a form of social support for parents of premature infants; to aid medical residents in reducing job-related stress in emergency psychiatry; and as a stress reduction technique for veterinarians forced to euthanize animals as part of their job functions. Journal writing has played an important role in many clinical settings for clients, such as programs for those who have experienced sexual abuse, those who attend 12-step programs, and individual psychotherapy.

On the professional level, certain types of autobiographical assignments are often given to residents and students in training for use as a form of stress relief. However, writing a personal journal carries less personal risk and less risk of exposing others, as the nature of journaling—a personal activity not to be shared with others—permits a sense of anonymity. The use of journals in clinical training settings can be a safe place to "dump" one's issues and fears. Journal entries written after therapy sessions can be methods for students in training to bridge back to their supervisors to discuss issues of erotic or aggressive countertransference reactions, for example. The privacy of journal writing exempts it from inclusion in the record of a resident's progress, although the writer may use the thoughts recorded in a journal as guides for productive discussions between interns and teaching faculty or supervisors.

On the personal level, journal writing can be a powerful tool for reflection and self-discovery in most life situations. It can measurably reduce depression and be a way to relieve anger, grief, and stress (Campbell, 1992). Keeping a journal can be a valuable process for gaining balance and clarity as well as recognizing emotional issues that may be difficult to verbalize. For families and individuals experiencing health-related crises, journal writing can help them participate more in care, enhance their relationships with healthcare providers, explore new issues, identify feelings, and improve their self-care.

Journals allow individuals to observe life, express personal feelings, reflect on life, and record insights and solutions to current life problems. This type of introspection is not common or widely known in U.S. culture, but a journal can be a powerful tool to document both positive and negative emotions and not be judged or shamed for expressing those feelings. Many therapists and counselors suggest that their clients keep journals in order to track their progress over time. Some patients write for healing and recovery, some to have a sounding board for complaints, and some as a method to explore emotional facets of their lives. In most journaling assignments, the person facilitating the experience (teacher, therapist, social worker, etc.) typically offers writing prompts so that client-authors have a general guideline as to issues they might wish to include in their personal writing; basically, these prompts can be used as a jumping-off point for people who are not accustomed to writing or simply do not know how to start. Other considerations include when to write, the writing environment, the rationale for writing, and how often to write. These will vary from person to person and depend on where the journaling impetus originates (self-initiated, therapist-initiated, healthcare facilitated, etc.).

COMMUNICATION

Although language is a primary form of communication and connection, it is only one form of communication. Humans express thoughts, feelings, experiences, and community in a variety of ways, including music and art (Chapter 32), dance, film, video, social media, and so on. We communicate in nonverbal ways; word language is something we may not acquire until a year or more after we are born. In the modern world, we communicate through different media and modes, each with its own benefits, costs, and risks. *How* we communicate is as important as *what* we want to say or express, because the medium we select embodies the message differently. Communicating effectively also improves assertiveness. Studies demonstrate that effective and positive communication has benefits in reducing stress (Floyd & Riforgiate, 2008; Floyd et al., 2007; Meyers, 1964).

—*Serena Wadhwa*

EXPRESSIVE WRITING

Writing about stress in a structured manner has been shown to reduce negative feelings associated with stressors over time (Smyth & Pennebaker, 2008). Another type of structured writing for stress reduction, called *expressive writing* or *emotional writing* (EW), is expression of strong emotions through structured writing exercises. Past research has revealed the connection of poor health and adverse life events, emotional upheaval, and trauma (Pennebaker, 1997). The scientific community has known for quite a while that any type of trauma—divorce, death of a spouse, loss of a job, accidents, physical trauma, and disease, among others—can produce stress. People are more likely to become sick, depressed, die from a heart attack, and gain or lose weight after an emotional upheaval (Pennebaker & Evans, 2014 . Connections between childhood trauma and poor health outcomes in adulthood due to childhood stressors were noted in a landmark study of more than 12,000 people (Stockdale, 2011).

One notable factor related to lived trauma and emotional stress is that those people who keep emotions bottled up inside are more likely to experience negative health outcomes than those who talk about and process their traumatic experiences (Pennebaker, 2014). Coping with stress using maladaptive strategies such as repressing emotion, and the inability to find or use language as a form of expression, can lead to an increase in stress-related disorders and chronic health conditions and disease (Cusinato & L'Abate, 2012; Stockdale, 2011). Failure to process trauma experiences is associated with sleep disruptions, alcohol and drug abuse, breakdowns in social networks, and an increased risk of additional traumatic experiences (Pennebaker & Chung, 2011). Expressive writing can often help prevent and interrupt the process of developing negative outcomes. So, the question of whether writing about emotional experiences would also improve health and reduce stress was posed. Since that time, more than 300 studies have garnered consistently positive results from structured, daily writing assignments that focused mainly on the emotional reactions to trauma and emotional events.

As with any type of emotional expression for stress reduction, results vary, and not every method of stress reduction has identical outcomes with individuals across gender, age, race, and socioeconomic status. In fact, with EW one of the immediate effects after engaging in writing often includes feeling worse, as the writer re-experiences the trauma while writing. Reports of feeling sad and weepy are common. Typically, this is generally short-lived, and may be compared to how a person might feel after watching a sad movie. Often people feel sad, yet have insights not previously available; this is critical to know when beginning to use EW, so as to allow time afterward to reflect on the experience and the results of writing.

Longer-term results are far more positive. People who engage in EW report feeling happier and better-adjusted over time as a result of processing their emotions through structured writing. Some studies have noted improvements in cognitive functioning and overall well-being; others found a decline in depression, general anxiety, and rumination about past events weeks to months after the intervention (Barclay & Skarlicki, 2009; Lepore, 1997). As people re-experience past trauma over and over, the power it holds over their social and emotional lives becomes smaller. This is one reason some researchers believe EW works: what is called *habituation*—the increased exposure to the trauma—works over time to decrease stress and depressive symptoms. Others believe that the benefits stem from identifying, labeling, and integrating negative emotions into the broader context of one's life (Baddeley & Pennebaker, 2011; Sloan, Feinstein, & Marx, 2009).

BENEFITS OF EW

Whatever the reasons for its effectiveness, the benefits of EW are noteworthy. Physiologically, reduced stress is documented (e.g., reduced muscle tension, lower blood pressure, lower heart rate, and other improved biological markers). Psychologically, mood improves; social interactions become more enjoyable; and symptoms of anger, PTSD, and depression are also reduced in a variety of stressful situations (Pennebaker & Graybeal, 2001; Snyder, Gordon, & Baucom, 2004). For some people, EW increases their working memory, which in turn enhances their performance on the job or at school. Stress interferes with cognitive functioning, so it is thought that EW assists in freeing up the working memory to focus more efficiently on complex thought processes (Pennebaker, 2014).

Expressive writing may simply allow people to understand their lives better and to better connect with others and benefit from social support. Rather than merely venting, expressive writing allows people to make sense of negative issues and put them into perspective. It may also promote better immune function and better sleep. Over time, many of a person's unhealthy behaviors may subside. As Dr. Michael C. Miller of Harvard Medical School noted in a 2014 article, expressive writing can help people in a number of ways. In his article, he gives instructions for EW, including setting a length of time to write, such as 15 or 30 minutes; setting a schedule; and focusing on a stressful experience, but letting it flow.

The timing matters when a person writes about emotional upheaval. It typically helps to wait a while after a traumatic or upsetting event before starting the expressive writing process. Writing too soon after the event does not allow the necessary psychological distance for perspective and reflection, and may actually make the person feel worse. It can take some time immediately following a traumatic event for an individual to fully process the emotions surrounding it. Writing as therapy is not recommended when the event is too recent for the person to have re-adjusted from the physical and/or psychological effects.

CONCLUSION

Dealing with emotional stress and trauma are part of the human experience. There are times when stressful experiences take people by surprise, so that the individuals involved do not have enough time to process those stressors or their associated implications. The idea of life correction has been perceived as a plausible explanation for why EW is effective. *Life correction* is related to perspective-taking, where a person steps back to get some distance between life events and lived reality. This perspective-taking is achieved by examining one's life through writing (McAdams, 2001). Autobiographical memory work is related to EW; in this memory work, people look back on their lived experiences and, by retrieving memories of the most intensive stressors, can identify, acknowledge, and process their most difficult memories (Neisser & Fivush, 1994). Utilizing EW as a method to evaluate what issues and events have shaped them, and why, can enable people to move forward and change their lives for the better. The ability to detach from associated stressors and life upheavals allows one to gain perspective and consider how one might move forward or cope in a different way (see also Chapter 36, "Cognitive Restructuring to Manage Stress"; and Chapter 37, "Language and Stress").

Writing creates a space for individuals to slow down and reevaluate their life situations. The act of writing also forces one to establish a structure in addition to the acknowledgment and labeling of one's emotions. A powerful characteristic of the writing process is that deep emotional experiences and feelings are transformed into words. Often, expressing emotion and naming past transgressions, trauma, and experiences allows people to heal from the pain of their pasts and move on to live healthier, less stressful lives.

REFERENCES AND FURTHER READING

Anderson, C., & MacCurdy, M. (Eds.). (2000). *Writing and healing: Toward an informed practice.* Urbana, IL: National Council of Teachers of English.

Baddeley, J. L., & Pennebaker, J. W. (2011). A postdeployment expressive writing intervention for military couples: A randomized controlled trial. *Journal of Traumatic Stress, 24*(5), 581–585.

Barclay, L. J., & Skarlicki, D. P. (2009). Healing the wounds of organizational injustice: Examining the benefits of expressive writing. *Journal of Applied Psychology, 94*(2), 511–523.

Campbell, J. (1992). Treating depression in well older adults: Use of diaries in cognitive therapy. *Issues in Mental Health Nursing, 13*(1), 19–29.

Cusinato, M., & L'Abate, L. (2012). *Advances in relational competence theory: With special attention to alexithymia.* New York, NY: Nova Science.

Floyd, K., Mikkelson, A. C., Tafoya, M. A., Farinelli, L., La Valley, A. G., Judd, J., . . . Wilson, J. (2007). Human affection exchange: XIV. Relational affection predicts resting heart rate and free cortisol secretion during acute stress. *Behavioral Medicine, 32*(4), 151–156.

Floyd, K., & Riforgiate, S. (2008). Affectionate communication received from spouses predicts stress hormone levels in healthy adults. *Communication Monographs, 75*(4), 351–368.

Folkman, S., & Lazarus, R. S. (1980). An analysis of coping in a middle-aged community sample. *Journal of Health and Social Behavior, 21*(3), 219–239.

Lepore, S. J. (1997). Expressive writing moderates the relation between intrusive thoughts and depressive symptoms. *Journal of Personality and Social Psychology, 73*(5), 1030–1037.

McAdams, D. O. (2001). The psychology of life stories. *Review of General Psychology, 5*(2), 100–122.

Meads, C. (2003). *How effective are emotional disclosure interventions? A systematic review with meta-analyses.* Paper given at the 3rd International Conference on the (Non) Expression of Emotions in Health and Disease, Tilburg, The Netherlands.

Meyers, M. E. (1964). The effect of types of communication on patients' reactions to stress. *Nursing Research, 13*(2), 126–131.

Miller, M. C. (2014). The mental health benefits of expressive writing. Retrieved March 1, 2015, from http://www.newsinmind.com/general-news/the-mental-health-benefits-of-expressive-writing.

Neisser, U., & Fivush, R. (1994). *The remembering self: Construction and accuracy in the self-narrative.* New York, NY: Cambridge University Press.

Pearlin, L. I., & Aneshensel, C. S. (1986). Coping and social supports: Their functions and applications. In L. H. Aiken & D. Mechanic (Eds.), *Applications of social science to clinical medicine and health policy* (pp. 417–437). New Brunswick, NJ: Rutgers University Press.

Pennebaker, J. W. (1997). Writing about emotional experiences as a therapeutic process. *Psychological Science, 8*(3), 162–166.

Pennebaker, J. W., & Chung, C. K. (2011). Expressive writing and its links to mental and physical health. In H. S. Friedman (Ed.), *Oxford handbook of health psychology* (pp. 417–437). New York, NY: Oxford University Press.

Pennebaker, J. W., & Evans, J. F. (2014). *Expressive writing: Words that heal.* Enumclaw, WA: Idyll Arbor.

Pennebaker, J. W., & Graybeal, A. (2001). Patterns of natural language use: Disclosure, personality and social integration. *Current Directions in Psychological Science, 10*(3), 90–93.

Sloan, D. M., Feinstein, B. A., & Marx, B. P. (2009). The durability of beneficial health effects associated with expressive writing. *Anxiety Stress Coping, 22*(5), 509–523.

Smith, M. A., & Segal, M. A. (2014). Stress management: How to reduce, prevent and cope with stress. Retrieved January 20, 2015, from http://www.helpguide.org/articles/stress/stress-management.htm.

Smyth, J. M. (1998). Written emotional expression: Effect sizes, outcome types, and moderating variables. *Journal of Consulting and Clinical Psychology, 66*(1), 174–184.

Smyth, J. M., & Pennebaker, J. W. (2008). Exploring the boundary conditions of expressive writing: In search of the right recipe. *British Journal of Health Psychology, 13*(pt. 1), 1–7.

Snyder, D. K., Gordon, K. C., & Baucom, D. H. (2004). Treating affair couples: Extending the written disclosure paradigm to relationship trauma. *Clinical Psychology: Science and Practice, 11*(2), 155–160.

Stockdale, B. (2011). Writing in physical and concomitant mental illness: Biological underpinnings and application for practice. In L. L'Abate & L. Sweeny (Eds.), *Research on writing approaches in mental health* (pp. 23–35). Bingley, UK: Emerald.

Ullrich, P. A., & Lutgendorf, S. L. (2002). Journaling about stressful events: Effects of cognitive processing and emotional expression. *Annals of Behavioral Medicine, 24*(3), 244–250.

35

Humor and Stress

Jimia Stokes

Humor has demonstrated efficacy in dealing with the various life situations that cause stress. The therapeutic use of humor enhances physical and mental well-being, and studies have shown how humor affects the brain.

There are a number of definitions that attempt to describe humor, and there is even a word to describe the study of laughter: *gelotology*. Kaduson and Schaefer (2004) define *humor* as the ability or quality of people, objects, or situations to evoke feelings of amusement in other people. McGhee (1980) states that the only prerequisites for humor are the capacity for play and the ability or "sense" to detect incongruities. Freud suggested that humor disguises aggressive impulses. A *sense of humor* is a person's ability to appreciate humor; a sense of humor also communicates a person's ability to use humor as a coping strategy for life situations (Martin, 2001).

People use humor for a variety of reasons and in many different situations. Wooten (1996) discussed how humor is utilized as a coping strategy for self-care. Wooten referenced a humor training course presented in 1990 by the 8th International Conference of Humor in England where she utilized several adult scales to determine the effects of humor among 231 nurses using the Adult Nowicki-Strickland Scale and Svebak's Sense of Humor Questionnaire, using only the subscales that have proven to be reliable and valid and Wilcoxon Matched Pairs Signed-Ranks Test. This study indicated that if one is encouraged and guided to use humor, they can gain a sense of control in their life work. In an article written by Dr Kounti-Zafeiropoulou Fotini (2014): *The contribution of humor in our lives* he referenced how Wooten divided therapeutic humor into three categories: hoping, coping, and gallows humor. *Hoping humor* allows individuals to hope for something better in spite of difficult circumstances. *Coping humor* helps people to change the way they think and regain control over their lives. *Gallows humor* allows people to recognize situations that they cannot control, and helps to change their perceptions of those situations into something that can be handled.

MEN AND WOMEN AND HUMOR

Cohan and Bradbury (1997) speculate that the more aggressive humor of men in times of turmoil adversely affects bonding between newlywed couples, compared with the more soothing humor favored by women. They analyzed the marriages of 60 couples over an 18-month time period and found that when men used humor to cope with stressful events, such as job loss or death, it led to a greater incidence of divorce and separation than when women used humor in those same stressful situations.

Though male humor may play a role in establishing romantic relationships, female humor appears to be more effective in maintaining them. Kohn, Kellermann, Gur, Schneider, and Habel (2011) looked at the difference in the brain activities of both men and women and found that in women, behaviors and cognitive processes were more activated in the processing of humor and emotions. This could mean that women have a distinct pattern of neural activity that occurs in a response to humor, with the left temporal gyrus experiencing the most activity. Women show greater activity in the left prefrontal cortex than men (Proceedings of the National Academy of Sciences, 2005). Azin, Mobbs, Booil, Menon, and Reiss researchers at Stanford University in California, suggested that women take significantly longer than men to decide whether or not they find something funny. The research found that women show a greater humor response in the limbic system of the brain than men, indicating that they feel a greater sense of reward and execute a greater degree of processing and language-based decoding. Simply put, the research indicates that women tend to be able to make light of situations that are often serious in nature, allowing them to feel better and helping others around them to relax.

In a study published in the *Proceedings of the National Academy of Sciences*, researchers found that in men, fiber pathways run back and forth within each brain hemisphere, whereas in women they tend to zig-zag between the left, or "logical," and right, or "creative," sides of the brain. One implication of this is that men tend to see issues and resolve them directly, due to the strong connections between the "perception" and "action" areas of their brains. In contrast, women might be more inclined to combine logic and intuition when solving a problem.

Another hypothesis about the expression of emotions is that women tend to be "externalizers" in their expressive domains and men "internalizers" in their psychophysiological domains. This may help explain the differences in how men and women deal with stress in personal and external situations. Three hormones in the brain are responsible for the responsive differences between men and women:

cortisol, epinephrine, and oxytocin. Cortisol and epinephrine raise a person's blood pressure and circulating blood sugar levels. Oxytocin, which promotes nurturing and relaxation, helps to counter the production of cortisol and epinephrine. Men secrete lesser amounts of oxytocin, and thus experience more stress than women. An influential study published in the July 2000 issue of *Psychological Review* reported that females were more likely to deal with stress by "tending and befriending"; that is, by nurturing those around them and reaching out to others. "Tending involves nurturing activities designed to protect the self and offspring that promote safety and reduce distress" (Taylor et al., 2000, pp. 411–429).

USING HUMOR AS A CONTROL MECHANISM

Many have found that humor is a healthy way to reframe a stressful situation. When we are faced with a difficult situation, incorporating laughter and humor into it can help us deal with difficulties and threats. Looking at our life situations with a sense of humor helps keep things in balance. One of the fathers of psychology, William James, wrote: "We don't laugh because we're happy; we're happy because we laugh" (Brehony, 2000, p. 228).

The stress level one experiences will continue to be out of one's control until one takes responsibility for the role that one plays in both creating and maintaining one's personal stress (Smith & Segal, 2014). Philosopher Alan Watts said, "The whole art of life is knowing how to transform anxiety into laughter" (Watts, 2014). Just as modern medicine provides a framework for how we treat individual illnesses, humor provides a basis for helping people get through their problems. Humor can be one of the essential tools for bringing about change and progress in helping individuals deal with their personal life issues.

When we experience challenges that go beyond our personal abilities, our anxiety levels increase, causing the situations we have encountered to become more difficult for us to handle (Hendry & Kloep, 2002). According to Susanne Jacobs (2009) of the Institute for Child, Adolescent and Family Studies, "humor can be taught and is used constructively as a coping mechanism in potentially harmful situations" (p. 498).

PHYSICAL HEALTH BENEFITS FROM HUMOR

Fry (1977) initiated the earliest studies on the effects of humor on human physiology, and garnered data to provide a basis for the use of humor in clinical settings. Rod Martin (1996) wrote an article referencing the work of Adler and Hillhouse's research on how a stressful life event adversely affects a person's immune system. While there is a need for more empirical studies to investigate and define the interplay between humor and the immune system, there have been a number of experimental studies that have examined the various aspects of immunity with regard to humorous stimuli. Martin (2001) cited laboratory experiments on the effects of exposure to comedy on a number of immune system components. The results of the studies provided little evidence that humor and laughter actually made health-related differences. With regard to immunity, the findings have been inconsistent: some studies have shown changes in multiple components of immunity when the subject is exposed to humor, some studies have shown immuno-enhancing effects, and others have shown immunosuppressive effects. There are significant limitations to most of these studies, particularly the absence of a control group, which make it hard to determine whether the detected changes in immunity were due to humor and laughter or to other factors such as common emotions.

However, there is evidence supporting the use of humor to improve physical health. Some studies showed an improvement in blood sugar levels, an increase in the production of natural killer (NK) cells that attack viruses and tumors, stimulation of organ functions, and increases in pain thresholds. In a study conducted by Berk and colleagues (1989), the researchers took blood samples from 10 male participants, half of whom watched a 60-minute comedic videotape; the other five did not view the tape, but instead sat in a room for 60 minutes. The results found that the participants who were exposed to humor had significantly lower levels of cortisol and higher levels of growth hormones and immuno-enhancing effects (an increase in the T-helper/suppressor ratio). Kamei, Kumano, and Masumura (1997) had opposite findings: they took blood samples from 8 male medical students who watched a comedic videotape (no time limit was mentioned). Blood samples were taken from the same participants 2 hours before and a week after they took a stressful physical examination; these findings differed from those of Berk et al., in that Kamei et al. found that humor had an *immunosuppressive* effect. However, researcher Rod Martin (2001) referenced a study conducted by Itami, Nobori, and Teshima, blood samples were taken from 19 participants before and after the participants watched a 3-hour comedy show; these researchers found significant increases in NK cell activity and CD4/CD8 ratio, indicating a "normalizing effect of laughter on immunity" (p. 509).

Physical health often serves as a guide in determining an individual's emotional well-being. Martin (2001, p. 515) stated that "humor is a complex phenomenon involving cognitive, emotional, behavior, physiological and social aspects." He hypothesized that laughter could possibly cause physiological changes in the body that improve circulation and respiration, and stimulate the production of the endorphins that help to reduce pain and stress-related hormones, thereby enhancing the person's immune system and response. The United States Department of Health and Human Services National Institute for Occupational Safety and Health (NIOSH, 1999) provided a pamphlet titled *Stress at Work* that suggested as to how employers can reduce work-related stress, stating that a relaxed work environment improves productivity. Employers have found that when they allow employees to take the time to have social gatherings where they smile and laugh together, there is a reduction in the number of sick days used.

In a research article written by Tait Trussell (2008) Dr. Michael Miller, a cardiologist at the University of Maryland Medical Center in Baltimore, took part in a research study that looked at how an active sense of humor can help guard the heart against heart attack; he stated: "We don't know yet why laughing protects the heart: but we know mental stress is associated with impairment of the endothelium, the protective barrier lining our blood vessels. This can cause a series of inflammatory reactions that lead to fat and cholesterol build-up in the coronary arteries and ultimately to a heart attack" (p. 88). Norman Cousins (1990) published an article titled "The Laughter Prescription," where he discussed the research of Dr. James Walsh, a medical director of the School of Sociology at Fordbam University in New York reported his research that demonstrated how hearty laughter stimulates internal organs, "making them work better through the increase of circulation that follows the vibrating massage that accompanies it, and heightens resistive vitality against disease" (p. 36) and wrote a number of articles and books on the subject of using humor to combat disease and reduce its effects, the most famous of which was *Anatomy of an Illness* (1979). There is some controversy among physicians and other scientists as to how well his techniques worked, but Cousins firmly believed that they did, and he lived approximately 25 years after being diagnosed with ankylosing spondylitis.

Cousins's story, and others like it, led scientists and doctors to conduct studies on ways to bring the efficacy of humor into therapeutic practice. In an article titled "Laughter Prescription" (2009), Dr. William Strean wrote about the conclusion of Dr. Morse and his use of humor to reduce stress and pain and enhance healing in the dental setting, nonliability inhering in the use of laughter in medicine, noting that "Laughter and humor are not beneficial for everyone, but since there are no negative side effects, they should be used to help reduce stress and pain and to improve healing" (8th Para.).

Researchers at the University of Maryland explored the effects of laughter on cardiac health and concluded that laughter appeared to cause the inner lining of blood vessels to dilate, thereby increasing blood flow and avoiding dangerous vessel constriction (Borchard, 2011). Cousins discussed how Dr. William Fry Jr., of the Department of Psychiatry at Stanford Medical School, believed that laughter was a form of exercise that caused spasmodic skeletal muscle contractions that are followed by postlaughter muscular relaxation. The pulse races, causing huffing and puffing, speeds up the heart rate, raises blood pressure, accelerates breathing, increases oxygen consumption, gives the muscles of the face and stomach a workout, and relaxes muscles not involved in laughing.

MENTAL HEALTH

Individual differences and personality traits largely determine how an individual will deal with a stressful situation, and people's cognitive reactions play a predominant role in how stressful a situation is for them. Some people are born with a temperament that predisposes them to higher or lower levels of tolerance to stress. In recognition of the individuality of these reactions, a number of studies have investigated the use of humor and laughter in psychotherapy. Marc Gelkopf (2009) states that research dating back 30 years suggests that humor positively affects mental health. Nevertheless, therapeutic humor is underutilized due to a discrepancy between research and clinical practice. Gelkopf listed reasons why he believes that humor is not used more often to treat individuals with mental health problems such as major depressive, bipolar, personality, substance use, conduct, reactive attachment, and posttraumatic stress disorders and traumatic brain injuries. He thinks it is due to what he calls the history of professional socialization in psychiatry, where practitioners are taught to believe that the use of humor would be risky, especially in dealing with clients who are schizophrenic and in populations with serious mental illness (SMI); also, clinicians do not want to incur liability for the inappropriate use of humor in clients with SMI. Gelkopf (2011) notes that individuals with SMI are traditionally considered as having impairment in their ability to enjoy humor. Other reasons Gelkopf mentions are that humor is not considered to be fully in the mainstream of therapy, having what he describes as a "new-age," unscientific connotation; thus, it is difficult to secure financial support for intervention and/or scientific studies concerning humor. Finally, Gelkopf theorizes that the psychiatric bias against humor in therapy dates back to the Middle Ages in Western European history, when the laugh of a madman was described as the laughter of death.

Multiple studies have provided a framework regarding the use of humor and laughter, as well as other psychotherapeutic approaches, in the treatment of medical patients, both children and adults. In *The Psychology of Humor* (Martin, 2007), the author states that humor helps to improve positive emotions and describes how humor may positively affect health. Skevington and White (1998) explored how humor seemed to have an effect on pain. A study conducted by Walter et al. (2007) compared humor to traditional therapy in the treatment of elderly patients diagnosed with late-life depression or Alzheimer's disease; there was an improvement in the patients with depression but very little to no improvement among individuals with Alzheimer's. They concluded that when the brain is damaged by Alzheimer's disease, humor has no effect, but suggested that humor could be used as a complementary tool with traditional therapy. The bottom line is that, while there is a need for a cost-effective ways of treating mental illness, clinicians are not ready to rely on humor to fill this gap, because of the lack of empirical studies, perceived methodological flaws, the lack of control groups, and the use of nonstandardized assessment tools.

Use of humor has also been explored in the areas of education and psychotherapy (Dziegielewski, Jacinto, Laudadio, & Legg-Rodriguez, 2003; Franzini, 2001). Dziegielewski et al. followed up on work by Buckman (1994), in which he set out 13 considerations for the therapeutic use of humor:

1. There must be a therapeutic relationship before humor is used in therapy.
2. Humor transcends and disarms the client's unconscious resistances, enabling the therapeutic exploration of painful conflict issues.
3. To be effective, humor, like any interoperation, must be timely.
4. By using all the healthy defense mechanisms, humor becomes the highest-level and healthiest functioning defense mechanism.
5. Humor bonds the client and the therapist in accomplishing the painful work of therapy.
6. Bypassing superego censorship, humor enhances ego functioning to manage and explore unconscious material.
7. Incongruity and surprise make humor enjoyable while executing its interpretive work.
8. Therapists' use of humor allows clients to become better aware of what might otherwise have been unconscious or beyond awareness.
9. The therapist's use of humor addresses transferential and countertransferential issues.
10. Humor enables regression in the service of the ego.
11. The therapist-client relationship determines the type, timing, and use of humor employed.
12. Thoughtful spontaneity is always the determinant for the therapeutic use of humor.
13. Humor = pain + distance.

There are both advocates and opposers of the use of humor in psychotherapy. A notable sense of humor can be discerned in the approaches of early theorists such as Albert Ellis, Erik Erikson, Virginia Satir, Carl Whitaker, and Carl Rogers. Gelkopf (2009) discusses how humor has impacted health care and how the application of humor has been shown to be beneficial within the framework of psychotherapy. He notes that therapists treating individuals with serious mental illnesses such as schizophrenia, bipolar disorder, obsessive compulsive disorder, posttraumatic stress disorder (among others) can utilize humor as an adjunct to conventional treatment, in both individual and group therapies. Major psychotherapy orientations that include behaviorists, cognitivists, family therapists, provocative therapists, existentialist therapists, and others have used humor in their therapeutic practices.

In *The Expression of the Emotions in Man and Animals,* Darwin (1899) speculated that the evolutionary basis of laughter was its function as a social expression of happiness and that because of this, humor creates or enhances group cohesion. Due to their apparent lack of social skills, individuals with SMI often experience high levels of social alienation; thus, the use of laughter and humor in groups of such patients has been shown to be significant. Individuals with SMI often find their way to groups through treatment referrals. Laughter is used in therapeutic groups to reduce stress. When we laugh, our muscles contract, stimulating the release of endorphins that help to reduce stress. Group facilitators often lead with opening statements that will cause laughter, recognizing that you don't need to have a good sense of humor or be happy to benefit from a good laugh.

Humor is a natural tension reducer and has been found to relieve somatic stress and facilitate therapeutic processes. The therapeutic relationship is enhanced by deepening the therapeutic alliance, strengthening the feeling of acceptance, enhancing empathy and a sense of belonging. For some, humor can also help overcome the overexaggerated seriousness that is sometimes used as a defense mechanism against uncertainty.

Humor helps to soothe the stress in people who have experienced trauma and other stress-generating conditions by creating distractions and social connections, relieving tension, and helping to change perspectives by releasing emotions. Trauma can be both physical and psychological, but in psychology and psychiatry *trauma* is a psychological or emotional injury caused by a deeply disturbing experience—and it can have lasting effects. Stress is a common product of trauma, often involved in addiction behaviors and posttraumatic stress disorder (PTSD). Cousins was quoted as saying: "If laughter can improve one's perspective on life and on pain, it follows that it might be helpful in combating unusual stress" (p. 37).

The members of the Association for Applied and Therapeutic Humor (AATH) come from various disciplines (teachers, psychotherapists, psychiatrists, counselors, nurses, and other health professionals). Their mission is to help promote health and well-being through the use of humor interventions. Monro (1988) described three theories associated with humor: the first was artificial empowerment resulting in feelings of superiority (Superiority Theory); the next a means of dealing with frustration or injustice through resorting to divergent logic and contradiction (Incongruity Theory); and the last (Relief Theory) as removing social restraint through the expression of the inexpressible. These theories could directly or indirectly contribute to lower anxiety and tension and creation of more positive mood or mental state.

Goldin et al. (2006) state that humor has to be used appropriately in counseling, as it may sometimes be perceived as disrespectful, as making light of the client's feelings, or as a way for the counselor to avoid dealing with a client's anxieties. If therapists avoid using humor in ways that could be misinterpreted, they will find that humor can often be beneficial when dealing with stressful topics in the therapeutic setting.

THE BRAIN AND HUMOR

Many of the various parts of the brain are involved in processing humor. The right hemisphere of the brain expresses and reads emotions. The occipital portion, at the back of the brain, is where the cerebral cortex, which is responsible for interpreting visual information, is located. It is within these structures that the appreciation for contradiction lies. However, it is the frontal lobe that makes sense of the difference between a script (stand-up comedy, cartoon, or joke) and a serendipitous situation that is unintentionally or inadvertently comedic.

The brain works hard to process humor, which Charles Darwin referred to as the "tickling of the mind." Humor can be visual, auditory, or both. The brain is responsible for processing the timing, order, and emphasis of humor. The frontal lobe makes the differentiation between a serious statement and a humorous statement. Research shows that with written material, persons with frontal-lobe injury are unable to distinguish between what is humor and what is serious; instead, they have a literal understanding of what is being read (Restak, 2013).

Neuroscientists continue to research the mechanics of the brain and the effects of humor. Certainly, the brain is the organ that regulates how we perceive, recognize, and interpret humor. Much of the research in this area seeks to identify the parts of the brain (hippocampus, occipital cortex, temporal lobe, limbic system, and the amygdala) involved and to describe the connections that yield the humor experience. Fry (1977) did several surveys and analyses intended to further research into humor and brain function. Fry described a type of laughter termed "mirthful laughter," which was said to have a physiological effect (Fry & Savin, 1988). This depends on brain functioning, as the brain not only participates in the physiological effects of mirthful laughter but also allows us to experience laughter and process humor (mirth).

Researchers continue to look at how the brain processes funny experiences, by acknowledging how positive emotions effect the brains mechanism. They identified three components of the brain as follows: cognitive thinking, the section of the brain that helps you comprehend the joke, the frontal lobe of the brain works along with the temporal lobe, and the hypothalamus helps move facial muscles that help contribute in laughter. Although the research of humor and its health benefits are relatively new, the researchers have identified a connection to the neuropsychological and physiological benefits of humor. *Gelotology* is the physiological study of humor. Martin's article concluded that while there is a continued need for further study in the effects of humor and laughter on our health, his article indicated that there is evidence that humor has some effect on the immune system and pain response. Allan Reiss (2008) and his colleagues at Stanford University conducted research on the effects of humor on the region of the nucleus accumbens of the brain that releases dopamine when there is a humorous experience. The procedure of responding to and appreciating humor begins with the launch of a script in the temporal lobes.

Humor creates substantial demands on the brain. For something to be perceived or interpreted as humorous, the timing, order, and emphasis must be right. Although humor can be utilized as an effective coping tool, at times it can create stressful experiences. Individuals who base their careers on making people laugh by using humor have experienced stress, and those careers have been shown to take a toll on their personal mental health.

It is well documented that stress causes disease or dis-ease. We know that when we are uncomfortable we often default to a joke or an expression that lightens the mood; this helps us to relieve our stress and feel better. So, why does psychology neglect the use of humor as an accepted technique?

CONCLUSION

This chapter was intended to review and contribute to the debate about the effects of humor, and whether it can legitimately be brought into the serious business of treating stress, improving physical and mental health, and so on. As yet, there is limited evidence for the therapeutic use of humor to reduce stress and improve health, though the amount of research continues to grow. Previous reviews suggest that humor has multiple effects on emotions, judgments, attitudes, and perceptions that may directly or indirectly benefit physical and psychological health. Humor can be a tool for discerning human development and gauging a person's level of socialization; it can also be integrated into professional development for knowledge and skills enhancement. However, further work must be done to demonstrate the efficacy of humor and develop proven approaches and techniques before humor is fully accepted and integrated into medical and mental health practices.

We hope that practitioners will experiment with using humor in therapy. Medical and mental health professionals take an oath to do no harm; along this line of thinking, Strean (2009, p. 965) states that "there are almost no negative side effects or undesirable ramifications associated with laughter as an intervention. Humor helps patients and nurses to distance themselves from negative emotions and consequently uplifts them as positive emotions are transferred."

REFERENCES AND FURTHER READING

Azin, E., Mobbs, D., Booil, J., Menon, V., & Reiss, A. (2005). Sex differences in brain activation elicited by humor. *Proceedings of the National Academy of Sciences, 102* (45). Retrieved June 4, 2014 from http:// http://www.pnas.org/content/102/45/16496.full.

Berk, L. S., Tan, S. A., Fry, W. F., Napier, B. J., Lee, J. W., Hubbard, R. W., . . . Eby, W. C. (1989). Neuroendocrine and stress hormone changes during mirthful laughter. *American Journal of Medicine and Science 298* (6), 390–396. Retrieved from, https://www.ncbi.nlm.nih.gov/pubmed/2556917.

Borchard, T. (2011). The healing power of laughter. *PsychCentral.* Retrieved June 4, 2014, from http://psychcentral.com/blog/archives/2011/05/17/the-healing-power-of-laughter.

Brehony, K. (2000). After the darkest hour. Retrieved June 4, 2014, from https:// http://www.goodreads.com/book/show/822791.After_the_Darkest_Hour.

Buckman, E. S. (1994). *Handbook of humor: Clinical applications in psychotherapy.* Melbourne, FL: Krieger.

Cohan, C. L., & Bradbury, T. N. (1997). Negative life events, marital interaction, and the longitudinal course of newlywed marriage. *Journal of Personality and Social Psychology, 73*(1), 114–128.

Cousins, N. (1979). Anatomy of an illness. In A. Monat, & R. S. Lazarus (Eds.), *Stress and coping: An anthology* (3rd ed., pp. 48–61). New York, NY: Columbia University Press.

Cousins, N. (1990). The laughter prescription. *Saturday Evening Post,* 262(6), 32–110.

Darwin, C. (1899). The expression of the emotions in man. Critical Inquiry [serial online]. September 2010; *37* (1):34–59. Available from: Academic Search Complete, Ipswich, Retrieved June 4, 2014.

Dziegielewski, S., Jacinto, G., Laudadio, A., & Legg-Rodriguez, L. (2003). Humor: An essential communication tool in therapy. *International Journal of Mental Health, 32*(3), 74–90.

Franzini, L. R. (2001). Humor in therapy: The case for training therapists in its uses and risks. *Journal of General Psychology, 128*(2), 170.

Fry, W. F. (1977). The respiratory components of mirthful laughter. *Journal of Biological Psychology, 19,* 39–50.

Fry, W. F., & Savin, W. M. (1988). Mirthful laughter and blood pressure. *HUMOR: International Journal of Humor Research 1*(1), 49–62.

Gelkopf, M. (2011). The use of humor in serious mental illness: A review. *Evidence-Based Complementary and Alternative Medicine* (Ecam), *8*(1), 1–8. http://dx.doi.org/10.1093/ecam/nep106.

Giuliani, N., McRae, K., & Gross, J. (2008). The up- and down-regulation of amusement: Experiential, behavioral, and autonomic consequences. *Emotion, 8*(5), 714–719.

Goldin, E., Bordan, T., Araoz, D., Gladding, S., Kaplan, D., Krumboltz, J., & Lazarus, A. (2006). Humor in counseling: Leader perspectives. *Journal of Counseling and Development, 84*(4), 397–404.

Hendry, L. B., & Kloep, M. (2002). *Lifespan development: Resources, challenges and risks.* London, UK: Thomson Learning.

Jacobs, S. (2009). Humour in gestalt therapy—curative force and catalyst for change: A case study. *South African Journal of Psychology, 39*(4), 498–506.

Kaduson, H., & Schaefer, C. (Eds.). (2004). *101 Favourite play therapy techniques.* Lanham, MD: Rowman & Littlefield.

Kamei, T., Kumano, H., & Masumura, S. (1997). Changes of immunoregulatory cells associated with psychological stress and humor. *Perceptual and Motor Skills, 84*(3 Pt. 2), 1296–1298.

Kohn, N., Kellermann, T., Gur, R., Schneider, F., & Habel, U. (2011). Gender differences in the neural correlates of humor processing: Implications for different processing modes. *Neuropsychologia, 49*(5), 888–897.

Kounti-Zafeiropoulou, F. (2014). The contribution of humor in our lives. *Studying Humour International Journal,* 1. Retrieved from https://ejournals.lib.auth.gr/humour/article/download/4344/4418.

Martin, R. (1996). Sense of humor and physical health: Theoretical issues, recent findings, and future directions. Retrieved from, http://www.msumcounselored.org/files/TheUseBenefitsofHumorinHealth/article_2.pdf.

Martin, R. (2001). Humor, laughter, and physical health: Methodological issues and research findings. *Psychological Bulletin, 127*(4), 504–519.

Martin, R. (2007). *The psychology of humor: An integrative approach.* Burlington, MA: Academic Press.

McGhee, P. E. (1980). Development of the sense of humor in childhood: A longitudinal study. In P. E. McGhee & A. Chapman (Eds.), *Children's humor* (pp. 213–236). Chichester, UK: John Wiley & Sons.

Monro, D. H. (1988). Theories of humor. In L. Behrens, & L. J. Rosen (Eds.), *Writing and reading across the curriculum* (3rd ed., pp. 349–355). Glenview, IL: Scott, Foresman and Company.

Reiss, A. L., Hoeft, F., Tenforde, A., Chen, W., Mobbs, D., & Mignot, E. (2008). Anomalous hypothalamic responses to humor in cataplexy. *PLoS ONE, 3*(5), e2225. doi:10.1371/journal.pone.0002225.

Restak, R. (2013, June 10). Laughter and the brain. *The American Scholar.* Retrieved from http://www.theamericanscholar.org/laughter-and-the-brain/#VQr7cY7F98E.

Saper, C. B. (1988). Humor in psychiatric healing. *Psychiatric Quarterly, 59*(4), 306–309.

Sauter, S., Murphy, L., Colligan, M., Swanson, N., Hurrell Jr., J., Scharf Jr., F., . . . Tisdale, J. (1999). *NIOSH approach to job stress* (Publication 99–101). Retrieved from http://www.cdcgov/niosh/docs/99-101/default.html.

Skevington, S. M., & White, A. (1998). Is laughter the best medicine? *Psychology and Health, 13*(1), 157–169.

Smith, M., & Segal, R. (2014). Stress management: How to reduce, prevent, and cope with stress. Retrieved May 14, 2014, from http://www.helpguide.org/articles/stress/stress_management.htm.

Strean, W. B. (2009). Laughter prescription. *Canadian Family Physician, 55*(10), 965–967. Retrieved May 14, 2014 from http://www.cfp.ca/content/55/10/965.full.pdf+html

Taylor, S. E., Cousino, L. K., Lewis, B. P., Gruenewald, T. L., Gurung, A., & Updegraff, J. A. (2000). Biobehavioral responses to stress in females: Tend-and-befriend, not fight-or-flight. *Psychological Review, 107*(3), 411–429. Retrieved May 14, 2014, from http:// http://scholar.harvard.edu/marianabockarova/files/tend-and-befriend.pdf.

Trussell, T. (2008). Healing humor. *Saturday Evening Post, 280*(4), 36–88.

United States Department of Health and Human Services. Stress at work. Rockville-NIH Publication No 99-10. Retrieved May 14, 2014, from http://www.cdc.gov/niosh/docs/99-101/default.html.

Walter, M., Hanni, B., Haug, M., Amrhein, I., Krebs-Roubicek, E., Muller-Spahn, F., & Savaskan, E. (2007). Humour therapy in patients with late-life depression or Alzheimers disease: A pilot study. *International Journal of Geriatric Psychiatry, 22*(1), 77–83.

Watts, A. (2014). The guy quote. *Dysonology—Word Press*. Retrieved May 14, 2014, from https://dysonology.wordpress.com/2014/01/03/the-guy-quote-alan-watts/.

Wooten, P. (1996). Humor an antidote for stress. *Holistic Nursing Practice. 10*(2), 1996, 49–55. Retrieved May 14, 2014, from http://pattywooten.com/images/HumorStress Antidote.pdf.

36

Cognitive Restructuring to Manage Stress

Kimberly S. Kut

Cognitive restructuring is a therapeutic process developed from the historical works of Albert Ellis and Aaron T. Beck, who pioneered rational emotive behavior therapy (1955) and cognitive therapy (early 1960s), respectively. It is also utilized in cognitive behavior therapy, cognitive processing therapy, schema therapy, and dialectical behavior therapy. Cognitive restructuring is the core mechanism in the promotion of positive change in these empirically validated, cognitive behavioral-based psychotherapies. This chapter first introduces the basics of cognitive therapy before describing the use of cognitive restructuring as a therapeutic tool in the management of stress and overall psychological symptomatology, because it is imperative to understand through cognitive theory how people's thought processes, emotions, and behaviors all influence each other and are reciprocally related. The interactions of how one thinks, feels, and behaves can cause or contribute to both distress and the intensity and maintenance or the alleviation and overall prevention of distress.

According to Beck (1995), the cognitive model of psychopathology postulates that rather than a situation itself causing distress, it is one's perceptions and interpretations (often expressed in immediate, automatic thoughts) during or about a situation that influence one's subsequent emotional, behavioral, and physiological reactions. Beck further states, "In a nutshell, the *cognitive model* proposes that distorted or dysfunctional thinking (which influences the patient's mood and behavior) is common to all psychological disturbances" (1995, p. 1). In addition, thoughts play a significant role in maintaining distressing and dysfunctional emotions and behaviors (Padesky & Greenberger, 1995). As stated by Freeman, Pretzer, Fleming, and Simon (2004), the cognitive model "also recognizes that emotions can influence cognitive processes and that behaviors can influence the evaluation of a situation by modifying the situation or by eliciting responses from others" (p. 6). Therefore, thoughts, emotions, and behaviors impact each other and affect the outcome of a situation. When a person is distressed by negatively experienced emotions (feeling overwhelmed, anxious, angry, depressed, etc.), many of the person's perceptions and interpretations of situations are often inaccurate and dysfunctional to some degree, if not completely (Beck & Bieling, 2004). If distortions arise during these interactive processes and it becomes a habitual way of thinking, feeling, and behaving in certain situations, a self-perpetuated, ongoing cycle may develop and generalize to other situations (Freeman et al., 2004). The result may not only be distress, but also possible failure in achieving desired outcomes or goals in the situation or in life itself.

DEFINITION OF COGNITIVE RESTRUCTURING

What is cognitive restructuring? Per Beck (1995), "[r]ealistic evaluation and modification of thinking produce an improvement in mood and behavior. Enduring improvement results from modification of the patient's underlying dysfunctional beliefs" (p. 1). Therefore, cognitive restructuring was developed as a multistep therapeutic process to increase awareness, and identify, challenge, test, and ultimately change the dysfunctional cognitive processes and patterns that result in faulty information processing, increased symptomatology, and overall distress (Leahy & Rego, 2012). During the cognitive restructuring process, irrational, distorted, and maladaptive thoughts, appraisals, and beliefs that are contributing to and maintaining psychological disturbance are modified into rational, realistic, and adaptive thought processes (Clark, 2013). Hence, mood improves and healthy behaviors tend to increase (Beck, 1995). Once rational, functional thought processes are intact and strong emotions are not driving thinking and behavior, one can more effectively problem-solve, cope, and make healthy choices and decisions.

As with many types of growth and change, cognitive restructuring can be a difficult, lengthy process, and it requires awareness, willingness, determination, and perseverance. Cognitive restructuring is not merely a coping tool: it is a life skill. The result of mastering this skill is less unwarranted cognitive, emotional, and behavioral distress, which paves the way for more pleasant overall experiences.

AUTOMATIC THOUGHTS, INTERMEDIATE BELIEFS, AND CORE BELIEFS

The cognitions that are targeted for modification during the cognitive restructuring process are the automatic thoughts, intermediate beliefs, and core beliefs (also called *schemas*) that are dysfunctional. *Automatic thoughts* are knee-jerk, raw thoughts, images, and memories that spontaneously arise in the moment and are situation specific (Beck, 1995; Freeman et al., 2004). They are the immediate interpretations one makes in a situation (Freeman et al., 2004). Automatic thoughts are unplanned and occur without apparent volition, but they influence one's emotions, physiological reactions, and behavior in response to events (Freeman et al., 2004; Padesky & Greenberger, 1995). For example, a highly dedicated and ambitious student named Tristan receives a "B" on a math exam and is devastated. He turns red, begins to sweat, feels embarrassed and depressed, breaks into tears, and refuses to go to any social events for weeks. Preceding his emotions and behavior were possibly the irrational automatic thoughts: "I really messed up," "I'm an idiot," "I'll never get into college!" Automatic thoughts are on a surface level, and thus are closest to conscious awareness—closer than intermediate and core beliefs. However, they flow so naturally and abruptly that individuals may not always be completely aware of their exact automatic thoughts, and may instead be more aware of the emotion(s) that the thoughts elicited and respond accordingly (Beck, 1995). Automatic thoughts are influenced by both intermediate and core beliefs.

Underlying one's automatic thoughts is a class of beliefs called *intermediate beliefs*. These beliefs consist of rules/expectations, attitudes, and assumptions that often are not articulated on a conscious level (Beck, 1995). They are conditional, cross-situational beliefs or rules that shape a person's response to experiences and situations and guide the individual's life (Padesky & Greenberger, 1995; Freeman et al., 2004). Intermediate beliefs often involve "if-then" and "should" statements (Padesky & Greenberger, 1995). Continuing with the previous example of Tristan, his irrational rules and expectations may be as follows: "I should (or must) get an 'A' on all tests," "Intelligent people always get perfect marks." His dysfunctional attitude may include: "It's bad to get anything less than an 'A'," "A 'B' is unacceptable." His maladaptive assumptions are likely: "If I get anything less than an 'A,' then I am stupid and incompetent, and I will not get into college"; "If I am stupid and incompetent, then no one will like me."

The most fundamental level of beliefs is *core beliefs/schemas,* which underlie and fuel both intermediate beliefs and automatic thoughts (Beck, 1995). Core beliefs are cognitive structures that function to organize, filter, and process incoming information and stimuli (Dobson & Dozois, 2010). They provide a basis on which a person screens, categorizes, interprets, and assigns meaning to experiences (Freeman et al., 2004). Core beliefs are unconditional, rigid, global, and overgeneralized beliefs about oneself, others, and the world that operate on an unconscious level (Beck, 1995; Padesky & Greenberger, 1995; Freeman et al., 2004). These beliefs develop early in childhood through life experiences and interactions with parents, caregivers, family members, friends, and overall significant others. People have both positive and negative core beliefs, with the latter mainly surfacing during times of distress (Beck, 1995). Negative core beliefs fall into three categories: helplessness, unlovability, and worthlessness. People may have core beliefs that fall into one, two, or all three realms (Beck, 2011). These beliefs are absolute and dichotomous (Padesky & Greenberger, 1995). In view of Tristan's aforementioned automatic thoughts and intermediate beliefs, his irrational, maladaptive core beliefs that are being stirred include: "I am incompetent"; "I am inadequate"; "I am stupid"; "I am a failure"; "I am bad." He also internally believes, as previously stated, that if he is stupid and incompetent then no one will like him; thus, he is unworthy of love. Therefore, his unconscious dysfunctional core beliefs are also dichotomous because they include: "I am unlovable"; "I am unworthy." Furthermore, given his faulty assumption that he will not get into college after receiving a "B," Tristan also likely has the distorted core beliefs: "I am helpless; I am powerless." In contrast, when Tristan receives an "A" on an exam, his negative, irrational core beliefs do not get activated and therefore do not trigger his dysfunctional intermediate beliefs and automatic thoughts. As a result, his self-esteem remains unthreatened, his stress level is low, his emotions and physiological responses are not distressing, and his maladaptive isolating behaviors do not occur.

It is important to note that positive core beliefs can also be irrational and dysfunctional. For instance, if Tristan has the core belief that all colleges will accept straight "A" students with no exceptions, then imagine his distress if he is denied admission after garnering an impeccable academic record. Another example is Karina, who has the irrational core belief that all people can be trusted. Imagine the dangerous implications of such a core belief about others!

Because core beliefs function outside of a person's awareness, they are rarely articulated clearly without therapeutic assistance (Beck, 1995). All three levels of these cognitive processes (automatic thoughts, intermediate beliefs, and core beliefs) are interconnected (Padesky & Greenberger, 1995). As shown in the example of Tristan, negative and irrational core beliefs can fuel distorted intermediate beliefs and automatic thoughts, thus driving negative emotion, unpleasant physiological reactions, and unhealthy behavior. Table 36.1 shows the three categories of negative core beliefs.

Table 36.1 Categories of Core Beliefs

Helpless Core Beliefs	
"I am helpless."	"I am trapped."
"I am powerless."	"I am inadequate."
"I am out of control."	"I am ineffective."
"I am weak."	"I am incompetent."
"I am vulnerable."	"I am a failure."
"I am needy."	"I am a loser."

"I cannot do anything right."	"I am defective" (i.e., I do not measure up to others).
"I am disrespected."	"I am not good enough" (have no achievements or poor quality of achievements).
"I am a victim."	
Unlovable Core Beliefs	
"I am unlovable."	"I am bad (so no one will love me)."
"I am unlikable."	"I am defective (so no one will love me)."
"I am undesirable."	"I am unworthy (to receive love)."
"I am unattractive."	"I am not good enough (to be loved by others)."
"I am unwanted."	"I am bound to (will always) be rejected."
"I am unworthy."	"I am bound to (will always) be abandoned."
"I am uncared for."	"I am bound to (will always) be alone."
"I am different."	
Worthlessness Core Beliefs	
"I am dangerous."	"I am immoral."
"I am worthless."	"I am toxic."
"I am unacceptable."	"I am evil."
"I am bad."	"I do not deserve to live."
"I am a waste."	

Source: "Categories of core beliefs." Adapted from *Cognitive Behavior Therapy: Basics and Beyond* (2nd ed., p. 233), by J. S. Beck, 2011, New York, NY: Guilford Press, Copyright 2011 by Guilford Press; Copyright 2005 by Judith S. Beck, PhD. Reprinted with permission of Guilford Press and Judith S. Beck, PhD; *Cognitive Therapy: Basics and Beyond* (p. 169), by J. S. Beck, 1995, New York, NY: Guilford Press, Copyright 1995 by Guilford Press; Copyright 1995 by Judith S. Beck, PhD. Reprinted with permission of Guilford Press and Judith S. Beck, PhD. Note: The table material was combined from both sources.

COGNITIVE DISTORTIONS

All human beings are susceptible to dysfunctional automatic thoughts, intermediate beliefs, and core beliefs. Beck (1976) termed these errors in logic or thinking errors *cognitive distortions* (also see Freeman et al., 2004). According to Freeman et al. (2004), these distortions can result in erroneous conclusions even if one perceives the situation correctly. If the initial situation is perceived inaccurately, additional distortions occur and magnify the overall misperceptions. Beck (1976) identified a variety of cognitive distortions that can create havoc for individuals, affecting the way they perceive, interpret, feel, and respond in situations. Once people learn to identify and evaluate their thoughts and beliefs, they often find that their cognitions during certain situations involve one or more concurrent cognitive errors. Once the distortions are identified, they can be challenged and modified as they occur in everyday thought processes. A list of common cognitive distortions is shown in Table 36.2.

Some of the most common include *all-or-nothing thinking* (also known as absolute, black-and-white, dichotomous, and polarized thinking): Oneself, others, or situations are viewed in two mutually exclusive categories with no "shades of gray" in between, instead of on a continuum. Another is *fortune-telling,* where one anticipates that a future event will turn out negatively, is convinced that this expectation/prediction is an established fact, and reacts accordingly without considering more likely outcomes. With the *mental filter* (also known as *selective abstraction*), undue attention or emphasis is focused on a particular aspect of a situation, especially a negative detail, while other relevant factors of the situation or evidence are ignored or dismissed; working under this error, the person is not seeing the whole picture.

COGNITIVE MODEL OF STRESS

When people experience stress, deviations in their thinking processes play a major role in their emotional, physiological, and behavioral reactions to the stressful event. According to the cognitive model of stress, people automatically appraise and assign meaning to the stressful event in terms of the demands the situation places on them and their perceived ability to effectively cope with the demands and stress. Stress is the result of a dynamic interaction between the individual and his or her environment, with cognitive processes playing a major role (Pretzer & Beck, 2007). Thus, one can see how automatic thoughts, intermediate beliefs, and core beliefs come into play during a stressful event and affect the emotions and behaviors that follow. If a person perceived and interpreted a stressful situation accurately, without distortions, problematic stress levels would occur only if objectively stressful events continued and the person was unable to escape the distressing situation or overcome it. However, people often fall prey to cognitive distortions during stressful events, resulting in misperceptions and misinterpretations of both the situations and their ability to cope with the situations (Pretzer & Beck, 2007).

COGNITIVE RESTRUCTURING TECHNIQUES

People are not always aware that some of their automatic thoughts and intermediate and core beliefs are distorted, irrational, and dysfunctional; this lack of

Table 36.2 Common Cognitive Distortions

1. *All-or-nothing thinking* (also known as absolute, black-and-white, dichotomous, and polarized thinking): Oneself, others, or situations are viewed in two mutually exclusive categories with no "shades of gray" in between, instead of on a continuum.

   Example: "If I'm not a total success or if I'm not perfect, then I'm a complete failure."

2. *Catastrophizing:* Current or future events are viewed or anticipated negatively and treated as intolerable catastrophes, rather than being viewed them in a realistic perspective.

   Example: "If he breaks up with me, I'll never be happy again."

3. *Fortune-telling:* One anticipates that a future event will turn out negatively, is convinced that this expectation/prediction is an established fact, and reacts accordingly without considering more likely or other outcomes.

   Example: "I know I will fail the test tomorrow, so I won't bother to study for it."

4. *Jumping to conclusions:* A negative interpretation is made without strong evidence or facts to convincingly support the conclusion.

   Example: "She's been in an accident—that's why she isn't home yet."

5. *Mind-reading:* The belief that one knows what others are thinking while failing to consider other possibilities.

   Example: "He's thinking that I'm incompetent and unfit for the project."

6. *Disqualifying or discounting the positive:* One treats positive experiences, deeds, or qualities as if they do not count, thereby maintaining a negative belief contrary to everyday experiences and evidence.

   Example: "I got an 'A' on the test, but that doesn't mean I'm smart; I got lucky."

7. *Emotional reasoning:* One assumes that one's emotions reflect the truth and ignores evidence to the contrary.

   Example: "I feel unattractive, therefore I am unattractive."

8. *Labeling:* One labels oneself or others in a fixed, global manner and fails to consider evidence that may lead to a more reasonable, less disastrous or definitive conclusion.

   Example: "He's a loser." "I'm a pig." "I'm a failure."

9. *Magnification/minimization:* When evaluating oneself, others, or a situation, an unreasonable magnification of the negative and/or minimization of the positive aspects (or vice versa), occurs.

   Example: (Magnification of the negative) "I stuttered once during my speech and now the speech is ruined"; (Minimization of the negative) "My partner only hits me in the stomach, not my face, so it's no big deal."

(*continued*)

Table 36.2 Common Cognitive Distortions (continued)

10. *Mental filter* (also known as *selective abstraction*): Undue attention is focused on a particular aspect of a situation, especially a negative detail, while other relevant factors of the situation or evidence are ignored or dismissed, causing inability to see the whole picture.

    Example: "I am doing a poor job at work because I got one low rating on my evaluation." (Yet, high ratings were received on the rest of the evaluation.)

11. *Tunnel vision:* One only sees the negative aspects of a situation, and is thus blinded to the whole picture.

    Example: "It's raining; what a depressing, awful day."

12. *Overgeneralization:* One makes a drastic, negative conclusion that extends far beyond the current situation, thereby viewing one event as being characteristic of life in general.

    Example: "My boyfriend lied to me; therefore he will always lie, as will all men."

13. *Personalization:* One takes the blame for others' negative behavior without considering more plausible explanations; one assumes that one is the cause of a certain external event when, in fact, other factors are responsible.

    Example: "I know my supervisor is being curt with me today because I did something wrong, and she doesn't like me." (However, the real reason the boss is being curt is because she is upset and preoccupied due to a loss in her family.)

14. *"Should" and "must" statements* (also known as *imperatives*): One has a precise, fixed idea of how one and/or others should behave, thus resulting in an overestimation of how bad it is that these expectations are not met. Includes the use of these rigid ideas/statements to provide motivation or control behavior.

    Example: "It's unacceptable that I made a mistake and received a 'B' on my term paper. I should never make a mistake, and I must have a straight 'A' academic record."

Source: Common cognitive distortions. Adapted from *Cognitive Therapy: Basics and Beyond* (p. 119), by J. S. Beck, 1995, New York, NY: Guilford Press; Copyright 1976 Aaron T. Beck, MD. Adapted with permission by Judith S. Beck, PhD.

Note: See also *Feeling Good: The New Mood Therapy* (rev. ed.), pp. 32–43, by D. D. Burns, 1999, New York, NY: Avon Books, for further cognitive distortion examples.

knowledge contributes to their stress and emotional distress. The lack of awareness also means that they are unlikely to challenge these thoughts and beliefs and seek evidence to contradict them without assistance. An experienced cognitive or cognitive-behavioral therapist will teach clients the art of cognitive restructuring along with other therapeutic tools. The cognitive restructuring process includes a variety of cognitive techniques, such as Socratic questioning, as well as behavioral experiments to evaluate and test the validity of the client's thoughts and beliefs (Beck, 1995). Cognitive restructuring techniques include, but are not limited to, the items shown in Table 36.3.

Before dysfunctional cognitions can be altered, they must first be identified. Therefore, the first step is *awareness* of automatic thoughts. In other words, one must pinpoint the automatic thought(s) that occurred after an event and before the distressing emotion occurred. As stated earlier, people are more aware of the emotions that arose than the thoughts that led up to the emotion. Therefore, it is often necessary in the beginning to first identify the unpleasant emotion that was stimulated by an event and then try to recall what thoughts accompanied the emotion and the thoughts that led to the distress. Recognizing automatic thoughts, let alone intermediate and core beliefs, can be difficult at first. However, with practice and dedication, one can learn to identify, challenge, and reframe irrational thoughts and beliefs in the moment, thus preventing undue emotional distress and unhealthy behavior or the escalation thereof. A highly useful tool in mastering this essential process is the dysfunctional thought record, more simply known as the daily thought record (Beck, 1995; Freeman et al., 2004). It is used to identify and record situations (events, memories, images, etc.) and the automatic thoughts, emotions, physiological responses, and behaviors that followed (see Table 36.4). In addition, it is used for recording the process of evaluating and challenging automatic thoughts, the reframing of the thoughts, and the new emotions and behaviors the new thoughts elicit.

When completing thought records, one's automatic thoughts, emotions, and physiological responses are rated from 1–100 (or 1–10, if easier) as to the degree of belief in the thought and degree or intensity of the emotions and internal responses. Once this is done, the thoughts are evaluated to determine whether they are rational or irrational. This entails examining whether cognitive distortions exist in the thoughts and what rational evidence exists to prove the thoughts true or refute them. Following this step is the reframing of the automatic thoughts without any cognitive distortions, thus replacing the dysfunctional thoughts with rational alternative thoughts. The rational thoughts are then rated as to degree of belief, as is the intensity of the emotions that the new thoughts elicit. The rational thoughts, as opposed to the irrational ones, likely result in a less distressing or overall pleasant emotion, with an assertive, healthy behavior following. A daily thought record can also help in identifying dysfunctional beliefs, and can then be used to guide the person in evaluating, challenging, and modifying them. The thought record not only aids in the cognitive restructuring process, but also provides individuals with an enhanced self-understanding of their thoughts, emotions, and behaviors.

Table 36.3 Cognitive Restructuring Techniques

1. Monitor and identify automatic thoughts that occur after events.
2. Evaluate and rate the degree of belief in the automatic thought and the degree of emotion that followed the thought.
3. Identify the cognitive distortions in the thought.
4. Ask what would it would mean if the thought were true: why would it be a problem, and what would happen? (Downward arrow technique: Continuing this line of questioning for each answer given will, in time, result in the discovery of intermediate beliefs and ultimately core beliefs.)
5. Identify the intermediate beliefs and core beliefs (and the distortions thereof).
6. Examine the costs and benefits of the thoughts and beliefs.
7. List the evidence supporting or refuting the thoughts and beliefs, as well as the weight and quality of evidence.
8. Place the event in perspective on a numbered continuum and ask what would truly happen if the event occurred: What would the worst- and best-case scenarios would be (and the probability of each), and what would the person still be able to do if the event did occur?
9. Examine the double standards involved. Would the person apply the same set of standards to others? Why or why not?
10. Argue back at the thought. Client and therapist take roles in arguing against the negative thoughts and beliefs.
11. Logically analyze the thoughts, beliefs, and conclusions.
12. Determine if there is sufficient information to draw such a conclusion.
13. Test the thoughts and beliefs with behavioral experiments.
14. Apply response-stimulus hierarchy and graded imaginal and in-vivo exposures to feared stimuli.
15. Are there alternative thoughts, beliefs, explanations, and conclusions?
16. Is there a problem to be solved? If so, how does the client plan to solve it?
17. Acceptance: Is there a reality that the client can learn to accept rather than trying to fix it or struggle with it?

Source: Cognitive restructuring techniques. Adapted from "Cognitive Interventions" (pp. 93–95), by R. L. Leahy, 1996, in R. L. Leahy (Ed.), *Cognitive Therapy: Basic Principles and Applications,* Northvale, NJ: Jason Aronson, Inc. Copyright 1996 by Jason Aronson, Inc. Adapted with permission of Jason Aronson, Inc.

Table 36.4 Sample Daily Thought Record

Event/ Situation (Date)	Automatic Thought	Emotion	Physiological Response	Behavioral Response/ Outcome	Evaluate and Challenge Automatic Thought (Rational/ Irrational)	Reframe Automatic Thought	New Emotion	New Behavioral Response/ Outcome
Specify the event/situation leading to distressing thought(s) and emotion(s).	Specify the thought(s) leading to the distressing emotion(s).	Specify the emotions (sad, anxious, angry, etc.) resulting from the thoughts.	Specify sweating, flushed, rapid heartbeat or respiration, etc., that are accompanying the thoughts and emotions.	Specify behavior(s) and outcome that followed.	Are there cognitive distortions in the thought? If so, which ones?	Reframe the thought(s) without cognitive distortions and/or list alternative, rational thoughts.	Specify the emotion(s) the new thought(s) elicits.	What adaptive behavior and outcome result from the new thought(s) and emotion(s)?
	Rate degree of belief in the thought, 1–100.	Rate intensity of emotion, 1–100.	Rate intensity of response, 1–100.		List any real evidence to prove the thought true or false.	Rate degree of belief in new thought(s), 1–100.	Rate intensity of emotion(s), 1–100.	
	If emotions are identified first, ask what thoughts arose before the emotion was experienced.							

Source: Daily Thought Record. Adapted from Cognitive Behavior Therapy Worksheet packet. Copyright 2011 by Judith S. Beck. Adapted with permission by Judith S. Beck, PhD.

EMPIRICAL EVIDENCE OF EFFICACY

For decades, cognitive restructuring has been empirically tested as either a stand-alone treatment or in conjunction with other cognitive and/or behavioral treatments for a variety of clinical disorders, as well as stress-related symptomatology. The results of past and present studies have suggested that cognitive restructuring is a highly effective treatment both in and of itself and alongside other treatment modalities (Leahy & Rego, 2012). Clark (2013) scrutinized a multitude of psychotherapy process studies conducted from 1996 to 2012 to determine the effectiveness of cognitive restructuring for symptom reduction. His review of these studies revealed that cognitive restructuring is an effective treatment intervention for depression and anxiety, including panic symptoms, social anxiety disorder, obsessive-compulsive disorder, and posttraumatic stress disorder. Because stress can often result in symptoms of anxiety and/or depression, it is advantageous to learn and incorporate cognitive restructuring skills into daily living. However, to ensure a full understanding and mastery of the necessary skills, it is important to seek guidance from a professional trained in psychology.

CONCLUSION

Cognitive restructuring is an empirically validated, effective therapeutic treatment for numerous psychological disorders and stress-related conditions. It is a multistep process in which dysfunctional cognitive processes that are contributing to distress are consciously identified, evaluated, challenged, and ultimately changed into rational and functional thought processes. The cognitive processes targeted in cognitive restructuring are automatic thoughts, intermediate beliefs, and core beliefs/schemas, all of which are interrelated and drive emotions and behavior. These levels of cognitions develop early in life and are the unique lens through which individuals view themselves, others, and the world. Unfortunately, a person's lens is not always clear, especially when he or she is distressed. In other words, an individual's thought processes can become distorted and maladaptive and can cause or contribute to cognitive, emotional, physiological, and behavioral distress and clinical psychiatric symptomatology. Fortunately, cognitive restructuring can help change dysfunctional thought processes with a variety of therapeutic strategies. It is best to seek assistance from a professional trained in psychology to fully learn and master the skills of cognitive restructuring.

REFERENCES AND FURTHER READING

Beck, A. T. (1976). *Cognitive therapy and the emotional disorders.* New York, NY: Meridian.
Beck, J. S. (1995). *Cognitive therapy: Basics and beyond.* New York, NY: Guilford Press.

Beck, J. S. (2011). *Cognitive behavior therapy: Basics and beyond* (2nd ed.). New York, NY: Guilford Press.

Beck, J. S., & Bieling, P. J. (2004). Cognitive therapy: Introduction to theory and practice. In M. J. Dewan, B. N. Steenbarger, & R. P. Greenberg (Eds.), *The art and science of brief psychotherapies: A practitioner's guide* (pp. 15–49). Arlington, VA: American Psychiatric Publishing.

Burns, D. D. (1999). *Feeling good: The new mood therapy* (rev. ed.). New York, NY: Avon Books.

Clark, D. A. (2013). Cognitive restructuring. In S. G. Hoffman (Ed.), *The Wiley handbook of cognitive-behavioral therapy* (1st ed.). [Online]. Retrieved January 5, 2014, from Wiley Online Library at http://onlinelibrary.wiley.com/doi/10.1002/9781118528563.wbcbt02/full. doi:10.1002/9781118528563.wbcbt02.

Dobson, K. S., & Dozois, D. J. A. (2010). Historical and philosophical bases for the cognitive-behavior therapies. In K. S. Dobson (Ed.), *Handbook of cognitive-behavioral therapies* (3rd ed., pp. 3–38). New York, NY: Guilford Press.

Freeman, A., Pretzer, J., Fleming, B., & Simon, K. M. (2004). *Clinical applications of cognitive therapy* (2nd ed.) New York, NY: Springer Science + Business Media.

Leahy, R. L. (1996). Cognitive interventions. In R. L. Leahy (Ed.), *Cognitive therapy: Basic principles and applications* (pp. 93–95). Northvale, NJ: Jason Aronson.

Leahy, R. L., & Rego, S. A. (2012). Cognitive restructuring. In W. T. O'Donohue & J. E. Fisher (Eds.), *Cognitive behavior therapy: Core principles for practice* (pp. 133–158). Hoboken, NJ: John Wiley & Sons.

Padesky, C. A., & Greenberger, D. (1995). *Clinician's guide to mind over mood.* New York, NY: Guilford Press.

Pretzer, J. L., & Beck, A. T. (2007). Cognitive approaches to stress and stress management. In P. M. Lehrer, R. Woolfolk, & W. E. Sime (Eds.), *Principles and practice of stress management* (3rd ed., pp. 465–496). New York, NY: Guilford Press.

37

LANGUAGE AND STRESS

Rae Noble

INTRODUCTION

"Human systems are language-generating and, simultaneously, meaning-generating systems" (Anderson & Goolishian, 1992, p. 26). We continuously rely on language in some form. Language allows us to make decisions and act upon those choices. This chapter explores our use of verbal and nonverbal language, informed by our thoughts and beliefs, and how we affect our own stress levels. We may be exacerbating and perpetuating the stress in our lives, or we may be effectively managing and calming ourselves. The language we choose plays an enormous role in the crescendo or decrescendo of that stress.

"The history of language clearly shows that complex thinking with all its peculiarities is the very foundation of linguistic development" (Vygotsky, 1962, p. 72). As the development of language is informed by a rich mixture of internal and external and experiences, language, then, manifests in multiple, concurrent processes.

> Language, as I mean the term, is a structural means to externalize internal, interpersonal, and perceptual experience. It is not only the spoken or written word. Language is also image, gesture, and tone. These aspects of language are encoded deeply in the individual psyche even before words become symbols and verbal language begins to dominate as a means to express now embedded and embodied concepts. (Lark, 2005, p. 25)

Spaniol and Cattaneo (1994, p. 266) assert that "language is a social instrument that is shaped by culture and also shapes culture." As language users and participants in multiple circles and communities, we are simultaneously affecting and being affected by our culture and related languages.

LANGUAGE AND CHOICE

As the previous paragraphs intimated, preceding our use of language are our thoughts and beliefs, which many have the privilege and faculty of choosing or working to understand. As Shakespeare wrote in the 1603 publication of *Hamlet,* "There is nothing either good or bad but thinking makes it so." In a philosophical lecture on thought and speech, Davidson (cited in Guttenplan, 1975) explained, "Having a thought requires that there be a background of beliefs" (p. 9). What we think and, later, how we speak is first influenced by a core set of beliefs, such as believing oneself to be worthy of love, or capable, or inadequate. It can be argued that one's core beliefs form as a direct result of the thoughts and language of others, received as messages when one is young; it becomes clear what an intricate web these concepts and applications create. Though outside the scope of this chapter, these questions demonstrate the complexity of language.

HOW DOES CHOICE AFFECT LANGUAGE AND STRESS?

As William James, the great American philosopher, physician, and psychologist noticed more than a century ago, "The greatest weapon against stress is our ability to choose one thought over another" (James, n.d.). Iyengar (2010) echoes, "It becomes clear that choice is an enormously powerful force, an essential determinant of how we live" (p. 4). Iyengar begins her book, *The Art of Choosing* (2010), with a powerful consideration from Archibald MacLeish, an American poet and recipient of the Pulitzer Prize, who wrote, "What is freedom? Freedom is the right to choose: the right to create for oneself the alternatives of choice. Without the possibility of choice . . . a man is not a man but a member, an instrument, a thing" (MacLeish, n.d.).

Dr. William Glasser (1998), author of *Choice Theory,* explains:

> [W]e choose all our actions and thoughts and, indirectly, almost all our feelings and much of our physiology. As bad as you may feel, much of what goes on in your body when you are in pain or sick is the indirect result of the actions and thoughts you choose or have chosen every day of your life. (p. 4)

Glasser (1998) describes misery as a democratic experience. This speaks to the nature of democracy and our ability, with language and action, to bring about the reality we choose. If we perpetuate stressful, hurried, tense speech, we will surely experience that as reality. Countering this, we can bring about positive changes when we embrace deliberate perspectives and calm narratives. Fredrickson (2009) reminds us, "Whatever your current circumstances, you've got what it takes to reshape your life and the world around you for the better" (p. 15).

Glasser (1998) discusses choice theory as an alternative to external control psychology, the way in which most people in today's society operate. Underlying external control psychology is the belief that people's thoughts, language, and actions are the result of stimuli in the world (e.g., a ringing telephone, a stop light), or are caused by the behavior of others (e.g., someone yelling at you, a crying child). Likewise, it is believed that one can control the behavior of others. "The foundation of these beliefs, that we are externally motivated, is wrong" (Glasser, 1998, p. 16). Glasser writes about his experience looking through a thesaurus to find entries expanding on words related to (1) this psychology of blaming external circumstances for one's experience and (2) choosing our perspectives regardless of what circumstances arise (choice theory). He discovered that far more entries existed to describe external control psychology than choice theory. "Since our language is a mirror of our culture, this is strong evidence that we live in a world that is attuned more to destroying relationships than to preserving them" (p. 21). One such relationship at risk of being destroyed is our perception of self and our capability.

Establishing choice as an integral element within our language experience allows us to look more closely at verbal and nonverbal systems, and how our stress level may be impacted by them. We move to a discussion of these intersections next.

VERBAL LANGUAGE AND STRESS MANAGEMENT

Fleagle (2010) explained, "The construct of verbal language involves any systematic linguistic structure that is based upon the usage of words, and is most likely agreed upon by a common group" (p. 10). We rely heavily on verbal communication:

> Verbal language is the most highly promoted form of interpersonal, cultural transmission of information and meaning among dominant voices in Western culture. As the prevailing form of communication, verbal language categorizes, codifies, symbolizes, and organizes perceived experience into a meaningful constellation of belief. (Lark, 2005, p. 25)

Perhaps it is for these reasons—verbal communication's access within groups and the emphasis we place on this form of communication—that common experiences such as daily stress can so thoroughly pervade our language system. In the English language alone, we have countless ways of naming and describing physical, emotional, and mental stress (e.g., wiped out, burned out, worn out, exhausted, peaked, sapped, frenzied, frazzled, overloaded, overwhelmed, harrowed, drawn, done, fried).

Clearly, language is a powerful tool; it can be honed and modified at will, and as needed. Wilson (1958) writes of the ambiguity of language, and provides examples of how the words *freedom* and *democracy* most likely would have meant four very different things between North America and Soviet Russia. He describes an anecdote in which a man argued his point using the words *normal* and *natural* interchangeably—no doubt a semantic exchange that not everyone could agree with. "It is the possibility of saying one and the same thing in several ways, it is synonymy, which permits language to divide itself up" (Barthes, 1986, pp. 106–107).

This may also reflect the range of individuals' perceptual differences. A common, stress-related example can be heard in the optimism vs. pessimism debate: is the glass half-empty or half-full? Losier (2009) writes about the option to reframe difficult situations, a practice involving the language we choose as well as perspective. He provides an example of someone complaining about a week full of rain, contrasted with someone noticing a week full of rain. The latter chose to speak with gratitude about a garden being watered as a result of the precipitation. In an article on occupational stress as an educator, Singer (2013) wrote, "Stress does not result from events that take place in your classroom, school, or life. Stress results from what you say to yourself about those events. You have a choice about how you direct your thinking" (paragraph 6).

In a recent personal conversation, this writer heard the story of a woman's traumatic stress, involving an account of an attack by a large dog. As she worked through her story, I realized that what she was describing felt and sounded very different from my own concept and working definitions of *stress* and *trauma*. The information she was sharing would have landed in my category of mild stress, or perhaps surprise. For this individual, however, the experience shook her deeply and she continues to code the experience as trauma. She has had an ongoing, severe fear of dogs since the event. The way we perceive an event, and choose language to recount the experience, solidifies our memory of that event. In a self-perpetuating cycle, this could affect the way we generate thoughts and more language regarding the event, in turn continuing to affect our emotions and stress level.

Putting verbal language into action as a tool against stress can look like positive self-talk or affirmations. Bourne and Garano (2003) discuss coping statements to use in a moment of anxiety or stress. The statements fall into one of three categories:

1. statements to prepare oneself to enter a difficult situation, such as:
   "Whatever I do, I'll do the best I can."
2. statements to use during the difficult situation in the present moment, such as:
   "I'm going to be all right. I've succeeded with this before."
   "I can think about being in a peaceful place as I undertake this."

3. statements to use to offset uncomfortable emotions while in the difficult situation:
   "This will pass soon."
   "I deserve to feel okay right now." (pp. 140–142)

Writing the statements on index cards or on a smartphone (something portable and accessible) can also be a helpful solution. The authors also note that these coping statements have to be practiced many times before they can be fully internalized (Bourne & Garano, 2003, p. 142).

Love and Domar (2009) suggest matching our internal resources against the external circumstances when something stressful arises. In practice, this could look like mentally sifting through a list of questions about the situation and whether we have faced something similar at any previous moment in life. Their classic example is managing a screaming child while you are attempting a grocery store run. The questions to be examined in the moment might sound like this: "Do [I] have the courage to ignore other shoppers' judgments about [my] child and [my] parenting skills? Do [I] have experience defusing explosive situations? Do [I] know a few stress management techniques, such as deep breathing?" (p. 70). Here again we see how verbal language in the form of self-talk can make or break a challenging, stressful moment.

In the development of self-talk, Singer (2013) emphasizes the importance of careful discernment when choosing one's "internal dialogue" (paragraph 7). Common examples of negative self-talk may begin with "I can't . . . What if . . . I don't think . . . I should not have" (paragraph 8). This narrative keeps us stressed out and focused on a hypothetical problem. Furthermore, this approach can limit the belief in self and one's capability. He writes that we have the option to replace these self-defeating, fear-based thoughts with "rational, healthy thoughts that are calming and reinforcing" (paragraph 8).

Losier (2009) discusses methods to master better communication; two of these can be used in self-talk and may therefore affect the level of stress we experience in a given moment. This can, in turn, have a positive impact on our interactions with others. He writes, "The more positively we see and talk about things, the more positive our communications will be. The more positively we communicate, the better we connect, and the more likely we are to receive a positive response" (p. 85). Those moments of praise, if noted and later incorporated into self-talk, could help to minimize stress when it occurs, using something like Bourne and Garano's (2003) aforementioned suggestion: "I'm going to be all right; I've succeeded with this before" (pp. 140–142).

Another way of using language to impact stress level is future pacing. As Losier (2009) describes, "Future pacing is a way to communicate to another person [or self] that whatever he or she may have been anticipating as a negative experience or outcome could very well turn out to be a positive one" (p. 88). Choosing to future pace while experiencing or combating stress could sound like, "I'm about to walk into a good situation" or "An exciting opportunity awaits." If coupled with a self-affirmation, this could take the form of, "I am capable of handling whatever I am about to encounter and it is going to help me grow as an individual."

NONVERBAL LANGUAGE AND STRESS MANAGEMENT

Despite our culture's emphasis on the spoken word, Sue and Sue (1990) note that only 30–40 percent of communicated material is transmitted verbally. In fact, body language is commonly regarded as an individual's primary language (Knapp, 1978; Kendon, 2004). We are communicating constantly. "Willingly or not, humans, when in co-presence, continuously inform one another about their intentions, interests, feelings and ideas by means of visible bodily action" (Kendon, 2004, p. 1).

Lark (2005) explains that "visual and kinesthetic languages provide equal or additional access to narrative discourse" (p. 26). The first type of nonverbal communication many can summon to mind is gesture. Thomas wrote:

> Gesture is an inseparable accompaniment of any spoken language. The difference between a face-to-face encounter and a telephone conversation is a reminder of the extent to which facial expression and bodily movements can amplify, modify, confirm, or subvert verbal utterance. Sorrow or happiness, deference or insult, are conveyed as effectively by gesture as by word. (1991, p. 6)

Thomas (1991) and Kendon (2004) discuss gesture as a partner to verbal expression. Not only can gestures supplement the spoken word, they also frequently substitute for the spoken word. Kendon (2004) defines *gesture* as "visible bodily action when it is used as an utterance or as a part of an utterance" (p. 7). In her thesis, Button (1997) writes, "A gesture, tone, inflection, posture or eye contact may enhance or negate the context of a message" (p. 12). Gesture can quickly and effectively communicate stress, perhaps even more clearly than verbal communication, as gesture transcends language barriers and is more difficult to disguise.

Another element of nonverbal communication is *paralanguage*. "The term paralanguage is used to refer to other vocal cues that individuals use to communicate. For example, loudness of voice, pauses, silences, hesitations, rate, inflections" (Sue & Sue, 1990, p. 56). Someone's forced or hurried speech could be an indication of stress. Note that paralanguage or other nonlinguistic communication may be incongruent with one's verbal presentation; when it is (as in sarcasm), the paralanguage controls the meaning.

Knapp (1978) writes about the impact that physical body type, clothing, eye behavior and movement, posture, physical behavior, and touch can have on a social interaction. Kendon (2004) expands upon this notion:

How people arrange their bodies and how they orient them and place them in relation to each other or to features in the environment, provides important information about how they are engaged with one another and about the nature of their intentions and their attitudes. (p. 1)

EMOTIONAL INTELLIGENCE

Emotional intelligence (EI or EQ) was popularized in the late 1990s when author Daniel Goleman wrote his book, *Emotional Intelligence: Why It Can Matter More Than IQ* (1995). This concept grew out of research conducted by Peter Salavoy and John Mayer, two American psychologists. The term describes the "ability to monitor one's own and others' feelings and emotions, to discriminate among them and to use this information to guide one's thinking and action" (Markulis & Strang, 2015, p. 184). According to Salavoy and Mayer (as cited in Samad, 2014), emotional intelligence is made up of four distinct components: identifying, using, understanding, and managing emotions. Research demonstrates that the lack of emotional intelligence increases an individual's experience of distress (Gohm, Corser, & Dalsky, 2005). Thus, when people have EI, they are able to cope with stress more effectively, as they strategize to regulate emotions. People with high EI may reach out to others for support or disclose what they are feeling/experiencing verbally or in writing. Other factors; however, also may affect one's use of emotional intelligence. As Gohm, Corser, and Dalsky (2005) pointed out, even though a person has the knowledge, skills, or awareness relating to EI, individual factors may affect a person's motivation to use these components.

There are mixed perspectives on whether EI is an ability or a disposition; nevertheless, emotional intelligence has been demonstrated to have positive benefits on psychological and physical health, relationships, and work and academic performances (Nelis, Quoidbach, Mikolajczak, & Hansenne, 2009; Gohm, Corser, & Dalsky, 2005; Samad, 2014). The emotional components discussed in EI are similar to the emotional regulation module taught in dialectical behavioral therapy (DBT), developed by Marsha Linehan (Gardner & Qualter, 2009), which was originally intended as a way of treating individuals who struggled with characteristics of borderline personality disorder. Although DBT is now used in treatment for a variety of maladaptive coping mechanisms, the module on emotional regulation assists people with developing awareness, knowledge, and skills about their emotions, thus increasing their emotional intelligence.

—*Serena Wadhwa*

Stress may show up in a person's harried demeanor, gaze, and so on; everything in a moment can act as a piece of information. Stress can thus be carried and communicated in a myriad of ways.

Perhaps the most detailed analysis of the intersection of stress and body language can be found in studies of the game of poker. Players often study and train extensively to master themselves, ensuring that their stress level (and, by extension, clues about their cards or strategies) is not betrayed by their physiological expression. "Stress can stop you thinking clearly and can also influence your body language" (James, 2007, pp. 77–78). "It changes your breathing patterns, blink rate, muscle tension and voice pitch, and that's just for starters." James (2007) explored the fine line of how much stress allows someone to function optimally and what tips that level of stress into a danger zone, where one begins to make poor decisions and lose control of emotions or behaviors. Stress can also impact cognition, with significant effects on concentration, distractibility, a reduction in short-term memory, and difficulty making decisions (p. 85). James posited that stress management is done most successfully using a combination of verbal self-talk and nonverbal body language control.

James (2007) outlined methods to effectively lower stress level, some involving conscious, intentional decisions about body posture. Two of these are "relax your jaw" and "relax your muscles" (p. 89). This is a prime example of choosing a nonverbal intervention and allowing it to act as the catalyst in lowering stress. The reverse can be true as well; we can effectively perpetuate our own stress levels when we do not check in with our bodies, keeping the shoulders knotted up and jaw tightly clenched. Perhaps it is for this reason that progressive muscle relaxation, with intentional focus given to relaxing all areas of the body, is so effective and commonly used as an intervention to lower stress levels.

Another way to alleviate stress in the body is making the choice to slow down. Kendall-Reed and Reed (2004) describe a former client seeking help with his stress levels. They helped him make small adjustments in his daily routine, including three-minute meditation sessions throughout the week, and saying "no" more often rather than taking on additional commitments. Soon this client reported feeling more relaxed as well as being more productive. Secondary benefits were "noted improvements in his interpersonal relationships and enjoyment of life" (p. 141). We can fool ourselves into believing that we have no time to pause or rest. However, those deliberate moments of quietness and stillness can provide excellent fuel for the mind and body to accomplish something more effectively. Numerous studies indicate that we accomplish more when we choose to take more breaks (Carr, 2014; Deutscher, 2013; Panepento, 2004).

Quality of life may also be positively affected when we tune in to our bodies and address any built-up stress, rather than powering through it or ignoring it.

Kendall-Reed and Reed (2004) describe dozens of techniques and movement practices aimed at lowering stress and improving one's daily experience (see also Chapter 25 on physical activity).

SUMMARY

Core beliefs and thoughts inform our perceptions and choice of language. This in turn has an impact on the ways in which we experience stress. We communicate our perceptions and perspectives of stress, both verbally and nonverbally, almost constantly. It is possible to shape our own experience of stress with intentional use of language and self-care options. We can, therefore, perpetuate stressful experiences by ruminating on and continuing to play them out. Conversely, we have the everpresent option of challenging ourselves to receive a potentially stressful situation as an opportunity for a shift in perspective.

Pinker (2007) eloquently pieces together a rich statement regarding our thoughts and experiences, informing infinite options of language and movements and, by extension, our lives with or without stress:

> The view from language shows us the cave we inhabit, and also the best way out of it. With the use of metaphor and combination, we can entertain new ideas and new ways of managing our affairs. We can do this even as our minds flicker with the agonists and antagonists, the points and lines and slabs, the activities and accomplishments, the gods and sex and effluvia, and the sympathy and deference and fairness that make up the stuff of thought. (p. 439)

See also Chapter 34, on writing and stress; and Chapter 36, "Cognitive Restructuring to Manage Stress."

REFERENCES AND FURTHER READING

Anderson, H., & Goolishian, H. (1992). The client is the expert: A not knowing approach to therapy. In S. McNamee & K. J. Gergan (Eds.), *Therapy as social construction* (pp. 25–32). Thousand Oaks, CA: Sage.

Barthes, R. (1986). *The rustle of language*. Toronto, Canada: Collins.

Bourne, E., & Garano, L. (2003). *Coping with anxiety: Ten simple ways to relieve anxiety, fear and worry*. Oakland, CA: New Harbinger Publications.

Button, S. (1997). *Cross cultural art therapy in a psychiatric hospital: Making a vital connection* (master's thesis). The School of the Art Institute of Chicago, Chicago, IL.

Carr, K. (2014). Why self-care isn't selfish. *Women's Health, 11*(3), 122.

Deutscher, A. (2013). Avoid burnout and maximize productivity. *Canadian Manager, 38*(3), 23–24.

Fleagle, R. (2010). *Examining the functions and interactions of verbal and nonverbal languages in art therapy at a multilingual community center* (master's thesis). The School of the Art Institute of Chicago, Chicago, IL.

Fredrickson, B. L. (2009). *Positivity: Groundbreaking research reveals how to embrace the hidden strength of positive emotions, overcome negativity, and thrive.* New York, NY: Crown.

Gardner, K., & Qualter, P. (2009). Emotional intelligence and borderline personality disorder. *Personality and Individual Differences, 47*(2), 94–98.

Glasser, W. (1998.) *Choice theory: A new psychology of personal freedom.* New York, NY: HarperCollins.

Gohm, C. L., Corser, G. C., & Dalsky, D. J. (2005). Emotional intelligence under stress: Useful, unnecessary, or irrelevant? *Personality and Individual Differences, 39*(6), 1017–1028.

Goleman, D. (1995). *Emotional intelligence: Why it can matter more than IQ.* New York, NY: Bantam.

Groberman, A. (2012, May 21). *Difference between stress and anxiety.* Retrieved from http://www.psyweb.com/articles/anxiety/difference-between-stress-and-anxiety.

Guttenplan, S. (Ed.). (1975). *Mind and language.* Oxford, UK: Oxford University Press.

Iyengar, S. (2010). *The art of choosing.* New York, NY: Twelve/Grand Central Publishing.

James, J. (2007). *Poker face: Mastering body language to bluff, read tells and win.* New York, NY: Marlowe.

James, W. (n.d.). Retrieved from http://www.brainyquote.com/quotes/authors/w/william_james.html

Kendall-Reed, P., & Reed, S. (2004). *The complete doctor's stress solution: Understanding, treating, and preventing stress and stress-related illnesses.* Toronto, Canada: Robert Rose.

Kendon, A. (2004). *Gesture: Visible action as utterance.* New York, NY: Cambridge University Press.

Knapp, M. (1978). *Nonverbal communication in human interaction* (2nd ed.). New York: Holt, Rinehart, & Winston.

Lark, C. V. (2005). Using art as language in large group dialogues: The TREC model. *Art Therapy: Journal of the American Art Therapy Association, 22,* 24–31.

Losier, M. J. (2009). *Law of connection: The science of using NLP to create ideal personal and professional relationships.* New York, NY: Wellness Group/Grand Central Publishing.

Love, S. M., & Domar, A. D. (2009). *Live a little! Breaking the rules won't break your health.* New York, NY: Crown.

MacLeish, A. (n.d.). Retrieved from http://quotes.liberty-tree.ca/quote_blog/Archibald.MacLeish.Quote.6B21.

Markulis, P., & Strang, D. (2015). Emotional intelligence: A demonstration. *Developments in Business Simulation and Experiential Learning, 42,* 184.

Matthews, G., Emo, A. K., Funke, G., Zeidner, M., Roberts, R. D., Costa Jr., P. T., & Schulze, R. (2006). Emotional intelligence, personality, and task-induced stress. *Journal of Experimental Psychology: Applied, 12*(2), 96–107.

Nelis, D., Quoidbach, J., Mikolajczak, M., & Hansenne, M. (2009). Increasing emotional intelligence: (How) is it possible? *Personality and Individual Differences, 47*(1), 36–41.

Panepento, P. (2004). Employee-wellness programs pay off in productivity and morale. *Chronicle of Philanthropy, 16*(18), 38–39.

Pinker, S. (1999). *Words and rules: The ingredients of language.* New York, NY: HarperCollins.

Pinker, S. (2007). *The stuff of thought: Language as a window into human nature.* New York, NY: Viking Penguin.

Samad, H. A. (2014). Emotional intelligence: The theory and measurement of EQ. *European Scientific Journal, 10*(10).

Singer, J. (2013). 7 super strategies for success over stress. *Educational Leadership, 70*(9), 24–28.

Spaniol, S., & Cattaneo, M. (1994). The power of language in the art therapeutic relationship. *Art Therapy: Journal of the American Art Therapy Association, 11*(4), 266–270.

Sue, D. W., & Sue, D. (1990). *Counseling the culturally different: Theory and practice.* New York, NY: John Wiley & Sons.

Thomas, K. (1991). Introduction. In J. Bremmer & H. Roodenburg (Eds.), *A cultural history of gesture* (pp. 1–14). Ithaca, NY: Cornell University Press.

Vygotsky, L. S. (1962). *Thought and language.* Cambridge, MA: Massachusetts Institute of Technology.

Wilson, J. (1958). *Language and the pursuit of truth.* London, UK: Cambridge University Press.

38

Substance Misuse and Stress

Jimia Stokes

INTRODUCTION

This chapter looks at how mind-altering substances affect the brain, and how use and misuse of these substances potentially cause medical, social, economic, and legal issues that influence everyday life situations and take a toll on the national economy. It explores how the use and abuse of alcohol and other drugs (AODs) can lead to addiction, with stressful and life-threatening consequences.

According to the Substance Abuse and Mental Health Services Administration's (SAMHSA's) "National Survey on Drug Use and Health," 19.9 million persons aged 12 or older needed treatment for an illicit drug or alcohol abuse problem in 2007 (SAMHSA, 2009). Illicit drug use is on the rise today among teens, so the statistics from 2009 are much higher in 2012: an estimated 23.9 million Americans age 12 or older (9.2 percent of the population) stated that they had used an illicit drug or abused a psychotherapeutic medication (such as a pain reliever, stimulant, or tranquilizer) in the past month. This is up from 8.3 percent from 2002 to 2009. The increase mostly reflects a rise in the use of marijuana, the most commonly used illicit drug (National Institutes of Health [NIH], 2014).

But why do people use drugs? Prescription drugs are used medically to treat illness, relieve pain, and cure disease; much of this use is legal, monitored, and approved. The use of alcohol and other substances on celebratory occasions, as a part of religious rituals, and for other social reasons goes back thousands of years. People also use drugs out of curiosity and peer influence. Individuals may use a substance to change the way they feel, change their mood, or alter their state of mind. There is no single reason why people use or abuse alcohol or other drugs.

Of interest in the context of stress, another reason individuals may use AODs comes from the National Institute on Drug Abuse (NIDA). In 2014, NIDA reported that some people use drugs to relieve stress, and that a number of people suffering from mood disorders, social anxiety, stress-related disorders, and depression first begin abusing drugs in an attempt to lessen feelings of distress.

FACTORS INFLUENCING ABUSE

Many factors influence the transition from use to abuse. This section provides a brief overview of some of these factors.

BIOLOGICAL/PHYSIOLOGICAL

A primary biological factor in drug abuse is the abuser being born with genes that create a predisposition for drug abuse; in actual abusers, this tendency is often accompanied by environmental factors, such as family and peer influence, and socioeconomic status. The developmental factor influences how early the person begins to use drugs: although drug use at any age can lead to addiction, drug use by persons in their early teens causes the underdevelopment of still-developing brain areas that govern decision making, judgment, and self-control. Because of this brain immaturity, adolescents may be especially prone to risk-taking behaviors, including trying drugs of abuse.

BRAIN RESPONSE

The brain is genetically wired to repeat activities that promote pleasure. The brain remembers the reward of the ingested substance and, over a period of time, tells the individual to repeat the action . . . again, and again, and again. This physical reaction can create an *addiction,* which is a condition in which an individual feels compelled to do something that he or she is unable to control. Volkow and Fowler (2000) ascribe this to the orbitofrontal cortex of the brain, which is involved in compulsive behavior and drives; with compulsive repetitive behaviors, its abnormal activation in the addicted individual could explain why individuals continue to use drugs even when they have developed a tolerance to the pleasurable drug effects and are suffering adverse reactions.

Northrop and Yamamoto (2013) conducted research on lab rats in which they exposed the rats to chronic stress by depriving them of food and water for 10 days, agitating their cages, exposing them to cold temperatures, and isolating them from other rats, while dosing them with methamphetamines. The authors found that methamphetamines acutely increased dopamine levels in the striatum part of the brain, which is responsible for movement of the body and cognitive and memory processes. Reynolds (2012) examined the link between early life stress and later drug abuse by identifying glucocorticoid receptors (GR) in mice. Her study found that when stress is present, the brain releases signals that cause the adrenal glands to release glucocorticoid hormones, which stimulate receptors that are found throughout the brain and the body. The receiving cells, in turn, alter their activity in ways that produce stress-related symptoms and behaviors.

Reynolds cited the works of Dr. Huda Akil and Dr. Stanley Watson, researchers at the University of Michigan, who conducted a study in which they augmented the GR receptors by giving the mice cocaine injections and continued to re-expose the mice to the drug for a period of 14 days during the early postnatal period. The study revealed that mice that received augmentation of their GR receptors showed increased anxiety and drug sensitivity; the mice that were not given GR augmentation did not exhibit increased anxiety or sensitivity. This research indicates that when an individual uses a drug, the GR receptors regulating the way the body responds to stress are suppressed by the drug; therefore, stress increases. The body's alarm response begins to work right away to help the body react better to the threat.

Other Factors

Many other factors influence the complex transition from substance use to misuse, and the differences between a moderate substance use disorder and a severe substance use disorder. These include co-existing mental health disorders and cultural and environmental influences (e.g., it's "normal" to drink to the point of blacking out; it's cool to be able to "out-drink" others [which may in fact indicate tolerance], and various other social, cultural, and environmental misperceptions). Additionally, individual coping mechanisms, maturity levels, self-esteem/self-efficacy levels, and thinking patterns also play a role in the progression of this phenomenon. The psychological model of addiction views substance use and abuse as a coping mechanism that people use to deal with stress, reduce tension, self-medicate, and decrease withdrawal-related distress. The psychological model of addiction highlights the critical role of the mind in the susceptibility to and the overall societal increase in addiction (Baker, Piper, McCarty, Majeskie, & Fiore, 2004).

In substance use/abuse research, several theories, such as the stress coping model of addiction, the transactional stress theory, and problem-solving theory, have been employed to explain the relationship between stress coping and substance use. Some evidence suggests that the utilization of effective problem-solving skills can minimize the psychological stress and unhealthy behaviors (e.g., substance use) often associated with stress coping. Other theories posit that spiritual issues and/or lack of purpose/unclear values may influence addiction. Societal issues and influences are explored later in this chapter.

LEGAL AND ILLICIT DRUGS AND THEIR EFFECTS

A substance that alters brain chemistry and stimulates behavioral change is called a *psychoactive substance*. There are a variety of substances with psychoactive properties, both legal and illegal. Some psychoactive drugs have the same effects as illicit drugs. The Centers for Disease Control and Prevention (CDC) classifies illicit drugs into a number of categories, the three most common of which are: sedatives/depressants, stimulants, and hallucinogens. One psychoactive drug that has been newly legalized in some states is marijuana (also known as ganja, grass, pot, skunk, and weed).

Other legal psychoactive drugs are tobacco and alcohol; OxyContin (oxycodone) and morphine are legal when prescribed by a licensed professional. According to NIDA, tobacco acts as a stimulant to the central nervous system, although some individuals argue that its effects are more relaxing. However, the mechanism of nicotine (the drug in tobacco) elicits the release of adrenaline (NIDA, 2012a), a stimulant hormone intimately involved in the stress response. Alcohol is a depressant, although some individuals may experience it initially as a stimulant, as it seems to provide initial energy and motivation by reducing inhibitions. Heroin and oxycodone are opioid narcotics that have the effect of relieving pain. Heroin is produced from morphine, which comes from the poppy plant. According to NIDA, about 23 percent of those who use heroin end up dependent upon it. Heroin abuse can affect both the brain's pleasure systems and its ability to perceive pain. When opioids are prescribed as a pain relievers, some research indicates that they are frequently misused or abused when not monitored. Cocaine (also known as big C, blow, coke, flake, and lady) is a stimulant. The general effects of stimulants are increased energy, increased physiological symptoms (heart rate, breathing, etc.), and sometimes euphoria (the euphoria from cocaine will vary in intensity from that of caffeine or methamphetamines). Cocaine also causes insomnia, restlessness, anxiety, and depression.

Other categories of substances that are subject to abuse include hallucinogens, steroids, synthetics, and inhalants. Effects range from hallucinations, to the enhancement of senses, to an instant euphoria. Understanding the effects of these drugs provides information about how the use and misuse of these drugs affect the brain and physical and cognitive behaviors (CDC, 2014).

Misuse is defined by the World Health Organization as the use of a substance for a purpose not consistent with legal or medical guidelines (also known as *hazardous use;* WHO, n.d.). The *Merriam-Webster Dictionary* defines *drug* as a substance that is used for medicine, but extends that definition to also include an illegal and often harmful substance (such as heroin, cocaine, LSD, or marijuana) that people take for pleasure. The term *drug use* can be defined as the use of prescription and illicit drugs with no negative consequences.

In 2014, the CDC noted that the *Dietary Guidelines for Americans* define "moderate alcohol consumption" as having up to 1 drink per day for women and up to 2 drinks per day for men. "Normal" drinking is subjective; many people believe that they have a higher tolerance for alcohol than others—and that can be true. However, what someone thinks is "normal" drinking may be considered "binge" drinking as described by the National Institute on Alcohol Abuse and Alcoholism (NIAA); the NIAA defines *binge drinking* as "a pattern of alcohol consumption that brings the blood alcohol concentration (BAC) level to 0.08% or more" (NIAA, 2012). This means that an individual, depending on what is being drunk and other contextual factors, potentially can have more than 4 or 5 drinks in one sitting and reach the legal limit.

It is easy to exceed the "normal drinking" limit for alcohol, just as it is easy to go from drug use to drug misuse or abuse. *Substance misuse* can be loosely defined as being on a continuum of use. At one end of this continuum is abstinence or no use; at the other end is loss of control and other consequences. Many people who try AODs go through an experimental phase and do not continue along the continuum to use of "harder" drugs. Some people are able to go through one or more of these earlier stages without developing negative consequences (Dugdale, 2012).

SOCIETAL ISSUES AND INFLUENCES

The National Institute on Drug Abuse (NIDA, 2012b) estimated that for the period 2000 through 2004, the total overall costs of substance abuse in the United States, including productivity, health, and crime-related costs, exceeded $600 billion annually. This includes approximately $193 billion for illicit drugs, $193 billion for tobacco, and $235 billion for alcohol.

Based on annual averages from the 2002, 2003, and 2004 National Surveys on Drug Use and Health, an estimated 1.2 million adults aged 18 or older were arrested for a serious violent or property offense in the past year. The Substance Abuse and Mental Health Services Administration (2003) estimates that 38 percent of homeless persons were dependent on alcohol and that 26 percent abused other drugs. These statistics illustrate how the excessive use of drugs influences (and may create) a variety of other challenges, including physical and mental health problems, legal issues, and homelessness.

DRUG USE AND STRESS

Everyday life events can be stressful. Stressful situations that are out of one's control cause a natural response to fight or flee (NIH, 2001). When most people feel stress, they experience physical symptoms that often precede emotional symptoms. Some physical symptoms of stress include headaches, stomach pains, lack of sleep, and lack of appetite, among others. Physiological stress is a response to hunger or food deprivation, sleep deprivation or insomnia, extreme hyper- or hypothermia, and drug withdrawal states. The use of psychoactive drugs creates what is called *pharmacological stress,* which causes cravings and a need to binge. When we "feel" stress, we are wired to do something to alleviate that stress.

Some substances may be used to alleviate some of what an individual experiences when stressed; often there is a "conditioning" for use of the substance to combat stress (e.g., "I really need a drink!"). Thus, an individual who initially uses a substance to cope with stress may, after a period of time, come to depend on the substance, leading to misuse and possibly abuse. Substance misuse has a domino effect on home life, school, and work. This is consistent with incentive conditioning models stating that exposure to drug-related cues produces conditioned responses, which in turn can cue subsequent drug-seeking behavior and use (Garavan, 2000). The bottom line is that once you start using drugs in response to a stress-related issue, and you feel better because of that drug use, the next time you are faced with a stressful situation, your brain remembers what you did and tells you to do that again.

However, drug use, misuse, and addiction have serious consequences. Users are often involved in domestic violence, workplace injuries, and drunk/intoxicated driving injuries and fatalities; they are also more prone to develop alcohol-related diseases (cancer, cardiovascular, and digestive disease) and sexually transmitted infections (STIs; Dugdale, 2012). A user's risky behavior may include changes such as ignoring responsibilities and losing focus on priorities. People who abuse drugs often withdraw from friends and family and isolate themselves, or they may make friends with other abusers. Users may believe that they don't have a problem and that they can quit any time they want.

Regardless of the substance, the important thing to recognize is that when people continue to use drugs in spite of the negative consequences, they have moved from the use of drugs to the misuse/abuse of drugs. The issue becomes the individual's inability to abstain from using the substance despite the increasing difficulty it causes. The negative consequences can be physical harm from accidents, fights, or illness (hepatitis C or HIV); financial ruin; and loss of job or expulsion from school, among others. The consequences of abuse are exacerbated by the loss of income, education, family, and so on.

Sometimes people begin using AODs because they have underlying emotional problems that they believe are helped by the substance use; they see their behavior as self-medicating. When people under stress are not managing that stress, substance use can create even more stress; depression, anxiety, or anger gain a foothold in the psyche, and a conditioned cycle may begin.

Certainly, there are "good" stressors. These may be experienced when individuals establish goals for themselves and seek to achieve those goals: stress is created by the need to master or accomplish something. The individual is excited and has feelings of pleasure, but the body still responds by releasing hormones that tell the brain something feels different. The greater the uncontrollability and unpredictability of the stressful situation, and the lower the sense of mastery or adaptability, the greater the magnitude of the stress response and risk for persistent homeostatic dysregulation will be. Thus, the dimensions of intensity, controllability, predictability, mastery, and adaptability are important in understanding the role of stress in increasing the risk of maladaptive behaviors such as addiction (Sinha, 2008). Volkow (2005) gave a good example of the link between stress and substance use. Some individuals who were affected by Hurricane Katrina—displaced from their homes, or lost loved ones—developed behavioral and emotional issues that influenced their desire for relief and prompted them to begin using substances. Eventually, some of these individuals' use increased to substance misuse and abuse. The report stated that the mass expansion of the displaced population made it more challenging to provide the needed mental health care. A lot of those victims turned to what was readily available to them—and unfortunately, drugs and alcohol were more accessible than treatment (Volkow, 2005). The study concluded that Katrina-related trauma and its psychological sequelae will remain a significant public health issue for years.

REFERENCES AND FURTHER READING

Baker, T. B., Piper, M. E., McCarty, D. E, Majeskie, M. R., & Fiore, M. C. (2004). Addiction motivation reformulated: An affective processing model of negative reinforcement. *Psychological Review, 111*(1), 33–51. Retrieved April 10, 2014, from http://www.ncbi.nlm.nih.gov/pubmed/14756584.

Centers for Disease Control and Prevention (CDC). (2014, March 14). *Frequently asked questions.* Retrieved from https://www.cdc.gov/.

Dugdale, D. (2012). Medline Plus: A service of the National Institute of Health. Retrieved May 7, 2014, from http://www.nlm.nih.gov/medlineplus/ency/article/001522.htm.

Garavan, H. (2000). Cue induced cocaine craving: Neuroanatomical specificity for drug users and drug stimuli. *American Journal of Psychiatry, 157*(11), 1789–1798.

Merriam Webster's Dictionary. (n.d.). s.v. *stress.* Retrieved April 10, 2014, from http://www.merriam-webster.com/dictionary/stress.

National Institute on Alcohol Abuse and Alcoholism (NIAA). (2012). Overview of alcohol assumption. Alcohol facts and statistics. Retrieved from NIAA website via GPO Access: https://www.niaaa.nih.gov/alcohol-health/overview-alcohol-consumption/alcohol-facts-and-statistics.

National Institute on Drug Abuse (NIDA). (2009). *Drug facts: Understanding drug abuse and addiction.* Retrieved April 16, 2014, from http://www.drugabuse.gov/publications/drugfacts/understanding-drug-abuse-addiction.

National Institute on Drug Abuse (NIDA). (2012a). Is Nicotine Addictive. Retrieved from NIH website via GPO Access: https://www.drugabuse.gov/publications/research-reports/tobacco/nicotine-addictive.

National Institute on Drug Abuse (NIDA). (2012b). Principles if drug addiction treatment: A research base guide (third edition) Retrieved April 16, 2014, from https://www.drugabuse.gov/publications/principles-drug-addiction-treatment-research-based-guide-third-edition/frequently-asked-questions/drug-addiction-treatment-worth-its-cost.

National Institute on Drug Abuse (NIDA). (2014). Drugs, brains and behaviors: The science of addiction. *Why do people take drugs? Research of the National Institute on Drug Abuse*. Retrieved from NIDA website via GPO Access: https://www.drugabuse.gov/publications/principles-drug-addiction-treatment-research-based-guide-third-edition/principles-effective-treatment.

National Institutes of Health (NIH). (2001). Post-traumatic stress disorder. Retrieved from NIH website via GPO Access: http://www.nimh.nih.gov/health/topics/post-traumatic-stress-disorder-ptsd/index.shtml.

National Institutes of Health (NIH). (2012). NIAA council approves definition of binge drinking. Retrieved from *NIAA Newsletter* via GPO Access: http://pubs.niaaa.nih.gov/publications/Newsletter/winter2004/Newsletter_Number3.pdf.

National Institutes of Health (NIH). (2014). Drug facts: Nationwide trends. Retrieved from NIDA website via GPO Access: http://www.drugabuse.gov/publications/drugfacts/nationwide-trends.

Northrop, N. A., & Yamamoto, B. K. (2013). Cyclooxygenase activity contributes to the monoaminergic damage caused by serial exposure to stress and methamphetamine. *Neuropharmacology, 72*, 96–105.

Reynolds, S. (2012). Stress receptor mediates lifelong consequences of early trauma. Retrieved April 14, 2014, from http://www.drugabuse.gov/news-events/nida-notes/2012/11/stress-receptor-mediates-lifelong-consequences-early-trauma.

Sinha, R. (2008). Chronic stress, drug use, and vulnerability to addiction. *Annals of the New York Academy of Sciences*, 1141, 105–130.

Substance Abuse and Mental Health Services Administration (SAMHSA). (2003). Homelessness–Provision of mental health and substance abuse services. Retrieved April 14, 2014, from http://mentalhealth.samhsa.gov/publications/allpubs/homelessness/.

Substance Abuse and Mental Health Services Administration (SAMHSA). (2009). Results from the 2008 national survey on drug use and health: National findings. Retrieved April 14, 2014, from http://www.dpft.org/resources/NSDUHresults2008.pdf.

Volkow, N. D. (2005). The effects of stress on drug abuse after Katrina. Retrieved from NIH Directors page via GPO Access: http://www.drugabuse.gov/about-nida/directors-page/messages-director/2005/09/effects-stress-drug-abuse-after-katrina.

Volkow, N. D., & Fowler, J. S. (2000). Addiction, a disease of compulsion and drive: Involvement of the orbitofrontal cortex. *Cerebral Cortex, 10*(3), 318–325. doi:10.1093/cercor/10.3.318.

World Health Organization. (n.d.). Lexicon of alcohol and drug terms published by the World Health Organization, s.v. *misuse, drug or alcohol*. Retrieved April 10, 2014, from http://www.who.int/substance_abuse/terminology/who_lexicon/en.

39

Eating Disorders: A Maladaptive Coping Mechanism

Joann V. Hendelman

Think of yourself going to the kitchen looking for a snack to eat. You start by opening the refrigerator. You look inside, searching for something that you feel like eating. Although there is plenty of food in the fridge, you come up empty. Next you move to the cupboard, also fairly well stocked, to continue your search. You again come up empty. Why do you think you cannot find anything you want to eat? The answer is that you are not hungry. Maybe you are looking to feed something else—perhaps boredom, sadness, anxiety, or anger—or maybe you are celebrating. You have now witnessed your own emotional eating. You are eating to numb or calm your feelings. You may engage in ritualistic behavior associated with eating; for example, taking a break from studying means it is time to get something to eat.

Eating disorders are considered to be coping strategies to manage and reduce stress (McFillan et al., 2012). Just as you might have been looking for food to reduce your boredom or anxiety or sadness, individuals struggling with eating disorders seek to numb their feelings with food, by binging and purging, or by restricting or avoiding food intake. This happens most often when these individuals lack healthy coping strategies, have difficulty tolerating stress, and feel out of control in one or more areas of their lives (Ball & Lee, 2000). In some cases, eating disorders can lead to death.

Emotional eating serves some significant functions. It can relieve (at least temporarily) negative emotions (anxiety, sadness, anger, etc.). It can also turn down the volume on negative devaluing and even abusive inner thoughts . . . at least temporarily. It has been shown that people are more likely to eat for emotional reasons they rely on emotion-oriented coping (focusing only on getting rid of or decreasing the negative affect rather than finding a long-term solution) and avoidance or distraction (coping through avoiding the situation, refocusing on something else but not focusing on a long-term solution) as their primary methods of handling emotions (Spoor, Bekkar, Van Strien, & Van Heck, 2007).

Some people learned to numb their emotions with food very early in life. When you fell down and skinned a knee as a child, your mother might have picked you up, dried your tears, and said, "Here, honey. Here's a cookie, this will make you feel better." If one cookie can help to make a child feel better about that skinned knee, then imagine what a whole box of cookies might do to make someone feel better after that exam they flunked, or how that carton of ice cream could make you feel after breaking up with your boyfriend or girlfriend!

No matter who we are, we have all had experiences with disordered eating in one form or another, whether it has been bingeing, restricting, or dieting. Let's now look at eating disorders and how they are used as coping mechanisms. First, we will investigate the three main eating disorders: anorexia nervosa, bulimia nervosa, and binge eating disorder. Then we will address how these eating disorders work as maladaptive coping mechanisms, and finally the implications for treatment.

We discuss the three main eating disorders here using a "transdiagnostic approach," which means that we view the core elements of all three disorders as essentially the same. In these illnesses, a person's shape and weight become overvalued, there is a strict focus on control over eating, body dissatisfaction is high, and there are difficulties in regulating emotions and similar attitudes (Brockmeyer et al., 2014). Notably, females and males are more similar than dissimilar when it comes to the core eating-disorder symptomatology (Streigel-Moore et al., 2009).

In the United States, 20 million women and 10 million men suffer from a clinically significant eating disorder at some time in their life, including anorexia nervosa, bulimia nervosa, binge eating disorder, or an eating disorder not otherwise specified (EDNOS) (Wade, Keski-Rahkonen, & Hudson, 2011). Eating disorders do not discriminate between age, gender, race, or class—no one is immune.

Eating disorders do not exist on their own. Commonly, they co-exist with other illnesses such as anxiety, depression, obsessive-compulsive disorder, personality disorders, substance use disorders, and the like. Anxiety disorders often precede the onset of eating disorders. In contrast, depression appears to come after the onset of an eating disorder and may actually be a consequence of an eating disorder (Bardone-Cone et al., 2010). The eating disorder is a symptom of underlying/coexisting problems that must be addressed in treatment.

ANOREXIA NERVOSA

Anorexia nervosa (AN) is self-imposed starvation resulting from a distorted body image and an intense fear of gaining weight. Around 50 percent of individuals with AN meet the criteria for restricting type AN, which means they engage in dieting, fasting, and/or excessive exercise; the other 50 percent meet criteria for binge-eating/purging type AN, which means they may also engage in self-induced vomiting, or misuse of laxatives, enemas, and/or diuretics (Siegel, Brisman, & Weinshel, 1997). Individuals with binge-eating/purging type AN are at higher medical risk of health complications (American Psychiatric Association, 2013). Persons with anorexia become physically emaciated as a result of eating very little and/or throwing up what they do eat. Additionally, it is also common for people with AN to lie or manipulate in order to not eat; for example, they may say that they have already eaten, that they have a stomach problem, or that they have special food, diet, or allergy requirements. Ironically, these individuals tend to be preoccupied with food, cooking, and calories. They may make gourmet meals for everyone else but eat none themselves—often using "I snacked the whole time I was cooking" as an excuse. Individuals with AN tend to be highly focused on control, not only over what they eat but in every facet of their lives (Siegel et al., 1997).

People with AN usually have a distorted image of their bodies, and expect themselves to meet unrealistic visions of slenderness. They view themselves as much heavier than they actually are. They may also develop and perform obsessive exercise routines so that they can lose more weight.

Additionally, those who struggle with AN are generally socially isolated. Almost every social event includes food in some way. That makes it very difficult for people struggling with AN to be involved in such occasions, due to their need to control their food intake. It is also common for individuals with AN to wear very loose-fitting clothes, in order to hide how thin they are from others. These individuals also tend to be cold, no matter what the external temperature is; they are often seen wearing more or heavier clothes than should be necessary for the weather because they are cold all the time (hypothermia) as a result of their poor circulation. They often have low blood pressure (hypotension) and may even have blue (cyanotic) discoloration of the hands and feet due to poor circulation stemming from low body weight and malnutrition (Siegel et al., 1997). Anorexia nervosa has the highest mortality rate of all psychiatric disorders (Sullivan, 1995).

Bulimia nervosa (BN) is a disorder in which an individual engages in episodes of bingeing and purging. *Bingeing* is the process of eating a significantly large amount of food in a short period of time. *Purging* is defined as any behavior meant to rid the body of calories. It can take the form of (self-induced) vomiting or misuse of laxatives, enemas, or diuretics, and may even take the form of overexercising or use of diet pills. Individuals with BN are normal weight to overweight. They tend to be secretive eaters, eating normal amounts of food when around other people, and bingeing and purging when alone. For individuals with BN, it is often not about the taste of the food; rather, the goal of bingeing is to numb their thoughts. Many people also describe themselves as feeling out of control or unable to stop their bingeing. After the binge, however, it is common for those with BN to feel guilty and depressed over the amount of food eaten, and many will become overly focused on the weight gain that they believe will result from the binge. To compensate and avoid weight gain, they purge the unwanted food/calories, through actions that often bring on strong feelings of shame and anxiety. These feelings of shame and anxiety may in fact cause the cycle of bingeing and purging to begin again as a way to avoid these emotions. This may go on for several hours until the individual is exhausted (Siegel et al., 1997).

As a result of this behavior, individuals with BN may have high blood pressure (hypertension), dehydration, and electrolyte imbalances. They may have swollen parotid glands ("chipmunk face"), puffy cheeks, broken blood vessels in the eyes, and/or a sore throat as a result of vomiting. They may also have dental erosion from the vomiting due to the action of stomach acids on the teeth (Siegel et al., 1997).

BINGE EATING DISORDER

Binge eating disorder (BED) is recurrent episodes of binge eating without the compensatory purging behavior found in BN. People with BED use food as a drug to self-medicate. As a result of their binges, they often experience rapid weight gain, which is often accompanied by feelings of disgust and shame. They will hide food in anticipation of a binge that they can perform secretly. They eat to the point of major discomfort and pain, and they feel totally out of control when it comes to food. They do not purge in any way. They only see success and failure in regard to their weight. When their weight drops, they feel successful; however, when their weight goes up, they experience a sense of failure, often accompanied by shame and anxiety (Siegel et al., 1997).

People with BED are overweight to morbidly obese. A majority of obese people are in fact dealing with BED (Clyne & Blampied, 2004). Like all eating disorders, BED is not "just about the food." Although eating is the primary behavior or symptom that people may see, it is the person's emotions and thoughts that drive his or her behavior. Therefore, simply stopping someone from eating may not be enough to "fix" the problem. For example, many people who have had weight loss surgery (and who can no longer binge because of the surgery) have turned to alcohol to replace their emotional eating and numb the negative emotions that still persist (Lent et al., 2013).

Eating disorders are determined by sociocultural, biological, and psychological factors contributing to the development and maintenance of the illness (Ball & Lee, 2000). Since the 1980s, family, twin, and adoption studies have consistently found genetic influences in the predisposition to eating disorders; in fact, eating disorders are considered to be primarily due to genetic factors (Zerwas & Bulik, 2011).

Not all "disordered eating" is bad, or even uncommon. It is not unusual to binge-eat on occasion (for example, on a Thanksgiving holiday) or to fast for a religious purpose. However, when the bingeing, purging, and/or restrictive eating become excessive, or the individuals do not want to or feel that they cannot stop, then it becomes a problem. As previously stated, eating disorders do not come from only one source; many factors contribute to the development and maintenance of these disorders. However, one common factor in all eating disorders is that the individual struggling with the disorder lacks healthy coping tools. As a result, life stressors often coincide with the onset and worsening of symptoms (Fairburn, Cooper, & Shafran, 2003).

REACTING TO STRESSORS

Reaction to a stressor depends on both internal mediators (one's coping ability, expectations about one's ability to cope, and experiences in coping with stressors in the past) and external mediators (one's support system, material resources, and social environment) (Cattanach & Rodin, 1988). People with eating disorders often have difficulty dealing with stress and negative emotions. Fairburn et al. (2003) call it *mood intolerance:* an inability to appropriately deal with negative or intense mood. Such individuals often have limited coping ability and limited coping skills, and generally rely on avoidant and emotion-focused coping strategies (namely, avoidance of painful emotions and thoughts) (Fitzsimmons & Bardone-Cone, 2010). Stressors may be significant in predisposing, precipitating, or maintaining an eating disorder (Cattanach & Rodin, 1988).

Those struggling with BN and BED use eating as an avoidant coping mechanism, using food as a distraction from their negative thoughts and feelings. However, because bingeing results in new negative emotions, use of this coping strategy is maladaptive, as it perpetuates the person's high level of distress (Latner & Clyne, 2008). Specifically, it has been found that the inability to withstand negative emotions, rather than a specific fear or anxiety, most often perpetuates disordered eating behavior (Anestis, Selvy, Fink, & Joiner, 2007). Therefore, an individual with an eating disorder is less likely to be able to handle a crisis than someone without an eating disorder (Brewerton, Lydiard, Ballenger, & Herzog, 1993). Overall, these individuals tend to be more passive, and find it difficult to express feelings (Troop, Holbrey, & Treasure, 1998).

In fact, the unique ways in which an individual with an eating disorder perceives, appraises, and interacts with the environment may be the most important determining factor in the development of the eating disorder—more so than the actual stressors the individual comes into contact with (Lazarus, 1966). The initial stress starts the ball rolling, but it is the person's inability to counter the stress in any meaningful way that is the ultimate problem precipitating and maintaining the eating disorder. People with eating disorders are hypersensitive to what is going on around them, usually seeing everything regarding themselves in a negative light. They are likely to perceive even minor situations as stressful (Fitzsimmons &

Bardone-Cone, 2010). They are more likely to blame themselves for anything that happens even when it may be obvious to an outsider that they had no responsibility for the event or situation (Troop, Holbrey, & Treasure, 1998). Troop, Holbrey, Trowler, and Treasure (1994) posed the possibility that disordered eating may in fact be a result of the lack of coping styles rather than the original stress itself.

It must be noted here that avoidant coping strategies are not always maladaptive. In fact, some (e.g., taking a walk or getting together with a friend) work well in the short term, meaning they help with immediate reduction of pain, stress, and anxiety. However, typically these short-term strategies are only used until a longer-term solution (also known as a *task-oriented strategy*) can be found; this is usually a strategy that involves actually changing something that caused the problem in the first place (Fitzsimmons & Bardone-Cone, 2010). However, the person with an eating disorder rarely gets to the long-term solution, instead becoming stuck in cycles of short-term solutions and thus never truly feeling better or having any real resolution of the pain.

USING FOOD (OR RESTRICTING FOOD) TO SELF-MEDICATE AND REGULATE EMOTIONS

Disordered eating behavior (binge eating, extreme food restriction) is used as a coping mechanism to reduce or escape from negative affect (Fitzsimmons & Bardone-Cone, 2010). Eating is a form of self-medication similar to an alcoholic's use of alcohol to numb inner thoughts and feelings. Eating is used to feel better, which can then lead to binge eating in order to maintain the improved mood and try to make it last (Raspopow, Matheson, Abizaid, & Anisman, 2012). As might be expected, binge eating is more likely to occur on days of sustained or increasing negative affect (Berg et al., 2013). Boredom, stress, extreme sadness, and anxiety are the emotions that will most likely lead to a binge (Clyne & Blampied, 2004).

Deaver et al. (2003) found that individuals with eating disorders report high negative emotions prior to bingeing, an improved emotional state during a binge, and deteriorating mood after the binge. In other words, the individual initially experiences positive emotions as a result of the binge, often because he just ate food that he does not usually "allow" himself to eat on a regular basis. After the binge, however, he is faced with the guilt of the binge and the subsequent consequence of the feared weight gain, resulting in his mood plummeting. Both binge eating and purging are used to diminish negative affect, regardless of whether the behaviors occur alone or in tandem (Berg et al., 2013). The use of binge eating to distract from a negative emotional state is similar to the avoidance function of self-injurious behavior like cutting. In fact, many people who struggle with binge/purge-type eating disorders also use self-injury (cutting) in their search for numbness by refocusing on physical pain that distracts them from the emotional pain. The cutting is also used as self-punishment (Anestis et al., 2007).

Significant weight loss through extremely restrictive eating, as seen in AN, is another means of emotional regulation resulting in a short-term decrease in negative affect. These individuals' continued weight loss is reinforced by their feelings of control and achievement, and the resultant self-esteem, based on this low-body-weight "success." Persons struggling with AN are extremely resistant to weight gain, feeling that they will lose this extremely important coping mechanism and the feeling of control, especially if they have no other coping tools or alternatives (Brockmeyer et al., 2012).

People struggling with eating disorders use less behaviorally focused coping. They lack problem-focused or social support-seeking skills. They tend to avoid confronting their own problems, and certainly avoid confronting someone else with whom they have a problem. They may live in isolation, as they may lack social skills and often experience social anxiety (fear of social situations) (Brewerton et al., 1993). They may perceive themselves as unable to cope, unable to tolerate stress, and unable to solve problems (Anestis et al., 2007).

People with eating disorders tend to be hypersensitive to everything and everyone around them. They paint every situation with a negative brush, relying on past experience to be the sole predictor of what the future will be. Therefore, these individuals often disregard or misread important social cues. The avoidant coping strategy (also known as the eating disorder behavior) is utilized to defend against the predicted rejection or psychological harm (McFillin et al., 2012). They are fearful of allowing themselves to be vulnerable to anyone, as they view vulnerability as being "out of control," and this blocks their ability to maintain friendships and have confidants on whom they can rely. Additionally, with AN, negative mood and distortions of perception are exacerbated by the bodily effects of starvation, malnutrition, and low blood pressure (Raspopow et al., 2012).

It is not uncommon for those suffering from an eating disorder to feel unworthy and undeserving of friends. Some may even see themselves as bad people, which can be a result of past experiences of abuse or trauma. Additionally, the lack of social interactions and failed attempts at social interaction further push people into using their disordered eating behaviors as methods for coping (Raspopow et al., 2012). To gain a bit of understanding into how hard social functioning is for someone with AN, for example, think of when you have not eaten for an extended period of time, or are extremely tired or ill: Are you easy to be around, or are you cranky? How able are you to make new friends in that state? What if that state were your everyday norm?

Blodgett Salafia and Lemer (2012) looked at disordered eating in middle-school girls and boys. Girls were found to experience more stress overall than boys, and the majority of this stress was found to be caused by interpersonal (relationships and family) and performance-related stressors. Boys experienced stress due to performance, relationship, education, financial, and family-related stressors. Further, they found that in both boys and girls, stress led to body dissatisfaction, which in turn led to dieting. In girls, they found that this propensity to diet when stressed led to bulimic symptoms of bingeing and purging. Overall, increased stress led to negative body image, which contributed to feelings of decreased self-worth.

Further, there appears to be a close connection between stress and perfectionism during adolescence. As a way to cope with or avoid stress, many individuals develop perfectionism as a way to "prevent" stress from occurring. (You may know from experience, however, that there is no way to prevent stress!) Particularly in girls, this need to be perfect can become internalized, and thus affect all of their daily choices. Restrictive eating and dieting were found to be a behavioral coping mechanism for the perceived lack of perfection (Hewitt et al., 2002).

Finally, stress itself can directly affect hunger levels; sustained stress may start a person down the road toward disordered eating even before these behaviors are used as coping tools. For example, have you ever been too upset to eat? Have you ever forgotten to eat because you were too busy? Have you ever eaten lots of junk food because it was finals week? These behaviors—which are considered relatively normal—can lead to changes in physical appearance, such as weight loss, sunken eyes and cheeks, and looking tired, which in turn can lead to a greater focus on body image (Blodgett Salafia & Lemer, 2012).

Individuals who have fully recovered from eating disorders behave similarly to non-eating disordered people when it comes to coping skills (Fitzsimmons & Bardone-Cone, 2000). This indicates the importance of developing coping strategies and emotional management skills during treatment. Proper treatment and therapy can help the individual learn to cope with distress in more adaptive ways and have success in tolerating and reducing stress over the long term (Corstorphine et al., 2007). It is important to teach distress tolerance skills to help replace maladaptive, disordered eating behaviors to assist these individuals in managing their emotions with more adaptive and less dangerous alternatives (Anestis et al., 2007).

If someone is battling an eating disorder, no one should ever deny to them that a problem exists. People who may have eating disorders need to seek specialized, professional help as soon as possible. There should be no shame in having an eating disorder; it is an illness that is no one's fault.

CONCLUSION

Eating disorders are a widespread problem, and they can be lethal. The three main eating disorders—anorexia nervosa, bulimia nervosa, and binge eating disorder—are maladaptive numbing techniques that some people use to handle the stress they encounter. The lack of effective coping mechanisms is a significant factor in the development and maintenance of eating disorders. People struggling with eating disorders primarily use emotion regulation and avoidance/distracting techniques rather than task-oriented problem-solving techniques that would create more effective, longer-term solutions to the problem that is causing or related to the stress. Treatment that helps the individual learn more effective coping strategies is an essential part of long-term recovery.

REFERENCES AND FURTHER READING

Academy for Eating Disorders. (2012). *Eating disorders: Critical points of early recognition and medical risk management in the care of individuals with eating disorders.* Deerfield, IL: Author. Retrieved from http://www.aedweb.org/downloads/Guide-English.pdf.

American Psychiatric Association. (2013). *Diagnostic and statistical manual of mental disorders, fifth edition.* Washington, DC: American Psychiatric Publishing.

Anestis, M., Selvy, E., Fink, E., & Joiner, R. (2007). The multifaceted role of distress tolerance in dysregulated eating behaviors. *International Journal of Eating Disorders, 40*(8), 718–726.

Ball, K., & Lee, C. (2000). Relationships between psychological stress, coping and disordered eating: A review. *Psychology and Health, 14,* 1007–1035.

Bardone-Cone, A., Harney, M., Maldonado, C., Lawson, M., Robinson, D., Smith, R., & Tosh, A. (2010). Defining recovery from an eating disorder: Conceptualization, validation, and examination of psychosocial functioning and psychiatric comorbidity. *Behaviour Research and Therapy, 48*(3), 194–202.

Berg, K., Peterson, C., Crosby, R., Cao, L., Engel, S., Mitchell, J., & Wonderlich, S. (2013). Facets of negative affect prior to and following binge-only, purge-only, and binge/purge events in women with bulimia nervosa. *Journal of Abnormal Psychology, 122*(1), 111–118.

Blodgett Salafia, E., & Lemer, J. (2012). Associations between multiple types of stress and disordered eating among girls and boys in middle school. *Journal of Child and Family Studies, 21,* 148–157.

Brewerton, T., Lydiard, R., Ballenger, J., & Herzog, D. (1993). Eating disorders and social phobia. *Archives of General Psychiatry, 50*(1), 70.

Brockmeyer, T., Grosse Holtforth, M., Bents, H., Kammerer, A., Herzog, W., & Friederich, H. (2012). Starvation and emotion regulation in anorexia nervosa. *Comprehensive Psychiatry, 53,* 496–501.

Brockmeyer, T., Skunde, M., Wu, M., Bresslein, E., Rudofsky, G., Herzog, W., & Friederich, H. (2014). Difficulties in emotion regulation across the spectrum of eating disorders. *Comprehensive Psychiatry, 55,* 565–571.

Cattanach, M., & Rodin, J. (1988). Psychosocial components of the stress process in bulimia. *International Journal of Eating Disorders, 7*(1), 75–88.

Clyne, C., & Blampied, N. (2004). Training in emotion regulation as a treatment for binge eating: A preliminary study. *Behaviour Change, 21*(4), 269–281.

Corstorphine, E., Mountford, V., Tomlinson, S., Waller, G., & Meyer, C. (2007). Distress tolerance in the eating disorders. *Eating Behaviors, 8*(1), 91–97.

Deaver, C., Miltenberger, R., Smyth, J., Meidinger, A., & Crosby, R. (2003). An evaluation of affect and binge eating. *Behavior Modification, 27*(4), 578–599.

Fairburn, C., Cooper, Z., & Shafran, R. (2003). Cognitive behaviour therapy for eating disorders: A transdiagnostic theory and treatment. *Behaviour Research and Therapy, 41,* 509–28.

Fitzsimmons, E., & Bardone-Cone, A. (2010). Differences in coping across stages of recovery from an eating disorder. *International Journal of Eating Disorders, 43*(8), 689–693.

Hewitt, P., Caelian, C., Flett, G., Sherry, S., Collins, L., & Flynn, C. (2002). Perfectionism in children: Associations with depression, anxiety, and anger. *Personality and Individual Differences, 32,* 1049–1061.

Latner, J., & Clyne, C. (2008). The diagnostic validity of the criteria for binge eating disorder. *International Journal of Eating Disorders, 41*(1), 1–14.

Lazarus, R. (1966). *Psychological stress and the coping process.* New York, NY: McGraw-Hill.

Lazarus, R., & Folkman, S. (1984). *Stress, appraisal, and coping.* New York, NY: Springer.

Lent, M., Hayes, S., Wood, G., Napolitano, M., & Argyropoulos, G. (2013). Smoking and alcohol use in gastric bypass patients. *Eating Behaviors, 14*(4), 460–463.

McFillin, R., Cahn, S., Salzer Burks, V., Peaslee Levine, M., Lane Loney, S., & Levine, R. (2012). Social information-processing and coping in adolescent females diagnosed with an eating disorder: Toward a greater understanding of control. *Eating Disorders, 20,* 42–59.

Raspopow, K., Matheson, K., Abizaid, A., & Anisman, H. (2012). Unsupportive social interactions influence emotional eating behaviors: The role of coping styles as mediators. *Appetite, 62,* 143–149.

Sherwood, N., Crowther, J., Wills, L., & Ben-Porath, Y. (2000). The perceived function of eating for bulimic, subclinical bulimic, and non-eating disordered women. *Behavior Therapy, 31*(4), 777–793.

Siegel, M., Brisman, J., & Weinshel, M. (1997). *Surviving an eating disorder: Strategies for family and friends.* New York, NY: Harper Perennial.

Spoor, S., Bekkar, M., Van Strien, T., & Van Heck, G. (2007). Relations between negative affect, coping, and emotional eating. *Appetite, 48,* 368–376.

Striegel-Moore, R., Rosselli, F., Perrin, N., DeBar, L., Wilson, G., May, A., & Kraemer, H. (2009). Gender difference in the prevalence of eating disorder symptoms. *International Journal of Eating Disorders, 42,* 471–474.

Sullivan, P. (1995). Mortality in anorexia nervosa. *American Journal of Psychiatry, 152*(7), 1073–1074.

Troop, N., Holbrey, A., & Treasure, J. (1998). Stress, coping, and crisis support in eating disorder. *International Journal of Eating Disorders, 24,* 157–166.

Troop, N., Holbrey, A., Trowler, R., & Treasure, J. (1994). Ways of coping in women with eating disorders. *Journal of Nervous and Mental Disease, 182,* 535–540.

Wade, T. D., Keski-Rahkonen A., & Hudson, J. (2011). Epidemiology of eating disorders. In M. Tsuang & M. Tohen (Eds.), *Textbook in psychiatric epidemiology* (3rd ed., pp. 343–360). New York, NY: John Wiley & Sons.

Zerwas, S., & Bulik, C. (2011). Genetics and epigenetics of eating disorders. *Psychiatric Annals, 41*(11), 532–538.

40

Self-Injury to Cope with Stress

Wendy E. Goetz, Laura Foster, and Sarah Sanders

Stress is a common human experience, and one that most people are taught or learn to manage through the use of effective and healthy coping skills. Some individuals, however, develop coping skills that are ineffective, unhealthy, and may perpetuate the cycle of stress. Nonsuicidal self-injury (NSSI) is one type of unhealthy coping skill that occurs in children, adolescents, and adults in various cultures and environments. Nonsuicidal self-injury is a mechanism for coping with stress by responding with behaviors that purposely harm the body, without suicidal intent and not done as part of culturally or socially accepted decorative practices (e.g., piercing, tattooing) (Breen, Lewis, & Sutherland, 2013). This behavior is also referred to as deliberate self-harm, self-hurting/wounding, self-mutilation, and parasuicide (Klonsky, 2007), but the term *nonsuicidal self-injury* or its abbreviation (NSSI) is often used as an accurate, general term for this kind of behavior. In this chapter, NSSI, self-injury, and self-harm are used interchangeably.

Often, self-injury is an attempt to self-soothe in times of significant emotional distress. While the act of engaging in self-injury is intended to alleviate the individual's stress, participating in these behaviors may contribute to the perpetuation of stress. Self-harm is typically a private and secretive act, and the physical marks left behind may have to be covered or hidden. Many self-injurers struggle with concealing their behaviors and marks. Skin cutting is the most commonly recognized form of self-injury, but scratching, burning, carving, pinching, hitting/banging, self-bruising, picking scabs and interfering with wound healing, biting, and excessive rubbing are also included in the category of nonsuicidal self-injury (Butler & Malone, 2013). The injuries may occur once or more often over time. They are frequently directed at the arms and wrists, which can be easily concealed with clothing, but multiple areas of the body may be harmed, including the hands, thighs, and stomach (Klonsky, 2007).

Although some forms of self-injury may be severe and cause significant damage to the body through deliberate actions, the intent and purpose of the self-injuring behavior notably differ from those of suicidal behavior. Nonsuicidal self-injury is distinct in that the individual's objective is not to end his or her life, but to change the emotional experience of life. As Butler and Malone (2013) state, NSSI can be understood as a signal of psychological distress because it is a maladaptive coping mechanism used in efforts to regulate overwhelming feelings so that an individual can endure life; suicide attempts reflect a desire to escape and end one's life completely.

DEVELOPMENTAL ISSUES AND LIFE SPAN PREVALENCE

Incidents of self-injury have been reported and treated in young children, adolescents, and adult populations. Few studies have been able to explore the prevalence of self-harm in children under the age of 12, due to children's lack of ability to self-report these behaviors and the absence of recorded hospital or emergency room (ER) visits in which the resulting injuries of NSSI are treated (Hawton, Saunders, & O'Connor, 2012). Children who are exposed to or experience early traumas may be more likely to self-injure as a way of coping and regulating emotion. *Trauma,* which is defined as a deeply distressing or disturbing encounter or event, can trigger a stress response in anyone who experiences it. Trauma may be related to violence, loss, natural disasters, real or perceived dangers, abuse, or neglect.

In addition to trauma, certain parenting styles can be a source of stress for children (Hudson, Dodd, & Bovopoulos, 2011). *Permissive parenting* is a style in which the parents demonstrate little interest in consistency of rules and expectations. *Authoritarian parenting* is parenting in which little or no explanation is given to the child about decisions being made by the parents, there is little flexibility in rules and routines, and children are restricted from making choices. Both of these parenting styles make appropriate boundaries difficult for children to identify and can create in them a sense of unpredictability, an inability to make decisions, or the unwillingness to make mistakes (Hay & Meldrum, 2010). The inability to predict others' behaviors and situational outcomes can be extremely stressful for young children, who may utilize self-harm to cope with the stress of these experiences. Children often self-injure by banging the head on a solid object or hitting themselves. Skin picking, hair pulling, and biting are also forms of self-harm that are commonly seen in children.

Self-injury is prevalent in adolescents, as they are in the process of forming individual identities and interpersonal boundaries. According to one study, approximately 15 percent of adolescents in the United States indicated that they have self-injured (Hay & Meldrum, 2010). The age of onset for self-injury is typically between the ages of 12 and 15 years, particularly in girls (Hawton et al., 2012). An increase in stress, including a variety of social, familial, and cultural factors, in combination with an adolescent's immature or ineffective emotional regulation, can create a scenario in which self-injury is utilized. The most common form of self-harm in this population is skin cutting or scratching, but poisoning, engaging in risk-taking behaviors, and hitting are also common. Self-harm increases rapidly during the early teenage years, with the female-to-male gender ratio being approximately 6:1, especially around the age of 13–15 years (Hawton et al., 2012). In later teenage years, the prevalence in boys increases and may be close to that of girls. The main gender differences concern methods of self-injury as opposed to types of stressor; females appear more likely to cut themselves, whereas males appear more likely to burn or hit themselves (Klonsky, 2007).

When adolescents believe that they are socially inferior to their peers, or of lower social status, they are more likely to experience stress (Gilbert et al., 2010). Adolescents from families where financial concerns interfere with the individual's life experience may also experience elevated levels of stress. Adolescents who are questioning their sexual orientation or who are uncertain about whether to disclose their orientation to others may experience an increased amount of stress (Hawton et al., 2012). Also, during adolescence, the stress associated with grief and loss could be triggered by death, a change in environment or school, or the end of a significant relationship. Being a victim of cyber-bullying or traditional bullying (Hay & Meldrum, 2010) is an extremely common experience for adolescents; these repeated verbal, physical, or electronic assaults increase self-doubt and shame in adolescents, thereby heightening stress. The adolescent may also experience stress from feeling a fear of actual physical harm or injury by another.

Experiencing sexual or physical abuse is an intrusion on an individual's interpersonal boundaries, and creates an environment of uncertainty, intimidation, and fear. Secrecy often accompanies abuse, and an adolescent may believe that he or she is responsible for hiding information or evidence of the abuse. The unpredictability that exists in a home where there is abuse can cause stress for the victim. Adolescents may feel stress associated with keeping younger siblings safe, as well as keeping the abuse secret so as not to jeopardize the parental union or incapacitate the primary caregiver by involving law enforcement or community agencies. Parental neglect, marital discord, and parental divorce also create stressful situations for adolescents. Teenagers who witness conflicted relationships between parents or experience the dissolution of their parents' marriage may feel significant distress.

Adolescents who believe that they must achieve high levels of success or perfect performance, or who live in a highly competitive culture or society, appear to be more susceptible to experiencing stress. In one survey conducted by the

American Psychological Association, 27 percent of American adolescents reported being under an extreme amount of stress during the school year, and 13.4 percent reported extreme stress during the summer (Johnson, 2014). However, restricted academic success can also negatively affect an adolescent's stress levels.

The prevalence of self-harm in adults is reported to be approximately 4 percent of the population (Klonsky, 2011). Many of these adults began self-injuring as adolescents and continued to use self-injury as a form of coping with adult stressors (Klonsky, 2007). Witnessing the act of self-injury in other family members or peers may provide a behavioral model that adolescents follow to cope with distress (Hawton et al., 2012), and they may carry the practice into adulthood. Marital struggles, caretaking of aging parents, financial concerns, and residual stress from childhood and adolescent experiences or trauma are all issues that may be continuous sources of distress in adulthood.

DIAGNOSTIC PRESENTATION

Engaging in a serious maladaptive coping strategy in response to stress, as is the case with self-injury, typically leads to the person being diagnosed with a psychiatric disorder. Currently there is no NSSI or self-injury diagnostic disorder; however, there are several commonly used diagnoses for those who in engage in self-harm. Disorders often diagnosed include depression, anxiety, eating disorders, substance use disorders, and posttraumatic stress disorders (Klonsky & Muehlenkamp, 2007; Miller & Pariseau, 2013). Interestingly, Klonsky and Muehlenkamp (2007) found that anxiety may be more associated with self-injury than with depression. They attributed this finding to the emotional arousal shared between self-injury and anxiety, which is also the same emotional arousal involved in the stress response.

While there is currently no NSSI diagnostic disorder, as noted earlier, self-harm was listed once as a symptom of a disorder in the *Diagnostic and Statistical Manual of Mental Disorders, Fourth Edition–Text Revision* (*DSM-IV-TR;* American Psychiatric Association, 2000), called borderline personality disorder (BPD). As Klonsky and Muehlenkamp (2007) stated, "the link between BPD and self-injury is not surprising because both have negative emotionality and emotion dysregulation as core features" (p. 1048). The similarities between BPD and self-harm may shed light on possible underlying personality dynamics, such as negative emotionality and emotional dysregulation that contribute to maladaptive coping in response to stress.

PERCEIVED FUNCTIONS OF SELF-HARM IN RESPONSE TO STRESS

For those who self-injure, the behavior may be a reaction to emotional distress and an attempt to self-soothe and cope, especially in times of stress and difficulty. Individuals who engage in self-injury may see their behavior in a positive way, as a means of relieving stress, tension, and emotional pain or expressing feelings they cannot otherwise manage. As Klonsky and Muehlenkamp (2007) note, emotional regulation is the most prevalent function of self-injury, as it is used to escape or alleviate intense and overwhelming negative feelings such as anger, anxiety, and frustration that these individuals experience before they self-injure; self-injurers often report feeling relief and calm after the self-injurious act.

In a study researching individuals' self-reported reasons for self-injuring, Horne and Csipke (2009) found that respondents sought either to decrease their distressing emotions or to increase certain feelings in order to combat the numbness associated with dissociation after a stressful event (as cited in Barton-Breck & Heyman, 2012). In dissociative episodes, individuals often describe feeling surreal, outside the body, or feeling numb or nothing at all, which can be especially difficult to explain if an individual has trouble identifying and understanding his or her emotions (Klonsky & Muehlenkamp, 2012). When in stressful situations, persons who self-injure may lack sufficient emotional skills to help them understand their experience, may not be fully aware of the range of feelings they have, or may struggle with the expression of complex feelings such as dissociation. Self-injury accompanied by the sight of blood and sensation of pain can, in a sense, "shock the system" and interrupt the experience of numbness or dissociation, and help the individual regain a sense of self and feel real or alive again (Klonsky & Muehlenkamp, 2012).

Some individuals perceive self-harm as a means of affirming their identity or autonomy. In Barton-Breck and Heyman's (2012) study, self-injurers reported the behavior as a way to move the focus away from their distress and sustain their well-being in difficult circumstances. Respondents noted that self-harm increased their sense of self-control and individuality, as they alone could control what happened to their own bodies. Similarly, respondents explained that self-injury helped to push feelings away and conceal emotional distress so that the individuals could present themselves as calm and normal, avoiding embarrassment or danger anticipated from communicating their anger or upset with others. Breen, Lewis, and Sutherland (2013) also found that self-injury can serve as a way to establish one's self as distinct from others, or allow individuals to take on "self-injurer" as part of their identity and achieve membership in groups of people who engage in the behavior. Some individuals may use self-injury to generate feelings of excitement or exhilaration akin to the "high" of risky behavior; unlike self-injury that serves other functions, which is performed in private and kept secret, this sensation-seeking type of self-injury likely occurs around friends or peers (Klonsky & Muehlenkamp, 2007).

When a person is in significant distress, NSSI may be seen as an option to elicit attention and care from others. Respondents in Barton-Breck and Heyman's (2012) study reported a desire for others to know how terrible they felt and that self-injury was a "cry for help" to family, friends, and authority figures. In some cases, self-injurers may seek to influence others' behavior by using self-injury to prevent perceived abandonment by a loved one, to be taken more seriously, or to provoke affection or reprimand (some sort of attention). For those seeking reprimand, self-injury may function as a means of self-punishment, to derogate or invalidate one's self, or as an expression of self-directed anger (Klonsky & Muehlenkamp, 2007).

Although the intent of self-injury often differs from suicidal behavior, self-injury can also serve as a way to replace, resist, or avoid impulses to engage in a suicide attempt (Klonsky, 2007). For individuals who use self-harm to prevent themselves from acting on suicidal thoughts, the behavior may help alleviate or express the intense negative emotions that lead to suicidal ideation without risking death (Klonsky & Muehlenkamp, 2007; Klonsky, 2007).

BIOLOGICAL MECHANISMS IN SELF-HARM

A significant reason why many individuals do not engage in self-injury is because of the anticipated physical pain that comes from inflicting harm on oneself. This, however, begs the question as to why the physical pain associated with self-injury discourages some and not others. Consistent with this line of questioning, researchers have wondered whether those who engage in self-injury experience pain differently. One finding that supports this idea is that individuals who engage in self-injury often report little or no pain associated with the self-injurious act (Nock & Prinstein, 2005, as cited in Nock, 2010). Several laboratory-based studies documented that individuals who engage in self-injury are slower to identify and experience pain and therefore can tolerate pain longer than those who do not engage in self-injury. Researchers have documented this finding as having a lower sensitivity to pain (Bohus et al., 2000, Kemperman et al., 1997, and Rouss et al., 1999, as cited in Nock, 2010).

In addition to experiencing little or no pain, paradoxically, individuals who engage in self-injury often describe experiencing a sense of calmness afterward (Miller & Pariseau, 2013). Research has suggested that this calmness is due to a release of endogenous opiates (endorphins) into the bloodstream subsequent to bodily injury. Endogenous opiates lessen the experience of pain—hence the lower pain sensitivity previously described—and can also induce a feeling of euphoria (Van Ree et al., 2000, as cited in Nock, 2010). Researchers have described the overall effect as analgesic and therefore "adaptive from an evolutionary perspective, as it allows an organism to continue to function following injury" (Nock, 2010, p. 355), which may explain why some continue to engage in self-harm despite the initial pain of injury.

Having a high threshold for pain and experiencing euphoria or calmness after pain are both associated with having elevated levels of endogenous opiates in the body (Nock, 2010). It is suggested that some individuals are predisposed to have higher bodily levels of endorphins. It is also suggested that repeated self-injury contributes to higher baseline levels of endorphins. Both situations lead to lower pain sensitivity and a reinforced desire to engage in self-harm to gain the benefit of increased feelings of calmness (Nock, 2010). Some researchers believe that individuals engaging in self-injury have significantly low opioid effect, and thus the act of self-injury is self-medicating, as it brings forth a more normative level (Miller & Pariseau, 2013).

INEFFECTIVE COPING THROUGH SELF-INJURY

For some individuals, nonsuicidal self-injury likely serves several functions simultaneously; thus, self-injurers may return to the behavior in times of distress because it is effective in attaining interpersonal resources or avoiding painful emotions and interpersonal demands (Muehlenkamp, Brausch, Quigley, & Whitlock, 2013). However, the continued utilization of self-injury as a means of coping with stress can inhibit the formation of healthier, proactive coping skills. As discussed previously, individuals who self-injure often lack sufficient awareness and understanding of their emotions and struggle with expressing these feelings. Studies have also found that self-injurers have more social skill deficits and poorer social problem-solving abilities than their noninjuring peers, which may contribute to a lack of meaningful social relationships and fewer people from whom to seek emotional support (Claes et al., 2010, and Nock & Mendes, 2008, as cited in Muehlenkamp et al., 2013). Interpersonal relationships may also suffer when individuals use self-injury to present themselves as being calmer or less emotional than they feel or when they escalate the behavior to achieve the desired social support or response. This creates a split between the private and public self, with neither being completely genuine, which may lead to deep interpersonal isolation from "living a lie" or even provoke hostile responses to self-injuring behavior (Barton-Breck & Heyman, 2012).

Research shows that those who report NSSI are more likely to cope through avoidance behaviors; exhibit poor problem-solving ability and greater emotional suppression (avoiding showing emotions); and have poor cognitive reappraisal (difficulty changing how one thinks about stressful situations in order to reduce distress) (Gross & John, 2003, as cited in Andrews, Martin, Hasking, & Page, 2013). If individuals have a limited repertoire of coping skills and perceive self-harm to be part of their identity, they may be more likely to resort to self-injury in stressful situations, because they identify self-harm as their primary coping strategy rather than other mechanisms for stress relief (Nock, 2008, and Nock & Banaji, 2007, as cited in Muehlenkamp et al., 2013). In this way, self-harm may become a passive response to stress that leads to brooding rumination and repetitious focus on negative feelings and experiences, or avoidance of interpersonal issues that could be resolved through effective communication, which contributes to a vicious cycle of despair (O'Connor, Rasmussen, & Hawton, 2012).

Although aversive feelings may temporarily be relieved through self-injury, self-conscious emotions such as guilt, shame, and disgust may increase significantly following the behavior. Overall, self-injurers report feeling more emotionally distressed, having lower self-esteem, increased antisocial behavior, and difficulty controlling anger (Laye-Gindhu & Schonert-Reichl, 2005; Butler & Malone, 2013). If self-injury behavior continues, it is also likely to become more serious, with more lethal and varied means of injury, and occur more frequently, while making little change in the injurer's learning how to cope actively with stressful situations or difficult emotions (Andrews et al., 2013).

Self-injury can cause distress not only to the individual engaging in the behavior, but also to his or her loved ones, and may cause severe physical damage to the body or even lead to death (Klonsky, 2007). This can be especially difficult for friends and family of persons who self-injure, as they may be secretive and resistant to seeking help while also being at increased risk for suicide, particularly if they engage in self-injury more frequently, for prolonged periods of time, and use multiple methods (Duggan, Heath, Lewis, & Baxter, 2012). Even without such escalation, continued use of self-injury as a coping mechanism is likely to leave individuals feeling worn out by the ongoing emotional issues that were not dealt with initially (Barton-Breck & Heyman, 2012).

CONCLUSION

Research done as a result of a dramatic increase in NSSI over the past several decades has provided more insight into this complicated, maladaptive coping behavior, including biological, psychological, and environmental contributing factors. Self-injury behaviors are seen in all age groups and races in response to a variety of stressors. Though NSSI may alleviate distress in the short term, for various reasons, it is ineffective in the long term, as it prevents the individual from learning how to cope with inevitable future stressors in a nondestructive and proactive manner.

REFERENCES AND FURTHER READING

American Psychiatric Association. (2000). *Diagnostic and statistical manual of mental disorders, fourth edition-text revision*. Washington, DC: Author.

Andrews, T., Martin, G., Hasking, P., & Page, A. (2013). Predictors of continuation and cessation of nonsuicidal self-injury. *Journal of Adolescent Health, 53*, 40–46.

Barton-Breck, A., & Heyman, B. (2012). Accentuate the positive, eliminate the negative? The variable value dynamics of non-suicidal self-hurting. *Health, Risk, and Society, 14*(5), 445–464.

Breen, A. V., Lewis, S. P., & Sutherland, O. (2013). Brief report: Non-suicidal self-injury in the context of self and identity development. *Journal of Adult Development, 20,* 57–62.

Butler, A. M., & Malone, K. (2013). Attempted suicide v. non-suicidal self-injury: Behavior, syndrome, or diagnosis? *British Journal of Psychiatry, 202,* 324–325.

Duggan, J. M., Heath, N. L., Lewis, S. P., & Baxter, A. L. (2012). An examination of the scope and nature of non-suicidal self-injury online activities: Implications for school mental health professionals. *School Mental Health, 4,* 56–67.

Gilbert, P., McEwan, K., Irons, C., Bhundia, R., Christie, R., Broomhead, C., & Rockliff, H. (2010). Self-harm in a mixed clinical population: The roles of self-criticism, shame, and social rank. *British Journal of Clinical Psychology, 49,* 563–576.

Hawton, K., Harriss, L., & Rodham, K. (2010). How adolescents who cut themselves differ from those who take overdoses. *European Child and Adolescent Psychiatry, 19,* 513–523.

Hawton, K., Saunders, K. E. A., & O'Connor, R. C. (2012). Self-harm and suicide in adolescents. *Lancet, 379,* 2373–2382.

Hay, C., & Meldrum, R. (2010). Bullying victimization and adolescent self-harm: Testing hypotheses from general strain theory. *Journal of Youth Adolescence, 39,* 446–459.

Horne, O., & Csipke, E. (2009). From feeling too little and too much, to feeling more and less? A nonparadoxical theory of the functions of self-harm. *Qualitative Health Research, 19,* 655–667.

Hudson, J. L., Dodd, H. F., & Bovopoulos, N. (2011). Temperament, family environment, and anxiety in preschool children. *Journal of Abnormal Child Psychology, 39,* 939–951.

Johnson, S. (2014, February 11). Teens feeling stressed, and many not managing it well. *USA Today.* Retrieved from http://www.usatoday.com/story/news/nation/2014/02/11/stress-teens-psychological/5266739/.

Klonsky, E. D. (2007). The functions of deliberate self-injury: A review of the evidence. *Clinical Psychology Review, 27,* 226–239.

Klonsky, E. D. (2011). Non-suicidal self-injury in United States adults: Prevalence, sociodemographics, topography and functions. *Psychological Medicine, 41,* 1981–1986.

Klonsky, E. D.. & Muehlenkamp, J. J. (2007). Self-injury: A research review for the practitioner. *Journal of Clinical Psychology: In Session, 63*(11), 1045–1056.

Laye-Gindhu, A., & Schonert-Reichl, K. (2005). Nonsuicidal self-harm among community adolescents: Understanding the "whats" and "whys" of self-harm. *Journal of Youth and Adolescence, 34*(5), 447–457.

Miller, C., & Pariseau, C. (2013). Deliberate self-harm in adolescents. In W. T. O'Donohue, L. T. Benuto, & L. Woodward Tolle (Eds.), *Handbook of adolescent health psychology* (pp. 481–493). New York, NY: Springer Science+Business Media.

Millon, T., Millon, C., Meagher, S., Grossman, S., & Ramnath, R. (2004). *Personality disorders in modern life* (2nd ed.). New York, NY: John Wiley & Sons.

Muehlenkamp, J. J., Brausch, A., Quigley, K., & Whitlock, J. (2013). Interpersonal features and functions of nonsuicidal self-injury. *Suicide and Life-Threatening Behavior, 43*(1), 67–80.

Muehlenkamp, J. J., Kerr, P. L., Bradley, A. R., & Larsen, M. A. (2010). Abuse subtypes and nonsuicidal self-injury: Preliminary evidence of complex emotion regulation patterns. *Journal of Nervous and Mental Disease, 198*(4), 258–263.

Nock, M. K. (2010). Self-injury. *Annual Review of Clinical Psychology, 6,* 339–363.

O'Connor, R. C., Rasmussen, S., & Hawton, K. (2012). Distinguishing adolescents who think about self-harm from those who engage in self-harm. *British Journal of Psychiatry, 200*(4), 330–335.

41

SUICIDE

Serena Wadhwa

Suicide is an uncomfortable topic for many. An estimated 9.4 million adults have had "serious thoughts" about suicide, which is about 3.9 percent of adults in the United States (Substance Abuse and Mental Health Services Administration [SAMHSA], 2015). According to SAMHSA, statistically, this percentage has not changed significantly since 2010. Given the high rate of adults who have seriously considered killing themselves (this figure does not include numbers for adolescents and children), thoughts and completed acts of suicide may, to some degree, be viewed as a maladaptive means of coping with one's life circumstances. As previous chapters discussed, stress experiences in the past or constant stressors can distort one's ability to cope with additional and present stressors. Physiological, psychological, environmental, and social stressors, among others, are all components that potentially factor into the result of thoughts and behaviors centering around ending one's life on one's own terms. This chapter explores the notion of suicide as a coping mechanism in response to stress. Although there are certainly many factors, considerations, and influences in suicide, much of that topic is beyond the scope of this chapter, which specifically examines the influence of stress on the thoughts, planning, and completed action of suicide.

DEFINITION

What is meant by the terms *suicide, suicide attempt,* and *suicidal ideation?* According to the Centers for Disease Control and Prevention (CDC), *suicide* is "death caused by self-directed injurious behavior with an intent to die as a result of the behavior." A *suicide attempt* is a "non-fatal, self-directed, potentially injurious behavior with an intent to die as a result of the behavior; might not result in injury." Lastly, *suicidal ideation*, according to the CDC, is "thinking about, considering, or planning suicide" (CDC, 2015a).

According to the American Foundation for Suicide Prevention, and based on 2014 statistics collected by the CDC, suicide is the 10th leading cause of death in the United States. For every completed suicide, an estimated 25 attempts occur. Annually, the financial costs of suicide are estimated at $44 billion. Daily, there is an average of 117 completed suicides (American Foundation for Suicide Prevention, 2016).

Suicide is a serious public health problem, and it usually occurs when people feel that they cannot cope with certain stressors and that only death can end their suffering. The major factors in suicide include serious depression or other mental illness(es); alcohol or drug abuse; physical illness that already negatively affects quality of life, especially with pain or lack of mobility; history of suicides in family (often linked to clinical depression); and feeling alone and isolated. Certain societal conditions may trigger more serious stress and thoughts of suicide. Modern society is fraught with constant changes. As technology, the economy, educational opportunities, and the population, as well as other factors, change and grow, the adaptability required may challenge many people. Additionally, as they try to adapt, adjust to, and accommodate these changes to continue to function within the modern culture, some people may find themselves cut off from traditional means of effective coping (for example, social support). Adaptation to change may require separation from routine and familiar means of support, coping, and rituals. As explored in previous chapters, this can become a source of stress for an individual, particularly if other coping mechanisms are not in place. For example, when an economic recession occurs, and the stress from loss of multiple financial buffers is overwhelming, some people may consider suicide as a means of coping (see Willis, Coombs, Cockerham, & Frison, 2002).

MISCONCEPTIONS ABOUT SUICIDE

Society as a whole has an interest in preventing suicide. It is important to understand that in order to decrease the use of suicide as the ultimate coping mechanism, it is necessary to understand an individual's contextual factors prompting this drastic consideration. However, what may be most important in curbing the presence and use of this maladaptive coping mechanism is validating its existence and circumstances.

There are several myths related to suicide that, paradoxically, prevent individuals from being forthcoming about their thoughts. These are presented here only briefly, and readers are encouraged to refer to the cited references for further elaboration and information. Among these misconceptions are the following (Caruso, n.d.):

1. Myth: Suicide occurs without warning. Reality: Not true; frequently there are warning signs, such as withdrawal from friends and family, increased abuse of alcohol or drugs, and/or changes in behavior and personality.
2. Myth: People who talk about suicide are only seeking attention. Reality: Not true; they are looking for help with their problems. They need help and should get it.
3. Myth: People who attempt suicide are weak. Reality: Not true; they usually have a mental illness, but are no more mentally or emotionally weak than other people who have other kinds of illnesses. In particular, they most often suffer from serious clinical depression, caused by chemical imbalances in the brain.
4. Myth: People who are suicidal want to die. Reality: Not always true; most simply want to stop their pain.
5. Myth: People who want to commit suicide are crazy. Reality: Not true; again, most suicidal people simply want to stop their pain. Although they may have the mental illness of serious clinical depression (or another disorder), they are not always disconnected from reality, as is someone who has a psychosis. They may also be traumatized, suffering from extreme grief or from physical pain for which there is no cure, and feel completely without hope.

These are some of the many myths about suicide. Society as a whole must recognize that these are misinformed, untrue beliefs about the process and the action of intended death at one's own hand. There are warning signs: People who talk about suicide are seeking help and are usually in what is known as "psychache." Individuals who are thinking about, planning, or attempt suicide do not always want to die; rather, they seek relief from emotional pain, physical pain, or both. Suicide may seem like the only option when someone feels hopeless, helpless, and worthless (Rivers & Noret, 2013; Hall, Platt, & Hall, 1999). Suicide itself is not a mental illness; rather, it is a consequential behavior of many factors (life circumstances, the environment, dispositions, present untreated mental health issues, use of substances, age, demographics, etc.). Research supports the identification of clinical depression as a predictable factor in suicidal behavior (Gomez, Miranda, & Polanco, 2011); these authors also cite review literature demonstrating the association of acculturative stress with clinical depression and suicidal behaviors emerging in adolescence and later adulthood.

Chiles and Strosahl (2008) explore the validation of pain as an important strategy for anyone experiencing suicidal thoughts. Having someone to talk with about the pain of depression (especially a trained, experienced therapist or counselor), and to explore the ambivalence relating to suicidal thoughts and intentions, can help an individual understand the role played by this behavior. Counseling and/or other therapy may assist these individuals to realize that suicidal thoughts and behaviors are an attempt to alleviate fear, desperation, and pain where it seems like there is "no way out." This view of suicidal thoughts provides a context in which to raise other options that may not be so clear.

As previous chapters explored, chronic stress produces a cascade of detrimental consequences, including limiting one's ability to deal with the stress. Some research also reveals that chronic stress changes an individual physiologically in ways that may contribute to suicidality. For example, enlarged adrenal cortices were seen in individuals who completed suicide (as cited in Feskanich et al., 2002). However, survival seeking is controlled by the "reptilian" part of the human brain (so called because it is the part most similar to the brain in reptiles, and has not changed much despite millions of years of evolution). A suicidal individual's prefrontal cortex (which is responsible for critical thinking, decision making, evaluation, execution, etc.) must override this more primitive instinct with conscious and deliberate intention.

In another study, early stressors in an individual's life were found to contribute to modified neurobiological development that made the person more vulnerable to suicide as a behavior (Mann & Currier, 2010). These authors also reported that production of serotonin, a "feel-good" neurotransmitter, tends to be lower in those contemplating or committing suicide, independent of clinical disorders. The process might work like this: An individual facing many stressors is overwhelmed by the depth and breadth of those stressors. The stress response still offers only the choice of fight or flight to this person, who has already proven unable to do either, so that individual may see suicide as the only way to eliminate the pain, or to "survive" it, as no other options appear to exist. In a sense, suicide is the ultimate expression of flight. Zhang, Wang, Xia, Liu, and Jung (2012) cite research demonstrating that individuals with deficient coping, including poor problem-solving skills, are more at risk of suicidal ideation and behavior. Part of the challenge is for doctors, therapists, and counselors to assist these individuals in developing other options. Support networks, crisis hotlines, and support groups can also help. Although there are many theories and perspectives and much research on the risk factors, protective factors, and triggers of suicidal thoughts and actions, discussion of these areas is beyond the scope of this chapter.

WHAT DO YOU DO?

The stress and pain experienced by some people may be in response to any number of stressors: whether deeply personal, caused by loss of loved ones or physical illness, and/or exacerbated by an uncertain economy, loss of job, or safety and security issues related to crime, war, and terrorism. Whatever their origin, this stress and pain demand to be validated. However, the suffering individual's stress reaction restricts his or her ability to see potential options for relief and hope. What does a person who is having suicidal thoughts or plans do? Most of the literature written by those who have studied suicide suggests that talking with someone about what's going on is the key first step for such a person. The literature on suicide suggests first recognizing and acknowledging that such thoughts and intentions of

AFTER SOMEONE COMMITS SUICIDE: POSTVENTION FOR SURVIVORS

Suicide is the 10th leading cause of death and the second most common cause of death for 15- to 24-year-olds (Centers for Disease Control and Prevention, 2015b). *Postvention* (*post* meaning "after") is the term for activities and interventions taken after a completed suicide (Callahan, 1996). According to Leenaars and Wenckstern (1998), postvention can be done for any trauma, as its focus is those who survived the occurrence of the trauma. In the past, when someone completed a suicide, the typical response was not to talk about it. However, according to Shneidman (1981), postvention guidelines suggest beginning intervention efforts within 24 hours after the event. Some individuals may be resistant to talking about a suicide, but many others may welcome the opportunity to have someone listen to them. Other considerations for postvention include recognizing that timing is important in exploring emotions (particularly negative ones); monitoring any declines in behavior/health; being realistic; providing prevention, intervention, and postvention health care; and recognizing that healing takes time. Leenaars and Wenckstern (1998) go into more detail about each of these factors, and discuss variations that will influence the manifestation of these factors, which Shneidman originally developed. According to King (1999), effective postvention activities in a school setting spread the responsibility to all the professionals involved and provide a means to prevent a cluster tragedy (in which more than one student commits suicide) from occurring.

troubled people may be a normal reaction to intense stress. Those who have thoughts of suicide must find someone they can work with to validate the emotions they are having and work with them in uncovering options. The following resource section lists some numbers to call for help.

RESOURCES

For Telephone Counseling with Free and Confidential Information

National Suicide Prevention Lifeline: 1-800-273-8255
Or, 1-800-273-TALK
Also a chat service: http://www.suicidepreventionlifeline.org/GetHelp/LifelineChat.aspx
www.suicidepreventionlifeline.org

Organizations with Helpful Information

American Foundation for Suicide Prevention: http://afsp.org/
International Association for Suicide Prevention (IASP): http://www.iasp.info/resources/Crisis_Centres
Suicide Prevention Resource Center: http://www.sprc.org/

REFERENCES AND FURTHER READING

American Foundation for Suicide Prevention. (2016). Suicide statistics. Retrieved from http://afsp.org/about-suicide/suicide-statistics.

Callahan, J. (1996). Negative effects of a school suicide postvention program—a case example. *Crisis, 17*(3), 108–115.

Caruso, K. (n.d.). Suicide myths. Retrieved from http://www.suicide.org/suicide-myths.html

Centers for Disease Control and Prevention (CDC). (2015a). Definitions: Self-directed violence. Retrieved from http://www.cdc.gov/violenceprevention/suicide/definitions.html.

Centers for Disease Control and Prevention (CDC). (2015b). Suicide facts at a glance: 2015. Retrieved from http://www.cdc.gov/violenceprevention/pdf/suicide-datasheet-a.pdf.

Chiles, J. A., & Strosahl, K. D. (2008). *Clinical manual for assessment and treatment of suicidal patients.* Washington, DC: American Psychiatric Publishing.

Feskanich, D., Hastrup, J. L., Marshall, J. R., Colditz, G. A., Stampfer, M. J., Willett, W. C., & Kawachi, I. (2002). Stress and suicide in the Nurses' Health Study. *Journal of Epidemiology and Community Health, 56*(2), 95–98.

Gomez, J., Miranda, R., & Polanco, L. (2011). Acculturative stress, perceived discrimination, and vulnerability to suicide attempts among emerging adults. *Journal of Youth and Adolescence, 40*(11), 1465–1476.

Hall, R. C., Platt, D. E., & Hall, R. C. (1999). Suicide risk assessment: A review of risk factors for suicide in 100 patients who made severe suicide attempts—evaluation of suicide risk in a time of managed care. *Psychosomatics, 40*(1), 18–27.

King, K. A. (1999). High school suicide postvention: Recommendations for an effective program. *American Journal of Health Studies, 15*(4), 217.

Leenaars, A. A., & Wenckstern, S. (1998). Principles of postvention: Applications to suicide and trauma in schools. *Death Studies, 22*(4), 357–391.

Mann, J. J., & Currier, D. M. (2010). Stress, genetics and epigenetic effects on the neurobiology of suicidal behavior and depression. *European Psychiatry, 25*(5), 268–271.

Rivers, I., & Noret, N. (2013). Potential suicide ideation and its association with observing bullying at school. *Journal of Adolescent Health, 53*(1), S32–S36.

Shallcross, L. (2010). Confronting the threat of suicide. *Counseling Today.* Retrieved from http://ct.counseling.org/2010/07/confronting-the-threat-of-suicide.

Shneidman, E. S. (1981). Postvention: The care of the bereaved. *Suicide and Life-Threatening Behavior, 11*(4), 349–359.

Substance Abuse and Mental Health Services Administration (SAMHSA). (2015). *Behavioral health barometer: United States, 2015* (HHS Publication No. SMA-16-Baro-2015). Rockville, MD: Author.

Willis, L. A., Coombs, D. W., Cockerham, W. C., & Frison, S. L. (2002). Ready to die: A postmodern interpretation of the increase of African-American adolescent male suicide. *Social Science and Medicine, 55*(6), 907–920.

Zhang, X., Wang, H., Xia, Y., Liu, X., & Jung, E. (2012). Stress, coping and suicide ideation in Chinese college students. *Journal of Adolescence, 35*(3), 683–690.

42

Stress and Violence

Kira Weidner

Research reveals a well-established relationship between anger and stress, showing that people who express high levels of anger also report high levels of stress. When examining the emotion of anger, it is important to distinguish between the experience of anger, the expression of anger, and one's control over that expression. Anger in itself is a common occurrence; however, it is the expression of anger through violent behavior that is most often the target of research efforts. Anger expression takes many forms, including aggressive or abusive language, threats of violence, physical and sexual abuse, and torture and murder. Violence also takes different forms, with people engaging in impulsive violence or instrumental violence. *Impulsive violence* refers to violence as a reaction to situations that are fear-inducing or perceived as threatening or dangerous; this is in contrast to *instrumental violence,* which refers to planned violence usually not engaged in as a reaction to intense or immediate emotion.

Despite research on the link between anger and stress, the field of psychology has historically struggled to describe the nature of this relationship. The *Diagnostic and Statistical Manual of Mental Disorders, Fifth Edition* (*DSM-5;* American Psychiatric Association, 2013) classifies posttraumatic stress disorder (PTSD) separately from other stress disorders. Similarly, diagnoses identifying violent behavior as a primary diagnostic concern are classified separately from stress. Yet, in the study of violence, stress and posttraumatic stress appear less distinct and more interrelated. For example, research suggests that traumatized individuals develop an array of additional mental health problems and struggle more than nontraumatized individuals to develop healthy coping skills in response to life stressors. There is a relationship between the traumatic experiences and stress; for some people this relationship manifests as impulsivity in anger expression and aggressive behavior. Because many traumatized individuals struggle to develop effective tools for identifying and tolerating distress, this inability can make them more likely to express anger in response to stressful situations: as a reaction to a perceived threat and because of a reduced capacity to tolerate distress and control behavior. In this context, this chapter examines impulsive violence in relation to stress, recognizing the contributions of posttraumatic stress and trauma in the development of maladaptive coping skills.

FROM VICTIM TO PERPETRATOR: LEARNING VIOLENCE AS A TOOL FOR COPING

Early research on social learning theory found that children who witness violence learn to behave violently. Subsequent research examining the relationship between victimization and perpetration of violence has generally supported this theory. Specifically, a growing body of evidence suggests there are long-term consequences to experiencing violence, which include externalizing behavior such as aggression, delinquency, and hyperactivity, and perpetrating violence against others. Research suggests that being a victim of violence is not the only predictor of violent behavior: witnessing violence as a child also predicts violent behavior.

Exposure to, or experience of, trauma does not cause violence; however, research shows that certain types of trauma exposure in childhood do predict certain types of violent behavior. Some research suggests that chaotic and violent childhood and community experiences increase violent and aggressive behavior in both children and adults. Similarly, some research with male sexual offenders found higher rates of childhood sexual abuse in male sexual abusers than in nonsexual abusers, but did not find higher rates of childhood physical abuse in male sexual abusers. Given that individuals exposed to violence may be more likely to learn to act violently, the finding that traumatized individuals may struggle more than nontraumatized individuals to cope with stress may indicate that they are more vulnerable to acting on their anger when they experience added stress. The distinction between impulsive and instrumental violence is important because it separates those who act out in response to stress from those who act out to cause deliberate harm. Consistent with the idea that some types of violence are associated with PTSD and some are not, one study on intimate partner violence found that men with PTSD reported less intimate partner violence than men without a diagnosis of PTSD, suggesting that violence in intimate relationships may be more instrumental than impulsive.

Traumatized individuals often demonstrate difficulty with identifying and expressing emotions, as well as tolerating distress. Among survivors of childhood trauma, two patterns of distress tolerance emerge developmentally: rigid overcontrol of behavior and undercontrolled behavior. It is the trauma survivors with an undercontrolled pattern of behavior who are particularly vulnerable to impulsive anger expression. This area of research supports the notion that traumatic stress contributes to the development of a reduced capacity for distress tolerance, thereby making vulnerable individuals less likely to cope well with stress and more likely to respond impulsively to anger-inducing situations.

MALADAPTIVE COPING AND VIOLENT BEHAVIOR

Although it is important to understand the life experiences, such as trauma, that cause or encourage the development of poor coping skills, a considerable amount of research focuses on how those poor coping skills (as well as other characteristics) make people more or less likely to respond to stressful life situations with anger or violence. Similarly, this area of research also examines the characteristics that help people cope with stressors so they can control anger effectively.

CONFLICT RESOLUTION

Conflict occurs both intrapersonally and interpersonally. Conflict that occurs within oneself can be a battle between two desired goals, immediate needs and long-term wants, or a host of other negotiations. Interpersonally, conflict arises when goals, expectations, desires, wants, needs, and so forth are different from those of another individual or organization with which the person is having some communication or relationship (for example, in a marriage). According to Mischel, DeSmet, and Kross (2006), when trying to resolve interpersonal conflict, stress management plays a role. Stress influences the ability to stay in control, to develop options regarding the conflict, and to maintain one's emotions. People can learn about conflict resolution through observation, role plays, or direct experience. Depending on the issue, a professional coach or therapist may be able to assist in the skill development aspect of conflict resolution. The concept of *conflict resolution,* according to Afzalur Rahim (2002, p. 208), "implies reduction, elimination, or termination of conflict." As noted in several chapters in this book, effectively resolving or coping with a conflict is one way to reduce the effects of the conflict itself. Conflict resolution is a problem-solving approach and may often require people with certain skills to assist in mediation of the conflict (Deutsch, 1994). There are several interventions that use these various skills to provide resolution of conflicts.

—*Serena Wadhwa*

Distress tolerance refers to a person's capacity to cope, both with difficult situations and with any resulting negative emotions. Thus, distress tolerance requires the development of adaptive coping skills in response to stressful situations. This includes managing impulses such as anger without having to act on them. Specifically, people with low levels of distress tolerance are sensitive to stress and have poor coping skills to manage that stress, and thus display higher rates of anger expression than those with higher distress tolerance (Hawkins, Macatee, Guthrie, & Cougle, 2013). The ability to tolerate distress and control impulses appears to be a key factor differentiating those who feel angry from those who act on their anger. This points to a need for people who struggle with expressing their anger, in response to distressing events and emotions, to learn effective tools to improve their ability to cope.

The experience of anger can range from irritation to rage. Depending on a person's ability to tolerate distress, an event that might be mildly irritating to a person with high distress tolerance might lead to rage and violence in a person with low distress tolerance. In general, people with low distress tolerance experience negative emotions more easily and act on those negative emotions with more maladaptive coping. In the case of anger, people with low distress tolerance who become angry quickly tend to express that anger and feel out of control when doing so.

Anger is a common emotion, yet there are clear differences between people who feel angry but let go of that anger quickly, and those who become angry and act on that anger immediately. This difference in anger is referred to as state versus trait anger. All people have the capacity to become angry; they are likely to experience *state anger,* which will come and go, though more quickly for some than others. Those with high levels of *trait anger* frequently become angry and are prone to expressing that anger. For people with trait anger, the expression of that anger through violence may feel like the only way to calm themselves down and get rid of the anger. Once they feel angry, they have serious difficulty calming themselves without acting on that anger. They may be at risk of harming others verbally or physically because they cannot control their anger. In a study of parents with grade-school-age children, high trait anger was found to be associated with expression of anger. In another study, college students with low distress tolerance and high trait anger were found to experience difficulty controlling their anger, even if they did not act on it (Tafrate, Kassinove, & Dundin, 2002). These authors found that although low distress tolerance and high trait anger co-occur, this co-occurrence does not appear to predict anger expression through violence in college students. Were this study to be replicated with a sample of offenders who are more likely than college students to have expressed anger through violence rather than only verbal hostility, the relationship between low distress tolerance and high trait anger might predict higher rates of violence or suggest additional factors that lead people to act violently. There may well be other factors contributing to violence in addition to high trait anger and low distress tolerance.

People who experience and express anger easily also report that their anger is associated with high levels of stress, and they may feel that the stress is to their detriment, as they often suffer psychological, interpersonal, legal, and financial consequences as a result of their angry or violent behavior. Some of the most common and most-studied types of violence occur within families, and abusers in these instances are often under significant stress. High stress among parents has been associated with higher rates of abusive parenting; and for parents with high trait anger, stress may make them uniquely vulnerable to anger expression, increasing the risk that they may be violent with family members. Further, parents with high levels of stress who tend to express their anger through overreactive discipline and physical aggression were found to have an externalized locus of control; that is, they felt that factors outside themselves controlled their behavior. These parents often feel they have no control, and this is demonstrated in both their lack of control over their feelings and their physical expression of anger. Overall, this evidence indicates that stress is a major factor contributing to maladaptive anger expression, especially in those with low distress tolerance, high trait anger, and externalized locus of control.

REDUCING MALADAPTIVE ANGER AND VIOLENCE

Witnessing and experiencing violence are associated with the development of maladaptive coping and PTSD symptoms, including the expression of anger through aggressive behavior and violence. Further, the evidence regarding the relationship between stress and anger suggests that there is a serious need for interventions to aid in the development of adaptive coping for anger and stress, to prevent victimizing future generations and teaching that violence is an acceptable form of coping with anger.

Fortunately, a number of methods and programs are available to aid in the development of adaptive and healthy ways to cope with both anger and stress. First, for individuals with trait anger, learning to cope more effectively with stress may help reduce the need to act on anger. Further, anger management programs exist in many communities to help teach people skills to identify experiences and emotions that lead to anger; teach skills for coping with anger once it is identified; and help people learn how their anger and violence may cause further stress in their lives.

Although many forms of violence can be prevented, once violence has occurred there are frequently legal repercussions. Despite legally mandated anger management treatment, few individuals successfully complete mandatory anger management or battering prevention programs, and no treatment models are known to be more effective than others. Despite the fact that research is unclear about the types of treatment that work for anger and violence, it appears that personal and individual factors better predict success in reducing violent behavior. One factor predicting success in treatment is readiness for treatment, which refers to a person's desire to make serious behavior change. For example, there is some evidence that intimate partner violence offenders who willingly acknowledge the impact of their behavior on their victims are more likely to participate in treatment and have some success than those who deny that their behavior caused harm. However, no such evidence exists for sexual offenders; research actually demonstrates that neither psychological distress nor denial of sexual violence is associated with sexual or violent recidivism.

Victim safety is a serious concern, as victims are often revictimized, and it appears that many of the psychological and behavioral symptoms that result from the original victimization may increase their vulnerability to revictimization. Thus, it is important that individuals who struggle with anger continue to seek treatment for coping with anger and stress, just as it is important for researchers to continue to identify factors and means to improve treatment success.

CONCLUSION

In general, research clearly shows that there are multiple factors in predicting anger, violence, and maladaptive coping. Given the relationship between stress and anger, it would seem that people who have both low distress tolerance and high trait anger should also be at increased risk of acting out violently because of their anger. Despite the fact that people who act on their anger with violence often report being under high levels of stress, stress alone does not appear to predict violence. This is likely because those who act violently often fall within one of two categories: those who act impulsively with anger in reaction to a highly distressing event, and those who premeditate their violence with relatively little emotion involved. Thus, the research on stress and violence likely highlights the stress and anger of those who act impulsively in response to emotion, not those who premeditate violence.

Despite some evidence from social learning theory and trauma research which suggests that violence begets violence, people frequently live in dangerous and violent conditions and do not act violently, no matter how angry they may become. Yet, even when the impact of exposure to violence in contributing to violent behavior is considered, there still appear to be other mediating factors, besides stress and imitation, that lead some people to become angry and act violently when others do not. Because of the complex relationships among developmental factors, life experiences, and individual differences, it is difficult to explicitly state how stress causes violence. Rather, it is likely that stress contributes to violence, because no matter how much stress people are under, they still have a choice in their behavior.

It is important to note that individuals suffering from mental illness and trauma are rarely responsible for the types of heinous violence depicted by media, and that people without mental illness are more frequently responsible for acts of violence. Individuals with trauma and mental illness often exhibit under- or overcontrolled behavior; it is the subset of people with mental illness who also exhibit undercontrolled behavior who are most vulnerable to acting impulsively and aggressively on feelings of anger. Because a discussion of instrumental violence is beyond the scope of this chapter, readers may wish to study instrumental violence or psychopathy to better understand how violence can be detached from emotion in some individuals.

Finally, researchers and policy makers acknowledge that exposure to violence in and of itself does not cause a person to become violent. Rather, research suggests that exposure to violence can increase psychological vulnerability and make it difficult for people to cope effectively with stressors. Acknowledging that people are responsible for their own behavior, and facilitating their recognition of this fact, may improve treatment outcomes and help people identify the reasons they will benefit from stress and anger management. See also Chapter 43, on posttraumatic stress disorder.

REFERENCES AND FURTHER READING

Afzalur Rahim, M. (2002). Toward a theory of managing organizational conflict. *International Journal of Conflict Management, 13*(3), 206–235.

American Psychiatric Association. (2013). *Diagnostic and statistical manual of mental disorders* (5th ed.). Arlington, VA: American Psychiatric Publishing.

Anakwenze, U., & Zuberi, D. (2013). Mental health and poverty in the inner city. *Health and Social Work, 38*(3), 147–157. doi:10.1093/hsw/hlt013.

Anger management: Williams' 12 strategies for controlling aggression. (n.d.). *Mind Tools*. Retrieved from https://www.mindtools.com/pages/article/newTCS_97.htm.

Arslan, C. (2010). An investigation of anger and anger expression in terms of coping with stress and interpersonal problem-solving. *Educational Sciences: Theory and Practice, 10*(1), 25–43.

Babcock, J. C., Green, C. E., & Robie, C. (2004). Does batterers' treatment work? A meta-analytic review of domestic violence treatment. *Clinical Psychology Review, 23*, 1023–1053.

Bandura, A. (1977). *Social learning theory*. New York, NY: General Learning Press. Retrieved from http://www.jku.at/org/content/e54521/e54528/e54529/e178059/Bandura_SocialLearningTheory_ger.pdf.

Bandura, A. (1978). Social learning theory of aggression. *Journal of Communication, 28*(3), 12–29. doi:10.1111/j.1460-2466.1978.tb01621.x.

Chan, Y. C. (1994). Parenting stress and social support in mothers who abuse their children in Hong Kong. *Child Abuse and Neglect, 18,* 261–269.

Cook, A., Spinazzola, J., Ford, J., Lanktree, C., Blaustein, M., Cloitre, M., . . . van der Kolk, B. (2005). Complex trauma in children and adolescents. *Psychiatric Annals, 35*(5), 390–398.

Deutsch, M. (1994). Constructive conflict resolution: Principles, training, and research. *Journal of Social Issues, 50*(1), 13–32.

Diong, S. M., & Bishop, G. D. (1999). Anger expression, coping styles, and well-being. *Journal of Health Psychology, 4,* 81–96.

Diong, S. M., Bishop, G. D., Enkelmann, H. C., Tong, E. M. W., Why, Y. P., Ang, J. C. H., & Khader, M. (2005). Anger, stress, coping, social support and health: Modelling the relationships. *Psychology and Health, 20*(4), 467–495.

Greeson, J. P., Briggs, E. C., Layne, C. M., Belcher, H. E., Ostrowski, S. A., Kim, S., . . . Fairbank, J. A. (2014). Traumatic childhood experiences in the 21st century: Broadening and building on the ACE studies with data from the National Child Traumatic Stress Network. *Journal of Interpersonal Violence, 29*(3), 536–556. doi:10.1177/08862 60513505217.

Hanson, K. R., & Morton-Bourgon, K. E. (2005). The characteristics of persistent sexual offenders: A meta-analysis of recidivism studies. *Journal of Consulting and Clinical Psychology, 73*(6), 1154–1163. doi:10.1037/0022-006X.73.6.1154.

Hawkins, K., Macatee, R. J., Guthrie, W., & Cougle, J. R. (2013). Concurrent and prospective relations between distress tolerance, life stressors, and anger. *Cognitive Therapy and Research, 37,* 434–445. doi:10.1007/s10608-012-9487-y.

How to control your anger. (2016). *NHS Choices.* Retrieved from http://www.nhs.uk /Conditions/stress-anxiety-depression/Pages/controlling-anger.aspx.

Hoyt, T., Wray, A. M., Wiggins, K. T., Gerstle, M., & Maclean, P. C. (2012). Personality profiles of intimate partner violence offenders with and without PTSD. *Journal of Offender Rehabilitation, 51*(4), 239–256. doi:10.1080/10509674.2011.650349.

Jespersen, A. F., Lalumière, M. L., & Seto, M. C. (2009). Sexual abuse history among adult sex offenders and non-sex offenders: A meta-analysis. *Child Abuse and Neglect, 33*(3), 179–192. doi:10.1016/j.chiabu.2008.07.004.

Lam, D. (1999). Parenting stress and anger: The Hong Kong experience. *Child and Family Social Work, 4*(4), 337–346. doi:10.1046/j.1365-2206.1999.00133.x.

Lila, M., Gracia, E., & Murgui, S. (2013). Psychological adjustment and victim-blaming among intimate partner violence offenders: The role of social support and stressful life events. *European Journal of Psychology Applied to Legal Context, 5*(2), 25–31. doi:10.5093/ejpalc2013a4.

Lila, M., Oliver, A., Galiana, L., & Gracia, E. (2013). Predicting success indicators of an intervention programme for convicted intimate-partner violence offenders: The Contexto programme. *European Journal of Psychology Applied to Legal Context, 5*(1), 73–95.

Liu, J. (2004). Childhood externalizing behavior: Theory and implications. *Journal of Child and Adolescent Psychiatric Nursing, 17*(3), 93–103.

Malinosky-Rummell, R., & Hansen, D. J. (1993). Long-term consequences of childhood physical abuse. *Psychological Bulletin, 114*(1), 68–79.

Mayo Clinic Staff. (2014). Anger management: 10 tips to tame your temper. Retrieved from http://www.mayoclinic.org/healthy-lifestyle/adult-health/in-depth/anger-management/art-20045434.

Mischel, W., DeSmet, A. L., & Kross, E. (2006). Self-regulation in the service of conflict resolution. In M. Deutsch, P. T. Coleman, & E. C. Marcus (Eds.), *The handbook of conflict resolution: Theory and practice* (pp. 294–314). San Francisco, CA: John Wiley & Sons.

Robinson, L., Smith, M., & Segal, R. (2016). How to reduce, prevent, and cope with stress. (2016). HelpGuide.org. Retrieved from http://www.helpguide.org/articles/stress/stress-management.htm.

Rodriguez, C. M., & Green, A. J. (1997). Parenting stress and anger expression as predictors of child abuse potential. *Child Abuse and Neglect, 21*(4), 367–377.

Rodriguez, C. M., & Richardson, M. J. (2007). Stress and anger as contextual factors and preexisting cognitive schemas: Predicting parental child maltreatment risk. *Child Maltreatment, 12*(4), 325–337.

Ruback, R., Clark, V. A., & Warner, C. (2014). Why are crime victims at risk of being victimized again? Substance use, depression, and offending as mediators of the victimization–revictimization link. *Journal of Interpersonal Violence, 29*(1), 157–185. doi:10.1177/0886260513504626.

Sayles-Cross, S. (1988). Profile of familial elder abuse: A selected review of the literature. *Journal of Community Health Nursing, 5*(4), 209–219.

Scarpa, A., & Raine, A. (2000). Violence associated with anger and impulsivity. In J. C. Borod (Ed.), *The neuropsychology of emotion* (pp. 320–339). New York, NY: Oxford University Press.

Scott, K. L., & Wolfe, D. A. (2003). Readiness to change as a predictor of outcome in batterer treatment. *Journal of Consulting and Clinical Psychology, 7*(5), 879–889. doi:10.1037/0022-006X.71.5.879.

Spielberger, C. (1999). *STAXI-2: State-trait anger expression inventory-2: Professional manual.* Odessa, FL: Psychological Assessment Resources.

Tafrate, R. C., Kassinove, H., & Dundin, L. (2002). Anger episodes in high- and low-trait anger community adults. *Journal of Clinical Psychology, 58*(12), 1573–1590.

Tweed, R. G., & Dutton, D. G. (1998). A comparison of impulsive and instrumental subgroups of batterers. *Violence and Victims, 13*, 217–230.

Webster-Stratton, C. (1988). Mothers' and fathers' perceptions of child deviance: Roles of parent and child behaviors and parent adjustment. *Journal of Consulting and Clinical Psychology, 56*, 909–915.

Youngstrom, E., Weist, M. D., & Albus, K. E. (2003). Exploring violence exposure, stress, protective factors and behavioral problems among inner-city youth. *American Journal of Community Psychology, 32*, 115–129.

43

Posttraumatic Stress Disorder

Amber N. Douglas

The view of traumatic stress reactions as clinical phenomena is deeply rooted within the history of psychology, psychiatry, and general observations of human behavior (Reyes, Elhai, & Ford, 2008). Perhaps the first description of a traumatic stress phenomenon was inscribed on clay tablets more than 5,000 years ago. Writings describing posttraumatic symptoms consistent with current diagnostic criteria can be found in various texts, including the Bible, ancient Greek plays, and Shakespeare's works. Despite these early writings, a formal definition of traumatic stress (disorder) was not articulated until the 18th century (Reyes, Elhai, & Ford, 2008). The constellation of experiences consistent with our current diagnosis of posttraumatic stress disorder (PTSD) was initially conceptualized by Breuer and Freud (1893/1955). Freud described it primarily as a disorder of memory, in that traumatic experiences become etched upon survivors' memories and cannot be forgotten, resulting in experiences of distress.

PTSD is a psychological disorder that may occur in a person of any age in response to a severe psychological stressor. Individuals with this syndrome exhibit a core set of symptoms characterized by the re-experiencing of the traumatic event, avoidance of memories of the traumatic event, and (hyper)arousal. Although both children and adults may experience PTSD, there are specific manifestations of symptoms that are distinct to children. According to the *Diagnostic and Statistical Manual of Mental Disorders, Fifth Edition* (DSM-5; American Psychiatric Association, 2013), diagnostic criteria for PTSD include:

> A history of exposure to a traumatic event that meets specific stipulations and symptoms from each of four symptom clusters: intrusion, avoidance, negative alterations in

> cognitions and mood, and alterations in arousal and reactivity. The sixth criterion concerns duration of symptoms; the seventh assesses functioning; and, the eighth criterion clarifies symptoms as not attributable to a substance or co-occurring medical condition.
>
> Two specifications are noted including delayed expression and a dissociative subtype of PTSD, the latter of which is new to DSM-5. In both specifications, the full diagnostic criteria for PTSD must be met for application to be warranted. (U.S. Department of Veterans Affairs, 2016)

As a diagnosis, PTSD is unique in that it requires an external event—a *traumatic stressor*—to meet the diagnostic criteria. It is estimated that almost 7 percent of American adults will experience PTSD at some point in their lives, with women being more than twice as likely as men to experience it (National Comorbidity Survey, 2005).

WHAT IS TRAUMA?

Trauma, as used in traumatic stress studies, is a broad concept that encompasses both physical and psychological experiences of extreme stress. Weathers and Keane (2008) observe that the term *trauma* is used to refer to (1) a stressor, (2) an individual appraisal of this stressor, and (3) an individual's response to the stressor. In part, the controversy surrounding PTSD and trauma itself is based on the accessibility of a broad definition. Interestingly, the current clinical diagnostic classification (criterion A) for PTSD is much narrower than what is commonly used. This criterion requires that a stressful event be or be perceived to be life-threatening and result in psychological experience of terror, horror, or helplessness. Some critiques of the *DSM-5* have suggested that the definition of trauma is too narrow and fails to encompass experiences of extreme stress that may not reach the threshold of fear for one's own life or the life of a loved one. Proponents of the criteria contend that the restrictions are necessary to reduce misuse of the diagnosis.

The *DSM-5* provides a list of potentially traumatic events that include war, kidnapping, torture, rape, domestic violence, child sexual abuse (without acknowledged fear of death), and terrorism. The inclusion of the term "potentially" acknowledges the high degree of individual variability in response to stressful events. In fact, far more people will experience extreme stress events and survive more or less intact than the small minority of those so exposed who will go on to experience PTSD. The factors that determine who eventually develops the syndrome are multifaceted.

ETIOLOGY OF PTSD

Etiology is the study of causation or origin of a disease. Several factors are related to the etiology and development of PTSD. Magnea and Lanius (2008) put these factors into three categories that are useful for classification: (1) pretrauma factors, including demographic, family history, and biological predisposition; (2) peritrauma factors, including emotional processing, cognitive appraisal, and dissociation; and (3) posttrauma factors, including type and availability of social support. This chapter examines each of these.

PRETRAUMA CHARACTERISTICS

Research on biological differences between individuals with PTSD and those without has produced contradictory findings. Initially, neuroendocrine researchers argued that the hypothalamic-pituitary-adrenocortical (HPA) axis was involved in the human stress response. Further findings indicated that cortisol, a hormone secreted at times of stress and fear, was the measurable output of this systemic response. Based on these findings, researchers contended that individuals with PTSD suffered from a hypersensitization of the HPA system, which decreased (inhibited) the levels of cortisol secretion as part of the stress response. However, more recent research indicates that in fact there are no differences in the HPA axes or cortisol levels between individuals with PTSD and controls (individuals without PTSD) (Carlson, Dalenberg, & Muhtadie, 2008). Behavioral neuroscientists have also examined differences in the hippocampus, a brain structure thought to play a vital role in memory, specifically autobiographical memory. Again, although early studies suggested that individuals with PTSD had significantly smaller hippocampi, more recent investigations (Carlson, Dalenberg, & Muhtadie, 2008) indicate that there are no consistent differences between these individuals and controls. However, research does indicate that despite the failure to observe differences in neurological structures as a result of stress exposure, there are in fact meaningful relationships between genetics and PTSD (Amstadter & Nugent, 2008).

The developmental period during which a traumatic event occurs is also an important factor in predicting the likelihood of development of PTSD (Carlson, Dalenberg, & Muhtadie, 2008). Specifically, events that occur earlier in development and are chronic have a more substantial impact on psychological development. Similarly, there is an important relationship between childhood trauma and attachment to primary caregivers that can exacerbate or ameliorate certain types of trauma (see Cloitre, Cohen, & Koenen, 2006).

Gender is another preexisting factor that is related to the development of PTSD. Although women on the whole are exposed to fewer traumatic events than men (Tolin & Foa, 2006), they are more likely to develop PTSD. It is also true that the nature of the traumatic event exposure differs as a function of gender. Theorists posit that differences in rates of PTSD between men and women are a function of the types of trauma and gender roles that place women at greater risk for development of PTSD. Given this, treatment interventions have attempted to examine both the nature of traumatic stress in the lives of women survivors and how those stressors interact with gender expectations (Kimerling, Ouimette, & Weitlauf, 2007).

Ethno-racial status is a strong predictor of PTSD: Higher rates of PTSD have been observed within African American, Latino, American Indian, and some Asian/Pacific Islander American subgroups (Pole & Triffleman, 2008). Causal explanations regarding these ethnic disparities are relatively new: some authors suggest that certain groups experience greater traumatic stress exposure; others indicate a cumulative impact of racial stress and race-based discrimination; and most recently, still others indicate that peritraumatic and posttraumatic processing (Pole & Triffleman, 2008) might account for the higher rates of PTSD in specific ethno-racial minority groups. In addition to differences in prevalence, ethnic and racial minorities are less likely to utilize existing mental health services as compared to their white counterparts. However, when those with PTSD engage in treatment, it appears that there are few differences in effectiveness as a function of ethnic status (Pole & Triffleman, 2008).

PERITRAUMA EXPERIENCES

Dissociation is the "disruption in the usually integrated functions of consciousness, memory, identity or perception of the environment" (American Psychiatric Association, 1994, p. 477). *Peritrauma dissociation* refers to dissociative experiences that occur during or immediately after a traumatic event, and it is linked to the development of PTSD (Van der Hart et al., 2008). Similarly, a growing body of literature indicates that the cognitive and emotional processing during and immediately following a traumatic event mediate the development of PTSD (e.g., Conway & Pleydell-Pearce, 2000; Ehlers & Clark, 2000; Jobson & O'Kearney, 2009; Rubin, Berntsen, & Bohni, 2008).

POSTTRAUMA CHARACTERISTICS

Social support, perceived support, received support, and social embeddedness are important determinants in the development of PTSD. Research on social support suggests that higher levels of each type of social support are predictive of lower posttrauma symptoms. Hence, treatment interventions attempt to maximize social networks after trauma exposure to improve psychological adjustment and resiliency (Kaniasty & Norris, 2008). Treatment is also a factor that determines the likelihood of developing PTSD, as discussed in the next section.

POSTTRAUMATIC GROWTH

Although the concept of posttraumatic growth is not new, with the concept of growth from tragedy having been explored through several means (see Frankl, 1963; Seligman, 1992), it is a relatively new area of clinical research that evolved to study the effects of trauma in relation to positive change. It is well known that many individuals who experience a traumatic event experience distress, and that some such individuals do so at levels that negatively affect their functioning. However, Tedeschi and Calhoun (1995) explored how traumatic experiences may also prompt the development of personal strength, openness to vulnerability, deeper relationships, and effective coping mechanisms. Tedeschi and Calhoun (2004) posit that posttraumatic growth occurs as a process in five areas: a greater appreciation for life, intimate relationships, personal strength, awareness of new possibilities, and spiritual development. Several meta-analyses (Dekel, Ein-Dor, & Solomon, 2012; Helgeson, Reynolds, & Tomich, 2006; Prati & Pietrantoni, 2009) provide statistical data on to the efficacy of these concepts. Turner and Cox (2004) offer suggestions on facilitating the process of posttraumatic growth.

—*Serena Wadhwa*

THEORETICAL PERSPECTIVES ON PTSD

Brewin and Holmes (2003) provide a thorough and comprehensive review of the psychological theory of PTSD. Psychodynamic theory offers one of the oldest perspectives on PTSD. Horowitz's stress response theory holds that PTSD is the result of two competing processes: the first is motivated to suppress traumatic stimuli and avoid triggers of the trauma; the second is motivated to promote resolution of the traumatic event. Conflict thus results as the mind fluctuates between these two modes of processing. Brewin and Holmes (2003) suggest that the psychodynamic stress response theory has been influential in the development of subsequent cognitive processing theories, as it was the first to examine the role of underlying schemas, cognitive appraisals, and environmental factors in influencing individual responses. Psychodynamic approaches to treatment of PTSD focus on examination of the psychological defense of an unacceptable wish that was triggered by a traumatic event. The goal of psychodynamic interventions for PTSD is to assist patients toward understanding this wish and working through past conflicts. According to psychodynamic theory, trauma has to be understood within the context of an individual's unique life experiences.

More recently, theories have attempted to isolate mechanisms that maintain core posttraumatic symptoms more explicitly. Foa and Rothbaum's (1998) emotion processing theory (EPT) points to specific cognitive schemas that are disrupted as a result of traumatic stress. At its core, EPT is an extension of fear network theories (e.g., Lang, 1979), which suggest that trauma memories are typical memories with a unique structure (Brewin & Holmes, 2003). Foa and her colleagues contend that traumatic events can erode one's previously established sense of safety. According to EPT, core PTSD symptoms are accompanied by a negative belief that is addressed through a treatment of prolonged exposure within a supportive therapeutic context. This approach allows participants to evaluate and examine negative beliefs, confront avoidance behaviors, and reprocess the traumatic memory.

Exposure therapies are consistent with emotion processing theory. These therapies include cognitive and behavioral interventions that, in a systematic, controlled, and measured format, present individuals with images, objects, and in vivo scenarios related to a past trauma to reduce fear response (Rothbaum, 2008). Exposure therapies are thought to go beyond extinction responses as observed in traditional learning paradigms and aid in emotional processing of traumatic events. To do this, exposure is combined with cognitive training that examines cognitions associated with avoidance and fear responses of trauma cues. In addition, the therapeutic context is thought to provide a safe environment where the person can reinterpret and relive past experiences (Rothbaum, 2008).

An alternative explanatory theory of PTSD suggests that the trauma memories causing the disorder are stored in a unique manner. Dual representation theory posits that traumatic memories are maintained within two parallel memory systems: verbally accessible memory and situationally accessible memory (Brewin & Holmes, 2003). Verbally accessible memory exists within the integrated autobiographical memory systems and can be deliberately retrieved (accessed). Conversely, situationally accessible memories are flashbacks and are triggered by environmental determinants. These memories exist without a verbal code and are not integrated into an individual's life narrative. According to this theory, effective treatment necessitates the evaluation of negative cognitions and creation of positive associations that build on the perceptions of alternative positive possible selves that sometimes develop following a traumatic event.

Finally, Ehlers and Clark (2000) presented a cognitive theory of posttraumatic stress disorder. The theory accounts for pretrauma appraisal processes, and peritraumatic evaluations as they predict negative appraisals and subsequent cognitions following a traumatic event. Similar to other theories, the Ehlers and Clark theory stresses that integration of the trauma memory is key; however, they highlight the circumstances that interact to predict the ease with which and the likelihood that this integration and processing will occur. The theory also points to specific therapeutic interventions. Both dual processing and the Ehlers-Clark cognitive theory focus on how trauma has affected the person's cognitions and beliefs. The treatment progresses toward challenging these beliefs and replacing distortions with more accurate and positive cognitive frameworks.

CONCLUSION

For adults, PTSD is associated with difficulty in social and family life, occupational instability, marital problems, and difficulty in parenting, among other things. Mental health care providers need to realize that these difficulties in living are affected not only by the patient's traumatic experiences, but also by his or her cultural environment, ethnic background, social relationships, spiritual worldview, and unique neurophysiology. When individuals experience a life-threatening encounter, they go into a survival and self-protection mode. Persons with PTSD do not readily return to a natural state; rather, they remain in a mode of self-protection and become hyperaware of their surroundings, always on guard against the source of the trauma. It is therefore important to understand the processes that keep individuals who remain haunted by their traumas from returning to a state of normalcy. Their usual means of coping (talking with friends, exercise, prayer, and other support methods) do not alleviate the stress for very long. The ability to cope depends as well on the maturity of the individual, his or her personality structure, and previous experiences. Effective treatment considers how a person responds to trauma and manages symptoms to reduce the debilitating effects of PTSD. See also Chapter 42 on violence and stress.

REFERENCES AND FURTHER READING

American Psychiatric Association. (1994). *Diagnostic and statistical manual of mental disorders* (4th ed.). Washington, DC: American Psychiatric Publishing.

American Psychiatric Association. (2013). *Diagnostic and statistical manual of mental disorders, fifth edition (DSM-5)*. Arlington, VA: American Psychiatric Publishing.

Amstadter, A., & Nugent, N. (2008). Genetics. In G. Reyes, J. D. Elhai, & J. D. Ford (Eds.), *The encyclopedia of psychological trauma* (pp. 294–295). Hoboken, NJ: John Wiley & Sons.

Breuer, J., & S. Freud. (1893/1955). On the psychical mechanism of hysterical phenomenon: Preliminary communication. In J. Breuer & S. Freud, *Studies on hysteria* (pp. 3–17). New York, NY: Basic Books.

Brewin, C. R., & Holmes, E. A. (2003). Psychological theories of posttraumatic stress disorder. *Clinical Psychology Review, 23,* 339–376.

Carlson, E. B., Dalenberg, C., & Muhtadie, L. (2008). Etiology. In G. Reyes, J. D. Elhai, & J. D. Ford (Eds.), *The encyclopedia of psychological trauma* (pp. 257–163). Hoboken, NJ: John Wiley & Sons.

Cloitre, M., Cohen, L., & Koenen, K. (2006). *Treating survivors of childhood abuse: Psychotherapy for the interrupted life.* New York, NY: Guilford Press.

Conway, M. A., & Pleydell-Pearce, C. W. (2000). The construction of autobiographical memories in the self-memory system. *Psychological Review, 107,* 261–288.

Dekel, S., Ein-Dor, T., & Solomon, Z. (2012). Posttraumatic growth and posttraumatic distress: A longitudinal study. *Psychological Trauma: Theory, Research, Practice, and Policy, 4*(1), 94–101.

Ehlers, A., & Clark, D. M. (2000). A cognitive model of posttraumatic stress disorder. *Behaviour Research and Therapy, 38,* 319–345.

Foa, E. B., & Rothbaum, B. (1998). *Treating the trauma of rape: Cognitive behavioral therapy of PTSD.* New York, NY: Guilford Press.

Frankl, V. (1963). *Man's search for meaning.* New York, NY: Pocket Books.

Helgeson, V. S., Reynolds, K. A., & Tomich, P. L. (2006). A meta-analytic review of benefit finding and growth. *Journal of Consulting and Clinical Psychology, 74*(5), 797–816.

Jobson, L., & O'Kearney, R. (2009). Impact of cultural differences in self on cognitive appraisals in posttraumatic stress disorder. *Behavioural and Cognitive Psychotherapy, 37*(3), 249–266.

Kaniasty, K., & Norris, F. H. (2008). Longitudinal linkages between perceived social support and posttraumatic stress symptoms: Sequential roles of social causation and social selection. *Journal of Traumatic Stress, 21*(3), 274–281.

Kimerling, R., Ouimette, P., & Weitlauf, J. (2007). Gender issues in PTSD. In M. J. Friedman, T. M. Keane, & P. A. Resick (Eds.), *Handbook of PTSD: Science and practice* (pp. 207–228). New York, NY: Guilford Press.

Lang, P. J. (1979). A bioinformational theory of emotional imagery. *Psychophysiology, 166,* 495–512.

Magnea, G., & Lanius, R. A. (2008). Biology, brain structure, and function, adult. In G. Reyes, J. D. Elhai, & J. D. Ford (Eds.), *The encyclopedia of psychological trauma* (pp. 84–90). Hoboken, NJ: John Wiley & Sons.

National Comorbidity Survey. (2005). NCS-R appendix tables: Table 1. Lifetime prevalence of DSM-IV/WMH-CIDI disorders by sex and cohort. Table 2. Twelve-month prevalence of DSM-IV/WMH-CIDI disorders by sex and cohort. Retrieved from http://www.hcp.med.harvard.edu/ncs/publications.php.

Pole, N., & Triffleman, E. (2008). Race and ethnic factors. In G. Reyes, J. D. Elhai, & J. D. Ford (Eds.), *The encyclopedia of psychological trauma* (pp. 560–564). Hoboken, NJ: John Wiley & Sons.

Prati, G., & Pietrantoni, L. (2009). Optimism, social support, and coping strategies as factors contributing to posttraumatic growth: A meta-analysis. *Journal of Loss and Trauma, 14*(5), 364–388.

Reyes, G., Elhai, J. D., & Ford, J. D. (Eds.). (2008). *The encyclopedia of psychological trauma.* Hoboken, NJ: John Wiley & Sons.

Roberts, C. A. (2011). *Coping with post-traumatic stress disorder: A guide for families.* Jefferson, NC: McFarland.

Rosen, G. M. (Ed.). (2004). *Posttraumatic stress disorder: Issues and controversies.* Hoboken, NJ: John Wiley & Sons.

Rothbaum, B. O. (2008). Exposure therapy. In G. Reyes, J. D. Elhai, & J. D. Ford (Eds.), *The encyclopedia of psychological trauma* (pp. 270–271). Hoboken, NJ: John Wiley & Sons.

Rubin, D. C., Berntsen, D., & Bohni, M. K. (2008). A memory-based model of post-traumatic stress disorder: Evaluating basic assumptions underlying the PTSD diagnosis. *Psychological Review, 5*(4), 985–1011.

Seligman, M. (1992). *Learned optimism*. Sydney, Australia: Random House.

Tedeschi, R. G., & Calhoun, L. G. (1995). *Trauma and transformation: Growing in the aftermath of suffering*. Thousand Oaks, CA: Sage.

Tedeschi, R. G., & Calhoun, L. G. (2004). Posttraumatic growth: Conceptual foundations and empirical evidence. *Psychological Inquiry, 15*(1), 1–18.

Tolin, D. F., & Foa, E. B. (2006). Sex differences in trauma and posttraumatic stress disorder: A quantitative review of 25 years of research. *Psychological Bulletin, 132*(6), 959–992.

Turner, de S., & Cox, H. (2004). Facilitating post traumatic growth. *Health and Quality of Life Outcomes, 2*(1), 34.

U.S. Department of Veterans Affairs. (2016, February 23). DSM-5 criteria for PTSD. Retrieved from http://www.ptsd.va.gov/professional/PTSD-overview/dsm5_criteria_ptsd.asp.

van der Hart, O., van Ochten, J. M., van Son, M. J., Steele, K., & Lensvelt-Mulders, G. (2008). Relations among peritraumatic dissociation and posttraumatic stress: A critical review. *Journal of Trauma and Dissociation, 9,* 481–505.

Weathers, F., & Keane, T. M. (2008). Trauma, definition. In G. Reyes, J. D. Elhai, & J. D. Ford (Eds.), *The encyclopedia of psychological trauma* (pp. 657–660). Hoboken, NJ: John Wiley & Sons.

44

Burnout

Serena Wadhwa

It's not uncommon to hear someone exclaim, "I'm burned out!" But what does this mean? Is this the same concept as stress? Do these people mean that they are completely overwhelmed, or does *burnout* mean something different? This chapter explores the concept and experience of burnout and how it differs from and relates to stress. The chapter covers what burnout is, symptoms of burnout, and strategies to manage it.

What comes to mind when you think of the word *burnout?* Chances are, regardless of the field or profession you are in (whether student, teacher, parent, plumber, engineer, health care professional, mechanic, or other), your conception of burnout is not confined to any particular field or group of people. Burnout is not a condition found in the *Diagnostic and Statistical Manual-5,* as it is not listed as a "clinical disorder" (Korczak, Huber, & Kister, 2010).

Partly due to this lack of a generally accepted definition, general statistics are not available on how many people experience burnout. However, one report has suggested that 21–67 percent of mental health workers may experience high levels of burnout (Miller, Hubble, & Mathieu, 2015). Other reports suggest that while nearly 2 percent of employees from a variety of backgrounds quit their jobs, the recovery rates of these jobs are slow; burnout may be one factor in this stagnant progression (Stern, 2012). Earlier reports show that 10–20 percent of employees are "burned out" (Golembiewski, Boudreau, Munzenrider, & Luo, 1996).

ORIGIN AND DEFINITION

The term *burnout* was coined in the 1970s by psychiatrist Herbert Freudenberger. Freudenberger worked as a psychiatrist at a free clinic for patients who abused drugs, and he observed over a period of time the development of physical and emotional symptoms in the health care professionals who worked there, most of them as volunteers. He adopted the term *burnout* for this condition, derived from a description of chronic substance abusers, but which he used to describe a condition where people had figuratively "burned out" and could no longer do their jobs well, having become cynical and disengaged with patients (Maslach & Schaufeli, 1993).

Around the same time, a social psychology researcher Christina Maslach was observing how human services employees coped with emotional arousal on the job. She later adopted the term *burnout* as well, as it was familiar to the individuals who participated in the interviews with her (Maslach & Schaufeli, 1993). While similar states of detachment, depletion, physical and emotional exhaustion, and other symptoms certainly existed prior to the 1970s, the cultural context was different, and there was much less interest in or recognition of the condition than there was beginning in the 1970s. Researchers in this area point out that many social, economic, occupational, and political factors were different after WWII, thus creating both higher incidence of the condition and interest in it. When scientific interest in the concept of burnout did arise, Maslach and Schaufeli indicate that there were two main disadvantages to the literature that appeared in this time period: there was a broader interpretation of *burnout* that sometimes extended beyond the actual scope of the definition; or, conversely, the research did not include necessary components of the definition. There was also a disconnect between research and practice: Researchers were not as interested in the concept as practitioners were. When Maslach and Jackson attempted to publish some initial theoretical research, it was stigmatized as "pop psychology" (Maslach & Schaufeli, 1993).

Nonetheless, in the late 1970 and 1980s, the Maslach Burnout Inventory (MBI) gained popularity as a reliable and valid instrument to measure *burnout,* which was defined as "a syndrome of emotional exhaustion, depersonalization and reduced personal accomplishment [that] can occur among individuals who do 'people work' of some kind" (Maslach & Jackson, 1981). Emotional exhaustion is evidenced by a lack of energy and a condition in which resources are used up (Cordes & Dougherty, 1993). *Depersonalization* refers to the experience of treating people as numbers or objects and approaching problems by the book rather than applying problem-solving skills to help individuals based on their particular conditions (Cordes & Dougherty, 1993). Reduced personal accomplishment is characterized by a decrease in one's sense of occupational and social competence (Cordes & Dougherty, 1993). The authors also note that burned-out employees' work performance may deteriorate; thus, employees may experience more reprimands from supervisors or bosses and get into more trouble on the job.

SYMPTOMS

There are many symptoms of burnout. People who are burned out may experience lethargy, cynicism, depressive symptoms, trouble getting out of bed, and changes in appetite (Golembiewski et al., 1996); fatigue, avoidance, disengagement, negative attitude, and withdrawal (Polman, Borkoles, & Nicholls, 2010); headaches, stomachaches, cognitive impairments, challenges with listening, quickness to anger, difficulty holding in feelings, resentment, apathy, rigidity, increased boredom, dullness, and guilt and a possible sense of failure (McElroy, 1982). Cordes and Dougherty (1993) cite several studies that include the characteristics of irritability, helplessness, anxiety, insomnia, tension, deterioration of social and family relationships, and decreased tolerance and increased impatience, as well as behavioral consequences such as absenteeism, decreased work performance, and substance use.

DIFFERENTIATING BURNOUT FROM STRESS

The concept of burnout may not seem much different from the conceptions of stress presented in earlier chapters. In fact, there is an overlap (Sears, Urizar, & Evans, 2000; Cordes & Dougherty, 1993). If we define *stress,* loosely, as a pressure or a demand that exceeds the organism's ability to cope with it, we can see that within an occupational or professional setting, there are many opportunities for stress. As a result, Sears, Urizar, and Evans (2000) theorized that the occurrence of this kind of work stress over a period of time can result in emotional exhaustion, one of the primary symptoms of burnout. Cordes and Dougherty (1993) suggested that burnout represents a pattern in response to a particular type of stress.

TIERED CHARACTERISTICS OF BURNOUT

The literature recognizes that several categories of factors play a role in the development of burnout. These include characteristics relating to the job and the job role, characteristics relating to the organization, and personal characteristics (Cordes & Dougherty, 1993).

Job and Role Characteristics

Job and role characteristics include factors such as the job environment and hours; the role of the individual in the job and the type of interactions the individual has at work (for example, interactions that are personally involving may increase the potential for burnout); the type of clients (if there are clients) with whom the employee interacts; whether role conflict or ambiguity is present; and whether the person feels overwhelmed by the job role (e.g., lacking skills) (Cordes & Dougherty, 1993).

ORGANIZATIONAL AND PERSONALITY CHARACTERISTICS

McElroy (1982) listed organizational factors that contribute to burnout, such as large caseloads; ineffective supervision, management, or leadership; lack of communication; and rigid job descriptions. Conflicted values and lack of realistic perception are other organization-related factors.

McElroy (1982) also identified personality types that may be more vulnerable to burnout, including those with strong dependency needs and achievement needs. Individuals with unresolved grief or adverse personal experiences within the chosen field may have difficulty with burnout. Also frequently affected are those who have trouble setting boundaries; those who lack support; and those who have difficulty communicating or voicing their needs and opinions. Someone who believes that he or she is controlled externally will also be more prone to burnout. Cordes and Dougherty (1993) also cite several of these factors; in addition, they report that unmet expectations can contribute to burnout.

VALUES: A STRESSOR WHEN WE ARE IN CONFLICT WITH THEM, OR A REINFORCEMENT WHEN WE CAN HONOR THEM

Situations that place uncomfortable demands upon us can result in tension and stress (Coletta, 1978). Exploring what values may be in conflict with work demands is one way to understand this type of trigger for the stress response, as well as an option to manage it. *Values* are those things that are important to us as individuals. Obviously, these vary from person to person. For example, one individual may value material things and money more than another. Another person may highly value freedom, and thus make decisions or seek opportunities that allow or enhance freedom. The inclusion of clarifying values to promote congruent behaviors toward a life of one's choosing, and as a means of increasing psychological well-being, has been a focus of study in two approaches: Acceptance and Commitment Therapy (ACT), developed by Dr. Stephen Hayes; and Dialectical Behavioral Therapy (DBT), developed by Dr. Marsha Linehan. Although the use of values may manifest in various ways, one of the similarities in these two therapies is the notion of the importance of value clarification for one's health. When individuals are clear about personal values and move toward living within this self-determined framework, there is a means of evaluating when and whether an individual is acting according to those values (Hayes, Strosahl, & Wilson, 1999; Wilson & Murrell, 2004). In DBT, value clarification is used in one of the sessions to define the concept of a "life worth living," and in one of the assignments to gain awareness about what is important to the individual. Readers are referred to Linehan's work for more information.

Values can be stressors for some individuals, particularly if they are unable to integrate their values into their lives. In contrast, values can also be mechanisms for effectively coping with stress, when individuals incorporate actions relating to their values in order to prevent, manage, and/or reduce stress.

REDUCING, MANAGING, AND PREVENTING BURNOUT

The concept of burnout is most often applied to occupational and institutional contexts, and the literature in this area suggests several strategies that can be utilized to effectively intervene to avoid or recover from burnout. According to Morse, Salyers, Rollins, Monroe-DeVita, and Pfahler (2012), there has been little research on interventions that differentiate between prevention and recovery efforts targeting burnout. According to these authors, this lack of differentiation may relate to the fact that burnout is conceptualized as a continuum; future research may perhaps clarify these issues and sharpen the distinction. Overall, Morse et al. were able to do a meta-analysis of studies on burnout that demonstrated a positive effect of prevention and intervention efforts; strategies that were utilized included cognitive restructuring, relaxation, assertiveness training, leadership training, social skills enhancement, and a few others. These authors also noted that there was a three-pronged approach in terms of where the interventions were directed: Interventions generally target the individual, the organization, or both.

ORGANIZATIONAL APPROACHES TO REDUCING BURNOUT AND ITS CONSEQUENCES

One of the main things that organizations can do to reduce employee burnout is to increase employees' choices. For example, as detailed in one article, when an agency allowed staff to determine their own hours within the time period the agency was open, staff turnover and the use of sick days declined (Miller et al., 2015). Thus, increasing the sense of an internal locus of control is an important factor in reducing burnout; notably, it can also reduce the sense of residual effects of stress overload.

There are not enough good studies of burnout in organizational settings (Morse et al., 2012). These authors also noted that in many organizations, there is a possibility that some burnout components can be reduced while others cannot. In these situations, a larger systematic or logistical change may be required.

INDIVIDUAL APPROACHES TO REDUCING BURNOUT

Much of the research focuses on what the individual can do to prevent, manage, and reduce the phenomenon of burnout, whether by increasing coping mechanisms or using support systems (Morse et al., 2012). Generally, these approaches, using a variety of cognitive behavioral interventions and relaxation skills, demonstrate efficacy at reducing levels of stress and burnout. A few specific strategies include reflection, limiting work hours, practicing gratitude, and taking time-outs (Zwack & Schweitzer, 2013). Several of these approaches are explored in other chapters of this book.

Miller, Hubble, and Mathieu (2015) explored the concept of "caring effectively." Their article was written to change how those in the helping professions, especially mental health professionals, currently view burnout and to examine what certain therapists (whom the authors call "Supershrinks") do differently than others. Miller et al. state that the bottom line, finally, is to recognize when caring is going nowhere. The supereffective therapists they interviewed have developed the ability to recognize when their work is not helping the patient or client and when to suggest that the patient/client should see another professional. They have found that this is an important aspect of preventing burnout. Although this article concentrated on those who are counseling professionals, it is possible that the principles the authors derived could be applied to many jobs, and even personal situations. Following the strategies described by Miller et al., the burned-out person might try a range of options: learning when to pull back with regard to certain duties or routines; trying other strategies or duties; and, if necessary, quitting.

CONCLUSION

Although the concept of burnout relates to stress in some ways, it also is vastly different from stress, incorporating the primary experiences of emotional exhaustion, depersonalization, and reduced personal accomplishment (Maslach & Jackson, 1981). Burnout manifests in individuals who work with others in a variety of contexts, whether these are personal or professional, at home or in the work setting. However, most of the research on the concept of burnout has been conducted within occupational and academic settings. Burnout manifests in ways similar to chronic stress, and symptoms will vary from individual to individual. This chapter explored a variety of factors that increase an individual's vulnerability to burnout, as well as factors that prevent the onset of it. Finally, it presented research exploring what an individual can do to prevent, reduce, and manage burnout, as well as what organizations can do to reduce employee burnout.

REFERENCES AND FURTHER READING

Coletta, S. S. (1978). Value clarification in nursing: Why? *AJN: The American Journal of Nursing, 78*(12), 2057.

Cordes, C. L., & Dougherty, T. W. (1993). A review and an integration of research on job burnout. *Academy of Management Review, 18*(4), 621–656.

Golembiewski, R. T., Boudreau, R. A., Munzenrider, R. F., & Luo, H. (1996). *Global burnout: A worldwide pandemic explored by the phase model.* Greenwich, CT: JAI Press.

Hayes, S. C., Strosahl, K. D., & Wilson, K. G. (1999). *Acceptance and commitment therapy.* New York, NY: Guilford Press.

Korczak, D., Huber, B., & Kister, C. (2010). Differential diagnostic of the burnout syndrome. *GMS Health Technology Assessment, 6,* Doc. 9.

Kraft, U. (2006, June/July). Burned out. *Scientific American Mind, 17*(3), 28–33.

Leiter, M. P., & Maslach, C. (2001). Burnout and quality in a sped-up world. *Journal for Quality and Participation, 24*(2), 48–51.

Maslach, C., & Jackson, S. E. (1981). The measurement of experienced burnout. *Journal of Occupational Behavior, 2,* 99–113.

Maslach, C., & Schaufeli, W. B. (1993). Historical and conceptual development of burnout. In W. B. Schaufeli, C. Maslach, & T. Marek (Eds.), *Professional burnout: Recent developments in theory and research* (pp. 1–16). Washington, DC: Taylor & Francis.

McElroy, A. M. (1982). Burnout: A review of the literature with application to cancer nursing. *Cancer Nursing, 5*(3), 211–218.

Miller, S., Hubble, M., & Mathieu, F. (2015, May/June). Burnout reconsidered: What supershrinks can teach us. *Psychotherapy Networker,* 19–23.

Morse, G., Salyers, M. P., Rollins, A. L., Monroe-DeVita, M., & Pfahler, C. (2012). Burnout in mental health services: A review of the problem and its remediation. *Administration and Policy in Mental Health, 39*(5), 341–352. doi:10.1007/s10488-011-0352-1.

Polman, R., Borkoles, E., & Nicholls, A. R. (2010). Type D personality, stress, and symptoms of burnout: The influence of avoidance coping and social support. *British Journal of Health Psychology, 15*(3), 681–696.

Sears, S. F., Jr., Urizar, G. G., Jr., & Evans, G. D. (2000). Examining a stress-coping model of burnout and depression in extension agents. *Journal of Occupational Health Psychology, 5*(1), 56.

Stern, G. (2012). Employee burnout: Around the corner? Already here. Retrieved August 1, 2015, from http://fortune.com/2012/05/21/employee-burnout-around-the-corner-already-here.

Stoyanov, D. 2014. *New model of burn out syndrome: Towards early diagnosis and prevention.* Aalborg, Denmark: River Publishers.

Wilson, K. G., & Murrell, A. R. (2004). Values work in acceptance and commitment therapy. In S. C. Hayes, V. M. Follette, & M. Linehan (Eds.), *Mindfulness and acceptance: Expanding the cognitive–behavioral tradition* (pp. 120–151). New York, NY: Guilford Press.

Zwack, J., & Schweitzer, J. (2013). If every fifth physician is affected by burnout, what about the other four? Resilience strategies of experienced physicians. *Academic Medicine, 88*(3), 382–389.

45

Psychological Stress Disorders

Serena Wadhwa

For a long time, with the goal of assisting in devising and applying effective treatments, experts have attempted to devise a systematic classification of medical disorders that accounts for the physical, mental, behavioral, emotional, spiritual, social, and other manifestations that occur in response to something abnormal happening to the body, whether that happening is an isolated event, a recurrent situation, a minor inconvenience, or a major hassle. The resulting mix of symptomatology, described in previous chapters, highlights the challenges inherent in separating and classifying these events. Stressors come from a variety of sources and have different impacts on individuals. However, individuals' genetics, vulnerabilities, perceptions, support, coping mechanisms, environments, and personality factors, among other factors, all figure into the possibility of an individual developing a disorder. This chapter explores some of these psychological/mental health stress-related disorders, basing the discussion on the *Diagnostic and Statistical Manual of Mental Disorders, Fifth Edition,* published by the American Psychiatric Association (2013). Certainly, many physical disorders can result from chronic stress (see Chapter 11 on the mind-body connection for more on physical disorders and stress); however, this chapter focuses on psychological disorders, specifically those that are stress related.

The onset of each identified psychological disorder is slightly different. Some individuals may experience a form of anxiety, which is a clinical disorder category unto itself. Anxiety can be triggered by stress and vice versa; however, this chapter focuses on disorders specifically related to experiences of acute and chronic stress experiences in adults. Several classifications are currently indicated for stress-related disorders. Some of these are categorized as trauma-related disorders, whereas others are considered to be "conditions" that are not disorders in the sense that they are classified in the same way; however, they have some influence or impact that caused the individual to have some distress, thus influencing the individual's development, neurodevelopment, and social, emotional, and cognitive developmental systems, as well as coping mechanisms. These conditions are discussed here as well. This chapter investigates some of the approaches, from both traditional medicine and alternative or complementary disciplines, that are utilized to treat and begin healing of some of these disorders.

This chapter includes brief overviews of a few of the other classifications not listed under the "Trauma and Stress Related Disorders" section of the *DSM-5*, but many recognized disorders are not covered here. Although the disorders in these other classifications can be stressful to those who have them, and potentially influence the onset of a psychological stress-related disorder, an in-depth review of these is well beyond the scope of both this chapter and this book.

The Diagnostic and Statistical Manual: Mental Disorders (*DSM-I*) was first published in 1952. Its primary purpose was to focus on the "clinical utility" of the descriptions offered; however, it did little in terms of providing definitions, one of the key criticisms by British psychiatrist Erwin Stengel ("History of the DSM," 2016). It was not until publication of the *DSM-III*, in 1980, that criteria for the disorders were specified (several other recommended changes were made as well). As revisions continued, the American Psychiatric Association (APA) worked with many professionals to assist in modifying upcoming manual revisions. The most recent revision, the *DSM-5*, was published in 2013.

TRAUMA- AND STRESS-RELATED DISORDERS

The *DSM-5* (APA, 2013) lists exposure to a traumatic or stressful event as the primary criterion for the categories of trauma- or stress-related disorders. "Traumatic or stressful event" can mean different things to different people, and includes occurrences such as natural disasters, exposure to violence, accidents, unexpected losses, medical procedures, and so on. Individuals who are exposed to such an event (or events) may experience a variety of symptoms and exhibit a wide variety of responses (Levine, 1997). Herman (1997) explores three general responses: hypervigilance, numbing, and avoidance. The *DSM-5* includes several manifestations of these in a variety of anxiety, depressive, and dissociative symptoms (APA, 2013). The following subsections discuss the seven disorders listed in this category, giving a synopsis of the criteria and some general information about each disorder. Note that our purpose here is not to enable diagnosis of any particular disorder; rather, it is to provide information about the disorder and its stress-related symptomatology. More detail about the criteria and diagnostic information for all of these disorders is available in the *DSM-5*.

Reactive Attachment Disorder

Generally, reactive attachment disorder is developed in childhood, although it is not commonly diagnosed (APA, 2013). According to Kay and Green (2013, research on this disorder is sparse. Features of this disorder include "inhibited and emotionally withdrawn behavior towards adult caregivers," which includes not seeking or responding to comfort when distressed and limited social/emotional and positive responsiveness to others. Children with this disorder have some history of neglect and/or are in environments with inconsistent exposure to care and that have frequent changes in caregivers. Kay and Green (2012) note that children exposed to severe neglect manifest symptoms characteristic of this disorder; these children tend to be institutionalized. Many studies have indicated the importance of physical touch in the development of the young. In a well-known study conducted by Harry Harlow, a psychologist who studied the effects of separation and isolation (among other factors), baby rhesus monkeys were separated from their mothers. Even though their physical needs were met, the monkeys displayed various social deficits as compared to monkeys reared by their mothers. Additionally, the deprived monkeys preferred clothed surrogates, whether or not the surrogates offered food. This demonstrated the need for comfort and safety to establish some bond.

Neglected children often do not obtain the necessary psychological benefits that comfort and nurturing provide, and the effects of this deprivation can be numerous (Crouch & Milner, 1993; Hanson et al., 2013). One of the potential effects relates to attachment problems, which lead children to be selective about whom they attach to or to be unable to attach at all.

Disinhibited Social Engagement Disorder

Disinhibited social engagement disorder also generally arises in childhood, although it may manifest throughout adolescence. Features of this disorder include a child's inhibition about approaching and interacting with unfamiliar adults in ways that are not consistent with culturally appropriate interactions. Children and adolescents with this disorder have some history of neglect and/or are raised in environments with inconsistent exposure to care and that have frequent changes in caregivers. The *DSM-5* (APA, 2013) indicates that this disorder is also related to severe neglect and shares similar features with reactive attachment disorder.

Posttraumatic Stress Disorder (PTSD)

Posttraumatic stress disorder (PTSD) may be present in individuals as young as 6 years of age (APA, 2013), and usually occurs up to a month after the precipitating event. Primary features of this disorder include direct exposure to or witnessing of a traumatic event or learning of such an event happening to a close friend or family member. McNally (2009) argued that while it is possible for an individual to experience anxiety symptoms after hearing about another's stressful experience, this is not the same as actually experiencing and having a memory of the event: An individual embodies a traumatic experience differently than the narrative of a trauma. Neuroscience demonstrates that the brain shifts into different developmental pathways as a result of unprocessed traumatic memories. Thus, recognizing that experienced and vicarious trauma are different in several ways is important. Other features of posttraumatic stress disorder include intrusive symptoms, avoidance, numbing, and/or hypervigilance. An individual's risk of developing PTSD varies depending on several factors described in the *DSM-5,* as well as several protective factors. These include social, environmental, genetic, developmental, and cultural factors, as well as others.

Acute Stress Disorder

Acute stress disorder may be present in children or adults. Like PTSD, there is a direct exposure to or witnessing of a traumatic event, or learning of such an event happening to a close friend or family member. To be diagnosed, individuals must meet 9 or more of 14 specified symptoms. The feature differentiating this disorder from PTSD is that the symptoms occur three days to one month after the stressor. Also different is the length of the symptoms: If they persist beyond a month, a diagnosis of PTSD is usually made (Gibson, 2016). An individual's risk of developing acute stress disorder varies depending on several factors as described in the *DSM-5,* as well as several protective factors. These include social, environmental, genetic, developmental, and cultural factors, among others.

Adjustment Disorders

Adjustment disorders present a cluster of behavioral and emotional symptoms, usually within three months of exposure to a specific stressor (a move, a new job, status change, etc.). These symptoms do not usually extend beyond six months and are not symptomatic of other mental health disorders or pre-existing conditions (APA, 2013). As other chapters have explained, various experiences can be stressful, and part of the stress experience revolves around whether or not a person perceives himself or herself as having the resources needed to meet the demands or pressures. For example, a person who relocates due to a job change may have the support of family and friends back home, as well as other resources to assist in the transition. As the individual adjusts to the new environment, job, social circles, town, and so on, there may be some experiences of anxiety, loneliness, and feeling overwhelmed. These may eventually dissipate. However, for someone who may not have these resources, who doesn't have others to rely on, or perhaps doesn't speak the language, or who has different customs and routines, this adjustment may be more intense, as there is so much more to know, learn, and shift, thus extending the experience of symptoms within the context of these major stressors.

Other Classifications

Other classifications exist for trauma- and stress-related disorders. For example, if something is causing significant impairment in various areas of the individual's life, but other criteria listed in the *DSM-5* are not met, it is possible that the person may be diagnosed with Other Specified Trauma- and Stressor-Related Disorder. If not enough information is presented to make a diagnosis, Unspecified Trauma- and Stressor-Related Disorder may be the appropriate diagnosis.

Other diagnostic disorders that develop in response to stress-related issues include disorders that meet depressive disorder criteria, anxiety disorder criteria, and dissociative disorder criteria. Though it does not discuss the criteria for all these various disorders, this chapter does explore the possible overlap of these clinical manifestations and their correlation with stress-related symptomatology.

Depressive disorders include a variety of disorders in which the primary feature is "the presence of a sad, empty, or irritable mood" that is accompanied by physical and cognitive changes that affect the individual's day-to-day functioning. Depending on the age of the individual, studies suggest that when a person experiences chronic stress for a period of time, often the person becomes lethargic and/or depressed due to exhaustion of the endocrine system. This may be misdiagnosed if other symptoms are perceived in the context of a depressive disorder rather than a stress reaction (Voelker, 2004). Additionally, increased cortisol levels in the bloodstream have been associated with depressive episodes (Burke, Davis, Otte, & Mohr, 2005). A thorough assessment is necessary, and it is important to recognize that symptoms may not all fit into one set of criteria.

Anxiety disorders are another classification of disorders in which the primary feature is fear of a real or perceived threat and anxiety is the anticipation of that threat. This classification includes disorders such as separation anxiety disorder, selective mutism (not speaking at times), specific phobias, social anxiety, panic disorders, agoraphobia (the fear of outside spaces), and generalized anxiety disorder. The *DSM-5* assigns each of these disorders specific criteria and time frames; however, the primary feature is that fear and anticipation of that fear are present and manifest as behavioral, emotional, physical, or other interfering, dysfunctional behaviors. As previous chapters have discussed, *stress* is the experience of adjusting or adapting to demands or pressure. If there is fear associated with that adjustment or adaptation, anxiety may also be present. Thus, it will be necessary to do a thorough assessment to ascertain if an individual has a clinical disorder as a result of a stressor that perhaps can be assuaged with appropriate coping mechanisms, or if the problem fits the clinical diagnosis in the classification as listed in the *DSM-5*.

The dissociative disorders include the primary feature of some piece of an experience being cut off at the time of the actual experience. Physically, some thoughts, emotions, the person's sense of identity, experience of being in "real time," or sense of being in control of behaviors, can be "cut off." The person does not experience this piece as a part of him or her. It is separate; hence "dissociated." Included in this category are dissociative identity disorder, dissociative amnesia, and depersonalization/derealization disorder. Again, although these disorders have specific criteria and time frames, it is not uncommon for individuals experiencing chronic or severe stress to "cut off" from part of their experience. Thus, it is necessary to do a thorough assessment to ascertain the extent of these symptoms to determine if they constitute a clinical disorder or if they are functioning in a different context.

Other conditions that may be a focus of clinical attention include events that may have been a stressor for an individual at one time or another. These may also be current stressors in the individual's life. These conditions do not require treatment in the sense that a disorder does; however, they are factors that potentially influence the prognosis, outcome, and treatment of manifested and unknown physical, emotional, relational, cognitive, and developmental issues. Many of these have been discussed in previous chapters as stressors that may arise for individuals, and they are situations that may affect individuals in a variety of ways. For our current purposes, the general categories are listed here; specific issues are elaborated upon in the *DSM-5*.

- Problems related to family upbringing. These include problems with upbringing, cognitive perceptions, affective issues, sibling problems, being raised in a foster home or by relatives; or being raised in a home where there was parental distress (APA, 2013).
- Other problems related to primary support groups. These include problems with the spouse or partner, divorce or separation, intense emotion, and/or bereavement.
- Child maltreatment and neglect problems, such as physical abuse, sexual abuse, child neglect, or psychological abuse.
- Adult maltreatment and neglect problems. This includes physical abuse toward a spouse or partner; sexual abuse toward a spouse or partner; neglect of a spouse or partner; psychological abuse of a spouse or partner; or abuse by a nonpartner/nonspouse.
- Educational and occupational problems, housing problems, economic problems, social environment problems, legal system problems, counseling, other circumstances, a history of trauma or self-harm, etc.

To summarize, the experience of stress, whether it be a result of one event, a multitude of events, or something that happens outside of one's everyday experience, can become encapsulated in a clinical disorder or a dysregulating experience that the individual's coping mechanisms cannot handle to resolve the experience.

TREATMENT

Several approaches have been explored in the resolution of trauma, as well as in managing anxiety, depression, and other stress-related disorders. A range of counseling and therapy approaches are used, depending on the target of treatment. For example, a mental health professional (a licensed therapist, counselor, psychologist, etc.) may have receive extensive training in psychoanalytic approaches and thus be able to utilize dreams, free association, and three or four talk sessions a week as a healing modality. Other treatment approaches also exist, each requiring specific training and, in some cases, certification. Reviewing all of these approaches is beyond the scope of this chapter, which instead gives an overview of those approaches considered to be evidence based. An *evidence-based approach* meets certain standards set by the federal government, and has demonstrated outcomes through research (Substance Abuse and Mental Health Services Administration, 2015).

THERAPY FOR STRESS DISORDERS

Therapy, according to the National Institute of Mental Health (NIMH, n.d.) is a way to treat people who have a mental disorder. *Psychotherapy* involves educating individuals about their mental health disorders, teaching coping mechanisms, and working through unresolved issues that may get in the way of effective daily functioning. NIMH describes various psychotherapeutic approaches, such as cognitive behavioral therapy, dialectical behavioral therapy, psychodynamic therapy, and family-focused therapy, among others.

Therapy addresses mental health issues that affect a person's ability to perform daily activities and to interact with others. Clinical disorders, such as clinical depression, clinical anxiety, personality disorders, and the like, tend to be focal points for therapy. This differs from coaching, including life coaching, or career coaching, in that coaching does not address mental health issues; rather, coaches assist clients in setting goals and gaining the skills to improve their lives and careers (Hart, Blattner, & Leipsic, 2001).

Successful therapy has many benefits for the client or patient, which include (1) gaining insight into problems; (2) developing skills for improvement; (3) learning how to overcome certain problems, such as social anxiety; and (4) obtaining solutions to the issues for which the client sought therapy in the first place (Brazier, 2016).

Somatic Experiencing: Developed by Peter Levine, this approach has clients explore various states of the experienced trauma, and its emotional-physiological components, while utilizing relaxation techniques. This allows the client to release the tension held over from the stress experience, similar to what an animal experiences when recovering from a stressed state (Whitehouse & Heller, 2008). When the autonomic nervous system releases this energy, the client experiences a shift toward connection and engagement. Some researchers state that the primary concept of somatic experiencing (interoception, or visceral internal sensations) has also been found effective in treating depression, anxiety, and other disorders, separately treated as distinct disorders (see Payne, Levine, & Crane-Godreau, 2015, for a review). This is necessary because some individuals do not have access to body experiences, for many reasons; when they "learn" to connect to their own body experiences, expressing and validating them, there is movement toward healing. A similar perspective is offered to support the use of somatic experiencing for trauma- and stress-related disorders.

Cognitive behavioral therapy (CBT): In a meta-analysis review conducted by Hofmann, Asnaani, Vonk, Sawyer, and Fang (2012), the authors confirmed the reliability of CBT approaches (which use interventions in maladaptive thought and behavior patterns) for treating anxiety, and also noted that it has some medium-size effects with PTSD. When using CBT with trauma- and stress-related disorders, the CB therapist generally examines the individual's beliefs and expectations relating to the situation itself, and the individual's perceptions of coping as factors playing a role within the disorder. By challenging some of these beliefs and exploring the meaning and context of the situation, an individual is able to gain additional clarity on what happened and his or her response (Resick, Nishith, & Griffin, 2003; Stergiopoulos, Cimo, Cheng, Bonato, & Dewa, 2011).

Medication: The results of a meta-analysis conducted by Ipser and Stein (2012) suggest that the appropriate medications at the appropriate dosages for about a year can potentially have positive results; however, there is not enough information to make any judgments about efficacy after this time period. The authors noted in their discussion that other factors are to be included when considering the use of medications (for example, the duration of PTSD symptoms). In general, this review supported short-term treatment of PTSD with some types of medications (see Chapter 33, on medications), although there are mixed results in terms of efficacy for the symptoms of posttraumatic stress. More research is needed in this area (Hoskins et al., 2015). Other research also demonstrates the effectiveness of medication for trauma- and other stress-related disorders. It is known that chronic stress and traumatic experiences can shift how the brain functions; therefore, medications that address these shifts and assist with restoring more balanced functioning can be effective (Hamblen, 2010).

Eye Movement Desensitization and Reprocessing (EMDR): Developed in the 1980s by Francine Shapiro, EMDR is a therapist-guided process in which an individual follows the side-to-side movements of the clinician's finger or a light source with the eyes. This bilateral stimulation in EMDR has been demonstrated to be efficacious with posttraumatic stress disorder (Nijdam, Gersons, Reitsma, de Jongh, & Olff, 2012; Bisson et al., 2007). Although there has been controversy over the eye moments as a component of healing, research suggests that they are in fact a central component of this treatment (McGuire, Lee, & Drummond, 2014).

Other approaches include hypnosis, creative art therapies, psychodynamic therapies, stress management, and (as mentioned earlier) a variety of specific therapy and counseling approaches.

REFERENCES AND FURTHER READING

American Psychiatric Association (APA). (2013). *Diagnostic and statistical manual of mental disorders, fifth edition.* Arlington, VA: American Psychiatric Publishing.

Bisson, J. I., Ehlers, A., Matthews, R., Pilling, S., Richards, D., & Turner, S. (2007). Psychological treatments for chronic post-traumatic stress disorder: Systematic review and meta-analysis. *British Journal of Psychiatry, 190*(2), 97–104. doi:10.1192/bjp.bp.106.021402.

Brazier, Y. (2016). What is psychotherapy? *Medical News Today.* Retrieved from http://www.medicalnewstoday.com/articles/156433.php.

Burke, H. M., Davis, M. C., Otte, C., & Mohr, D. C. (2005). Depression and cortisol responses to psychological stress: A meta-analysis. *Psychoneuroendocrinology, 30*(9), 846–856.

Crouch, J. L., & Milner, J. S. (1993). Effects of child neglect on children. *Criminal Justice and Behavior, 20*(1), 49–65.

Gibson, L. E. (2016). Acute stress disorder. Retrieved from http://www.ptsd.va.gov/professional/treatment/early/acute-stress-disorder.asp.

Hamblen, J. (2010). Treatment of PTSD: A handout from the National Center for PTSD. Retrieved from http://newriver.edu/images/stories/library/Stennett_Psychology_Articles/Treatment%20of%20PTSD%20-%20A%20Handout%20from%20the%20National%20Center%20for%20PTSD.pdf.

Hanson, J. L., Adluru, N., Chung, M. K., Alexander, A. L., Davidson, R. J., & Pollak, S. D. (2013). Early neglect is associated with alterations in white matter integrity and cognitive functioning. *Child Development, 84*(5), 1566–1578.

Hart, V., Blattner, J., & Leipsic, S. (2001). Coaching versus therapy: A perspective. *Consulting Psychology Journal: Practice and Research, 53*(4), 229–237.

Herman, J. L. (1992). Complex PTSD: A syndrome in survivors of prolonged and repeated trauma. *Journal of Traumatic Stress, 5*(3), 377–391.

Herman, J. L. (1997). *Trauma and recovery* (Vol. 551). New York, NY: Basic Books.

History of the DSM. (n.d.). Retrieved July 1, 2015, from http://www.psychiatry.org/practice/dsm/dsm-history-of-the-manual.

Hofmann, S. G., Asnaani, A., Vonk, I. J., Sawyer, A. T., & Fang, A. (2012). The efficacy of cognitive behavioral therapy: A review of meta-analyses. *Cognitive Therapy and Research, 36*(5), 427–440.

Hoskins, M., Pearce, J., Bethell, A., Dankova, L., Barbui, C., Tol, W. A., . . . Bisson, J. I. (2015). Pharmacotherapy for post-traumatic stress disorder: Systematic review and meta-analysis. *British Journal of Psychiatry, 206*(2), 93–100. doi:10.1192/bjp.bp.114.148551.

Ipser, J. C., & Stein, D. J. (2012). Evidence-based pharmacotherapy of post-traumatic stress disorder (PTSD). *International Journal of Neuropsychopharmacology, 15*(6), 825–840.

Kay, C., & Green, J. (2013). Reactive attachment disorder following early maltreatment: Systematic evidence beyond the institution. *Journal of Abnormal Child Psychology, 41*(4), 571–581.

Levine, P. A. (1997). *Waking the tiger: Healing trauma—The innate capacity to transform overwhelming experiences.* Berkeley, CA: North Atlantic Books.

McGuire, T. M., Lee, C. W., & Drummond, P. D. (2014). Potential of eye movement desensitization and reprocessing therapy in the treatment of post-traumatic stress disorder. *Psychology Research and Behavior Management, 7*, 273–283.

McNally, R. J. (2009). Can we fix PTSD in DSM-V? *Depression and Anxiety, 26*(7), 597–600.

National Institutes of Mental Health. (n.d.). Psychotherapies: What is psychotherapy? Retrieved from http://www.nimh.nih.gov/health/topics/psychotherapies/index.shtml.

Nijdam, M. J., Gersons, B. R., Reitsma, J. B., de Jongh, A., & Olff, M. (2012). Brief eclectic psychotherapy v. eye movement desensitization and reprocessing therapy for post-traumatic stress disorder: Randomised controlled trial. *British Journal of Psychiatry, 200*(3), 224–231. doi:10.1192/bjp.bp.111.099234.

Payne, P., Levine, P. A., & Crane-Godreau, M. A. (2015). Somatic experiencing: Using interoception and proprioception as core elements of trauma therapy. *Frontiers in Psychology, 6*(93), 1–18.

Resick, P. A., Nishith, P., & Griffin, M. G. (2003). How well does cognitive-behavioral therapy treat symptoms of complex PTSD? An examination of child sexual abuse survivors within a clinical trial. *CNS Spectrums, 8*(5), 340–355.

Shalev, A. Y., Bonne, O., & Eth, S. (1996). Treatment of posttraumatic stress disorder: A review. *Psychosomatic Medicine, 58*(2), 165–182.

Stergiopoulos, E., Cimo, A., Cheng, C., Bonato, S., & Dewa, C. S. (2011). Interventions to improve work outcomes in work-related PTSD: A systematic review. *BMC Public Health, 11*(1), 838.

Substance Abuse and Mental Health Services Administration. (2015). NREPP submission process. Retrieved from http://nrepp.samhsa.gov/04f_reviews_submission.aspx.

Voelker, R. (2004). Stress, sleep loss, and substance abuse create potent recipe for college depression. *JAMA, 291*(18), 2177–2179.

Whitehouse, B., & Heller, D. P. (2008). Heart rate in trauma: Patterns found in somatic experiencing and trauma resolution. *Biofeedback, 36*(1), 24–29.

46

The Prevention, Management, and Reduction of Stress

Michele Ferraro

Is it possible to prevent stress? Although stress affects everyone differently, because individual tolerance levels differ, stress begins with a physiological response that cannot be prevented, as discussed in previous chapters. Stress is blamed for a huge amount of human devastation that is recorded by the medical community on a daily basis in the form of physiological (body), psychological (mind), and spiritual (spirit) symptoms. Most people can identify with sleepless nights, excessive worry, the experience that there is never enough time to complete tasks, relationship issues, and so on. One might assume that if it were possible to eliminate the negative effects of stress, that practice or technique would be widespread and touted globally. And yet, there are many practitioners who claim to know the secrets of stress prevention, maintenance, and reduction, and preach their version of it to hopeful (or desperate) clients. There is no shortage of research on the subject, and it is presented in a myriad of venues, from medical institutions, houses of worship, institutions of higher learning, and small healing centers to online practitioners, in print, in person, through infomercials, and through distance learning. Is all this a money-making scam, or can stress really be prevented?

Answering that question is complex, and really depends on semantics. In other words, the meaning of an "overabundance" of stress is an individual matter: what is stressful for each person, what one does to offset the negative effects of stress, or even what is not recognized as stressful but nonetheless has deleterious effects on one's body, mind, and spirit. Certainly, it is possible to reduce stress, and through diligence and determination to maintain that reduction. The manner in which stress affects a particular human being is better comprehended by reviewing the human being in a holistic manner, as this allows examination of the body, mind, and spirit.

By assessing these areas through environmental, genetic, and epigenetic layers, a complex process may be simplified. "There are no lions coming," said Dr. Janis Frankel, of the Association for Advanced Training in the Behavioral Sciences, to the students who participated in a 2010 four-day review as they studied for the Examination for Professional Practice in Psychology (EPPP; an exam that grants licensure as a psychologist to eligible persons who pass it). While that was true in the literal sense, almost every student nevertheless continued to experience a high degree of stress that caused exhaustion, racing heart, inability to concentrate, memory difficulty, sleep issues, and digestive problems. These students were aware of many ways to combat the effects of stress; however, their knowledge did not eliminate the problem. Human beings and other animals are physiologically designed to respond to stress in the form of threats with fight, flight, or freeze. What happens when humans are exposed to a threat is a complex sequence of physiological and psychological responses. Although there may be no lions actually in hot pursuit, our bodies, minds, and spirits are deleteriously affected when danger is sensed—real or imagined.

Stress as defined by the National Institutes of Health (NIH) is "the brain's response to any demand" (NIH, 2014). Not all demands create havoc in the body. A moderate amount of stress may be positive and even desirable. What happens physiologically is important to understand. When the body senses a threat that is prolonged, or a series of successive threats or threats that overlap, the physiological function responding to the stress cannot return to homeostasis, and the chronic stress state causes the resulting and unrelenting release of hormones to produce negative effects on the body. In contrast, when stress is a positive motivating factor, the body returns to homeostasis without being constantly taxed or restimulated by a continuous flood of hormones that compromises the immune system. Positive stress is moderate and short-lived or temporary. This is the kind of stress that aids development in stable, favorable relationships. Moreover, there is enough hormonal assistance for the system to become activated and get the job done. Good stress is not the subject here, as it does not cause problems; the intention is to draw the distinction between good stress and bad stress.

THE QUESTION OF PREVENTION

If, as the NIH suggests, stress is the result of any demand, then prevention is not possible, because demands are always present and will continue to be present. Even Henry David Thoreau at Walden's pond felt stress. It is easy to identify stress that is connected to basic physiological needs, such as safety, food, shelter, and economic security, but a myriad of other stressors are also present in everyday life. Deadlines, an overload of obligations, financial concerns, frustrations, conflicts, and illness are present in an increasingly overwhelming combination in day-to-day existence. Demands may take the form of relationship interactions, illness, political change, global events, climate change, war, weather events, terrorism, and on and on. It may be more a question of surviving stress than preventing it.

In the modern world, we are assaulted by stress in ways that we seldom think consciously about anymore. For example, road rage may be nothing more than a 21st-century response to intense stress in the form of traffic, which can be a life-or-death situation. Crowded streets, cities, venues, schools, busses all create stress—this is the known psychological effect of crowding. Research suggests that women become depressed and men become more aggressive in crowded situations. Although Deaux and Wrightsman (1988) claim that a crowd enhances a positive situation, crowds make the negative situations that do occur more stressful. At football games or concerts, crowding may be expected and acceptable, but in the normal hustle and bustle of daily city living it appears not to be. Other effects of crowding, such as pollution, also increase the effects of stress in multiple ways. For example:

- Air pollution has negative effects on health and is associated with lower cognitive performance and decreased sensitivity to social clues (Gatto et al., 2014).
- High temperatures have been linked to a number of negative consequences, including frustration, aggressiveness, and a tendency to make risky decisions (Bushman, 2013).
- Noxious or excessive noise exposure can cause stress and irritability, interfere with the ability to concentrate, and increase aggressiveness, especially among individuals who are already angry or annoyed. Some research has found, however, that the negative effects of noise are reduced when people believe they can stop or control the noise, even when they do not actually do so (Donnerstein & Wilson, 1976).

Physiological Overview

In a stressful event, the hypothalamus activates several systems: the sympathetic nervous system (SNS) activates the adrenal medulla, releasing norepinephrine and epinephrine into the bloodstream; the impulses from the SNS activate the glands and smooth muscles; the adrenal cortex system releases CRF and the pituitary gland secretes the hormone ACTH; ACTH arrives at the adrenal cortex and releases approximately 30 other hormones into the bloodstream. At this point the neural activity combines with hormones in the bloodstream to produce the fight-flight-freeze response. This is explained in more complete detail in other chapters.

If the stress does not subside, chronic stress develops as cortisol continues to be manufactured and released into the system. Daniela Kaufer, an associate professor of integrative biology at the University of California-Berkeley, is a renowned researcher, who states that her research program "focuses on the molecular events that underlie the plasticity of the brain in the face of stress and neurological insults, bridging the gap between the gross physiological effects, and the molecular and cellular events that underlie them" (Kaufer, n.d.). Her main subject is the hippocampus, an area of the brain that is a part of the limbic system and is primarily associated with memory formation, spatial navigation, and emotion. One of Kaufer's studies found that chronic stress causes the brain to generate fewer neurons and more myelin-producing cells than normal. This results in more white matter in certain areas of the brain, disrupting the balance and timing of communication within the brain, and the reduced number of neurons has a negative effect on memory and learning. Current research also suggests that when stress is prolonged, creating a chronic condition, a neural connection between the hippocampus and the hypothalamus develops, weakening the pathway to the prefrontal cortex. Kaufer thinks this could moderate the fight-or-flight response, resulting in a faster fear response and a lowered ability to return to homeostasis (Friedman & Kaufer, 2013). As stress increases and becomes chronic, physiological changes may also occur in the development of hippocampal stem cells (Kaufer et al., 2004).

Preventing stress from doing further damage requires serious, dedicated effort and lifestyle change, because the result of chronic stress can be physical, mental, and spiritual illness. The physical symptoms include a compromised immune system, as well as headaches, body aches, pains, digestive issues, nausea, diarrhea, and constipation. The chronically stressed person is also frequently subject to illnesses such as colds, sinus infections, high blood pressure, herpes breakouts, loss of sex drive, chest pains, and rapid heartbeat. A continually compromised immune system may also lead to serious physical disease such as heart disease, diabetes, and cancers.

Psychological Overview

Psychological issues of stress include anxiety, nervousness, loneliness, anger, mood disorders, sleep disturbances, eating disorders, isolation, and loss of interest in pleasurable activities. These symptoms create memory and concentration problems, poor judgment, negative and racing thoughts, and overwhelming worry. Treatment from primary care physicians and psychiatrists often includes anxiolytics, such as benzodiazepines and antidepressants, which come with their own sets of side effects. These can include addiction, sexual dysfunction, and an assortment of physical maladies, thus producing additional psychological stress.

Spiritual Overview

The spirit, as one of the three human "bodies" that make up the whole of a human being (the others being the physiological body and the psychological body), is the body that creates meaning in and of day-to-day life or existence. Physiological and psychological stress, especially chronic stress, may have a deleterious effect on the spirit. Spiritual symptoms of excess stress include feelings of despair, inner

AVOIDANCE IS INEFFECTIVE FOR HANDLING STRESS

Avoidance is for the most part an ineffective—and usually harmful—coping mechanism for handling stress. Although there is some research indicating that initial avoidance, including denial, can act as a psychological benefit, it is only helpful when it is not a prolonged, continued, or habitual response. Avoidance can take many forms: procrastination, people-pleasing, and engagement in other passive behaviors; ignoring the stress-producing factors; or wishing that certain issues, struggles, and problems would just "go away."

Coping by avoidance can actually deplete a person's internal resources to be effective in self-regulation and reduce the ability to solve problems (Langlois, 2013). When an individual employs avoidance strategies, the stress experienced from the initial source of avoidance usually increases, and may even precipitate additional struggles due to lingering emotions, thoughts, behaviors, interactions, reactions, and other factors.

—*Serena Wadhwa*

worthlessness, hopelessness, emptiness, the sense that life has no meaning, and a sense that the future is doomed. Keeping the spiritual body healthy is another defense against stress and a foundation for developing a feeling of well-being.

In 1959, after studying for 18 years at the Sera monastic university in Lhasa, Lama Thubten Yeshe escaped from Tibet with a number of other refugees. He is credited with bringing Tibetan Buddhism to Westerners and founding the Foundation for the Preservation of the Mahayana Tradition. His many lectures were captured in the Lama Yeshe Wisdom Archive.

> I hope that you understand what the word "spiritual" really means. It means to search for, to investigate, the true nature of the mind. There's nothing spiritual outside. My rosary isn't spiritual; my robes aren't spiritual. Spiritual means the mind, and spiritual people are those who seek its nature. (Yeshe, 2003, p. 89)

Peter Russell, faculty member at the Institute of Noetic Sciences, puts it in a slightly different way:

> The essence of spirituality is the search to know our real self, to discover the true nature of consciousness.
>
> If consciousness is human awareness of our existence, the more it is nurtured and developed the more we are able to fight off physiological and psychological stress. (Russell, 2006)

Yet another description comes from Len Sperry, a psychiatrist, clinical psychologist, and professor of graduate counseling at Florida Atlantic University. In the inaugural issue of *Spirituality in Clinical Practice,* he identified areas in which psychotherapists engage in the discussion of spirituality:

> (1) as a spiritual resource for coping with a serious health problem, personal or professional loss, or interpersonal conflict; (2) in situations involving betrayal, death of a child, or other loss resulting in symptoms reflecting a crisis of faith or meaning in life; and (3) for the spiritual quest of increased well-being and awareness. (Sperry & Shafranske, 2005)

Sperry claims the third point is the most frequent reason clients bring up spirituality in the clinical setting. As clients desire ways to grow and become more aware, they are drawn to spiritual practices to alleviate suffering and struggle.

Spirit, as one of a human being's three holistic bodies, includes human consciousness or awareness. To be a whole person, one needs health in all of the bodies. Working on improving one part assists the other parts, but strengthening all of the bodies achieves the greatest overall results. Ken Wilbur, a great American philosopher and writer, describes awareness like this:

> Across the board, the sense of being any sort of Seer or Witness or Self vanishes altogether. You don't look at the sky; you are the sky. You can taste the sky. It's not out there. As Zen would say, you can drink the Pacific Ocean in a single gulp, you can swallow the Kosmos whole—precisely because awareness is no longer split into a seeing subject in here and a seen object out there. There is just pure seeing. Consciousness and its display are not-two. (Wilbur, 2000, p. 342)

In this context one is purely in the present, so there is no stress, judgment, or expectations.

THE BIG PICTURE FOR STRESS

Stopping the onslaught of stress is impossible in this physical world, so mitigating the negative effects of future stress and existing stress damage may be the best approach. Learning what demands are within one's control is the first step. The stress demand may come from traumatic events or daily stress that burgeons into chronic stress from work, school, family obligations, financial concerns, driving, being overextended socially, a failure to say "no" to increased demands, and interpersonal conflicts, to name just a few. While those demands will continue in a fast-paced lifestyle, one can learn to change one's physiological, psychological, and spiritual responses to those daily events by utilizing evidence-based interventions. Other demands exist that most of us have no control over, such as global warming, terrorism, war, economic fluctuations, environmental and political changes, and weather conditions. These are situations that we must adapt to; however, they may continue to create stress even when we recognize that they are outside of our control.

Seven Lifestyle Interventions

Mitigation of the damage of stress in the areas we can control includes seven basic elements: (1) sleep, (2) exercise, (3) meditation and mindfulness, (4) proper nutrition and hydration, (5) stress inoculation and the acquisition of stress coping mechanisms, (6) trauma release, and (7) supportive relationships. This combination of measures allows one to design a healthy, holistic lifestyle, which will assist in offsetting the ravages of stress and utilize stress to one's advantage. When one is already overwhelmed by stress, this magnitude of lifestyle change may appear daunting and stressful in and of itself. Incorporating one element at a time and then making small incremental changes in other areas assists in adopting and adapting to a healthier lifestyle.

Sleep

This exploration of stress prevention, maintenance, and reduction measures begins with sleep. Sleep is the first line of defense in stress reduction. Sufficient sleep keeps the body, mind, and spirit functioning optimally. Furthermore, sleep is a process in human beings that supports life. It is necessary for learning, memory, and problem solving. Sleep plays a vital role in good health and well-being throughout the life span. Getting enough quality sleep at the right times can help protect mental health, physical health, quality of life, and safety.

> The way you feel while you're awake depends in part on what happens while you're sleeping. During sleep, your body is working to support healthy brain function and maintain your physical health. In children and teens, sleep also helps support growth and development. (National Heart, Lung, & Blood Institute [NHLBI], 2012)

The National Institutes of Health state that adults require 7 to 9 hours of sleep per night, and teenagers require 8 to 9¼ hours per night for optimal functioning. Younger children and infants require even more hours of sleep. Interestingly, as adults age, the requirement for sleep does not decrease. The National Institutes of Health conducted research which indicated that most Americans do not get the recommended amount of sleep each night. For example, here are some significant findings compiled by the NIH:

- 50 to 70 million American adults have sleep or wakefulness disorders.
- One-third of Americans get less than 7 hours of sleep per night.
- 12 to 18 million U.S. adults have sleep apnea.
- Insufficient sleep and insomnia are more prevalent in women.
- 70 percent of high school students are not getting enough sleep on school nights.
- Memory and cognitive impairment: Decreased alertness and excessive daytime sleepiness impair your memory and your cognitive ability—your ability to think and process information.
- Automobile injury: The National Highway Traffic Safety Administration (NHTSA) estimates conservatively that each year drowsy driving is responsible for at least 100,000 automobile crashes, 71,000 injuries, and 1,550 fatalities.
- Decreased performance and alertness: One-third of adults are sleepy during daylight hours on a daily basis. Sleep deprivation induces significant reductions in performance and alertness. Reducing your nighttime sleep by as little as 1½ hours for just one night could result in a reduction of daytime alertness by as much as 32 percent.
- $50 billion a year is lost in productivity due to sleep problems. Excessive sleepiness also contributes to a greater than twofold increased risk of sustaining an occupational injury.
- Research shows that sleeping less than 7 to 8 hours each night, irregular sleep schedules, or poor-quality sleep are associated with many health risks, such as:
  - Heart failure
  - Stroke
  - Obesity
  - High blood pressure
  - Psychiatric problems, including depression and other mood disorders
  - Attention deficit disorder (ADD)
  - Mental impairment
  - Fetal and childhood growth retardation
  - Injury from accidents
  - Disruption of bed partner's sleep quality
  - Poor quality of life (NHLBI, 2013).

All the evidence shows that sufficient sleep is necessary to reduce the negative effects of stress. Paradoxically, sleep deprivation may be the result of chronic stress, an untreated sleep disorder, an illness, insomnias, or a myriad of other problems. A professional should assess the causes of insufficient sleep and a plan should be developed and implemented to resolve sleep challenges. Sleep deprivation has also been linked to adverse effects on both brain function and structure, resulting in mood disorders, psychoses, emotional dysregulation, and instability. Consistent inadequate sleep deleteriously affects the neural pathways, neurotransmitter communication, and chronic stress.

A discussion of sleep is incomplete without mention of the circadian rhythm. Researchers have been studying the effects of a "biological clock" for more than 50 years. What is known is that almost all organisms, even down to algae, possess some type of inner biological rhythm. In humans, the suprachiasmatic nuclei (SCN), located in the anterior hypothalamus, modulates the circadian clock. According to Vitaterna, Takahashi, and Turek (2001):

> Nearly all physiological and behavioral functions in humans occur on a rhythmic basis, which in turn leads to dramatic diurnal rhythms in human performance capabilities. Regardless of whether it results from voluntary (e.g., shift work or rapid travel across time zones) or involuntary (e.g., illness or advanced age) circumstances, a disturbed circadian rhythmicity in humans has been associated with a variety of mental and physical disorders and may negatively impact safety, performance, and productivity. Many adverse effects of disrupted circadian rhythmicity may, in fact, be linked to disturbances in the sleep-wake cycle. Some rhythmic processes are more affected by the circadian clock than by the sleep-wake state, whereas other rhythms are more dependent on the sleep-wake state.

Sleep in the appropriate amount is a primary ingredient in preventing stress from becoming chronic. When it is elusive, an assessment by a professional will assist in determining the causes of insomnias. It is challenging, because the question of which came first—the sleep issue or the stress issue—may be difficult to answer. Lack of sleep may be caused by depression or a physical illness, which may be caused by chronic stress and lack of sleep.

> The conservation of sleep across all animal species suggests that sleep serves a vital function. Sleep is reported to have a critical function in ensuring metabolic homeostasis. Using real-time assessments of tetramethylammonium diffusion and two-photon imaging in live mice, natural sleep or anesthesia associated with a 60% increase in the interstitial space, resulting in a striking increase in convective exchange of cerebrospinal fluid with interstitial fluid. In turn, convective fluxes of interstitial fluid increased the rate of β-amyloid clearance during sleep. Thus, the restorative function of sleep may be a consequence of the enhanced removal of potentially neurotoxic waste products that accumulate in the awake central nervous system. (Xie et al., 2013)

Exercise/Physical Activity

Exercise is an additional stress buster and an overall health enhancer. Even the addition of 30 minutes a day of movement is beneficial, and the 30 minutes can be broken up into two 15-minute segments, or even three 10-minute segments. Mayo Clinic Staff writers report that exercise can improve sleep. Exercise can reduce stress, and improve cardiovascular function, mood, and self-confidence. Whether it is taking the stairs instead of an elevator or escalator, parking at a far corner of the parking lot, taking walking breaks, gardening, or housecleaning, the idea is to just move. Physical activity doesn't have to just take place in a fitness facility. Make physical activity fun: for example, bicycle riding, swimming, skating, playing tennis, and everything in between are also options (Mayo Clinic, 2014).

The National Institutes of Health note that exercise is one of the most important things we can do to improve and safeguard our health. Everyday we are inundated with studies finding links between inactive behavior and increased health risks, such as weight gain, type 2 diabetes, heart disease, chronic stress, anxiety, pain, dementia, and early death. First Lady Michelle Obama started an initiative called Let's Move, encouraging children and their families to eat nutritiously and exercise more often. The World Health Organization (WHO) reports:

> Globally, around 31% of adults aged 15 and over were insufficiently active in 2008 (men 28% and women 34%). Approximately 3.2 million deaths each year are attributable to insufficient physical activity. (WHO, 2016)

Nicholas Pimlott, MD, CCFP, scientific editor of the *Canadian Family Physician,* calls exercise the miracle drug:

> The evidence for the health benefits of physical activity in adults is overwhelming. Regular physical activity reduces the risk of chronic diseases such as coronary artery disease, diabetes, and obesity. Regular physical activity also helps improve mental health . . . . (Pimlott, 2010)

According to the American Psychological Association (APA, 2012):

> The research keeps growing—exercise benefits your mind just as well as your body. We keep hearing about the long-term benefits of a regular exercise routine. But even a 20-minute walk, run, swim or dance session in the midst of a stressful time can give an immediate effect that can last for several hours.

Meditation

Jon Kabat-Zinn, Professor of Medicine Emeritus and founding director of the Stress Reduction Clinic and the Center for Mindfulness in Medicine, Health Care, and Society at the University of Massachusetts Medical School, is the author of *Full Catastrophe Living: Using the Wisdom of Your Body and Mind to Face Stress, Pain, and Illness* (1991). He emphasizes the importance of mindfulness meditation in stress reduction and healthy living, citing studies conducted at the clinic.

This is what some other popular healthcare physicians say about mindfulness meditation:

- Deepak Chopra: "Benefits of meditation are stress reduction, better sleep, lower blood pressure, improved cardiovascular function, improved immunity, and the ability to stay centered in the midst of all the turmoil that's going on around you. Meditation helps you do less and accomplish more" (Chopra Center, n.d.).
- Andrew Weil, MD, says mindfulness meditation is a way to "achieve personal peace and healing."
- The Mayo Clinic says: "Meditation is simple and inexpensive. It requires only your time and effort, and the risks are minimal. If you're interested in stress reduction, give meditation a try."
- Joan Borysenko, PhD, says: "Physiological research shows that at least three 20 minute periods of meditation weekly are necessary to experience long-term reduction in heart-rate, blood pressure, anxiety and other stress-related problems" (Borysenko, n.d.).

Neuroplasticity and Mindfulness Meditation

The idea that the "brain can change its structure through experience" (Siegel, 2012, p. 8.1)—rewire itself by creating new neural pathways (Begley, 2007)—provides us with additional information for healing. In 1980, Jon Kabat-Zinn founded the Stress Reduction Clinic and the Center for Mindfulness in Medicine, Health Care, and Society at the University of Massachusetts Medical School. He and his students, residents, and interns conducted 34 years of well-developed research studies whose results detail the benefits of meditating. Some of the benefits include:

- Reduction in depression and anxiety
- Lower blood pressure
- Improvement in sleep quality and quantity
- Pain reduction
- Increase in concentration and attention
- Reduced cardiovascular disease
- Improvement in overall feeling of well-being (Center for Mindfulness in Medicine, Health Care, and Society, 2014)

The word *mindfulness* appears everywhere in popular vernacular, with research confirming its uses in everything from acne reduction to improving attention and concentration in schoolchildren with ADHD. The intention to attend to a specific thing (like one's breath, a word, a phrase, a raisin) holds in it an opportunity to link neurons and create new networks. For example, Sara Lazar (2006), wrote: "Meditation can have a serious impact on your brain long beyond the time when you're actually sitting and meditating, and this may have a positive impact on your day-to-day living." Research funded by the NIH and CDC found measurable changes in the brains of people who meditate routinely. Chittaranjan and Radhakrishnan (2009) claim, "Prayer is a special form of meditation and may therefore convey all the health benefits that have been associated with meditation."

Prayer

Research studies on the healing power of prayer are numerous. The National Institutes of Health classified prayer as a mind-body intervention. "Religious traditions across the world display beliefs in healing through prayer" (Chittaranjan & Radhakrishnan, 2009). These authors also make the following statement:

> We must keep in mind that religion is based on faith and not on proof. This implies that, if God exists, he's indifferent to humanity or has chosen to obscure his presence. Either way, he would be unlikely to cooperate in scientific studies that seek to test his existence.
>
> Where does this leave us? God may indeed exist and prayer may indeed heal; however, it appears that, for important theological and scientific reasons, randomized controlled studies cannot be applied to the study of the efficacy of prayer in healing. In fact, no form of scientific enquiry presently available can suitably address the subject. Therefore, the continuance of such research may result in the conducted studies finding place among other seemingly impeccable studies with seemingly absurd claims . . . . Whereas, we have attempted to be scientifically and politically correct in our critique, other authors, such as Dawkins, . . . [have] been humorous, nay even scathing, in their criticism.

In *Complementary and Alternative Medicine for Psychologists* (Shale, Elkins, & Fisher, 2014) say, "Within each culture, some form of spirituality and prayer has served as the institutionalized means of seeking assistance from a supreme being or beings perceived as powerful enough to alter nature, health, and disease. Different religions hold different beliefs about a supreme being" (p. 3). On the next page they claim, "The mechanisms through which spirituality and prayer may work are unknown; however, the underlying mechanisms have been the topic of some scientific study." Despite a plethora of research, there is not any significant scientific evidence that prayer heals.

Nutrition and Hydration

Research studies continuously identify the importance of proper nutrition and hydration. Eating fatty and sodium-laden foods can cause fatigue issues, in addition to obesity and other diseases. The Physicians Committee for Responsible

Medicine reports that Americans tend to eat comfort food when we are stressed. They suggest that, instead of ice cream and high fat, we try:

> low-fat, high-fiber, carbohydrate-rich meals with plenty of fruits and vegetables. They soothe us without sapping our energy and give us the nutrients we need to boost our immune system. (Physicians Committee for Responsible Medicine, n.d.)

Dehydration can cause decreased alertness, abdominal pain, anxiety, confusion, dizziness, and lightheadedness. Eating nutritious foods and staying hydrated is an important way of warding off stress.

Stress Inoculation

Donald Meichenbaum, PhD, first wrote specifically about Stress Inoculation Training (SIT) in 1985. The clinical references describing the approach date primarily from the 1980s.

> The theory is based on the premise that successful coping with stress in the present strengthens the ability to cope with stress in the future. When using this technique a person acquires a variety of skills to help him/her cope with the current problem as well as future problems. The assumption is that successful coping with stress in the present will reduce its impact in the future. (Meichenbaum, 1996)

SIT is a form of cognitive behavioral therapy implemented in a three-phase intervention that can be as short as a 20-minute session before surgery or as long as 40 weekly or biweekly sessions followed by boosters and follow-ups. The first phase identifies the demands or stressors that create problems. The patient is encouraged to look at the issues in a way that accommodates a problem-solving approach. The second phase develops skill acquisition and rehearsal. The third phase involves application of the coping skills and follow-through.

In *The Happiness Advantage,* writer and former Harvard educator Shawn Achor claims:

> [P]ositive psychology researchers finished a meta-analysis study of nearly every scientific happiness study available—over 200 studies on 275,000 people worldwide. Their findings exactly matched the principles I was teaching—that happiness leads to success in nearly every domain, including work, health, friendship, sociability, creativity, and energy. (Achor, 2010, p. 21)

Cognitive Reframing

Stress can be overwhelming. During times of intense stress, people may develop many negative thoughts. *Cognitive reframing* refers to changing the way you think about something by looking at it through a positive lens. An example of this way of thinking is seeing the glass as half full instead of half empty. This involves taking a negative situation and attempting to find opportunities to turn it into a positive situation. A negative thought like "I am so overloaded with work, I will never be free from it" is a perfect example of a defeatist thought. Changing the thought by looking at it as an opportunity to become a positive thinker may change the thought to "I have an overabundance of work, and I am going to become a better organizer by prioritizing what I can accomplish each day." Or perhaps a caregiver feels stressed and overwhelmed by caring for a family member who has Alzheimer's disease. Repeating the same instructions or listening to the same stories over and over may be frustrating, but if you turn the negative into a positive it may be an opportunity to bring a little daily happiness into the life of a frightened, confused loved one and experience some happiness yourself.

In *The Happiness Advantage*, Shawn Achor describes seven principles of positive psychology, of which three are listed here:

- The Tetris Effect: how to retrain our brains to spot patterns of possibility, so we can see and seize opportunities wherever we look.
- The Zorro Circle: how to channel our efforts on small, manageable goals, to gain the leverage to gradually conquer bigger and bigger ones.
- Social investment: how to reap the dividends of investing in one of the greatest predictors of success and happiness—our social support network (Achor, 2010)

Eric Karpinski is a happiness coach who works with Shawn Achor at GoodThinkInc. They have created a program that Karpinski describes as three steps to rethinking stress, or a stress-enhancing mindset:

Step 1—Acknowledge your stress.
Step 2—Welcome your stress.
Step 3—Use your stress.

Here's why recognizing your stress is important. When you are unconsciously stressed, you process that stress in the limbic centers of your brain which drive you into a reactive, unthinking fight-or-flight mode. By recognizing and acknowledging your stress, on the other hand, your brain shifts where it processes that stress to the prefrontal cortex. This is the rational, thinking part of your brain, which allows you to pause, evaluate your options and consciously choose how you respond to the stress (Karpinski, 2013).

Trauma Release

Stressful or traumatic events create not only acute but also chronic forms of stress. The memories, thoughts, feelings, and images trigger a traumatic response.

Trauma is defined by the American Psychological Association (APA, 2016) as "an emotional response to a terrible event like an accident, rape or natural disaster. Reactions such as shock and denial are typical. Longer-term reactions include unpredictable emotions, flashbacks, strained relationships and even physical symptoms."

A disturbing event may be as damaging as a traumatic experience to some individuals. Regardless of the magnitude of the trauma—physiological, psychological, and/or spiritual—it culminates in a stress response or reaction. Instead of the experience being processed and released, trauma responses tend to stay around for a long time. Neuropsychologist Dr. Rick Hansen (2011) claims it is the way a trauma is held in memory that keeps it returning to the present in the form of flashbacks. Many times, one is never able to actually process through the trauma memories, because they are stuck.

Dr. Hansen claims that the stress response of cortisol release kills neurons in the hippocampus (up to 25 percent of them) until the trauma is released (2011); the stress response thus causes "a deterioration of the brain" that makes the person unable to form new memories, "which is a key factor in depression or PTSD." So, the stress of trauma changes the brain and mind in a negative manner. Trauma release is vital to breaking this cycle of re-experiencing the stressful event. Evidence-based interventions for doing so include Exposure Therapy (based on cognitive behavioral therapy [CBT]), Eye Movement Desensitization and Reprocessing (EMDR; Shapiro, 2001), and Focusing.

Exposure therapy

Exposure Therapy involves several steps that include exposure to the feared stimulus through flooding or implosive therapy. The idea is to desensitize the patient to the traumatic memories while providing a supportive therapeutic relationship. First, the individual talks to the therapist about the experience in detail, discussing all of the associated memories, thoughts, and feelings. Second, the therapist has the patient bring up all of the memories simultaneously, experiencing the trauma afresh and discussing the responses. Usually this is an overwhelming experience, but the repeated exposures help to desensitize the patient to the trauma. The third step is to create strategies to help in coping with the memories. Many times, putting cognition with the memory is helpful, such as, "This was not my fault," or "I didn't do anything to bring this on." Directed Therapeutic Exposure (DTE) is another term to describe implosive therapy. The goal is not to erase the memories but to reduce the intrusive quality of the memories.

EMDR

EMDR is another evidence-based intervention, initially used to reduce distress in veterans with PTSD. It also employs exposure, but includes eye movements, tones, or taps which, according to Dr. Francine Shapiro, "allow the spontaneous emergence of insights, emotions, physical sensations, and other memories." Shapiro introduced EMDR in 1989. This eight-phase approach has been heavily researched, and now is used for a myriad of disorders, as well as for performance enhancement (Barker & Barker, 2007). WHO listed it as a first-line therapy for PTSD (WHO, 2013). Collecting the appropriate information is vital in EMDR so that the target may be accurately identified. Safety is also important, and this therapy installs or strengthens the client's sense of safety. Then a three-pronged protocol is implemented. With each series of eye movements, the client is given a Subjective Units of Distress Scale (SUDS) charting the strength of the distress until it neutralizes. Then a new action is installed. When EMDR is used after a Focusing session, it is not necessary to go through all eight phases, because safety has already been established, the target has been identified, the client has had a bodily felt sense of the issue requiring attention, the body has given a solution, and the client's resources or positive cognitions have been strengthened (Shapiro, 2001).

Focusing

Focusing is supported by a long series of operational research studies conducted first at the University of Chicago and then internationally. Focusing is a mode of inward bodily attention that most people do not yet know about. It is more than being in touch with your feelings and different from bodywork (The Focusing Institute, 2016). Focusing occurs exactly at the interface of body-mind. It consists of specific steps for getting a body sense of how you are in a particular life situation. The body sense is unclear and vague at first, but if you pay attention it will open up into words or images and you will experience a felt shift in your body. In the process of Focusing, one experiences a physical change in the way that the issue is being lived in the body. One learns to live in a deeper place than just thoughts or feelings. The whole issue looks different and new solutions arise.

Supportive Relationships

Abraham Maslow's hierarchy of needs lists belongingness on the third level of human needs, after physiological and safety needs. In other words, people need people to survive. Our relationships can play a significant role in reducing our stress or in compounding and complicating stress. *Supportive relationships* are the relationships that can reduce incoming stress: "Empirical evidence supports the hypothesis that intrinsically motivated individuals will move in a direction of increasing relatedness with others" (Joseph & Patterson, 2008).

A social support network provides many benefits, the most important of which is a psychological feeling of well-being that accompanies that sense of belongingness. Friends, family, pets, and buddies help cope with stress, increase a sense of self-worth, and make one feel secure. Supportive relationships feel good. It helps to trust someone enough to access their information and advice, as well as dispense it. One way of increasing a network of supportive relationships may be to find areas of interest and get involved. It will make a big difference in reducing stress. Many people are close to family members, old friends, coworkers, and neighbors. A supportive relationship is friend and confidante. If the list is short or nonexistent, look for people who share the same interests and values by volunteering, joining a church and/or fitness center, taking a class, or pursuing a hobby.

MAINTAINING HEALTHY WAYS TO HANDLE STRESS

Over the past half-century, stress has been widely studied, used as a variable in models of behavior and disease, and achieved prominence in the lay public that few other biobehavioral concepts have attained (Baum, 1990). However, the insertion of stress into the public consciousness has not always been accompanied by concrete, useful suggestions on handling it. This section briefly summarizes the best of the existing advice on maintenance of a stress-busting lifestyle.

Maintaining a healthy lifestyle is a choice one makes to mitigate the effects of stress. Even with a healthy lifestyle and a good start down the path to stress prevention, maintenance challenges can be daunting. The obstacles may seem overwhelming. For some, getting 8 hours of sleep, in addition to 8 hours of work, 2 hours of commuting, and 2 hours for exercise and meditation, leaves only 4 hours a day for eating, family time, socializing, errands, and some personal time. For many people, a 40-hour workweek is just a dream, so the week can easily get cluttered with time-consuming tasks. Most people dislike being so rigidly scheduled, and being a student, parent, or a caregiver really makes adhering to a time schedule even more challenging. Most people, more often than not, play multiple roles.

Revisiting the seven basic elements—sleep, exercise, meditation, proper nutrition and hydration, stress inoculation and the acquisition of stress coping mechanisms, trauma release, and supportive relationships—is crucial at this juncture. If one had nothing to do but attend to one's prevention strategy, perhaps it would be possible to maintain a modicum of calm. However, this is rarely the case. By the time we are stressed "to the max," physical and psychological symptoms may be overtaking our lives, and few options for immediate relief are available. The simplest solution is usually to maintain what healthy lifestyle elements currently exist and keep refining and working toward a sustainable reduction in stress.

Environmental reduction measures may be one step. Stress is a demand on the system, and people are bombarded with demands on their systems in the form of environmental attacks, so research suggests that being aware of your environment may help in avoiding or managing stressors. Learn about air and water pollutants

TIME MANAGEMENT

Time management is a set of behaviors that decrease the effect of stressors on an individual. According to Macan, Shahani, Dipboye, and Phillips (1990, as cited in Jex and Elacqua, 1999), there are three dimensions to time management. The first is goal setting and prioritization. This includes what to accomplish in the day and what is the top priority. The second dimension concerns the mechanics of time management, which include actions such as preparing materials to take to work/school or making one's lunch the night before. The final dimension is establishing a preference for organization; this basically means starting one's work session with a clean work space. In one study (Macan, 1994), the author found that engagement with these behaviors led to decreased tension and increased satisfaction. The Centers for Disease Control and Prevention suggest keeping a time log to determine how you actually spend your time, and recommend that you use this log as a guide to assist in functions in the dimensions previously mentioned.

—*Serena Wadhwa*

in your area, and find out how to guard against them. For example, try not to run next to the highway and breathe car exhaust fumes. Don't eat fish with high mercury content, such as mackerel (King), marlin, orange roughy, shark, swordfish, tilefish, and tuna (bigeye, ahi). Dr. Jane Hightower and other health professionals have concluded that high mercury levels are reversible: Cutting consumption of mercury-contaminated fish causes mercury levels in the body to drop, though it can take 6 months or more to achieve this (Menon, 2016).

Choose a few other high-impact preventive methods to get going. Sleep should be number one, as it has the largest influence on the system as a whole. Choose to eat healthy foods: give up the sugar, processed foods, soda, and high-sodium, high-calorie snacks. Introduce more fruits and vegetables—organic if possible, and home-grown is even better. Move more: walk, take the stairs, park farther away from your destination, stand up and stretch. Walk with your friends and family for fun. Laugh.

Be consciously aware of all of the stressors that impact your life, both the good and the bad ones, and remember that there will be many of them. Be systematic in your categorizing and listing; it is not just work, home, and relationships. Stress or demand on the whole being takes many forms, and reducing stress involves knowing where it comes from. Sometimes, there are limited or no options for reduction.

REFERENCES AND FURTHER READING

Achor, S. (2010). *The happiness advantage*. New York, NY: Crown.

American Psychological Association (APA). (2012). Five tips to help manage stress. Retrieved from http://psycnet.apa.org/psycextra/518762012-001.pdf.

American Psychological Association (APA). (2016). Trauma. Retrieved from http://www.apa.org/topics/trauma/.

Australian Government Department of Health. (2014). Australia's physical activity and sedentary behaviour guidelines. Retrieved from http://www.health.gov.au/internet/main/publishing.nsf/Content/health-pubhlth-strateg-phys-act-guidelines.

Barker, R. T., & Barker, S. B. (2007). The use of EMDR in reducing presentation anxiety. *Journal of Family Psychotherapy, 15*, 47–61.

Barnett, J. E., Shale, A. J., Elkins, G., & Fisher, W. (2014). Spirituality and prayer. In A. Shale, G. R. Elkins, & W. I. Fisher (Eds.), *Complementary and alternative medicine for psychologists: An essential resource* (pp. 119–132). Washington, DC: American Psychological Association.

Baum, A. (1990). Stress, intrusive imagery, and chronic distress. *Health Psychology, 6*, 653-675.

Begley, S. (2007). *Train your mind, change your brain: How a new science reveals our extraordinary potential to transform ourselves*. New York, NY: Mind and Life.

Ben-Zur, H. (2009). Coping styles and affect. *International Journal of Stress Management, 16*(2), 87.

Borysenko, J. (n.d.). Meditation and inner peace. Retrieved from http://www.joanborysenko.com/mind-body-balance/stress-reduction/meditation-and-staying-centered/.

Bushman, B. J. (2013, July 18). Global warming can also increase aggression and violence. *Psychology Today*. Retrieved from https://www.psychologytoday.com/blog/get-psyched/201307/global-warming-can-also-increase-aggression-and-violence.

Center for Mindfulness in Medicine, Health Care, and Society. (2014). Mobilize your own inner resources for learning, growing, and healing. Retrieved from http://www.umassmed.edu/cfm/stress-reduction/.

Centers for Disease Control and Prevention. (n.d.). Lifestyle coach facilitation guide: post-core. Stress and time management. Retrieved from http://www.cdc.gov/diabetes/prevention/pdf/postcurriculum_session12.pdf.

Chittaranjan, A., & Radhakrishnan, R. (2009, October–December). Prayer and healing: A medical and scientific perspective on randomized controlled trials. *Indian Journal of Psychiatry, 51*(4), 247–253.

The Chopra Center. (n.d.). Why meditate. Retrieved from http://www.chopra.com/ccl/why-meditate.

Deaux, K., & Wrightsman, L. (1988). *Social psychology*. Pacific Grove, CA: Brooks/Cole.

Donnerstein, E., & Wilson, D. W. (1976). Effects of noise and perceived control on ongoing and subsequent aggressive behavior. *Journal of Personal and Social Psychology, 34*(5), 774–781.

EMDR Institute. (2016). What is EMDR? Retrieved from http://www.emdr.com/what-is-emdr/.

The Focusing Institute. (2016). What is focusing? Retrieved from http://focusing.org/.

Friedman, A. R., & Kaufer, D. (2013, December). Emerging roles for hippocampal adult neural stem cells in memory. *Colloquium Series on Stem Cell Biology, 2*(2), 1–39. doi:10.4199/C00100ED1V01Y201311SCB005.

Gatto, N. M., Henderson, V. W., Hodis, H. N., St John, J. A., Lurmann, F., Chen, J-C., & Mack, W. J. (2014, January). Components of air pollution and cognitive function in middle-aged and older adults in Los Angeles. *Neurotoxicology, 40,* 1–7. Retrieved from http://www.ncbi.nlm.nih.gov/pmc/articles/PMC3946571/.

Hansen, R. (2011). *The enlightened brain: The neuroscience of awakening.* Boulder, CO: Sounds True.

Jex, S. M., & Elacqua, T. C. (1999). Time management as a moderator of relations between stressors and employee strain. *Work & Stress, 13*(2), 182–191.

Joseph, S., & Patterson, T. G. (2008). The actualising tendency: A meta-theoretical perspective for positive psychology. In B. E. Levitt (Ed.), *Reflections on human potential: Bridging the person-centered approach and positive psychology* (p. 10). Ross-on-Wye, UK: PCCS Books.

Kabat-Zinn, J. (1982). An outpatient program for chronic pain. *General Hospital Psychiatry, 4*(1), 33–47.

Kabat-Zinn, J. (1991). *Full catastrophe living: Using the wisdom of your body and mind to face stress, pain, and illness.* New York, NY: Random House.

Karpinski, E. (2013, June) Three steps to rethink stress. Retrieved from http://thehappinesscoach.biz/the-three-steps-to-rethink-stress/.

Kaufer, D. (n.d.). Integrative biology: Research description. Retrieved March 14, 2014, from https://ib.berkeley.edu/people/faculty/kauferd.

Kaufer, D., Ogle, W., Pincus, Z., Clark, K., Nicholas, A., Dinkel, K., . . . Sapolsky, R. (2004). Restructuring the neuronal stress response with anti-glucocorticoid gene delivery. *Nature Neuroscience, 7,* 947–953.

Langlois, J. C. (2013). *The influence of avoidance coping and stressors on depression risk* (Doctoral dissertation). Alliant International University, California.

Macan, T. H. (1994). Time management: Test of a process model. *Journal of Applied Psychology, 79,* 381–391.

Massachusetts General Hospital. (2011, January). Mindfulness meditation training changes brain structure in eight weeks. *Science Daily News.* Retrieved from https://www.sciencedaily.com/releases/2011/01/110121144007.htm.

Mayo Clinic. (2014). Stress management: Stress basics. Retrieved from http://www.mayoclinic.org/healthy-lifestyle/stress-management/basics/stress-basics/hlv-20049495.

Meichenbaum, D. (1996). Stress inoculation training for coping with stressors. *The Clinical Psychologist, 49,* 4–7.

Menon, S. (2016). Mercury guide. Retrieved from https://www.nrdc.org/stories/mercury-guide.

National Heart, Lung, and Blood Institute. (n.d.). Guide to physical activity. Retrieved from http://www.nhlbi.nih.gov/health/public/heart/obesity/lose_wt/phy_act.htm.

National Heart, Lung, and Blood Institute. (2012). Why is sleep important? Retrieved from http://www.nhlbi.nih.gov/health/health-topics/topics/sdd/why.

National Heart, Lung, and Blood Institute (NHLBI). (2013). Sleep disorders & insufficient sleep: Improving health through research. Retrieved May 1, 2014, from https://www.nhlbi.nih.gov/news/spotlight/fact-sheet/sleep-disorders-insufficient-sleep-improving-health-through-research.

National Institutes of Health (NIH). (2014). Fact sheet on stress. Retrieved from https://www.nimh.nih.gov/health/publications/stress/index.shtml/index.shtml.

Physicians Committee for Responsible Medicine. (n.d.). How to eat right to reduce stress. Retrieved from http://www.pcrm.org/health/health-topics/how-to-eat-right-to-reduce-stress.

Pimlott, N. (2010, May). The miracle drug. *Canadian Family Physician, 56*(5), 407.

Russell, P. (2006). What is spirituality? Retrieved from http://www.peterrussell.com/Weaver/WeaverSpirituality.php.

Shale, A., Elkins, G. R., & Fisher, W. I. (Eds.). (2014). *Complementary and alternative medicine for psychologists: An essential resource.* Washington, DC: American Psychological Association.

Shapiro, F. (2001). *Eye movement desensitization and reprocessing: Basic principles, protocols and procedures.* New York, NY: Guilford Press.

Siegel, D. J. (2012). *Pocket guide to interpersonal neurobiology.* New York, NY: Mind Your Brain.

Sperry, L., & Shafranske, E. P. (Eds.). (2005). *Spiritually oriented psychotherapy.* Washington, DC: American Psychological Association.

Stroebe, M., Boelen, P. A., Van Den Hout, M., Stroebe, W., Salemink, E., & Van Den Bout, J. (2007). Ruminative coping as avoidance. *European Archives of Psychiatry and Clinical Neuroscience, 257*(8), 462–472.

Vitaterna, M. H., Takahashi, J. S., & Turek, F. W. (2001). Overview of circadian rhythms. *Alcohol Research and Health, 25*(2), 85–93.

West, D. (2013). Meditation the rise of futuristic medicine from an ageless practice. Retrieved from http://www.wakingtimes.com/2013/10/17/meditation-rise-futuristic-medicine-ageless-practice/.

Wilbur, K. (2000). *A brief history of everything.* Boston, MA: Shambala.

World Health Organization (WHO). (2013). Guidelines for the management of conditions specifically related to stress. Geneva: WHO.

World Health Organization (WHO). (2016). Physical inactivity: A global public health problem. Retrieved from http://www.who.int/dietphysicalactivity/factsheet_inactivity/en/.

Xie, L., Kang, H., Qiwu, X., Chen, M., Yonghong, L., Meenakshisundaram, T., . . . Nedergaard, M. (2013, October). Sleep drives metabolite clearance from the adult brain. *Science, 342*(6156), 373–377. doi:10.1126/science.1241224.

Yeshe, L. T. (2003). *Becoming your own therapist.* Boston, MA: Lama Yeshe Wisdom Archive.

47

Trends and Future Directions in Stress Research

Serena Wadhwa

Stress is such a broad topic that there is both plenty of research to conduct and plenty to explore within the subject itself. As the content in these volumes demonstrates, there are many vantage points from which to view this concept. The evolution of *stress,* from its origins in the early 1900s as a term adopted from physics; to the recognition of the physiological mechanisms of the body and brain; to modern concepts of appraisal and assessments, stressors, the influence of nature and nurture, the psyche, and mental health disorders; as well as the plethora of strategies to manage stressors, perceptions, and effects of stress, gives an idea of the diverse nature of what we call stress. So, what's left? What is research focusing on when it comes to stress? What's trending regarding stress in the modern world?

Complementary and alternative medicine (CAM) approaches are becoming more the norm as the modern world evolves. In a literature search on PsycINFO from 1964 to 1999, only 69 articles surfaced for the subjects of complementary and alternative medicine and stress. From 2000 to 2016, 3,366 articles appeared. The desire to explore the pros and cons of non-Western medicine—to discover and understand what works for others—is something continuously piquing interest, not only of individuals who conduct research, but also of people who may want to pursue CAM as a healing modality. For example, according to Heather Shannon, a counselor and health coach, one trend that may be on the rise is the exploration of nutrition as an alternative to medications (Irving, 2013). Research also suggests that some medical doctors are learning how to navigate the many new options available when prescribing for healthier lifestyles (Khan, Weller, & Blair, 2011; Jonas & Philips, 2012). Integrating lifestyle medicine into medical school training

ANIMAL-ASSISTED THERAPY

Animal-assisted therapy, or pet therapy, is relatively new to the field of therapy, although human relationships with animals have existed for thousands of years. Historically, animals were used as a means of facilitating a calmer environment, particularly in asylums in the late 1700s and during distressing events in the 1800s (Brodie & Biley, 1999). Considering that more than 60 percent of American households currently have a pet (Herzog, 2010), it's not surprising that pet therapy offers benefits to reduce and/or manage the negative effects of distress. In the 21st century, we call it *pet-facilitated* or *animal-assisted therapy* when an animal is intentionally introduced to a treatment milieu or to an individual as part of treatment (Nimer & Lundahl, 2007). Brodie and Biley (1999) provide an overview of the benefits of pet therapy, most of which fall into the categories of physical/general health, social benefits, and psychological benefits. Some of these benefits include fewer doctor visits during times of stress; decreased blood pressure; a source of companionship; increased interactions with others; some reduction in depression, hopelessness, and irritability; and an increase in humor and play. Although there are not yet enough studies to recommend specific methodologies, a 2013 review of research by Levine et al. on the effects of pet ownership on human cardiovascular disease showed enough evidence to suggest that pet ownership, especially of dogs, is probably associated with decreased incidence and severity of cardiovascular disease. Grants have been awarded to the American Humane Association to launch research studies in a *"Canines and Childhood Cancer (CCC)"* project.

Animals are also used as part of physical or occupational therapy in which the animals are walked, groomed, or otherwise tended to; these behaviors help the individual work muscles and improve motor skills (Nimer & Lundahl, 2007). Additionally, animals have been utilized as therapy in clinical and medical populations and treatment settings, including skilled nursing facilities for elderly people. Equine-assisted therapy involves horses and people in treatment of psychological issues (Klontz, Bivens, Leinart, & Klontz, 2007); results demonstrated that the effects of the therapy were stable six months later.

is being examined. As cited in Philips, Pojednic, Polak, Bush, and Trilk (2015), the World Health Organization predicts that disease caused by poor lifestyle choices may eventually account for about 66 percent of all disease occurrence. Medical students do not have training in incorporating lifestyle changes within their scope of practice. Philips et al. (2015) explore this as an area of curriculum development, where medical students could be taught guidelines for prescribing and advocating for healthier lifestyle choices that range from improved sleep, physical activity, and nutrition to relaxation, including leisure and having fun. Health and wellness are in the forefront in the modern world, against a background of complex individual, community, and global stressors.

Another current trend is exploration of the social, global, economic, and political influences on the experience of stress. Traditionally, as Becker (2013) points out, the experience of stress is considered something to which the individual needs to adapt and adjust. In her latest book, she challenges the traditional view of stress being an individual problem and applies a broader perspective to the experience of and responsibility for stress. She disputes the notion that only the individual holds this responsibility, and asks questions about the amount of responsibility that could be assigned to society at large, including the economic, global and political aspects of society. Some critics point out that some of her hypotheses and contentions require much more empirical support, but the notion that we need to look at additional and larger factors and influences in the processes that keep stress cycling is valid. For example, research has focused on the impact of stress on children and how these experiences affect the development of the brain, which in turn affects how children learn to operate and function in the world. Neglect, abuse, and other chronic stressors can influence the brain and thus individuals' subsequent thoughts, emotions, and actions. Policy makers are also mindful of these factors and effects as they search for ways to more effectively help individuals struggling with chronic (toxic) stress and means of treating and navigating these effects. Closing the gap between research and practice is another part of this trend. Although research demonstrates that the continuance of certain social events and conditions elevates detrimental stress hormone levels in the body (e.g., domestic violence, poverty), there is only so much an individual can do to "manage" what his or her body experiences; it is not 100 percent a personal matter. As long as these detrimental social/societal factors remain, the person will still experiences the stress therefrom. Thus, implementation of programs and other services to address these needs from a public health perspective is being explored.

Another area of interest is posttraumatic growth. More research is being conducted in this area to gain an understanding of how individuals "bounce back" from perceived traumatic situations; that is, how they integrate changes and move forward. This area focuses on various aspects of growth, including the acceptance of limitations, the development of philosophical perspectives, and resiliency. All of these areas are currently receiving attention, in contrast to previous research that focused primarily on the subjectivity of the stress experience and its impact on the individual's functionality. For example, Bicknell and Liefooghe (2006) study interactions and relationships between individuals and the environment; disharmony resulting from individuals' own psychological processes and their experience; and the dilemmas that exist within an individual and between the individual and external factors. These processes are being explored within an overarching conceptualization for understanding the experience of stress and how stress can be effectively managed. The "adaptology" field involves and integrates the structural, functional, and biopsychosocial components (Derevenco, 2009) relating to posttraumatic growth and resiliency, even while it recognizes that maladaptation leads to stress disorders, trauma reactions and responses, and a host of other complications. According to some researchers, adaptology offers a broader view of stress that integrates many aspects of the human experience.

Neural functioning, particularly its role in coping mechanisms, is coming to the forefront as well. In a keynote lecture at the National Conference of the College of Counseling Psychologists, Dr. Pierre Rossouw presented long-term research about the evolving nature of neural functioning and the study of its role within the psychological fields. Applied neuroscience examines how this field could enhance wellness in the modern world. Related to neural functioning, there is an explosion of research on neurotoxicity, neuroplasticity, and neural growth. For example, in a literature review on the topic of neuroscience and stress on Google Scholar, from 2006 to 2016, there were more than 1 million citations on the topic. A search from 1994–2005 yielded slightly more than 600,000 citations. This research suggests that because the brain can develop new connections, thus offering an alternative path of response, individuals who suffer with reactive and intense responses to stressful situations may have a new mechanism to develop new connections. The longstanding belief that the brain does not develop any more beyond the age of 25 is wrong. More and more research is investigating how the brain, when exposed to new experiences, new skills, and different feedback, makes new and different connections. According to Todd Hare, a researcher at the University of Zurich (Maier, Makwana, & Hare, 2015), an area to be explored in further research on stress is how some coping mechanisms that protect the structural brain from the damage of stress affect decision-making processes under moderate stress. This is exciting stuff in the realm of stress.

As the modern world continues to make technological advancements, there will be more research focused on technostress and social media, particularly regarding the influence of social media on mental health (a 2016 commercial on the SyFy cable channel advertised a television show called *The Internet Ruined My Life*). There is also concern about individuals in the "sandwich" generation, who are caught in the middle of taking care of both their parents and their children. The fluctuating demands on the various generations, and the resources needed to maintain, manage, and improve quality of life, are an ongoing concern in the field of stress, as is the influence of economic shifts, generational values, and global factors relating to quality of life. Personal factors, such as sleep, physical activity, nutrition, and other lifestyle aspects are increasingly being influenced by larger factors. For example, someone who is working for a company with headquarters in another part of the world may be required to work very different hours from others in the physical vicinity, due to the nature of the job and the differences in time zones. This individual may subsequently encounter challenges with sleep, eating patterns, and the like that have a detrimental effect on health; in turn, the stress-related health issues may lead to the individual losing or quitting the job. If as a result of unemployment this individual must move in with parents or other relatives, the new demands placed on all parties involved can create yet another layer of stress, fatigue, and dysfunction.

Stress disorders will certainly continue to be a focus of research, as will approaches to reduce the experience of stress disorders within certain populations. More research is being conducted on veterans and how to effectively assist them in increasing post-service quality of life, particularly for individuals who have post-traumatic stress disorder or other mental health impairments. Physical disorders are also being examined, as brain research explores ways to assist individuals who have experienced traumatic brain injury or other organic disorders. As mindfulness and other alternative approaches for regulating emotions and shifting perceptions of situations come to the forefront of research and interest, we may see a surge of application in these areas. For example, there is already some current literature on the utilization of nonverbal therapies, such as expressive therapies, movement therapies, and body-oriented therapies, as treatments for stress disorders.

Another area that may become increasingly important is the role of international and global factors in stress. As the world becomes smaller due to modern advances in technology, communications, and media exposure, we may also become more observant of cultural aspects worldwide. We may start to explore the world in a different way as we observe and recognize how other cultures and countries conceptualize experiences of stress differently than we do in the Western world. As more individuals are traveling abroad and students take study-abroad opportunities, we are all being exposed to a wider world. International students coming to the United States for academic opportunities bring with them different systems of healing and contexts; likewise, Western students who study abroad also expose their host cultures and individuals to different systems of healing and contexts.

Stress is a part of the modern world—so much so that stress is a part of our evolving understanding of the modern world. In contrast to when the term was first applied to individual experience, more than 60 years ago, our current concept of stress is much more involved and complex, and many of its components still remain mysterious, loosely defined, poorly understood, or even unknown.

Research and questions will continue to investigate how experiences shape us, how we shape our experiences, and how each of these influences figures in the complex neuroscience of stress. As individuals attempt to navigate stress more effectively, and search for tools to increase health, well-being, and quality-of-life, we continually open ourselves to the who, what, when, how, and why of the stress experience and all the fields involved in answering these questions.

REFERENCES AND FURTHER READING

American Humane Society. (2013). Canines and childhood cancer (CCC): Examining the effects of therapy dogs with childhood cancer patients and their families. Retrieved from http://www.americanhumane.org/interaction/programs/animal-assisted-therapy/canines-and-childhood-cancer.html.

Becker, D. (2013). *One nation under stress: The trouble with stress as an idea.* New York, NY: Oxford University Press.

Bicknell, M., & Liefooghe, A. (2006). The art of stress. *Journal of Occupational and Organizational Psychology, 79*(3), 377–394.

Boyczuk, A. M., & Fletcher, P. C. (2015). The ebbs and flows: Stresses of sandwich generation caregivers. *Journal of Adult Development, 23*(1), 51–61. doi:10.1007/s10804-015-9221-6.

Brodie, S. J., & Biley, F. C. (1999). An exploration of the potential benefits of pet-facilitated therapy. *Journal of Clinical Nursing, 8*(4), 329–337.

Derevenco, P. (2009). New approaches to adaptation. *Physiology, 19*(3), 4–6.

Herzog, H. (2010). *Some we love, some we hate, some we eat: Why it's so hard to think straight about animals.* New York, NY: Harper Perennial.

Irving, D. (2013). Counselor career stories: Taking a holistic approach to mental health. *Counseling Today,* 28.

Jonas, S., & Phillips, E. M. (2012). *ACSM's exercise is medicine: A clinician's guide to exercise prescription.* Philadelphia, PA: Lippincott Williams & Wilkins.

Khan, K. M., Weller, R., & Blair, S. N. (2011). Prescribing exercise in primary care: Ten practical steps on how to do it. *British Medical Journal, 343*(d4141), 806.

Klontz, B. T., Bivens, A., Leinart, D., & Klontz, T. (2007). The effectiveness of equine-assisted experiential therapy: Results of an open clinical trial. *Society & Animals, 15*(3), 257–267.

Levine, G. N., Allen, K., Braun, L. T., Christian, H. E., Friedmann, E., Taubert, K. A., . . . Lange R. A.; on behalf of the American Heart Association Council on Clinical Cardiology and Council on Cardiovascular and Stroke Nursing. (2013). Pet ownership and cardiovascular risk: A scientific statement from the American Heart Association. *Circulation, 2013,* 127. Retrieved from http://circ.ahajournals.org/content/127/23/2353.full.

Maier, S. U., Makwana, A. B., & Hare, T. A. (2015). Acute stress impairs self-control in goal-directed choice by altering multiple functional connections within the brain's decision circuits. *Neuron, 87*(3), 621–631.

Nimer, J., & Lundahl, B. (2007). Animal-assisted therapy: A meta-analysis. *Anthrozoos: A Multidisciplinary Journal of the Interactions of People and Animals, 20*(3), 225–238.

Phillips, E., Pojednic, R., Polak, R., Bush, J., & Trilk, J. (2015). Including lifestyle medicine in undergraduate medical curricula. *Medical Education Online, 20.* Retrieved from http://med-ed-online.net/index.php/meo/article/view/26150.

Part IV
Personal Accounts

The 20 personal accounts that follow were written by people who have had to confront, overcome, or learn to work with the stresses in their lives. Whether the stress comes from work, school, family, relationships, lack of money, serious illness, death, or just too much to do, the writers express—honestly, poignantly, and sometimes humorously—how they have successfully and at times unsuccessfully handled stressors in their lives. Because of the personal nature of these stories, some of the writers have chosen to be anonymous or identified by first name or initials only; however, all essays are true accounts written by real people facing difficulties.

Reaching Goals While Reducing Stress

I've learned that pursuing goals allows me the opportunity to challenge myself by stretching my capabilities while ultimately fulfilling dreams. When personal or professional goals are managed appropriately, they can be invigorating. I've often found that pursuing a goal without planning or aligning expectations can be stressful. Using detailed and focused goals can become a powerful tool in managing stress.

I was a master of giving 100 percent at my current job. But I was not one to tell myself: "Wow, I really enjoy helping people learn something new. I should become a trainer." I was better at: "Stay in this job because you have been here for awhile and you are good at doing the same thing you have been doing." I was not an initiator of my own development. Once I realized I could achieve other things—things that were not already on my "I did this"—list, the world opened up to me. I was now asking, "Why not?" It was invigorating.

As I read about goal setting, I realized that others could experience stress while working on goals due to a lack of knowledge and experience in developing detailed and focused goals. I was determined to identify a framework to follow in order to use goals as a development tool.

The keys to successful goal management allow the goal-seeker to operate with less stress and more accomplishment. Combining the practices of creating S.M.A.R.T. (Specific, Measurable, Attainable, Relevant, Time-bound) goals, being flexible, and sharing individual encouragement assist in keeping the goal-seeker on the path to completion with reduced stress.

Drafting S.M.A.R.T. goals has been a staple in the self-improvement world for years. In 1968, Dr. Edwin Locke published *Toward a Theory of Task Motivation and Incentives*. MindTools.com summarizes Locke's theory: goals provide a source of motivation, linking "how difficult and specific a goal was and people's performance of a task" (Mind Tools, n.d.). Typically, a goal-seeker is best motivated with a specific, complex goal instead of a simple goal without structure. Likewise, the article "Motivation in Their Work Reduces Stress Among IT Consultants" notes that "consultants experience less stress when they carry out assignments in a working environment that motivates them" (University of Gothenburg, 2011). From my personal experience, once I establish goals that are an extension of my future plans, my motivation for pursuing those future plans increases. Ultimately, being motivated to pursue those goals also reduced my stress levels. I was focused on the process of reaching the goals, which helped me avoid the stressful situation of being lost in the mystery of what to do next.

The success of S.M.A.R.T. goals lies in planning and organization. Each element in S.M.A.R.T. (Specific, Measurable, Attainable, Relevant, and Time-bound) allows the goal-seeker to think purposefully while organizing the goal with focused details that propel motivation. Staying motivated regarding a goal reduces stress because the organized details remove ambiguity or fear about the process. This propels the goal-seeker into action with specific steps and a defined timeline, instead of only seeing an entire, overwhelming goal. Organization around the goal reinforces the individual steps, time frame, and focus needed for motivation.

I have worked on projects where I struggled to progress due to unclear objectives and fluctuating timelines (stress). Making sense of the project (goal) was difficult and stopped me from making progress at all. Eventually, my motivation dwindled. It was difficult to stay on task. Now, when faced with projects without structure, I step back and build a framework to focus on the smaller chunks instead of wallowing in the disorganization. This framework creates a path for motivation throughout the project.

I also learned the value of flexibility while progressing through a goal's life span. Many things can derail a goal, many of which are out of our control. After continually trying to control those elements, I finally truly understood that I could not. In fact, the more I tried to control them, the more stress I felt. A pivotal moment occurred when I was able to identify the element that halted progress as something I could control or not. If I could control it, I went back to the goal details and realigned as necessary. This refueled my motivation and put me back on track. If I could not control it, I released my need to restrain the element. This helped me focus on revising the goal for my new scenario. Either way, I needed flexibility to accept the new conditions. The revision provided a new perspective with a better path to follow. The result was better attention to and motivation toward the goal with less stress.

One extraneous benefit of working on goals is the perspective on what it takes to complete them. Understanding the steps you completed, and what you learned about yourself, provides insight for others. I was thankful when people asked about my progress toward my goals. That positive energy added motivation and encouragement. If this was how I felt when asked about my goals, I assumed others would benefit from the reciprocity as well.

I see my role as a fellow goal-seeker and as a cheerleader. I make a point to inquire about others' desires to pursue their goals and what initiated their goal-seeking in the first place. I schedule reminders to check in with goal-seekers to inquire about their progress and to remind them that someone is cheering for their success. This activity provides positive reinforcement for all involved. The goal-seeker receives encouragement, which translates into motivation and lower stress. I, too, am encouraged to continue reaching for my own goals due to the interaction. Goals are, of course, contagious.

Although stress is something that can derail progress as we work on professional and personal goals, there are methods to manage the stress. When pursuing goals, it's imperative to develop and use a detailed and focused plan, such as the S.M.A.R.T. method. Exhibiting flexibility and sharing your goals and encouragement with others also help to reduce stress. Goals are dynamic and inspiring when the goal-seeker develops and utilizes these techniques. All of this, coupled with a positive outlook, leads to effort that can only produce positive results.

Joelyne Marshall

REFERENCES AND FURTHER READING

Harvard Mental Health Letter. (2011, March). Understanding the stress response. Retrieved from http://www.health.harvard.edu/staying-healthy/understanding-the-stress-response.

Lipkin, N. (2013, September 18). The role stress plays in stupidity. Retrieved from http://www.thoughtleadersllc.com/2013/09/the-role-stress-plays-in-stupidity/.

Mind Tools. (n.d.). Locke's goal setting theory. Retrieved from https://www.mindtools.com/pages/article/newHTE_87.htm.

University of Gothenburg. (2011, March 1). Motivation in their work reduces stress among IT consultants. *ScienceDaily*. Retrieved from https://www.sciencedaily.com/releases/2011/03/110301091340.htm.

Perfectionism and Stress

I am worthy if . . .

Anyone striving for perfection can tell you this: Perfection is itself the single biggest obstacle to obtaining it. Perfectionism is an ideal that becomes a way of being, created to ensure that we achieve success. This ideal can place intense pressure on an individual. Its pursuit, however, is the experience over and over again of failure. It is the origin of discontent and the one of the biggest obstacles to happiness, creativity, and achievement. It evokes the idea of strength, but its fuel is our own sense of weakness. However, we have created a culture in which the stress to be perfect is extremely high. We see this in our work culture and in our educational system. Our hyperjudgments on how to parent and the pressure for our children to achieve and accomplish at extremely high levels are creating barriers to well-being. Perfectionism is a huge stressor, and most individuals do not have the resources to meet its demands. The stress of feeling imperfect may be debilitating and is often one of the main obstacles or detriments to our mental health.

Those of us who struggle with perfectionism share a deep need to avoid any sense of shame, vulnerability, or connection that opens us to anger, disappointment, or reproach, because at our core we believe we are unworthy and not good enough. To have that externally validated shatters us like glass. The millions of pieces we must collect and put back together are sharp, cutting our fingers in an arduous and painful process.

If we appear perfect, we are safe from feeling the wounds that others inflict with their judgments. Judgments from others are perceived as a threat, which can trigger a fight-or-flight response. We are beyond feeling vulnerable and ashamed. It catapults us to a place where we feel we can breathe stress free, where there is no worry of another's judgment, harmful words, actions, anger, irritation, or disappointment because we have done nothing wrong. We acted perfectly and no one can find fault. We have risen above any fear of experiencing difficult emotions or of feeling shame or guilt. We are safe.

If this were true, why do so many of us who strive for perfection often not feel safe? Perhaps it's because we cultivate perfection not as a way to manage and be present with the truth, but as a way to avoid it. Perfectionism is our invisible cloak, hiding the deep, painful deprivation of our own sense of worth, acceptance, and relevance.

The difficulty lies in the fact that no one is immune to mistakes, mishaps, and bad choices; thus, we are not able to avoid these feelings. The pieces of glass cut and this creates a desperate need to stop the pain and discomfort. The need to avoid, along with a core belief that we are unworthy, does not open us to the movement and growth that taking responsibility and owning our mistakes allow. It short-circuits compassion and forgiveness. Instead, we are consumed by our need to stop the pain, and to do this we turn to numbing, disconnection, blaming others, withdrawal, isolation, and anger/lashing out.

Perfectionism is correlated with many disorders, such as depression, anxiety, eating disorders, self-injury, and obsessive-compulsive disorder (OCD). As a clinician, I also see it in areas many of us wouldn't expect: for example, how one is allowed to grieve. When I work with individuals who struggle with the need to be perfect, we frequently find its pursuit rooted in their childhood and the expectations, whether overt or more subtle, that they felt from their parents. As parents, our own need to be perfect undermines our ability to fully see and attune to our children, let alone ourselves as individuals and partners. Some say that instilling a need for perfection in our children is perhaps the worst lesson we teach them, because the lesson is this: love is conditional. Their belief is "I am worthy if . . ."

This is not to say that we only develop a need for perfectionism from our parents; as mentioned earlier, we live in a culture that demands perfection. There is also one's own personality traits, and recent research in such areas as neuroscience and functional nutrition are illuminating aspects of biochemistry and our ability to think and act rationally.

Regardless of its origin, perfectionism is painfully confusing because the pursuit of it involves wanting one thing (success and safety), but experiencing another (failure and insecurity). In therapy, it is healing for individuals to feel validation of their experiences and normalize their responses. A key insight is to realize that the thoughts they hold about themselves and their perfectionist behaviors served a valuable function, but have now become a way of being that cultivates painful disconnection from others, and most importantly, from themselves. Once they are able to recognize the insecurities of perfectionism, I find that we start to organically weave in cognitive behavioral tools to increase their knowledge of distorted expectations. This brings with it an awareness of how they have developed a sense of who they are attached to them. A story emerges: every story is unique, but a common thread beyond the pressure to prove their worthiness is the emptiness these individuals experience in not feeling understood. People are surprised by this; it is often an "aha" moment in therapy. They recognize that without feeling understood and heard, it is difficult to experience a sense of genuine connection and acceptance.

One of the most beneficial aspects of therapy is the experience of feeling understood and heard. It validates us just as we are, and it can shift how we understand ourselves, both as ourselves and in relation to others. This sense of validation can reduce an individual's perception that something is threatening or stressful. A connection between a therapist and the client is built that provides clients with enough safety to risk letting go of their perfectionist judgments, space to understand how it has disrupted their lives, and the ability to make knowledgeable choices about how they want to choose to be. They become disentangled from the stress of perfectionism and, most importantly, feel safe learning, growing, and connecting in healthy ways. The conditional "if" dissolves, and they are simply worthy. This becomes wonderfully enough.

Jamie Pekarek Krohn, LCPC

Optimal Balance with Pain

When I was a full-time student, during my graduate program I also worked full time and had a part-time graduate assistantship (this entailed assisting professors in the psychology department with projects, research, and whatever psychology-department-related tasks were needed). This was in addition to an active social life and dating. While there were a lot of things going on, at the time I didn't realize how much pressure this lifestyle put on me. There were many weeks I found myself at the student health clinic, complaining of feeling feverish, ringing in my ears, pains, aches, fatigue, and a host of other ailments. The doctors and nurses were not able to find the origin of these symptoms and basically told me it was "all in my head" (and hearing that was stressful). One of the nurses asked me about my stress levels, and I told her everything that was going on. She suggested I try to relax. I never went back there.

Instead, I started doing a lot of research on stress and its management. I found several things that I was already doing (like exercise, relaxation, and social support) were supposed to be helpful; I discovered new strategies, like good nutrition (especially drinking more water), hobbies (I love playing pool), and journaling, and those worked well. Although these strategies didn't "cure" my symptoms, I did find myself not feeling as stressed. As time went on, I continued to have these symptoms, but felt that I was able to manage them more effectively.

In 2002, I was diagnosed with a chronic pain syndrome. While it was a relief to have a label for the plethora of symptoms I experienced, it was also stressful, for several reasons. One, it was a new thing that I had limited information about at the time (so it kind of freaked me out); two, having a diagnosed pain syndrome in and of itself is stressful (not to mention adding one more thing to an already full plate); and three, there was the not knowing and uncertainty of what it meant for me (what's going to happen, etc.). At the time of the diagnosis, I didn't have resources or support to work with this new pressure of coping with a chronic pain syndrome and didn't know if I was going to be able to do that.

Despite that, I was determined. I wanted to figure out how I could still do and be the person I am/want to be while managing this experience. I didn't want it to stop me from living my life. I liked doing the things I was doing. I mean, I was completing an advanced graduate degree, had an active life, enjoyed it, it was a *good* life. So I did more research on the chronic pain syndrome. I talked with others and listened to what they did to help themselves. I tried some of those things; sometimes they worked and sometimes they didn't. (That trial-and-error thing, not the most fun thing to do, although sometimes the most necessary.) I did try medications—several, in fact—and the side effects did not make them worth it for me. Enduring the pain was something I chose over the side effects, and it wasn't about being strong or coming from a "see me roar" side. It was humbling to experience that pain and realize I was choosing it.

After a couple of years of trying various things and using many of the things that I knew from my stress management days, I found a place of optimal balance. This is my personal space where I thrive. It doesn't mean I don't experience pain; I do. However, it's a place where I am able to continue to function and know that I come first. Being able to "schedule" things as my mind, body, spirit, and the other parts of me need, in order to ensure that I'm not overdoing something or underdoing something, is an important part of my balancing act. And it's not that I'm *always* able to do it. Most days, yes. What I've recognized is that my pain and stress levels are immensely connected. If I don't regulate my stress, my pain increases and gets in the way of my sleep, fun, and other pieces that are central and necessary for me to function. This—managing and regulating my stress system, my stress levels—is an important part of maintaining my optimal balance.

Anonymous

Managing Stress: My Holistic Journey

Stress . . . it seems to be a part of daily life these days. Sadly, it is more prevalent in our society and comes at earlier ages. Society today is an "instant results," "can't wait," "do better," "be number one," "in a hurry" mode, and more. Because of this mindset, more and more people are having physical signs of stress and more medication is being prescribed to help for a Band-Aid fix.

Stress comes in many forms, and some stress is actually good for us. But chronic stress can be harmful in many ways. Being in the health and wellness field for more than 16 years, I have learned various coping mechanisms that can help combat the effects of stress on the body. We can't live in a bubble, but we can arm ourselves with some simple tools through diet, exercise, music, massage therapy, and more.

Having gone through many things in a short span of time—from near financial ruin, a long divorce, children going to college, a job that was completely toxic, aging parents, and more—stress was something I woke up with and went to bed with. Not exactly a healthy living pattern at all. Sleep was difficult, eating sometimes became an issue, too much or too little. Pain in my muscles due to chronic tension, frequent migraine headaches, lack of energy, high blood pressure, and not enough hours in my day to complete everything I thought I had to finish. Any of this sound familiar to you?

For my symptoms, I decided to first try natural, nonprescription methods of treatment. I first started with taking walks to clear my head and get the natural endorphins going. Those are the hormonal compounds made by the body to combat pain. I found that my migraines were lessened, and that even though I was increasing my heart rate as I walked briskly, over a period of time it gave me more energy, and the pain seemed to subside as well.

I knew my diet wasn't always the best, being "on the run" all day long, so I decided to try some good supplements and even ones specifically for stress and to help promote sleep. I used botanically based substances, including essential oils. I used lavender oil sometimes on my pillow and near my nose and temples to breathe in. Essentials oils have long been used to help alter a person's mind, mood, and health in a positive way. I started learning all about essential oils and finding their therapeutic properties, which ranged from pain management to even cleaning my house. Taking a hot bath with some essential oils is very soothing to tired muscles and relaxed me as well. Surrounding myself with a decluttered room with simple pleasures like clean fluffy towels and a soft bathrobe gives me that comfy feeling. I do things that make me happy—anything to lift my spirits.

Our world is full of noise, and sometimes more noise, including music, was still too much for me. However, soothing music in a quiet room with dim lights promotes relaxation as well. Just like water running gently; there are many types of devices that use water or even just the sound of water to help calm the body and mind of stress. This helped me soothe my overstimulated senses, allowing me to quiet my mind and relax.

I also sought a massage therapist to help with my pain in my upper arms, back, and neck. Stress seems to settle in these areas for me and make the muscles tighten up, thereby restricting the natural blood flow and causing pain. In the beginning, I had gentle massage therapy, which appears to help with chronic pain. I could feel how tight my muscles were, which at one point affected my raising my arms or just doing normal tasks. That's what chronic stress did to my body.

Eating a diet rich in fresh vegetables and fruits and good lean protein also helps. Processed foods, fast food, sugary foods and drinks, and fried food are not helpful to a healthy body. I learned that by bettering my eating habits, the more energy I had, and the less susceptible to illness I was. Eating healthily helps prevent disease, such as diabetes and heart disease.

Doing what I love and loving what I do help a lot! Working in a toxic work environment made me recognize that I needed to look for something else, or, at the least, do something that made me happy. Hobbies, dancing, reading a good book, owning a pet, or even gardening all help with stress relief. I love to garden and harvest my own vegetables. Being outside and breathing fresh air is great, too. I love being one with nature and watching the fruits of my labor bloom into beautiful things and edible nutrition . . . this can all be done without chemicals as well. I also took my passion and started to help others.

So, do you see a pattern here yet? I've learned that there are many ways to help battle stress. But, first I had to find out the root cause of it and determine how I could deal with it by removing it, toning it down, and dealing with it in a positive way. Results can happen quickly, even if some may take a little longer. But the more I understood why I was stressed, the easier it was to begin to deal with it in a healthy way to eventually rid myself of the side effects that it gave me. And that might help you when reducing it in your life.

Stress comes and goes as part of daily living; it all depends how long you deal with it and how you deal with it. Talk with a trusted friend . . . you'll be amazed how helpful that is. To your health!

Karen McNab

What the Stress!

Most of my life I have had to be the strong one, the fixer, and sometimes even the mother figure. Since this was my reality, there was no way for me to understand what people meant when they said "I'm so stressed out." To me it seemed they were being lazy, or complaining: How could something (compared to what I was doing as the fixer, mother figure, etc.) be stressful to them? "They must not be managing their time well," or "Why would they let someone stress them out?" I always said to people, "Stress! What is that?!"

The day after my 10th birthday, my 6-year-old sister passed away in my dad's arms on the way to the hospital. A few months after my 13th birthday, my father passed away 2 days after my sister's birthday. It was not until I was older that I realized that for a child, I was stressed. I had my menstrual cycle for 1 month at age 10 and did not have it again for 2 years. Talk about stress!

At such a young age, I had to grow up fast. I was keeping the house in order, going to school, taking care of a depressed mother, and still trying to be a child. This was the norm for me. I managed through all of this to attend college; I earned my bachelor's degree in 4 years, and began my career in the education field.

Now in my early 30s, I am beginning to feel and understand the stress in my life. Honestly, I have never recognized or acknowledged it until recently. I began working as an academic advisor at a university in 2007. It was great at first, and then I hated to even come in to work. In early 2010 I was rushed to the hospital after passing out in the bathroom at work. The doctors found nothing wrong with me and I was discharged after 8 hours.

In December 2011, I got married on my sister's birthday, and closed on a house three weeks later. The wedding was not stressful. It was small and at the courthouse. However, purchasing a home took a toll on me, and that is when I began to notice stress, but I still had not acknowledged it. My hair was falling out, I was grinding my teeth in my sleep, and not sleeping much at all some nights.

In 2013, I finally came to the realization that all of these things in my life were stressful, and my body was reacting to it. I am currently finishing my thesis for my master's degree, and for the summer semester I went to my advisor for help. I told her that I was having headaches, feeling tired, and just could not focus. I was afraid that I wouldn't finish what I started. She suggested that I take a meditation course with her. Along with her meditation course, I took an empowerment-over-stress course. The combination of the two courses has changed my life completely.

During the summer of 2013, I practiced several different methods of meditation. The meditation that has best worked for me is mindfulness meditation. The ability to connect with my body and actually pay attention to what is going in and with it is absolutely incredible. It is amazing how just taking a few minutes a day to devote to yourself, and focus on your well-being and growth, can be so liberating. I find that I am much more pleasant and have an abundance of energy. Along with the meditation I began to make other life changes. I had to remove things in my life that were stressful, which included taking on other people's issues and stress. Remember, I was always the problem solver! When I began to back down and let people know that I could no longer be the "middle man," they took it a lot better than I thought.

The stress empowerment course was when everything came full circle for me. All of these things that had happened to me over the course of my life (early menstrual cycle, hair falling out, etc.) were all a result of stress, and I had had no clue! Our bodies are well-oiled machines and will work in mint condition if we pay attention to them and take care of them. I did not know what could have happened in the long run if I had continued to ignore the signals my body was giving me, beginning as early as age 10. Heart attack, stroke, or even dying were all very strong possibilities for me. Well, not anymore. Knowledge is power and I am armed with the knowledge on how to deal with stress, good or bad.

Now, this will take some work. I am willing to do the work to better my life. I want to live a long and healthy life, not only for myself, but also for my family. Not only have I incorporated meditation into my daily routine, I have included my husband as well. Each morning we have a positive chant that we say on the way out the door: "Today will be a good day, today I will be positive." Waking up and starting our days off on a positive note has made a great impact.

We make choices every day in all the things we do. I am choosing every day to live a positive, healthy, and happy life. I chose what food I put in my body, what mood I will be in today, and how I feel in any given situation. If I choose the positive path, it will work out every time. I am happy that I am at this place in my life now and that I learned this information now rather than later, when it could possibly have been too late. I feel empowered, strong, healthy, and stress-free.

Shavron Kelley

Clearing Unconscious Stress

Most of us are not aware of how stressed-out we are. We are likely unconscious of the presence of stress. I, for one, have been completely stressed-out without even realizing it. I take care of myself, find work/life balance, avoid compassion fatigue, exercise and relax regularly, and have a daily meditation practice. Yet my mind is rarely in the moment. Future worries are only temporarily relieved with past memories.

When in the moment, I am usually looking to respond to something in my environment: to answer an email, to fix something, or lose myself in the next task or distraction. In fact, the stress that I am under is a completely unconscious, self-manufactured, numbing haze that I have used to cover more painful and difficult realities of being alive. For it is the mystery of life that can ultimately be the most stressful dilemma we encounter. The root of stress lies in our avoidance of existential anxieties. We evoke worry and stress in order to avoid greater painful realities that are usually unsolvable.

I am not alone in this self-inflicted, unconscious stress miasma. Many of my clients complain of unconscious anxiety. They make all the right choices in their lives, are mindful of how they treat others, strive toward satisfaction in relationships, and are conscious of world events. Yet over and over I see twisted faces in my office, worn-down bodies, and weary souls that ache from ongoing unconscious stress. Theirs is a tale of a relentless internal drumbeat that drives them toward more and more activity. They lose themselves in endless tasks and are whisked away out of their bodies and into their to-do lists.

Their stress-driven drumbeat is stronger than the beating of their own hearts. What gets lost in the daily demands of their schedule is the quiet and deep passion that brings meaning to their lives. Little by little their focus turns away from the quiet beating of their hearts toward the endless worries driving them into the fear-based, hurried future.

The stress in their lives did not get created in a day. It formed little by little, as they turned their attention away from what they truly loved. These clients started to forget who they are and what their grander purposes are in the world. Instead, their deadlines, schedules, rushing, and anxiety captured the headlines of their souls. Once the administrative demands of life are prioritized, then the quiet, sweet moments of life get lost. This is how we end up unconsciously stressed.

Identifying stress helps. When I know that my body is tight or that I am worried, I can consciously tell myself to relax or that I need to go for a walk. Yet the unconscious nature of stress is its most insidious element. I take a break if I am aware of being overwhelmed, but stress is a program that subtly drives our minds and bodies. It is related to a primitive fight-or-flight response to perceived environmental threats. Stress becomes the operating system hard-wired into our day-to-day lives, quietly running the show in the background.

What the stressed-out among us need to do first is to recognize and remove this toxic operating system. Then we need to install a more mindful intention that runs our lives. Self-awareness and intention are the keys that help people cope with stress.

Recognizing unconscious stress is the first step. We need to notice when we show signs of tension. Typically this includes a mild depressed feeling, worrying about the future, a preoccupation with tasks, and an overabundance of irritability. When we recognize that we are in this state of stress, we must find a way to ground ourselves into the present. I recommend that clients "come to their senses" in these moments. I ask them to notice what they are observing through the five senses. What do they see, smell, taste, feel, and hear? One's body is always in the moment, yet one's mind may not be. Coming to one's senses can help focus away from worry and stress and into the present moment.

Continually noticing one's senses and physical presence in space and time helps clear out the unconscious stress. It also might put us in touch with painful memories or unsettling mysteries, but at least we are not operating under stress. We can ground ourselves in existential realities rather than living in unconscious stress. After we ground ourselves, it can then help to clarify an intention upon which we want to focus. Often the best way to cope with stress is to get focused on our intentions.

When we resist stress, it persists. If we fight against stress, we get embroiled with it and stuck more in it. What is effective is to cut through the stress by first coming into the present moment and then refocusing on our priorities. Is life really about the to-do lists? Do we really believe that if we are late to the next meeting, something terribly bad will happen? Most of the things we worry about never happen, yet unconscious stress still can run us like a turbulent wave. Instead, continually reminding yourself of your intentions and your goals can help steer the ship.

Perhaps your intention is to be more connected to the love that is inside of you and to share that with others, while bringing them more in touch with their own hearts. Or maybe you are here to find joy and amusement and make others laugh. Or perhaps peace is what your intention is all about. Whichever the case, clarifying your purpose and connecting to it regularly is a powerful antidote to stress.

My purpose has changed over time. I lose sight of it often and then get filled in with stressful demands. Yet when I reconnect with a sense of a purpose, then stress starts to move out of me. It stands no chance against the power of my mission.

David Klow, LMFT

Relying on God in the Stressful Times

Being a mom, or for that matter being human, I have that list of things that weigh on me day after day. Work, church obligations, my blog, being a divorced parent, a lawsuit, and being recently diagnosed with fibromyalgia and hypothyroidism all take up the top spots on that list for me. Can we say stress multiplied by 10 boys and girls?

Oh, and add being a transgender woman on top of it all.

Stress is an everyday part of my life. There are times when the world seems to bear down on me like a crushing weight, day after day the same thing. I try to keep my head above water but fail more times than I care to admit.

There is one thing I have learned that rises above all the crap that is thrown at me: It is my faith, a faith in something higher and greater than myself, a faith in something stronger and more powerful than myself, a faith in someone who craves for the times I ask for help, a faith in the one true God.

Since I was a baby, I was raised in a Christian home, raised in the Christian church. I came to a saving knowledge of Christ at a very early age, around 7 years old. But all these years later, it is just now I am learning the importance of how my faith, or lack thereof, affects the stress level I feel.

Faith isn't just something you have or don't have, it is a journey. It is a step-by-step process. Faith is an intangible. You can't see it, smell it, hear it, or taste it. But as your faith grows, you feel it.

Faith is not an easy thing to have, and it certainly is not an easy journey. Anyone who tries telling you otherwise is selling you a bill of goods. I will be the first to tell you that I fall short time and time again—much more than I ever care to discuss. When I fail to have faith, I fail to stop trying to control my life. I take the control away from God. I fail to remember all the times He was the one who had the power, the strength, the insight to help me through the stressful times in my life. I fail to put my faith in God and His ability and desire to hold my hand and guide me through the life He has for me. I fail to let Him lift me up over the obstacles that life lays down in my path.

I'm one of those types who like to have control, and it's not easy to release that control over to anyone else. But having faith in my God means just that: giving God, my Father in Heaven, control of my life. No longer am I trying in vain to solve every problem that comes my way. No longer am I expending energy trying to walk through life when God Himself wants us to lean on Him.

Prior to when I was first diagnosed with fibromyalgia, with all the pain, with all the fatigue, with all the memory issues, there was one thing that got me through it. I finally understood Philippians 4:6–7, "Be anxious for nothing, but in everything by prayer and supplication with thanksgiving let your requests be made known to God. And the peace of God, which surpasses all comprehension, will guard your hearts and your minds in Christ Jesus." I had a peace that I felt in my innermost being, a peace that words cannot describe, a peace that I know could only come from putting my faith in God.

This was a situation that was beyond my control, beyond anything I could even comprehend. Prayer is a powerful weapon against stress. I had no choice but to come to God on my knees for the answers. On those days when I could barely stand, I had faith that God would give me strength and would carry me. On those days I suffered from pain, I had faith that God understood because of the pain Christ suffered on the cross. On the day I heard the diagnosis, I had faith that God, the Great Physician, had me in His hands.

In addition, faith was the one of the few things that got me through when I took the steps to transition from the male life I had pretended at for so long and started living an authentic life as a woman. After much prayer, I had faith that God had finally opened the door for me. After 40 years, I knew God would see me through the transition and had big things for me on the other side.

Like any journey, it has not been easy, and it's not that I lean on faith and nothing else. God wants us to bring everything to Him, and in turn I trust that God will provide the tools for me to handle the events in my life and overcome the stress I feel. It can come in the way of friends, a pastor, and even professional help.

In the New Testament, Romans 8:28 reminds me that no matter what circumstances I may find myself in, I can have faith in knowing "that in all things God works for the good of those who love him, who have been called according to his purpose."

Finally, Philippians 4:12–13 pretty much sums it all up for those who put their faith in God: "I know what it is to be in need, and I know what it is to have plenty. I have learned the secret of being content in any and every situation, whether well fed or hungry, whether living in plenty or in want. I can do all this through him who gives me strength."

Meggan Sommerville

Mystery Afflictions: Can It Be Stress?

I hate going to the doctor. I don't know if this feeling is just a holdover from childhood, or simply a desire to control my own health, but I try to avoid it unless I am absolutely desperate. About 10 years ago, I got to that point of desperation when my face had swollen up for what felt like the millionth time. My upper lip had blown up so big that my cubicle neighbor at work told me I looked like a Dr. Seuss character. That was it! I had to call on the professionals to solve this problem. My doctor referred me to an allergist, who ran through all the tests and asked me about my eating habits and other environmental factors that might be causing the swelling. The results came back and . . . nothing. The cause of the swelling was officially unknown, so the allergist joked, "I guess you're just allergic to yourself." I did not find this funny.

That joke might have been funny if this swelling nonsense hadn't been such a disruptive part of my life for the past few years. There were only so many ways for me to arrange my hair to cover up the facial mutations that would attack me for seemingly no reason at all. It felt as if I were holding a ticking time bomb with no timer. I never knew when the next time would be. Would it happen right before a job interview? Or during a first date? The impending doom of waking up with a swollen face created a constant state of panic for me.

My first encounter with this affliction was about 5 years earlier when the bottoms of my feet began to swell. No matter how much I padded my feet, it felt like I was walking barefoot on jagged rocks. I was getting over an illness at the time, so I attributed the foot torture to my immune system getting thrown off. However, when the illness went away, the swelling did not. For years afterward, I would randomly blow up. Sometimes it would be the side of my face, other times it was the squishy part of my hand between my thumb and index finger. My bottom lip would blow up so big that it would hang down, exposing my lower gums to the world. The most invasive, the most frequent, and the most feared swelling occurred in my eyelids. This began in the morning, with a bruised feeling in the outer corner of my eye, then over the next few hours the eyelid would inflate to the point where I could no longer see. The upside was that it only happened in one eye at a time. The downside was that it left me looking like Sloth from *The Goonies,* and I could not figure out why.

I had my suspicions, though. The swelling always happened when I didn't want it to happen. It always happened when I had some important place to be, or when I traveled. I believed that it was caused by stress. Believing in this theory didn't help me, though. When important events like job interviews came up, I was so afraid that any related anxiety would cause me to wake up looking like a cyclops, that I would get even more stressed out. And once the swelling started, there was no stopping it. So I went to the doctor, hoping that she could just wave her magic prescription pad and solve my problem.

I had expressed my theory to both my physician and allergist, but they shrugged it off. I don't blame them, though, because stress is such a hard diagnosis to prove. Medicine is very evidence based and I had no evidence on which to base my theory. So, the allergist gave me a prescription for some heavy-duty antihistamines and sent me on my way. The daily antihistamine regimen didn't last long, because they made me wake up every morning feeling hung over. I'm not a big fan of having a hangover that isn't preceded by an evening of fun, so I discontinued the medication.

After that, I tried to test my theory that stress was causing my problem, so I desperately tried to relax. I got into yoga, practiced deep breathing, and took morning jogs. The episodes of swelling did decrease, but they still popped up when I least expected them. As time went on, I started taking an antidepressant medication, known as a selective serotonin reuptake inhibitor (SSRI) for an unrelated problem. I didn't notice at first (because it's hard to notice something that's not happening), but my swelling problem went away. After a couple of years on the antidepressant, I felt that it had served its purpose, so I weaned myself off of them. Lo and behold, the swelling came back. After doing some research, I learned that SSRI antidepressants have an off-label use for anxiety disorders. Serotonin is useful in regulating the body's stress response, and this medication increases the amount of usable serotonin in the body. Problem solved! I went back on the medication and haven't had a single episode of exploding face since. That was 7 years ago.

While there may not be any diagnostic test that proves a problem is related to stress, there is plenty of physiological havoc that can result from stress. Although there was some truth in the allergist's joke that I was allergic to myself, she could offer no practical solution without causal evidence. What good is a diagnosis that has no solution?

One thing I learned from this situation is that we are each the biggest experts on our own health. Many of us are inclined to rely fully on a physician's assessment, and to discount or completely disregard our gut feelings on the issue. However, when it comes to our own lives, we are the experts. We live with ourselves every day, so that gut feeling has value. Sometimes a hunch can lead to the right diagnosis. We just need to give ourselves enough credit to become our own health advocates. If I had been persistent in trying to convince my doctor that my problem was related to stress, I might have arrived at a solution sooner. Luckily, I stumbled across one by accident.

Molly

Let the Music Play and Read for the Knowledge

There is nothing in life that I like less than stress. Life, as I have told my three children, is neither fair nor kind, and it has thrown me more challenges than I could possibly understand. "Life is what you make of it" has been my serendipitous belief, and that seems to be how I have coped with stress for the major part of my life. How have I kept myself on somewhat of an even keel? Let me begin.

Work, family, marriage, children, and death all seem to spin out of control and collide like a great meteor, fracturing my life into a thousand pieces. The anger and stress just seem to build inside, while the masks of wit, charm, and self-confidence appear on the outside. I find that music and learning soothe the savage beast that hides within me. It seems to defuse the tension, at least for a little while, and allows me to regain my control and keep the beast at bay. However, I'm not a fool: I recognize that seeking professional help is necessary at times, and I do so.

My past experiences have a profound effect on my present state of being. Marriage is a stressor. My marriage was a roller-coaster ride with wonderful highs and frightful lows. According to friends, my husband and I were polar opposites. It's not easy for two individuals to become one collective entity when their individual lives have been somewhat established. My husband was 10½ years older than I, a soldier, and an alcoholic. We moved overseas right after the wedding. Not only did I leave all that I was accustomed to (family, friends, job, and city), but now I had to adjust to a new husband, an Army life, a new country . . . and the list could go on. Making it a bit more stressful, we became pregnant within three months after the wedding. Crying seemed to make me feel better, but I don't know if that was actually a relief mechanism or hormones. Once again, music seemed to calm the rage that still hid within me, as did reading. Not the romance novels that so many other

Army wives seemed to embrace, not me: I found that psychology books were far more fascinating, along with history. Spending hours at the base library did inspire me to think about going back to school, which I did years later, when we left the Army.

My husband had been sober for 8 years when yet another "stress" occurred. Our family moved to another state when two of my three children were in high school (a cardinal sin in parenting) and the other in middle school. This was stressful, but manageable, and I had learned not to sweat the small stuff (like hair color; I even helped dye one daughter's hair blue). These were all things my husband and I did not make into major issues, and the girls moved beyond their rebellious teens unscathed by drugs or alcohol (they saw enough with their father). Outwardly, I appeared to be taking this all in stride; however, deep down the stress of these years was daunting. The stress drove me back into the classroom and I finished college, of course listening to music and keeping my sense of humor through it all.

The day I sat in the ER hearing the doctor say to my husband, "You have a tumor in your lung and it doesn't look good," my life stopped as I tried to process these words. The fear and anguish were palpable. Nothing that had happened in my life was as crushing as this. This was the man I had spent the past 27 years with, the father of my children, the love of my life. We were just starting our phase of life as empty nesters, looking forward to travel and time at the ocean. Dreams shattered by one sentence. I went into medical mode (as my husband called it), taking charge of the coordination of his treatment with the doctors and manipulating my work schedule so I could take care of him. He was my husband and I would do anything for him—and did when he said, "You know, the one thing we haven't done is build a house." So, while going through treatment for cancer, we built a house. He was in it 10 days before he died, but it was in his bed, in his home, surrounded by those he loved. Can I honestly say how I handled the stress? Not really. All of it seems like a blur with the few memories I have, but I do remember the music. The songs I sang to him and those playing on the radio. I moved from our new home 6 months later because of a more substantial position in another state. I knew it was the right move to secure my future now that I was alone and needed the income, but it wasn't easy.

Since that move, my youngest daughter and 90-year-old mother have moved in with me. My other two daughters live in two different states back East, allowing my frequent flyer miles to come in handy. All different kinds of stresses, but stress nonetheless. What have I done to deal with this? Earned my master's degree and am in the dissertation phase of my doctorate, all done while listening to music, keeping a smile on my face, and a sense of humor. I've learned that the more I know, the more empowered I become and the better I handle life's situations.

Nancy Burley

Mind, Body, Spirit: What Are They Really?

Focusing, a way to bring one's attention inside the body to listen to more than left-brain chatter, allows the body to be recognized and acknowledged, thereby creating a meaningful inner dialogue at the intercept of mindbodyspirit. *Clearing a space,* the first stage of focusing, is a method of moving issues and concerns out of consciousness, so what really needs attention may be acknowledged and then released. This allows for something more to emerge, which one experiences viscerally.

I recently had a dream that allowed me to utilize my focusing skills. In the dream, I am sitting in an overstuffed rocking chair. I hear a woman's agitated voice in an emotional conversation. She walks into my office, animatedly continues without pause a monologue clearly intended to produce a defensive response. Gesticulating wildly, she instructs an invisible entity to take a seat. I don't recognize her. A moment of silence ensues, she sits, then continues in serious dialogue. I am not allowed an opportunity to participate: to reflect, acknowledge, question, or summarize what I have witnessed. I have effectively been silenced.

She rises dramatically, stares challengingly at me, and then at the sofa. Suddenly, from the place the woman had been directing her diatribe, a clear, cold, shooting fluid strikes me, covering me head to toe. Before I can react, I am frozen. I cannot speak or move. I am stuck. The woman leaves the office, presumably followed by the presence of a polyurethane-projecting, invisible entity.

Wondering if I will be rescued, I attempt to call out, but the words do not materialize into sound. I think I must be dreaming and time has slowed to a tortured pace. Who is scheduled to come in next? How long before I am found? Will my husband search for me? Who will make dinner? What happens if I need the toilet?

With nothing to do but think, I reconstruct the events leading up to my stuck stage. I meditate, I clear a space, I breathe. . . .

After an interminable period; I hear the door. My officemate sticks her head into my office and greets me, but I don't move or respond. She stares at me, touches me, and pulls away quickly. Soon paramedics arrive, taking me to a hospital, but the doctors are mystified. They cannot break through the substance covering my body. After examinations at various facilities, I am taken to the National Institutes of Health (NIH), where a scientist manages to laser off a tiny piece of hardness, then places it under a powerful microscope. I panic when I notice the clear fluid oozing onto the scientist's eyewear, his face, and soon enveloping his entire body, freezing him.

The door bursts open, my husband enters with outstretched arms. I am filled with fear that he will touch me and also become frozen. Suddenly, my right hand pushes into a stop sign; I begin singing "STOP IN THE NAME OF LOVE"—Okay, it is a dream, you know! I woke up, wondering what it meant.

Shortly thereafter, it hit me: I am stuck and no one can help me—except me. It was a felt sense; I felt it viscerally as soon as I recalled the images. I asked the questions Dr. Gendlin outlined in his 1986 book, *Let Your Body Interpret Your Dream*. I've used this method of dream interpretation with my clients. Gendlin says the body is more than the physical, it also includes behaviors and cultural patterns that are innate. My dream is metaphorical, viscerally showing me in images what is happening in my life and the answer to my dilemma.

Approaching the interpretation in a holistic, systematic manner is enlightening. Past and present merge symbolically. I realize for the last 18 months, I have left an issue unresolved. I have identified this many times over the past months. With this dream, I had a bodily felt sense that I was stuck and that only I could break through. The frustration, the inability to move forward, the fear of it spreading were palpable.

I became aware that I am consumed with this feeling of "stuckness," yet am unable to move out of it. I examined the story line outlining current concerns. I pondered who the unknown woman was, and what she represented. The woman was bossy and dictatorial, very much like me with this issue—perhaps even unreasonable.

Gendlin suggests becoming the character to empathize with that perspective. The felt quality of that woman is like my heart racing, breathless, nauseated—very much how I feel on many days when the ramifications of this issue come to mind. Revisualizing the end of the dream, I am even more convinced no one can assist me, because I have what I need inside to change this issue. The polyurethane projecting from an invisible entity is my creation. I am stuck, and I am doing it to myself. My frozen body correlates to my belief that my entire life is stuck, but that is not true. I choose to not allow anyone to help me—because how could anyone know more than I do about what is happening? (My throat tightens and my belly clutches with this sensing.)

The dream interpretation process went quickly; I frequently checked with my body to note its reaction. Answering questions brought a deeper meaning to the interpretation. When I say, "I will work on this issue until it is resolved," I sigh and notice the truth of it. This realization resonates deep within me. I feel lighter. I acknowledge that I can ask for help with some things. I am awash in relief inside and out. This dream interpretation process works.

We often carry around unresolved issues—sometimes for years, even decades. We believe we have moved forward, but the issues reappear. Sitting with the whole of it, identifying what is there, acknowledging its presence, cognitively choosing to release it, and then filling that space of loss with something positive prevents its return and reduces the stress that may be associated with it.

Michele Ferraro, PsyD

Stressful Situations

Stress comes in many forms for me. I have been self-reliant since I was 13 years old, when my father suddenly passed away from heart disease. I have little memory of my time in high school and college at this point in my life, with the exception of my anxiety around taking exams and writing papers (such as the one being penned now). I dealt with my academic stress by calling on my sole confidant, my mother, and a routine of two #2 pencils, a can of soda, and a candy bar for the big test.

College passed, and I entered the working world as a technologist for a Chicago-based engineering company. My entry into the working world was quiet and uneventful. I joined some of my co-workers when they formed their own company and stayed with them for almost four years.

The new position gave me opportunities to travel abroad to experience other countries and cultures—and exposed one of my deepest fears, of air travel. The anxiety started after my trip overseas and continues today with both physical and emotional anguish. I sleep very little prior to any trip, tend to be more forgetful of responsibilities, and on the day of the flight experience physical weakness and digestive disruption.

I have tried watching movies, listening to audio books, and reading, but the feeling of anxiety prevents me from concentrating on the stories and enjoying them. Another technique I have tried is deep breathing, and focusing on the breath to help calm me. The breathing does help ease the stress, and it's been successful several times during short flights. Sleep medication is another remedy that eases my anxiety, and has been successful on longer flights, but I try to avoid medications whenever possible. The last attempted remedy was alcohol, which seems to increase the anxiety and only make the situation worse. I continue to take one or more trips during the year that require me to fly, and to employ one or more of these remedies with success. I avoid medications and alcohol, and focus on healthy methods to reduce my anxiety and stress.

Years of long hours working and enjoying the technology bubble, the crash, and resurgence have taken a toll on my body. I have worked hard on eating healthily, exercising, and seeing the doctor on a regular basis. I was diagnosed with a defective bicuspid heart valve when I was a child, and with age this type of deformity can cause other problems. My diagnosis requires me to see my doctor and cardiologist once or more during the course of the year to ensure that nothing significant has changed since the last visit.

There is a great deal of stress that occurs prior to seeing either doctor, because I know one day the message will not be good. Preventive medicine should make this easier, as any changes will be caught early, but it has the opposite effect, causing the same intense stress effect as air travel. I have failed to deal with the stress, most recently by rescheduling appointments to avoid going, and I have also become lost while traveling to a new office and ended up being an hour late. I avoid thinking about the pending appointment to prevent focusing on it, and instead focus on positive things that will improve my health, such as a healthy diet and exercising regularly. On the day of the appointment, I've found that being close to the hospital or doctor's office helps reduce both the stress regarding arriving on time and the stress of the appointment. These two remedies, combined with breathing techniques, have helped me deal with the stress related to these visits, and ultimately make me a healthier person.

Overall, my health and exercising have become an intense focus over the past few years, and a new source of stress. My weight has varied more than 60 pounds, and I've trained for more than a dozen endurance events. The focus I had in the beginning has waned the past few months and made it difficult to regain the success of the past. The impact is felt both physically and emotionally, and will affect the remainder of my life. My health is based on getting enough sleep, healthy eating, and regular exercise. If one of these components is not balanced, then my health is ultimately compromised.

The right amount of sleep is affected by several factors, including work, life, and social obligations. I make an effort to keep a regular schedule during the week to help balance the irregular sleep patterns during the weekend. The negative effects of not enough sleep lead to little or no exercise and poor food choices. Healthy eating is my biggest weakness, because food has served as a stress reliever during my adult life. I improve on this by learning about healthy foods, and limiting myself to natural foods instead of processed foods. Physical activity is my strongest attribute, and I have always enjoyed putting in the time to improve myself physically. The repetitive nature of some activities causes me to refocus on new ones to keep my program fresh and exciting. These three areas are the foundation of my health and lead to reducing the stress I experience in my life.

Stress enjoys a significant role in my life by motivating me to improve, travel the world, and monitor my health to live a full life. I have made risky professional decisions that have been questioned by my peers, but ultimately I have been validated. I have attempted hiking segments of the Appalachian Trail, mountain-biked the north rim of the Grand Canyon, and ran with 11 other people from Madison, Wisconsin, to Chicago to prove to myself that I am capable of more than I believe. I like to challenge myself by taking on situations that cause me stress in order to improve on how I react to stress, and grow as an individual. Stress does affect me, and has hindered my success, but it will not take me over or prevent me from achieving success.

Garrett W. Starke

Overcoming Me

As far back as I can remember, I have had a number of strange ailments that doctors have not always been able to understand the cause of. As a child, nosebleeds were a regular occurrence, which continued until middle school. I grew up in a home with an alcoholic father where children were meant to be seen and not heard. I found a confidante in middle school when my parents separated, and was finally able to talk about everything I had been feeling for so long. The nosebleeds stopped and it was smooth sailing for a period of time, as I was not keeping things as bottled up as I had in the past. Freshman year of college, at age 18, I moved away and had never been so far away from home. My father passed away during my second semester, and I did my best to stuff my emotions down in order to try and "be normal." I was diagnosed with colitis and made a 3-hour drive home nearly every weekend to try and get some relief and relaxation from the anxiety I was feeling living away from home for the first time. I watched as my friends at school were having an amazing time, and outwardly I appeared to be as well, but it was nearly intolerable and I dropped out and went back home my sophomore year.

At age 22, I was working for a trucking company and had quite a bit of responsibility. While the money was great at that time, I was left unfulfilled. I wanted an education and to do so many different things in my life. Things seemed bleak, as I had failed at school already and was unsure how to get my life back on track. It didn't take long with this negative thinking for me to be sporting a new accessory, a heart monitor. My heart was beating irregularly and would stop, for only a second, but long enough for me to be sure that I was dying. My doctor ran every test imaginable, but there was no explanation for the heart palpitations, which continued for years. While living with my long-term boyfriend, around the age of 27, I returned to school. I worked as a waitress 40-plus hours a week and completed my undergraduate work in 3 years. It was then that I was struck with a pain that left me bedridden for days. It felt as if there was an ice pick lodged in the side of my head, and I was unable to move. My boyfriend finally was able to get me to the doctor, where they were sure that I had a brain aneurysm. Going through another battery of tests, it was determined that I was having severe migraines. These mind-numbing headaches occurred often during the course of our troubled relationship, and dissipated at the end of the relationship.

For a few years I lived life by the seat of my pants, without a care in the world. I had a job making great money, but did not use much brainpower. While I was feeling great physically, I quickly tired of the monotony and lack of personal responsibility. I wanted more from life. I found a job in the helping field, which I loved, and eventually returned to school to begin graduate school. I was again back to working 40-plus hours and being a full-time student. During my first semester, I ended up in the hospital with tonsillitis so severe that my airway was blocked, and I was put on morphine and steroids. A year into graduate school, I had ACL surgery and ended up with a pulmonary embolism. It seemed that these ailments were never-ending. Looking back, with a different mindset, I see the cause of these ailments all too clearly: STRESS!

I never really thought that stress could have so much power over me, because I felt that it was nonsense: I was in complete control over the stress in my life, and it had no major effect on me. WRONG!! My mind was convinced of this notion, but my body knew better. I have been given signals all throughout my life from my body that something needed to change. It was as if my body was screaming at me to take a time out and relax, to breathe and find an outlet, to take care of myself. For so many years I didn't understand what effect stress was having on me—until I finally stopped to listen to my body. I finally began to learn what it is that I need to become centered in order to better cope with stress. Unfortunately, I cannot banish stress altogether, but I can learn how to gain control and power over the stress in my life so as not to let it cause illness, as I had been doing for so many years.

Learning to deal with personal stress is just that: personal. If there were a quick fix for it, there would not be so many books written on the topic or so many medications to help with varying symptoms. I have learned that to manage my stress, one thing that helps is to STOP! Stop what I am doing for just five minutes out of the day, take a personal inventory and listen to my body. At first this was very difficult for me, as my mind raced and filled with all of the things that I should be doing instead. After a few times of "taking five," I noticed that the air was stuffy and my breathing was shallow. I changed my location and went outside and took a deep breath. It was better but not completely. I got into my car and drove to the closest national park. The minute I got out of my car, I took another deep breath. Here was my calm and my serenity. I walked many miles that day, stopping to literally smell the flowers along the path, and I felt my soul fill back up as I just stopped to finally take a breath.

Kerry Knowles

I Am So Not "Zen"

I must admit that my stress is often self-inflicted, and most of it is a reaction to feeling less powerful and knowledgeable than I want to be in certain parts of my life. For example, when I am puzzled by someone else's behavior, I tend to analyze the possible motivations behind their words and actions. This analysis can be very frustrating and doesn't consistently lead me to solutions or greater understanding. Yet I keep analyzing and beating my brain against the unyielding wall of "why do they do that?" I want to gain or reclaim my power in relationships and situations by being better prepared for different outcomes and by understanding other people. When I set emotional boundaries within relationships, I want them to be respected, and I feel stress when the opposite happens. As I've learned, humans are unpredictable creatures and I can never be fully prepared for every possibility.

Reminding myself that I cannot control much in life except my reactions is one of my attempts to minimize stress, but often it doesn't work. I have high standards, both for myself and the people in my life, and sometimes I stubbornly cling to my own unwritten rules. I don't want to fall short of those standards and disappoint myself. I also don't want to disappoint or hurt others. I could be setting myself up to be upset by the clash between unreasonable expectations and reality. When I encounter this dilemma, I have to decide whether or not to adjust my expectations so that I don't feel discontented or resentful.

In a more practical sense, I find that I repeat daily patterns that cause me stress, such as being disorganized in the mornings. I dislike feeling rushed and harried while searching for my glasses, keys, or phone, but I continue to scramble each day. Although better routines would eliminate most of those stressors, for some reason I don't make the necessary changes. On some level, I must be weighing the stress of the status quo versus the stress of change and choosing to continue the pattern.

When I plan an event or project at work or in my personal life and it doesn't go smoothly, I find it very stressful. For example, when guests are late to a social gathering or when someone acts inconsiderately or rudely, I feel stressed. I question whether I could have done anything differently to prevent the problem, or I search for someone to blame. These questions lead to a negative and unproductive thought cycle, which I try to stop as soon as I recognize it.

Conflict and confrontation are very powerful stressors for me, so I usually avoid them whenever possible. However, this avoidance frequently leads to physical tension. If I don't find a way to release the tension, I carry it around with me, leading to headaches and other health problems. Fortunately, going for a walk and breathing outdoor air often clear my head, adjust my thinking, and help me relax. I'm learning to pay attention to my body's needs and signals and take better care of it.

To cope with bad news, I focus on the positive contributions that I can make within my circle of influence, however small it may be. I volunteer or donate goods or money, and work to raise awareness of issues that bother me. I also use humor and positive stories to balance against whatever negativity I encounter.

Another coping method I learned, particularly during the time I was unemployed/underemployed, was to be proactive about earning money in creative ways. As a result, I felt both empowered and useful. I also decided to adopt a dog and took risks in new areas that I hadn't explored before.

In a moment of extreme stress or crisis, I try to remember to breathe deeply and refocus on whatever is most important at the time. If I ask myself whether the problem is as dire as I perceive it to be, and if it will truly matter in a year (or long into the future), then I can often put it into perspective. In the midst of a tough situation, it helps to be gentle with myself. I allow myself to feel emotions and notice them in the moment without judging them harshly, since that judgment would only add another layer of stress. If I chide myself that I "should" or "should not" feel a certain way, it's not helpful or healthy. Taking a walk, listening to music, and removing myself from the situation temporarily are some of my favorite strategies to relieve the stress. Pleasure reading, working on creative projects, and taking naps are also ways I manage my reactions to stress.

I frequently discuss my problems with others and through their eyes learn to look at stressors from different angles. Sometimes I find that I can react more calmly in the future after I have talked about a recurring stress pattern. Hopefully, I can recognize the patterns when I encounter them again and approach them differently. It's helpful to remember that others share the same stressors and struggles, whether it's something overwhelming like the death of a loved one, or a much less significant disappointment.

I have found that stress can be a great teacher. It reveals where my priorities lie and where I am directing my energy. When I find myself feeling upset, I may realize that my standards are unrealistic in a given situation. By becoming aware of this, I have the opportunity to accept what's happening and release those negative feelings. I've also found that stress forces me to take a closer look at how I am spending my limited time and energy. I can identify the stressors and decide whether the ultimate goal or desired outcome is worth the price of dealing with them. Stress can be a red flag that I'm heading in the wrong direction and not following my intuition, or it can be a motivator to change and challenge myself in new ways.

Lynn

Stress Is from Within

This is my story . . .

Among the prevailing myths regarding stress is that stress comes from external sources. My view, however, is that stress originates from within the individual experiencing the stress. I believe the many spiritual leaders who write about the need for individuals to recognize that they are the authors of their own lives. Nothing happens *to* individuals. It happens *from* within individuals. For example, I'm walking down the street and approach something that resembles a snake. If I'm deathly afraid of snakes, I begin to get uncomfortable. I feel anxiety building and may even begin to breathe heavily and feel some moisture in the palms of my hands. I prepare to cross the street. However, as I get closer, I notice that it's not a snake, it's only a shoe string. Immediately my anxiety begins to decrease and I start feeling better. The snake was not real and did not cause stress; rather, it was my perception of a situation that caused stress. Upon seeing the situation for what it was, my stress dissipated. With this being said, I want to share a personal experience with you.

One day, I showed up to work and much of EVERYTHING was falling apart. It was 32 below zero (wind chill factor) in Chicago, and I was the ONLY person who came to my work office on this day. There were three messages (my entire staff) stating that trouble with car, trouble at home, and being sick prevented them from coming into work. I also received a voicemail from my boss, stating, "We're going to go in a different direction with the new project." The project that I had been researching for two weeks had to be redone. Did I mention that the project proposal was due by the close of business on the next day? I started the coffee maker and headed over to the hospital to make my daily rounds. I worked at a detoxification program for patients who wanted to begin their addiction recovery journey, and this was the beginning of what I perceived as a stressful day.

After my rounds, I headed back to my office and met a young lady, a nurse. She told me about a medication, and how it was able to allow patients who were desperately trying to overcome opioid dependence to have a better chance of success at recovery. The information was compelling to me, because not only was I working at a hospital trying to help people begin or restart their journeys to recovery, I was also working at home to try to save my father's life.

His journey had begun with pills after a violent encounter with a robber when I was 6 years old. He was attempting to protect himself and was shot in the pancreas. The bullet was never removed and caused him severe pain forever after. His pain was so excruciating that I can still hear him moaning in my head. I remember many times being scared and hiding under the bed. His doctor gave him pills to numb the pain, which turned into more pills, which turned into tolerance, and eventually into habitual use and pill dependency. Fast-forward to more than 30 years later of opioid dependence for my father, when I proposed to him the medication that I learned about from the nurse. He agreed to give it a try, and for a few months we had a relationship that was free of illicit drugs, free of not having to secure drugs for him, free of worrying about a knock on the door from a drug dealer, free of overdose, and free of the pain of withdrawal. During this time he gave me the best gift that I could ever ask for: he gave me freedom. During this time he shared with me that he was proud of me, proud of my choice to be a counselor and to help people like him. He also told me that he wasn't ready to "quit." Shortly thereafter (about three years ago), he lost his life to the very thing that I fight to overcome daily for clients and others: a heroin overdose. The streets of Chicago had become, according to CBS News (June 29, 2010), the heroin overdose capital of the nation.

I have a clear definition of what stress is, or at least an understanding of what it feels like. I have come up with my own definition based on my experiences: A physical response to an emotional surprise. A unique opportunity to fuel personal growth and change. Today, as I know it and understand it, stress will not change. My circumstances will continue to challenge me and even produce symptoms. Some symptoms include an inability to sleep, a general feeling of anxiety, a lack of patience, headaches, depression, and so on. At the same time, stress can also produce symptoms of courage, strength, focus, and the like. I've learned that I have the individual freedom to decide. As a young woman who was born to teenage parents and a father who struggled with alcoholism and addiction, I had no idea that life could be any different than my experience. During that time, I had no idea that anything was wrong, nor did I believe that my life was not a good one. My experience has taught me that it is better to face my fears or troubles and overcome them. Avoidance has never been a positive solution for me. The result is an earned maturity and a realistic view of the world, a spirit that is not easily disrupted and a laser-like focus on solutions.

My reward is within my individual journey. Stress and tension are as much a part of everyday life as joy and peace. Since I cannot control what is outside of my control, my only recourse is to manage my stress symptoms. Symptom relief comes in many forms for me, including prayer, meditation, relaxation, medication, "letting go," hypnosis, self-actualization, and gratitude, to name a few. Gratitude is an efficient and effective approach because I believe everything in this life happens for a reason. Gratitude helps me identify and understand my personal goals and develop a plan to reach them. Once I have gained an understanding of what my goals are, I can decide which stress management techniques are appropriate for me. So far, gratitude has been the most effective tool in combating my personal stress.

I AM grateful.

Jamelia Hand

It's the Most ~~Wonderful~~ Stressful Time of the Year

December is the most stressful month of the year for me. I will mention to anyone who will listen that all three of my children have birthdays in December. I know! Three birthdays, combined with the holidays and all they entail, usually mean my head is spinning by mid-month. And by mid-month, I mean October. So when my friend Serena asked me to write an essay on stress, in December, a week before Christmas, I, of course, said, "Yes."

My thought process was, "Well, why the heck not?" I mean, how much *more* stressful can one month possibly get? Plus, one advantage in agreeing to add an essay to my December to-do list is that I will be under plenty of stress when I write it, and will therefore be able to put all my stress-busting techniques to use. Real-time testing!

First, a little about me, so you can understand where I'm coming from when I talk about the stressors in my life. I am the mother of three teenagers. I suppose I could stop right there, but that's not nearly enough about me. What do you think of me? Don't answer that. It might cause me stress. My three teens consist of twin boys, 16, and a daughter, 14. Have I mentioned in this paragraph that all three of them have birthdays in December?

I've been married to a wonderful man for almost 25 years, so thankfully not much stress in the relationship department, except it is difficult as hell to get him to peel me a grape anymore. I'm also a writer—novels and screenplays and a blog. (And essays for friends when they ask.) My day job? I fly jets. Big ones. For a major airline. People often ask me about the stress involved in piloting an airliner. *Do you worry about all the passengers in back?* Honestly? Not as much as you might think. I worry about getting my own butt safely from A to B and then C and then eventually, back home to my family. If I'm successful at that, then the rest sort of takes care of itself. Yes, of course there is plenty of stress involved in flying the plane, but the ironic truth is, my day job causes me much less stress than all the rest of my life combined. I believe this is mostly because jets can't cop an attitude.

I remember one particularly rough day as a junior co-pilot. Bad weather, mechanical delays. It was stressful. Until the captain asked me, "Are they shooting at us, Kim?" Of course, the answer was *no*. We were on the ramp at O'Hare. You see, Captain Dan (really) had flown helicopters in Vietnam, where during the course of just doing his job, he got shot at all the time. I'm not a huge advocate of trying to make yourself feel better about your current situation by considering how much worse it could be, but still . . . whatever works. *Are they shooting at us?* has become a go-to phrase that puts most of my everyday stressors in perspective.

Another thing I find myself doing, which creates self-induced stress, is running my "I'm overwhelmed" program. (This idea of "running a program" was borrowed from Tony Robbins, just FYI.) I usually do it on a particularly harrowing day or week or month, like December (let me take this opportunity to remind you, all three of my teenagers have birthdays in December. This was not the result of poor family planning, what with two of them being twins and the fact that my daughter is adopted. So please don't judge me for being a poor family planner. It will cause me additional stress.). You probably know what I'm talking about when I say the "I'm overwhelmed program," though. It's when you keep repeating to yourself, over and over, "I'm swamped," or "I'm stressed out," or "I don't have enough time." As a firm believer in New Age woo-woo philosophy, I think just the act of *saying* or even *thinking* you're overwhelmed can actually make you overwhelmed. So when I notice I'm running "I'm overwhelmed" on a loop in my head, I have to find a way to shut it off. Chocolate helps.

My two favorite stress reducers (since I don't think they'll let me talk about chocolate and Chardonnay) are running and Bikram Yoga, which I began so I could keep running—because if I ever had to stop running completely, my family would move away. You can set your watch to my achieved level of cranky, determined by how long it has been since my last run. Nothing clears out my stress-induced orneriness like going out for a jog. We can talk about endorphins and detoxing the lymph system, etc., but meh. All I know is, after a 45-minute run along the lake or a yoga class, I am high on life, the universe, and everything. I believe it is absolutely true what the experts say about stress and the effects of exercise. If only those experts would create a stress-busting study on the effects of chocolate and Chardonnay. Sigh.

Practicing Bikram Yoga for the past 12 years has also taught me to breathe. I know what you're thinking. You're thinking, what kind of idiot needs to be taught how to breathe? But here's what I learned about breathing from Bikram Yoga: calm, even breathing can get me through almost anything. When I can remember my breath during a 90-minute workout in 105-degree heat, I can remember it anywhere. Landing a plane in a rainstorm. Making dinner when I haven't been to the grocery store in a week. Or every single day in the month of December, when the holidays are bearing down, I haven't started my cards, and all three of my children have birthdays. And I decide to write an essay on stress for a friend who asks, because, seriously, why the heck not?

Inhale. Exhale. Piece of cake. And no one's shooting at me.

Kim Strickland

Coping in the Midst of Cancer

This has been the story of stress in my life. I've been through 20 moves, survived a flood, lost a parent, been involved in a major lawsuit, been divorced, and suffered a miscarriage. I have also remarried, had a child, been promoted, and sold and purchased several houses. While my story of stress has ebbed and flowed, the stress-driven anxiety and its consequent productivity have helped me accomplish quite a bit. Anxiety has been my companion and, oddly, a coping mechanism. As anxiety ratchets up—it is like a living being inside my head and chest—my energy increases. I seek out more caffeine and more activity. Stress leads to anxiety and anxiety leads to action. I clean, bake, exercise, organize, run errands.

Last year, however, I was diagnosed with bladder cancer. My primary doctor sent me to the emergency room after taking a urine sample that was more blood than urine. After a series of tests, I was told that I needed a cystoscopy, which is a scope used to look into the bladder. It is an invasive but routine test. My urologist was not there to do the procedure, but his partner was. He refused to come to my hospital room to describe the procedure, and when they took me downstairs I realized I was being taken to an operating room. An anesthesiologist greeted me and asked me to sign a consent form. I insisted on seeing the doctor, whom I'd never met before, and he told me I had cancer and that he would be removing the tumor.

I was alone in an operating-room prep area without my family and had not been told before that moment that I had a tumor or that it was likely cancer. Instead of stress-fueled anxiety, I encountered fear. If anxiety is a living being, fear is a mushroom cloud. I found that I had few internal resources for facing my own mortality. Restless activity, projects, and chores were no longer comforting. In fact, they were almost impossible because fear made it difficult to focus.

Anxiety and my drug of choice, caffeine, provided an intense focus to cope with stress, but fear was immune to these comforts. My attention was transfixed by cancer. It felt like a roaring in my ears that drowned out any other sound. If I tried to turn away, look at something else, the fear just followed. It was a bag over my head, a tunnel, a spotlight aimed directly at me, a wailing siren.

I was in a constant state of fighting to get my head out of the water. Cancer was the hand pushing me back under. From surgeries to treatments to diagnostic tests, and from doctors to nurses and technicians, I experienced a world out of my control. Even the most mundane of tests feels like a prologue to doom. An X-ray or an ultrasound, even for an unrelated symptom, seems like the prologue to another chapter in cancer. Every pain shouts "metastases."

A year later, I have traveled to a very different place. The passage of time and a good prognosis have clearly enabled me, but I have also learned some new ways of coping. My local cancer support center offers a huge variety of classes and groups and counseling at no cost to cancer patients. After discovering them, I took complete advantage of what they offer, and still regularly participate.

Here are some of the healthier coping strategies that I've learned:

- Nutrition: After consulting with a nutritionist and reading several cookbooks, I have immersed myself in new eating habits. The cancer community has been inspiring in the way that they frame nutrition. Rather than a series of don'ts, I have learned about what I can eat. My daughter and I have had so much fun learning new recipes and trying foods that we'd never tried. I have a much better sense of how food can provide healthy comfort and healing.
- Support Group: I am not a group sort of person, and have avoided everything from the Girl Scouts to the PTA. However, when you're drowning, you reach for what can save you. I reached for the support group, and they have changed my world. Talking to people who have been through and are going through exactly what I am experiencing is invaluable. My friends and family are very supportive, but they don't always understand, and I'm not always comfortable talking about my feelings. It's easier to get "tough love" from other cancer patients, too.
- Meditation/Relaxation: I took a six-week beginning yoga class and I am still participating in a guided imagery group. In the midst of panic and anxiety, these activities have offered me a time-out. The structure of a class/group activity encouraged me to fully participate. As the weeks have gone on, I've learned to physically relax and mentally relax. I have also gotten a relaxation-related iPhone app that I have used at work and home.
- Counseling: I am a good student, a learner. Working in a one-to-one relationship with someone I trust has been transformative. I find that my counselor helps me integrate most of the aspects of my cancer journey. She has provided insight about talking to my doctors, living with my family, working, and coping.

Working with the Cancer Support Center in my community, I have developed a sense of belonging and empowerment for me. Though cancer was the catalyst for seeking help, the center has provided me with help for all of the stressful aspects of my life.

Traveling the bumpy road of a cancer diagnosis, buckling up through hairpin turns and steep climbs, has offered many opportunities to feel vulnerable and powerless, to realize how little control I have. But relaxation and counseling have offered me strategies to respond to the need for control.

I'm learning how to let go of some of these bad emotions. I'm learning that I *can* let go. I'm learning that I have more strength inside than I ever knew.

I've realized lately that I've lived through some difficult experiences and have more than survived them. I am thriving in the face of cancer. I'm healthier and more at peace than I've ever been. I'm more invested in my work and my family. And, I feel empowered and better able to face the normal stresses of everyday life.

Kerri K. Morris

My Tornado of Stress

My mom was a single parent, and by the time I was 11 years old I was given the responsibility to take care of myself and my brother. Having to make sure that we woke up in time to go to school, get our homework done, and even learn to cook basic meals so we could eat created what I call my *tornado of stress*. With these responsibilities came a bombardment of worry. These worries led to the stress that I experienced in my daily life. For me, it is like I live with burdens that seem to swirl above my head uncontrollably and endlessly. These burdens are a combination of a stream of tasks, dealing with personal or professional situations, and the deep sense of responsibility for those around me. These stressors lead me to a constant state of anxiety, so when a new problem arises, the stress is stronger and it leads me to have mood swings, which leave me tired and unable to think logically. I try to address these stressors by breaking them down, but addressing these stressors is a challenge for me. I understand that I have a constant set of stressors that I need to deal with. So, I focus on one stressor before me, and inevitably, another stressor diverts my attention and sets me back to the beginning, which leaves me emotionally exhausted. My feelings of accomplishment are diminished by these newly added stressors and by the constant way my mind diverts my attention. Stress not only causes me emotional distress, but also leads to me to have various physical ailments. Understanding both the emotional and physical symptoms helps me manage the source of my stress.

Trying to function when I am at a high stress level causes one or more physical reactions within me. I understand these physical reactions, but I have been unable to prevent them entirely. My initial symptom is developing eczema in my scalp, which indicates to me that I am starting to feel a higher level of anxiety. When my anxiety intensifies, the eczema spreads to other areas of my body, like my hands and feet. I treat the eczema, but forget to deal with what is causing the stress. I also suffer from high blood pressure, and during high levels of tension it rockets and results in terrible, debilitating headaches, anger, and moodiness. I treat the headaches with medication and ignore the stressor. The final major indicator of maximum stress level is my constant feeling of hunger. During this time, I can eat everything and anything under the sun, but nothing satisfies my hunger. This is the point when I recognize loss of control and need to bring myself back down from this craziness. The constant physical reaction to this tornado of stress has left me overweight and feeling physically tired in fighting the stress battle.

What I've learned from identifying my physical reactions to stress is that in order to prevent myself from crashing and burning into the ground, I need to make an effort to control my environment and my reaction to stress. I know I am a stress eater, and I tried every diet under the sun, but I was still overweight and physically tired. I came to the conclusion that it causes me additional stress to diet. Therefore, I began cooking meals that are good for my body and discovered that cooking is a positive way for me to relax. I plan out my meals and look for recipes that are delicious and nutritious; I have inner peace in knowing I am feeding my body wholesome, healthy meals. Eating healthy meals has had a positive impact on my blood pressure and overall health. When I cook, I feel like a conductor directing a wonderful melody, and this brings me joy and helps me get relief from my stress. Trying new healthy recipes has changed me into a healthy food advocate among my friends, and has influenced my friends to want to be healthy. As my friends and I get together as a group, we can make smarter, healthier decisions and this, along with the camaraderie, seems to make my tornado of stresses lessen.

I also realized that exercise is my friend; it is another key to relieving my stress. I focus on a daily routine of going to the gym, and when I do this, I am able to cope with most everything. Exercising daily helps me relax and be able to focus on my stressors individually instead of being overwhelmed by them. It has helped my mind to not be diverted by new stressors. I am able to keep focus. Setting goals also helps relieve my anxiety about my weight, knowing that I am working toward a healthier me. I use yoga to learn breathing and relaxation techniques, so, when I feel a higher stress level, I try to remind myself to take deep breaths and focus on one issue at a time. I use the endorphins produced by exercise to continually feel good all day so that stress doesn't take over.

When my tornado of stress overpowers me, I reach out to friends and family for support in working through the difficult situation. When sorting through my stress, my initial reactions are sometimes negative. I may raise my voice in aggravation, have intense disagreements with loved ones, or become unable to patiently deal with my son's issues. To help prevent these negative reactions, I seek out the opinion of one or more people, and discuss the issues to help diffuse the situation, which leads to a more positive outcome. Talking through my issues also helps me break down the stress, discern the root causes, and prevent them from getting worse. I know that with each passing day, I learn more about myself and how to recognize and cope with stress in my life, and I hope to continue to notice patterns that help me address my tornado of stress.

Lisbett R. Lee

My Trials and Triumphs of Graduate School

My years in graduate school were filled with both trials and triumphs. The triumphs brought happiness into my life, but the trials brought feelings of uncertainty about pursuing a master's degree, which elevated my stress level. Before entering the master's program, I had plenty of time to do what I wanted, despite working a full-time job. I would go the gym five to six times a week for an hour, and I would spend quality time with my daughter and my dogs. But when I started school full time, I had little to no opportunity to go to the gym, or to spend time with my daughter or dogs. It seemed as if there were not enough hours in the day to do what I needed or what I wanted to do. It didn't bother me initially, because I was so excited to be on the journey of pursuing a lifelong goal. Who would have thought, me, Teri Thompson, in a graduate program?

The graduate program was fast paced. My days and nights were filled with reading books and writing papers. My time at the gym had been replaced with hours at the library. My classmates had become my new best friends and they didn't even know it. We met up occasionally to discuss various school projects while drinking caffeinated drinks to keep us alert and focused. It was around this time that I began to realize that my stress level was increased because I started experiencing heart palpations and I was short-tempered with my loved ones. My body usually gives me these types of warning signs when I need to slow down, but this time I ignored them because my classmates had relayed to me that their stress levels had increased as well. I assumed that this was the norm, because they had validated my feelings, but deep down inside I didn't feel like myself. I felt restless and tired. I had decreased the amount of days and time that I spent at the gym, and it seemed as if I only saw my daughter and dogs in passing.

I don't know how I maintained a relationship, but I did. I actually got engaged. My fiancé appeared to understand my time constraints, but I often felt guilty. We could no longer go out on Saturday nights because I had to meet a Sunday paper deadline. For the majority of my classes, my papers had to be turned in by midnight on Sunday, and I am a procrastinator. I would start my paper the day before it was due, which means my weekends were filled with writing papers. By choosing to write my papers on the weekends, I missed out on valuable time that I could have spent with my family and going to the gym.

What kept me going was that there was end date in sight, also known as graduation, and I was not on this journey alone. Although I did not do it, my classmate Kerry would count down the days. I could not wait to see her every week so she could tell me how many days we had left. My last two semesters were extremely tough because I decided to do a double internship. I had a 52-hour work week excluding travel and homework. This is when things began to fall apart. A month into my double internship, I was exhausted. I felt tired, cranky, and irritable. In addition, I was no longer in the classroom except for my weekly meeting with my instructor for supervision. My days consisted of going to an internship site, where I was treated like an employee minus the pay. I traveled one hour to and from my internship site, favorable traffic conditions and weather permitting, and I was not compensated for any of it. Oh, yeah: I was not supposed to be—at least that is what I kept telling myself to ease my stress and anxiety. I also had a tough time dealing with being out of the classroom and in the field. You see, it was easy for me to be in the classroom and discuss hypothetical cases, but now I was no longer in the classroom. I was dealing with real-life cases and I was expected to perform. I could not wait until my weekly supervision meeting with my instructor to discuss my issues at the internship site and my feeling of uncertainty. Looking back, I realize that it was not my competence I was struggling with, it was the fact that I was stressed out, and it was manifesting in different ways. I recognized I was no longer making time for things that I enjoyed doing.

I really enjoy working out at the gym and spending quality time with my family and my dogs, but when I neglected to do these things my stress level increased. I neglected to do the things I needed the most, as I focused on a desired goal. I now realize that although I was not spending as much time as I would have liked to going to the gym and being with my family, the little time that I did helped me make it through. I remember the relief I felt after just taking a walk with my dogs. I learned that when things are stressful, I cannot stop doing the things that I enjoy, and that I need to keep some time for myself. I always knew that self-care was important, but I didn't realize just how important until my stress level became unmanageable. Up until this point I had never had anything push both my physical and mental limits simultaneously, so I was unaware of the effects of being stressed out.

In hindsight, I know having these things in place before graduate school was why I never felt stressed out. Getting enough exercise and spending time with the people and animals I love were all things that I had neglected while pursuing higher learning. However, they were still there when I needed them to help me get my stress level back under control when it became unmanageable.

And, yes, I graduated!

Teri Thompson

The Intuitive Side of My Stress

It's 2:00 a.m. on a Saturday night and I'm on my fourth cup of coffee for the day. I normally drink one cup per day, but during times like these, it's always more. There's a blizzard outside, and the holidays are just around the corner. Will I do well on all five of my exams, so that I can enjoy the break? Will I pass them all? My mind is all over the place. I'm thinking about Christmas shopping, transportation concerns, and how fast I can memorize 10 lectures. My stress level is higher than ever. Will my internal resources meet the demands required of me? Will I be able to make it through my first week of finals in college?

Stress is something I have struggled with all my life. I've always been an idealist and a visionary, which led me to have high standards for myself. I found myself having a vision of something that "should" be a certain way and being disappointed when my expectations were not met. This led me to be constantly stressed, because I always expect myself to meet my inner standards. To prevent the stress caused by something that doesn't match up to my vision of myself, I would procrastinate, avoid the situation, and numb my feelings by eating. I remember the times when I was given the assignment to write a paper; I had a topic and a vision of what I wanted to express, but struggled with ways to express exactly what I wanted to say. It would take me days to finish that paper, and in the end I was never completely satisfied with the results. That night, when I was cramming 10 weeks' worth of lectures to learn for test day, I was rarely confident that I knew enough of the material to do well.

What I've learned about my stress is that my stress is really *fear.* Fear caused by uncertainty of the outcome. When I'm not in control of a situation and don't know its outcome, I spend more time anticipating the situation. Not only that, I am also scared of the uncertainty of not knowing if my internal resources will meet the demands of a situation. I've learned that stress is highly based on my personality type and perception of an event. For me, having a slightly neurotic personality type increases my triggers for stressful situations. I've found that I have more trouble managing stress because of my natural anxiety and apprehensiveness.

Managing my stress has been a huge challenge for me, but a great learning experience as well. Stress has been with me throughout my entire life and the various stages of life I have gone through. For example, in middle school I would be stressed about a certain boy not talking to me. As I grew older and schoolwork became more challenging, my sources of stress changed to worries about keeping up in my studies, and dealing with my parents as an adolescent. Now that I'm working, my stress stems from managing my time and maintaining a work-life balance. As my sources of stress became more complex, I have coped with the help of the resiliency I have formed through dealing with the stress in all my different stages of life.

I've learned that managing stress is a very intuitive process for me. The first time I realized that was during the most stressful times in my life in graduate school. I started to notice that stress was taking a toll on me because I did not feel like myself. I didn't wish to socialize with others, I wasn't taking care of myself physically, and my thoughts were disorganized. I couldn't describe the feeling, but it was a general uneasiness. It was almost like an out-of-body experience. The overwhelming amount of work that needed to be done in a short amount of time, in addition to dealing with family and health problems, had me at a breaking point.

Since then, I have learned to listen to my body and my inner voice to guide me in ways to take care of myself and maintain wellness. Listening to my body helps me to set limits for myself, and reminds me that I need to practice some self-care. During difficult and stressful times, I use a lot of self-talk and positive affirmations. I tell myself that this is only temporary and that I can get through it. Exercising regularly and getting enough sleep are some of my most important and reliable coping skills. Aromatherapy, massage, and relaxation techniques are some newer skills I discovered after I started working and needed something to help me relax after a long day at work. Using my intuition to manage my stress has taught me to search within and to stop looking outside for comfort and validation. When I listen to my body, I can prevent a full-blown "stress relapse" by using my internal resources and coping methods to pick myself back up again.

Sometimes I react in the moment and turn to negative coping skills such as emotional eating and procrastination. I try not to beat myself up for it, and move on by reminding myself to make healthier choices in the future. Of course, it is also a reminder to stay on track by exercising, eating nourishing foods, getting enough rest, and maintaining my social networks. Staying positive helps me to get back up, brush myself off, and keep going. The stress I experience now is a lot different from the stress I experienced that Saturday night before my final exams. At that time, stress was new, and my toolbox of coping skills was not as full as it is now. The challenging life experiences I have had since then have taught me how to cope, what works and what doesn't, and I am grateful for these experiences. I have become more resilient because of these stressful events. As I continue to grow older, and my life experiences become more complex, I hope to manage my stress intuitively as it comes, by listening to my body, using my internal resources, and staying positive.

Neha

Overcommitted to Stress: My Way Out

I have always thought of myself as being tough and able to cope with challenges I face in life; as a result, I never appreciated the impact stress could have on me. I viewed stress to be something that is always avoidable and never understood the gravity of it until I had a firsthand experience with it that nearly broke me down. Although I have misused the word and the phrase "I am stressed" in several ways, I have come to realize that being stressed is not just a cliché, but a reality that can break even the toughest Marine if the person does not handle it well and in a timely manner.

It all started as I climbed higher on life's ladder and started facing challenges and demanding circumstances. I graduated from college with two younger siblings still in high school when the sole provider of my family then, my dad, suffered a stroke that made him lose his job. I found myself assuming his role and trying to keep things together and care for my younger siblings. Within the same time frame, I had enrolled in graduate studies and had a lot of other commitments. In spite of all the challenges and predicaments, I tried to manage to the best of my ability all that was going on around me. The only problem: I wasn't doing it the right way.

Like a sailboat being tossed on a raging sea, the extent of loss or damage depends on the crew's preparation for such a situation and the strength of the anchor. In the same way, I am better able to manage stressful situations when I'm prepared and have preplanned for the unforeseen challenges that may be associated with change. These demanding circumstances I found myself in began to weigh down on me at a steady but a consistent pace without my noticing the impact they were having on me. Eventually, my stress reached the threshold point where it began to invade all aspects of my life in what I can best describe as a cascade of negative processes. I started eating less and unhealthily because I was almost always busy and didn't have much time on my hands. This began to tell on my physical appearance. At the end of the day, I was so exhausted and stressed out that I didn't feel like eating anything. There were times that I was too restless and couldn't sleep, and times when I overslept because I had been stressed for a long period of time without a break. There were days when I couldn't do anything or even get out of bed. Once my eating pattern and sleeping patterns were affected, my output at school and work was also negatively impacted. I was feeling overwhelmed all the time. But the negative aspect was that I wasn't getting anything done.

I say stress is better addressed not only by managing it well and making necessary changes, but also by making those changes in a timely manner, because I believe the duration of being stressed was proportional to the impact it had on me. I was lucky to have identified what was going on and made a timely attempt to address it. I had reached the point of being burned out from all the overwhelming demands around me, and almost lost many important relationships and was at the brink of losing a part-time job when it dawned on me that I had been stressing myself out with so many commitments and responsibilities but had nothing positive to show for it. It was as though my whole life revolved around the commitments I had entangled myself with and I had no personal or social life. On top of that, it seemed only a matter of time before I had a major nervous breakdown.

It was at that point, where everything seemed to be falling apart, that I began to question myself as to how I had ended up in such a difficult situation. I began to wonder if there was a way to undo all, or at least most, of the damage that had been done. This made me take a step back to re-evaluate my life and daily activities—a decision that saved me from getting to a point of no return.

Two things I identified as the most important factors in managing stress were proper time management and prioritizing. Once I sat down to document my daily activities, I was able to identify which activities I was spending too much time on. I found out that certain activities, such as wasting time surfing the Internet, watching late-night television shows, and not having a consistent bedtime could be replaced with taking short naps and taking a break to relax. Also, allotting some time from these activities to create an extended and relaxing sleep at night was not only possible but rewarding.

Again, I was also able to prioritize my activities within the day and learned how to speak up when my workload was too much or ask for assistance when necessary. I was surprised by the impact these had on lowering my stress. I woke up each morning feeling rejuvenated and ready to approach the challenges of the day with a fresh mind. This increased my output at work, made me less busy, and helped me take care of my health. Once I was able to focus on things I could control and faced life one day at a time, I was able to give myself the break I needed, regain the things I had lost, and get my life back on track.

Lastly, this taught me an important lesson: I cannot carry the world's problems on my shoulders. As much as I will want to help out, cutting down on the number of commitments and approaching life one step at a time is very important to preventing stress. Although this was not an easy road, I believe I learned a vital lesson that has helped me immensely in being able to live and perform effectively in today's fast-paced society with all its demands—without having to stress myself out.

M.O.N.

Recommended Resources

BOOKS

Alberti, R. E., & Emmons, M. L. (1974). *Your perfect right: A guide to assertive living.* San Luis Obispo, CA: Impact.

Arieti, S. (1976). *Creativity: The magic synthesis.* New York, NY: Basic Books.

Assagioli, R. (2000). *Psychosynthesis: A collection of basic writings.* Amherst, MA: Synthesis Center Inc. (in cooperation with the Berkshire Center for Psychosynthesis).

Assagioli, R., & Firman, D. T. (2007). *The act of will.* New York, NY: Association for the Advancement of Psychosynthesis.

Auerbach, S. M., & Gramling, S. E. (1997). *Stress management: Psychological foundations* (1st ed.). New York, NY: Pearson.

Bach, G. R., & Goldberg, H. (1974). *Creative aggression: The art of assertive living.* Issaquah, WA: Wellness Institute.

Bailey, C. (1996). *The new fit or fat.* Boston, MA: Houghton Mifflin.

Benson, H., & Klipper, M. Z. (2009). *The relaxation response.* New York, NY: HarperCollins e-Books.

Bieliauskas, L. A. (1981). *Stress and its relationship to health and illness.* Boulder, CO: Westview Press.

Bloomfield, H. H., & Cooper, R. K. (1995). *Power of five: Hundreds of 5-second to 5-minute scientific shortcuts to ignite your energy, burn fat, stop aging and revitalize your love life.* Emmaus, PA: Rodale.

Bonny, H. L., & Savary, L. M. (1990). *Music and your mind: Listening with a new consciousness* (rev. ed.). Barrytown, NY: Station Hill Press.

Borysenko, J. (1990). *Guilt is the teacher, love is the lesson: Lessons in loving one person for life.* New York, NY: Warner Books.

Borysenko, J. (1993). *Fire in the soul: A new psychology of spiritual optimism*. New York, NY: Warner Books.

Borysenko, J. & Borysenko, M. (1994). *The power of the mind to heal: Renewing body, mind, and spirit*. Los Angeles, CA: Hay House.

Borysenko, J. Z., & Rothstein, L. (2007). *Minding the body, mending the mind*. Cambridge, MA: Da Capo Press.

Bower, S. A. A., & Bower, G. H. (2004). *Asserting yourself: A practical guide for positive change*. Cambridge, MA: Da Capo Life Long.

Brennan, B. (2011). *Hands of light: A guide to healing through the human energy field* (reissue ed.). New York, NY: Bantam/Random House.

Brigham, D. D., Davis, A., & Cameron-Sampey, D. (1996). *Imagery for getting well: Clinical applications of behavioral medicine*. New York, NY: W.W. Norton.

Brown, B. B. (1978). *Stress and the art of biofeedback*. New York, NY: Joanna Cotler Books.

Brown, B. B. (1983). *New mind, new body: Bio-feedback; new directions for the mind*. New York, NY: Harper & Row.

Brown, D. W. (2007). *Teach yourself aromatherapy* (4th ed.). London, UK: Teach Yourself Books.

Burns, D. D. (2000). *10 days to great self-esteem: 10 easy steps to brighten your moods and discovering the joy in everyday living*. London, UK: Vermilion.

Cameron, J. (1993). *The artist's way: Meeting your creative myths and monsters*. Boulder, CO: Sounds True Recordings.

Cameron, J. (1997). *The vein of gold: A journey to your creative heart*. London, UK: Pan Books.

Cameron, J., & Lively, E. (2016). *It's never too late to begin again: Discovering creativity and meaning at midlife and beyond*. New York, NY: TarcherPerigee.

Cannon, W. B. (1963). *Wisdom of the body*. New York, NY: W.W. Norton.

Castleman, M. (1991). *The healing herbs: The ultimate guide to the curative power of nature's medicines*. Emmaus, PA: Rodale Press.

Chaitow, L. (1992). *The stress protection plan: How to stay healthy under pressure*. London, UK: Thorsons.

Charlesworth, E. A., & Nathan, R. G. (2004). *Stress management: A comprehensive guide to wellness*. New York, NY: Random House.

Chopra, D. (2007). *Perfect health: The complete mind body guide* (rev. ed.). New York, NY: Three Rivers Press.

Chopra, D. (2010). *Ageless body, timeless mind: A practical alternative to growing old*. London, UK: Ebury Digital.

Cooper, K. H. (1970). *The new aerobics*. New York, NY: Bantam Doubleday Dell.

Cotton, D. H. G. (1999). *Stress management: An integrated approach*. New York, NY: Brunner-Mazel.

Cousins, N. (2005). *Anatomy of an illness as perceived by the patient* (20th anniversary ed.). New York, NY: W.W. Norton.

Covey, S. R. (2004). *The 7 habits of highly effective people: Powerful lessons in personal change*. New York: Simon & Schuster Adult Publishing Group.

Cox, T. (1978). *Stress CB*. Baltimore: Lippincott Williams and Wilkins.

Csikszentmihalyi, M. (2008). *Flow: The psychology of optimal experience.* New York, NY: Harper Perennial Modern Classics.

Curtis, J., & Detert, R. (1981). *How to relax: Holistic approach to stress management.* Palo Alto, CA: Mayfield.

Davis, M., Eshelman, E. R., McKay, M., & Fanning, P. (2008). *The relaxation & stress reduction workbook* (6th ed.). Oakland, CA: New Harbinger Publications.

Davis, R. E. (1995). *An easy guide to meditation.* Lakemont, GA: Csa Press.

Diamond, H., & Diamond, M. (1987). *Fit for life II: Living health.* New York, NY: Warner.

Dossey, L. (1989). *Recovering the soul.* New York, NY: Bantam Books.

Dossey, L. (1991). *Meaning & medicine: Lessons from a doctor's tales of breakthrough and healing.* New York, NY: Bantam Dell.

Dossey, L. (1993). *Healing words: The power of prayer and the practice of medicine.* San Francisco, CA: HarperCollins.

Douglass, M. E., & Douglass, D. N. (1993). *Manage your time, your work, yourself.* New York, NY: AMACOM.

Eliot, R. S., Breo, D. L., & Debakey, M. E. (1989). *Is it worth dying for? A self-assessment program to make stress work for you, not against you.* New York, NY: Bantam Doubleday Dell.

Eller, D. (1999). *Power up: 101 ways to boost your energy.* New York, NY: Avon Books.

Ellis, A., Harper, R. A., & Powers, M. (1975). *A new guide to rational living.* Hollywood, CA: Melvin Powers, Wilshire Book.

Everly, G. S., & Lating, J. M. (2002). *A clinical guide to the treatment of the human stress response* (2nd ed.). New York, NY: Kluwer Academic/Plenum.

Everly, G. S., & Rosenfeld, R. (1981). *The nature and treatment of the stress response: A practical guide for clinicians.* New York, NY: Kluwer Academic/Plenum.

Fadiman, J., & Gordon, J. S. (1981). *Health for the whole person: Complete guide to holistic medicine.* Boulder, CO: Westview Press.

Fanning, P. (1994). *Visualization for treating cancer* (2nd ed.). Oakland, CA: New Harbinger.

Fensterheim, H., & Baer, J. (1975). *Don't say yes when you want to say no.* New York, NY:Dell.

Fischer-Rizzi, S., Ebenhoch, P., Hartmann, G., & Reinersmann, E. E. (1991). *The complete aromatherapy handbook: Essential oils for radiant health.* New York, NY: Sterling.

Frankl, V. E. (1959). *Man's search for meaning: An introduction to logotherapy.* Boston, MA: Beacon Press.

Gawain, S. (2002). *Creative visualization: Use the power of your imagination to create what you want in your life* (25th ed.). San Rafael, CA: Nataraj/New World Library.

Gill, J. L. (2005). *Personalized stress management* (2nd ed.). United States: Pagefree.

Girdano, D. A., Dusek, D. E., & Everly, G. S. (2012). *Controlling stress and tension* (9th ed.). San Francisco, CA: Benjamin-Cummings.

Goldberger, L., & Breznitz, S. (1993). *Handbook of stress: Theoretical and clinical aspects* (2nd ed.). New York, NY: Free Press.

Goldstein, J. & Kornfield, J., with the Dalai Lama & Robert K. Hall. (1987). *Seeking the heart of wisdom: Path of insight meditation.* Boston, MA: Shambhala.

Goleman, D. (1978). *The varieties of the meditative experience.* New York, NY: John Wiley & Sons.

Gordon, J. S. (1990). *Stress management.* New York, NY: Chelsea House.

Greenberg, J. S., & Greenberg, J. (2008). *Comprehensive stress management* (11th ed.). New York, NY: McGraw-Hill Higher Education.

Hanson, P. (1988). *The joy of stress.* London, UK: Pan Books.

Hendricks, G., Hendricks, K., & Bradshaw, J. (1980). *Conscious loving: The journey to co-commitment: A way to be fully together without giving up yourself.* New York, NY: Random House.

Hewitt, J. (1990). *The complete yoga book: Yoga of breathing, yoga of posture, and yoga of meditation/Three volumes in one.* New York, NY: Schocken Books.

Holland, N. N., & Holl, N. N. (1982). *Laughing: A psychology of humor* (23rd ed.). Ithaca, NY: Cornell University Press.

Inlander, C. B., & Moran, C. K. (1996). *Stress: 63 ways to relieve tension and stay healthy.* New York, NY: Walker Books.

Jacobson, E. (1974). *Progressive relaxation: A physiological and clinical investigation of muscular states* (3rd ed.). Chicago, IL: University of Chicago Press.

Kabat-Zinn, J. (2004). *Wherever you go, there you are: Mindfulness meditation for everyday life.* London, UK: Piatkus Books.

Kabat-Zinn, J. (2013). *Full catastrophe living: Using the wisdom of your body and mind to face stress, pain, and illness* (2nd rev. ed.). New York, NY: Bantam/Random House.

Kanfer, F. H., & Goldstein, A. P. (1990). *Helping people change: A textbook of methods.* New York, NY: Pergamon Press.

Katch, V. L., McArdle, W. D., & Katch, F. I. (2010). *Essentials of exercise physiology* (4th ed.). Philadelphia, PA: Wolters Kluwer/Lippincott Williams & Wilkins Health.

Kemper, D. W. (1986). *Pathways: A success guide for a healthy life* (2nd ed.). Boise, ID: Healthwise.

Klein, A. (2000). *The healing power of humor: Techniques for getting through loss, setbacks, upsets, disappointments, difficulties, trials, tribulations and all that.* Los Angeles, CA: Penguin Group (USA).

Lakein, A. (1990). *How to get control of your time and your life.* New York, NY: Penguin Books Australia.

Lamott, K. (1974). *Escape from stress.* New York, NY: Putnam.

LaRoche, L. (2009). *Relax: You may only have a few minutes left: Using the power of humour to overcome stress in your life and work.* Carlsbad, CA: Hay House.

Lazarus, A. A. (1984). *In the mind's eye: The power of imagery for personal enrichment* (2nd ed.). New York, NY: Guilford Press.

Lazarus, R. S., & Folkman, S. (1984). *Stress, appraisal, and coping.* New York, NY: Springer.

Leatz, C. A., & Stolar, M. W. (1992). *Career success/personal stress: How to stay healthy in a high-stress environment.* New York, NY: McGraw-Hill.

Lefcourt, H. M., & Martin, R. A. (2011). *Humor and life stress.* New York, NY: Springer-Verlag.

Leshan, L. (1999). *How to meditate: A guide to self-discovery.* New York, NY: Little, Brown.

Levine, S. (1987). *Healing into life and death.* New York, NY: Anchor Books/Doubleday.

Leyden-Rubenstein, L., & Leyden-Rubenstein, S. S. T. (1998). *The stress management handbook: Strategies for health and inner peace.* New York, NY: McGraw-Hill.

Lidell, L., Dorelli, F., Maxwell-Hudson, C., Thomas, S., & Beresford-Cooke, C. (2001). *The book of massage: The complete step-by-step guide to eastern and western techniques.* New York, NY: Simon & Schuster Adult.

Locke, S., & Cousins, N. (1987). *The healer within: The new medicine of mind and body.* New York, NY: New American Library.

Love, S. (1982). *Mastery and management of time.* New York, NY: Simon & Schuster.

Lowen, A. (1994). *Bioenergetics: The revolutionary therapy that uses the language of the body to heal the problems of the mind.* New York, NY: Penguin Group (USA).

MacKenzie, A. R. (1975). *The time trap.* New York, NY: McGraw-Hill.

Madders, J. (2004). *Stress & relaxation.* Abingdon, UK: Taylor & Francis.

Mahoney, M. J., & Thoresen, C. E. (1974). *Self-control: Power to the person.* Monterey, CA: Brooks/Cole.

Maslach, C., & Leiter, M. P. (1997). *The truth about burnout: How organizations cause personal stress and what to do about it.* San Francisco, CA: Jossey-Bass.

Maslach, C., & Zimbardo, P. G. (1982). *Burnout: The cost of caring.* New York, NY: Prentice Hall.

McQuade, W., & Aikman, A. (1993). *Stress: What it is, what it can do to your health, how to handle it.* New York, NY: Signet/New American Library.

Meichenbaum, D. (1992). *Stress inoculation training: Psychology practitioner guidebooks.* New York, NY: Pergamon Press.

Metcalf, C. W. W., & Felible, R. (1993). *Lighten up: Survival skills for people under pressure.* New York, NY: Basic Books.

Miller, J., Miller, L. H., Smith, A. D., & Rothstein, L. (1994). *The stress solution: An action plan to manage the stress in your life.* New York, NY: Pocket Books.

Millman, D. (2007). *Wisdom of the peaceful warrior: A companion to the book that changes lives.* Tiburon, CA: H. J. Kramer.

Mitchell, S. (2011). *The complete illustrated guide to massage: A step-by-step approach to the healing art of touch.* London, UK: Thorsons/Element.

Mitchell, S., & Christie, C. (1998). *I'd kill for a cookie: A simple six-week plan to conquer stress eating.* New York, NY: New American Library.

Morse, D. R., Furst, L., & Carrington, P. (1979). *Stress for success.* New York, NY: Van Nostrand Reinhold.

Moyers, B. (1993). *Healing and the mind.* New York, NY: Knopf Doubleday.

Myss, C., Myss, C., & Shealy, N. (1997). *Anatomy of the spirit: The seven stages of power and healing.* New York, NY: Crown.

Nucho, A. O. (1988). *Stress management: The quest for zest.* Springfield, IL: Charles C. Thomas Publisher.

Nuernberger, P., & Brown, B. B. (1990). *Freedom from stress: A holistic approach.* Honesdale, PA: Himalayan Institute Press.

Ornish, D. (1990). *Dr. Dean Ornish's program for reversing heart disease: The only system scientifically proven to reverse heart disease without drugs or surgery.* New York, NY: Ballantine Books.

Patel, C. (1996). *The complete guide to stress management.* London, UK: Vermilion.

Pearsall, P. (1997). *The pleasure prescription.* MacMillan Audio.

Pelletier, K. R. (1984). *Healthy people in unhealthy places: Stress and fitness at work.* New York, NY: Delacorte Press/Seymour Lawrence.

Pelletier, K. R. (1984). *Mind as healer, mind as slayer: A holistic approach to preventing stress disorders.* New York, NY: Bantam/Doubleday.

Pennington, M. B. (1980). *Centering prayer: Renewing an ancient Christian prayer form.* Garden City, NY: Doubleday Religious.

Pennington, M. B., Kushner, L., & Moran, M. T. (1999). *Centered living: The way of centering prayer.* Liguori, MO: Liguori/Triumph.

Perls, F. S. (1989). *The gestalt approach and eye witness to therapy.* Palo Alto, CA: Science and Behavior Books.

Powell, J. R., & George-Warren, H. (1994). *The working woman's guide to managing stress.* Upper Saddle River, NJ: Prentice Hall.

Prilleltensky, I. (2016). *The laughing guide to well-being: Using humor and science to become happier and healthier.* Lanham, MD: Rowman & Littlefield.

Prochaska, J. O., Norcross, J. C., & DiClemente, C. C. (1994). *Changing for good: The revolutionary program that explains the six stages of change and teaches you how to free yourself from bad habits.* New York, NY: Quill.

Raber, M. F., Dyck, G., & Crisp, M. (1993). *Managing stress for mental fitness.* Menlo Park, CA: Crisp.

Ratcliff, J. D. (1976). *The body and how it works: Reader's Digest home doctor library.* London, UK: Reader's Digest Association.

Rice, V. H. (2000). *Handbook of stress, coping, and health: Implications for nursing research, theory, and practice.* Thousand Oaks, CA: Sage.

Robertson, J. (1990). *Humor, the magic of genie.* Houston, TX: Rich.

Roy, A. (1992). *Commonsense time management* (1st ed.). New York, NY: American Management Association.

Sapolsky, R. M. (2004). *Why zebras don't get ulcers: The acclaimed guide to stress, stress-related diseases, and coping* (3rd ed.). New York, NY: Henry Holt.

Schutz, W. C. (1989). *Joy: Twenty years later.* Berkeley, CA: Ten Speed Press.

Seaward, B. L. (1997). *Stand like mountain, flow like water: Reflections on stress and human spirituality.* Deerfield Beach, FL: Health Communications.

Seligman, M. E. P., & Rubenstein, J. (2005). *Learned optimism: How to change your mind and your life.* New York, NY: Simon & Schuster.

Selye, H. M. D. (1974/1991). *Stress without distress.* New York, NY: New American Library.

Shealy, N. C. (2002). *90 days to stress-free living: A day-by-day health plan, including exercises, diet, and relaxation techniques.* London, UK: Vega Books.

Shealy, N. C., & Myss, C. M. (1992). *The creation of health: Merging traditional medicine with intuitive diagnosis.* New York, NY: New American Library.

Shephard, R. J. (1998). *Aerobic fitness and health.* Champaign, IL: Human Kinetics.

Siegel, B. S. (1999). *Love, medicine and miracles.* London, UK: Rider & Co.

Silva, J. (1986). *The Silva mind control method for business managers.* New York, NY: Pocket Books.

Simmons, R. (1998). *Stress: Your questions answered* (The Element Guides Series). Shaftesbury, UK: Element Books.

Simonton, O. C., Matthews-Simonton, S., & Creighton, J. (1992). *Getting well again*. New York, NY: Bantam.

Smith, M. J. (1980). *When I say no, I feel guilty*. New York, NY: Bantam Books.

Somer, E., & Snyderman, N. L. (1999). *Food and mood: The complete guide to eating well and feeling your best* (2nd ed.). New York, NY: Henry Holt.

Stein, D. (1995). *Essential reiki: A complete guide to an ancient healing art*. New York, NY: Crossing Press.

Stevens, J. O. (1989). *Awareness: Exploring, experimenting, experiencing*. London, UK: Eden Grove Editions.

Storr, A. (2005). *Solitude*. New York, NY: Free Press.

Tannen, D. (1990). *You just don't understand*. New York, NY: HarperCollins.

Tanner, W. B. (1989). *The mystical, magical, marvelous world of dreams*. n.p.: Wild Comet.

Tisserand, R., & Tisser, R. (1977). *The art of aromatherapy*. London, UK: Random House.

Van Toller, S., & Dodd, G. H. (Eds.). (1993). *Fragrance: The psychology and biology of perfume*. New York, NY: Kluwer Academic.

Veninga, R. L., & Spradley, J. P. (1982). *Work stress connection: How to cope with job burnout*. Boston, MA: TBS The Book Service.

Weil, A. (1990). *Natural health, natural medicine*. Boston, MA: Houghton Mifflin.

Williams, R. (1991). *The trusting heart: Great news about type A behavior.* New York, NY: Random House.

Wolpe, J. (1982). *The practice of behavior therapy* (3rd ed.). Elmsford, NY: Pergamon Press.

Woodham, A., & Peters, D. (2000). *Encyclopedia of natural healing: The definitive home reference guide to treatments for the mind and body* (2nd ed.). London, UK: Dorling Kindersley.

ARTICLES

Bennett, M. P., & Lengacher, C. A. (2006). Humor and laughter may influence health. I. History and background. *Evidence-Based Complementary and Alternative Medicine, 3*(1), 61–63. doi:10.1093/ecam/nek015.

Berk, L. S., Tan, S. A., Fry, W. F., Napier, B. J., Lee, J. W., Hubbard, R. W., . . . Eby, W. C. (1989). Neuroendocrine and stress hormone changes during mirthful laughter. *American Journal of the Medical Sciences, 298*(6), 390–396. doi:10.1097/00000441-198912000-00006.

Ekman, P., Levenson, R., & Friesen, W. (1983). Autonomic nervous system activity distinguishes among emotions. *Science, 221*(4616), 1208–1210. doi:10.1126/science.6612338.

Griffin, K. (1992). A whiff of things to come. *Health (Time Inc. Health), 6*(7), 34.

Guerra, P. (1998). Team of researchers reach depressed youths through music therapy. *Counseling Today*. Retrieved from http://www.counseling.org/Resources/Library/Selected%20Topics/Depression/musictherapy.htm.

Landau, R., & Litwin, H. (2000). The effects of extreme early stress in very old age. *Journal of Traumatic Stress, 13*(3), 473–487. doi:10.1023/a:1007737425260.

Lazarus, A. A., & Mayne, T. J. (1990). Relaxation: Some limitations, side effects, and proposed solutions. *Psychotherapy: Theory, Research, Practice, Training, 27*(2), 261–266. doi:10.1037/0033-3204.27.2.261.

Levine, I. S. (2008). Mind matters: Get moving. *Science.* doi:10.1126/science.caredit.a0800113. Retrieved from http://www.sciencemag.org/careers/2008/07/mind-matters-get-moving.

Pew, K. (2000). Forgive an enemy—you'll feel better. *Self, 21*(2), 67.

Savacool, J. (2000). Stress: What really sets you off? *Self,22*(12), 108.

Schwerin, R. (1996). Natural stress relief, natural health. *PC Computing,9*(8), 220.

Zvi, A. (1988). Using humor to develop creative thinking. *Journal of Children in Contemporary Society, 20*(1-2), 99–116.

AGENCIES AND ORGANIZATIONS

Following is a list of agencies and organizations that provide a number of helpful resources relating to stress, health, and many of the topics covered in this book. They are arranged under these broad topics:

- General Health Resources
- Alternative Health Care and Complementary Medicine
- Addiction, Anxiety, Stress, and Other Mental Health Issues
- Diseases and Disorders
- Environmental Health
- Exercise and Weight Control
- Life Cycle and Health (Aging)
- Prevention of Stress
- Women's Health

GENERAL HEALTH RESOURCES

American Medical Association
515 N. State St
Chicago, IL 60654
800-621-8335
www.ama-assn.org

This association provides resources for physicians with additional information aimed at the general consumer. The site also offers related links to various health issues and a members-only area.

American Red Cross
2025 E St, NW
Washington, DC 20006

202-303-5000
www.redcross.org

The website for this world-renowned emergency response organization features information about volunteering, classes, assistance, and news.

Centers for Disease Control and Prevention (CDC)
1600 Clifton Rd
Atlanta, GA 30333
www.cdc.gov

This government agency is part of the U.S. Department of Health and Human Services; its website offers information to consumers on all aspects of health and disease.

Healthfinder/U.S. Department of Health and Human Services
PO Box 1133
Washington, DC 20013-1133
www.healthfinder.gov

This government agency site, from the Department of Health and Human Services, covers everything from breastfeeding to nutrition information from federal and state agencies. The site also includes information about support and self-help groups.

Health Resources and Services Administration
5600 Fishers Ln
Rockville, MD 20857
301-443-3376
www.hrsa.gov

This U.S. Department of Health and Human Services site links to a great deal of government health information, including information about transplants, HIV/AIDS, and the National Health Service Corps, as well as public health links.

Mayo Clinic
200 First St SW
Rochester, MN 55905
904-953-2000
www.mayoclinic.org

The Mayo Clinic, a nonprofit worldwide leader in medical care, research, and education, developed this website to provide information to medical professionals, patients, and their families in the form of past articles and current research, as well as a question-and-answer format search.

Medical Library Association
65 East Wacker Pl, Suite 1900
Chicago, IL 60601-7246
312-419-9094
www.mlanet.org

This nonprofit, educational organization of health sciences information professionals supports research and works to promote the importance of quality information for improved health in the community. Their MLA's resources section includes recommended, authoritative sites for consumers and for these specific conditions: cancer, diabetes, heart disease (http://www.mlanet.org/resources/userguide.html). Especially useful is the site's Consumer and Patient Health Information Section (CAPHIS) at http://caphis.mlanet.org/, which includes the top websites you can trust for health information (http://caphis.mlanet.org/consumer/index.html).

Medline Plus
8600 Rockville Pike
Bethesda, MD 20894
www.nlm.nih.gov/medlineplus

A service of the U.S. National Library of Medicine through the National Institutes of Health, this online resource connects consumers with the latest research in health topics, drugs, supplements, and other health facts.

National Health Information Center
PO Box 1133
Washington, DC 20013-1133
800-336-4797
http://health.gov/about-us/

Sponsored by the U.S. Department of Health and Human Services, this health referral service answers questions for professionals and consumers on all kinds of health issues. It also provides support through the Healthfinder website, another government resource for consumer health information.

National Institutes of Health (NIH)
9000 Rockville Pike
Bethesda, MD 20892
301-496-4000
www.nih.gov/health

This government site provides a comprehensive list of resources on health issues from ADHD to stress and viruses. The NIH is under the U.S. Department of Health and Human Services.

National LGBT Health Education Center
Ansin Building, 8th Floor
1340 Boylston St
Boston, MA 02215
617-927-6354
www.lgbthealtheducation.org/lgbt-education/lgbt-health-resources/

Essentially a clearinghouse of material on LGBT health, this site provides access to numerous other sites, directories, associations, articles, and courses, on topics ranging from discrimination in LGBT health to training for health professionals, violence and trauma support, parenting resources, and more.

National Library of Medicine
8600 Rockville Pike
Bethesda, MD 20894
888-346-3656
www.nlm.nih.gov

Located on the campus of the National Institutes of Health, the National Library of Medicine is the world's largest medical library, with a collection of material that is available for research in all areas of medicine and health care. The various reading rooms are open during the week for research or for those interested in learning more about diseases, drugs, clinical trials, and other medical resources.

Physicians Committee for Responsible Medicine
5100 Wisconsin Ave, NW, Suite 400
Washington, DC 20016
www.pcrm.org

The PCRM promotes nutrition and preventive medicine and supports research programs for diabetes, cancer, and other issues. This site offers restaurant reviews, physician referrals, and other resources for students and educators.

World Health Organization (WHO)
525 23rd St, NW
Washington, DC 20037
202-974-3000
www.who.int

This website emphasizes international health issues and offers reports, research, and information on issues from eradicating polio to advances in medications. There is a great deal of information for those interested, but it is not geared for the casual browser.

ALTERNATIVE HEALTH CARE AND COMPLEMENTARY MEDICINE

American Academy of Medical Acupuncture
5820 Wilshire Blvd, Suite 500
Los Angeles, CA 90036
800-521-2262
www.medicalacupuncture.org

This medical physician-only professional organization works to promote the integration of acupuncture with Western medical training. The organization is only open to physician acupuncturists.

American Association of Acupuncture and Oriental Medicine
PO Box 162340
Sacramento, CA 95816
866-455-7999
www.aaaomonline.org

Formed in 1981, the AAAOM is a national association providing professional standards in the practice of acupuncture and Oriental medicine in the United States, with the goal of promoting excellence and integrity in the profession.

American Association of Naturopathic Physicians
4435 Wisconsin Ave NW, Suite 403
Washington DC 20016
866-538-2267
www.naturopathic.org

This site provides consumer information and the ability to search for a naturopathic doctor by zip code. There is also a database of members and information concerning professional education for members.

American Botanical Council
PO Box 144345
Austin, TX 78714-4345
512-926-4900
www.herbalgram.org

This nonprofit research and information organization is dedicated to providing accurate and reliable information for consumers about the use of herbs and medicinal plants.

American College for Advancement in Medicine
24411 Ridge Rte, Suite 115
Laguna Hills, CA 92653
949-309-3520
www.acam.org

This not-for-profit corporation is dedicated to the education of physicians and other health care professionals in complementary, alternative, and integrative medicine. The site offers a public connection to physicians who use integrative medicine as well as information on integrative treatment options.

American Holistic Medical Association
PO Box 2016
Edmonds, WA 98020
425-967-0737
www.aihm.org

This organization serves its members and provides advocacy concerning the use of holistic and integrative medicine by licensed health care providers. It also provides links to patients interested in choosing a holistic provider.

Association for Applied and Therapeutic Humor
220 E. State St, Floor G
Rockford, IL 61104
http://www.aath.org

Offers resources and information about the therapeutic benefits of humor.

Association of Accredited Naturopathic Medical Colleges
4435 Wisconsin Ave NW, Suite 403
Washington DC 20016
202-237-8150
www.aanmc.org

This site provides information about naturopathy and naturopathic medicine, including a list of schools offering the program, admission and application information, career information, and open house and campus tour details.

Ayurvedic Institute
PO Box 23445
Albuquerque, NM 87192
www.ayurveda.com

This nonprofit organization features a school and spa. Its website links to information about the practice of Ayurvedic medicine, along with education, membership information, an events calendar, and other online resources.

Biofeedback Certification International Alliance
5310 Ward Rd, Suite 201
Arvada, CO 80002
http://www.bcia.org/i4a/pages/index.cfm?pageid=1

Created in 1981, the Biofeedback Certification International Alliance (BCIA) is a non-profit organization providing certification to individuals meeting specific standards within the biofeedback field. It provides resources to professionals relating to biofeedback and information on certification. There is also a database available to locate a practitioner.

Center for Mind-Body Medicine
5225 Connecticut Ave, NW, Suite 414
Washington, DC 20015
202-966-7338
www.cmbm.org

This nonprofit educational organization offers facts about resources, research, a list of CMBM certified practitioners, and a job and internship list.

Conscious Living Foundation
http://consciouslivingfoundation.org

Offers resources and classes to enhance awareness and consciousness for living.

International Institute of Stress Management and Allied Sciences
http://www.iismaas.com

Offers programs and resources to manage stress more effectively.

National Ayurvedic Medical Association
620 Cabrillo Ave
Santa Cruz CA 95065
800-669-8914
www.ayurveda-nama.org

This website links Ayurvedic medical professionals from across the country and works to promote the science and practice of Ayurveda.

National Center for Complementary and Integrative Health (NCCIH)
9000 Rockville Pike
Bethesda, MD 20892
888-644-6226
https://nccih.nih.gov/

The NCCIH, formerly known as the National Center for Complementary and Alternative Medicine, is the U.S. government's lead agency for scientific research on unconventional or complementary medical practices, research, and products. The website offers information as well as links to research, grants, training, and legislative updates.

National Commission for Certification of Acupuncture and Oriental Medicine
76 South Laura St, Suite 1290
Jacksonville, FL 32202
904-598-1005
www.nccaom.org

This nonprofit organization evaluates entry-level programs and competency in the practice of acupuncture and Oriental medicine through its program of professional certification.

ADDICTION, ANXIETY, STRESS, AND OTHER MENTAL HEALTH ISSUES

Alcoholics Anonymous
475 Riverside Dr, 11th Floor
New York, NY 10115
www.aa.org

Alcoholics Anonymous is an organization for individuals who are working to achieve sobriety from alcohol. The site offers general information, directions on how to find an AA meeting, and information for family members. The organization, which was founded in the 1950s, is self-supporting through contributions. There are no dues or fees for membership.

American Anorexia/Bulimia Association
165 West 46th St, Suite 1108
New York, NY 10036
212-575-6200
http://orgs.tigweb.org/american-anorexia-bulimia-association

The AABA is a nonprofit organization dedicated to the treatment of eating disorders. The information on this site is geared toward the general public.

American Institute of Stress
6387B Camp Bowie Blvd #334
Fort Worth, TX 76116
682-239-682
http://www.stress.org/

The American Institute of Stress is a nonprofit organization established in 1978 at the request of Hans Selye, who first investigated stress in modern life. Its serves as a clearinghouse for information on all stress-related subjects.

American Psychiatric Association
http://www.psychiatry.org

Provides information for individuals and families on various mental health disorders; supplies resources for finding a psychiatrist and understanding mental health.

Anxiety and Depression Association of America
8730 Georgia Ave, Suite 600
Silver Spring, MD 20910
240-485-1001
www.adaa.org

Along with resources for professionals, this site offers helpful information about anxiety, self-help publications, ways to find a therapist, and explanations of treatment options.

Attention Deficit Disorder Association
PO Box 7557
Wilmington, DE 19803
800-233-4050
http://www.add.org

The ADDA site offers information, resources, and networking opportunities for adults with ADHD. It offers facts, articles, research, support group information, and links to other helpful resources.

Depression and Bipolar Support Alliance
730 N. Franklin St, Suite 501
Chicago, IL 60654-7225
800-826-3632
www.dbsalliance.org

The website for this national organization, which serves patients with mental illness, offers support, information about mood disorders, links to research and clinical trials, and a calendar of educational programs and events.

Dressing Room Project
PO Box 834
Black Mountain, NC 28711
828-318-4438
https://www.facebook.com/The-Dressing-Room-Project-182888068397362/

This facebook page supports the promotion of a positive body image for girls and women, and was developed through the Emerging Women Projects (EWP), a nonprofit organization that works to empower teen girls. The project offers girls and women opportunities to create positive body image cards and post them in public places.

Hospice Foundation of America
1621 Connecticut Ave, NW, Suite 300
Washington, DC 20009
800-854-3402
www.hospicefoundation.org

This organization conducts professional development for hospice providers, offers research and publications, and assists individuals who are coping with caregiving, terminal illness, and grief through links on its website.

International OCD Foundation
337 Notch Hill Rd
North Bramford, CT 06471
203-315-2190
www.iocdf.org

This international not-for-profit organization, founded in 1986, works to link individuals who have obsessive-compulsive disorder or related disorders with health care professionals and information to assist them in their treatment. The website lists resources, programs, research, and legislative updates for interested individuals.

Mental Health America
500 Montgomery St, Suite 820
Alexandria, VA 22314
703-684-7722
800-969-6642
http://www.mentalhealthamerica.net/about-us

This nonprofit organization addresses all aspect of mental health and illness and supports reform and education to improve treatment and conditions for Americans with mental illness.

National Alliance on Mental Illness (NAMI)
2107 Wilson Blvd, Suite 300
Arlington, VA 22201-3042
800-950-6264
www.nami.org

This advocacy organization works to improve treatment of and quality of life for individuals with mental illness. Founded in 1979, the organization supports research and awareness of mental illness, offering resources to patients and their families. There is also a link to legislative information, a magazine, a blog, and a ranking of states and the quality of their mental health services.

National Association of Anorexia Nervosa and Associated Disorders
PO Box 640
Naperville, IL 60566
www.anad.org

The ANAD, which is among the country's oldest nonprofit organizations, offers access to a wealth of resources for persons with eating disorders and their families.

National Center for PTSD
U.S. Department of Veterans Affairs
810 Vermont Ave, NW
Washington DC 20420
Veterans Crisis Line: 1-800-273-8255 (Press 1)

The U.S. Department of Veterans Affair has worked to improve service, including more focus and resources on posttraumatic stress disorder (PTSD) treatment and interventions for returning veterans. This website offers outreach and resources for veterans, their families, and those treating them.

National Institute of Mental Health (NIMH)
Science Writing, Press, and Dissemination Branch
6001 Executive Blvd, Room 8184, MSC 9663
Bethesda, MD 20892-9663
301-443-4513
www.nimh.nih.gov

This organization, under the U.S. National Institutes of Health, supports basic and clinical research to prevent and cure mental illness. The website offers links to research and funding, news, and legislative updates, as well as basic mental health information.

National Mental Health Association
See Mental Health America

National Suicide Prevention Lifeline
1-800-273-8255
Or, 1-800-273-TALK
Also a chat service: http://www.suicidepreventionlifeline.org/GetHelp/LifelineChat.aspx
www.suicidepreventionlifeline.org

A site that offers 24-hour confidential resources (phone counseling and chat lines) to help those struggling with thoughts of suicide. Also provides articles, blogs, and other resources to help young adults, those who are facing bullying, and veterans. Help in Spanish is available.

DISEASES AND DISORDERS

AIDSinfo: National Institutes of Health (NIH)
PO Box 6303
Rockville, MD 20849-6303
http://aidsinfo.nih.gov

This government site is provided by the U.S. Department of Health and Human Services to offer information on HIV/AIDS treatment, prevention, and research. It also provides information on related health topics and a link to clinical trials.

AllergyKids Foundation
PO Box 20236
Boulder, CO 80308
www.allergykids.com

This organization works to provide information about additives used in food. It is run entirely by volunteers and donations are put toward research on the role of food in the health of children.

Alliance for Lupus Research
28 West 44th St, Suite 501
New York, NY 10036
212-218-2840 or 800- 867-1743
www.lupusresearch.org

The ALR is a national health organization founded in 1999 by Robert Wood Johnson IV. Its focus is to discover better treatments and ultimately to prevent and cure systemic lupus erythematosus (SLE).

Alzheimer's Association
225 N. Michigan Ave, Floor 17
Chicago, IL 60601-7633
800-272-3900
www.alz.org

This nonprofit association seeks to improve care for patients with Alzheimer's disease on a national and international level. The website offers links to support groups, a 24-hour "Helpline," and links to information on clinical trials.

American Academy of Allergy, Asthma & Immunology
555 East Wells St, Suite 1100
Milwaukee, WI 53202-3823
800-822-2762
www.aaaai.org

The AAAAI is a professional medical specialty organization that represents allergists, physicians, clinical immunologists, and health professionals. Its online site offers consumers a referral directory and resource center, along with information.

American Autoimmune Related Diseases Association
22100 Gratiot Ave, East
Detroit, MI 48021
800-598-4668
www.aarda.org

The AARDA is a national, nonprofit health agency dedicated to eradication of autoimmune diseases through education, public awareness, research, and patient services.

American Cancer Society
250 Williams St
Atlanta, GA 30303
800-227-2345
www.cancer.org

The ACS is a national voluntary health organization whose goal is to assist those with cancer by providing information and by supporting research.

American Diabetes Association
1701 North Beauregard St
Alexandria, VA 22311
www.diabetes.org

This association works to prevent and cure diabetes through funding research and by providing information for diabetics and others interested in the disease.

American Heart Association
7272 Greenville Ave
Dallas, TX 75231
www.americanheart.org

This association provides clear, concise information on heart disease as well as on nutrition, exercise and stroke-related illness for a general audience.

American Lung Association
1301 Pennsylvania Ave NW, Suite 800
Washington, DC 20004
www.lungusa.org

This organization has been in operation for more than 100 years, according to its website, and continues its efforts to improve lung health and prevent lung disease by supporting education and research.

Arthritis Foundation
1330 West Peachtree St.
Atlanta, GA 30309
800-283-7800 or 404-872-7100
www.arthritis.org

This organization is dedicated to improving the lives of people with arthritis through information, access to health care, advocacy, and research support.

Autism Society of America
7910 Woodmont Ave, Suite 300
Bethesda, MD 20814-3067
800-AUTISM
www.autism-society.org

The site for this grassroots organization features its quarterly journal, publications, and programs; it continues to advocate for the rights of all people with autism.

Celiac Disease Foundation
13251 Ventura Blvd, Suite 1
Studio City, CA 91604
818-990-2354
www.celiac.org

This website is designed to provide resources, information, diet and lifestyle suggestions, and treatment information for those suffering from celiac disease.

CFIDS Association of America
See Open Medicine Foundation.

Christopher & Dana Reeve Foundation
636 Morris Tpke, Suite 3A
Short Hills, NJ 07078
800-225-0292
www.christopherreeve.org

This international website, which can be accessed in eight different languages, is designed to provide information for those dealing with spinal cord injury as well as resources for those working with spinal injury patients. Links to the Quality of Life grants program and the Paralysis Resource Center will help readers find additional information.

Crohn's and Colitis Foundation of America
386 Park Ave S, 17th Floor
New York, NY 10016
800-932-2423
www.ccfa.org

This website provides information about the nonprofit organization and its resources aimed at assisting those living with Crohn's disease and ulcerative colitis. There are links to research, disease management choices, and even a youth and teen page.

Gluten Intolerance Group of North America
31214 124th Ave, SE
Auburn, WA 98092
253-833-6655
www.gluten.org

The website for this nonprofit organization provides medical information, a recipe database, links to gluten-free restaurants, and a list of local branches across the United States for those suffering from gluten intolerance.

Immune Deficiency Foundation
40 W. Chesapeake Ave, Suite 308
Towson, MD 21204
800-296-4433
www.primaryimmune.org

Although immunodeficiency diseases are considered relatively rare, this organization provides accurate information on research, treatment, and patient needs to an international audience.

International Association for Chronic Fatigue Syndrome CFS/ME
27 N. Wacker Dr, Suite 416
Chicago, IL 60606
847-258-7248
www.iacfsme.org

This not-for-profit organization, started in 1992, works to support those with CFS by providing information for researchers, clinicians, health care workers, and support groups. Membership is also available internationally for those interested in the organization.

Juvenile Diabetes Research Foundation International
120 Wall St
New York, NY 10005-4001
800-533-2873
www.jdrf.org

This international organization works with other groups around the world to provide information, research, and assistance in developing new and better treatments for patients with juvenile (Type 1) diabetes. The site features research, publications, and information about advocacy.

Learning Disabilities Association of America
4156 Library Rd
Pittsburgh, PA 15234-1349
412-341-8077
www.ldaamerica.org

This nonprofit organization, started in the 1960s, now serves tens of thousands of members with learning disabilities, as well as their families and the professionals who assist them. The site offers resources for teachers, parents, adults, and professionals, as well as links to a bookstore, resources, state chapters of the organization, and legislative updates.

Leukemia & Lymphoma Society
1311 Mamaroneck Ave
White Plains, NY 10605
800-955-4572
www.lls.org

This organization supports and funds researchers who are working to find a cure for leukemia, lymphoma, Hodgkin's disease, and melanoma. It offers information that links individuals with clinical trials, and to services they need as they manage their disease.

Lupus Foundation of America
800-558-0121
www.lupus.org

This interactive website offers basic information about lupus and also connects individuals to local chapters of this national nonprofit health organization and support groups. It sponsors a Walk for Lupus fundraiser.

March of Dimes Foundation
1275 Mamaroneck Ave
White Plains, NY 10605
888-663-4637
www.marchofdimes.org

This organization was started by President Franklin D. Roosevelt to help fight the disease of polio. Over the years, the mission of the organization has shifted to support research in finding and curing the causes of premature birth and birth defects.

MRSA Survivors Network
PO Box 241
Hinsdale, IL 60522
630-325-4354
www.mrsasurvivors.org

This network was founded in early 2003 to inform consumers and health providers about the serious health issues associated with serious infection contracted from MRSA. The organization lobbies for change in national policy concerning MRSA and public health.

National Center for Learning Disabilities
381 Park Ave S, Suite 1401
New York, NY 10016
212-545-7510
www.ncld.org

This organization advocates for U.S. children, adolescents, and adults with learning disabilities. Its site offers a resource locator, age-related content, a blog to connect members, and a newsletter.

National Eye Institute
31 Center Dr
Bethesda, MD 20892-3655
301-496-5248
www.nei.nih.gov

Established in 1968 by President Lyndon B. Johnson, this government organization is dedicated to promoting research and finding a cure for human eye diseases and disorders. The website links to jobs, training, resources, research, news, and health information.

National Institute of Allergy and Infectious Diseases
6610 Rockledge Dr, MSC 6612
Bethesda, MD 20892
866-284-4107
www.niaid.nih.gov

Sponsored by the Department of Health and Human Services and its National Institutes of Health, this organization is designed to improve research and understanding of treatment and responses to immunologic, infectious, and allergic diseases. There are links to scientific resources, funding sources, research, and news and legislative updates.

Open Medicine Foundation
29302 Laro Dr
Agoura Hills, CA 91301
http://www.openmedicinefoundation.org/

A nonprofit organization whose mission is to "[s]upport collaborative medical research to find effective treatments and diagnostic markers for difficult-to-treat neuro-immune illnesses"; currently focusing on an "End ME/CFS Project" that is designed to find biomarkers and effective treatments for myalgic encephalomyelitis/chronic fatigue syndrome.

PCO (Polycystic Ovary Syndrome) Support
PO Box 3403
Englewood, CO 80155-3403
www.pcosupport.org

This site, sponsored by the Polycystic Ovarian Syndrome Association, Inc., is dedicated to serving women who have been diagnosed with PCOS. The website offers information on medical treatments and supplements, and also offers a message board for women who need support, a newsletter, and links to recent research in PCOS and its treatment.

Solve ME/CFD Initiative
PO Box 220398
Charlotte, NC 28222-0398
704-365-2343
http://solvecfs.org/

The SMCI is a charitable organization dedicated to conquering chronic fatigue and immune dysfunction syndrome. Its site offers links to research, free brochures, and a youth home page, along with patient support and advocacy.

U.S. Department of Veterans Affairs
810 Vermont Ave, NW
Washington, DC 20420
http://www.va.gov/

The U.S. Department of Veterans Affairs provides patient care and federal benefits to veterans and their dependents.

ENVIRONMENTAL HEALTH

National Institute of Environmental Health Sciences (NIH)
111 T.W. Alexander Dr
Research Triangle Park, NC 27709
www.niehs.nih.gov

This environmental organization promotes the health of the community and supports research under the umbrella of the National Institutes of Health. The website offers information on a large variety of issues ranging from carcinogens like formaldehyde and aristolochic acids, to cell phone health concerns, environmental diseases, and a follow-up on the environmental impact of the Gulf oil spill.

Occupational Safety and Health Administration (OSHA)
200 Constitution Ave, NW
Washington, DC 20210
800-321-6742 (OSHA)
www.OSHA.gov

A rich resource for employees as well as employers, this government agency ensures safe and healthful working conditions by setting and enforcing standards and by providing training, outreach, education, and assistance. The website gives information on how to work more safely, from working at a desk that is set up ergonomically to working in more hazardous settings; it also provides a mechanism to investigate and file complaints about potential work safety hazards, along with information about OSHA standards and other resources.

U.S. Environmental Protection Agency (EPA)
1200 Pennsylvania Ave, NW
Washington, DC 20460
www3.epa.gov

This highly interactive website provided by the U.S. government offers an A-to-Z index of environmental issues facing Americans, including acid rain, mold, radon, and climate change. The website includes news and announcements, additional research, and contact information, as well as a map of the United States that offers a breakdown of environmental issues unique to each state.

EXERCISE AND WEIGHT CONTROL

Aerobic and Fitness Association of America (AFAA)
1750 E. Northrop Blvd, Suite 200
Chandler, AZ 85286
www.afaa.com

The AFAA website offers fitness education for professionals and upholds the Basic Exercise Standards and Guidelines for safe fitness practice.

American College of Sports Medicine (ACSM)
PO Box 1440
Indianapolis, IN 46206
317-637-9200
www.acsm.org

This professional organization provides access to research, as well as education and advocacy for certified professionals, graduate students, and undergraduate students in the field of applied exercise science and clinical sports medicine.

American Council on Exercise (ACE)
4851 Paramount Dr
San Diego, CA 92123
800-825-3636
www.acefitness.org

This nonprofit organization is a resource for fitness professionals and consumers. Its website provides research on fitness products and programs and offers certification and continuing education standards for fitness professionals.

President's Council on Physical Fitness, Sports, and Nutrition
1101 Wootton Pkwy, Suite 560
Rockville, MD 20852
www.fitness.gov

This government site, which is part of the U.S. Department of Health and Human Services, provides information about the history of the President's Council, along with exercise and nutrition tips.

Shape Up America
6707 Democracy Blvd, Suite 306
Bethesda, MD 20817-1129
www.shapeup.org

This site features information about the national initiative to promote healthy weight called Shape Up America. There is advice from fitness and nutrition experts as well as practical tips and support plus a tool to determine body mass index (BMI).

LIFE CYCLE AND HEALTH (AGING)

American Society on Aging
833 Market St, Suite 512
San Francisco, CA 94103
415-882-2910
www.asaging.org

This website is geared toward the researchers, educators, health practitioners, and others who work with older adults.

National Clearinghouse on Families & Youth
5515 Security Ln
North Bethesda, MD 20852
301-608-8098
http://ncfy.acf.hhs.gov

This information resource, offered through the U.S. Department of Health and Human Services, seeks to assist individuals and organizations that with work at-risk youth and families.

National Council on Aging
1901 L St, NW, 4th Floor
Washington, DC 20036
202-479-1200
www.ncoa.org

The NCOA is a nonprofit service and advocacy organization that works to serve older Americans through their community organizations by bringing together other nonprofits, businesses, and government to improve the lives of older adults.

National Resource Center on LGBT Aging
c/o Services & Advocacy for GLBT Elders (SAGE)
305 Seventh Ave, 6th Floor
New York, NY 10001
212-741-2247
http://www.lgbtagingcenter.org/

The National Resource Center on LGBT Aging provides information about the services and support available for lesbian, gay, bisexual, and transgender (LGBT) older adults. The website offers numerous articles that cover general health and aging concerns, as well as legal and social issues facing LGBT seniors.

PREVENTION OF STRESS

Academy of Nutrition and Dietetics
120 South Riverside Plaza, Suite 2000
Chicago, IL 60606-6995
800-877-1600
312-899-0040
http://www.eatright.org/

The Academy of Nutrition and Dietetics, an organization of food and nutrition professionals, provides wide-ranging, accurate, and sensible information on how to shop, eat, and prepare food for the best health. This site includes information on nutrition throughout life, weight control, disease prevention and management, keeping or attaining a healthy weight, prevention and management of diseases, and a searchable database of registered dietitian nutritionists.

American Meditation Institute
PO Box 430
Averill Park, NY 12018
518-674-8714
www.americanmeditation.org

The AMI is a nonprofit education organization working to improve training and education in mind-body medicine by offering information, as well as a speaker's bureau and links to other organizations.

American Yoga Association
PO Box 19986
Sarasota, FL 34276
912-927-4977
www.americanyogaassociation.org

The site offers information about yoga, its history and types, and how to choose a qualified teacher.

National Center for Complementary and Integrative Health (NCCIH)
Meditation
https://nccih.nih.gov/health/meditation

This section of the NCCIH website offers numerous articles, tips, and information on meditation and mindfulness as a health and stress prevention tool.

National Center on Sleep Disorders Research
6701 Rockledge Dr
Bethesda, MD 20892
301-435-0199
www.nhlbi.nih.gov/about/ncsdr

This branch of the National Institutes of Health offers links to research, patient information, and training for health professionals related to sleep disorders.

National Sleep Foundation
1010 N. Glebe Rd, Suite 420

Arlington, VA 22201
703-243-1697
https://sleepfoundation.org/

The National Sleep Foundation is a nonprofit organization whose website provides education on sleep and advocacy for better health. It provides resources on sleep science, healthy sleep habits, and sleep disorders to medical professionals, patients, and the public.

WOMEN'S HEALTH

National Women's Health Information Center
8270 Willow Oaks Corporate Dr
Fairfax, VA 22031
800-994-9662
http://www.idph.state.il.us/about/womenshealth/prevguide2003.pdf

This federal government source for information on women's health is sponsored by the U.S. Department of Health and Human Services and its Office on Women's Health. The office was established in 1991 to improve the health and well-being of U.S. women and girls by sponsoring programs that focus on health, by providing information to the public, and by educating physicians and researchers.

National Women's Health Network
1413 K St, NW, 4th Floor
Washington, DC 20005
202-682-2646
www.nwhn.org

This membership-based organization, founded in 1975, works to influence health policy by promoting women's health issues. It monitors the actions of the federal government and funding agencies as well as industry and health professionals and supports grassroots action to improve health care outcomes for women.

U.S. Department of Health and Human Services, Office on Women's Health
200 Independence Ave, SW
Washington, DC 20201
800-994-9662
http://womenshealth.gov/

Womenshealth.gov is operated by the U.S. Department of Health and Human Services' Office on Women's Health. The site includes a large range of health topics, e-publications, and news.

About the Editor and Contributors

EDITOR

Serena Wadhwa, PsyD, LCPC, CADC, RYT, is assistant professor of Addictions Studies and Behavioral Health at Governors State University, University Park, Illinois. Her published work includes *Substance Use in the Workplace: Problem or Not?* (2013); *Grief and Loss in the Workplace* (2015); and *Stress Intelligence* (forthcoming), as well as several articles. Dr. Wadhwa works in a variety of roles as a consultant, creator, presenter, trainer, lecturer, radio talk show host, stress coach, yoga instructor, and blogger.

CONTRIBUTORS

Chapter Contributors

Thomas C. Anderson, PhD, is a clinical psychologist in Oak Park, Illinois. His clinical work and research help clients understand and manage complex thoughts, feelings, and behaviors associated with illness, difficult life events, and mood disorders. Dr. Anderson received his training at Loyola University of Chicago, Indiana University, and Arizona State University.

Raven Lynn Badger, PhD, is a sexologist and associate professor in addictions studies at Governors State University, University Park, Illinois. She has several publications to date including book chapters, research articles, and her book *Sexuality and Addiction: Making Connections, Enhancing Recovery* (Praeger, 2012).

Dr. Badger is currently conducting sexual health research with women in substance abuse treatment in Chicago.

Kirsten Levin Belzer, LCSW, CHT, is a licensed clinical social worker in private practice in Chicago, specializing in issues of stress, anxiety, depression, trauma, and grief. She graduated from Northwestern University's Medill School of Journalism and received a master's degree in social work from the University of Chicago's School of Social Service Administration.

Judy Berglund, PhD, LCSW, teaches research, social welfare policy, diversity and social justice, and practice in social work. She has worked with families and children in mental health, schools, and hospital settings since 1983, and worked for state governments as a trainer on mental health policies. She currently teaches in the BSW program at Western Illinois University, in Macomb, Illinois.

Erin Conway, PsyD, CADC, BCB, specializes in forensic and neuropsychology. She is board certified in biofeedback and is a certified alcohol and drug counselor. She has a strong interest in complementary therapies and currently works with children, adolescents, and adults in a private practice setting in the greater Chicago area.

Joseph Day, DrPH, is an assistant professor and coordinator of the Community Health program at Governor's State University, University Park, Illinois. Research experiences include studying chronic disease prevention, racial and ethnic health disparities, and substance abuse in youth. Current projects include students' responses to contextual stress and substance use, psychological distress, and risk behavior.

Amber N. Douglas, PhD, is associate professor of psychology and education and associate professor of gender studies at Mount Holyoke College in South Hadley, Massachusetts. Her research interests include psychological trauma and the psychology of ethnic minorities.

Rachel Dubrow, MSW, LCSW, is a psychotherapist in private practice in Skokie, Illinois. She specializes in helping adults work through life's stressors and find balance so they can live happier, more fulfilled lives. In addition to her practice, she is an adjunct faculty member and teaches master of social work courses online.

Lydia Falconnier, PhD, is an assistant professor at Governors State University, University Park, Illinois. She completed her doctorate at the University of Chicago in 2003. Dr. Falconnier teaches social work practice and human behavior courses.

Her research interests focus on the service needs of low-income mothers involved in the child welfare system.

Jonathan Fenton is a psychotherapist at a women's health center in the Chicago area. He graduated cum laude from the University of Baltimore and earned his master's degree from Adler University, Chicago. He has treated mood, anxiety, psychotic, personality, substance-use, and trauma disorders, and has conducted research on alternative therapies, harm reduction, nutrition, and evolutionary psychology.

Michele Ferraro, PsyD, MBA, is the founder of a wellness clinic promoting mind-body-spirit medicine. She works with individuals who experience high levels of pain, trauma, depression, and anxiety by sharing focusing, meditation, and EMDR. Her website is www.BeingInSpirit.com.

Laura Foster, LCPC, ATR-BC, is a licensed clinical professional counselor and board-certified art therapist. She is the founder of a private psychotherapy practice in Chicago, Illinois. She received her master's degree in counseling and art therapy from the Adler School of Professional Psychology in Chicago.

Wendy E. Goetz, PsyD, is a licensed clinical psychologist in private practice in Chicago, Illinois, focusing on relationship and communication issues with adults, couples, and families. Her clinical work is informed by systemic, interpersonal, dynamic, multicultural, and emotion-focused theories and perspectives.

Joann V. Hendelman, PhD, MA, BSN, RN, FAED, CEDRN, CEDS-S, is clinical director/postdoctoral training director for the Alliance for Eating Disorders Awareness headquartered in West Palm Beach, Florida. She is a Fellow in the Academy for Eating Disorders, and a Certified Eating Disorders Specialist and Supervisor. She does training for universities, military, and multispecialty physicians, dentists, and community forums.

Janis Clark Johnston, EdD, is a family psychologist in Oak Park, Illinois. She has worked as a school psychologist, supervising psychologist, employee assistance therapist, and private practice psychologist. Her publications include journal articles, book chapters, and a book, *It Takes a Child to Raise a Parent: Stories of Evolving Child and Parent Development* (2013).

Meetu Khosla, PhD, MPhil, MA, BA(Hons), in psychology from the University of Delhi. She has been a Fulbright-Nehru Fellow, Erasmus Mundus Fellow, Shastri Fellow, and ICSSR fellow, and has served as an associate professor in psychology at the University of Delhi for 21 years. She has published more than 35 research papers, several book chapters, and a book on physiological psychology.

Yoo Jung Kim is a research fellow at the National Institutes of Health and a recent graduate of Dartmouth College. She is a staff writer for the SCI-ED Blog hosted by the Public Library of Science. She is one of the coauthors of a book titled *What Every College Science Student Should Know,* to be published in 2016 by the University of Chicago Press.

Kimberly S. Kut, PsyD, holds a doctoral degree in clinical psychology from the Illinois School of Professional Psychology at Argosy University, Chicago. She is a multifaceted psychologist specializing in evidence-based treatment for anxiety-related disorders and issues. She is employed at a counseling center in Illinois and is preparing to found a private practice.

Ioulia Maimari, MSc, is a registered clinical psychologist and a cognitive behavioral therapist in private practice in Paphos, Cyprus. She also teaches cognitive behavioral therapy in postgraduate training programs, provides psychoeducational workshops and career counseling, and publishes extensively in local papers and websites.

Rae Louise Mazzei, PsyD, CADC, BCB, is a clinical psychologist, certified alcohol and drug counselor, and certified hypnotherapist; she is also board certified in biofeedback. In her private practice in Schaumburg, Illinois, she provides counseling to adolescents, adults, couples, and families. Additionally, she offers psychological assessment, behavioral health, and supervision services.

Cheryl L. Mejta, PhD, is the chair of the Department of Addictions Studies and Behavioral Health at Governors State University, as well as a clinical health psychologist. She teaches a course on comparative and complementary alternative medicine. Additionally, she works in a primary care setting with patients who have chronic illnesses.

Robert R. Moss, PhD, ABN, ABPP, a former associate professor in clinical psychology, currently works at North Mississippi Medical Center's Regional Pain Consultant in Tupelo, Mississippi. He is the founding editor-in-chief of *AIMS Neuroscience.* He originated the Clinical Biopsychological Model of psychotherapy integration. He is board certified in clinical psychology (ABPP) and neuropsychology (ABN).

Rae Noble, LCPC, ATR, is an art therapist serving as clinical manager of an eating recovery center residential program in Chicago, Illinois. Rae works primarily with survivors of trauma, eating and mood disorders, and addiction; she aligns with a person-centered, strengths-based model of therapy.

Samantha Reif, PhD, received her MS and PhD degrees from Rosalind Franklin University of Medicine and Science, North Chicago, Illinois. She has completed advanced training in behavioral medicine and cognitive behavior therapy at Harvard/Massachusetts General Hospital in Boston, and at the University of Chicago Hospitals. She is also an experienced professor and lecturer, and has conducted research in human behavior, health, and decision making.

Tara C. Samples, PhD, is a licensed clinical psychologist in the state of Illinois, a nationally certified health service psychologist, an assistant professor of clinical mental health counseling with Lincoln Christian University (LCU), Lincoln, Illinois, and a clinical supervisor for the Student Counseling and Consultation Center at LCU and a nearby community college. Her clinical and scholarly interests include trauma spectrum disorders, mood and anxiety disorders, and primary, secondary, and tertiary interventions to foster resilience in trauma-exposed populations.

Sarah Sanders, PsyD, is a licensed clinical psychologist specializing in the treatment of anxiety, eating disorders, depression, and life transition issues. In addition to research experience on the topic of self-harm, she also coauthored a research article on procrastination rates among adults with ADHD. She practices in Chicago, Illinois.

Cynthia Schroeder, MHS, is a doctoral candidate in neuroscience at Rush University Medical Center, Chicago, focusing on neurodegenerative movement disorders. She is also an adjunct professor of addiction studies at Governors State University, University Park, Illinois.

Heather Shannon, LCPC, is a psychotherapist, certified health coach, and the owner of a private practice in Chicago specializing in helping "Type A" professionals and entrepreneurs. Her holistic approach incorporates nutrition, positive psychology, and mindfulness to help individual clients and groups strengthen self-care, improve relationships, and address compulsive behaviors.

Doug Smith, MD, is a forensic psychiatrist who served in the role of medical director for three Ohio state psychiatric hospitals until mid-2012, when he became Medical Director for the Summit County Alcohol, Drug Addiction, and Mental

Health Services Board. He is an associate professor of psychiatry at the Northeast Ohio Medical University (NEOMED), Rootstown, Ohio, where he directs community psychiatry and co-directs an integrated care fellowship. Dr. Smith serves as a member of the board of trustees of NAMI Ohio.

Gage Stermensky II, PsyD, is a licensed clinical psychologist, is the director of behavioral health at the Community Action Partnership of Western Nebraska, and has his own professional practice in Scottsbluff, Nebraska. Dr. Stermensky's scholarly activities include publishing articles, making presentations at international conferences, acting as grant chair and writer, and serving as an undergraduate faculty member. He has more than 10 years of clinical experience.

Jimia Stokes, MHS, received the 2015 National Board Certified Counselors (NBCC) Minority Fellowship Award in Addiction Counseling. She is an experienced facilitator, with more than 20 years of social service experience that has addressed community-level health and social issues in the Chicago area. She is a strong advocate for the underserved population.

Ingrid M. Tiegel, PhD, is a professor in the department of psychological sciences at Carthage College, Kenosha, Wisconsin. She received her doctorate from the University of Minnesota. She previously taught at SUNY-Stony Brook and California Lutheran University. She designed and teaches the course "Psychology of Stress" at Carthage College.

Quenette L. Walton is a postdoctoral fellow at the UCLA Center for Health Services and Society in Los Angeles. Her research aims to understand the complex interaction of race, social class, gender, and cultural context as factors in behavioral health disparities among middle-class African American women.

Kira Weidner, PsyD, is a licensed clinical psychologist based in Chicago, Illinois. She is the clinical psychologist for a youth center and teaches as a adjunct faculty member at The Chicago School of Professional Psychology. She utilizes harm-reduction, trauma-informed, and multicultural approaches in her work. Her background also includes work with incarcerated youth and adults.

Julia Yang, PhD, is a professor in Taiwan. She is the author of a number of books and articles.

Personal Account Contributors

Some personal account authors are not listed if they wanted to be known only by initials or as "Anonymous."

Nancy Burley wears many hats. She is a widow, mother, daughter, grandmother, student, administrator, teacher, and researcher, who experiences stress on a daily basis.

Jamelia Hand is an MHS, CADC, MISA I therapist with 15 years of clinical practice and pharmaceutical/ addictions treatment consultant work. In her current role, she is an associate director of a health provider center. She is also an educator on addictions topics and owner of both a clinical consulting firm and a handwritten greetings company.

Shavron Kelley is an academic advisor at Governors State University. She has a bachelor's degree in psychology and a master's degree in communications and training. She has worked in the field of education for the past 14 years.

David Klow is the founder and owner of a counseling center in Chicago. He is a Licensed Marriage and Family Therapist. David is also a clinical lecturer through the Department of Psychology for Northwestern University's Master of Science in Marital and Family Therapy Program at The Family Institute.

Kerry Knowles is a graduate of the master's program in addiction studies counseling concentration at Governors State University. She owns a successful art business as well as being a mental health therapist. Her true passion lies in her volunteer work, which she does both in the United States with local organizations and the Marine Corps and in India where she spent time teaching.

Jamie Pekarek Krohn is a psychotherapist in private practice in Madison, Wisconsin. She received her master's degree from DePaul University in counseling and human services, received a certification in adult psychoanalytic psychotherapy at the Chicago Institute of Psychoanalysis, and completed a 200-hour yoga teacher training. In addition, she serves on the advisory board for Erasing the Distance and is an alumni mentor and professional advisor for DePaul University. Prior to moving to Madison, she was in private practice in Chicago, Illinois, a therapist at Alexian Brothers Behavioral Health Hospital in their PHP for Eating Disorders, and adjunct faculty at The Chicago School of Professional Psychology.

Lisbett R. Lee has more than 15 years of experience in product support, strategic planning, training users, and managing client projects.

Karen McNab is a self-taught wellness consultant who has practiced for almost 18 years. She specializes in natural and holistic methodologies for health and continues to learn about better ways to achieve greater health holistically.

Joelyne Marshall a strategic and creative professional, has worked in learning and development for 20-plus years in a variety of sectors. She couples her MBA and fine arts degree in electronic media to assist and empower organizations and individuals in reaching higher performance while using training and coaching interventions.

Kerri K. Morris has been teaching writing and rhetoric courses since completing her PhD in 1989. She is associate professor of English and director of writing across the curriculum at Governors State University. She also has a blog at ChicagoNow, "Cancer Is Not a Gift."

Meggan Sommerville is a Christian writer, blogger, and transgender advocate. In 2012, she began Trans Girl at the Cross, a blog that tries to bridge the gap between the transgender community and the Christian church, in hopes of healing and educating people on different sides of this issue.

Garrett W. Starke has experience developing consumer-oriented interactive experiences for Fortune 500 companies. He also has experience in the software design process, and management experience including interviewing, mentoring, scheduling, estimates, and annual reviews.

Kim Strickland is the author of two novels, *Wish Club* and *Down at the Golden Coin*. She also writes "A City Mom," a blog at www.ChicagoNow. She received a B.S. in journalism with an English minor from the University of Illinois at Urbana-Champaign, where she also obtained her pilot training at the University of Illinois Institute of Aviation. A native Chicagoan, she still lives in the city with her husband and three children. When she is not being a mom or a writer, she flies for a major airline as a captain on Boeing 767 aircraft.

Teri Thompson LPC, NCC, CADC, was born in the inner city of Chicago to a single mother who worked full time to support Teri and her two brothers. The only one in her family to receive a college education, she has worked in the helping professions for more than a decade.

INDEX